THE CONCISE

ORIYA-ENGLISH DICTIONARY

THE CONCISE ORIYA-ENGLISH DICTIONARY

REV. R. J. GRUNDY

BASED ON

REV. AMOS SUTTON AND WILLIAM BROOKS

SECOND EDITION

GYAN

Published by

GYAN

Gyan Publishing House
5, Ansari Road
Daryaganj, New Delhi-110002
Phone: 011-47034999, 9811692060
E-mail: books@gyanbooks.com

Distribution Network
gyanbooks.com
India, USA, Canada, UK, Australia, France

ISBN : 978-81-212-4277-6 (PB)
First Published, Cuttack, 1928

2nd Impression 2020

Printed at: Gyan Press, Delhi.

The Concise Oriya-English Dictionary
Author: Rev. R. J. Grundy

THE CONCISE

ORIYA-ENGLISH DICTIONARY

DESIGNED

FOR THE USE OF EUROPEAN AND INDIAN STUDENTS AND SCHOOLS.

COMPILED BY

REV. R. J. GRUNDY

With the help of Indian Assistants.

SECOND EDITION

CUTTACK

ORISSA MISSION PRESS

1928

PREFACE.

In publishing this Oriya-English Dictionary a few words of introduction appear necessary. It is a new compilation based on those of Rev. Amos Sutton and Mr. William Brooks. Those who are acquainted with Mr. Brooks' book will find that many words not in ordinary use have been omitted and a large number of other useful words introduced. The book has been increased by about 40 pages. It is not claimed that the present compilation is in any way exhaustive, but it is hoped that it may be found more useful than its predecessors. In giving the English equivalents of the Oriya words an attempt has been made to put the one *mainly* used in the first place, those following being in order of importance, as far as possible. Thus, in some cases, the root meaning of a word may be given the last place. This plan has been adopted so that non-Oriyas consulting the book may be able to know, with some amount of certainty, when several equivalents are given for one Oriya word, which of them is in common use.

It is often difficult to know what words may be used in ordinary polite conversation and what words are only used in literature. As a guide in this direction some words have an asterisk (*) against them. The words with the * are not generally used in conversation, but are to be met with in literature. It is hoped this will be found helpful to the student.

Great care has been taken and a large amount of time expended in the endeavour to give the right shades of meaning in English, but success may not have been attained in all cases.

The Compiler wishes to place on record the very valuable assistance he has received from Pandit Ram Krishna Panda and the Rev. Joyananda Singh. But for their help he could not have got through the work satisfactorily. Words and their meanings have been discussed with them and the greatest care has been taken to give the most useful equivalents and to express the exact shades of meaning.

Cuttack, January, 1916. THE COMPILER.

THE CONCISE ORIYA-ENGLISH DICTIONARY.

ଅ.

ଅ. The first vowel. A *prefix*, meaning *un-*, *in-*, **not**; before a vowel it becomes ଅନ୍.

ଅଁଅଳା, ଅଁଉଳା, *n.* a medicinal tree and its fruit

ଅଇ, *n.* vomiting, sickness.

ଅଁଇଠା, ଅଇଣ୍ଠା, *n.* orts, remains of a meal.—*a.* that which has been tasted, as ଅଇଣ୍ଠା ଅନ୍ନ ।

ଅଇନା, *n.* a mirror.

ଅଇର, *n.* enemy.

ଅଋଣୀ, *a.* out of debt, not in debt.

ଅଂଶ, *n.* a share, part, portion.

* ଅଂଶକ, *n.* one share or part; one who divides into shares.

ଅଂଶତଃ, *ad.* partly.

* ଅଂଶାଂଶ, *n.* distinct shares, allotment.

ଅଂଶିତ୍ୱ, *n.* right to a share, partnership.

ଅଂଶୀ, *n.* a partner, sharer, co-partner.

* ଅଂଶୁ, *n* a ray of light; an atom.

* ଅଂଶୁକ, *n.* fine cloth; cassia leaf.

* ଅଂଶୁଧର, *n.* the sun.

* ଅଂଶୁମତ୍, ଅଂଶୁମାନ୍, ଅଂଶୁମାଳୀ, *a.* radiant, shining, bright.—*n.* the sun.

ଅଃ, *inter.* an exclamation of fatigue, surprise, or displeasure.

ଅକଉଡ଼ିଆ, *a.* penniless, very poor, no value.

ଅକଟା, *a.* whole, uncut.

ଅକଠିନ, *a.* not hard or difficult; soft.

ଅକଠୋର, *a.* not severe, rigid or cruel; gentle, mild.

ଅକଣ୍ଟକ, *a.* thornless; without an enemy.

ଅକଣ୍ଡା, *a.* uncleansed (rice).

ଅକଥନୀୟ, ଅକଥ୍ୟ, *a.* unspeakable; obscene.

ଅକଥା, *n.* bad word, obscene language.

ଅକଥିତ, *a.* unspoken, undivulged.

ଅକପଟ, *a.* sincere, frank, ingenuous.

ଅକରକରା, *n.* a medicinal tree and its fruit.

ଅକରୁଣ, *a.* unmerciful, unfeeling.

ଅକର୍କଶ, *a.* tender, soft, mild.

ଅକର୍ତ୍ତବ୍ୟ, *a.* improper, impracticable.

ଅକର୍ମ, *n.* a bad action.

ଅକର୍ମକ, *a.* intransitive (in *Gram.*)

ଅକର୍ମଣ୍ୟ, ଅକର୍ମା, *a.* lazy, useless, worthless.

ଅକଳ, *a.* difficult, hard to accomplish.

ଅକଳଙ୍କ, *a.* unstained, unblemished.

ଅକଳଣା, *a.* boundless or limitless.

ଅକଳନ୍ତା, ଅକଳିତ, *a.* boundless, limitless.

ଅକଲ୍, *n.* understanding, intellect.

ଅକଲ୍ୟାଣ, *n.* misfortune, malediction.

ଅକଳ୍ପନା, *n.* a want of contrivance.

ଅକଳ୍ପିତ, *a.* true, genuine, real, unfeigned.

ଅକସ, *n.* enmity, hatred, malice.

ଅକସ୍ମାତ୍, *ad.* suddenly, unexpectedly.

ଅକାଟ, *n.* a magical liquid.

ଅକାଣ୍ଡିଆ, *a.* uncleansed (rice).

ଅକାତ, ଅକାତକାତ, *a.* unfathomable, very deep water.

ଅକାତରେ, *ad.* fearlessly, liberally, freely.

ଅକାପଟ୍ୟ, *n.* sincerity, honesty.

ଅକାମ, ଅକାମୀ, ଅକାମୁକ, *a.* not sensual, not lustful, chaste, void of lust.

ଅକାମୀ, *a.* idle, useless.

ଅକାର, *n.* (in *Gram.*) the letter ଅ; vomiting.

ଅକାରଣ, *a.* without cause or reason; —*ad.* uselessly.

ଅକାରାନ୍ତ, *a.* ending with ଅ.

ଅକାର୍ଯ୍ୟ, *n.* an improper act.

ଅକାଳ, *n.* unseasonable time; a famine; *a.* premature.

ଅକାଳଫଳ, *n.* untimely fruit, untimely birth.

ଅକାଳେ, *ad.* untimely.

ଅକାଲ୍ପନିକ, *a.* real, proper.

ଅକିଞ୍ଚନ, *a.* destitute, poor, needy.

ଅକିଞ୍ଚିତ୍କର, *a.* insignificant.

ଅକୀର୍ତ୍ତି, *n.* infamy, blasphemy, bad name, defamation.

ଅକୁଟିଳ, *a.* plain, sincere.

ଅକୁଣ୍ଠିତ, *a.* undaunted, fearless, unflinching.

* ଅକୁତୋଭୟ, *a.* fearless.

ଅକୁଳା, *a.* illegitimate.

ଅକୁଳାନ, *a.* deficient, lacking, wanting.

ଅକୁଳୀନ, *a.* low-born, destitute of fame or renown.

ଅକୁଶଳ, *n.* misfortune, ill-luck.

* ଅକୂପାର, *n.* the sea, the ocean.

ଅକୂଳ, *a.* without banks, *i.e.* the banks or shore being out of sight.

ଅକୃତକାର୍ଯ୍ୟ, *a.* unsuccessful, fruitless.

ଅକୃତଜ୍ଞ, *a.* ungrateful, unthankful.

* ଅକୃତଦାର, *a.* unmarried; —*n.* a bachelor.

ଅକୃତ୍ରିମ, *a.* inartificial, genuine.

ଅକୃପା, *n.* mercilessness, cruelty.

ଅକ୍ରମ, *n.* want of order, irregularity.

ଅକ୍ରିୟା, *n.* inaction; improper action.

ଅକ୍ରୋଧୀ, *a.* not angry, placid, tranquil.

ଅକ୍ଳାନ୍ତ, *a.* unwearied, not fatigued.

ଅକ୍ଳେଶ, *n.* absence of distress or fatigue.

ଅକ୍ଷ, *n.* an axle-tree.

ଅଖଞ୍ଜ, ଅଖଞ୍ଜିଆ, *a.* inconvenient.

ଅଖଣ୍ଡ, *a.* unbroken, whole ; unrefuted.

ଅଖଣ୍ଡନୀୟ, *a.* infrangible, not to be broken ; unconfutable.

ଅଖଣ୍ଡିତ, *a.* unbroken, whole ; unconfuted.

ଅଖଳ, *a.* without hypocrisy.

ଅଖା, *n.* a sack, gunny.

ଅଖାଡୁଆ, *a.* without conscience.

ଅଖାତ, *a.* undug ;—*n.* a natural pond.

ଅଖାଦ୍ୟ, *a.* not fit for food.

ଅଖିଆ, *a.* not having eaten.

* ଅଖିଳ, *a.* all, entire, the whole.

ଅଖୁଣ, *a.* undefiled, without blemish, without defect or deformity.

ଅଖ୍ୟାତି, *n.* dishonour, disgrace, obloquy, slander.

ଅଗ, *n.* the point or top of any thing long or tall.

ଅଗଣନୀୟ, ଅଗଣ୍ୟ, *a.* incalculable, innumerable; unworthy of notice.

ଅଗଣା, *n.* a court-yard or private enclosure ;—*a.* uncounted.

ଅଗଣିତ, *a.* not calculated.

ଅଗଡବଗଡ, *n.* a medley, odds and ends.

* ଅଗତି, ଅଗତିକ, *a.* helpless.

ଅଗତିଆ, *ad.* having no choice left, without resource, desperately.

* ଅଗଦ, *n.* physic, medicine ;—*a.* healthy, without sickness.

ଅଗମ୍ୟ, *a.* inaccessible, impassable, incomprehensible.

ଅଗସ୍ତ, *n.* a low thorny plant, a thistle.

ଅଗାଡ, *n.* ear (of rice) without grain ;–*a.* worthless, vain, block-headed.

ଅଗାଡଆ, *a.* blighted.

ଅଗାଧ, *a.* very deep, bottomless.

ଅଗାଧୁଆ, *a.* unbathed.

ଅଗାଧୁଆହାଟ, *n.* an early market before bathing.

ଅଗୁରୁ, *n.* a sweet-scented wood;—*a.* light, unimportant.

ଅଗୁଣ, *n.* bad quality ;—*a.* useless, worthless.

ଅଗୁପ୍ତ, *a.* not hid, clear, or manifest.

ଅଗୋଚର, *a.* imperceptible, unknown.

ଅଗ୍ନି, *n.* fire ; digestive power.

ଅଗ୍ନିକଣ, ଅଗ୍ନିକଣା, *n.* a spark of fire.

* ଅଗ୍ନିକାର୍ଯ୍ୟ, *n.* purification by fire, burning the dead.

* ଅଗ୍ନିକୋଣ, *n.* the south-east quarter.

* ଅଗ୍ନିକ୍ରୀଡା, *n.* a display of fireworks.

* ଅଗ୍ନିଦ, *n.* an incendiary ; the person entitled to apply fire to the corpse.

ଅଗ୍ନିପରୀକ୍ଷା, *n.* trial by fire.

ଅଗ୍ନିପ୍ରସ୍ତର, *n.* a flint.

ଅଗ୍ନିବୃଦ୍ଧି, *n.* strengthening of digestion.

ଅଗ୍ନିମଣି, *n.* a chrystal, a gem.

ଅଗ୍ନିମୟ, *a.* abounding with fire, fiery.

ଅଗ୍ନିମାନ୍ଦ୍ୟ, *n.* indigestion, the want of appetite.

ଅଗ୍ନିଶିଖା, *n.* a flame of fire; the name of a poisonous plant.

* ଅଗ୍ନ୍ୟବତାର, *n.* a furious person, *lit.* an incarnation of fire.

* ଅଗ୍ନ୍ୟସ୍ତ୍ର, *n.* gun, fire-arms.

ଅଗ୍ନ୍ୟୁତ୍ପାତ, *n.* an eruption of fire.

ଅଗ୍ର, *n.* front, forepart, tip of any thing;—*ad.* before: further, onward.

ଅଗ୍ରଗଣନୀୟ, ଅଗ୍ରଗଣ୍ୟ, *a.* chief, entitled to precedence.

ଅଗ୍ରଗାମୀ, *a.* foregoing;—*n.* forerunner, leader.

* ଅଗ୍ରଜ, *a.* first-born;—*n.* an elder brother; Brahmin caste.

ଅଗ୍ରଣୀ, *n.* a leader, chief;—*a.* leading.

ଅଗ୍ରତେ, *ad.* in front.

ଅଗ୍ରପଶ୍ଚାତ୍, *ad.* backwards and forwards, sooner or later.

ଅଗ୍ରବର୍ତ୍ତୀ, *a.* preceding, going or standing before.

ଅଗ୍ରଭାଗ, *n.* top, end, the forepart of a thing.

* ଅଗ୍ରମାଂସ, *n.* an induration of the liver; flesh in the heart.

ଅଗ୍ରସର, *a.* preceding, moving in front.

* ଅଗ୍ରହାୟଣ, *n.* a Hindu month (Nov. & Dec.)

ଅଗ୍ରାହ୍ୟ, *a.* unacceptable, inadmissible.

ଅଗ୍ରିମ, *a.* first, best, chief.

ଅଗ୍ରେ, *ad.* in front, before, formerly, forward.

* ଅଘ, *n.* guilt, wickedness, sin.

ଅଘଟଣ, *n.* a misfortune;—*a.* ugly; impossible.

ଅଘାଟ, *n.* a part of the bank of a river which is not used as a landing or bathing place.

ଅଘିପୂର୍ଣ୍ଣିମା, *n.* the full moon in February.

* ଅଘୋର, *n.* a name of *Siva.*

ଅଘୋରୀ, *n.* a wild fanatic living on human flesh and filth.

ଅଙ୍କ, *n.* a figure, mark, cypher, the flank or side; *fig.* the bosom, the heart.

ଅଙ୍କନ, *n.* drawing, marking.

* ଅଙ୍କପୂରଣ, *n.* multiplication.

ଅଙ୍କବିଦ୍ୟା, *n.* arithmetic.

ଅଙ୍କବୃଦ୍ଧି, *n.* addition, multiplication, the increasing of a sum, increasing the price or demand.

ଅଙ୍କହରଣ, *n.* division, a decreasing of numbers.

ଅଙ୍କିତ, *a.* marked, paged, drawn.

ଅଙ୍କିବା, *a.* to draw, to mark.

ଅଙ୍କୁର, *n.* a germ, sprout, seed-bud.

ଅଙ୍କୁରିତ, *a.* germinated, sprouted.

ଅଙ୍କୁଶ, *n.* an iron hook or goad.

ଅଙ୍ଗ, *n.* a limb, member; the body.

ଅଙ୍ଗଚ୍ଛେଦ, ଅଙ୍ଗଚ୍ଛେଦନ, *n.* mutilation, amputation.

ଅଙ୍ଗଠା, *n.* a chafingdish, a portable fire-pan.

*ଅଙ୍ଗନ, *n.* a court-yard, an enclosed area.

ଅଙ୍ଗପ୍ରତ୍ୟଙ୍ଗ, *n.* all the limbs.

ଅଙ୍ଗଭଙ୍ଗୀ, *n.* a distorting of the body, gesticulation.

ଅଙ୍ଗରଖା, ଅଙ୍ଗା, *n.* a coat, cloak, a wrapper for the body.

*ଅଙ୍ଗରାଗ, *n.* adorning of the body; a cosmetic.

ଅଙ୍ଗସଙ୍ଗ, *n.* close contact; coition.

ଅଙ୍ଗହୀନ, *a.* mutilated, maimed, defective.

ଅଙ୍ଗାଧ, *n.* half a (bahungy) load.

ଅଙ୍ଗାର, *n.* charcoal, coal cinders.

ଅଙ୍ଗାମ୍ଳ, *n.* carbonic acid.

ଅଙ୍ଗୀକାର, *n.* acquiescence, agreeing to a proposal; confessing.

ଅଙ୍ଗୀକୃତ, *a.* agreed to, promised, engaged to do.

ଅଙ୍ଗୁଟ, *n.* misinterpretation, a perverted or distorted idea.

ଅଙ୍ଗୁର, *n.* grape, rasin.

ଅଙ୍ଗୁରୀ, ଅଙ୍ଗୁରୀୟ, ଅଙ୍ଗୁରୀୟକ, *n.* a ring for the finger or toe.

ଅଙ୍ଗୁଳିସନ୍ଧି, *n.* space between the fingers or toes.

ଅଙ୍ଗୁଳୀ, *n.* a finger or toe.

ଅଙ୍ଗୁଷ୍ଠ, *n.* the thumb, great toe.

ଅଙ୍ଗୁଷ୍ଠାନା, *n.* a thimble.

ଅଚକିତ, *a.* not startled, not alarmed, steady.

ଅଚଞ୍ଚଳ, *a.* unwavering, steady, not quick.

ଅଚତୁର, *a.* dull, inactive, not clever.

ଅଚଳ, ଅଚଳନ୍ତି, *a.* motionless, unable to move; decrepit;—*n.* a mountain.

ଅଚଳାଚଳ, *a.* immovable; abundant.

ଅଚ୍ଛବ, ଅଚ୍ଛନବ, *n.* cholera, plague.

ଅଚିକିତ୍ସା, *n.* quackery, neglect of medicine.

ଅଚିନ୍ତନୀୟ, *a.* incomprehensible.

ଅଚିନ୍ତା, *n.* irresponsibility.

ଅଚିର, *a.* transient, finite, transitory.

*ଅଚିନ୍ତିତ, *ad.* suddenly, unexpectedly.

ଅଚିହ୍ନା, *a.* unknown, not acquainted with, unrecognised.

ଅଚେତନ, *a.* void of sensation, insensible.

ଅଚେଷ୍ଟ, *a.* without exertion, inactive.

ଅଚୈତନ୍ୟ, *a.* inanimate, without sensation.

*ଅଚ୍ୟୁତ, *a.* indestructible, imperishable.

ଅଛତ୍ର, *a.* without a king;—*n.* interregnum.

ଅଛେଦ୍ୟ, *a.* indivisible.

ଅଛୁଆଁ, *a.* untouchable.

ଅଜଗର, *n.* a large serpent, the boa-constrictor.

ଅଜଟ, *a.* pertinacious, opinionated.

ଅଜୀର୍ଣ, *n.* indigestion.

ଅଜାଡ଼ା, *a.* poured out.

ଅଜଣା, *a.* unknown.

ଅଜର, *a.* not subject to decay or decrepitude, imperishable.

ଅଜଣ, *a.* ill-born (term of abuse); not purified (used in reference to poisonous drugs).

* ଅଜସ୍ର, *ad.* incessantly, continually.

ଅଜା, *n.* maternal grandfather; a she-goat.

ଅଜାଗ୍ରତ, *a.* careless, unwatchful.

ଅଜାଡ଼ିବା, *v.* to pour out.

ଅଜାତ, *a.* unborn, unproduced.

ଅଜାତି, ଅଜାତିଆ, *n.* an outcast;—*a.* without caste.

ଅଜାଶୁର, *n.* a wife's or husband's grandparents.

ଅଜିତ, *a.* unconquered;—*n.* *Vishnu*, *Siva*.

ଅଜିତେନ୍ଦ୍ରିୟ, *a.* incontinent, lascivious.

ଅଜୀବ, *a.* inanimate, lifeless.

ଅଜୀର୍ଣ୍ଣ, *a.* undigested, not old or worn out;—*n.* indigestion.

ଅଜେୟ, *a.* invincible, unconquerable.

ଅଝଡ଼ା, *a.* unswept.

ଅଝାଡ଼ୁଆ, *n.* any snake whose bite is fatal.

ଅଜ୍ଞ ଅଜ୍ଞାନ, ଅଜ୍ଞାନୀ, *a.* ignorant, uninformed, without knowledge.

ଅଜ୍ଞତା, ଅଜ୍ଞାନତା, *n.* ignorance.

ଅଜ୍ଞାତ, *a.* unknown.

ଅଜ୍ଞାତକୁଳଶୀଳ, *a.* unknown (spoken of a person whose birth and family customs are not known).

ଅଜ୍ଞାତରେ, *ad.* unknowingly.

ଅଜ୍ଞାତସାର, *a.* without the knowledge of a thing.

ଅଜ୍ଞାତସାରେ, *ad.* unknowingly.

ଅଜ୍ଞାନ, *n.* ignorance, false knowledge;—*a.* ignorant, unwise.

ଅଜ୍ଞାପିତ, *a.* unpublished.

* ଅଜ୍ଞେୟ, *a.* incomprehensible.

ଅଞ୍ଚଳ, *n.* that part of a cloth which is thrown over the shoulder, outskirt, a district.

ଅଞ୍ଜନ, *n.* collyrium, black pigment for the eyes.

ଅଞ୍ଜଳି, *n.* two handsful, the open hands joined.

ଅଟକ, *n.* a hindrance, impediment, obstruction.

ଅଟକଳ, *n.* a guess, a supposition.

ଅଟକାଇବା, *v.* to obstruct, to hinder; to detain.

ଅଟକାଳି, *n.* overboiled rice, cooked pulse or *dáli*.

* ଅଟନ, *n.* a journey.

* ଅଟବୀ, *n.* a forest, a thicket.

ଅଟଳ, *a.* immovable, unchangeable, incontrovertible, permanent.

ଅଟଳବଚନ, *n.* an unrefutable proposition or argument.

ଅଟା, *n.* flour

ଅଟାଳ, ଅଟେଳ, *n.* an enclosure for cattle; a granary.

* ଅଟ୍ଟହାସ, *n.* immoderate laughter.

* ଅଟ୍ଟାଳୀ, ଅଟ୍ଟାଳିକା, *n.* a palace, an upper-roomed house.

ଅଠଚାଳିଶ, *a.* and *n.* forty-eight; 48, XLVIII.

ଅଠତିରିଶ, *a.* and *n.* thirty-eight; 38, XXXVIII.

ଅଠର, *a.* and *n.* eighteen; 18, XVIII.

ଅଠଷଠି, *a.* and *n.* sixty-eight; 68, LXVIII.

ଅଠସ୍ତରି, *a.* and *n.* seventy-eight; 78, LXXVIII.

ଅଠା, *n.* gum, any glutinous substance.

ଅଠାଇଶ, *a.* and *n.* twenty-eight; 28, XXVIII.

ଅଠାକାଠି, ଅଠାକାଣ୍ଡିଆ, *n.* point of a reed covered with bird-lime.

ଅଠାନବେ, *a.* and *n.* ninety-eight; 98, XCVIII.

ଅଠାବନ, *a.* and *n.* fifty-eight; 58, LVIII.

ଅଠାଳିଆ, *a.* glutinous.

ଅଠାଶୀ, *a.* and *n.* eighty-eight; 88, LXXXVIII.

*ଅଠୋଲ, *a.* complete, full.

ଅଡଙ୍ଗ, *n.* a place where salt is manufactured or stored.

ଅଡା, *n.* a station, a place where bearers change or where cowherds meet.

ଅଡାଇବା, *v.* to drive cattle, to turn out.

ଅଡି, *n.* determination, pertinacity, obstinacy.

ଅଡିବା, *v.* to jibb (said of a horse), to be obstinate.

ଅଡିବାଳ, *a.* pertinacious, obstinate.

ଅଡୁଆ, *a.* unsettled, in confusion.

ଅଡ଼ୌଲ, *a.* out of shape, awry, crooked.

ଅଢଣ, *n.* a small raised verandah.

ଅଢଙ୍ଗ, ଅଢଙ୍ଗା, *a.* shapeless, ill-made, ugly.

*ଅଢା, *s.* a measure of capacity.

ଅଢାଇ, ଅଢେଇ, *n.* two and a half.

ଅଢେଇଆ, *n.* a measure of two and a half seers.

ଅଲ୍ପଦିନିଆ, *a.* temporary.

ଅଣ, *n.* broth, juice, gravy.

ଅଣଓସାର, *a.* narrow.

ଅଣକ, *n.* a ladle made of a cocoanut shell.

ଅଣକଦଳିଆ, *n.* fruitless plantain tree.

ଅଣସଲା, ଅଣଶିଲା, *n.* a peg or wooden pin for fastening a cart wheel.

ଅଣଚାଳିଶ, *a.* and *n.* thirty-nine; 39, XXXIX.

ଅଣଚାଶ, *a.* and *n.* forty-nine; 49, XLIX.

ଅଣନବେ, *a.* and *n.* eighty-nine; 89, LXXXIX.

ଅଣନାତି, *n.* great-grandson.

ଅଣପୁରୁଷା, *n.* a eunuch, an effeminate person.

ଅଣଲେଉଟ, *a.* not liable to fail, infallible, efficacious.

ଅଣବାପୁଆ, *n.* an illegitimate child, a bastard.

ଅଣଶୁଦ୍ଧିଆ, *a.* in a state of ceremonial impurity.

ଅଣସର, *n.* fifteen days before the car festival.

ଅଣହେଲା, *n.* disrespect, disregard, contempt.

ଅଣା, *n.* an anna, sixteenth part of a rupee.

ଅଣାଅଶୀ, *a.* and *n.* seventy-nine; 79, LXXIX.

ଅଣାଇବା, *v.* to cause to be brought.

ଅଣାଏ, ଅଣାଟ, *n.* one anna.

ଅଣାୟତ୍ତ, *a.* powerless, helpless.

ଅଣାବଣା, *a.* all of a litter, here and there.

ଅଣି, *n.* a nickel coin value one [anna.

* ଅଣିମା, *n.* superhuman power; minuteness.

ଅଣୁ, *n.* an atom, a particle.

ଅଣୁବୀକ୍ଷଣ, *n.* a microscope.

ଅଡେଣି, *ad.* turned on one side (always used with a verb as ଅଡେଣି ଶୋଇବା, sleeping on one side).

ଅଣ୍ଟା, *n.* the loins, the waist.

ଅଣ୍ଟାଇବା, ଅଣ୍ଟେଇବା, *v.* to raise up, to support.

ଅଣ୍ଟାଶୋଷା, ଅଣ୍ଟାଯଷା, *n.* a bribe.

ଅଣ୍ଟାବନ୍ଧା, *n.* a girdle, a bandage for the loins.

ଅଣ୍ଟାସୂତା, *n.* a string or chain worn round the loins.

ଅଣ୍ଟି, *n.* a kind of pocket formed by tucking up the cloth.

ଅଣ୍ଟିବା, *v.* to last or hold out, to suffice

ଅଣ୍ଡ, ଅଣ୍ଡା, *n.* an egg, roe, spawn.

ଅଣ୍ଡକୋଷ, *n.* testicle.

ଅଣ୍ଡଜ, *a.* produced from an egg, oviparous.

ଅଣ୍ଡାକାର, ଅଣ୍ଡାକୃତ, *a.* oval, elliptical; —*n.* an ellipsis, an oval.

ଅଣ୍ଡିଆ, *n.* a bull calf.

ଅଣ୍ଡିରା, *a.* a male, (applied to children) and animals.

ଅଣ୍ଡିରାଚଣ୍ଡୀ, *n.* a shameless and masculine woman.

* ଅତଃପର, *ad.* afterwards, subsequently.

ଅତଏବ, *conj.* therefore, wherefore.

ଅତଡ଼ା, *n.* the banks of a pond or river; a fire-heap.

ଅତଥ୍ୟ, *a.* not real, uncertain, false, inaccurate.

ଅତର, *n.* attar of roses, perfume.

ଅତରଦାନ, *n.* a vessel used to hold essence of roses, etc.

ଅତର୍କିତ, *a.* unexpected, careless.

ଅତର୍ଷ, *a.* greatly afraid.

ଅତଳ, *a.* bottomless.

ଅତଳସ୍ପର୍ଶ, *a.* unfathomable.

ଅତି, a *prefix* denoting excess, usually expressed by the words very, exceedingly.

ଅତିକ୍ରମ, *n.* exceeding the boundaries, transgression.

ଅତିକ୍ରାନ୍ତ, *a.* transgressed, surpassed.

ଅତିଗର୍ହିତ, *a.* despicable, vile.

ଅତିଥି, *n.* a guest, a stranger.

ଅତିଥିଶାଳା, *n.* a house or room for guests.

ଅତିଥିସତ୍କାର, ଅତିଥିସେବା, *n.* hospitality.

ଅତିଦାନ, *n.* excessive generosity.

* ଅତିପାତ, *n.* passing away, lapse (of time).

* ଅତିବାଦ, *n.* exaggeration; reproof; [hyperbole.

ଅତିବାହିତ, *a.* spent (time spent).

ଅତିବୃଷ୍ଟି, *n.* excessive rain, a deluge.

ଅତିବ୍ୟୟ, *n.* prodigality, profusion.

ଅତିରଞ୍ଜିତ, *a* exaggerated.

ଅତିରିକ୍ତ, *a.* superabounding.

ଅତିରେକ, *n.* a surplus, excess.

ଅତିଶୟ, *a.* much, exceeding.

ଅତିସାର, *n.* diarrhœa, dysentery.

ଅତୀତ, *a.* past, elapsed, gone.

ଅତୀତକାଳ, *n.* the time past; (in *Gram.*) the past tense.

ଅତୀବ, *a.* excessive, immeasurable.

* ଅତୀକ୍ଷ୍ଣ, *a.* blunt, dull.

ଅତୁଲ, ଅତୁଲନୀୟ, ଅତୁଲ୍ୟ, *a.* incomparable, peerless.

ଅତୃପ୍ତ, *a.* unsatisfied.

ଅତୃପ୍ତି, *n.* dissatisfaction.

ଅତ୍ୟନ୍ତ, *a.* excessive, great;—*ad.* very.

* ଅତ୍ୟୟ, *a* surpassing;—*s.* excess, violence, death, destruction.

ଅତ୍ୟଳ୍ପ, *a.* very few, very small.

ଅତ୍ୟାଚାର, *s.* unprincipled conduct, violence.

ଅତ୍ୟାଚାରୀ, *a.* oppressive, violent.

* ଅତ୍ୟାଜ୍ୟ, *a.* unrelinquishable.

ଅତ୍ୟାଶା, *n.* unreasonable hope or desire.

ଅତ୍ୟୁକ୍ତି. *n.* verbosity, profuse speech, tattle, hyperbole.

ଅତ୍ୟୁତ୍ତମ, *a.* best, excellent, superlative.

ଅତ୍ର, *ad.* here.

ଅତ୍ରତ୍ୟ, *a.* of this place.

ଅଥଚ, *conj.* also, and.

ଅଥବା, *conj.* otherwise, or else, or, alias.

ଅଥୟ, *a.* unsettled, troublesome.

ଅଥିରା, *a.* unsteady, fickle.

ଅଥର୍ବ, *n.* fourth *Veda.*

ଅଥଳ, *a.* unfordable.

ଅଥୁରୁପଥୁରୁ, *n.* the entire belongings of a person.

ଅଦଣ୍ଡ୍ୟ, *a.* unpunishable.

ଅଦତ୍ତ, *a.* not given in marriage;—*n.* a spinster.

ଅଦମ୍ୟ, *a.* unsubduable, impracticable, intractable.

* ଅଦର୍ଶନ, *n.* out of sight, disappearance.

ଅଦଳବଦଳ, *n.* exchange, permutation, barter.

ଅଦା, *n.* ginger.

ଅଦାଉତ, ଅଦୌତ, *n.* enmity, malice.

ଅଦାତା, *a.* penurious, stingy.

ଅଦାନ୍ତିଆ, ଅଦାନ୍ତୁଆ, *a.* without teeth, toothless.

ଅଦାଲତ, *n.* a court of justice.

ଅଦଥ, *n.* a miser;—*a.* miserly.

ଅଦିତି, *n.* mother of the gods, wife of *Kashyapa.*

ଅଦିନ, *a.* unseasonable.

* ଅଦୀକ୍ଷିତ, *a.* unconsecrated.

ଅଦୂରଦର୍ଶୀ, *a.* improvident, without care for the future.

ଅଦୃଶ୍ୟ, *a.* invisible, not to be seen.

ଅଦୃଷ୍ଟ, *a.* unseen, unperceived;—*n.* fate, destiny.

ଅଦୃଷ୍ଟବାନ୍, *a.* fortunate.

ଅଦେଖା, *a.* unseen, unperceived.
ଅଦ୍ଭୁତ, *a.* supernatural, marvellous, strange.
ଅଦ୍ୟ, *ad.* to-day. [to to-day.
* ଅଦ୍ୟତନ, *a.* of this day, belonging
ଅଦ୍ୟାପି, *ad.* to this day, still. [day.
ଅଦ୍ୟାବଧି, *ad.* from to-day ; till this
* ଅଦ୍ରି, *n.* a mountain, a rock.
ଅଦ୍ୱିତୀୟ, *a.* unique, peerless, sole, only-begotten. [second.
* ଅଦ୍ୱୈତ, *a.* single, having no
* ଅଦ୍ୱୈତବାଦୀ, *a.* asserting the unity of God ;—*n.* Unitarian.
* ଅଧଃ, *ad.* below, Hades.
ଅଧଃପତନ, ଅଧଃପାତ, *n.* a downfall.
ଅଧଃସ୍ଥ, ଅଧସ୍ଥ, *a.* subject to, situated below.
ଅଧ, ଅଧା, ଅଧେ, *n.* half, a half.
ଅଧକ, *n.* a half.
ଅଧକପାଳି, ଅଧାକପାଳି, *n.* a pain on one side of the head.
ଅଧପେଟ, *a.* half a meal.
ଅଧମ, *a.* vile, base, mean, wicked.
* ଅଧମର୍ଣ୍ଣ, *n.* a debtor, a borrower.
ଅଧମାଧମ, *a.* lowest of the low, excessively low or vile
* ଅଧର, *n.* the lower lip.
ଅଧରାମୃତ, *n.* the nectar of the lower lip, remains from a holy man's meal.
ଅଧର୍ତ୍ତବ୍ୟ, *a.* not subject to criticism, not cognizable, not seizable.

ଅଧର୍ମ, *n.* irreligion, impiety, unrighteousness.
ଅଧର୍ମାଚରଣ, *n.* unrighteous conduct.
ଅଧର୍ମୀ, *a.* unrighteous, irreligious.
ଅଧଲା, *n.* a half-pice. [value.
ଅଧଲାକିଆ, ଅଧଲକିଆ, *a.* half-a-pice
ଅଧସ୍ତନ, *a.* equal to the prefix *sub* (as sub-judge) ; lying beneath.
ଅଧାଅଧି, *n.* almost half.
ଅଧାର, *n.* food of birds.
ଅଧାର୍ମିକ, *a.* ungodly, unrighteous.
ଅଧି, *n.* (in *Comp.*) a prefix implying possession, more, etc.
ଅଧିକ, *a.* more, much, more than.
ଅଧିକନ୍ତୁ, *conj.* especially, particularly, moreover. [case.
ଅଧିକରଣ, *n.* (in *Gram.*) the locative
* ଅଧିକାଙ୍ଗ, *a.* having a superfluous member or limb.
ଅଧିକାଂଶ, *n.* greatest part, majority.
ଅଧିକାର, *n.* possession, right, estate.
ଅଧିକାରୀ, *n.* one having a right ; proprietor, owner, lord.
ଅଧିକୃତ, *a.* possessed as a right.
ଅଧିତ୍ୟକା, *n.* table-land of a mountain.
* ଅଧିନାୟକ, *n.* a leader, a teacher.
ଅଧିପତି, * ଅଧିପ, *n.* a king, master, lord, commander.
* ଅଧିବାସ, *n.* a ceremony preliminary to a festival, marriage, &c., a dwelling-place.
ଅଧିବାସୀ, *n.* a dweller.

ଅଧିବେଶନ, *n.* a meeting.
* ଅଧିମାସ, *n.* an intercalary month.
* ଅଧିରାଜ, *n.* an emperor, a sovereign.
* ଅଧିରୂଢ, *a.* mounted (as on a horse).
* ଅଧିରୋହଣୀ, *n.* a ladder or steps.
ଅଧିଷ୍ଠାତ୍ରୀ, *a.* presiding, governing, ruling.
ଅଧିଷ୍ଠାନ, *n.* abiding; presence. [ed.
* ଅଧୀତ, *a.* read, studied, instruct-
ଅଧୀନ, *a.* subject to, dependent.
ଅଧୀନତା, *n.* servitude, subjection.
ଅଧୀର, *a.* hasty, fickle; not slow.
ଅଧୀଶ୍ୱର, *n.* a sovereign, a lord.
ଅଧୁଁଅଧା, *a.* half-and-half.
ଅଧୁଆ, *a.* unwashed, uncleansed.
* ଅଧୁନା, *ad.* now, lately, recently.
* ଅଧୁନାତନ, *a.* of to-day, (to-day's).
ଅଧୁଲି, *n.* an eight-anna piece.
ଅଧୈର୍ଯ୍ୟ, *n.* impatience, rashness.
ଅଧୋଗତି, *n.* downfall.
* ଅଧୋଗମନ, *n.* a descending, going down.
ଅଧୋବଦନ, *a.* downcast, ashamed, dejected.
ଅଧୋମୁଖ, *n.* hanging the head through shame.
ଅଧ୍ୟବସାୟ, *n.* perseverance, devotedness to an object.
ଅଧ୍ୟୟନ, *n.* reading, study. [ruler.
ଅଧ୍ୟକ୍ଷ, *n.* a superintendent, chief,
ଅଧ୍ୟାତ୍ମ, *a.* spiritual.
ଅଧ୍ୟାପକ, *n.* a teacher, an instructor.
ଅଧ୍ୟାପନ, ଅଧ୍ୟାପନା, *n.* instruction, teaching. [lesson.
ଅଧ୍ୟାୟ, *n.* a chapter, a section; a
* ଅଧ୍ୟାସିତ, ଅଧ୍ୟୁଷିତ, *a.* thickly peopled, inhabited.
ଅଧ୍ୟାହାର, *n.* (in *Gram.*) an ellipsis.
* ଅଧ୍ୟେତା, *n.* a student.
* ଅନଘ, *a.* sinless, innocent, pure.
ଅନଙ୍ଗ, *n.* a name of Cupid.
ଅନଟନ, *n.* need, necessity.
ଅନତିଦୂର, *n.* a short distance.
ଅନଦ୍ୟତନ, (in *Gram.*) a tense indicating from 12 o'clock midnight to 12 o'clock the following midnight.
ଅନଧିକ, *a.* not much.
ଅନଧିକାରଚର୍ଚ୍ଚା, *n.* unwarranted interference. [herited.
ଅନଧିକୃତ, *a.* unpossessed, unin-
* ଅନଧୀନ, *a.* free, independent.
ଅନନ୍ତ, *a.* endless, eternal;—*n.* *Vishnu*; a deified serpent.
ଅନନ୍ତର, *ad.* after, afterwards.
* ଅନନ୍ୟ, *a.* the same, identical, sole.
* ଅନନ୍ୟଗତି, ଅନନ୍ୟଗତିକ, *a.* unable to move, helpless.
* ଅନନ୍ୟବୃତ୍ତି, *a.* of one trade or profession; steady.
ଅନନ୍ୟମନାଃ, *a.* having the mind fixed on one object, attentive.
* ଅନନ୍ୟସାଧାରଣ, *a.* uncommon.
* ଅନପତ୍ୟ, *a.* childless. [for.
ଅନପେକ୍ଷିତ, *a.* unexpected, unlooked

* ଅନବକାଶ, *s.* want of leisure.

* ଅନବଦ୍ୟ, *a.* not contemptible, unexceptionable.

* ଅନବଧାନ, *a.* inattentive, inadvertent :—*n.* inattention, inadvertence.

ଅନବରତ, *a.* incessant, perpetual, constant.

* ଅନବଲମ୍ବନ, *a.* without refuge or defence.

* ଅନବସର, *n.* see ଅନବକାଶ.

* ଅନବସ୍ଥିତ, *a.* unsteady, unsettled.

ଅନଭିଜ୍ଞ, *a.* ignorant, stupid.

ଅନଭ୍ୟାସ, *n.* want of practice.

* ଅନମ୍ବର, *n.* atomosphere, the sky.

ଅନର୍ଗଳ, *a.* unrestrained, free.

ଅନର୍ଥ, *a.* useless, answering no purpose;—*n.* a reverse, evil, calamity.

ଅନର୍ଥକ, *a.* unmeaning, useless, vain.

ଅନର୍ଯାପ, *a.* immense.

* ଅନଳ, *n.* fire.

* ଅନଳସ, *a.* industrious, not indolent.

* ଅନଶନ, *n.* abstinence from food, fasting.

* ଅନଶ୍ୱର, *a.* imperishable.

ଅନା, *inter.* see ! behold !

ଅନାଇବା, *v.* to look, to observe wistfully.

* ଅନାକାଂକ୍ଷୀ, *a.* destitute of wish or desire.

ଅନାକାର, *a.* without form, incorporeal.

* ଅନାକୁଳ, *a.* unperplexed, unembarrassed.

* ଅନାଗତ, *a.* not yet come, future.

ଅନାଚାର, *n.* misconduct, impurity.

ଅନାଜ, *n.* corn, edible vegetables.

ଅନାଡ଼ି, *a.* clumsy, awkward, stupid.

* ଅନାତୁର, *a.* healthy, not afflicted or distressed.

ଅନାଥ, *a.* unprotected, forlorn ;—*n.* orphan.

* ଅନାଥନାଥ, *n.* friend of the friendless, patron of the poor, God.

ଅନାଥା, *a. fem.* forlorn, unprotected ;—*n.* a widow.

ଅନାଦର, *n.* disrespect, incivility.

ଅନାଦି, *a.* eternal, without beginning.

ଅନାଦୃତ, *a.* disrespectful, disregarded.

ଅନାବନା, *a.* in confusion, mixed up.

ଅନାବଶ୍ୟକ, *a.* unnecessary, needless.

* ଅନାବିଳ, *a.* clean, pure.

* ଅନାବିଷ୍ଟ. *a.* not fully engaged, inattentive.

ଅନାବୃତ, *a.* uncovered, unclothed, exposed.

ଅନାବୃଷ୍ଟି, *n.* drought, want of rain.

ଅନାମ, *a.* without a name, nameless; —*n.* a proper name.

* ଅନାମକ, *a.* anonymous.

ଅନାମତୁ, *a.* the whole, entire, all.

* ଅନାମୟ, *n.* good health ;—*a.* without sickness.

ଅନାମିକା, * ଅନାମା, *n.* the fourth or ring finger.

ଅନାୟତ୍ତ, *a.* untamed, not mastered, not under subjection; incapable.

ଅନାୟାସ, *n.* ease, facility ;—*a.* easy.

ଅନାର, *n.* pomegranate.

ଅନାରସ, ଅନାରସ, *n.* a pine-apple.

ଅନାର୍ଯ୍ୟ, *n.* non-Aryan ;—*a.* born of a low family; unworthy, despicable.

ଅନାଲାପୀ, *a.* unfriendly.

ଅନାସ୍ଥ, *a.* see ଅନାଥ ।

ଅନାସ୍ଥା, *n.* carelessness, incredulity, want of confidence.

* ଅନାସ୍ୱାଦ, *a.* tasteless, insipid;—*n.* insipidity.

ଅନାହତ, *a.* not smitten ; useless.

ଅନାହାର, *n.* fasting ; abstinence.

* ଅନାହାର୍ଯ୍ୟ, *a.* not fit for food, rotten.

ଅନାହୂତ, *a.* uncalled, uninvited.

ଅନିଚ୍ଛା, *n.* disrelish, aversion, reluctance.

ଅନିଚ୍ଛୁକ, ଅନିଚ୍ଛୁ, * ଅନିଚ୍ଛ, *a.* averse, unwilling, indifferent.

ଅନିତ୍ୟ, *a.* temporary, fugitive, transitory.

ଅନିଦ୍ର, *a.* sleepless, awake, watchful.

ଅନିଦ୍ରା, *n.* want of sleep, sleeplessness.

ଅନିନ୍ଦିତ, ଅନିନ୍ଦ୍ୟ, *a.* not censurable, irreproachable.

ଅନିବାରିତ, *a.* not hindered, not resisted.

ଅନିବାର୍ଯ୍ୟ, *a.* irresistible, stubborn.

ଅନିୟମ, *n.* absence of rule or fixed order, irregularity, uncertainty.

ଅନିୟମିତ, *a.* irregular ; unfixed.

ଅନିମିଷ, ଅନିମେଷ, *a.* without winking, vigilant.

ଅନିର୍ଦ୍ଦିଷ୍ଟ, *a.* unsettled, unfixed.

ଅନିର୍ବଚନୀୟ, *a.* indescribable.

ଅନିର୍ବାଣ, *a.* inextinguishable.

ଅନିର୍ମଳ, *a.* impure, unclean.

* ଅନିଳ, *n.* the wind, air.

ଅନିଶ୍ଚିତ, *a.* undetermined, not appointed, uncertain.

ଅନିଷ୍ଟ, *a.* undesired, ominous, evil.

ଅନୀତି, *n.* injustice, immorality.

* ଅନୀଶ୍ୱରବାଦ, *n.* atheism, a denial of God.

* ଅନୀଶ୍ୱରବାଦୀ, *a.* denying God ;—*n.* an atheist.

ଅନୁ, a *prefix*, implying after, along.

* ଅନୁକମ୍ପା, *n.* pity, compassion, tenderness.

ଅନୁକରଣ, *n.* an imitation.

* ଅନୁକାରୀ, *a.* imitating, mimicking.

ଅନୁକୂଳ, *a.* friendly to, assisting, favourable ;—*n.* a beginning.

* ଅନୁକ୍ତ, *a.* unmentioned, unspoken.

ଅନୁକ୍ରମ, *n.* a succession, order, series.

ଅନୁକ୍ରମଣିକା, *n.* preface, an index, table of contents.

ଅନୁଗତ, *a.* attached to, dependent on.

ଅନୁଗମନ, *n.* a following ; the *Sati* rite.

ଅନୁଗାମୀ, *a.* devoted ;—*n.* a follower.

ଅନୁଗୃହୀତ, *a.* favoured, honoured.

ଅନୁଗ୍ରହ, *n.* grace, favour, kindness.

* ଅନୁଗ୍ରାହକ, ଅନୁଗ୍ରାହୀ, *a.* merciful.

ଅନୁଚର, *n.* an attendant, a follower.

ଅନୁଚିତ, *a.* unfit, improper, wrong.

* ଅନୁଚ୍ଚ, *a.* not high, low, lowly.

* ଅନୁଜ, *n.* younger brother ;—*a.* junior.

* ଅନୁଜା, *n.* younger sister.

ଅନୁଜୀବୀ, *a.* living upon, dependent.
* ଅନୁଜ୍ଞା, *n.* a command, permission.
* ଅନୁଜ୍ଞାତ, *a.* commanded.
* ଅନୁଜ୍ଞାପତ୍ର, *n.* written authority or command.
ଅନୁତପ୍ତ, *a.* repentant.
ଅନୁତାପ, *n.* repentance, regret, remorse.
ଅନୁତ୍ତମ, (1) *a.* inferior, not good.
*ଅନୁତ୍ତମ, (2) *a.* peerless, unsurpassed.
*ଅନୁଦୟ, *a.* early, before sunrising ;—*n.* degradation.
ଅନୁଦାର, *a.* niggardly, mean.
ଅନୁଦିନ, *ad.* daily, every day.
ଅନୁଦେଶ, *a.* absent from home and whereabouts unknown.
*ଅନୁଦ୍ବେଗ, *n.* freedom from care or perplexity.
ଅନୁଦ୍ୟତ, *a.* effortless, idle, inactive.
ଅନୁଦ୍ୟୋଗ, *n.* indolence, inactivity ; —*a.* lazy.
ଅନୁଧାବନ, *n.* running after ; reflection.
ଅନୁନୟ, *n.* submission, entreaty, humility.
ଅନୁନାସିକ, *a.* nasal.
ଅନୁପକାର, *n.* want of assistance, neglect ;—*a.* unassisted, neglected.
ଅନୁପମ, *a.* peerless, incomparable, unrivalled.
ଅନୁପଯୁକ୍ତ, *a.* unfit, improper, inconsistent.
ଅନୁପଯୋଗୀ, *a.* unfit,
ଅନୁପସ୍ଥିତ, *a.* absent, not present.

ଅନୁପାତ, *n.* proportion, arithmetical proportion.
ଅନୁପାନ, *n.* anything in which medicine may be taken (as honey or sugar, etc.)
ଅନୁପ୍ରାଣିତ, *a.* animated, inspired.
*ଅନୁପ୍ରାସ, *n.* alliteration, repetition of similar letters, syllables or sounds.
ଅନୁବର୍ତ୍ତୀ, *a.* following, attendant upon.
ଅନୁବାଦ, *n.* translation.
ଅନୁବାଦକ, *n.* translator.
ଅନୁବାଦିତ, *a.* translated.
*ଅନୁବୋଧ, *n.* recollection, afterthought.
ଅନୁଭବ, *n.* experience, experimental knowledge.
ଅନୁଭବୀ, *a.* experienced.
ଅନୁଭୂତ, *a.* experienced, felt, guessed, enjoyed.
ଅନୁମତ, *a.* permitted, allowed.
ଅନୁମତି, *n.* consent, permission.
*ଅନୁମନ୍ତା, *n.* one who gives permission.
ଅନୁମାନ, *n.* guess, an inference, a hypothesis.
*ଅନୁମିତ, *n.* an inference, a guess.
ଅନୁମୋଦନ, *n.* assent, as in seconding a resolution.
ଅନୁଯାୟୀ, *ad.* according to ;—*a.* like.
ଅନୁଯୋଗ, *s.* reproof, reprehension.
ଅନୁରକ୍ତ, *a.* attached to, fond of.
ଅନୁରାଗ, *n.* attachment, fondness.

ଅନୁରୂପ, *a.* corresponding with, like.

ଅନୁରୋଧ, *n.* recommendation, agreeing (to move a resolution).

*ଅନୁଶାସନ, *n.* order, law, discipline.

ଅନୁଶୀଳନ, *n.* study, attention.

ଅନୁଶୋଚନା, *n.* repentance. [ment.

*ଅନୁଷଙ୍ଗ, *n.* attachment, agree-

ଅନୁଷ୍ଠାନ, *n.* practice; beginning; topic of discourse. [ed.

ଅନୁଷ୍ଠିତ, *a.* begun; practised; arrang-

*ଅନୁଷ୍ଣ, *a.* not hot, cold. [aim.

ଅନୁସନ୍ଧାନ, *n.* search, investigation,

ଅନୁସନ୍ଧାନୀ, *a.* searching, investigating, looking after.

ଅନୁସରଣ, *n.* following a person.

ଅନୁସରଣୀୟ, *a.* deserving to be followed or attended.

ଅନୁସାରେ, *ad.* accordingly.

*ଅନୁସୂଚକ, *a.* reflecting, indicating.

*ଅନୁସୂଚନା, *n.* reflection, indication.

ଅନୁସ୍ୱାର, the nasal character (ଂ).

ଅନୁକ୍ଷଣ, *ad.* every moment, incessantly. [lor.

*ଅନୂଢ, *a.* unmarried;—*n.* a bache-

*ଅନୂଢା, *a. fem.* unmarried;—*n.* a spinster. [marshy.

*ଅନୂପ, *a.* rich in water, wet,

ଅନୃଣୀ, *a.* not in debt.

*ଅନୃତ, *a.* untrue;—*n.* falsehood.

ଅନେକ, *a.* many, abundant. [ous.

*ଅନେକଧା, *a.* of many sorts, vari-

ଅନୈକ୍ୟ, *n.* want of unity, discord.

*ଅନୌଚିତ୍ୟ, *n.* unfitness, impropriety.

ଅନ୍ତଃ, a *prefix.* inward, inner.

ଅନ୍ତଃକରଣ, *n.* the heart, will.

ଅନ୍ତଃପାତୀ, *a.* included, internal;—*n.* vicinity.

ଅନ୍ତଃପୁର, *n.* inner apartment, a seraglio.

ଅନ୍ତଃସତ୍ତ୍ୱା, *a.* pregnant.

*ଅନ୍ତଃସଲିଳା, *a.* with water (flowing) underground.

ଅନ୍ତଃସ୍ଥ, ଅନ୍ତସ୍ଥ, *a.* being between or at the end.

ଅନ୍ତଃସ୍ଥବର୍ଣ୍ଣ, *n.* the letters ଯ, ର, ଲ, ବ ।

ଅନ୍ତ, *n.* end, extremity; death.

*ଅନ୍ତକ, *a.* fatal, destructive;—*n.* death, *Yama.*

ଅନ୍ତକାଳ, *n.* the time of death.

ଅନ୍ତକୋଷ, *n.* hernia, hydrocele.

ଅନ୍ତତଃ, *ad.* at last, in the end, finally.

ଅନ୍ତବୁଜୁଳା, *n.* the bowels.

ଅନ୍ତର, *n.* the midst; a distance; difference, a remainder; an interval;—*a.* separated, departed; (at the end of a word) other, another (as ଦେଶାନ୍ତର, ସ୍ଥାନାନ୍ତର) ।

ଅନ୍ତରକରିବା, *v.* to subtract; to deprive of favour, love or affection.

ଅନ୍ତରଙ୍ଗ, *n.* a friend;—*a.* intimate.

ଅନ୍ତରଫଳ, *n.* a remainder.

ଅନ୍ତରସ୍ଥ, *a.* internal, situated within.

* ଅନ୍ତଃସତ୍ତ୍ୱା, *a.* pregnant.
ଅନ୍ତରାତ୍ମା, *n.* the soul, the spirit.
ଅନ୍ତରାୟ, *n.* impediment, obstacle.
ଅନ୍ତରାଳ, *n.* included space, gap.
ଅନ୍ତରିତ, *a.* inward, internal; departed, separated; dead.
* ଅନ୍ତରିନ୍ଦ୍ରିୟ, *n.* the mind.
ଅନ୍ତରୀପ, *n.* a cape, a promontory.
* ଅନ୍ତରୀକ୍ଷ, *n.* the sky, atmosphere.
ଅନ୍ତରେ, *ad.* in, within, out of.
ଅନ୍ତର୍ଗତ, *a.* included.
* ଅନ୍ତର୍ଜଳୋତ୍ସ, *n.* artesian fountain.
ଅନ୍ତର୍ଜାତୀୟ, *a.* international.
ଅନ୍ତର୍ଦାହ, *n.* inward burning.
ଅନ୍ତର୍ଦ୍ଧାନ, *n.* disappearance, exit.
ଅନ୍ତର୍ବର୍ତ୍ତୀ, *a.* internal, inward, interior, included.
ଅନ୍ତର୍ଭୁକ୍ତ, ଅନ୍ତର୍ଭୂତ, *a.* taken in, internal, inner; reduced.
ଅନ୍ତର୍ଯାମୀ, *a.* regulating the internal feelings;—*n.* Supreme Spirit as guiding and regulating mankind.
ଅନ୍ତର୍ହିତ, *a.* vanished, disappeared.
ଅନ୍ତି, *n.* the inside of melons, &c., the core.
* ଅନ୍ତିକ, *a.* near, contiguous, adjacent.
ଅନ୍ତିମ, *a.* extreme, final, last, very near.
ଅନ୍ତୁଡ଼ିଶାଳ, *n.* a lying-in room.
ଅନ୍ତେ, *a.* at last, in the end.
* ଅନ୍ତେବାସୀ, *n.* a pupil, a disciple.
ଅନ୍ତ୍ୟ, *a.* last, final, ultimate.

ଅନ୍ତ୍ୟଜ, *a.* born of one of the lowest caste;—*n.* a low-caste person.
ଅନ୍ତ୍ୟେଷ୍ଟି, *n.* a funeral sacrifice.
ଅନ୍ତ୍ର, *n.* the entrails, viscera.
ଅନ୍ଦର, *a.* inner.
ଅନ୍ଦରମହଲ, *n.* inner apartment.
ଅନ୍ଦାଜ, *n.* a guess, a supposition.
ଅନ୍ଦଶା, ଅନ୍ଦେଶା, *n.* expectation.
ଅନ୍ଧ, *a.* blind, sightless.
ଅନ୍ଧକାର, *n.* darkness; dark, obscure.
ଅନ୍ଧକାରମୟ, *a.* dark, cloudy.
ଅନ୍ଧକୂପ, *n.* a dark hole or well overgrown by weeds; hell.
* ଅନ୍ଧତମସ, *n.* gross darkness.
ଅନ୍ଧପୁଟଲି-ଦେବା ବା ଲଗାଇବା, *v.* to cover the eyes; (figuratively) to throw dust in the eyes, to divert the attention of.
ଅନ୍ଧଲା, *a.* blind, sightless.
ଅନ୍ଧାଯୁକ୍ତି, *a* unreasonable, unjust.
ଅନ୍ଧାର, *n.* see ଅନ୍ଧକାର ।
ଅନ୍ଧାରକଣା, *a.* unable to see in the dark;—*n.* night-blindness.
ଅନ୍ଧାରପକ୍ଷ, *n.* wane of the moon.
ଅନ୍ଧାରୁଆ, *a.* nearly blind;—*n.* the twilight.
ଅନ୍ଧିକନ୍ଧି, ଅନ୍ଧିସନ୍ଧି, *n.* a chink, crevice, flaw.
ଅନ୍ଧୁଣୀ, *n.* a blind girl or woman.
ଅନ୍ନ, *n.* food, boiled rice.
ଅନ୍ନକଷ୍ଟ, *n.* famine, scarcity.
ଅନ୍ନଛତ୍ର, *n.* a place where food is bestowed.
ଅନ୍ନଜଳ, *n.* board, maintenance.

ଅନ୍ନଦାତା, *n.* a supporter, a charitable man.

ଅନ୍ନଦାସ, *n.* one who serves for food.

ଅନ୍ନପ୍ରାଶନ, *n.* the ceremony of giving a child rice for the first time.

ଅନ୍ନବସ୍ତ୍ର, *n.* food and clothing, maintenance.

ଅନ୍ନନାଳୀ, ଅନ୍ନବହନାଳୀ, *n.* alimentary canal.

ଅନ୍ନଭୋକ୍ତା, *n.* a vegetarian.

ଅନ୍ନମୟକୋଷ, *n.* the gross material body.

* ଅନ୍ନଯୋଗ, *n.* providing of food.

* ଅନ୍ନରସ, *n.* chyle.

ଅନ୍ନାର୍ଥୀ, *a.* begging for food, hungry.

ଅନ୍ୟ, *a.* and *pron.* another, other, different.

ଅନ୍ୟଗାମୀ, *a.* adulterous; going after others.

ଅନ୍ୟତଃ, *ad.* by or from another.

ଅନ୍ୟତମ, *n.* one of many.

ଅନ୍ୟତର, *pron.* one of two;—*a.* either, other; different.

ଅନ୍ୟତ୍ର, *ad.* elsewhere, in another place.

ଅନ୍ୟଥା, *ad.* otherwise, differently;—*n.* change, alteration;—*a.* changed, altered.

ଅନ୍ୟଦେଶୀୟ, *n.* a foreigner; (in the Bible) a Gentile.

ଅନ୍ୟମତ, *n.* another manner; another sect;—*ad.* otherwise.

ଅନ୍ୟମନସ୍କ, ଅନ୍ୟମନା *a.* absentminded.

ଅନ୍ୟାନ୍ୟ, *a.* others.

ଅନ୍ୟାଯ୍ୟ, *a.* improper, unlawful.

ଅନ୍ୟାୟ, *a.* unjust, wrong;—*n.* injustice, outrage.

ଅନ୍ୟାୟୀ, *a.* unjust.

ଅନ୍ୟୋନ୍ୟ, *a.* reciprocal, mutual.

ଅନ୍ୟୂନ, *a.* not deficient, not less (may be equal or more).

ଅନ୍ୱୟ, *n.* (in *Gram.*) the government of words in a sentence, parsing; * race, lineage.

* ଅନ୍ୱିତ, *a.* formed to, connected with.

ଅନ୍ୱେଷଣ, *n.* inquiry, search, research.

ଅପ, a *prefix*, implying detraction.

ଅପକର୍ଷ, *n.* an evil tendency, a wrong bias.

ଅପକଳଙ୍କ, *n.* an indelible stain, a blot.

ଅପକାର, *n.* an injury, damage.

ଅପକାରକ, ଅପକାରୀ, *a.* mischievous.

ଅପକୀର୍ତ୍ତି, *n.* ill-fame, infamy.

ଅପକୃଷ୍ଟ, *a.* low, bad, debased, inferior.

ଅପକ୍ୱ, *a.* unripe, raw, immature.

* ଅପଘାତ, *n.* a violent death, murder.

ଅପଚୟ, *n.* detriment, waste, loss.

ଅପକ୍ୱର, *n.* indigestion;—*a.* undigested.

* ଅପଚିତ, *a.* lost, dispersed, wasted

* ଅପଚ୍ଛାୟା, *n.* a phantom, spectre.

ଅପଟାନ୍ତର, *a.* peerless, matchless, unique.

ଅପଟୁ, *a.* incapable, unskilled; diseased.

ଅପଠ, *n.* contention, quarrel.

ଅପଣ୍ଡିତ, *a.* unlearned, ignorant.
ଅପତ୍ୟ, *n.* a child ; off-spring.
ଅପତ୍ନୀକ, *a.* wifeless;—*n.* a widower.
ଅପଥ, *n.* a bad road, no road.
ଅପଥ୍ୟ, *a.* unwholesome, unsuitable.
ଅପଦସ୍ଥ, *a.* degraded, insulted.
ଅପଦାର୍ଥ, *a.* unsubstantial, empty;—*n.* a nonentity.
* ଅପଦେଶ, *n.* a pretext, pretence.
ଅପନୟନ, *n.* removing, extracting, destroying. [pulled off.
* ଅପନୀତ, *a.* taken away, removed,
ଅପନୋଦନ, *n.* removing.
ଅପଲୁଣ୍ଠ, *n.* desert.
ଅପବର୍ଗ, *n.* emancipation of the soul.
ଅପବାଦ, *n.* censure, accusation, libel
ଅପବାଦଜନକ, *a.* libellous.
ଅପବିତ୍ର, *a.* unholy, impure, unclean.
ଅପବ୍ୟୟ, *n.* prodigal expenditure.
ଅପବ୍ୟୟୀ, *a.* prodigal;—*n.* a squanderer, a prodigal. [age.
* ଅପଭାଷା, *n.* low or vulgar langu-
* ଅପଭ୍ରଂଶ, *n.* low term, vulgar talk ; a fall. [disrespect.
ଅପମାନ, *n.* dishonour, disgrace,
ଅପମୃତ୍ୟୁ, *n.* unnatural or untimely death. [fame.
ଅପଯଶ, *n.* disgrace, infamy, ill-
ଅପର, *a.* and *pron.* another, other.
ଅପରରାତ୍ର, *n.* the end of the night.
ଅପରଲୋକ, *n.* other people ; another world. [feated.
ଅପରାଜିତ, *a.* unconquered, not de-
ଅପରାଜିତା, *n.* *Doorga* ; the name of a creeping plant.
ଅପରାଧ, *n.* guilt, sin, fault, crime.
ଅପରାଧୀ, *a.* criminal, guilty, sinful.
ଅପରାହ୍ନ, *n.* the afternoon. [known.
ଅପରିଚିତ, *a.* unacquainted with, un-
ଅପରିଷ୍କୃତ, *a.* impure, undressed.
ଅପରିଚ୍ଛିନ୍ନ, *a.* unlimited.
ଅପରିପକ୍ୱ, *a.* unripe.
ଅପରିମିତ, *a.* immoderate; unmeasured, unlimited.
ଅପରିଷ୍କାର, *a.* impure, unclean.
ଅପରୀକ୍ଷିତ, *a.* untried, unexamined.
ଅପରୂପ, *a.* queer, distorted, ugly.
ଅପର୍ତ୍ତିଅଣି, *n.* a child left in a family whose elder brothers and sisters and one or more younger ones have died. [unlimited.
ଅପର୍ଯ୍ୟାପ୍ତ, *a.* more than sufficient,
* ଅପଲାପ, *n.* denial, evasion ; low discourse.
ଅପଶବ୍ଦ, *n.* rustic or low language.
ଅପସାରିତ, *a.* driven off, removed.
ଅପସ୍ମାର, *n.* epilepsy, falling sickness.
ଅପହରଣ, *n.* robbing, purloining.
ଅପହାରକ, *n.* a robber, a plunderer.
ଅପହୃତ, *a.* stolen, gained by plun- [der.
ଅପକ୍ଷପାତ, *n.* impartiality.
ଅପା, *n.* eldest sister. [uncooked.
ଅପାକ, *n.* indigestion ;—*a.* unripe;
ଅପାଙ୍ଗ, *n.* outer corner of the eye; * a cripple.

ଅପାଠ, *n.* a corrupt reading, unauthentic writing.

ଅପାଠୁଆ, *a.* ignorant, unlettered, stupid.

ଅପାତ୍ର, *a.* unfit, unworthy ;—*n.* unworthy person.

ଅପାଦାନ, *n.* (in *Gram.*) Ablative case.

* ଅପାନ, *n.* one of the five life-winds in the body.

* ଅପାବୃତ, *a.* opened, laid bare.

ଅପାମାର୍ଗ, *n.* the name of a medicinal plant.

* ଅପାୟ, *n.* destruction; hindrance.

ଅପାର, *a.* impassable, boundless, shoreless.

ଅପାରକ, ଅପାରଗ. *a.* incapable, incompetent.

ଅପାଳକ, *n.* want of rain ;—*a.* not maintaining or cherishing.

ଅପାଲଟି, *a.* see ଅଣଲେଉଟି ।

ଅପି, *conj.* (used as *prefix* or *suffix*), moreover, likewise, also, and.

ଅପିଚ, *conj.* moreover, also.

ଅପିତୃକ, *a.* fatherless.

ଅପୁତ୍ର, ଅପୁତ୍ରକ, *a.* sonless, without progeny.

ଅପୁରୁଷ, *n.* an eunuch ;—*a.* unmanly.

ଅପୂଜା, ଅପୂଜ୍ୟ, *a.* unworthy of worship.

ଅପୂର୍ଣ୍ଣ, *a.* unfilled.

ଅପୂର୍ବ, *a.* unprecedented, uncommon, excellent.

* ଅପେୟ, *a.* not fit to be drunk.

ଅପେକ୍ଷା, *n.* expectation, waiting for, hope ;—*conj.* than.

ଅପେକ୍ଷାକୃତ, *ad.* comparatively.

ଅପେକ୍ଷିତ, *a.* looked for, expected ; expectant, anxious.

* ଅପୋଗଣ୍ଡ, *n.* a child from five to sixteen years.

ଅପୌରୁଷ, ଅପୌରୁଷେୟ, *a.* superhuman ; unmanly, cowardly.

ଅପ୍ରକାର, *a.* bad, vile, disagreeable.

ଅପ୍ରକାଶିତ, *a.* secret, private, not manifest.

ଅପ୍ରକୃତ, *a.* spurious, improper.

ଅପ୍ରତିକାର୍ଯ୍ୟ, *a.* irremediable, irretrievable.

* ଅପ୍ରତିଭ, *a.* abashed, nonplussed.

* ଅପ୍ରତିମ, *a.* unparalleled, peerless.

ଅପ୍ରତିହତ, *a.* unaffected; unobstructed.

* ଅପ୍ରତୁଳ, *n.* want, need, exigency.

ଅପ୍ରତ୍ୟୟ, *n.* unbelief, mistrust.

ଅପ୍ରଧାନ, *a.* inferior, small.

ଅପ୍ରମାଣ, ଅପ୍ରମାଣିତ, *a.* not trustworthy, unproved.

ଅପ୍ରମାଦ, *n.* caution, safety, heed.

* ଅପ୍ରମେୟ, *a.* incapable of proof, improbable ; immeasurable.

ଅପ୍ରୟୋଜନ, *a.* needless, unnecessary.

ଅପ୍ରଶସ୍ତ, *a.* narrow, scanty, strait.

ଅପ୍ରସନ୍ନ, *a.* unpropitious, displeased.

ଅପ୍ରସ୍ତୁତ, *a.* not ready, unprepared, abashed, confounded, nonplussed.

ଅପ୍ରାକୃତ, *a.* uncommon.

ଅପ୍ରାପ୍ତ, *a.* unobtained.

ଅପ୍ରାପ୍ତବୟସ୍କ, ଅପ୍ରାପ୍ତବ୍ୟବହାର, *a.* under age, minor ;—*n.* a minor.

ଅପ୍ରାପ୍ତି, *n.* non-attainment. [be got.
ଅପ୍ରାପ୍ୟ, *a.* unobtainable, difficult to
ଅପ୍ରାମାଣିକ, *a.* unproved, incredible.
ଅପ୍ରିୟ, *a.* unamiable; not beloved.
ଅପ୍ରୀତି *n.* want of love, dislike, disgust. [sive.
ଅପ୍ରୀତିକର, *a.* disagreeable, offen-
ଅପ୍ସରସ, *n.* courtesans of the Hindu heaven.
ଅପୂର୍ବାଚର, *a.* surprising.
ଅଫଳନ୍ତ, *a.* fruitless, sterile, barren.
ଅଫିମ, *n.* opium. [away.
ଅବ, *prefix.* implying from, off,
ଅବକଳନା, *n.* an incorrect calculation.
ଅବକାଶ, *n.* leisure, opportunity.
ଅବକ୍ତବ୍ୟ, *a.* not fit or proper to be spoken, unutterable.
ଅବଖୁର, *n.* a small water vessel made of brass.
ଅବଗତ, *a.* known, acquainted with.
ଅବଗମ, *n.* knowledge, comprehension, perception. [ablution.
ଅବଗାହନ, *n.* immersion, bathing,
* ଅବଗୁଣ୍ଠନ, *n.* a veil (for the face).
* ଅବଗୁଣ୍ଠନବତୀ, *a.* (a woman) covered with a veil.
ଅବଚ୍ଛିନ୍ନ, *a.* limited.
ଅବଚ୍ଛେଦ, *n.* a limit, boundary.
ଅବଜ୍ଞା, *n.* contempt, despite, disregard.
ଅବଜ୍ଞାତ, *a.* despised, contemned. [ed.
ଅବଟା, *a.* not pulverized or pound-

ଅବଢ଼ା, *n.* boiled rice sold at Puri.
* ଅବତରଣ, *n.* the descending from a situation.
ଅବତରଣିକା, preface. [gem.
* ଅବତଂସ, *n.* a crest, an ear-ring,
ଅବତାର, *n.* a descent, incarnation.
ଅବତାରଣା, *n.* preface or introduction (to a work).
ଅବତୀର୍ଣ୍ଣ, *a.* descended, incarnate.
* ଅବଦ୍ୟ, *a.* unspeakable; blamable, faulty.
ଅବଧାନ, *n.* a schoolmaster; attention; care. [sis.
ଅବଧାରଣ, *n.* determining; empha-
ଅବଧାରିତ, *a.* emphatic, settled, fixed on, ascertained.
ଅବଧାର୍ଯ୍ୟ, *a.* fixable, determinable.
ଅବଧି, *n.* extreme limit; from—to.
*ଅବଧୀରଣା, *n.* disregard, disrespect.
ଅବଧୂତ, *n.* a class of devotee, free from ceremonial rules.
ଅବଧ୍ୟ, *a* not deserving of death, not to be slain. [graded.
ଅବନତ, *a.* bowed, bent down, de-
ଅବନତି, *n.* degradation.
* ଅବନୀ, ଅବନି, *n.* the earth, the world.
ଅବନ୍ତୀ, *n.* ancient name of Malabar; used as the name of a female and meaning everlasting.
* ଅବବୋଧ, *n.* perception, judgment, discrimination.
* ଅବବୋଧକ, *a.* indicating, showing.

ଅବମାନ, *n.* dishonour, disgrace.
ଅବମାନନା, *n.* disrespect, disesteem.
ଅବମାନିତ, *a.* despised, disregarded.
ଅବୟବ, *n.* a limb, part, feature.
ଅବରୁଦ୍ଧ, *a.* beseiged, imprisoned ; obstructed.
ଅବରୋଧ, *n.* inner apartment, seraglio ; a beseiging ; obstacle.
* ଅବରୋହ, *n.* a descent, the roots of the banyan tree hanging from its branches.
ଅବରୋହଣ, *n.* descending, alighting.
ଅବର୍ତ୍ତମାନ, *a.* non-existent, absent, dead, not present.
ଅବର୍ଣ୍ୟା, *a.* ugly, nasty. [fulcrum.
ଅବଲମ୍ବ, ଅବଲମ୍ବନ, *n.* a prop, support,
ଅବଳା, *n.* a young woman. [merrily.
ଅବଲୀଳାକ୍ରମେ, *ad.* easily, playfully,
* ଅବଲେହ, *n.* a medicine taken by lapping. [lapping.
* ଅବଲେହନ, *n.* act of licking or
ଅବଲୋକନ, *n.* looking at, viewing.
ଅବଶ, *a.* unsubjected ; benumbed.
ଅବଶିଷ୍ଟ, *a.* remaining, left.
ଅବଶେଷ, *n.* remainder, residue, balance. [necessary.
ଅବଶ୍ୟ, *ad.* certainly ;—*a.* certain,
ଅବଶ୍ୟମ୍ଭାବୀ, *a.* inevitable, sure to happen. [hausted.
ଅବସନ୍ନ, *a.* wearied, fatigued, ex-
ଅବସର, *n.* leisure, opportunity.
ଅବସରକ୍ରମେ, *ad.* leisurely, opportunely.

ଅବସରପ୍ରାପ୍ତ, *a.* retired. [dejection.
ଅବସାଦ, *n.* weariness, lassitude,
ଅବସାନ, *n.* extinction, conclusion, decline (as of the day).
ଅବସ୍ତୁ, *a.* vain, unsubstantial.
ଅବସ୍ଥା, *n.* condition, state, plight ; distress. [fixed state.
ଅବସ୍ଥାନ, *n.* a lodging, residence; a
ଅବସ୍ଥାନ୍ତର, *n.* different state or condition.
ଅବସ୍ଥାପନ୍ନ, *a.* holding a good position, influential.
ଅବସ୍ଥାପିତ, *a.* fixed or settled by.
ଅବସ୍ଥିତ, *a.* situated, settled.
ଅବସ୍ଥିତି, *n.* a dwelling, settlement.
* ଅବହିତ, *a.* attentive, careful.
ଅବହେଳା, *n.* neglect, disregard.
ଅବା, *conj.* or, perhaps, otherwise.
ଅବାକ୍, *a.* speechless, mute.
* ଅବାଚୀ, *n.* the south.
* ଅବାଚ୍ୟ, *a.* not fit to be spoken.
ଅବାଟ, *n.* the wrong way. [ly.
ଅବାଧରେ, ଅବାଧେ, *ad.* easily, smooth-
ଅବାଧ୍ୟ, *a.* disobedient, uncontrollable, obstinate.
ଅବାନ୍ତର, *a.* secondary ; extra ; situated between.
* ଅବାରଣୀୟ, *a.* irresistible.
ଅବାରିତ, *a.* unimpeded, free.
ଅବିକଳ, *a.* exact, correct.
ଅବିକା, *ad.* now;—*a.* unsold. [ness.
ଅବିଗୁଣ, *n.* injuriousness, harmful-
ଅବିଚଳିତ, *a.* fixed, steady.

ଅବିଚାର, *n.* injustice, unjust judgment.

ଅବିଚ୍ଛେଦ୍ୟ, *a.* inseparable.

ଅବିଜ୍ଞ, *a.* unlearned, ignorant.

ଅବିଘ୍ନ, *n.* freedom from impediment or obstruction ;–*a.* unhindered.

ଅବିଦିତ, *a.* unknown, unacquainted.

* ଅବିଦ୍ୟ, *a.* unlearned, uninstructed.

ଅବିଦ୍ୟମାନ, *a.* unperceived, absent.

ଅବିଦ୍ୟା, *n.* lack of science or wisdom ; illusion.

ଅବିଦ୍ୱାନ୍, *a.* unlearned, ignorant.

ଅବିଧି, *a.* lawless, illegal.

ଅବିନୟ, *n.* want of humility, arrogance, pride.

ଅବିନଶ୍ୱର, *a.* everlasting.

ଅବିନୀତ, *a.* immodest, wicked.

* ଅବିପନ୍ନ, *a.* not involved in misfortune.

ଅବିବାହିତ, *a.* unmarried (man).

ଅବିବାହିତା, *a.* unmarried (woman).

ଅବିବେକ, ଅବିବେକୀ, *a.* indiscriminative ; thoughtless.

ଅବିବେଚକ, *n.* one who does not discriminate;–*a.* unthinking, rash.

ଅବିବେଚନା, *n.* want of consideration or thought, rashness.

ଅବିଭକ୍ତ, *a.* undivided, entire.

ଅବିଭାଜ୍ୟ, *a.* indivisible.

ଅବିର, *n.* red powder used at *hori* festival.

ଅବିରତ, *a.* incessant, perpetual ;–*ad.* incessantly, perpetually.

ଅବିରଳ, *a.* dense, thick, plentiful, abundant.

ଅବିଶ୍ରମ, *a.* incessant, continuous ;–*ad.* incessantly.

ଅବିରୋଧ, *n.* peace, concord, harmony.

ଅବିଳମ୍ବ, *a.* prompt, without delay.

ଅବିଶ୍ରାନ୍ତ, *a.* untiring, unrested, incessant.

ଅବିଶ୍ୱସ୍ତ, - *a.* unfaithful, dishonest, treacherous.

ଅବିଶ୍ୱାସ, *n.* distrust, incredulity.

ଅବିଢ଼ା, ଅଢ଼ିଅଡ଼ା, *a.* unmarried (man).

ଅବିଢ଼ାଣୀ, ଅଢ଼ିଅଣୀ, *a.* unmarried (woman).

ଅବିହିତ, *a.* improper.

ଅବୁଝା, *a.* headstrong, obstinate, stupid, refusing to understand.

ଅବେଳ, *n.* an inconvenient time.

ଅବୈତନିକ, *a.* unpaid, honorary.

ଅବୈଧ, *a.* forbidden ; illegal.

ଅବୋଧ, *a.* stupid, senseless, ignorant.

ଅବ୍ଦ, *n.* a year, an era.

ଅବ୍ୟକ୍ତ, *a.* unpublished, indistinct, latent.

ଅବ୍ୟବସ୍ଥିତ, *a.* fickle, unstable, unmethodical.

ଅବ୍ୟବହାର୍ଯ୍ୟ, *a.* impracticable, unfit to be brought into common use.

ଅବ୍ୟବହିତ, *a.* immediate, following.

ଅବ୍ୟବହୃତ, *a.* not commonly used, not practised.

ଅବ୍ୟୟ, *a.* undiminishable ; (in Gram.) indeclinable (part of speech).

ଅବ୍ୟର୍ଥ, *a.* infallible, effectual.

* ଅବ୍ୟାଜ, *n.* honesty, simplicity, sincerity.
ଅବ୍ୟାଜରେ, *ad.* sincerely, naturally.
ଅବ୍ୟାପାର, *n.* interference in another's business.
* ଅବ୍ୟାହତ, *a.* unobstructed, free.
ଅବ୍ୟାହତି, *n.* release, freedom.
ଅଭକ୍ତି, *n.* want of devotion, irreverence ; unbelief, incredulity.
ଅଭଦ୍ର, *a.* impolite, evil, bad.
* ଅଭବ୍ୟ, *a.* uncivil, rude. [less.
ଅଭୟ, *n.* security, safety;—*a.* fear-
ଅଭକ୍ଷ୍ୟ, *a.* unfit for food, uneatable.
ଅଭାଗା, *a.* unfortunate, unlucky, wretched, forlorn, destitute.
ଅଭାଗିନୀ, *a.* unlucky (woman).
ଅଭାଗ୍ୟ, *n.* misfortune;—*a.* unlucky.
ଅଭାଜନ, *a.* unfit, not trustworthy.
ଅଭାବ, *n.* want, non-existence.
ଅଭି, a *prefix*, towards, to ; over, above, etc.
ଅଭି, ଅଭିଟା, *ad.* now, instantly.
ଅଭିଜ୍ଞ, *a.* learned, skilful, wise.
ଅଭିଜ୍ଞାନ, *n.* certainty ; a token, signal.
ଅଭିଜ୍ଞାନପତ୍ର, *n.* a certificate. [lary.
ଅଭିଧାନ, *n.* a dictionary, a vocabu-
* ଅଭିଧେୟ, *a.* explainable ;—*n.* a name. [lation, praise.
ଅଭିନନ୍ଦନ, *n.* welcome, congratu-
ଅଭିନବ, *a.* new, recent, modern.
ଅଭିନୟ, *n.* a play, a theatrical representation.
ଅଭିନିବିଷ୍ଟ, *a.* intent on, engaged in, occupied with.
ଅଭିନିବେଶ, *n.* intentness, application.
ଅଭିନୀତ, *a.* represented dramatically, performed.
ଅଭିନେତା, *n.* an actor.
ଅଭିନ୍ନ, *a.* unseparated, whole, entire ; identical.
ଅଭିପ୍ରାୟ, *n.* purpose, meaning, design, aim. [signed.
ଅଭିପ୍ରେତ, *a.* intended, aimed at, de-
* ଅଭିବନ୍ଦନ, *n.* salutation ; addressing, etc.
ଅଭିବାଦନ, *n.* reverential salutation, respectful obeisance.
* ଅଭିବ୍ୟକ୍ତ, *a.* declared, revealed, expressed.
ଅଭିଭାବକ, *n.* a guardian, protector.
ଅଭିଭୂତ, *a.* aggrieved, defeated, subdued.
ଅଭିମତ, *a.* approved, wished, chosen; —*n.* meaning, design.
ଅଭିମାନ, *n.* pride, self-esteem.
ଅଭିମାନୀ, *a.* proud.
ଅଭିମୁଖ, *a.* facing;—*n.* front.
ଅଭିଯାନ, *n.* marching against, attack, assault. [blamed.
ଅଭିଯୁକ୍ତ, *a.* accused in a court,
* ଅଭିଯୋକ୍ତା, *n.* a plaintiff, an assailant.
ଅଭିଯୋଗ, *n.* a plaint, an accusation.
* ଅଭିରାମ, *a.* beautiful, pleasing.
ଅଭିରୁଚି, *n.* relish, inclination, taste.

ଅଭିଳାଷ, *n.* a wish, a desire, lust.

ଅଭିଲଜ୍ଜ, *a.* shameless.

* ଅଭିଲେଖନ, *n.* writing down, copying.

ଅଭିଶପ୍ତ, *a.* cursed, imprecated.

ଅଭିଶାପ, *n.* a curse, imprecation.

ଅଭିଷିକ୍ତ, *a.* installed to office, anointed.

ଅଭିଷେକ, *n.* installation to office, anointing.

ଅଭିସନ୍ଧି, *n.* purpose, object; deceit.

ଅଭିସମ୍ପାତ, *n.* a curse; * confluence, meeting together.

ଅଭିସାର, *n.* secret meeting of lovers.

ଅଭିସାରିକା, *n.* a woman who either goes to meet her lover or keep a secret appointment.

ଅଭିହିତ, *a.* spoken, disclosed.

ଅଭୀଷ୍ଟ, *a.* desired, beloved.

* ଅଭୁକ୍ତ, *a.* unfed, without food; uneaten.

ଅଭୂତପୂର୍ବ, *a.* without previous existence, wonderful.

ଅଭେକ, *a.* undressed, undisguised.

ଅଭେକା, *a.* destitute of food or clothing.

ଅଭେଦ, *n.* identity, similarity.

ଅଭେଦ୍ୟ, *a.* impenetrable, inseparable.

ଅଭ୍ୟନ୍ତର, *n.* the inside, the middle; —*a.* internal, inward.

ଅଭ୍ୟର୍ଥନା, *n.* a welcome, a request.

ଅଭ୍ୟସ୍ତ, *a.* having learned by practice, habituated; expert, exercised.

ଅଭ୍ୟାଗତ, *n.* a guest, visitor.

ଅଭ୍ୟାସ, *n.* practice, study, a habit.

ଅଭ୍ୟାସୀ, *a.* studious, practising, exercising.

ଅଭ୍ୟୁତ୍ଥାନ, *n.* rise, exaltation; rising in honour of.

* ଅଭ୍ୟୁଦୟ, *n.* prosperity, welfare.

ଅଭ୍ର, *n.* talc mineral; * the sky, cloud.

ଅଭ୍ରଙ୍କଷ, *a.* touching the clouds, very high.

ଅଭ୍ରାତୃକ, *a.* having no brothers.

ଅଭ୍ରାନ୍ତ, *a.* not mistaken.

ଅମଙ୍ଗ, *a.* averse, reluctant, unwilling.

ଅମଙ୍ଗଳ, *n.* evil, disaster, calamity.

ଅମଡ଼ା, *a.* not trodden, fresh.

ଅମଣିଆ, *a.* not trained, not broken in.

ଅମତ, *a.* not agreed;—*n.* disapproval, dislike.

ଅମନୁଷ୍ୟ, *a.* inhuman, vile.

ଅମପା, *a.* unmeasured.

ଅମର, *a.* immortal, undying.

ଅମରତ୍ୱ, *n.* immortality.

ଅମରାବତୀ, *n.* the residence of *Indra.*

ଅମର୍ଯ୍ୟାଦା, *n.* dishonour, disgrace, disrespect.

* ଅମର୍ଷ, *n.* anger, displeasure, impatience.

ଅମଲ, *n.* intoxicating drugs or spirits; jurisdiction.

ଅମଲୀ, *n.* one who uses intoxicating drugs or spirits.

ଅମାତୃକ, *a.* motherless, not maternal.

ଅମାତ୍ୟ, *n.* minister of state; an attendant.

ଅମାନକ, *a.* disobedient, regardless, arrogant.
ଅମାନତ, *n.* a deposit.
ଅମା'ନିଆ, *a.* disobedient. [pectable.
ଅମାନ୍ୟ, *a.* disrespectful, not res-
ଅମାପ, *a.* unmeasured.
ଅମାବସ୍ୟା, ଅମାବାସ୍ୟା, ଅମାସ୍ୟା, ଅମାସିଆ, *n.* the change of the moon.
ଅମାୟିକ, *a.* sincere, without guile.
ଅମାର, *n.* storehouse for grain.
ଅମାରି, ଅମାରୀ, *n.* a *houda* with a hood.
ଅମାର୍ଜିତ, *a.* not cleansed, not scour-
ed. [ed.
ଅମିତ, *a.* unmeasured, unnumber-
ଅମିତ୍ର, *n.* an enemy;—*a.* friendless.
ଅମିନ, *n.* Amin, one who measures land.
ଅମିଶ୍ର, *a.* pure, unadulterated; a whole (number).
ଅମୀର, *n.* a rich man.
ଅମୁକ, ଅମୁକେର, *pron.* a certain person or thing. [door.
ଅମୁହାଁ, *a.* without an opening or
ଅମୂଳକ, *a.* unfounded, baseless.
ଅମୂଲ୍ୟ, *a.* invaluable, priceless.
ଅମୃତ, *a.* not dead;—*n.* water of life, nectar. [Jagannath.
ଅମୃତମଣୋହି, *n.* property offered to
*ଅମେଧ୍ୟ, *a.* unholy. [union.
ଅମେଳ, *n.* the want of union, dis-
ଅମୋଘ, *a.* infallible, effectual.
* ଅମ୍ବର, *n.* the sky, a cloud; * ap-
*ଅମ୍ବୁ, *n.* water. [parel.
* ଅମ୍ବୁକଣା, *n.* a drop of water, rain.
*ଅମ୍ବୁଜ, *n.* an aquatic plant, a lotus.
*ଅମ୍ବୁଦ, *n.* a cloud.
* ଅମ୍ବୁଧି, *n.* the sea.
* ଅମ୍ବୁରାଶି, *n.* sea, ocean.
ଅମ୍ଭୋଦାରା, *a.* very generous.
ଅମ୍ଳ, *a.* acid, sour, tart;—*n.* sour thing.
ଅମ୍ଳପିତ୍ତ, *n.* an acidity of the stomach.
ଅମ୍ଳାନ, *a.* unfading, imperishable.
ଅଲ୍ଲଣିଆ, *a.* offered to gods.
ଅଯତ୍ନ, *n.* want of care or diligence.
ଅଯଥା, *a.* unlike, improper. [per.
ଅଯଥାର୍ଥ, *a.* untrue, unjust, impro-
*ଅୟନ, *n.* sun's course north or south of the equator, a going.
ଅଯଶଃ, *n.* dishonour, infamy.
*ଅୟସ୍କାନ୍ତ, *n.* a loadstone, magnet.
ଅଯାଚିତ, *a.* unasked, unsolicited.
ଅୟି, ଅୟେ, *interj.* oh! ah!
ଅଯୁକ୍ତ, *a.* unconnected, incompatible. [even.
ଅଯୁଗ୍ମ, *a.* single, separate; odd, un-
ଅଯୁତ, *a.* ten thousand.
ଅଯୋଗ୍ୟ, *a.* unfit, unworthy, improper, unsuitable
ଅଯୋଧ୍ୟା, *n.* name of a city, *Oude.*
ଅଯୌକ୍ତିକ, *a.* unreasonable.
ଅର, *n.* felloe of a wheel.
ଅରଟ, *n.* a spinning-wheel.
ଅରଖ୍, ଅରଖି, *n.* spirituous liquor.
ଅରଣ, ଅରଣା, *n.* a wild buffalo.
ଅରଣ୍ୟ, *n.* a forest, a wilderness.

* ଅରଣ୍ୟାନୀ, *n.* a large forest or desert.

* ଅରବିନ୍ଦ, *n.* a water-lily, lotus.

ଅରମା, *a.* overgrown by weeds, dirty.

ଅରମାନ, *n.* dishonour, distress.

ଅରସିକ, *a.* not witty, dull.

ଅରକ୍ଷକ, *a.* without a keeper or shepherd.

ଅରକ୍ଷିତ, *a.* friendless, forlorn, wretched.

ଅରାଜକ, *a.* anarchical, without a king.

ଅରାଜକତା, *n.* anarchy.

* ଅରାତି, *n.* an enemy, adversary.

* ଅରି *n.* an enemy, a foe.

* ଅରିନ୍ଦମ, *a.* victorious, conquering.

* ଅରିଷ୍ଟ, *n.* good or bad luck; a sign of death.

ଅରୁଆ, *n.* dry-husked rice.

ଅରୁଚି, *n.* disgust for food; aversion, dislike.

ଅରୁଚିକର, *a.* producing disrelish or disgust.

ଅରୁଣ, *n.* aurora ; the dawn.

ଅରୁଣିମା, *n.* redness, reddish colour.

ଅରୁଣୋଦୟ, *n.* first peep of day.

* ଅରୁନ୍ଧତୀ, *n.* the name of a planet ; the name of the wife of *Basistha.*

ଅରୁଦ୍ଧ, *a.* uncovered, open, not screened.

ଅରୂପ, *a.* shapeless; deformed, ugly, distorted.

ଅର୍ଗଳ, *n.* a bar, a bolt.

ଅର୍ଗଳା, *n.* a small door, a window.

* ଅର୍ଘ, *n.* price.

* ଅର୍ଘ୍ୟ, *n.* an oblation consisting of purified water, sundried rice and *Durba* grass;—*a.* worshipful.

* ଅର୍ଚ୍ଚକ, *n.* a worshipper.

ଅର୍ଚ୍ଚନା, *n.* worship, homage, adoration.

ଅର୍ଚ୍ଚିତ, *a.* worshipped, adored.

ଅର୍ଜ୍ଜକ, *a.* acquiring, earning, procuring ;—*n.* earner.

ଅର୍ଜ୍ଜନ, *n.* earnings, gain, acquisition of wealth.

ଅର୍ଜ୍ଜିତ, *a.* earned, acquired.

ଅର୍ଜି, ଅରଜି, *n.* a petition, a plaint.

ଅର୍ଜ୍ଜୁନ, *n.* the name of the third son of *Pándu.*

ଅର୍ଣ୍ଣବ, *n.* the ocean, sea.

* ଅର୍ଣ୍ଣବତରୀ, ଅର୍ଣ୍ଣବପୋତ, ଅର୍ଣ୍ଣବଯାନ, *n.* a ship.

ଅର୍ଥ, *n.* meaning ; wealth ; object.

ଅର୍ଥକର, *a.* money-making.

ଅର୍ଥଦଣ୍ଡ, *n.* a fine, penalty.

ଅର୍ଥପ୍ରୟୋଗ, *n.* using, the application of wealth as to trade, &c.

ଅର୍ଥପ୍ରାପ୍ତି, *n.* profit, gain; interest of money.

* ଅର୍ଥବିତ୍, *a.* discriminating, wise.

ଅର୍ଥଶାସ୍ତ୍ର, *n.* the science of ethics.

ଅର୍ଥାଗମ, *n.* substantial income.

ଅର୍ଥାତ୍, *ad.* namely, that is to say, viz.

ଅର୍ଥାନ୍ତର, *n.* another meaning.

ଅର୍ଥୀ, *n.* a plaintiff, a petitioner, a beggar.

ଅର୍ଥେ, *ad.* (in Composition used as an *affix*) for the purpose of, with a view to.

ଅର୍ଦ୍ଧ, *a.* half, a moiety.

ଅର୍ଦ୍ଧଚନ୍ଦ୍ର, *n.* a crescent, a half-moon; a slap, a push with the hand at the back of the neck.

ଅର୍ଦ୍ଧରାତ୍ର, *n.* midnight.

ଅର୍ଦ୍ଧାଙ୍ଗ, *n.* half the body; a wife (better-half).

ଅର୍ଦ୍ଧାଂଶ, *n.* a half-share, a half.

ଅର୍ପଣ, *n.* bestowing, a delivering up.

ଅର୍ପିତ, *a.* delivered, consigned, placed.

ଅର୍ବୁଦ, *a.* and *n.* a hundred millions, 100,000,000; * a wen.

ଅର୍ଣ୍ଣା, *a.* overrun with weeds or creepers, (see ଅରଣ୍ୟା).

ଅର୍ଶୀ, *n.* (see ଅର୍ଶ).

ଅର୍ଶ, *n.* hemorrhoids or piles.

ଅଳକା, *n.* a woman's hair brought low over the forehead, a side curl; an ornament for holding the bair on the forehead; * city of *Kubera*.

ଅଳଙ୍କାର, *n.* ornaments for personal adornment; also used rhetorically.

ଅଳଙ୍କୃତ, *a.* adorned, decorated.

ଅଳତା, *n.* a red dye used by women to paint their feet; lac.

ଅଳନ୍ଧୁ, ଅଳନ୍ଧୁମ, *n.* a spider's web turned black with smoke, soot.

ଅଳସ, ଅଳସୁଆ, *a.* indolent, slothful, lazy.

* **ଅଲକ୍ତ, ଅଲକ୍ତକ**, *n.* lac;—*a.* saturated with lac.

ଅଲଗା, *a.* separate, distinct, different, unconnected.

ଅଲଗୁଣା, *n.* a clothes-horse, something to hang clothes on, clothes-rack.

ଅଲଗ୍ନ, *a.* unconnected, not in contact.

ଅଲଙ୍ଘନ, *n.* breaking the fast.

ଅଲଙ୍ଘ୍ୟ, *a.* inviolable, not to be disobeyed with impunity.

ଅଲଜ୍ଜ, *a.* destitute of shame, shameless.

ଅଲଣା, *a.* not salted, insipid.

ଅଲଣାକଥା, *n.* useless talk.

ଅଲକ୍ଷଣ, *n.* bad omen, evil signs.

ଅଲକ୍ଷିତ, *a.* unseen, unperceived, unmarked.

ଅଲକ୍ଷ୍ମୀ, *n.* misfortune, the goddess of misfortune.

ଅଲକ୍ଷ୍ୟ, *a.* undistinguishable.

ଅଲଜ୍ଜକ, *a.* shameless.

* **ଅଲାବୁ, ଅଲାବୂ**, *n.* gourd, bottle-gourd.

ଅଲାଭ, *n.* loss, detriment.

ଅଲାଇଚ, *n.* cardamoms.

ଅଲାଇବଲାଇ, ଅଲେଇବଲେଇ, *n.* the good or ill that befalls man; disturbance, calamity; responsibility.

ଅଲାଣି, *n.* an unworthy or useless fellow.

ଅଲଗେଇବା, *a.* separate, distinct.

ଅଳି, *n.* importunity; * humble-bee.

ଅଳିଅ, *a.* unswept, untidy ;—*n.* scattered rubbish, litter.

ଅଳୀକ, ଅଲୀକ, *a.* false, vain, useless.

ଅଲେଖ, *n.* the name of a religious sect that recognise no written scripture, but worship the sun as Supreme God.

ଅଲେଖା, *a.* unwritten.

ଅଲୌଢତ, *a.* surprising, astonishing.

ଅଲୌକିକ, *a.* supernatural.

ଅଳ୍ପ, *a.* a few, little, small.

ଅଳ୍ପାୟୁ, *a.* short-lived.

ଅଲ୍ଲଳ, *a.* fondled, caressed, spoilt, (said of children or women).

ଅଶକ୍ତ, *a.* unable, weak, infirm.

ଅଶକ୍ୟ, *a.* impossible, impracticable.

* ଅଶନ, *n.* act of eating ; food.

* ଅଶନି, *n.* thunder-bolt, lightning.

ଅଶରଣ, *a.* helpless, forlorn.

ଅଶରୀରୀ, *a.* incorporeal, immaterial; * *n.* the name of the God of love.

ଅଶାନ୍ତ, *a.* not placid, turbulent, distressed.

ଅଶାନ୍ତି, *n.* want of tranquility, disturbance, restlessness.

ଅଶାସ୍ତ୍ର, *a.* unorthodox, unlawful.

ଅଶାସ୍ତ୍ରୀୟ, *a.* inconsistent with the written law or scripture.

ଅଶିଷ୍ଟ, *a.* rude, ill-bred, clownish.

ଅଶିଷ୍ଟାଚାର, *n.* rude behaviour, wickedness.

ଅଶିଷ୍ଟାଚାରୀ, *a.* impolite, rude.

ଅଶିକ୍ଷିତ, *a.* untaught, unlearned.

ଅଶୀ, ଅଶୀତି, *n.* and *a.* eighty, 80, LXXX.

ଅଶୁଚି, *a.* impure, unclean, foul.

ଅଶୁଦ୍ଧ, *a.* impure; inaccurate, incorrect.

ଅଶୁଭ; *a.* unpropitious, bad, evil.

ଅଶୁଭଲକ୍ଷଣ, *n.* ill-omen.

ଅଶୁଭଦର୍ଶନ, *n.* a portentious look or aspect.

ଅଶେଷ, *a.* boundless, endless, infinite.

ଅଶେଷବିଧ, *a.* entire, universal.

ଅଶୋକ, *a.* free from grief ;—*n.* the name of a tree.

ଅଶୋକାଷ୍ଟମୀ, *n.* a Hindu festival.

ଅଶୌଚ, *n.* uncleanness, impurity.

ଅଶ୍ରଦ୍ଧା, *n.* distrust, disregard, sneer.

ଅଶ୍ରାନ୍ତ, *a.* unwearied, not fatigued.

ଅଶ୍ରାବ୍ୟ, *a.* not fit to be heard, bad (language).

ଅଶ୍ରୁ, *n.* a tear.

ଅଶ୍ରୁତ, *a.* unheard, unheard of.

ଅଶ୍ରୁତପୂର୍ବ, *a.* not heard of before, unprecedented.

ଅଶ୍ରୁପାତ, *n.* weeping, shedding tears.

ଅଶ୍ରେଷ୍ଠ, *a.* inferior, not the best, common.

ଅଶ୍ଳୀଳ, *a.* coarse, vulgar (language).

ଅଶ୍ଳେଷା, *n.* the ninth stellar mansion.

* ଅଶ୍ୱ, *n.* a horse.

* ଅଶ୍ୱଚିକିତ୍ସା, *n.* farriery, the treatment of horses when sick.

* ଅଶ୍ୱତର, *n.* a mule.

ଅଶ୍ୱତ୍ଥ, *n.* the peepul tree. [syce.
* ଅଶ୍ୱପାଳ, ଅଶ୍ୱପାଳକ, *n.* a groom, a
ଅଶ୍ୱମେଧ, *n.* the sacrificing of a horse.
* ଅଶ୍ୱଶାଳା, *n.* a stable.
ଅଶ୍ୱାରୂଢ଼, ଅଶ୍ୱାରୋହୀ, *a.* mounting a horse ;—*n.* a horseman.
ଅଶ୍ୱିନୀ, *n.* the first stellar mansion.
ଅଶ୍ୱିନୀକୁମାର, *n.* the physicians of heaven.
* ଅଶ୍ୱା, ଅଶ୍ୱୀ, *n.* a mare. [bladder.
* ଅଶ୍ମରୀ, *n.* stone or gravel in the
ଅଷାଢ଼, *n.* the Hindu month corresponding to parts of June and July. [in curry.
ଅଷାଢ଼ୁଆ, *n.* a wild vegetable used
ଅଷ୍ଟ, *n.* and *a.* eight, 8, VIII.
ଅଷ୍ଟକ, *a.* eight-fold ;—*n.* a book consisting of eight poetical verses.
ଅଷ୍ଟଦିକ୍, ଅଷ୍ଟଦିଗ, *n.* the eight cardinal points of the compass.
ଅଷ୍ଟଧା, *a.* divided into eight parts.
ଅଷ୍ଟଧାତୁ, *n.* the eight metals. [footed.
* ଅଷ୍ଟପଦ, *n.* a spider ;—*a.* eight-
ଅଷ୍ଟପ୍ରହର, *n.* the eight watches;—*ad.* incessantly.
ଅଷ୍ଟମ, *a.* the eighth, 8th.
ଅଷ୍ଟମଙ୍ଗଳା, *n.* the eighth day after marriage.
ଅଷ୍ଟମୀ, *n.* eighth day of the moon.
ଅଷ୍ଟାଙ୍ଗ, *n.* eight members of the body.

ଅଷ୍ଟାଙ୍ଗପ୍ରଣାମ, *n.* salutation by prostrating one's self. [XVIII.
ଅଷ୍ଟାଦଶ, *n.* and *a.* eighteen, 18,
ଅଷ୍ଟାଦଶାଙ୍ଗ, *n.* a popular medicine composed of eighteen ingredients.
ଅଷ୍ଟାବିଂଶତି, *n.* and *a.* twenty-eight, 28, XXVIII. [28th.
ଅଷ୍ଟାବିଂଶତିତମ, *a.* twenty-eighth,
ଅସଙ୍କୀର୍ଣ୍ଣ, *a.* wide. [able.
ଅସଂଖ୍ୟ, *a.* innumerable, incalcul-
ଅସଂଯୁକ୍ତ, *a.* unconnected, not in contact.
ଅସଂଯୋଗ, *n.* disunion, disjunction.
ଅସଂଲଗ୍ନ, *a.* unconnected, disjoined.
ଅସଂଶୟ, *a.* undoubted, certain, sure.
ଅସଂସ୍କୃତ, *a.* unconsecrated.
ଅସଙ୍ଗତ, *a.* absurd, improper, unlikely, inconsistent.
ଅସଜ, *a.* inconvenient, difficult.
ଅସତ୍, *a.* untrue, ungodly, non-existent.
ଅସତର୍କ, *a.* inattentive, inadvertent.
ଅସତୀ, *a.* unchaste, impure.
ଅସତ୍ୟ, *a.* untrue, false, useless.
ଅସଦାଚାର, *n.* evil conduct, bad behaviour.
ଅସଦୃଶ, *a.* unlike, dissimilar. [ship.
ଅସଦ୍ଭାବ, *n.* dislike, want of friend-
ଅସନା, *a.* slovenly, untidy, filthy.
ଅସନ୍ତୁଷ୍ଟ, *a.* displeased, dissatisfied.
ଅସନ୍ତୋଷ, *n.* displeasure, dissatisfaction.

ଅସନ୍ଦିଗ୍ଧ, *a.* undoubted, unsuspected, sure.

ଅସବାବ୍, *n.* goods, furniture, accoutrements, baggage.

ଅସଭ୍ୟ, *a.* rude, uncivilized.

ଅସଭ୍ୟତା, *n.* rudeness, impoliteness.

ଅସମ, *a.* uneven, unlike, not level

ଅସମୟ, *n.* inconvenient time, adversity ;—*a.* premature.

ଅସମର୍ଥ, *a.* unable, incapable, feeble.

* ଅସମସାହସିକ, *a.* very courageous, very bold.

ଅସମାନ, *a.* unequal, not smooth or level.

ଅସମାପ୍ତ, *a.* unfinished, unended.

ଅସମାପ୍ତି, *n.* incompleteness.

ଅସମ୍ପର୍କୀୟ, *a.* destitute of relationship or connection.

ଅସମ୍ପୂର୍ଣ୍ଣ, *a.* incomplete, imperfect, unfulfilled.

ଅସମ୍ଭବ, *a.* impossible, improbable, astonishing, strange.

ଅସମ୍ଭ୍ରମ, *n.* disgrace, dishonour, indignity.

ଅସମ୍ମତ, *a.* dissentient, averse, reluctant.

ଅସମ୍ମାନ, *n.* dishonour, disrespect, irreverence.

ଅସରନ୍ତି, *a.* endless, (as an endless store of rice or other goods).

ଅସରପା, *n.* a cockroach.

ଅସରଫି, *n.* a gold mohur.

ଅସର, *n.* a shower.

ଅସଲ, *a.* original, genuine, real, principal (money).

ଅସହନୀୟ, ଅସହ୍ୟ, *a.* unbearable, intolerable.

ଅସହିଷ୍ଣୁ, *a.* impatient, unable to bear.

ଅସାଧାରଣ, *a.* particular, uncommon, extraordinary.

ଅସାଧୁ, *a.* unrighteous, bad, immoral.

ଅସାଧ୍ୟ, *a.* impossible, impracticable ; incurable.

ଅସାବଧାନ, *a.* careless, thoughtless, unguarded.

ଅସାବଧାନତା, *n.* thoughtlessness, carelessness.

ଅସାମୟିକ, *a.* untimely, unseasonable.

ଅସାମର୍ଥ୍ୟ, *n.* inability, want of power.

ଅସାମାନ୍ୟ, *a.* uncommon, particular, special.

ଅସାର, *a.* worthless, unfit.

ଅସାକ୍ଷାତରେ, *ad.* out of sight, behind one's back.

* ଅସି, *n.* a sword, scimitar.

* ଅସିକୋଷ, *n.* a scabbard.

ଅସିଝା, *a.* under-boiled.

* ଅସିତ, *a.* not white, black.

ଅସିଦ୍ଧ, *a.* not completed or perfected, not proven.

ଅସୀମ, *a* boundless, limitless.

ଅସୁଖ, *a.* unhappy, uncomfortable; —*n.* pain, sorrow, displeasure.

ଅସୁଚିସ୍ଥ, ଅସୁସ୍ଥ, *a.* unclean (place).

ଅସୁନ୍ଦର, *a.* ugly.

ଅସୁବିଧା, *n.* inconvenience ;—*a.* inconvenient.

ଅସୁମାର, ଅସୁମାରି, *a.* innumerable.

ଅସୁର, *n.* demon, an evil spirit.

ଅସୁଲ, *n.* collection, realization of taxes, etc.

ଅସୁସାର, *a.* unwell ; inconvenient.
ଅସୁସ୍ଥ, *a.* ill, sick, uncomfortable.
* ଅସୂୟା, *n.* slander, detraction, malice.
ଅସୃଷ୍ଟ, *a.* uncreated.
ଅସ୍ତ, *n.* setting of the heavenly bodies ;—*a.* set below the horizon.
ଅସ୍ତଗତ, *a.* set, gone below the [horizon.
ଅସ୍ତଗିରି, *n.* the western mountains.
ଅସ୍ତବଲ, ଅସ୍ତାବଲ, *n.* a stable.
ଅସ୍ତବ୍ୟସ୍ତ, *a.* unsteady, fickle, capricious, troubled, confused.
ଅସ୍ତାଚଳ, *n.* see ଅସ୍ତଗିରି ।
ଅସ୍ତିତ୍ୱ, *n.* existence.
ଅସ୍ତୁ, *v.* amen, be it so.
ଅସ୍ତ୍ର, *n.* a weapon, a sword, a tool.
ଅସ୍ତ୍ରକାରକ, *n.* an armourer.
ଅସ୍ତ୍ରଚିକିତ୍ସକ, *n.* a surgeon.
ଅସ୍ତ୍ରଚିକିତ୍ସା, *n.* surgery.
ଅସ୍ତ୍ରଜ୍ଞ, *a.* skilled in arms.
ଅସ୍ତ୍ରଧାରୀ, *a.* taking arms, bearing [arms.
ଅସ୍ତ୍ରାଗାର, *n.* arsenal, armoury.
ଅସ୍ତ୍ରାଘାତ, *n.* the stroke of a weapon.
ଅସ୍ତ୍ରୀକ, *a.* without a wife, unmarried.
ଅସ୍ଥାନ, *n.* a bad place, wrong place; [the privy parts.
ଅସ୍ଥାବର, *a.* movable, not fixed.
ଅସ୍ଥାୟୀ, *a.* temporary, fleeting.
ଅସ୍ଥି, *n.* a bone.
ଅସ୍ଥିଚର୍ମ, *n.* skin and bone.
ଅସ୍ଥିପଞ୍ଜର, *n.* a skeleton.
ଅସ୍ଥିର, *a.* unstable, wavering, capri- [cious.
ଅସ୍ଥିରତା, *n.* fickleness ; anxiety.
ଅସ୍ଥିସମର୍ପଣ, *n.* committing of the bones of the dead to the river Ganges.
* ଅସ୍ଥୈର୍ଯ୍ୟ, *n.* irresolution, fickleness.
ଅସ୍ନାତ, ଅସ୍ନାନୀୟ, *a.* unbathed, impure.
ଅସ୍ପର୍ଶ୍ୟ, ଅସ୍ପୃଶ୍ୟ, *a.* untouchable, unholy.
ଅସ୍ପଷ୍ଟ, * ଅସ୍ଫୁଟ, *a.* indistinct, inarticulate, obscure.
ଅସ୍ୱଚ୍ଛ, *a.* not clear, turbid, impure.
ଅସ୍ୱାଦୁ, *a.* insipid, ill-flavoured.
ଅସ୍ୱାମିକ, *a.* having no husband.
ଅସ୍ୱାସ୍ଥ୍ୟ, *n.* illness, indisposition.
ଅସ୍ୱୀକାର, *n.* non-acquiescence, denial.
ଅସ୍ୱୀକୃତ, *a.* not agreed, not acquiesced in, not acknowledged.
ଅହଃ, *n.* a day, (used as a *prefix* and *suffix*).
ଅହଙ୍କାର, *n.* pride, self-importance.
ଅହଂକାରୀ, *a.* proud, haughty, self-conscious.
ଅହମ୍ମା, *n.* quarrelling, resentment.
ଅହରହ, *ad.* daily, every day.
ଅହର୍ନିଶ, *ad.* day and night.
* ଅହର୍ମଣି, *n.* the sun, the genii or lord of the day.
* ଅହି, *n.* a snake, a serpent.
* ଅହିନକୁଳଭାବ, *n.* mortal enmity.
* ଅହିଫେନ, *n.* opium.
ଅହିରାଜ, *n.* a large snake, a python.
ଅହିଂସକ, *a.* harmless, not injurious.

ଅହିଂସା, *n.* harmlessness, without malice, not injuring.

ଅହିତ, *n.* disadvantage, injury.

ଅହୋ, *inter.* alas! wonderful! O brave!

ଅହୋରାତ୍ର, *ad.* day and night.

ଅହ୍ନିଆ, *n.* an offering prepared for presenting to gods.

* ଅହୟ, *n.* a married woman (not a widow).

ଅହ୍ୟା, ଅହୁଆ, *n.* a small fire-place.

* ଅକ୍ଷ, *n.* dice; axle-tree.

ଅକ୍ଷକ୍ରୀଡା, *n.* play at dice.

ଅକ୍ଷତ, *a.* unhurt, uninjured;—*n.* dry husked rice.

ଅକ୍ଷ ଦଣ୍ଡ, *n.* (in *Geog.*) axis.

ଅକ୍ଷବୃତ୍ତ *n.* (in *Geog.*) parallel of latitude.

ଅକ୍ଷମ, *a.* incapable, impotent.

ଅକ୍ଷୟ, *a.* imperishable, durable.

ଅକ୍ଷୟତୃତୀୟା, *n.* the third day of moon's increase in *Bysakha.*

ଅକ୍ଷର, *n.* letter, character, type.

* ଅକ୍ଷରଜୀବୀ, *a.* gaining a livelihood by writing or by letters;—*n.* a writer, a copyist.

ଅକ୍ଷରଯୋଜକ, *n.* a compositor.

ଅକ୍ଷରେଖା, *n.* (in *Geog.*) lines of latitude.

ଅକ୍ଷାଂଶ, *n.* a degree of latitude or longitude.

* ଅକ୍ଷି, *n.* an eye, the eyes.

ଅକ୍ଷୁଣ୍ଣ, *a.* not perplexed, sad, or distressed; full, undiminished.

* ଅକ୍ଷୁବ୍ଧ, *a.* unexcited, not agitated. quiet, composed.

ଅକ୍ଷୌହିଣୀ, *n.* a complete army consisting of 109,350 foot, 65,610 horse, 21,870 chariots and 21,870 elephants.

ଆ.

ଆ, the second vowel; a call, come: (as a *prefix*) up to, even to;—*inter*, aye! true!

ଆଂଶିକ, *a.* partly.

ଆଃ, *inter.* aye, aye! Oh! aye! ah! alas!

ଆଁ, *n.* opening the mouth.

ଆଁଶ, ଆଁଶୁ, *n.* roughness.

ଆଇଁଷ, *n.* fish, flesh.

ଆଇଁଷକାତି, *n.* the scales of a fish.

ଆଇଁଷିଣିଆଁ, *a.* fishy or fleshy (smell).

ଆଇନ, *n.* a law, an act of the legislature.

ଆଇନସିଦ୍ଧ, *a.* legal, lawful.

ଆଇମା, *n.* see ଅଇମା.

ଆଈ, *n.* a maternal grandmother.

ଆଉଁସା, *n.* a caress or endearment.

ଆଉଁସା-ଆଉଁସି, *n.* a mutual stroking or caressing; patting one another.

ଆଉଁସିବା, *v.* to stroke lovingly or gently, to caress.

ଆଉ, *ad.* more, other, another;—*conj.* and.

ଆଉଜାଇବା, *v.* to cause to lean or recline against.

ଅଉଜିବା, *v.* to lean or recline against.

ଅଉଟା, *a.* melted, molten; boiled.

ଅଉଟିବା, *v.* to melt; to boil.

ଅଉଡାଇବା, *v.* to repeat; to read.

ଅଉଡ, *n.* a hiccup, hiccough.

ଅଉଣ୍ଡେଇବା, *v.* to search or feel for.

ଅଉଲ, ଅହୁଲ, *n.* an oar.

ଅଏଲା, *a.* coming; future.

ଅକଟ, *n.* discipline, punishment.

ଅକଣ୍ଠ, *ad.* up to the throat.

* ଅକର, *n.* a mine, quarry, source.

* ଅକରଜ, ଅକରସ୍ଥ, *a.* mineral.

* ଅକର୍ଣ୍ଣ, *ad.* up to the ears.

ଅକର୍ଷକ, *a.* attractive;—*n.* that which attracts.

ଅକର୍ଷଣ, *n.* attraction.

* ଅକର୍ଷଣୀୟ, *a.* attractive.

ଅକସ୍ମିକ, *a.* unexpected, sudden.

ଅକାଙ୍କ୍ଷା, *n.* wish, desire, expectation.

ଅକାର, *n.* form, shape, figure, statue; (in *Gram.*) the letter ଅ and its sign 'ା'

ଅକାରବନ୍ତ, *a.* having a shape or bodily form; comely.

ଅକାରାନ୍ତ, *a.* (in *Gram.*) ending with the letter ଅ or its symbol 'ା'

ଅକାଶ, *n.* the sky, firmament, space.

ଅକାଶକୁସୁମ, *n.* falsity, vain hope, building castles in the air.

* ଅକାଶଚର, *a.* moving in the air, ærial.

ଅକାଶବାଣୀ, *n.* a voice from heaven, divine communication.

ଅକାଶମଣ୍ଡଳ, *n.* the firmament.

* ଅକାଶଯାନ, *n.* that which floats in the air, a balloon.

ଅକୁଞ୍ଚନ, *n.* contortion, contraction.

ଅକୁଞ୍ଚିତ, *a.* curled, contorted, tortuous.

ଅକୁଳ, ଅକୁଳିତ, *a.* troubled, distressed, agitated.

ଅକୃତି, *n.* a form, shape, figure.

ଅକୃଷ୍ଟ, *a.* attracted, drawn, charmed.

ଅକ୍ରମଣ, *n.* a seizing, an attack, invasion; assault.

ଅକ୍ରାନ୍ତ, *a.* invaded, seized, held.

ଅକ୍ରୋଶ, *n.* resentment, hatred.

ଅଙ୍କିବା, *v.* to draw.

ଅଙ୍କୁଡା, ଅଙ୍କୁଡ, ଅଙ୍କୁଶା, ଅଙ୍କୁଶୀ, *n.* a hooked stick; tendril of a creeper.

ଅଖଡା, *n.* a gymnasium; an orchestra, a place where persons meet to dance and sing, &c.

ଅଖପାଖ, *ad.* on all sides;—*n.* vicinity.

ଅଖର, *n.* the end, a termination.

ଅଖି, ଅକ୍ଷି, *n.* the eye, (see ଚକ୍ଷୁ).

ଅଖୁ, *n.* sugar-cane.

ଅଖୁରୋଲୁଷ, *n.* juice of the sugar-cane.

ଅଖୁନ, *n.* a Muhammadan teacher.

ଅଖୁପେଡବା, *v.* to press the sugar-cane.

*ଆଖେଟ, *n.* a hunting, pursuit.
ଆଖ୍ୟା, *n.* a name, title, term.
ଆଖ୍ୟାତ, *a.* titled, named; (in Sanskrit *Gram.*) Etymology.
ଆଖ୍ୟାନ, *n.* a word, a saying, a tale.
ଆଖ୍ୟାୟିକା, *n.* a short tale, narrative, history.
ଆଗ, *ad.* first, before, front, forward.
ଆଗଭଲା, *a.* forward, self-assertive.
ଆଗତ, *a.* come, arrived; future.
ଆଗଉଡ, ଆଗଲୁଡ, *a.* (payment) in advance; future.
ଆଗନ୍ତୁକ, *ଆଗନ୍ତୁ, *a.* arrived at a place;—*n.* an uninvited guest.
ଆଗପଛ, *ad.* before and behind, first and last.
ଆଗବଢ଼ି, *ad.* forestalling.
*ଆଗମ, *n.* a coming; the *Vedas*; Hindu ritual.
ଆଗମନ, *n.* a coming, an arrival.
*ଆଗମବକ୍ତା, *n.* a prophet.
ଆଗହୁଁ, ଆଗୁଁ, *ad.* before (time), first of all.
ଆଗାମୀ, *a.* coming, preceding, future.
*ଆଗାର, *n.* a house, a receptacle.
ଆଗିଲା, *a.* previous.
ଆଗୁଁସାର, *a.* forward, preceding.
ଆଗେ, *ad.* first, forward, before.
ଆଗୋ, *n.* a vocative particle used in addressing females.
ଆଗ୍ନେୟଗିରି, *n.* a volcano.
ଆଗ୍ନେୟାସ୍ତ୍ର, *n.* fire-arms, a rocket.
ଆଗ୍ରହ, *n.* zeal, eagerness, urgency.
ଆଙ୍ଗଠା, *n.* a chafingdish, (see ଅଙ୍ଗଠା).
ଆଙ୍ଗୁଠି, *n.* a finger or toe; a ring for either.
ଆଙ୍ଗୁଳି, *n.* a finger or toe.
ଆଘାତ, *n.* a blow, hurt, injury.
ଆଗୁଁ, (same as ଆଗହୁଁ), *ad.* before, in time past.
*ଆଘୂର୍ଣ୍ଣନ, *n.* a whirling round, rolling.
ଆଘ୍ରାଣ, *n.* a smelling, a scent.
*ଆଚମନ, *n.* rinsing the mouth after eating.
ଆଚମ୍ବିତ, *a.* amazed, astonished; sudden.
ଆଚରଣ, *n.* behaviour, usage; habit.
ଆଚାର, *n.* custom, conduct, practice; pickle.
ଆଚାରଭ୍ରଷ୍ଟ, *a.* apostatized, apostate.
ଆଚାରୀ, *a.* virtuous, ceremonious, (in these two senses used of a certain sect in Hinduism); behaving, conducting.
ଆଚାର୍ଯ୍ୟ, *n.* a teacher, a tutor; a teacher of religion.
ଆଚାର୍ଯ୍ୟାଣୀ, *n.* a female teacher, preceptress.
ଆଚ୍ଛନ୍ନ, *a.* dressed, covered.
ଆଛ, ଆଛା, *a.* good, unexceptionable; —*ad.* well.
ଆଚ୍ଛାଦନ, *n.* covering; a cover.
ଆଚ୍ଛାଦିତ, *a.* dressed, covered, concealed.
ଆଜି, *ad.* to-day.
ଆଜିକ, ଆଜିକି, *ad.* this day, this day only.
ଆଜନ୍ମ, *ad.* from one's birth.
ଆଜିଶର, *n.* to-night, this night.

ଆଜାନୁ, *ad.* reaching from the shoulder to the thigh or knee.

ଆଜି, *ad.* to-day.

ଆଜିକାର, *a.* belonging to this day.

ଆଜିକାଲି, *ad.* now-a-days; in these days; at the present time.

ଆଜୀବନ, *ad.* as long as one lives.

* ଆଜ୍ଞପ୍ତ, *a.* ordered, commanded.

ଆଜ୍ଞା, *n.* a command, a precept.

ଆଜ୍ଞାକାରୀ, *a.* obedient, obsequious; —*n.* one who obeys.

ଆଜ୍ଞାଦାତା, *n.* one who commands; —*a.* permitting.

ଆଜ୍ଞାପତ୍ର, *n.* a written command, a mandate.

ଆଜ୍ଞାପିତ, *a.* commanded, ordered.

ଆଜ୍ଞାବହ, ଆଜ୍ଞାବାହକ, *a.* obedient.—*n.* messenger.

ଆଞ୍ଜୁଳା, ଆଞ୍ଜୁଳି, *n.* the hands joined together like a cup, (see ଅଞ୍ଜଳି)।

ଆଞ୍ଜୁଳାଏ, ଆଞ୍ଜୁଳିଏ, *n.* a handful (as much as can be held in the hands when joined as a cup).

ଆଜୁଁ, (same as ଆଜିଠୁଁ) *ad.* from this day, from to-day.

ଆଟି, *n.* a sheaf, bundle, wisp.

ଆଟିକା, *n.* a small earthen cooking-pot.

ଆଠ, *a.* and *n.* eight, 8, VIII.

ଆଠଣା, ଆଠଅଣା, *n.* an eight-anna piece (see ଅଧୁଲି).

ଆଠବାଙ୍କ, *a.* crooked, deformed.

ଆଡ଼, *n.* side, direction; width.

ଆଡ଼କାଠ, *n.* a cross-beam, a beam.

ଆଡ଼ଘିଅ, *n.* remains of *ghee* after making sweetmeats.

ଆଡ଼ଣି, *n.* a large hand-punkah when being carried before rajahs; a cross-beam.

ଆଡ଼ବାୟା, *a.* half-deranged, cracked.

ଆଡ଼ମ୍ବର, *n.* much ado; empty noise; a pomp, a show.

ଆଡ଼ ହେବା, ଆଡ଼େଇ ହେବା, *v.i.* to move aside.

ଆଡ଼ା, *n.* a small regular gathering of people; breadth; a perch; cross-beam.

ଆଡ଼ାଆଡ଼ି, *ad.* athwart, diagonally.

ଆଢ଼, *n.* a hiding place (for hunting).

ଆଢ଼ୁଆଳ, ଆଡ଼ୁଆଳ, *n.* a partition, a curtain.

ଆଢ଼ୁଆଳରେ, ଆଡ଼ୁଆଳରେ, *ad.* secretly.

ଆଡ଼େଇ ଦେବା, *v.* to remove to one side.

ଆଢ଼ି, *n.* a measuring vessel.

ଆଢ୍ୟ, *a.* rich, affluent.

ଆଣ, *n.* dough.

ଆଣିବା, *v.* to bring.

ଆଣ୍ଠ, *n.* pride;—*a.* tough, hard, firm.

ଆଣ୍ଠେ, *ad.* tightly.

ଆଣ୍ଠୁଆ, *a.* strong, powerful, rich, influential.

ଆଣ୍ଠିଏ, ଆଣ୍ଠୁଆଣି, *a.* knee-deep.

ଆଣ୍ଠୁ, *n.* the knee.

ଆଣ୍ଠୁଅ, *n.* a kick with the knee.
ଆଣ୍ଠୁକୁଡ଼ା, *a.* without any issue.
ଆଣ୍ଠୁକୁଡ଼ି, *n.* fem. of above.
ଆଣ୍ଠୁଇବା, ଆଣ୍ଠୋଇବା, *v.* to kneel, to walk on the knees.
ଆତ, *n.* the custard-apple.
ଆତଙ୍କ, ଆତଙ୍ଗ, *n.* fear, alarm; disease.
*ଆତତାୟୀ, *a.* ready to murder or injure, ready to smite;—*n.* an enemy.
*ଆତପ, *n.* sunshine, heat.
*ଆତପତ୍ର, *n.* an umbrella.
ଆତଯାତ, *n.* coming and going.
ଆତସବାଜି, *n.* fireworks.
ଆତିଥେୟ, *a.* hospitable.
ଆତିଥ୍ୟ, *n.* hospitable reception, hospitality.
ଆତିଶଯ୍ୟ, *n.* excessiveness.
ଆତୁର, *a.* diseased, distressed.
ଆତ୍ମଜାତ, *a.* produced in one's mind.
ଆତ୍ମଗର୍ବ *n.* pride, arrogance.
ଆତ୍ମଗ୍ଳାନି, *n.* remorse.
ଆତ୍ମଘାତକ, ଆତ୍ମଘାତୀ, *a.* self-murder, suicide.
ଆତ୍ମଘାତ, *n.* committing suicide.
*ଆତ୍ମଜ, *n.* a son;—*a.* springing from self.
*ଆତ୍ମଜା, *n.* a daughter.
ଆତ୍ମଜ୍ଞାନ, *n.* self-knowledge.
*ଆତ୍ମଦେବତା, *n.* a guardian or family god.
ଆତ୍ମଦ୍ରୋହୀ, *a.* self-tormenting, bringing trouble upon one's self.
ଆତ୍ମପ୍ରସାଦ, *n.* self-satisfaction.
ଆତ୍ମବଞ୍ଚନା, *n.* self-deception.
ଆତ୍ମବଶ, *a.* under one's own power or control, subject to one's self.
ଆତ୍ମବିସ୍ମୃତ, *a.* forgetful of one's self.
*ଆତ୍ମମ୍ଭରି, *a.* selfishly voracious.
ଆତ୍ମଶ୍ଳାଘା, *n.* self-applause, egotism.
ଆତ୍ମସଂଯମ, *n.* self-restraint, stoicism.
ଆତ୍ମସାତ୍, *a.* own, proper, one's own.
ଆତ୍ମହତ୍ୟା, *n.* self-murder, suicide.
ଆତ୍ମା, *n.* spirit, soul, mind, self.
ଆତ୍ମାଧୀନ, *a.* independent.
ଆତ୍ମାଭିମାନୀ, *a.* self-applauding, vain.
ଆତ୍ମାର୍ଥୀ, *a.* selfish, egotistic.
ଆତ୍ମୀୟ, *a.* related to one's own self;—*n.* a friend.
ଆତ୍ମୀୟତା, *n.* friendship, intimacy.
ଆତ୍ୟନ୍ତିକ, *a.* excessive, infinite.
ଆଦତ୍, *n.* a bad habit, custom or usage.
ଆଦର, *n.* respect, esteem, veneration.
ଆଦରଣୀୟ, *a.* worthy of esteem or respect, respectable.
ଆଦର୍ଶ, *n.* a likeness, pattern, sample; an original; *a mirror.
*ଆଦାନ, *n.* receiving, taking.
ଆଦାୟ, *n.* obtaining payment, receiving anything, realising payment.
ଆଦାଲତ୍, *n.* a court of justice.
ଆଦି, *a.* the beginning, first, prior.
ଆଦିକାରଣ, *n.* the first or primary cause; God.
*ଆଦିତ୍ୟ, *n.* the sun; a deity.
ଆଦିଭୂତ, *a.* first-existent.

ଆଦିମ, *a.* first, primary.

ଆଦିମୂଳ, *n.* original cause ; God.

ଆଦିଷ୍ଟ, *a.* commanded, directed.

ଆଦୃତ, *a.* honoured, respected, esteemed.

ଆଦେଶ, *n.* a command, an injunction.

ଆଦୌ, *ad.* in the first place.

ଆଦ୍ୟ, *n.* the beginning ;—*a.* first, preceding, prior.

ଆଦ୍ୟନ୍ତ, *a.* first and last ;—*n.* the beginning and the end.

ଆଦ୍ୟୋପାନ୍ତ, *n.* the beginning and the end ;—*ad.* from first to last, all along.

ଆଧାର, *n.* a receptacle, vessel, holder.

ଆଧି, *n.* mental distress ; a pledge.

ଆଧିକ୍ୟ, *n.* abundance, excess.

ଆଧିପତ୍ୟ, *n.* sovereignty, lordship.

ଆଧୁନିକ, *a.* recent, modern.

* ଆଧେୟ, *a.* fit to be supported or contained.

ଆଧ୍ୟାତ୍ମିକ, *a.* internal, inherent.

ଆନ, *a.* another, other (a poetical from of ଅନ୍ୟ).

ଆନତ, *a.* gently bowed, modest.

* ଆନନ, *n.* the face, countenance.

ଆନନ୍ଦ, *n.* joy, felicity, happiness.

ଆନନ୍ଦଜନକ, *a.* joy-inspiring, pleasure-giving.

ଆନନ୍ଦିତ, *a.* glad, pleased.

ଆନମନା, *a.* otherwise-minded, absent-minded.

ଆନୟନ, *n.* bringing.

ଆନୀତ, *a.* brought.

ଆନୁକୂଲ୍ୟ, *n.* assistance, patronage.

* ଆନୁଗତ୍ୟ, *n.* obedience, submissiveness.

ଆନୁପୂର୍ବ, *ad.* according to order.

ଆନୁପୂର୍ବିକ, *a.* following in regular order.

ଆନୁମାନିକ, *a.* probable, inferable, hypothetical.

ଆନୁଷଙ୍ଗିକ, *a.* grafted, joined, connected ; secondary.

ଆନ୍ତରିକ, *a.* inward, internal; hearty.

ଆନ୍ଦୋଳନ, *n.* act of swinging, agitation.

ଆପଟ, *n.* a partition, a sheath.

ଆପଣ, *pron.* you, your honour.

ଆପଣା, *pron.* one's own, one's self.

ଆପତ୍, *n.* misfortune, calamity.

ଆପତ୍କାଳ, *n.* a time of adversity.

ଆପତ୍ତି, *n.* objection, excuse.

ଆପଦ, *n.* danger, misfortune, adversity.

ଆପଦ୍‌ଗ୍ରସ୍ତ, *a.* engulfed by adversity, unfortunate, distressed.

ଆପନ୍ନ, *a.* seized by, possessed of.

ଆପାତତଃ, *ad.* for the present, now, instantly, immediately.

ଆପାଦମସ୍ତକ, *ad.* from head to foot.

ଆପାମର, *ad.* from the highest to the lowest, all.

ଆପିଲ୍, *n.* (*English*), an appeal.

ଆପୁ, *n.* opium.

ଆପୁଆ, *a.* addicted to opium;—*n.* a sot.

ଆପେ, *pron.* self, one's self.

ଆପେକ୍ଷିକ ଗୁରୁତ୍ୱ, *n.* specific gravity.

ଆପୋସ୍ତ, *pron.* self, one's self.
* ଆପ୍ତବାକ୍ୟ, *n.* a revelation, authentic testimony. [satisfied.
ଆପ୍ୟାୟିତ, *a.* pleased, refreshed,
* ଆପ୍ଲାବନ, *n.* an overflowing, a flood.
ଆବଡାଖାବଡା, *a.* undulating, uneven.
ଆବଦ୍ଧ, *a.* responsible, pledged, bound. [cal.
ଆବର, *ad.* again, moreover, (poeti-
ଆବରଣ, *n.* a covering, a screen.
ଆବର୍ଜନା, *n.* sweepings, rubbish.
ଆବର୍ତ୍ତ, *n.* a whirlpool, an eddy.
ଆବଳି, ଆବଳୀ, *n.* line, range, row.
ଆବଶ୍ୟକ, ଆବଶ୍ୟକୀୟ, *a.* necessary, indispensable.
ଆବଶ୍ୟକତା, *n.* need, necessity.
ଆବହମାନ, *a.* customary, usual, uniform. [ted.
ଆବାଦ, ଆବାଦୀ, *a.* cultivated; popula-
ଆବାଳ, *a.* childish;—*ad.* from a child.
ଆବାଳବୃଦ୍ଧ, *ad.* both young and old.
ଆବାଳବୃଦ୍ଧବନିତା, *ad.* congregationally, the whole people including young and old.
ଆବାଲ୍ୟ, *ad.* from infancy.
ଆବାସ, *n.* a residence, a home.
* ଆବାହନ, *n.* an approach, invitation. [lopment.
ଆବିର୍ଭାବ, *n.* a manifestation, a deve-
ଆବିର୍ଭୂତ, *a.* unfolded, evolved, developed.
* ଆବିଳ, *a.* foul, sinful, guilty.

ଆବିଷ୍କାର, *n.* discovery. [displayed.
ଆବିଷ୍କୃତ, *a.* discovered, manifested,
ଆବିଷ୍ଟ, *a.* engaged in, devoted to.
ଆବୁ, *n.* a wen.
ଆବୁରିବା, ଆବୋରିବା, *v.* to take care of one's own work or things; to cover.
ଆବୃତ, *a.* concealed, covered.
ଆବୃତ୍ତ, *a.* circulated, revolved, stirred; repeated.
ଆବୃତ୍ତି, *n.* revolving; mental repetition; repetition. [fickleness.
ଆବେଗ, *n.* hurry, unsteadiness,
ଆବେଦକ, *a.* making known his case;—*n.* onↄ who enters a suit. [tion.
ଆବେଦନ, *n.* a representation, peti-
ଆବେଦନକାରୀ, *n.* a petitioner.
ଆବେଶ, *n.* intentness, close attention; inspiration.
ଆଭରଣ, *n.* an ornament, a jewel
ଆଭା, *n.* brilliancy, splendour.
ଆଭାଷ, *n.* a preamble, prologue, preface. [tion.
* ଆଭାଷଣ, *n.* addressing, conversa-
ଆଭାସ, *n.* brilliancy; design; a semblance.
ଆଭିଜାତ୍ୟ, *n.* high birth, nobility.
ଆଭିମୁଖ୍ୟ, *n.* a front position.
ଆଭ୍ୟାସିକ, *a.* eminent in studying.
ଆମ, *n.* mucous slime;—*a.* raw.
ଆମଦାନି, *n.* importation;—*a.* imported.

ଆମନ୍ତ୍ରଣ, *n.* invitation, calling.
ଆମନ୍ତ୍ରିତ, *a.* called, invited.
ଆମବାତ, *n.* rheumatism.
ଆମରକ୍ତ, *n.* dysentery.
ଆମଲକ, ଆମଲକୀ, *n.* name of a medicinal plant and its fruit, phyllanthus emblica.
ଆମଲା, *n.* a clerk.
ଆମଶୂଳ, *s.* the colic, griping.
ଆମାତିସାର, *n.* dysentery.
* ଆମାନ୍ନ, *n.* uncooked rice.
ଆମାଶୟ, *s.* dysenteric diarrhœa; the stomach.
ଆମିଷ, *s.* flesh, fish.
ଆମିଷାଶୀ, *a.* carnivorous.
* ଆମିକ୍ଷା, *s.* curds, cheese.
ଆମୂଳ, *ad.* radically, to the root.
ଆମୂଳଚୂଳ, *ad.* from beginning to end.
ଆମୋଦ, *n.* enjoyment, delight; fragrance.
ଆମ୍ପୁଡା, *n.* a rending, a scratching.
ଆମ୍ପୁଡିବା, *v.* to rend, to scratch.
ଆମ୍ବ, ଆମ୍ର, *n.* a mango.
ଆମ୍ବସଢ଼ା, *n.* dried mango juice.
ଆମ୍ବିଲ, *n.* a sour thing.
ଆମ୍ବିଳା, *a.* sour, acid.
ଆମ୍ବିଲିତ, *n.* a wild herb, ocalis monodelpha.
ଆମ୍ବିଲିପିତ୍ତ, *n.* syphilis, venereal disease.
ଆମ୍ରାତକ, ଆମଡା, *n.* the hog plum.
*ଆମ୍ରେଡିତ, *n.* tautology, repetition.
ଆୟ, *n.* income, gain, receipts.
ଆୟତ, *n.* oblong;—*a.* extended, long.
ଆୟତନ, *n.* extent, size, measure; * an altar.
ଆୟତ୍ତ, *a.* subject to, docile.
ଆୟତ୍ତତା, *n.* subjection.
ଆୟବ୍ୟୟ, *n.* income and expenditure.
ଆୟା, *n.* a waiting maid, a nurse-maid.
ଆୟାତ, *n.* an arrival;—*a.* arrived.
ଆୟାସ, *n.* labour, fatigue, exertion.
ଆୟୁଃ, *n.* life, life-time, age.
ଆୟୁଧ, *n.* a weapon, arms, armour.
ଆୟୁର୍ବେଦ, *n.* the science of medicine.
ଆୟୁର୍ବେଦୀ, *s.* a physician, a doctor.
ଆୟୁଷ, *s.* the period of life, age.
* ଆୟୁଷ୍ୟ, *a.* life-preserving, vital.
ଆୟୁଷ୍ମାନ୍, *a.* long-lived, long life.
ଆୟୋଜନ, *n.* collecting, procuring.
ଆୟୋଜିତ, *a.* collected, procured.
* ଆୟୋଧନ, *n.* war, battle, conflict.
ଆର, *pron.* other, another.
ଆରକ, *pron.* another one.
ଆରକ୍ତ, *a.* reddish, flesh-coloured.
ଆରଣ୍ୟ, *a.* wild, belonging to a forest, sylvan.
ଆରଣ୍ୟକ, *n.* a forest-dweller.
ଆରତି, *n.* waving lamps to an idol.
ଆରବ୍ଧ, *a.* begun, commenced.
ଆରମାନ, *n.* revenge; a desire, a wish; dishonour, distress.
ଆରମ୍ଭ, *n.* commencement, a beginning.
ଆରାଧନ, *n.* the act of worshipping.
ଆରାଧନା, *n.* worship, prayer.

ଆରାଧନୀୟ, ଆରାଧ୍ୟ, *a.* fit to be propitiated by prayer or worship, placable.

ଆରାମ, *n.* ease, health; a pleasure-garden.

ଆରିଷ, ଆରିଷା, *n.* the piles or hemorrhoids.

ଆରଶୀ, *n.* a looking-glass, mirror.

ଆରିସା, *n.* a kind of cake.

ଆରୂଢ଼, *a.* mounted or riding on.

ଆରେ, an inferior vocative particle used in calling a person, oh, you ho.

ଆରେକ, *pron.* other, another, (poetical).

ଆରୋଗ୍ୟ, *n.* health.

ଆରୋପ, *n.* attributing to, imputation.

ଆରୋପିତ, *a.* imputed.

ଆରୋହଣ, *n.* mounting, climbing, ascending, embarking, entering a conveyance.

ଆରୋହୀ, *a.* ascending, climbing; —*n.* a rider.

ଆର୍ତ୍ତ, *a.* pained, distressed.

ଆର୍ତ୍ତଧ୍ୱନି, ଆର୍ତ୍ତନାଦ, *n.* a groan, a cry of distress.

ଆ*ର୍ତ୍ତବ, *n.* the menses;—*a.* menstruous.

* ଆର୍ତ୍ତି, *n.* pain, distress, disease.

ଆର୍ଥିକ, *a.* pecuniary.

ଆର୍ଦ୍ର, *a.* wet, moist, clammy.

* ଆର୍ଦ୍ରକ, *n.* ginger.

ଆର୍ଦ୍ରା, *n.* the sixth planet.

ଆର୍ଯ୍ୟ, *a.* respectable, venerable, noble; of noble extraction.

ଆର୍ଯ୍ୟାବର୍ତ୍ତ, *n.* India proper, Hindusthan

ଆର୍ଶା, *n.* disease of women (menorrhagia).

ଆର୍ଶୀ, *n.* a looking-glass, a mirror.

ଆଲକାତରା, *n.* coal-tar.

ଆଳତି, *n.* waving of lamps before an idol.

* ଆଲମ୍ବ, *n.* a prop, fulcrum, support.

* ଆଲମ୍ବନ, *n.* depending on or resting on, dependence.

ଆଲୟ, *n.* a house, habitation.

ଆଲସ୍ୟ, *n.* indolence, laziness.

ଆଲାପ, *n.* friendly intercourse.

ଆଳି, ଆଳୀ, *n.* a female companion; a class.

ଆଳୁ, *n.* a yam, a potatoe.

ଆଲପିନ, *n.* a small nail.

ଆଲମାରି, *n.* a bookcase, an almirah.

ଆଲିଙ୍ଗନ, *n.* a hugging or embracing.

ଆଲୁଅ, *n.* light, brightness.

ଆଲେଖ୍ୟ, *a.* fit to be written, fit to be painted;—*n.* a painting, a writing.

ଆଲୋ, a vocative addressed to women.

ଆଲୋକ, *n.* light, brightness.

ଆଲୋଚନା, *n.* investigation, consideration, a seeking.

* ଆଲୋଡନ, *n.* stirring up, agitating.

ଆଶଂସା, *n.* doubt, supposition, desire.

ଆଶଙ୍କା, *n.* fear, dread, terror, peril.

ଆଶପାଶ, *ad.* on all sides, all around.

ଆଶୟ, *n.* an aim, scope, intention.

ଆଶା, *n.* hope, expectation, trust.
ଆଶାଭଙ୍ଗ, *n.* disappointment, defeat of hope.
ଆଶିଷ, *n.* a blessing, benediction.
ଆଶୀର୍ବାଦ, *n.* a blessing, benediction.
ଆଂଶୁ, *n.* the edge or prickles of leaves.
* ଆଶୁ, *ad.* quickly, soon, speedily.
ଆଶ୍ଚର୍ଯ୍ୟ, *a.* marvellous, miraculous, supernatural.
ଆଶ୍ଚର୍ଯ୍ୟାନ୍ୱିତ, *a.* struck with wonder, surprised.
ଆଶ୍ରମ, *n.* a hermitage, monastery.
* ଆଶ୍ରମୀ, *a.* residing in a hermitage.
ଆଶ୍ରୟ, *n.* a refuge, asylum, shelter.
ଆଶ୍ରିତ, *a.* protected, dependent.
ଆଶ୍ୱସ୍ତ, *a.* consoled, comforted, cheered. [comfort.
ଆଶ୍ୱାସ, *n.* encouragement, hope,
ଆଶ୍ୱିନ, *n.* part of September and October.
ଆଶ୍ଳେଷ, *n.* an embrace, a hug.
ଆଷାଢ଼, *n.* part of June and July.
ଆସକ୍ତ, *a.* attached to, enamoured.
ଆସକ୍ତି, *n.* attachment, love.
* ଆସଙ୍ଗ, *n.* attachment, society, fellowship.
* ଆସଙ୍ଗଲିପ୍ସା, *n.* the desire to remain together, love of company.
ଆସନ, *n.* a seat, chair, stool, act of sitting.
* ଆସନ୍ନ, *a.* approaching, near.
ଆସନ୍ନକାଳ, *n.* the time of death.
ଆସନ୍ତା, *a.* future ; *pp.* of ଆସିବା ।
* ଆସବ, *n.* rum, distilled spirits.
ଆସାନ, *a.* alleviating, easy.
ଆସାମୀ, *n.* defendant, respondent.
ଆସିବା, *v.t.* to come.
ଆସୀନ, *a.* seated.
* ଆସୁର, ଆସୁରିକ, ଆସୁରୀ, *a.* demoniacal, barbarous.
* ଆସେଧ, *n.* custody, imprisonment.
ଆସ୍‌ବାବ୍‌, *n.* baggage, furniture, apparatus. [clothes.
ଆସ୍ତରଣ, *n.* a carpet, a bed, bed
ଆସ୍ତେ, *ad.* slowly, gently, faintly.
ଆସ୍ଥା, *n.* reverence, faith, reliance, trust.
ଆସ୍ଥାନ, *n.* a place, a site.
ଆସ୍ତିକ, *n.* believing in the existence of God.
* ଆସ୍ପଦ, *a.* object, place.
ଆସ୍ପର୍ଦ୍ଧା, *n.* emulation, rivalry, a boast.
* ଆସ୍ଫାଳନ, *n.* (sword) exercise, stwitching.
* ଆସ୍ୟ, *n.* face, countenance, visage.
ଆସ୍ୱାଦ, *n.* taste, savour, relish.
ଆହତ, *a.* smitten, beaten, injured ; *pp.* of ଆଘାତ-କ ।
* ଆହବ, *n.* war, combat. [together.
ଆହରଣ, *n.* a collecting, bringing
ଆହରିବା, *v.t.* to collect, to bring together.
* ଆହର୍ତ୍ତା, *n.* an eater ; a bringer.
ଆହା, *inter*, ah ! alas ! aha !

ଆହାବ, *n.* courage, confidence.
ଆହାର, *n.* food, a meal, repast.
ଆହାରାର୍ଥୀ, *a.* hungry, desirous of food.
ଆହାରୀ, *a.* feeding, gluttonous (used with a noun before it).
ଆହାରୋପଯୁକ୍ତ, ଆହାରୋପଯୋଗୀ, ଆହାର୍ଯ୍ୟ, *a.* fit for food, eatable.
ଆହୁତି, *n.* a burnt-offering.
ଆହୁରି, *ad.* more, much more, again.
ଆହୁଲି, *n.* an oar.
ଆହୁଲିମାରିବା, *v.i.* to row.
ଆହୂତ, *a.* called, invited, summoned.
ଆହୃତ, *a.* taken, brought; eaten, *pp.* of ଆହରିବା ।
ଆହେ, *inter.* a vocative particle, oh!
ଆହୋ, *inter.* oh! ho!;—*v.* come, come here.
*ଆହ୍ନିକ, *a.* daily, belonging to a day.
ଆହ୍ନିକଗତି, *n.* diurnal motion.
ଆହ୍ଲାଦ, *n.* joy, gladness, delight.
ଆହ୍ଲାଦିତ, *a.* delighted, glad, merry.
ଆହ୍ୱାନ, *n.* a call, invitation, summons.
ଆକ୍ଷି, *n.* an eye, the eyes.
ଆକ୍ଷିଠାର, *n.* conveying a message by winking the eyes.
ଆକ୍ଷିଠାରିବା, ଆକ୍ଷିମାରିବା, *v.* to wink.
ଆକ୍ଷିରୋଗ, *n.* eye-disease.
ଆକ୍ଷିପତା, *n.* eye-lid.
ଆକ୍ଷେପ, *n.* reproach, grief, sarcasm.
ଆକ୍ଷେପକ. *n.* a reprover, he who reproaches.

ଇ.

ଇ, the third vowel: an affix, even, indeed, very.
ଇଃ, *inter.* expressive of anger, distress, &c.
ଇଂକାର, *n.* refusal, denial.
ଇଂରାଜ, ଇଂରେଜ, *n.* Englishman.
ଇଂରାଜୀ, *a.* English.
ଇକାର, *n.* the vowel symbol (ି).
ଇକଡ, ଇକର, *n.* a sort of reed from which rough pens are made.
ଇଙ୍କାର, *n.* refusal, denial, (see ଇଂକାର).
ଇଙ୍ଗୁଣ୍ଡି, *n.* a door-sill.
ଇଙ୍ଗିତ, *n.* a hint, nod, wink, signal.
ଇଚଡ, *n.* an unripe jack-fruit.
ଇଚ୍ଛା, *n.* wish, desire, will, choice.
ଇଚ୍ଛାନ୍ୱିତ, *a.* desirous of, wishing for.
ଇଚ୍ଛାପୂର୍ବକ, *ad.* voluntarily.
ଇଚ୍ଛାମତେ, *ad.* according to the will.
ଇଚ୍ଛାମୟ, *n.* the supreme God.
ଇଚ୍ଛୁକ, *a.* desirous, solicitous, willing.
ଇଜତ୍, ଇଜ୍ଜତ, *n.* respect; chastity, modesty.
ଇଜମାଲି, *a.* joined, undivided.
ଇଜରା, ଇଜାରା, *n.* a farm; revenue of a farm.
ଇଜରାଦାର, ଇଜାରାଦାର, *n.* a leaseholder, farmer, a zemindar.
ଇଜହାର, ଇଜାହାର, *n.* a plaint.
ଇଜ୍ୟା, *n.* a sacrifice, oblation.
*ଇଞ୍ଜିଲ, *n.* the Gospel, New Testament.
ଇଟା, *n.* brick.

ଇଟାଭାଟୀ, *n.* a brick-kiln.
ଇଡିବା, *v.t.* to pour out.
ଇତର, *a.* other ; common, vulgar.
ଇତରବିଶେଷ, *n.* distinction.
ଇତରଭାଷା, *n.* common or low language.
* ଇତରେତର, *a.* mutual, both.
ଇତସ୍ତତଃ, *ad.* hither and thither.
ଇତ୍ତଲା, *n.* information, intelligence.
ଇତି, *ad.* thus far, thus, the end.
ଇତଃପରେ, *ad.* after this.
* ଇତିକର୍ତ୍ତବ୍ୟ, *a.* indispensable.
ଇତିମଧ୍ୟରେ, *ad.* during this, meanwhile, in the interim.
ଇତିବୃତ୍ତ, *n.* history, that which has happened.
ଇତିହାସ, *n.* history, narrative, legend.
* ଇତ୍ୟନୁସାରେ, *ad.* according to this.
ଇତ୍ୟବସରେ, *ad.* in the meantime, at this opportunity.
ଇତ୍ୟାଦି, *ad.* etcetera, and so forth.
ଇଦାନୀଂ, *ad.* now, recently, lately.
* ଇଦାନୀନ୍ତନ, *a.* recent, modern, new.
ଇନ୍‌ସାଫ, *n.* decision of a case, right, justice, equity.
ଇନାମ୍, *n.* a reward, gift of land.
* ଇନ୍ଦିବର, ଇନ୍ଦୀବର, *n.* the blue lotus.
* ଇନ୍ଦୁ, *n.* the moon.
* ଇନ୍ଦୁର, *n.* a rat, a mouse.
ଇନ୍ଦ୍ର, *n.* sovereign of the gods, *Indra.*
* ଇନ୍ଦ୍ରଗୋପ, *n.* an insect, lady-bird.
ଇନ୍ଦ୍ରଜାଲ, *n.* juggling, deception.
ଇନ୍ଦ୍ରଜାଲିକ, *a.* magical, deceptive.

ଇନ୍ଦ୍ରଧନୁ, *n.* rain-bow.
* ଇନ୍ଦ୍ରନୀଳ, *n.* a sapphire.
ଇନ୍ଦ୍ରପ୍ରସ୍ଥ, *n.* the ancient name of Delhi.
ଇନ୍ଦ୍ରାଣୀ, *n.* consort of *Indra* ; a shrub (vital negundo).
* ଇନ୍ଦ୍ରାୟୁଧ, *n.* *Indra's* bow, the rain-bow.
ଇନ୍ଦ୍ରିୟ, *n.* organs of sensation and perception.
* ଇନ୍ଦ୍ରିୟଗୋଚର, *a.* perceptible to the senses.
ଇନ୍ଦ୍ରିୟଦମନ, *n.* self-control, self-denial
ଇନ୍ଦ୍ରିୟଦୋଷ, *n.* evil propensity, concupiscence.
* ଇନ୍ଦ୍ରିୟବଶତ୍ୱ, *n.* subjection of the senses.
* ଇନ୍ଦ୍ରିୟପରାୟଣ, *a.* devoted to the senses, carnal, sensual.
* ଇନ୍ଧନ, *n.* fuel, firewood.
ଇମ୍‌ତିହାନ, *n.* an examination, proof, trial.
ଇମାନ୍, *n.* faith, conscience, religion.
ଇୟତ୍ତା, *n.* fixed quantity, limit.
ଇୟାର, (vulgar), *n.* paramour, lover.
ଇରାବତୀ, *n.* a river in the Punjab.
ଇଲତ୍, *n.* filth, dirt ;—*a.* filthy, nasty.
ଇଲମ୍, *n.* learning, teaching, knowledge, qualification.
ଇଲାକା, *n.* jurisdiction.
ଇଲାକାଦାର, *n.* one possessing jurisdiction or authority.
ଇଲାଜ୍, *n.* remedy, medicine.
ଇଲିଶ, ଇଲ୍ଲିଶ, ଇଲ୍ଲୀଶ, *n.* the hilsa fish.

ଇଶାମୀ, *a.* witnessing.

ଇଶାରା, *n.* a nod or wink, a sign or token.

ଇଷ୍, ଇସ୍, *inter.* expression of anger, pain, or surprise.

ଇସବଗୋଲ, *n.* a medicinal seed.

* ଇଷୁ, *n.* an arrow.

* ଇଷୁଧର, *n.* an archer.

* ଇଷୁଧି, *n.* a quiver.

ଇଷ୍ଟ, *a.* desired, cherished, worshipped.

* ଇଷ୍ଟକ, ଇଷ୍ଟକା, *n.* a brick.

ଇଷ୍ଟକର୍ମ, *n.* a wished-for work.

ଇଷ୍ଟଦେବ, *n.* a tutelary deity.

ଇଷ୍ଟଦେବତା, *n.* a chosen god.

ଇଷ୍ଟାଳାପ, *n.* profitable conversation.

ଇସ୍ତଫା, *n.* resignation.

ଇସ୍ତମରାର, *a.* permanent, perpetual.

ଇସ୍ତିହାର, *n.* a proclamation, notice.

ଇସ୍ତ୍ରୀ, *n.* a smoothing-iron.

ଇସ୍ପାତ, *n.* steel.

* ଇହ, *pron.* this, here.

ଇହକାଳ, *n.* the present life.

ଇହଲୋକ, *n.* the present world.

* ଇକ୍ଷୁ, *n.* sugar-cane.

* ଇକ୍ଷୁରସ, *n.* juice of the sugar-cane.

ଇକ୍ଷ୍ୱାକୁ, *n.* father of the race of the sun.

ଈ.

ଈ, the fourth vowel; an exclamation of grief or anger.

ଈଃ, *interj.* expressive of contempt or sorrow.

ଈକାର, *n.* (in *Gram.*) the letter ଈ, the vowel symbol (ୀ).

ଈକାରାନ୍ତ, *a.* ending with the letter ଈ or the vowel symbol (ୀ); having a final ଈ.

ଈତି, *n.* agricultural calamity.

* ଈଦୃଶ, ଈଦୃକ୍, *ad.* thus, such, like this.

ଈର୍ଷା, ଈର୍ଷ୍ୟା, *n.* envy, spite, malice.

ଈର୍ଷାଳୁ, ଈର୍ଷ୍ୟାଳୁ, *a.* spiteful, malicious.

* ଈଶ, *n.* lord, master; *Siva.*

ଈଶାନକୋଣ, *n.* north-east.

ଈଶ୍ୱର, *n.* God, the Creator, Lord.

ଈଶ୍ୱରବାଦ, *n.* theism.

ଈଶ୍ୱରବାଦୀ, *a.* theistic.

ଈଶ୍ୱରତ୍ୱ, *n*, Godhead, the attributes of God.

ଈଶ୍ୱରନିଷ୍ଠ, *a.* firmly relying on God.

ଈଶ୍ୱରନିଷ୍ଠା, *n.* devotion to God, trust.

ଈଷ, ଈଶ, *n.* the beam of a plough.

ଈଷତ୍, *a.* a little, somewhat.

ଈଷଦୁଷ୍ଣ, *a.* lukewarm.

* ଈଷଦ୍ଦର୍ଶନ, *n.* a glance, a slight view.

* ଈଷଦ୍ଧାସ୍ୟ, *n.* slight laugh, a smile.

* ଈଷଦ୍ବକ୍ର, *a.* somewhat crooked, bent.

* ଈକ୍ଷଣ, *n.* the eye; seeing, looking at.

ଉ.

ଉ, the fifth vowel; an exclamation, oh!

ଉଃ, *interj.* an exclamation, oh! aye! ha!
ଉଆଁସ, *n.* change of the moon.
ଉଆ, *n.* rice not boiled before husking.
ଉଆଉ, *n.* a tree and its acid fruit.
ଉଆରସ୍, *n.* heir.
ଉଆସ, *a.* cheap.
ଉଆସ, *n.* a royal residence, a palace.
ଉଇଁବା, *v.* to rise into view.
ଉଇ, *n.* a termite, white-ant.
ଉଇହୁଙ୍କା, *n.* a white-ant hill.
ଉକାର, *n.* (in *Gram.*) the letter ଉ; the vowel symbol (ୁ).
ଉକାରାନ୍ତ, *a.* ending with the letter ଉ or the vowel symbol (ୁ).
ଉକାଳିବା, *v.* to vomit.
ଉକିଲ, *n.* an attorney, a pleader.
ଉକୁଚେଇବା, *v.* to hang.
ଉକୁଟାଇବା, *v.* to anoint, to apply to.
ଉକୁଟିସିବା, *v.* to go bad or rotten.
ଉକୁଣିଆପୋକ, *n.* a black insect mostly found in rice.
ଉକୁଣୀ, *n.* a louse.
ଉକ୍ତ, *a.* said, spoken, aforesaid.
* ଉକ୍ତି, *n.* a word, a saying, a reply.
ଉଖାଡିବା, *v.* to uproot.
ଉଖୁଡା, *n.* rice parched in molasses and ghee.
ଉଖାରିବା, ଉଖୁସାଇବା, *v.* to scratch, to wound slightly; to poke.
ଉଖୁସାଉଖୁର, *n.* mutual scratching (*i.e.* in the sense of quarrelling).
ଉଖୁରିଆ, *n.* a poker.
ଉଗାଳିବା, *v.* to block the way with outstretched arms.
ଉଗୁଡାଇବା, ଉଗୁଡେଇବା, *v.* to turn upside down.
ଉଗୁର, *n.* arrogance, pride.
ଉଗ୍ର, *a.* pungent, passionate, surly.
ଉଗ୍ରତା, *n.* surliness, pride.
ଉଗ୍ରଗନ୍ଧ, *a.* strong-scented.
ଉଘାଡ, *n.* a platform with thatched cover erected for the detection of wild animals in any field bearing crops.
ଉଘେଇବା, *v.* to cast in the teeth.
ଉଙ୍ଘାଇବା, *v.* to begin to speak.
ଉଙ୍ଘେଇବା, *v.* to nod, to be drowsy.
ଉଚିତ, *a.* morally right, proper.
ଉଚ୍ଚ, *a.* high, tall, lofty, elevated.
ଉଚ୍ଚତା, *n.* height.
ଉଚ୍ଚନୀଚ, *a.* uneven, high and low.
* ଉଚ୍ଚରିତ, *a.* uttered, pronounced.
ଉଚ୍ଛଳିତ, *a.* overflowing.
ଉଚ୍ଚାଟନ, *n.* disquietude, sadness; incantations that cause ruin.
ଉଚ୍ଚାବଚ, *a.* uneven, multiform.
ଉଚ୍ଚାରଣ, *n.* pronunciation, utterance.
ଉଚ୍ଚାରିତ, *a.* uttered.
* ଉଚ୍ଚାକୃତ, *a.* raised, elevated.
ଉଚ୍ଚୈଃ, *ad.* loud, aloud, on high.
ଉଚ୍ଚୈଃସ୍ୱର, *n.* a loud voice.
ଉଛୁଣି, *ad.* now, just now.
ଉଛୁର, *a.* late, behind time.
ଉଛୁଳିବା, *v.* to overflow.
ଉଜଡ଼ା, *a.* ruined, laid waste.

ଉଚ୍ଛିଷ୍ଟ, *n.* left, remaining, orts.
ଉଚ୍ଛୃଙ୍ଖଳ, *a.* self-willed. [age.
ଉଚ୍ଛେଦ, *n.* devastation, ruin, dam-
ଉଚ୍ଛ୍ୱାସ, *n.* a sigh. [&c.
ଉଞ୍ଛିବା, *v.* to prune trees, plants,
ଉଜାଗର, *a.* awake.
ଉଜାଡ଼, *a.* laid waste, destroyed, desolate. [pulate.
ଉଜାଡ଼ିବା, *v.* to root up, to depo-
ଉଜାଣି, *ad.* against the stream.
ଉଜିର, *n.* a counsellor of state.
ଉଜୁଡ଼ିବା, ଉଜୁଡ଼ିଯିବା, *v.i.* to lay waste, to waste, to destroy.
ଉଛେଁଳିବା, *v.* to finish, to complete.
ଉଜ୍ଜ୍ୱଳ, *a.* luminous, light, clear.
ଉଝାଳିବା, *v.* to clear out (a well or a tank); to repair (a house).
ଉଦ୍ଧଟ, *a.* self-willed, boastful.
ଉଟ, *n.* a camel.
* ଉଟଜ, *n.* a hut of leaves.
ଉଠାଇବା, *v.* to raise, to stir, to make get up. [up.
ଉଠାଉଠି, *n.* act of raising or taking
ଉଠାଣ, *n.* taking goods on credit; the passing of clouds from the sea. [tion.
ଉଠାଣୀ, *n.* steepness, height, eleva-
ଉଠିଆ, *a.* cultivated.
ଉଠିଆର, *n.* the day on which the rite of purification by bathing of the mother and new-born infant is performed,—about the seventh day after birth.

ଉଠିବା, *v.* to get up, to rise, to mount.
ଉଡ଼ଣା, ଉଢ଼ଣା, *n.* a sheet, a flowing upper garment.
ଉଡ଼ନ୍ତା, *a.* flying.
ଉଡ଼ା, *n.* flying;—*a.* rumoured.
ଉଡ଼ାଣିଆ, *a.* extravagant, prodigal; rumoured. [the air.
ଉଡ଼ିବା, *v.* to fly, to move through
ଉଡ଼ିଶା, *n.* Orissa. [flying.
ଉଡ଼ୁଉଡ଼ୁ, *ad.* ready to fly, while
ଉଡ଼ୁମ୍ବର, *n.* a wild fig-tree.
ଉଡ୍ଡୟନ, *n.* flying, flight.
ଉଡ୍ଡୀନ, ଉଡ୍ଡୀୟମାନ, *a.* flying.
ଉଣ୍ଡିବା, *v.* to grope, to search for.
* ଉର୍ଣ୍ଣନାଭ, *n.* a spider.
* ଉର୍ଣ୍ଣା, *n.* wool;—*a.* woollen.
ଉତାକ୍ତ, *a.* impatient, troubled, uneasy.
ଉତୁରିବା, *v.* to alight, to arrive; to bubble up.
ଉତ୍କଟ, *a.* painful; excessive; oppressive.
* ଉତ୍କଣ୍ଠା, *n.* regret, care, anxiety.
ଉତ୍କଣ୍ଠିତ, *a.* eager, anxious.
ଉତ୍କଳ, *n.* the country of Orissa.
ଉତ୍କର୍ଷ, *n.* excellence, abundance.
ଉତ୍କୃଷ୍ଟ, *a.* excellent, elevated, best.
* ଉତ୍କୋଚ, *n.* a bribe.
ଉତ୍କ୍ରମ, *n.* a departure from order, a leap, a bound.
ଉତ୍କ୍ରାନ୍ତ, *a.* leaped up, transgressed.
ଉତ୍କ୍ରୋଶ, *n.* an osprey, an eagle.

* ଉତ୍ଖାତ, *n.* eradication, destruction.

* ଉତ୍କ୍ଷିପ୍ତ, *a.* thrown up, tossed up.

ଉତ୍କ୍ଷେପ, ଉତ୍କ୍ଷେପଣ, *n.* a tossing up.

ଉତ୍ତପ୍ତ, *a.* heated, hot, excited.

ଉତ୍ତମ, *a.* very good, excellent, best.

ଉତ୍ତମର୍ଣ୍ଣ, *n.* a creditor, money-lender.

ଉତ୍ତମା, *n.* a beautiful or excellent woman.

ଉତ୍ତମାଙ୍ଗ, *n.* the head, chief member.

ଉତ୍ତର, *n.* an answer; the north;—*a.* northern; future.

ଉତ୍ତରକାଳ, *n.* the future, time to come.

ଉତ୍ତରକେନ୍ଦ୍ର, *n.* (in *Geog.*) North Pole.

* ଉତ୍ତରକ୍ରିୟା, *n.* funeral rites.

ଉତ୍ତରଖଣ୍ଡନ, *n.* a refutation, rejoinder.

ଉତ୍ତରଣ, *n.* arriving, alighting, landing.

ଉତ୍ତରପକ୍ଷ, *n.* reply to an argument, refutation.

ଉତ୍ତରପ୍ରତ୍ୟୁତ୍ତର, *n.* conversation, a dialogue, an altercation.

* ଉତ୍ତରଫାଲ୍ଗୁନୀ, *n.* the twelfth mansion in the Hindu Zodiac.

ଉତ୍ତରମେରୁ, *n.* North Pole

ଉତ୍ତରବୃତ୍ତ, *n.* (in *Geog.*) Arctic Circle.

* ଉତ୍ତରସାକ୍ଷୀ, *n.* one who testifies upon what he has heard.

* ଉତ୍ତରସାଧକ, *n.* an auxiliary, a helper, a prompter.

ଉତ୍ତରା, *n.* a copy of any writing.

ଉତ୍ତରାଧିକାର, *n.* an inheritance.

* ଉତ୍ତରାଧିକାରପତ୍ର, *n.* a will, a testament.

ଉତ୍ତରାଧିକାରୀ, *n.* an heir, a successor.

ଉତ୍ତରାୟଣ, *n.* (in *Astron.*) the sun's north declination.

ଉତ୍ତରାୟଣାନ୍ତବୃତ୍ତ, *n.* (in *Geog.*) the Tropic.

ଉତ୍ତରିବା, *v.* to arrive at a place, to alight.

ଉତ୍ତରୀ, ଉତ୍ତରୀୟ, *n.* light upper garment worn as a shawl.

ଉତ୍ତରୋତ୍ତର, *ad.* more and more, again and again.

* ଉତ୍ତାନ, *a.* spread out, lying on the back with the face upwards.

ଉତ୍ତାପ, *n.* heat, ardour, fervour, zeal.

ଉତ୍ତାପିତ, *a.* heated.

ଉତ୍ତାର, *n.* an antidote.

ଉତ୍ତାରିବା, *v.* to copy a writing.

ଉତ୍ତାରେ, *ad.* afterwards.

ଉତ୍ତୀର୍ଣ୍ଣ, *a.* arrived; passed (the exam.); got over, escaped.

* ଉତ୍ତୁଙ୍ଗ, *a.* high, lofty, elevated.

ଉତ୍ତେଜନା, *n.* inducement, excitement, incitement, enthusiasm.

ଉତ୍ତୋଳନ, *n.* a lifting, a raising.

ଉତ୍ତୋଳିତ, *a.* raised, lifted.

* ଉତ୍ତ୍ୟକ୍ତ, *a.* rejected, disgusted, vexed.

ଉଥଳନ, *n.* overflowing, boiling over.

ଉତ୍ଥାନ, *n.* a rising, a getting up.

ଉତ୍ଥାପନ, *n.* the act of raising up.

ଉତ୍ଥିତ, *a.* risen, raised, exalted.

ଉତ୍ପତ୍ତି, *n.* production, a product.

ଉତ୍ପନ୍ନ, *a.* produced, arisen from.

* ଉତ୍ପଳ, *n.* a water-lily, a lotus.

ଉତ୍ପାଟନ, *n.* a rooting up, an eradicating.

ଉତ୍ପାତ, *n.* ruin, outrage, violence.

ଉତ୍ପାଦକ, *a.* productive, effective; —*n.* generator, producer, originator, father.

ଉତ୍ପାଦନ, *n.* a bringing forth, a producing.

ଉତ୍ପୀଡ଼ନ, *n.* oppression, pressing, pressure.

* ଉତ୍ପ୍ରେକ୍ଷା, *n.* similitude, resemblance, illustration.

* ଉତ୍ପ୍ଳୁତ, *a.* disordered, reversed.

ଉତ୍ଫୁଲ୍ଲ, *a.* expanded, blown, gladdened.

ଉତ୍ସ, *n.* a spring, fountain, cascade.

ଉତ୍ସଙ୍ଗ, *n.* the bosom, lap, hips.

ଉତ୍ସନ୍ନ, *a.* destroyed, ruined.

ଉତ୍ସବ, *n.* a festival, holiday, festivity.

ଉତ୍ସର୍ଗ, *n.* a gift, oblation, offering, dedication.

ଉତ୍ସାହ, *n.* promptness, energy, zeal.

ଉତ୍ସାହିତ, *a.* excited, encouraged, cheered, emboldened.

ଉତ୍ସାହୀ, *a.* resolute, courageous, persevering.

ଉତ୍ସୁକ, *a.* zealous, eager, energetic.

* ଉତ୍ସୃଷ୍ଟ, *a.* offered, given in sacrifice, dedicated.

ଉଦ୍, a *prefix*, meaning superiority, up, on, over, apart, power, etc.

ଉଦଧି, *n.* the sea, the ocean.

ଉଦନ୍ତ, *n.* tidings, report, intelligence.

ଉଦୟ, *n.* a rising into view.

ଉଦୟକାଳ, *n.* time of sun-rising, time of prosperity.

ଉଦୟଗିରି, ଉଦୟାଚଳ, *n.* the eastern mountains.

ଉଦୟାସ୍ତ, *ad.* from sunrise to sunset.

ଉଦର, *n.* the belly, bowels.

* ଉଦରମ୍ଭରି, *a.* gluttonous, greedy.

ଉଦରାମୟ, *n.* dysentery, diarrhœa.

ଉଦରୀ, *a.* dropsical.

* ଉଦାନ, *n.* the air supposed to be in the throat.

ଉଦାର, *a.* generous, munificent.

ଉଦାରତା, *n.* generosity, liberality, nobility.

ଉଦାସ, *a.* stoical, sad;—*n.* solitude.

ଉଦାସୀ, ଉଦାସୀନ, *a.* indifferent, cynical;—*n.* a mendicant, a recluse.

ଉଦାହରଣ, *n.* an example, illustration.

ଉଦିତ, *a.* risen into view; * spoken.

* ଉଦୀଚୀ, *n.* the north quarter.

ଉଦୁମ୍ବର, *n.* a species of fig-tree.

* ଉଦ୍ଗତ, *a.* risen, ascended, vomited.

* ଉଦ୍ଗମ, *n.* ascension, going upwards.

* ଉଦ୍ଗାର, *n.* vomiting, belching.

* ଉଦ୍ଗ୍ରୀବ, *a.* with outstretched neck.

ଉଦ୍ଘାଟନ, *n.* an opening, an unbarring.

* ଉଦଂଶ, *n.* a gadfly, mosquito, gnat.

ଉଦାମ, *a.* unfettered, unbridled; unrestrained, free, unconfined.

ଉଦ୍ଦିଷ୍ଟ, *a.* regarded, designed.

ଉଦ୍ଦୀପକ, *a.* luminous; stimulating, exciting.

ଉଦ୍ଦୀପନା, ଉଦ୍ଦୀପନ, *n.* a blazing up; a glowing; revival, awakening.

ଉଦ୍ଦୀପ୍ତ, ଉଦ୍ଦୀପିତ, *a.* inflamed, lighted, illuminated; excited, animated.

ଉଦ୍ଦେଶ, *n.* aim, motive; search, vestige, trace.

ଉଦ୍ଦେଶ୍ୟ, *n.* aim, motive;—*a.* recognizable, traceable.

ଉଦ୍ଧତ, *a.* audacious, bold, rude.

* ଉଦ୍ଧରଣ, *n.* deliverance, salvation.

ଉଦ୍ଧାର, *n.* deliverance, rescue; the extracting of matter from a book.

ଉଦ୍ଧୃତ, *a.* quoted, extracted; * delivered, rescued.

* ଉଦ୍ଗାର, *n.* vomiting or belching out.

* ଉଦ୍ବାହ, *n.* a marriage, matrimony.

ଉଦ୍ବାର୍ଷ, *a.* excessive, proud.

ଉଦ୍ବିଗ୍ନ, *a.* perplexed, uneasy, anxious, troubled.

* ଉଦ୍ବିଡାଳ, *n.* an otter.

ଉଦ୍ବୃତ୍ତ, *a.* left as a surplus or remainder.

ଉଦ୍ବେଗ, *n.* anxiety, uneasiness, care.

* ଉଦ୍ବୋଧ, *n.* recollection, sentiment arising in the mind.

ଉଦ୍ଭବ, *n.* production, birth.

ଉଦ୍ଭାବନ, *n.* invention, discovery.

ଉଦ୍ଭିଦ୍, ଉଦ୍ଭିଦ, ଉଦ୍ଭିଜ୍ଜ, *n.* vegetable substances.

ଉଦ୍ଭିଦବିଦ୍ୟା, *n.* the science of botany.

* ଉଦ୍ଭୂତ, *a.* born of, produced.

ଉଦ୍ୟତ, *a.* prepared to do (an act), about to do (a thing), ready.

ଉଦ୍ୟମ, *n.* promptness, exertion, effort.

ଉଦ୍ୟମୀ, *a.* active, busy, prompt.

ଉଦ୍ୟାନ, *n.* a garden, a park, a grove.

* ଉଦ୍ୟାନପାଳ, *n.* a gardener.

ଉଦ୍ୟୋଗ, *n.* effort, endeavour, exertion, zeal, enterprise.

ଉଦ୍ୟୋଗୀ, *a.* active, industrious, energetic, endeavouring.

ଉଦ୍ରେକ, *n.* appearance; increase; beginning.

ଉଧ, ଓଧ, *n.* an otter.

ଉଧାର, *n.* a loan, a debt.

ଉନ୍ୟାୟ, *a.* without justice or reason, (see ଅନ୍ୟାୟ).

ଉନ୍ନତ, *a.* elevated, exalted, arisen.

ଉନ୍ନତାନତ, *a.* risen and fallen, elevated and depressed, rugged.

ଉନ୍ନତି, *n.* increase, prosperity, advancement.

ଉନ୍ନିଦ୍ର, *a.* sleepless, waking.

ଉନ୍ମତ୍ତ, *a.* frantic, mad, infatuated, deranged.

* ଉନ୍ମନା, *a.* absent in mind, vexed, regretting.

ଉନ୍ମାଦ, *n.* madness, mania.

ଉନ୍ମୀଳନ, *n.* opening; expansion.

* ଉନ୍ମୁଖ, *a.* prompt, looking up, eager. [up.

* ଉନ୍ମୂଳନ, *n.* eradication, rooting

ଉନ୍ମେଷ, *n.* opening (of the eyes), winking ; expansion. [loosing.

ଉନ୍ମୋଚନ, *n.* act of untying, un-

ଉପ, a *prefix* meaning towards, near to, by the side of, under.

ଉପକରଣ, *n.* apparatus, implements; materials ; insignia of royalty.

ଉପକାର, *n.* assistance, help, benefit.

ଉପକାରକ, *n.* helper ;–*a.* beneficent.

ଉପକାରିତା, *n.* efficacy, usefulness.

ଉପକାରୀ, *a.* helpful, assisting.

ଉପକୂଳ, *n.* shore, bank.

ଉପକୃତ, *a.* helped, assisted, benefitted, favoured. [tempt.

ଉପକ୍ରମ, *n.* commencement, an at-

ଉପକ୍ରମଣିକା, *n.* a preface.

ଉପଗତ, *a.* arrived, approached, attached to. [cess.

* ଉପଚୟ, *n.* abundance, plenty, ex-

* ଉପଚାର, *n.* service, a practice, usage. [ance, a trade.

* ଉପଜୀବିକା, *n.* livelihood, mainten-

ଉପଜୀବୀ, *a.* used only in conjunction with other words and signifies living upon, dependent on.

* ଉପଢୌକନ, *n.* a present, gift, largess. [a hill.

ଉପତ୍ୟକା, *n.* a valley at the foot of

ଉପଦର୍ଦ, *n.* oppression, tyranny.

* ଉପଦଂଶ, *n.* venereal disease.

* ଉପଦିଷ୍ଟ, *a.* instructed, taught.

* ଉପଦେବତା, *n.* a demigod, a phantom. [sermon.

ଉପଦେଶ, *n.* instruction, advice,

ଉପଦେଶକ, * ଉପଦେଷ୍ଟା, *n.* a teacher, a preacher.

ଉପଦ୍ରବ, *n.* calamity, ruin, outrage.

ଉପଦ୍ରବୀ, *a.* oppressive, tyrannical.

ଉପଦ୍ୱୀପ, *n.* a small island, a peninsula.

* ଉପନାମ, *n.* a surname, nickname.

ଉପନିବେଶ, *n.* colony.

ଉପନିଷତ୍, ଉପନିଷଦ୍, *n.* the philosophical part of the *Veda.*

ଉପନୀତ, *a.* arrived; invested.

ଉପନ୍ୟାସ, *n.* a novel, a prologue, tale, story, an entertaining story.

ଉପପତି, *n.* a paramour, a gallant.

ଉପପତ୍ତି, *n.* (in *Geom.*) the proof, demonstration. [woman.

* ଉପପତ୍ନୀ, *n.* a concubine, a kept

ଉପପଦ, *n.* (in *Gram.*) a compound, an adverbial phrase.

ଉପପାଦ୍ୟ, *n.* (in *Geom.*) a theorem.

* ଉପବନ, *n.* an artificial forest, a park. [fast.

ଉପବାସ, *n.* a religious or voluntary

ଉପବାସୀ, *a.* fasting, practising voluntary fastings.

ଉପବିଷ୍ଟ, *a.* seated, entered.

ଉପବୀତ, *n.* the sacred thread, *poitá.*

* ଉପବେଶନ, *n.* act of sitting.

* ଉପଭୋଗ, *n.* luxurious enjoyment,
gratification. [ness.
ଉପମା, *n.* comparison, simile, like-
* ଉପମାତା, *n.* a wet-nurse, a foster-
mother. [ture.
* ଉପମିତ, *n.* simile, likeness, pic-
* ଉପମେୟ, *a* comparable. [coming.
ଉପଯୁକ୍ତ, *a.* proper, suitable, fit, be-
ଉପଯୋଗୀ, *a.* suitable, worthy, fit,
proper. [upon, over.
ଉପର, *n.* the top, height ;—*ad.*
ଉପରଓଳି, ଉପରବେଳା, *n.* afternoon.
ଉପରମହଲ, *n.* an upper storey.
* ଉପରାଗ, *n.* an eclipse ; a calamity.
ଉପରି, *ad.* on, upon, above;–*a.* extra.
ଉପରିଭାଗ, *n.* the upper part. [lity.
ଉପରୋଧ, *n.* favour, support, partia-
* ଉପର୍ଯ୍ୟୁପରି, *ad.* one above another,
higher and higher.
* ଉପଲ, *n.* a stone, a small stone.
* ଉପଲବ୍ଧ, *a.* obtained, received,
guessed.
* ଉପଲବ୍ଧି, *n.* understanding, percep-
tion ; gain, profit.
* ଉପଲକ୍ଷ, * ଉପଲକ୍ଷଣ, *n.* an indica-
tion, illustration. [ing.
ଉପଶମ, *n.* alleviation, relief, abat-
ଉପଶାନ୍ତି, *n.* alleviation, tranquility.
ଉପସର୍ଗ, *n.* (in *Gram.*) a prefix ; a
symptom, portent. [destruction.
ଉପସଂହାର, *n.* finishing, conclusion;
ଉପସାଗର, *n.* gulf, bay.
* ଉପସ୍ତ୍ରୀ, *n.* a concubine.

* ଉପସ୍ଥ, *n.* the genitals;—*a.* near.
ଉପସ୍ଥାନ, *n.* attendance, presence ;
arrival.
ଉପସ୍ଥାପିତ, *a.* placed near to.
ଉପସ୍ଥିତ, *a.* arrived, present, at hand.
ଉପସ୍ଥିତି, *n.* see ଉପସ୍ଥାନ.
* ଉପସ୍ୱତ୍ୱ, *n.* profit, revenue, income.
ଉପହାର, *n.* an offering, present,
gift.
ଉପହାସ, *n.* ridicule, joke, jest.
* ଉପାଖ୍ୟାନ, *n.* a narrative, tale,
story.
* ଉପାଙ୍ଗ, *n.* a subordinate member.
ଉପାଡିବା, *v.* to uproot, to eradicate.
* ଉପାଦାନ, *n.* the element or sub-
stance of which a thing is made.
* ଉପାଦେୟ, *a.* excellent; acceptable.
ଉପାଧି, *n.* surname, a title, an attri-
ଉପାଧିପତ୍ର, *n.* a diploma. [bute.
* ଉପାଧ୍ୟାୟ, *n.* an instructor, teach-
er, tutor.
* ଉପାଧ୍ୟାୟାନୀ, * ଉପାଧ୍ୟାୟୀ, *n.* an in-
structress or teacher
* ଉପାନ୍ତ, *a.* near, proximate.
ଉପାୟ, *n.* an expedient, a remedy,
means. [ents.
ଉପାୟୀ, *a.* making use of expedi-
ଉପାର୍ଜନ, *n.* gain, earnings, savings.
ଉପାର୍ଜିତ, *a.* acquired, laid up.
ଉପାସ, *n.* a fast.
ଉପାସକ, *n.* a worshipper, servant;
—*a.* supplicatory. [plication.
ଉପାସନା, *n.* service, worship, sup-

ଉପାସ୍ୟ, *a.* adorable, worshipful.

ଉପୁଡ଼ିପଡ଼ିବା, ଉପୁଡ଼ିବା, ଉପୁଡ଼ିଯିବା, *v.* to be rooted up, to be destroyed.

ଉପୁରି, *a.* extra.

ଉପୁରିମୂଲ, *n.* extra wages.

ଉପୁରିମୂଲିଆ, *n.* extra cooly.

* ଉପେନ୍ଦ୍ର, *n.* a name of *Krishna.*

ଉପେକ୍ଷା, *n.* neglect, disregard, contempt.

* ଉପେକ୍ଷିତ, *a.* neglected, disregarded.

* ଉପ୍ତ, *a.* sown, disseminated, scattered.

ଉବାର, *a.* concealed, unknown.

ଉବୁଡ଼, *a.* prostrate (with the face down to the ground).

ଉଭୟ, *pron.* both, two together.

ଉଭୟଚର, *a.* amphibious.

ଉଭୟତ୍ର, *ad.* in both places.

ଉଭା, *a.* erect, standing upright.

ଉଭାଇଯିବା, ଉଭେଇବା, ଉଭେଇଯିବା, *v.* to disappear.

ଉଭୁଜବା, *v.* to dry wet rice by the fire.

ଉମର, *n.* age, the life-time.

* ଉମା, *n.* *Doorgá.*

* ଉରଃ, *n.* the breast, bosom, chest.

* ଉରଗ, *n.* a snake, reptile ;—*a.* crawling.

* ଉରଜ, *n.* the breast, paps, teat.

* ଉରୋଗାମୀ, *a.* creeping, crawling.

ଉର୍ବର, *a.* arable, fertile.

ଉଲୁଗୁଣାଦେବା, *v.* to cast in one's teeth, to upbraid, to twit.

ଉଲଙ୍ଗ, *a.* naked, unclothed, bare.

ଉଲଙ୍ଗତା, *n.* nakedness.

ଉଲଟ, ଉଲଟା, *a.* upside-down, reversed.

ଉଲଟପାଲଟ, *n.* topsy-turvy, disorder.

ଉଲଟାଇବା, *v.* to upset, to overturn.

ଉଲଟିବା, ଉଲଟିପଡ଼ିବା, ଉଲଟିଯିବା, *v.* to be upset, to be overturned.

ଉଲାସ, *n.* address, superscription.

ଉଲାରିପକାଇବା, ଉଲାରିବା, *v.* to loose.

ଉଲୁରିବା, ଉଲୁରିଯିବା, ଉଲୁରିପଡ଼ିବା, *v.* to get loose, to be elated.

* ଉଲ୍କା, *n.* a meteor ; torch, firebrand.

ଉଲ୍କାପାତ, *n.* a meteor falling.

* ଉଲ୍କାମୁଖୀ, *n.* a fox.

ଉଲ୍ଲଙ୍ଘନ, *n.* the act of transgressing or violating, transgression.

ଉଲ୍ଲାସ, *n.* joy, delight, exultation.

ଉଲ୍ଲୁ, ଓଲ୍ଲୁ, *n.* a stupid fellow, a bumpkin, *Eng.* an ass.

ଉଲ୍ଲେଖ, *n.* speechifying, mentioning, enunciating, allusion.

* ଉଶୀର, ଉଷୀର, *n.* roots of *bená* grass, *Khaskhas.*

* ଉଷା, *n.* the dawn of day.

ଉଷାକାଳ, *n.* the dawn, morning.

ଉଷୁନା, *n.* paddy or rice boiled in the husk.

ଉଷୁମ, *a.* warm, lukewarm.

* ଉଷ୍ଟ୍ର, *n.* a camel, dromedary.

* ଉଷ୍ଟ୍ରିକା, *n.* a female camel.

ଉଷ୍ଣ, *a.* warm, hot, sultry; passionate.

ଉଷ୍ଣକଟିବନ୍ଧ, *n.* (*Geog.*) torrid zone.

ଉଷ୍ଣତା, *n.* heat, warmth, passion.

* ଉଷ୍ଣୀଷ, *n.* a turban, a diadem.

ଉଷ୍ମାଇବା, ଉଷୁମାଇବା, *v.* to make warm, to warm, to incubate, to brood.

ଉସ୍କାଇବା, ଉସ୍କେଇବା, *v.* to excite, to agitate, to encourage.

ଉସ୍ୱାସ, *a.* light, easy, pleasurable.

ଉହା, *n.* a file; a polypus.

ଉହାଡ, *n.* a place out of sight, a hiding place; cover.

ଉହୁଁ, *interj.* expressing refusal or negation.

ଉହ୍ଲାଲ, ଉହ୍ଲେଲ, *n.* an earthen pot for carrying fire from place to place.

ଊ.

ଊ, the sixth vowel.

ଊଃ, *inter.* expressive of sudden pain; oh!

ଊକାର, *n.* (in *Gram.*) the letter ଊ or that character which (ୂ) indicates the sound of ଊ

ଊଣା, *a.* less, decrease.

ଊଣାଧିକ, *a,* less or more.

ଊଣେଇଶ, *n.* and *a.* nineteen, 19, XIX.

* ଊରୁ, *n.* the thigh.

* ଊରୁଜ, *n.* the Baishya caste;—*a.* born in the thigh.

* ଊର୍ଣ୍ଣନାଭ, *n.* a spider.

* ଊର୍ଣ୍ଣା, *n.* wool or fur.

ଊର୍ଦ୍ଧ୍ୱ, *a.* high, lofty, elevated, up.

ଊର୍ଦ୍ଧ୍ୱଗାମୀ, *a.* ascending.

ଊର୍ଦ୍ଧ୍ୱତନ, *a.* superior, higher, upper.

ଊର୍ଦ୍ଧ୍ୱଦୃଷ୍ଟି, *a.* looking upward.

ଊର୍ଦ୍ଧ୍ୱବାହୁ, *n.* a devotee with up-lifted arm.

ଊର୍ଦ୍ଧ୍ୱରେତା, *n.* a devotee who observes strict chastity.

ଊର୍ଦ୍ଧ୍ୱଲୋକ, *n.* heaven of the gods.

ଊର୍ଦ୍ଧ୍ୱସ୍ଥ, *a.* superior, above, upper.

ଊର୍ଦ୍ଧ୍ୱଶ୍ୱାସ, *n.* expiration, difficult breathing.

* ଊର୍ମି, *n.* a wave, a billow.

* ଊଷର, *a.* saline;—*n.* saline earth.

ଊହ୍ୟ, *a.* (in *Gram.*) elliptical, requiring to be investigated.

ଋ.

ଋ, the seventh vowel.

ଋକ୍, *n.* the first *Veda.*

ଋକାର, *n.* (in *Gram.*) the letter ଋ or the character (ୃ) which indicates the sound of ଋ

* ଋଜୁ, *a.* straight, upright, sincere.

ଋଣ, *n.* a loan, debt.

ଋଣଗ୍ରସ୍ତ, *a.* involved in debt, indebted.

ଋଣଗ୍ରହଣ, *n.* borrowing of money.

ଋଣମୁକ୍ତ, *a.* becoming free from debt.

ଋଣୀ, *a.* indebted;—*n.* a debtor.

ଋତ, *affix,* affected with.

ଋତୁ, *n.* a season; the menses.

ଋତୁମତୀ, *a.* menstruous.

ଋତୁରାଜ, *n.* the spring, season of spring.

ଋତୁସନ୍ଧି, *n.* between the seasons.

* ଋତୁସ୍ନାତା, *a.* bathed after the menses.

ଋତୁସ୍ନାନ, *n.* ablution after menstruation.
* ଋଦ୍ଧି, *n.* riches, opulence, wealth.
ଋଷି, *n.* a sage.
* ଋକ୍ଷ, *n.* a bear ; the constellation Ursa minor.

ଏ.

ଏ, the eighth vowel.
ଏ, *pron.* this.
ଏଥକୁ, *ad.* henceforth. [hither.
ଏଆଡ଼େ, *ad.* this way, on this side,
ଏଉତ୍ତାରୁ, *ad.* after this, from this time.
ଏକ, *a.* and *n.* one ; 1, I ; same.
ଏକଇ, *a.* the same, sole, identical.
ଏକଏକ, *ad.* severally, each, one by one.
ଏକକ, *a.* one, single, alone ;—*n.* units (in *Arith.*)
ଏକକାଳୀନ, *a.* contemporaneous, at the same time. [ously.
ଏକକାଳେ, *ad.* at once, simultane-
ଏକଗୁଁଆ, *a.* obstinate, self-willed.
ଏକଘରିଆ, *a.* unsocial, secluded, outcaste. [XLI.
ଏକଚାଳିଶ, *a.* and *n.* forty-one ; 41,
ଏକଚିତ୍ତ, *a.* unanimous, attentive.
ଏକଚେଟିଆ, ଏକଚାଟିଆ, *a.* monopolised.
* ଏକତମ, *a.* one among many.
* ଏକତର, *a.* one of two, either.
ଏକତରଫା, *a.* one-sided.
ଏକତା, *n.* union, oneness, sameness.
ଏକତାନ, *a.* of one voice or tune, intent on one object only ;—*n.* harmony.
ଏକତାଲ, *n.* harmony, unison.
ଏକତିରିଶ, *a.* and *n.* thirty-one ; 31, XXXI.
ଏକତୁମ୍ବା, *n.* a kind of lute.
ଏକତ୍ର, *ad.* in one place, together.
ଏକତ୍ୱ, *n.* oneness, sameness, identity.
* ଏକଦା, *ad.* once, at one time.
* ଏକଧା, *a.* single, one kind only.
ଏକପଟା, *n.* the upper cloth, a sheet.
ଏକପରାମର୍ଶ, *a.* unanimous. [party.
ଏକପକ୍ଷ, *n.* an ally ;—*a.* of the same
ଏକପିଟିଆ, *a.* one-sided. [sel.
ଏକଯୋଟ, *a.* united in plot or coun-
ଏକପ୍ରକାର, *a.* uniform, of one sort, after a fashion; passable. [age.
ଏକବୟସିଆ, *a.* of the same year or
ଏକବାଗିଆ, *a.* dogmatical, obstinate.
ଏକବାର, *ad.* once; altogether.
* ଏକବିଂଶ, *a.* twenty-one.
ଏକମତର, *a.* see ଏକପରାମର୍ଶ । [object.
* ଏକଲକ୍ଷ୍ୟ, *a.* having the same
ଏକଜିଦିଆ, *a.* self-willed, opinionated, obstinate.
ଏକଲକ୍ଷ, *a.* of the same intention ; —*n.* unity of purpose.
* ଏକଭୁକ୍ତ, *a.* united, collected under one head, classified.
ଏକମନା, ଏକମତ, *a.* unanimous, of one accord.

* ଏକମତାବଲମ୍ବୀ, *a.* following the same opinion; professing the same religion. [mutinous.

ଏକମେଳ, ଏକମେଳି, ଏକମେଳିଆ, *a.* united;

ଏକଯୋଟ, *a.* of the same party or plot, united together.

ଏକରୂପ, *a.* similar, like, same.

ଏକଲା, *a.* alone, solitary, single.

ଏକସଙ୍ଗ, ଏକସଙ୍ଗୀ, *a.* belonging to the same company, united, collected, compact.

ଏକଶିରା, *n.* hydrocele. [LXI.

ଏକଷଠୀ, *a.* and *n.* sixty-one; 61,

ଏକସମାନ, *a.* uniform, alike. [LXXI.

ଏକସ୍ତରି, *a.* and *n.* seventy-one; 71,

ଏକହାରା, *a.* single, not double; thin.

ଏକା, *a.* alone, solitary. [LXXXI.

ଏକାଅଶୀ, *a.* and *n.* eighty-one; 81,

ଏକାକାର, *a.* of one form, uniform.

ଏକାକୀ, *a.* alone, solitary, single.

* ଏକାଗ୍ର, *a.* intent on one thing.

* ଏକାଗ୍ରତା, *n.* the pursuit of one sole object.

ଏକାଙ୍ଗ, *a.* becoming one, become as one body.

ଏକାଟିଆ, *a.* single, alone.

ଏକାଠି, *ad.* in one place, together.

ଏକାତ୍ମ, *n.* intimacy of kindred spirits;—*a.* intimate.

* ଏକାଦଶ, *a.* eleven.

ଏକାଦଶୀ, *n.* the eleventh day of the moon (applied to first and second half of the moon).

* ଏକାନୁକ୍ରମେ, *ad.* in numerical order, successively.

* ଏକାଧିପତି, *n.* a sovereign, monarch.

ଏକାନ୍ତ, *a.* excessive; private;—*ad.* * certainly. [family.

ଏକାନ୍ନ, *a.* living together in joint

ଏକାବନ, *a.* and *n.* fifty-one; 51, LI.

ଏକାର୍ଣ୍ଣବ, *n.* a deluge, an extensive flood; a mixed mob.

ଏକାର୍ଥ, ଏକାର୍ଥକ, *a.* having the same meaning or scope.

ଏକାନବେ, ଏକାନବତି, *a.* and *n.* ninety-one; 91, XCI.

ଏକାର, *n.* (in *Gram.*) the vowel ଏ, or its symbol େ [fore.

ଏକାରଣ, *ad.* on this account, there-

* ଏକାହିକ, *a.* occurring every other day.

ଏକୁଆ, *n.* a kind of fever; partially-cleansed rice. [alone.

ଏକୁଟିଆ, *a.* one, only one;—*ad.*

ଏକୁନ, *n.* sum, total, aggregate.

ଏକେତ, *ad.* on the one hand, in the first place.

ଏକେଶର, *a.* self-dependent, alone.

ଏକୋଇ, *n.* intermittent fever.

ଏକୋଦର, ଏକୋଦରା, *a.* born of the same mother, uterine.

* ଏକୋପମ, *a.* similar, resembling.

ଏଗାର, *a.* and *n.* eleven; 11, XI.

ଏଜନ, *pron.* ditto, the same.

ଏଜାହାର, *n.* a deposition, affirmation.

ଏଠା, *n.* this place.

ଏଠାରେ, *ad.* here, in this place.
ଏଠି, ଏଠିକି, *ad.* here.
ଏଡ଼ି, *n.* the heel.
ଏଡ଼େଇବା, ଏଡ଼ିବା, *v.* to avoid, to disobey.
ଏଡ଼କ, ଏଡ଼େ, *a.* such, so.
ଏଣିକି, *ad.* here, hither; henceforth.
ଏଣୁ, ଏଣୁକରି, *ad.* therefore, on this account.
ଏଣେ, *ad.* hither.
ଏଣେତେଣେ, *ad.* hither and thither.
ଏଣ୍ଡୁଅ, *n.* a garden lizard.
ଏଣ୍ଡୁରି, *n.* a kind of cake.
* ଏତତ୍, ଏତଦ୍, *pron.* this.
* ଏତଦନନ୍ତର, *ad.* afterwards, after this.
* ଏତଦର୍ଥେ, *ad.* for this, for this reason.
* ଏତଦବଧି, *ad.* so far, from or to this.
ଏତଦ୍ଭିନ୍ନ, *ad.* beside this, except this.
* ଏତନ୍ମାତ୍ର, *ad.* merely this, only this.
* ଏତାଦୃଶ, *a.* such;—*ad.* like this.
* ଏତାବତ୍, *ad.* thus much, thus far.
ଏତେକ, ଏତକ, *ad.* so many, so much.
ଏତକମାତ୍ର, *ad.* simply this.
ଏତେ, *ad.* so much, so long, so many.
ଏତେକ, *ad.* so many, so much, so long.
ଏତେଲା, ଏତଲା, *n.* notice, news, information.
ଏଥର, *ad.* this time, this once.
ଏଥକୁ, *ad.* therefore.
ଏନିମନ୍ତେ, *ad.* wherefore, for this cause.
ଏପରି, *ad.* thus, in this manner.
ଏପର୍ଯ୍ୟନ୍ତ, *ad.* thus far, hitherto.
ଏପ୍ରକାର, *ad.* thus, such; this kind.

ଏବଂ, *conj.* and, also, likewise.
ଏବକୁ, *ad.* from now, now-a-days.
ଏବେ, *ad.* now, at this time.
ଏଭଳି, ଏମନ୍ତ, *ad.* thus, in this manner.
ଏରକମ୍, *ad.* this kind;—*a.* of this kind.
* ଏରଣ୍ଡ, *n.* the castor-oil tree and its seed.
ଏରଣ୍ଡା, ଏରୁଣ୍ଡି, *n.* lower piece of a door frame, a door-sill.
ଏରୂପ, *ad.* thus, this form.
* ଏଲା, *n.* cardamom.
ଏଲେକା, *n.* connection, jurisdiction.
ଏସକାଶୁ, *ad.* because of this, on this account.
ଏହା, ଏହି, *pron.* this.
ଏହିପରି, *ad.* thus, in this manner.
ଏହିମାତ୍ର, *ad.* merely this.
ଏହିକ୍ଷଣି, *ad.* now, immediately, instantly.
ଏହେତୁ, *ad.* on this account, therefore.
ଏକ୍ଷଣି, *ad.* now, immediately, instantly.

ଐ.

ଐ, the ninth vowel in the Oriya alphabet.
* ଐକମତ୍ୟ, *n.* confederacy, sameness.
* ଐକାନ୍ତ୍ୟ, *n.* consistency, perseverance.
ଐକାର, *n.* (in *Gram.*) the letter ଐ, the character ୈ which expresses the sound of ଐ ।

* ଐକାହିକ, *a.* on alternate days; tertian, quotidian.

ଐକ୍ୟ, *n.* unity, amity, oneness.

* ଐନ୍ଦ୍ରଜାଲିକ, *n.* jugglery, juggler;—*a.* magical.

* ଐରାବତ, *n.* *Indra's* elephant.

ଐଶାନ୍ୟ, *n.* the north-east quarter.

* ଐଶ୍ୱର, ଐଶ, ଐଶିକ, *a.* divine, relating to God. [Godly.

ଐଶ୍ୱରିକ, ଐଶ୍ୱ, ଐଶ୍ୱର୍ୟ୍ୟ, *a.* divine,

ଐଶ୍ୱର୍ଯ୍ୟ, *n.* grandeur, state, glory.

ଐହିକ, *a.* pertaining to this world.

ଓ.

ଓ, the tenth vowel in the Oriya [alphabet.

ଓଃ, *interj.* Oh! O!

ଓଁ, *n.* the sacred syllable denoting the Hindu trinity, *Om.*

ଓଉ, *n.* a kind of sour fruit.

ଓକର, ଓକାର, *n.* secret shame, domestic trouble or evil conduct which it is desired to keep secret in the home.

ଓକାର, *n.* (in *Gram.*) the letter ଓ, the character େ । which expresses the sound of ଓ ।

ଓକାଲତି, ଓକଲତି, *n.* the profession of an attorney.

ଓକାଲତନାମା, ଓକଲତନାମା, *n.* a writing constituting a person the attorney of another, *vakalatnama,* power of attorney.

ଓକିଲ, *n.* a law-pleader, an attorney, vakil.

ଓକିଲଖାନା, *n.* 'pleaders' room, bar [library.

ଓଗାଳିବା, *v.* to stop, to detain, to intercept.

ଓଗେର, *n.* etcetera, and the like.

ଓଜନ, *n.* weight, measure.

ଓଜର, *n.* an excuse, a pretence.

* ଓଜସ୍, ଓଜଃ, *n.* vitality, light, strength.

ଓଝ, *n.* (in *Math.*) square root.

ଓଝା, *n.* a schoolmaster; a surname.

ଓଝାଳିବା, *v.* to clean a well or tank.

ଓଟ, *n.* a camel.

ଓଟଘଓଟର, *n.* a mutual dragging or [pulling.

ଓଟାରିବା, *v.* to pull, to drag, to stretch.

ଓଠ, *n.* the lip, lower lip and chin.

ଓଡ଼, *n.* the aborigines of Orissa.

ଓଡ଼ଶ, *n.* a bed-bug.

ଓଡ଼ାଙ୍କ, *n.* (in *Arith.*) addition by means of a fixed rule.

ଓଡ଼ିଆ, ଓଡ଼ିଅ, *n.* an Oriya.

ଓଡ଼େ, *ad.* once (only used in connection with ploughing, as [ଓଡ଼େ ଚଷ) ।

* ଓଡ୍ରଦେଶ, *n.* Orissa.

ଓଢ଼, *n.* the thread (of a cloth) lengthwise.

ଓଢ଼ଣା, *n.* a veil worn by ladies.

ଓଦ, *n.* dampness, moisture.

ଓଦା, *n.* the upper cloth of a man,

ଓଧସ, *a.* unmarried, bachelor (abusive).

*ଓଦନ, *n.* food, boiled rice.

ଓଦର, *n.* a large oblong basket used for carting loose material, such as grain, sand, etc.

ଓଦା, *a.* damp, wet, moist.

ଓଧ, *n.* an otter.

ଓର, *n.* clue, trace, hint.

ଓରଫ୍, ଓରଫେ, *ad.* alias.

ଓଲମ, *n.* a plumb-line.

ଓଳାଇବା, ଓଳେଇବା, *v.* to sweep, to clean.

ଓଳି, *n.* half-a-day; the slope of the roof.

ଓଳିଆ, *n.* grain packed in bundles of straw.

ଓଳିଏ, *n.* a half-day.

ଓଳିକ, ଓଳଗି, *n.* a salutation, a bow.

ଓଲ, ଓଲୁଅ, *n.* an edible root.

ଓଲଉଠା, ଓଲଝଡ଼ା, *n.* cholera.

ଓଲୁଆ, *a.* gluttonous, greedy.

ଓଲୁ, *n.* an ignoramus.

ଓଲଟପାଲଟ, ଓଲଟାପାଲଟା, *ad.* upside down, topsy-turvy.

ଓଲଟା, ଓଲଟା, *n.* disorder, confusion; —*a.* turned over.

ଓସାର, *a.* wide, broad; —*n.* width, breadth.

ଓସାରିଆ, *a.* broad, wide.

ଓଷଧ, ଓଷଧି, ଔଷଧି, *n.* medicine.

ଓଷା, *n.* a festival or vow.

* ଓଷ୍ଠ, *n.* the chin, the lip.

ଓଷ୍ଠ୍ୟ, *a.* (in *Gram.*) labial, pronounced by the lips.

ଓଷ୍ଠାଗତ, *a.* expiring breath (on the lips).

ଓଷ୍ଠାଧର, *n.* upper and lower lips.

ଓହଳ, *n.* the roots of the banyan tree hanging from its branches.

ଓହଳିବା, *v.* to be hanging.

ଓହଳାଇବା, *v.* to suspend, to hang.

ଓହୋ, *inter.* O ho! take care! mind!

ଓହ୍ଲାଇବା, *v.* to come down, to descend, to lower.

ଔ.

ଔ, the eleventh vowel.

ଔକାର, *n.* (in *Gram.*) the letter ଔ, the chracter ୌ which expresses the sound of ଔ।

* ଔଚିତ୍ୟ, *n.* fitness, propriety.

ଔଦୁମ୍ବର, *n.* the sacrificial fig-tree.

* ଔତ୍କଟ୍ୟ, *n.* excessiveness, fury.

* ଔତ୍କର୍ଷ୍ୟ, *n.* excellency, superiority.

ଔତ୍ସୁକ୍ୟ, *n.* zeal, ardour, anxiety.

* ଔଦରିକ, *a.* gluttonous, voracious.

* ଔଦାର୍ଯ୍ୟ, *n.* munificence, candour, liberality.

ଔଦାସୀନ୍ୟ, ଔଦାସ୍ୟ, *n.* indifference, misanthropy; solitude, loneliness.

* ଔଦ୍ଧତ୍ୟ, *n.* violence, tyranny, a tumult.

* ଔଦ୍ୱାହିକ, *n.* a marriage-gift to a woman.

ଔପନିବେଶିକ, *a.* colonial.

* ଔପାଧିକ, *a.* relating to qualities.

* ଔପୟିକ, *a.* expedient, fit, proper.

ଔରସ, ଔରସ୍ୟ, *n.* legitimate descent; —*a.* lawfully begotten, natural.

* ଔର୍ଦ୍ଧ୍ୱଦେହିକ, *a.* due to a deceased person, funereal.

ଔଷଧ, *n.* medicine, drug, a remedy.

ଔଷଧାଳୟ,*n.* medicine shop, hospital.

କ.

କ, the first consonant.

କଅଁଳ, *a.* soft, mild, tender.

କଅଁଳା, *a.* new, young, tender.

କଅଁଳାଇବା, *v.* to coax, to encourage; to cause to sprout.

କଅଁଳାକଅଁଳି, *n.* coaxing, encouraging; enticing to evil. [infant.

କଅଁଳାପିଲା, *n.* an infant, a tender

କଅଁଳାବାଛୁରି, *n.* a very young calf.

କଅଁଳିବା, *v.* to bud, to send out a young shoot.

କଅଣ, କଣ, *pron.* what. [sob.

କଇଁ, *n.* the red or white lotus; a

କଇଁକଇଁ *a.* sobbed;-*ad.* sobbingly.

କଇଁଆ, *n.* tamarind fruit.

କଇଁଚି, *n.* a pair of scissors.

କଇଁଛ, *n.* a turtle.

କଇଁଥା, *a.* half-boiled.

କଇ, *n.* vomiting.

କଇଥ, *n.* the wood-apple.

କଇଦଖାନା, *n.* jail, a prison.

କଇଦୀ, *n.* prisoner;—*a.* imprisoned.

କଇର, *n.* a basket for keeping paddy.

କଉ, *n.* a kind of fish.

କଉଡ଼ି, *n.* a small shell current as money—a cowrie shell. [ment.

କଏଦ୍, *n.* imprisonment, confine-

କଏଦ୍‌ଖାନା, *n.* see କଇଦଖାନା।

କଏଦୀ, *n.* see କଇଦୀ।

କଁକଁ, *n.* an imitative sound.

କଂସା, *n.* white brass or bell-metal; a bowl made of mixed metals.

କଂସାଇ, *n.* a butcher.

କଂସାରି, *n.* a brazier, coppersmith.

କକଡ଼ା, *n.* sign of the Zodiac (Cancer); the crab. [uncle.

କକାଇ, କକେଇ, *n.* junior paternal

* କକୁଦ, *n.* a hump, a peak.

କଖାରୁ, *n.* a pumpkin.

* କଙ୍କ, *n.* a heron, a crane.

* କଙ୍କତିକା, *n.* a comb. (see କକୁଆ).

କଙ୍କଡ଼ା, *n.* a crab, the sign Cancer,

କଙ୍କଡ଼ାବିଛା, *n.* a scorpion.

* କଙ୍କଣ, *n.* a bracelet. [small bells.

* କଙ୍କଣୀ, *n.* anklet ornamented with

* କଙ୍କର, *n.* gravel.

କଙ୍କାଳ, *n.* the waist, loins; skeleton.

କଜି, କଜୀ, *n.* a dragon-fly.

କଙ୍ଗାଳ, *a.* poor, indigent, needy.

କଚ୍‌କଚ୍, କଚରକଚର, *n.* a quarrel.

କଚଡ଼ା, *n.* the act of falling or throwing; paddy straw cut close to the ground; all kinds of rubbish.

କଚଡ଼ାକଚଡ଼ି, *n.* dashing or casting down repeatedly. [washerman).

କଚା, *a.* washed, cleansed (by

କଚାଇବା, କଚେଇବା, *v.* to cause to be dashed against anything—(as washermen dash clothes).

କଚ୍‌କଚି, *n.* dashing or beating clothing, etc. [down.

କଚ୍‌ଡ଼ିବା, *v.* to dash down, to cast

କଚୁ, *n.* an edible root, class *arum.*

କଚୁରି, *n.* a kind of cake. [of justice.

କଚେରି, *n.* *cutchery*, an office, court

କଚ୍ଚା, *a.* *kutcha,* inferior, temporary.

କଛ, *n.* a measure, model, pattern.

କଚ୍ଛ *n.* the end of the *dhoti* which is tucked into the waistband.

କଚ୍ଛମାରିବା, *v.* to tuck the end of the *dhoti* into the waistband.

କଚ୍ଛଦୁରୁ, *a.* fearful, timorous.

କଛିବା, *v.* to measure.

କଚ୍ଛପ, *n.* a tortoise, a turtle.

* କଚ୍ଛୁ, *n.* the itch, a scale.

କଜଳପାତି, *n.* an iron case used to hold eye-paint; a kind of black bird resembling the Indian cuckoo.

କଜ୍ଜଳ, କଜ୍ୱଳ, *n.* collyrium, eye-paint.

କଜିଆ, *n.* a quarrel, contention.

କଜିଆଖୋର, *a.* quarrelsome, contentious.

କଞ୍ଚା, *a.* unripe, raw, not well done.

କଞ୍ଚି, *n.* a key, a branch or twig of bamboo.

* କଞ୍ଚୁକୀ, *n.* an attendant or overseer of women's apartments, chamberlain.

* କଞ୍ଚୁଳିକା, *n.* a woman's bodice.

କଟ, *n.* a pledge; a mat; a fixed time.

କଟକ, *n.* a royal city, a camp; Cuttack.

କଟକଟ, *n.* a throbbing sensation.

କଟକଣା, *n.* an agreement; discipline; an engagement.

କଟ-କବାଲା, *n.* a private deed of sale.

କଟକୀ, କଟକିଆ, *a.* belonging to Cuttack.

କଟଣ, *n.* a copper or brass cup.

କଟା, *a.* cut, hacked, chopped.

କଟାଇବା, *v.* to cause to be cut, to cause to spend time; to spend time.

କଟାକଟି, *n.* the act of cutting or hacking, operation; reaping, harvesting. [a knife.

କଟାରି, କଟାରୀ, *n.* a dagger, a poniard,

କଟାଳ, *n.* a weight used by goldsmiths; the spring tide.

କଟାଳ କରିବା, କଟାଳିବା, *v.* to demand, to insist on, to persistently beg, to tease.

କଟାଳି, କଟାଳୀ, *n.* a reaper.

କଟାଶ, *n.* a wild cat.

* କଟାହ, *n.* a boiler, a cauldron.

କଟାକ୍ଷ, *n.* a glance, an indirect glance.

କଟି, କଟିତଟ, କଟିଦେଶ, କଟୀ, *n.* the waist, loins, hips. [loins.

କଟିବନ୍ଧ, କଟିବନ୍ଧନୀ, *n.* a girdle for the

କଟୁ, *a.* harsh, bitter, pungent, hot.

* କଟୁଆଳ, *n.* a constable or town officer.

କଟୁଫଳ, *n.* a vegetable used in curries. [harsh words.

କଟୁବାକ୍ୟ, *n.* acrimonious language,

କଟୁବାଗୀ, କଟୁଭାଷୀ, *a.* speaking harsh or abusive language.

କଟୁରି, *n.* a gorse-hook, bill-hook.

କଟୁଙ୍ଗ, *n.* a medicinal tree.

କଟୁଫଳ, *n.* a medicinal nut.

କଠା, *n.* unripe jack-fruit; a small measuring vessel.

କଠାଉ, *n.* wooden clogs or sandals.

କଠିନ, *a.* hard, solid, harsh, severe.

କଠିନତା, *n.* hardness, solidity, severity.

କଠୋର, *a.* cruel, morose, austere.

କଡକଡ, *n.* a rustling sound.

କଡବା, *n.* a fasting. [gnashing.

କଡମଡ, *n.* a grinding, grating,

କଡା, *n.* one cowrie; a metal ring or link;—*a.* bitter, hard. [*kada.*

କଡାକଉଡ଼ି, *n.* only one cowrie or

କଡାକଡ, *n.* heated argument.

କଡାର, *n.* tawny colour; cement.

କଡ, କଡକାଠ, *n.* a beam, a rafter.

କଡୁଆ, *a.* acrid, bitter, pungent.

କଡେଇହେବା, *v.* to go to one side.

କଢ, କଢି, *n.* a bud.

କଢା, *n.* a ring, link; cauldron.

କଢାଇବା, *v.* to guide, to lead in the way; to cause to be extracted or removed.

କଣ, *n.* a corner; a particle, atom; a spark or sparkle, eye of a seed.

କଣ? *inter. pron.* what?

କଣଫଣା, *n.* a whitlow. [rent.

କଣା, *n.* blind of one eye; a hole or

କଣି, *n.* the branch of the bamboo; a particle of grain.

କଣିକା, *n.* a particle, grain, atom.

କଣ୍ଟ, *n.* measure, size, guage; the time agreed upon.

କଣ୍ଟକ, *n.* a thorn, prickle; an enemy, a foe.

କଣ୍ଟକିତ, *a.* full of thorns, thorny; with hair standing on end.

କଣ୍ଟା, *n.* a thorn, fork, nail, pin, spike, fish-bone. [plough.

କଣ୍ଟି, *n.* the wooden part of a

କଣ୍ଟିବା, *v.* to measure, to take dimensions. [out scales.

କଣ୍ଟିଆମାଛ, *n.* a species of fish with-

କଣ୍ଠ, *n.* the throat, Adam's apple.

କଣ୍ଠଗତ, କଣ୍ଠାଗତ, *a.* (life) come up into the throat, *e.g.* କଣ୍ଠାଗତ ପ୍ରାଣ।

କଣ୍ଠନଳୀ, *n.* throat, gullet.

* କଣ୍ଠଭୂଷା, *n.* a necklace, a neck ornament. [neck.

* କଣ୍ଠମଣି, *n.* a jewel worn round the

କଣ୍ଠସ୍ଥ, *a.* in the throat, learned by

* କଣ୍ଠମାଳା, *n.* a necklace. [heart.

କଣ୍ଠାଗତ, *a.* up to the throat, the last gasp; ready to utter. [vicle.

କଣ୍ଠାସ୍ଥି, *n.* the collar-bone, the cla-

କଣ୍ଠିଧାରୀ, *a.* wearing a necklace.

କଣ୍ଠୀ, *n.* a necklace.

କଣ୍ଠ୍ୟ, *a.* guttural.

କଣ୍ଠ୍ୟବର୍ଣ୍ଣ, *n.* (in *Gram.*) the class of guttural letters.

କଣ୍ଡରା, *n.* the village watchman caste.

କଣ୍ଡା, *a.* cleansed (rice or other grain) ;—*n.* a weaver's shuttle.

କଣ୍ଡରୁଣୀ, *n.* a woman of the watchman caste.

କଣ୍ଡୁ, *n.* the itch, an itching.

କଣ୍ଢେଇ, କଣ୍ଢେଇ, *n.* a toy, a doll.

କତରା, *n.* an old torn mat.

କତା, *n.* husk or fibre of the cocoa-nut.

କତି, *a.* close, not distant, near.

* କତିପୟ, *a.* a few.

କତୁରା, *n.* cutting with scissors, shearing ;—*a.* sheared.

କତୁରିବା, କତୁରାକରିବା, *v.* to cut, to trim (with scissors).

କତୁରୀ, *n.* scissors, shears.

* କଥକ, *n.* a speaker, an orator

କଥନ, *n.* a speaking, narrating ; a word.

କଥନୀୟ, *a.* fit to be spoken.

କଥା, *n.* a word, sentence, saying, a story.

କଥାଏ, *n.* one word.

କଥାଏକଥାଏ, *ad.* word by word, at every word.

କଥାପ୍ରସଙ୍ଗ, *n.* discourse, topic of conversation.

କଥାବାର୍ତ୍ତା, *n.* conversation, chit-chat.

କଥିତ, *a.* spoken, mentioned, expressed.

କଥୋପକଥନ, *n.* conversation, free intercourse.

କଦମ୍ବ, *n.* a trot, a foot-step.

କଦମ୍ବ, *n.* the *kadamba* tree.

କଦର୍, *n.* a trick, contrivance, plan, means.

କଦର୍ଯ୍ୟ, *a.* base, disagreeable, worthless, illegible.

କଦଳୀ, *n.* the plantain tree and fruit.

କଦଳୀପଟୁଆ, କଦଳୀପଟୁକା, *n.* fibre of the plantain tree.

କଦକ୍ଷର, *n.* bad writing, a scrawl.

କଦାକାର, *a.* ugly, ill-shaped, uncouth.

କଦାକୃତି, *a.* deformed, ugly.

କଦାଚ, *ad.* scarcely ever, seldom, at some time.

କଦାଚାର, *n.* bad conduct.

କଦାଚାରୀ, କଦାଚାରା, *a.* wicked, profligate.

କଦାଚିତ୍, *ad.* rarely, scarcely ever.

କଦାପି, *ad.* at some time, sometimes.

* କଦୁକ୍ତି, *n.* abuse, bad language.

* କଦୁଷ୍ଣ, *a.* lukewarm, tepid.

* କନକ, *n.* gold, gold colour.

କନଡା, *n.* air of a tune or song.

କନ୍କନ, *n.* a throbbing pain.

କନା, *n.* a rag, a piece of old cloth.

* କନାଟ, *n.* a tent fence, walls of a tent.

କନିକା, *n.* the croton seed.

କନିଷ୍ଠ, *a.* least, youngest, junior.

କନିଷ୍ଠତା, *n.* minority, inferiority.

କନିଷ୍ଠା, *n.* the little finger.

କନିୟର, *n.* the oleander tree.

* କନୀନିକା, *n.* the pupil of the eye.

* କନୀୟାନ୍, *a.* youngest, junior.

କନ୍ଥଡା, କନ୍ଥା, *n.* a garment of shreds.

କନ, *n.* raw sugar.

କନ୍ଦମୂଳ, *n.* the sweet potatoe.

କନ୍ଦର, କନ୍ଦରା, *n.* glen, defile.

କନ୍ଦର୍ପ, *n.* the name of the god of love, Cupid.

କନ୍ଦଳ, *n.* a quarrel, a dispute, contention.

କନ୍ଦଳିଆ, *a.* quarrelsome.

କନ୍ଦା *n.* a young tender sprout of the palm tree; a kind of eczema.

କନ୍ଦାଇବା, କନ୍ଦେଇବା, *v.* to cause to cry.

କନ୍ଦି, କନ୍ଦୀ, *n.* an alley, a street, a narrow passage.

କନ୍ଦୁକ, *n.* a ball.

କନ୍ଧ, *n.* a mountaineer, a *Kond.*

* କନ୍ଧର, *n.* the neck, shoulder; a cloud.

କନ୍ଧା, *n.* a kind of skin disease, eczema.

କନ୍ଧି, କନ୍ଧୀ, *n.* an alley, a street, a narrow passage.

କନ୍ୟା, *n.* a virgin, daughter, bride; the sign Virgo.

କନ୍ୟାସ୍ତ୍ରୀ, *n.* a new wife, youngest wife.

କନ୍ୟାମା, *n.* a step-mother.

କନ୍ୟାଶାଶୁ, *n.* husband's or wife's step-mother-in-law.

କପଟ, *n.* deceit, trickery, hypocrisy; —*a.* deceitful.

କପଟତା, *n.* deceitfulness, knavery.

କପଟବେଶ, *n.* an assumed part or character.

କପଟରଚନା, *n.* hypocritical or deceitful conduct; forgery.

କପଟୀ, *n.* a hypocrite, deceiver;—*a.* hypocritical.

କପଡ଼ା, *n.* cloth.

* କପର୍ଦ୍ଦ, କପର୍ଦ୍ଦକ, *n.* a cowrie; *Sira's* matted hair.

କପା, *n.* raw cotton.

କପାଟ, *n.* a door, a shutter.

କପାଳ, *n.* the forehead; fate, destiny.

କପାଳିଆ, *a.* fortunate, lucky.

* କପାଳୀ, *n.* a lintel.

କପି, *n.* a pulley; a monkey, an ape.

କପିକଳ, *n.* a pulley.

* କପିତ୍ଥ, *n.* the wood-apple.

କପିଳ, *a.* tawny, brown;—*n.* the name of a sage.

କପିଳବାସ୍ତୁ, *n.* the name of *Buddha's* birthplace.

କପୁଡ଼ିଆ, *n.* a seller of cloth, cloth-dealer.

କପୂର, *n.* camphor.

କପୂରଦାନା, *n.* a kind of spice used in *pán* and curry.

କପୋତ, *n.* a pigeon, a dove.

କପୋଳ, *n.* the cheek, temple.

କପୋଳକଳ୍ପିତ, *a.* fictitious, invented, fabricated.

କଫ, *n.* phlegm, a cold, catarrh.

କଫଝୁଲ, *n.* a medicinal plant.

କଫୀ, *n.* coffee.

* କଫୋଣି, *n.* the elbow.

କବଚ, *n.* coat of mail; a charm, an amulet.

କବ୍ଜା, *n.* hinge for doors, the wrist.

କବଟା, *n.* a piece of a cloth.

* କବନ୍ଧ, *n.* a headless trunk, a demon.

କବର, *n.* a grave, a tomb.

* କବରୀ, *n.* a braid or knot of hair.

କବଳ, *n.* a mouthful, a morsel.

କବଳିତ, *a.* swallowed, eaten.

କବାଟ, *n.* a door, a window-shutter.

କବାବ, *a.* roasted.

କବାବ୍‌ଚିନି, *n.* a small spicy berry which is stimulating and purgative, the seed of *piper cubeba.*

କବାଲା, *n.* a deed of transfer, a bill of sale.

କବି, *n.* a poet, a writer of taste.

କବିରପନ୍ଥୀ, *a.* professing the doctrine of *Kavira* ;—*n.* a disciple of [*Kavira.*

କବିତା, *n.* poetry, verse.

କବିଲା, *n.* a wife, a family.

କବିରାଜ, *n.* a native physician.

କବୁତର, *n.* a pigeon, a dove.

କବୁଲ୍, *n.* a confession, an acknowledgment.

କବୁଲାଇବା, *v.* to cause to confess.

କବୁଲିୟତ୍, *n.* a written acknowledgment.

କମ, *n.* ornamented work ; brace- [let.

* କମଠ, *n.* a tortoise, a turtle.

କମଣ୍ଡଳୁ, *n.* a devotee's water-pot.

* କମନୀୟ, *a.* beautiful, agreeable.

କମର, *n.* the loins, waist.

କମର୍‌ବନ୍ଦ, *n.* a belt.

କମର୍‌ବନ୍ଦୀ, *n.* a girding of the loins, preparedness.

* କମଳ, କମଳିନୀ, *n.* a lotus ; water.

* କମଳା, *n.* *Lakshmi.*

କମଳା, କମଳାଲେମ୍ବୁ, *n.* an orange.

* କମଳିନୀ, *n.* an assemblage of water lilies.

କମାଇବା, *v.* to earn by labour, to gain ; to make less.

କମାଣ, *n.* a cannon ; a cross-bow.

କମାଣି, *n.* a bow (for playing the violin).

କମାର, *n.* a blacksmith, a mechanic.

କମାରଶାଳ, *n.* a smithy.

କମିନା, କମଣା, *a.* vile, mean, licentious;—*n.* a term of abuse.

କମ୍, *a.* less, deficient, lacking.

କମତି, *n.* a diminution, a defect.

କମ୍ପ, କମ୍ପନ, *n.* a trembling, a quaking.

କମ୍ପମାନ, *a.* trembling, quivering.

କମ୍ପାସ, *n.* compass.

କମ୍ପିତ, *a.* shaken, agitated.

କମ୍ବଳ, *n.* a blanket.

କଁଷ୍ୱା, *n.* unripe tamarinds.

* କଷ୍ୱାଳ, *n.* a dealer in salt.

କର, *n.* revenue ; the hand ; *a ray of light.

କରକଚ, *n.* salt obtained by solar [evaporation.

କରକଟ୍, *n.* road metal.

* କରକା, *n.* hail; an ascetic's water- [pot.

* କରକୋଷ୍ଠୀ, *n.* lines in the palm of the hand, palmistry.

କରଗତ, *a.* come to the hand, ob- [tained.

* କରଗ୍ରହ, *n.* receiving tribute ; a marriage.

କରଗ୍ରାହୀ, *n.* a taxgatherer.

କରଚୁଲ୍, କରଛୁଲ୍. *n.* a ladle.

କରଜ, କର୍ଜ୍ଜ, କର୍ଜ, *n.* a loan, a debt.

କରଜଆ, କର୍ଜିଆ, କର୍ଜ୍ଜଆ, *a.* in debt, in- [debted.

କରଞ୍ଜ, *n.* an acid fruit.

* କରଟ, କରଟକ, *n.* a crow.

କରଡା, *a.* strong, hard, tough.

କରଣ, *n.* a writer, writer caste ; * a doing or making.
କରଣକାରକ, *n.* (in *Gram.*) the instrumental case.
କରଣୀ, *n.* power, greatness; trowel; Oriya swift hand-writing.
କରଣୀୟ, * କରଣାର୍ହ, *a.* proper to be done, proper.
କରତ, *n.* a saw, a cutting instrument with a toothed edge.
କରତଳ, *n.* palm of the hand; * sub-
କରତାଳ, *n.* a cymbal. [jection.
କରତାଳି, *n.* clapping the hands.
କରତିବା, *v.* to saw.
କରତୀ, *n.* a sawyer.
କରଦ, *a.* tributary, revenue paying.
* କରପତ୍ର, *n.* the palms ; blade of a saw.
* କରପଲ୍ଲବ, *n.* a finger, the hand.
କରପୀଡନ, *n.* a hand-shake.
କରପୁଟ, *n.* the hands joined respectfully like a cup.
* କରବାଳ, *n.* a sword, scimitar.
* କରମର୍ଦ୍ଦନ, କରମର୍ଦ୍ଦ. *n.* see କରପୀଡନ.
କରମାଳା, *n.* a rosary, bead-roll.
କରାଇବା, *v.* to cause to do,
କରଣ୍ଡ, *n.* a small brass box.
କରାର, *n.* a promise, engagement.
କରାର୍‌ନାମା, *n.* a written engagement.
କରାଳ, *n.* a kind of pitch;–*a.* frightful, huge, high.
* କରିଣୀ, *n.* a female elephant.
କରିବା, *v.* to do, to make.

କରିଷ, *n.* a weight weighing nearly $1\frac{1}{2}$ tola.
* କରୀ, *n.* an elephant.
* କରୀନ୍ଦ୍ର, *n.* leader of a herd of elephants.
* କରୀଷ, *n.* dried cow-dung.
କରୁଣା, *n.* clemency, mercy, pity.
କରୁଣାନିଧାନ, *a.* merciful ;—*n.* a sea of mercy—God.
କରୁଣାମୟ, *a.* merciful ;—*n.* God.
କରେଇହେବା, *v.* to go to one side, to turn on one side.
କରାହି, କରଇ, *n.* a caldron. [crab.
କର୍କଟ, *n.* the Zodiac Cancer ; *a
କର୍କଟକ୍ରାନ୍ତି, *n.* Tropic of Cancer.
କର୍କର, *n.* a grating noise ; * gravel.
କର୍କଶ, *a.* hard, rough; unkind.
କର୍ଜ, *n.* a loan, debt.
କର୍ଜଦାର, *n.* a debtor, one who owes.
କର୍ଣ୍ଣ, *n.* the ear ; (in *Geom.*) a diagonal line ; * a rudder.
* କର୍ଣ୍ଣକୁହର, *n.* the cavity of the ear.
କର୍ଣ୍ଣଗୋଚର, *a.* within hearing, heard (*i.e.* came to the knowledge).
କର୍ଣ୍ଣଡେରିବା, *v.* to listen to.
କର୍ଣ୍ଣଫୁଲ, *n.* earing, eardrop. [man.
* କର୍ଣ୍ଣଧାର, *n.* a helmsman, a steers-
* କର୍ଣ୍ଣବେଧ, *n.* boring of the ear.
କର୍ଣ୍ଣମଳ, *n.* ear-wax.
କର୍ଣ୍ଣଶୂଳ, *n.* ear-ache.
* କର୍ଣ୍ଣିକା, କର୍ଣ୍ଣିକାର, *n.* pericarp of a lotus. [perer.
* କର୍ଣ୍ଣେଜପ, *n.* a talebearer, whis-

କର୍ତ୍ତନ, *n.* deduction; cutting, clipping.
* କର୍ତ୍ତରୀ, *n.* a pair of scissors.
କର୍ତ୍ତବ୍ୟ, *a.* fit to be done, necessary, proper.
କର୍ତ୍ତବ୍ୟତା, *n.* practicability, fitness.
କର୍ତ୍ତବ୍ୟନିଷ୍ଠ, *a.* firm in duty.
କର୍ତ୍ତବ୍ୟପରାୟଣ, *a.* dutiful.
କର୍ତ୍ତା, *n.* master, agent, doer.
କର୍ତ୍ତାକାରକ, *n.* (in *Gram.*) the nominative case.
କର୍ତ୍ତାପଣ, *n.* mastership, authority.
କର୍ତ୍ତୃକ, *a.* by, by the agency of.
କର୍ତ୍ତୃତ୍ୱ, *n.* authority, agency.
କର୍ତ୍ତୃପକ୍ଷ, *n.* head official.
କର୍ତ୍ତୃବାଚ୍ୟ, *n.* (in *Gram.*) the active voice.
କର୍ତ୍ତ୍ରୀ, *n.* mistress, governess.
* କର୍ଦ୍ଦମ, *n.* mud, mire.
* କର୍ପଟ, *n.* old and patched garments.
କର୍ପଟୀ, *n.* strip of cloth over the privities.
କର୍ପୂର, *n.* camphor.
* କର୍ବୁର, *a.* variegated, speckled.
କର୍ମ, *n.* work, deed, an action.
କର୍ମକର୍ତ୍ତା, *n.* a manager.
* କର୍ମକାର, *a.* a mechanic, a smith.
କର୍ମକାରକ, *n.* (in *Gram.*) the accusative case.
କର୍ମକାରୀ, କର୍ମକାରକ, *a.* effecting, doing business;—*n.* the person who does any work.
କର୍ମଚାରୀ, *n.* an officer, a workman, a steward;—*a.* engaged in a work.
କର୍ମଚ୍ୟୁତ, *a.* cashiered, dismissed.
* କର୍ମଠ, *a.* industrious, clever.
କର୍ମଣିବାଚ୍ୟ, *n.* (in *Gram.*) the passive voice.
* କର୍ମଣ୍ୟ, *a.* fit for work, serviceable.
କର୍ମଦୋଷ, *n.* evil consequence of human acts, sin, vice, error.
କର୍ମଧାରୟ, *n.* (in *Gram.*) name of a compound.
* କର୍ମନିଷ୍ଠ, *a.* active.
କର୍ମପାରକ, କର୍ମପାରଗ, *a.* capable of any work, clever.
କର୍ମଫଳ, *n.* moral results, fruit of actions.
କର୍ମବିପାକ, *n.* consequence of human actions, consequence (mainly suffering) of acts done in a previous birth.
କର୍ମଭୂମି, *n.* place of work or service.
କର୍ମଭୋଗ, *n.* bearing the consequences of good or bad conduct.
କର୍ମଶୀଳ, *a.* industrious, diligent.
* କର୍ମଶୂର, *n.* a hero in action;—*a.* industrious, clever.
* କର୍ମସଚିବ, *n.* a minister, a counsellor.
କର୍ମସାଧନ, *n.* accomplishing or effecting any work.
କର୍ମକ୍ଷମ, *a.* capable of work, able to work.
* କର୍ମୋଦ୍ୟତ, *a.* industrious, diligent, busy.
କର୍ମିଷ୍ଠ, *á.* industrious, skilful.
* କର୍ମୀ, *a.* ingenious;—*n.* an artist.
କର୍ମେନ୍ଦ୍ରିୟ, *n.* the organs of action.

* କର୍ଷ, *n.* a weight nearly 1½ tola (see କରଷ).

* କର୍ଷକ, *n.* a cultivator.

କର୍ଷଣ, *n.* ploughing or drawing.

କର୍ଷଣକାରୀ, *n.* and *a.* a cultivator, a ploughman.

* କର୍ଷଣୀ, *n.* the bit of a bridle.

କର୍ଷିତ, *a.* ploughed, drawn.

କଲ, *n.* any kind of machinery, an engine; the inside of the cheek.

* କଲକଣ୍ଠ, *n.* black cuckoo; a duck; a pigeon.

କଲକଲ, *n.* a hum, buzz, hubbub.

କଳଙ୍କ, *n.* rust, stain, stigma, slander.

କଳଙ୍କିତ, *a.* stained, rusty, spotted; disgraced.

କଳଙ୍କୀ, *n.* rust;—*a.* *stained, blemished, charged with crime.

* କଲତ୍ର, *n.* a wife.

କଲଧ୍ୱନି, *n.* a low sweet tone (such as made by a pigeon, cuckoo, etc.).

କଳନା, *n.* a guess, a supposition.

କଲମ, *n.* a pen; a graft or cutting.

କଲମ୍‌ତରାଶ, *n.* a penknife, pen-cutter.

କଲମ୍‌ଦାନ, *n.* a standish, pen-rack.

କଲମ୍ବ, *n.* an edible water plant, a plant-stalk.

କଲରବ, *n.* a murmur, clamour, buzz.

କଳଶ, କଳଶୀ, କଲ୍‌ଶ, କଲ୍‌ଶୀ, କଳସ, କଳସୀ, କଲ୍‌ସ, କଲ୍‌ସୀ, *n.* a water-pot, pitcher, jar.

କଲହଂସ, *n.* a species of duck.

କଳହ, *n.* a quarrel, brawl, contention.

କଳହୀ, କଳେହୀ, *n.* a quarrelsome woman.

କଳା, *a.* black;—*n.* lamp-black, moon's digit.

* କଳାଧର, କଳାନିଧି, *n.* the moon.

* କଳାପ, *n.* a peacock's tail; a zone; a multitude.

କଳାପାଢ, *n.* a long iron box in which women keep lamp-black for the eyes.

* କଳାପୀ, *n.* a peacock.

କଳାଲୁଣ, *n.* black salt.

କଳାଶିର, *n.* a disease of children when the veins become livid.

କଳି, *n.* quarrelling, fighting; the fourth *juga* or age of the world.

* କଳିକା, *n.* a bud, an unblown flower.

କଳିକାଳ, *n.* the present or iron age.

କଳିଙ୍ଗ, *n.* ancient name of a part of India to the south.

କଳିଚୂନ, *n.* shell-lime, white-wash.

କଳିଜା, *n.* the liver.

କଳିଯୁଗ, *n.* the fourth age of the world consisting of 432,000 years.

କଳିହା, କଳିହୁଡା, *n.* a quarrelsome person, a brawler.

କଳିହୁଣ୍ଡି, *n.* a quarrelsome noisy woman.

କଲୁଷ, *n.* sin, guilt, moral defilement.

କଲେଇ, *n.* tinning.

* କଳେବର, *n.* the body.

* କଳ୍କ, *n.* sediment, filth.

କଲ୍କୀ, *n.* tenth and last incarnation of *Vishnu.*

କଳ୍ପ, *n.* a period of 432,000,000 years; * a contrivance, scheme, purpose.

କଳ୍ପତରୁ, *n.* a fabled tree yielding whatever fruit one many desire ; figuratively a very generous man.

କଳ୍ପନା, *n.* a scheme, a plot.

କଳ୍ପାନ୍ତ, *n.* end of the age or world.

କଳ୍ପିତ, *a.* fictitious, invented, imaginary.

* କଲ୍ମଷ, *n.* sin, filth, moral impurity.

* କଲ୍ୟ, *ad.* yesterday ; to-morrow.

କଲ୍ୟାଣ, *n.* prosperity ; a benediction ; blessing.

କଲ୍ୟାଣକର, *a.* prosperous.'

କଲ୍ୟାଣୀୟ, *a.* deserving of success, or blessing.

* କଲ୍ଲୋଳ, *n.* roar of the sea, tumult.

କଷା, କଶା, କସା, *a.* close-fisted ;—*n.* a niggard ; * a whip.

କଶାଘାତ, *n.* whipping.

କସୁର୍, କସୂର୍, *n.* a fault ; a coming short.

* କଶେରୁ, କସେରୁ, କଶେରୁକା, କସେରୁକା, *n.* the backbone, vertebræ.

କଷ, *a.* tight;—*n.* a rope; * a touch-stone.

କଷଣ, *n.* trouble, a testing; tanning of leather.

କଷା, *n.* an astringent ;—*a.* astringent ; tanned.

କଷାଇବା, *v.* to cause to tan.

* କଷାୟ, *n.* an astringent taste.

କଷି, *n.* fruit only just formed.

କଷ୍ଟ, *n.* pain, distress, difficulty.

କଷ୍ଟକର, *a.* troublesome.

କଷ୍ଟସାଧ୍ୟ, *a.* difficulty accomplishable.

କଷ୍ଟି, କଷ୍ଟିପଥର, *n.* a touch-stone.

କସ୍‌ବୀ, *n.* a whore, a prostitute.

କସ୍‌ବୀବାଜ, *n.* a whoremonger.

କସମ୍, *n.* an oath, an asseveration.

କସରତ୍, *n.* gymnastics.

କସାଇ, କଂସାଇ, *n.* a butcher.

କସୁର୍, *n.* fault.

କସ୍ତୁରା, *n.* an oyster.

କସ୍ତୁରୀ, *n.* musk.

କସ୍ମିନ୍‌କାଳେ, *ad.* when ? at what time ?

କହାକହି, କୁହାକୁହି, *n.* a dialogue, disputation.

କହିବା, *v.* to speak, to teil.

କହୁଣ୍ଡ, *n.* a large basket made of split bamboos in which to store grain.

କହୁଣି, କହୁଣୀ, *n.* the elbow.

କହୁଣିଆ, *a.* deserving to be beaten.

କହ୍ଲାର, *n.* the white water-lily.

* କକ୍ଷ, କକ୍ଷଦେଶ, *n.* the arm-pit ; a room ; a corner; orbit.

କକ୍ଷା, *n.* contention ; * girdle.

କାଂକ, କାଁକ, କାଙ୍କ, *n.* a hoe or tool for digging earth.

କାଂକଡ, କାଙ୍କଡ, *n.* edible fruit of a species of creeper.

* କାଂସ୍ୟ, *n.* bell-metal.

*କାଂସ୍ୟକାର, *n.* a brazier, brass-founder.

କାଉଁଚ, କାଉଞ୍ଚ, କାଉଁଶ, *n.* a plant the straw of which is used to make fine baskets.

କାଉଁଚ, କାଉଞ୍ଚ, *n.* a small red seed.

କାଇ, *n.* starch.

କାଇ, କାଇପୋକ, *n.* a large red ant infesting mangoe trees.

କାଇଘର, କାହୁଘର, *n.* a thatched house.

କାଇଲ୍, *a.* convinced, confounded, faulty ;—*n.* fault.

କାଇମ, *n.* an aquatic bird.

କାଇମାଟି, *n.* a reddish chalk used for colour-washing.

କାଉଁରିଆ, *n.* the pith of the plant from which jute is obtained.

କାଉଁଳିଆ, *n.* a small cloud ;—*a.* cloudy.

କାଉ, *n.* a crow.

କାଉକାଉ, କାଉଁକାଉଁ, *n.* noisy contention of a crowd. [tution.

କାଏଦା, *n.* a rule, a law, a consti-

* କାକ, *n.* crow. [named.

କାକଚରିତ, *n.* a prophetical book so

*କାକନିଦ୍ରା, *n.* a nap, a doze.

*କାକତାଳୀୟ, *a.* sudden, unexpected.

*କାକଭୁଣ୍ଡ, *a.* crow-like, crafty.

କାକପଦ, *n.* the sign (∧) caret.

* କାକବନ୍ଧ୍ୟା, *n.* a woman who has borne only one child.

କାକର, *n.* dew.

କାକସ, *n.* a kind of cake.

କାକା, *n.* father's younger brother, uncle.

କା-କା, *n.* the noise of a crow.

କାକାତୁଆ, କକାତୁ, *n.* a cockatoo.

କାକୀ, *n.* wife of father's younger brother, aunt; * a female crow.

କାକୁଡ଼ି, *n.* a species of cucumber.

କାକୁସ୍ତି, କାକୁତି, *a.* a cry of distress, a scream.

କାଖ, *n.* the arm-pit, the side.

କାଖେଇବା, *v.* to carry on the hip, to embrace.

କାଗଜ, *n.* paper.

କାଗଜି, କାଗଜିଲେମ୍ବୁ, *n.* a small lime.

କାଙ୍ଗାଳ, *a.* poor, needy, wretched.

କାଚ, *n.* glass, crystal, earthenware.

କାଚପାତ୍ର, *n.* a glass plate or dish.

କାଚମଣି, *n.* a crystal.

କାଚସ, *n.* a dealer in glass bangles; name of a caste.

*କାଚଲବଣ, *n.* black salt. [dashing.

କାଚିବା, *v.* to wash or cleanse by

କାଛ, କାଛୁଆ, *n.* a small cloth.

କାଛୁ, *n.* the itch, scab, scabies.

କାଛୁଆ, *a.* constantly suffering from itch, itchy. [magistrate.

କାଜି, *n.* a Muhammadan judge or

*କାଞ୍ଚନ, *n.* gold. [of a city.

*କାଞ୍ଚୀ, *n.* a woman's girdle ; name

କାଞ୍ଚୁଲି, କାଞ୍ଚଲା, *n.* a woman's bodice.

କାଞ୍ଜି, *n.* sour rice-water.

କାଞ୍ଜିଆ, *a.* rotten (egg). [pound.

କାଞ୍ଜିହାଉସ୍, କାଞ୍ଜିହାଉଦା, *n.* a cattle-

କାଟ, *n.* a cut, a sample.
କାଟଣା, *n.* making thread, spinning.
କାଟିବା *v.* to cut, to clip; to deduct.
କାଟୁଣୀ, *n.* (*fem.*) a spinner.
କାଠ, *n.* wood, firewood, timber.
କାଠଘୋଡ଼ା, *n.* a clothes-horse.
କାଠପେଡ଼ି, *n.* a wooden box.
କାଠକୁଟା, *n.* a woodpecker; cutting of wood.
କାଠି, *n.* a splinter, a twig.
କାଠିନ୍ୟ, *n.* severity, harshness, hardness.
କାଠୁଆ, *n.* a small wooden cup; a small canoe, a trough; a dealer in wood;–*a.* thick(consistency).
କାଢ଼ିଅ, *n.* credit, debt.
କାଢ଼ିବା, *v.* to take out, to extract.
* କାଣ, *a.* one-eyed, blind of one eye.
କାଣୀ, *n.* (*fem.*) blind of one eye.
କାଣୀଫଳ, *n.* (in *Math.*) a rule or process for measuring the area of land.
କାଣ୍ଟି, *n.* refuse or sediment of oil.
କାଣ୍ଡ, *n.* an arrow; a stalk or stem; a section or chapter.
କାଣ୍ଡଜ୍ଞାନ, *n.* discretion, sense of fitness of things, the perception of things in their true light, idea.
* କାଣ୍ଡାର, *n.* a helmsman, steersman.
କାଣ୍ଡି, କାଣ୍ଡୀ, *n.* a heap, stack, pile.
କାଣ୍ଡିଅ, *a.* cleansed (rice).
କାଣ୍ଡିବା, *v.* to cleanse rice or grain by the *dhenki*.
କାଣ୍ଡ, *n.* lechery, lasciviousness.
କାଣ୍ଡିଅ, *n.* a lecher;—*a.* libidinous.
କାଣ୍ଡୋଇ, *n.* a lustful woman;—*a.* whorish.
କାତ, *n.* a boat-pole.
କାତର, *a.* troubled, distressed, anxious.
* କାତରୋକ୍ତି, *n.* lamentation, complaint.
କାତି, *n.* fish scales, a snake's skin; knife.
କାଦୁଅ, *n.* mud, mire, soft clay.
କାଦୁଆ, *a.* muddy, dirty, sloppy.
କାନ, *n.* the ear, hearing.
କାନକୁଟୁରା, କାନକୁଟୁରୀ, କାନକୋଟରୀ, *n.* a kind of earwig.
କାନକୋଳି, *n.* an edible wild plum.
କାନଖଡ଼କା, *n.* an ear-pick.
କାନପୂଜ, *n.* earwax or dirt.
କାନଗୋଇ, *n.* a record-keeper.
କାନଟଣା, *n.* ear-ache.
* କାନନ, *n.* a thicket, forest, wood.
କାନପଚ, *n.* a running from the ear.
କାନପତା, *n.* the lobe of the ear.
କାନପାତଳା, *a.* quick of hearing.
କାନଫୋଡ଼ା, *n.* boring the ear.
କାନମୋଡ଼ା, *n.* wringing the ears.
କାନି, କାନ୍ଥି, *n.* the corner of the *sari* or any cloth.
କାନିବା, *n.* a small oval-shaped earthen jar.
* କାନୀନ, *n.* child of an unmarried woman.
* କାନ୍ଦୁଡ଼, *n.* a lily.

କାନୁନ୍, *n.* a law, statute, regulation.

କାନୁନ୍‌ଗୋ, *n.* a record-keeper.

* କାନ୍ତ, *n.* a husband, lover ;—*a.* beloved, dear.

କାନ୍ତ୍ରସ୍ଟ, *n.* contractor (a corruption of the English word).

କାନ୍ତଲୁହା, *n.* steel, bright iron.

* କାନ୍ତା, *n.* a wife; a beautiful woman.

* କାନ୍ତାର, *n.* a dangerous road ; a forest.

* କାନ୍ତି, *n.* beauty, light, brilliancy.

କାନ୍ଥ, *n.* a wall.

କାନ୍ଥକୁଣ, *n.* a recess in a wall.

କାନ୍ଥଭା, *n.* a house in ruins, a broken wall.

କାନ୍ଦଣା, *n.* weeping, bewailing.

କାନ୍ଦବୋବାଳି, *n.* a loud cry, a bellowing.

କାନ୍ଦିବା, *v.* to cry, to weep.

କାନ୍ଦୁଣିଆ, *a.* always crying (crying baby.

କାନ୍ଧ, *n.* the shoulder.

କାନ୍ଧଧରାଧରି, *n.* holding one another by the shoulder.

କାନ୍ଧି, କାନ୍ଦି, *n.* a bunch of plantains or other fruit.

କାନ୍ଧିଆପରଭ, *n.* a palky bearer.

କାନ୍ଧେଇବା, *v.* to carry on the shoulders.

କାପ, *n.* an ear-ornament.

* କାପଟ୍ୟ, *n.* hypocrisy, dissimulation.

କାପୁଡ଼ିଆ, କାପିଡ଼ା, *n.* a hawker of cloth.

କାପୁରୁଷ, *n.* a scamp, a coward.

କାପ୍ତା, *n.* a pigeon, a dove.

କାଫଳ, କାଫଲ, *n.* medicinal bark.

କାଫୀ, *n.* coffee ;—*a*, useful, good.

କାଫ୍ରି, *n.* an Affrican.

କାବା, *a.* startled, wonderful.

କାବୁ, *n.* control, power, authority.

କାବ୍ୟ, *n.* poetry, a poem.

କାମ, *n.* work, object; * desire, lust.

* କାମଜ, *a.* arising from lust.

କାମରା, *n.* a room, an apartment, split bamboos when used to bind a hedge.

* କାମଦ, *a.* gratifying, giving rise to desire.

କାମଧେନୁ, *n.* a fabulous cow which grants whatever is desired by the possessor.

କାମନା, *n.* a wish, desire, prayer, supplication.

* କାମରୂପ, *a.* beautifully formed ; —*n.* a district in Assam.

* କାମରୂପୀ, *a.* assuming any shape at will.

କାମଳ, *n.* the jaundice.

କାମାତୁର, *a.* sick with love, lustful.

* କାମାର୍ତ୍ତ, * କାମାର୍ଥୀ, *a.* lewd, lascivious, wanton.

କାମିନୀ, *n.* name of a flowering shrub ; * a beautiful woman, a lascivious woman.

* କାମାନ୍ଧ, *a.* blinded by lust or love.

* କାମୀ, କାମୁକ, *a.* lascivious, lustful, lewd.

* କାମୁକୀ, *n.* a lustful woman.

କାମୁଡା, *n.* a bite, sting ;—*a.* bitten, biting.

କାମୁଡିବା, *n.* to bite, to sting.

କାମୋଦ, *n.* the air of a tune.

କାଞ୍ଜି, *n.* a miser, a grasper ;—*a.* miserly, stingy, grasping.

* କାୟ, କାୟା, *n.* the body.

କାୟସ୍ଥ, *n.* the name of a caste in Bengal;—*a.* * corporeal.

କାୟିକ, *a.* bodily, corporeal.

କାରକ, *n.* (in *Gram.*) case; an agent, a doer;—*a.* doing, effecting, (with the exception of its use in Grammar this word is only used joined to another noun).

କାରଖାନା, *n.* a manufactory, a workshop.

କାରଣ, *n.* cause, reason, motive.

କାରବାର, *n.* business, trade ; use.

କାରବାରି, *a.* useful ; commercial ; —*n.* merchant, tradesman.

କାରସାଜ, କାରସାଦ *n.* artifice, trickery.

* କାରା, *n.* prison.

* କାରାଗାର, *n.* a jail, prison.

* କାରାବଦ୍ଧ, *a.* imprisoned.

* କାରାବାସ, *n.* imprisonment.

କାରଗର, *n.* a mechanic, an artizan.

କାରଗରି, କାରଗିରି, *n.* mechanical labour, mechanics.

* କାରୁକାର୍ଯ୍ୟ, *n.* mechanical work.

* କାରୁଣ୍ୟ, *n.* mercy, compassion, pity.

* କାର୍କଶ୍ୟ, *n.* hard-heartedness, unfeelingness, rudeness.

କାର୍ତ୍ତିକ, *n.* a Hindu month, part of Oct. and Nov.; name of a god.

* କାର୍ପଣ୍ୟ, *n.* parsimony, stinginess.

* କାର୍ପାସ, *n.* cotton, cotton-plant (shrub).

* କାର୍ମୁକ, *n.* a bow.

କାର୍ଯ୍ୟ, *n.* work, labour, affair, effect.

* କାର୍ଯ୍ୟକର, *a.* useful, advantageous.

* କାର୍ଯ୍ୟକର୍ତ୍ତା, *n.* an agent, a manager.

କାର୍ଯ୍ୟକାରୀ, *n.* a worker;—*a.* useful ; accomplishing, doing a work well.

* କାର୍ଯ୍ୟକୁଶଳ, *a.* skilful, clever, doing a work well.

କାର୍ଯ୍ୟଦକ୍ଷ, *a.* clever in work.

କାର୍ଯ୍ୟାର୍ଥୀ, *a.* desirous of employment.

କାଳ, *n.*, time; death ;—*a.* * black.

କାଳଶତ୍ରୁ, *n.* an enemy.

କାଳକୂଟ, *n.* deadly poison, venom.

କାଳକ୍ରମେ, *ad.* in process of time.

କାଳଗ୍ରାସ, *n.* death.

* କାଳଧର୍ମ, *n.* effects proper to the time, behaviour suited to any particular time or season.

କାଳପୁରୁଷ, *n.* an evil spirit or spectre ; death.

* କାଳପ୍ରାପ୍ତ, *a.* dead, deceased.

କାଳବେଳା, *n.* an unpropitious time.

କାଳଯାପନ, କାଳକ୍ଷେପ, କାଳକ୍ଷେପଣ, କାଳାତିପାତ, *n.* the spending of time.

କାଳସର୍ପ, *n.* the black cobra.

* କାଳାନ୍ତକ, *n.* death.
କାଳି, *n.* ink ; a stain.
କାଳିଆ, *a.* black, dark.
* କାଳିମା, *n.* blackness, darkness.
କାଳିକା, କାଳୀ, *n.* goddess *Káli.*
* କାଳୀନ, *a.* relating to time (always used in conjunction with a noun).
କାଳେ, *ad.* haply, perhaps, lest.
କାଲ, *a.* deaf ;—*n.* a deaf man.
କାଲି, *ad.* yesterday, to-morrow.
କାଲୁଣୀ, *a. fem.* deaf ;—*n.* a deaf woman.
* କାଳ୍ପନିକ, *a.* feigned, artificial, fictitious.
କାଶ, *n.* a cough ; * a kind of grass.
କାଶିବା, *v.* to cough.
କାଶୁନ୍ଦି, *n.* mango chutney or pickle.
କାଶୀ, *n.* city of Benares.
କାଶୁଆ, କାସୁଆ, *a.* afflicted with a cough.
* କାଷ୍ଠ, *n.* wood, timber, fuel.
* କାଷ୍ଠଫଳକ, *n.* wooden plank, a board, a black-board.
* କାଷ୍ଠମୟ, *a.* wooden, made of wood.
କାସ, *n.* a cough, rheum.
କାସନ୍ଦ, କାସିନ୍ଦ, *n.* mango pickle (see କାଶିନ୍ଦ).
କାହାଣ, *n.* sixteen *páns*, or 1280 units.
କାହାଣୀ, *n.* a tale, story, legend.
କାହାଳ, *n.* the low bearer caste.
କାହାଳି, *n.* a leaf formed into a tube from which to smoke tobacco ; a long brass trumpet.
କାହିଁ, *ad.* where ? in what place ?
କାହିଁକି, *ad.* why ? wherefore ?
କାହିଁପାଇଁ, *ad.* wherefore ? why ?
କାହୁଁ, *ad.* whence? from whence?
* କିଂଶୁକ, *n.* a flowering tree (*Butea frondosa*).
କି, *pron.* what ?—*conj.* or.
କିଆଁ, *ad.* why? what? wherefore ?
କିଆ, *n.* a large thorny long-leafed shrub frequently used for hedges.
କିଆପଟ, *n.* fibre obtained from the roots of the above shrub.
କିଆରି, କିଆରୀ, *n.* divisions or plots of a cultivated field.
* କିଙ୍କର, *n.* a slave, servant.
* କିଙ୍କର୍ତ୍ତବ୍ୟବିମୂଢ, *a.* not knowing what to do.
କିଙ୍କିଣୀ, *n.* a girdle of small bells.
କିଚିରି, କିଚିରିମିଚିରି, *n.* the chirping sound made by a flock of small birds ; the chattering of monkeys.
କିଛି, *a.* and *pron.* some, a little, a few, any.
କିବାଢ, *ad.* what sort ! what kind ? also implying how changed !
କିଞ୍ଚିତ, *a.* and *pron.* some, any, a a few, little.
* କିଞ୍ଚିନ୍ମାତ୍ର, *ad.* a very little, very few.
କିଟକିଟ, କିଟିକିଟିଆ, *a.* dirty, filthy, squalid ; pitch dark.
କିଡକିଡ, କିଡମିଡ, *n.* the grinding or gnashing of teeth.

କିଣା, *a.* bought, purchased ;—*n.* buying.

କିଣାବିକା, *n.* a buying and selling.

କିଣିକିଣି, *n.* twinkling sound of an ornament.

କିଣିଖିଆ, *a.* and *n.* one who lives on bought food, one who is not a farmer.

କିଣିବା, *v.* to buy, to purchase.

କିତାବ, କିତାବ୍, *n.* book.

କିନ୍ଖାପ୍, *n.* a kind of ornamental dress.

କିନାର୍, କିନାରା, *n.* a shore, an edge, a margin.

କିନାରି, *n.* a selvedge ; a border on cloth.

କିନ୍ତୁ, *conj.* but.

* କିନ୍ନର, *n.* fabled beings with horses' heads.

କିପରି, *ad.* how ? in what way ?

କିପର୍ଯ୍ୟନ୍ତ, *ad.* how far ? how long ?

କିପାଇଁ, କିପାଁ, *ad.* why ? wherefore ?

କିପ୍ରକାରେ, *ad.* how ? in what manner?

କିବା, *conj.* or, otherwise.

କିମତି, କିମ୍ମତି, *n.* value, price, rate, worth.

କିମତେ, କେମନ୍ତେ, *ad.* how ? in which way ?

କିମିଆ, *n.* magic, enchantment ; chemistry.

କିମିଆଗାର, *a.* a magician.

* କିମ୍ବଦନ୍ତୀ, *n.* rumour, common report.

କିମ୍ବା, *conj.* or, else, otherwise, either.

* କିମ୍ଭୂତ, *ad.* how ? what kind of ?

* କିଞ୍ଚିତ୍, *pron.* some, a few, a little.

କିରଣ, *n.* a ray, a sunbeam.

କିରାଣୀ, କିରାନି, କେରାଣି, କେରାନି, *n.* clerk, Eurasian.

* କିରାତ, *n.* a hunter, bird catcher ; a savage.

କିଳିକିଳିଷ, *n.* loud laughter.

କିରିଚ, *n.* a dagger, poniard, dirk.

* କିରୀଟ, *n.* a crown, diadem, tiara.

କିରୂପ, *a.* what sort ? what kind ?

କିରୂପେ, *ad.* how ? in what way ?

କିରେ, a low or familiar *vocative.*

କିଲେ, କିଲୋ, a *vocative* addressed to women.

କିଲ୍ଲା, କିଲ୍ଲ, *n.* fort, district.

* କିଶଲୟ, କିସଲୟ, *n.* new leaves.

* କିଶୋର, *n.* a child under fifteen years of age ; a colt, a young one.

କିସ, *pron.* what ?

କିସମତ, *n.* a part, division ; fortune, fate.

କିସ୍ମିସ୍, କିଶ୍ମିସ୍, *n.* raisins, currants, dried grapes.

କିସମ୍, *n.* sort, kind.

କିସ୍ତ, କିସ୍ତି, *n.* an instalment.

କିସ୍ତଖିଲାପ, କିସ୍ତିଖିଲାପ, *n.* failure to pay by instalments, default in payment.

କିସ୍ତବନ୍ଦ, କିସ୍ତିବନ୍ଦୀ, *n.* agreement to pay by instalments.

କିସ୍ତି, *n.* a boat.

କିହୋ, an honorific *vocative* particle (masculine).

କିହେତୁ *ad.* why ? for what cause ?

କୀଟ, *n.* an insect, worm, maggot.

* କୀଟଜା, *n.* lac.

କୀଟମୟ, *a.* full of insects.
କୀଟାଣୁ, *n.* bacillus, germs. [vorous.
* କୀଟାଦ, *n.* insect-eater;—*a.* insecti-
* କୀଦୃକ୍, କୀଦୃଶ, *ad.* how? of what sort?
କୀର୍ତ୍ତନ, *n.* singing, praise, celebration.
କୀର୍ତ୍ତି, *n.* renown, celebrity, fame.
କୀର୍ତ୍ତିମାନ୍, *a.* renowned, celebrated.
କୀର୍ତ୍ତିସ୍ତମ୍ଭ, *n.* a pillar erected to commemorate some event.
* କୀଲ, * କୀଲକ, *n.* a bolt, pin, rivet, peg; the fist.
କୀଳଣା, କୀଳିଣି, *n.* a bolt; fastening of a door.
କୀଳା, *n.* a stake, peg, tent-peg.
କୀଳିବା, *v.* to bolt a door.
କୁ, a *prefix*, meaning bad, inferior.
କୁଅଁ, *n.* a leaf-bud, a sprout.
କୁଅଁ, କୁଅଁକୁଅଁ, *n.* the cry of a new-born child.
କୁଅଁରପୂର୍ଣ୍ଣିମା, କୁଅଁରପୁର୍ଣ୍ଣିମା, *n.* the full moon of *Aswina.*
କୁଅଁରୀ, *n.* a virgin, a girl from ten to twelve years.
କୁଆ, *n.* a crow. [star.
କୁଆତର, କୁଆତାର, *n.* the morning
କୁଆପଥର, *n.* hail, hailstones.
କୁଆଶା, *n.* a mist, a fog; vain hope.
କୁକର୍ମ, *n.* an evil action, wicked-
କୁକର୍ମୀ, *a.* wicked, sinful. [ness.
କୁକାର୍ଯ୍ୟ, *n.* wickedness, sin.
କୁକୁଡ଼ା, * କୁକ୍କୁଟ, *n.* a domestic fowl, a cock.
କୁକୁର, କୁକ୍କୁର, *n.* a dog. [gate.
* କୁକ୍ରିୟ, *a.* wicked, sinful, profli-
କୁକ୍ରିୟା, *n.* a bad action, a crime, a sin.
କୁଙ୍କୁଚିବା, *v.* to be contracted, to be shrivelled, to shrink.
* କୁଙ୍କୁମ, *n.* saffron.
କୁଦ, *n.* a turner's lathe.
କୁଦବାଠ, *n.* the wood which is fixed in a lathe to be turned; also the two upright posts of the lathe.
* କୁଚ, କୂଚ, *n.* a woman's breast.
* କୁଚକ୍ର, *n.* bad company, conspiracy.
* କୁଚାଗ୍ର, *n.* the nipple of the breast.
କୁଟେଇବା, *v.* to cut in pieces, to chop.
* କୁଛନ୍ଦ, *n.* doggerel poetry.
କୁଜ, *n.* a hump; * the planet Mars.
କୁଜା, *a.* hump-backed, deformed, crooked. [garment.
କୁଞ୍ଚ, *n.* the front or border of a
କୁଞ୍ଚକୁଞ୍ଚିଆ, *a.* curly; insincere, perverse.
କୁଞ୍ଚା, *n.* a measure; fourth part of a seer; the front or border of a garment.
କୁଞ୍ଚି, *n.* a sort of key.
କୁଞ୍ଚିକାଠି, *n.* a key or instrument to fasten or open a lock. [ed.
କୁଞ୍ଚିତ, *a.* warped, shrivelled, curl-
କୁଞ୍ଜ, *n.* a bower, an arbour.

* କୁଞ୍ଜର, *n.* an elephant.

କୁଞ୍ଜୁଆ, *a.* low, base;—*n.* a low-caste.

* କୁଟଜ, *n.* name of a plant.

କୁଟା, *n.* loose straw, stubble, old thatch;—*p.a.* pounded, beaten.

କୁଟାଇବା, *v.* to cause to be pounded, to cause to be beaten.

କୁଟାକୁଟି, *n.* pounding, chopping up.

କୁଟିକମ, *n.* ornamented work.

କୁଟିବା, *v.* to pound, to beat.

କୁଟିଳ, *a.* crooked, insincere.

କୁଟିଳବନ୍ଧନୀ, *n.* a bracket as { }

* କୁଟୀ, କୁଟୀର, * କୁଟି, କୁଟିର, *n.* a hovel, booth, hut, a small room.

କୁଟ୍ଟଣୀ, *n.* a woman who pounds rice, etc.; a bawd, a procuress.

କୁଟୁମ୍ବ, *n.* a relative by marriage or birth.

କୁଟୁମ୍ବୀ, କୁଟୁମ୍ବୀୟ, *a.* related by birth.

* କୁଠାର, *n.* an axe, a hatchet.

କୁଡ଼ିଆ, *n.* a hut, a cottage.

କୁଡୁଆ, *n.* a long kind of earthen pot only found in Puri and Bhubaneswar.

କୁଢ, *n.* a small heap; a sweet-scented drug.

କୁଢାଇବା, *v.* to pour out, shower down.

କୁଢିଆ, *a.* lazy, indolent; leprous; —*n.* a leper.

କୁଢୀ, *n.* a leper;—*a.* leprous.

କୁଣିଆଁ, *n.* a guest.

କୁଣ୍ଠିତ, *a.* niggardly, miserly; unwilling.

କୁଣ୍ଡ, *n.* an earthen water vessel; a sacrificial pit; *a bastard.

କୁଣ୍ଡଳ, *n.* an ear-ring.

କୁଣ୍ଡଳାକାର, *a.* circular, spiral.

* କୁଣ୍ଡଳୀ, *a.* wearing ear-rings; coiling, winding;—*n.* a snake.

କୁଣ୍ଡା, *n.* the husk or bran of rice; combing the hair.

କୁଣ୍ଡାଇବା, କୁଣ୍ଡେଇବା, *v.* to comb; to scratch.

କୁଣ୍ଡାଇହେବା, କୁଣ୍ଡେଇହେବା, *v.* to itch, to have an eager desire impelling to something.

କୁଣ୍ଡାପଥର, *n.* soft sandstone.

କୁଣ୍ଡି, *n.* a stone cup.

କୁଣ୍ଡିଆ, *n.* the itch.

କୁଣ୍ଢ, *n.* the space that can be enclosed by arms joined as in embracing.

କୁଣ୍ଢାଇବା, କୁଣ୍ଢେଇବା, *v.* to embrace, to enfold in the arms.

କୁଣ୍ଢାକୁଣ୍ଢି, *n.* mutual embrace.

କୁତ, *n.* letting for a fixed period at a fixed rental.

କୁତୁକୁତାଇବା, *v.* to tickle.

କୁତୁକୁତୁ, *v.* tickling.

କୁତୂହଳ, *n.* pleasure, delight in; sport, gratification, eagerness; surprise.

* କୁତୂହଳୀ, *a.* sportive, playful, excited.

* କୁତ୍ର, *ad.* where? in what place?

* କୁତ୍ରାପି, *ad.* wherever, anywhere, somewhere.

କୁକୁର, *n.* a dog, a cur. [dal.

* କୁତ୍ସା, *n.* censure, calumny, scan-

କୁତ୍ସିତ, *a.* ugly, mean, vile, or deformed.

କୁଥଳୀ, *n.* a small wallet used by Hindus for holding sacred flowers.

କୁଦ, *n.* an elevation, a sand-hill.

କୁଦା, *n.* a leap, jump.

କୁଦାଇବା, *v.* to trample down.

କୁଦାକୁଦ, *n.* a jumping, dancing, leaping. [dance.

କୁଦାମାରିବା, କୁଦିବା, *v.* to jump, to

କୁଦାଳ, *n.* a digging-hoe.

କୁନୀତ, *n.* low or perverted morals.

* କୁନ୍ତ, *n.* a stab, a pierce.

* କୁନ୍ତଳ, *n.* hair of the head.

କୁନ୍ଥାଇବା, *v.* to groan.

କୁନ୍ଥାଣ, କୁନ୍ଥା, *n.* a groaning, a straining at stool.

କୁନ୍ଦ, *n.* a lathe; name of a flower; frankincense.

କୁନ୍ଦକାଠ, *n.* the wood which is fixed in a lathe to be turned; also the two upright posts of the lathe. [lathe.

କୁନ୍ଦାଇବା, *v.* to cause to turn in a

କୁନ୍ଦିବା, *v.* to turn in a lathe.

କୁପଥ, *n.* a bad road; evil conduct.

କୁପଥ୍ୟ, *a.* unwholesome, hurtful (as diet).

କୁପିତ, *a.* angry, vexed, provoked.

କୁପୁତ୍ର, *n.* a bad son.

କୁବାକ୍ୟ, *n.* an evil speech, obscene word.

* କୁବାଦ, *n.* accusation, libel.

କୁବାସ, *n.* a disagreeable scent.

କୁବୁଦ୍ଧି, *n.* a perverted understanding.

କୁବେର, *n.* the god of wealth.

କୁବୃତ୍ତି, *n.* an evil profession, subsistence obtained by bad living.

କୁବ୍ଜ, *mas.* କୁବ୍ଜା, *fem.*, *a.* hump-backed, crook-backed.

କୁମର, *n.* a son, a boy.

କୁମନ୍ତ୍ରଣା, *n.* evil counsel, intrigue.

କୁମାର, *n.* a son, a prince (unmarried). [girl.

କୁମାରିକା, *n.* a virgin, a girl, a young

କୁମାରୀ, *n.* a girl, a virgin; * *Doorgá.*

* କୁମୁଦ, କୁମୁଦିନୀ, *n.* the red-and-white lotus.

* କୁମୁଦିନୀ ନାୟକ, *n.* the moon.

କୁମେରୁ, *n.* South Pole.

କୁମ୍ପା, *n.* a narrow-necked bottle.

କୁମ୍ପି, *n.* a small narrow-necked bottle.

କୁମ୍ଭ, *n.* a jar, pitcher; the Zodiac Aquarius.

* କୁମ୍ଭକାର, *n.* a potter. [bird.

କୁମ୍ଭାଟିଆ, କୁମ୍ଭାଟୁଆ, *n.* a species of

କୁମ୍ଭାର, *n.* a potter.

କୁମ୍ଭିପଟିଆ, କୁମ୍ଭିପଟୁଆ, *n.* a sect who worship only one God.

କୁମ୍ଭୀପାକ, *n.* one of the Hindu hells.

କୁମ୍ଭୀର, *n.* a crocodile, an alligator.

* କୁରଙ୍ଗ, *n.* a deer, an antelope.
* କୁରଙ୍ଗୀ, *n. fem.* deer, antelope.
କୁରରୀ, *n.* a female eagle. [appetite.
କୁରୁଚି, *n.* disgust, distaste, loss of
କୁରୁଣ୍ଡ, *n.* hydrocele.
କୁରୁମ, *n.* a species of wood.
କୁରୁଳିବା, *v.* to shout with joy.
କୁରୂପ, *a.* ugly, deformed;—*n.* an ugly appearance.
କୁର୍ତ୍ତି, କୁର୍ତ୍ତା, *n.* a coat, a jacket.
କୁଳ, *n.* lineage, caste, family.
କୁଳକଣ୍ଟକ, *n.* a thorn or plague in the family. [station.
କୁଳକ୍ରିୟା, *n.* duties of one's rank or
କୁଳଚ୍ୟୁତ, *a.* fallen from family or caste privileges. [family.
କୁଳଜାତ, * କୁଳଜ, *a.* born of a good
* କୁଳଜ୍ଞ, *n.* a genealogist.
* କୁଳଟା, *n.* a prostitute. [caste.
କୁଳଧର୍ମ, *n.* duties of a family or
* କୁଳପତି, *n.* the head of a family or caste. [family.
କୁଳବତୀ, *a.* (a woman) of good
କୁଳବଧୂ, *n.* a virtuous and good wife.
କୁଳବଦ୍ୟା, *n.* traditional calling.
କୁଳବୁଡା, *a.* disgraceful or destructive to the family;—*n.* one who is a disgrace to the family.
କୁଳଭ୍ରଷ୍ଟ, *a.* fallen from family rank.
କୁଳଶ୍ରେଷ୍ଠ, *a.* of good caste, of high rank, of good family. [family.
କୁଳାଙ୍ଗାର, *n.* a disgrace to the

* କୁଳାଚାର୍ଯ୍ୟ, *n.* a family priest.
କୁଳାଚାର, *n.* family usage or custom.
କୁଳି, କୁଳୁକୁଞ୍ଚା, *n.* gargling the mouth.
* କୁଳିଶ, *n.* *Indra's* thunderbolt.
କୁଳୀନ, *a.* of noble descent;—*n.* a nobleman. [cattle.
କୁଳ୍ଟି, *n.* bruised paddy boiled for
କୁଲେଇବା, କୁଳେଇବା, *v.* to suffice.
କୁଲକ୍ଷଣ, *n.* an evil sign, evil conduct.
କୁଲା, *n.* a kind of bamboo tray used as a winnowing-fan.
* କୁଲାଳ, *n.* a potter.
କୁଲି, *n.* a labourer, a cooly.
କୁଲୁପ, *n.* a lock, a padlock.
କୁଶ, *n.* a sacred grass.
କୁଶଳ, *n.* welfare, peace, happiness.
କୁଶଳକାରୀ, *n.* a benefactor.
* କୁଶାସନ, *n.* bad management; a mat of *Kushá* grass, a hassock.
କୁଣ୍ଡୁଲୀ, *n.* a small boat.
କୁଷ୍ଠ, *n.* leprosy.
କୁଷ୍ଠୀ, *n.* a leper;—*a.* leprous.
* କୁଷ୍ମାଣ୍ଡ, *n.* a gourd.
କୁସଂସର୍ଗ, *n.* bad company.
କୁସଂସ୍କାର, *n.* prejudice, superstition, a wrong notion. [est.
* କୁସୀଦ, *n.* usury, lending at inter-
* କୁସୀଦଜୀବୀ, *n.* a money-lender, a usurer.
କୁସୁମ, *n.* a kind of wood; * a flower; the menses.

* କୁସୁମାଞ୍ଜଳି, *n.* the joined hands filled with flowers for offering to the gods ; the last chapter in the book of Hindu philosophy.
* କୁସୁମିତ, *a.* in flower, blooming.
କୁସ୍ତି, *n.* a wrestling. [mare.
କୁସ୍ୱପ୍ନ, *n.* ominous dream, night-
କୁସ୍ୱଭାବ, *n.* evil nature, bad conduct.
* କୁହର, *n.* a cavity, a hole. [speak.
କୁହାଇବା, କୁହାଇଦେବା, *v.* to cause to
କୁହାକୁହି, କୁହାକୋହି, *n.* speaking with one another.
କୁହାଟ, *n.* a loud call.
କୁହାଟମାରିବା, କୁହାଟିବା, *v.* to call aloud.
କୁହୁକ, * କୁହକ, *n.* sorcery, magic, delusion.
କୁହୁଣ୍ଡା, *n.* a staple.
କୁହୁରବ, * କୁହୁ, *n.* the cuckoo's note.
କୁହୁଡ଼, *n.* a mist, fog, haze.
କୁରାଢ଼, *n.* an axe, a hatchet.
* କୁକ୍ଷି, *n.* the belly, the abdomen.
କୂଅ, *n.* a well.
* କୂଜନ, *n.* the chirping of a bird.
କୂଟ, *n.* illusion, deceit, * a mountain peak.
* କୂଟଯନ୍ତ୍ର, *n.* a deer-trap, snare, net.
* କୂଟସାକ୍ଷୀ, *n.* a false witness.
* କୂଟସ୍ଥ, *a.* uniform, unchangeable; —*n.* the soul. [attic.
* କୂଟାଗାର, *n.* the topmost room,
* କୂଟାର୍ଥ, *n.* obscurity, ambiguity, a double-meaning, fiction.

* କୂପ, *n.* a well.
* କୂର୍ମ, *n.* a tortoise, a turtle.
କୂଳ, *n.* a shore, coast, bank.
କୂଳବର୍ତ୍ତୀ, * କୂଳସ୍ଥ, *a.* situated by the sea shore or river bank.
* କୃକଲାସ, *n.* a lizard, chameleon.
କୃତ, *affix*, done, made, effected.
* କୃତକର୍ମା, *a.* successful, skilful.
କୃତକାର୍ଯ୍ୟ, *a.* successful ;—*n.* completed work.
କୃତଘ୍ନ, *a.* ungrateful, unthankful.
କୃତଘ୍ନତା, *n.* ingratitude, thanklessness.
କୃତଜ୍ଞ, *a.* grateful, thankful. [ness.
କୃତଜ୍ଞତା, *n.* gratitude; thankful-
* କୃତଦାର, *n.* married, wedded.
* କୃତନିଶ୍ଚୟ, *a.* determined.
କୃତାଞ୍ଜଳି, କୃତାଞ୍ଜଳିପୁଟ, *a.* with the hands joined in a suppliant manner.
* କୃତାନ୍ତ, *n.* a name of *Jama*, death.
* କୃତାଭିଷିକ୍ତ, * କୃତାଭିଷେକ, *a.* inaugurated.
କୃତାର୍ଥ, *a.* successful, prosperous.
* କୃତି, *n.* an act, action, deed, work. [ness.
* କୃତିତ୍ୱ, *n.* talent, ability, clever-
* କୃତୀ, *a.* learned, accomplished, clever. [nurse.
କୃତ୍ତିକା, *n.* the Pleiades ; *Kartick*'s
* କୃତ୍ୟ, *n.* duty, a work ;—*a.* proper to be done.
କୃତ୍ରିମ, *a.* artificial, counterfeit.

କୃଦନ୍ତ, *a.* (in *Gram.*) (words) formed by the addition of suffixes to the root.

କୃପଣ, *a.* stingy, penurious; * poor-spirited—*n.* a miser.

କୃପଣତା, *n.* niggardliness, parsimony.

କୃପା, *n.* mercy, pity, compassion.

* କୃପାଣ, *n.* a sword, a dagger.

କୃପାବାନ୍, କୃପାଳୁ, *a.* gracious, merciful, pitiful.

କୃପାମୟ, *a.* full of compassion or mercy.

କୃପାସିନ୍ଧୁ, *n.* an ocean of grace or mercy, God.

କୃପାଶୂନ୍ୟ, *a.* unkind, hard-hearted.

କୃମି, *n.* a worm, maggot, an insect.

କୃମିନାଶକ, * କୃମିଘ୍ନ, *a.* worm-destroying, vermifuge, anthelmintic.

* କୃଶ, *a.* lean, thin, emaciated.

* କୃଶାଙ୍ଗୀ, *n.* a woman of slender or delicate shape.

କୃଷକ, *n.* a farmer, husbandman, an agriculturist.

କୃଷି, *n.* ploughing, agriculture.

କୃଷିକର୍ମ, *n.* agriculture, husbandry.

କୃଷିଜୀବୀ, * କୃଷିବଳ, *n.* a cultivator.

କୃଷ୍ଣ, *a.* black, blue-black, dark-blue ;—*n.* *Krushna.*

* କୃଷ୍ଣତା, *n.* blue-blackness.

କୃଷ୍ଣପକ୍ଷ, *s.* wane of the moon.

କୃଷ୍ଣବର୍ଣ୍ଣ, *a.* black, dark blue ;—*n.* black or dark blue colour.

* କୃଷ୍ଣସାର, *n.* the black antelope.

କେଁକାଁ, କେଁକେଁ, *n.* a creaking sound.

କେ, *pron.* who? what person? someone, (used only in poetry).

କେଉଁ, *pron.* which?

କେଉଁଟା, କେଉଁଟି, *pron.* which one?

କେଉଟ, *n.* a fisherman.

* କେକା, *n.* the call of a peacock.

କେଞ୍ଚ, କେଞ୍ଚା, *n.* a thrust, a stab ; a spear or pike ; defeat.

କେଜାଣି, କିଜାଣି, *ad.* who knows? perhaps, lest, it may be.

କେଡେ, *ad.* how large? of what size?

କେଣେ, କେଣିକି, *ad.* where, whereto, to what place?

କେତକୀ, *n.* a thorny long-leafed shrub bearing a strong scented yellow flower.

କେତେ, କେତେକ, *pron.* how many, how much? some.

* କେତନ, *n.* a banner, flag.

କେତାବ୍, *n.* a book

କେତୁ, *n.* a flag, * ninth planet, comet.

* କେଦାର, *n.* divided parts or plots of a field; a cornfield.

କେନା, *n.* branch or twig of a tree.

କେନ୍ଦରା, *n.* a kind of musical instrument.

କେନ୍ଦୁ, *n.* a kind of jungly tree and its edible fruit.

କେନ୍ଦୁଆ, *n.* a wolf.

କେନ୍ଦ୍ର, *n.* (in *Astro.*) the poles; centre of a sphere.

* କେନ୍ଦ୍ରାପସାରିଣୀଶକ୍ତି, *n.* centrifugal force.

* କେନ୍ଦ୍ରାଭିକର୍ଷଣୀଶକ୍ତି, *n.* centripetal force.

କେବଳ, *ad.* only, merely.

କେବଣ, *pron.* what? (used only in poetry).

କେବା, *pron.* who? (used only in poetry).

କେବେ, କେବକୁ, *ad.* when? at what time?

କେମନ୍ତ, *ad.* is it so?

କେମତ, କେମିତ, କେମନ୍ତ, *ad.* how? what sort?

କେଣ୍ଟା, *a.* crooked-armed, (*fem.* କେଣ୍ଟୀ).

କେସ, *n.* a tuft; domiciled Bengali (of Orissa).

କେସଏ, କେଉଏ, *n.* one tuft.

କେସଣ୍ଡ୍ରି, *n.* a species of small fish.

କେସଣି, *n.* a scribe, a clerk; a Eurasian.

କେସ୍ୱା, କେରେସ୍ୱା, *n.* hire, rent.

କେଳା, *n.* Hindu gipsy tribe.

କେଳି, *n.* amorous sport.

କେଳୁଣୀ, *n.* a gipsy woman.

କେଶ, *n.* hair of the head.

* କେଶପାଶ, *n.* plaits of hair.

କେଶବ, *n.* *Vishnu.*

* କେଶମାର୍ଜ୍ଜନୀ, *n.* a comb, hair-brush.

କେଶର, *n.* the filaments of flowers; the yoke of an egg; a lion's mane.

* କେଶରୀ, *a.* having a mane;—*n.* a [lion.

କେହୁ, *pron.* anybody, someone.

କେଁ କେଁ, *n.* a sob or cry.

କେଁ ଫୁଲ, *n.* white waterlily.

କେଁସିକାଫଳ, *n.* fruit of the *bimba* tree.

* କୈତବ, *n.* deceit, fraud, craft.

କୈଫିୟତ, *n.* an official statement or explanation, remarks, report, reply.

* କୈବର୍ତ୍ତ, *n.* a fisherman; a caste.

* କୈବଲ୍ୟ, *n.* emancipation; *mahá-prasád.*

* କୈରବ, *n.* the lotus, waterlily.

କୈଳାସ, *n.* in *mytho.* residence of *Kubera* and *Siva*, one of the highest sumits of Himalaya mountains (*Gourishikhara*).

କୈଶିକାକର୍ଷଣ, *n.* capillary attraction.

* କୈଶୋର, *n.* boyhood, youth.

କୋଇ, *n.* a crucible, a fining-pot.

କୋଇଲ, *n.* Indian cuckoo.

କୋଇଲା, *n.* charcoal, coal.

କୋଉଠି, କୋଠି, *ad.* where?

କୋକିଳ, *n.* Indian cuckoo.

କୋକିଶିଆଳି, କୋକ, *n.* a fox.

କୋଚଟ, କୋଚଟିଆ, *a.* dirty; hard-hearted, miserly.

କୋଚଣୀ, କୋଚୁଣୀ, *n.* female hawker.

କୋଚ, *n.* retail trading.

କୋଚିଆ, *n.* an eel.

କୋଚିଲା, *n.* nux vomica and its tree.

କୋଚିଲାଖାଇ, *n.* a toucan or eater of the nux vomica fruit.

* କୋଜାଗର, *n.* the day of full moon in *Aswina.* [den.

କୋଟର, *n.* the hollow of a tree; a

କୋଟି, କୋଟୀ, *n.* a crore or ten millions; the upright side of a triangle; * the curved end of a bow; * the edge or point of a weapon.

କୋଟିକମ, *n.* ornamented work.

କୋଠ, *a.* common. [of a raja.

କୋଠକରଣ, *n.* an agent or steward

କୋଠରି, କୋଠରୀ, *n.* a room, cabin, an apartment.

କୋଠା, *n.* a brick-built or pucca house, a mansion.

କୋଠିଅ, *n.* a farm servant.

କୋଠି, କୋଠୀ, *n.* a bungalow; a granary, a factory.

କୋଡ, *n.* the lap, an embrace.

କୋଡା, *n.* a whip, a scourge; digging with a spade;—*a.* dug with a spade.

କୋଡ଼, *n.* a native spade. [20, xx.

କୋଡ଼ିଏ, *a.* and *n.* a score, twenty;

କୋଢ଼, *n.* leprosy.

କୋଢ଼ୀ, *n.* a leper;—*a.* leprous.

କୋଣ, *n.* a corner, an angle.

କୋଣାକୋଣି, *ad.* diagonally, corner to corner. [jar.

କୋତ, *n.* a large earthen vessel or

କୋଢଣ, *a.* dirty.

କୋଥମିରି, *n.* coriander plant.

କୋଥଳୀ, *n.* a small bag (to carry sacred flowers or utensils).

*କୋଦଣ୍ଡ, *n.* a bow.

କୋଦା, *a.* fat, corpulent.

କୋଦାଳ, *n.* a digging hoe (see କୋଡ଼).

କୋପ, *n.* anger, rage, wrath.

କୋପାଳୁ, *a.* wrathful, furious.

କୋପାନ୍ୱିତ, କୋପିତ, *a.* angry, passionate, irritated.

କୋବା, *n.* a sort of wooden hammer used to beat floors and roofs.

କୋବାକୋବି, *n.* a beating, beating one another.

କୋବି, *n.* a cabbage. [pundit.

* କୋବିଦ, *a.* learned, wise;—*n.* a

କୋମଳ, *a.* tender, soft, mild, gentle.

କୋରକ, *n.* distraint of goods; a flower-bud.

କୋରକଦାର୍, *n.* a distraining officer.

କୋରଟ, *n.* the rind of the branch of the *tal* palm. [den.

କୋରଡ, *n.* the hollow of a tree; a

କୋରଡା, *n.* a scourge, whip, cat-o'-nine-tails.

କୋରଣା, କୋରଣୀ, *n.* a scraper.

କୋରା, *n.* sweetmeat balls;—*a.* grated, rasped.

କୋରାନ, *n.* the Moslem *Koran.*

କୋରାଲୁଗା, *n.* unbleached calico.

କୋରିବା, *v.* to grate, to rasp, to scrape. [etc).

କୋଲୁପ, *n.* sediment (of ghee, milk,

କୋଳ, *n.* the lap, an embrace.

କୋଳଥ, କୁଳଥ, *n.* gram, a small bean, *kultha.*

କୋଳାକୋଳି, *n.* a mutual embracing.

କୋଳାହଳ, *n.* noise, shouting, tumult.
କୋଳି, *n.* the various kinds of wild plum.
କୋଳପ, *n.* a lock, a padlock.
କୋଶ, *n.* a *koss*, two miles, eight thousand cubits ;* a sheath, a scabbard.
କୋଶଲା, *n.* name of a vegetable.
କୋଷ, *n.* scrotum ; a store ; a treasury ; *a receptacle ; a sheath, a scabbard ; a vocabulary.
କୋଷ୍ଠ, *n.* bowels ; inner apartments.
କୋଷ୍ଠୀ, *n.* a horoscope; fate, destiny.
କୋହ, *n.* a sobbing, moan, cry.
କୋହଳ, *a.* loose, light.
* କୌଟିଲ୍ୟ, *n.* deceit, guile, insincerity.
କୌଡ଼ି, *n.* a shell current as money, a cowrie.
କୌଣସି, *pron.* any, some.
କୌତୁକ, *n.* sport, fun, diversion.
କୌତୁକୀ, *a.* sportive, jocular, funny; —*n.* a jester.
କୌତୂହଳ, *n.* curiosity, pleasure.
କୌପୀନ, *n.* a small loin cloth.
କୌମାଛ, କଉ, *n.* a species of fish.
* କୌମାର, *n.* youth, childhood.
* କୌମୁଦୀ, *n.* moonlight, lunar rays.
କୌରବ, *n.* the race of king *Kuru.*
କୌଳିକ, *a.* relating to a family.
* କୌଳୀନ୍ୟ, *n.* family honour, nobility.
କୌଶଳ, *n.* means, device, policy.
କୌଶଳକ୍ରମେ, *ad.* by a contrivance or stratagem.

* କୌଶେୟ, କୌଷେୟ, *a.* silken, made of silk.
କୌସ୍ତୁଭ, *n.* name of a breast-jewel of *Vishnu.*
କ୍ରନ୍ଦନ, *n.* a weeping, wailing.
* କ୍ରବ୍ୟ, *n.* flesh, raw-flesh, meat.
କ୍ରମ, *n.* a step, degree, series, order.
କ୍ରମଶଃ, *ad.* gradually, in regular order.
କ୍ରମାଗତ, *a.* successive, regular, continuous ;—*ad.* successively, orderly.
କ୍ରମାନ୍ୱୟ, *n.* regular order, succession ;—*a.* successive, serial ; —*ad.* successively, orderly.
କ୍ରମାନ୍ୱୟେ, *ad.* successively, in rotation.
କ୍ରମିକ, *a.* serial, successive, gradual.
କ୍ରମେ, କ୍ରମେ-କ୍ରମେ, *ad.* by degrees, gradually.
କ୍ରୟ, *n.* a purchase, act of buying.
* କ୍ରୟକର୍ତ୍ତା, *n.* a purchaser, a buyer.
କ୍ରୟବିକ୍ରୟ, *n.* buying and selling.
କ୍ରାନ୍ତି, *n.* one-third of a cowrie in value ; ecliptic-declination ; *ascension, surmounting.
କ୍ରିୟା, *n.* an action, work, affair ; (in *Gram.*) a verb.
କ୍ରିୟାକଳାପ, *n.* works, deeds, religious acts.
କ୍ରିୟାବାଚକ ବିଶେଷ୍ୟ, *n.* (in *Gram.*) a verbal noun.
କ୍ରିୟାବାନ୍, *a.* performing religious rites ; active ; abounding in works.

କ୍ରିୟାବିଶେଷଣ, *n.* (in *Gram.*) an adverb.

* କ୍ରୀଡନକ, *n.* play-things, toys.

କ୍ରୀଡା, *n.* sport, play.

* କ୍ରୀତ, *a.* bought, purchased.

କ୍ରୀତଦାସ, *n.* a slave.

କ୍ରୁଦ୍ଧ, *a.* enraged, angry, vexed.

କ୍ରୂର, *a.* cruel, harsh.

କ୍ରେତା, *n.* a purchaser, a customer.

* କ୍ରେତବ୍ୟ, କ୍ରେୟ, *a.* purchasable.

କ୍ରୋକ୍, *n.* a distraint, attachment (legal).

କ୍ରୋକଦାର୍, *n.* a baliff, one who distrains.

କ୍ରୋଡ, *n.* the lap, an embrace.

କ୍ରୋଡପତ୍ର, *n.* an appendix, a supplement.

କ୍ରୋଧ, *n.* anger, wrath, passion.

କ୍ରୋଧୀ, *a.* passionate, angry, wrathful.

କ୍ରୋଡ଼ି, *n.* ten millions, crore.

କ୍ରୋଶ, *n.* a *koss*, 4000 yards.

କ୍ରୌଞ୍ଚ, *n.* a species of heron ; name of a mountain.

କ୍ରୌଞ୍ଚଦ୍ୱୀପ, *n.* one of the seven continents.

କ୍ଳାନ୍ତ, *a.* wearied, fatigued, tired.

କ୍ଳାନ୍ତି, *n.* weariness, fatigue.

* କ୍ଳିନ୍ନ, *a.* wet, damp, moist, musty.

* କ୍ଳିଷ୍ଟ, *a.* distressed, pinched.

କ୍ଳୀବ, *a.* neuter, impotent ;—*n.* an eunuch.

କ୍ଳୀବଲିଙ୍ଗ, *n.* (in *Gram.*) the neuter gender.

* କ୍ଳେଦ, *n.* moisture, pus, filth in a liquid state.

କ୍ଳେଶ, *n.* trouble, distress, perplexity.

କ୍ଳେଶିତ *a.* afflicted, pained.

କ୍ଳେଶକର, *a.* troublesome, afflictive.

କ୍ୱଚିତ୍, *ad.* somewhere ; seldom, rarely.

* କ୍ୱଣିତ, *a.* sounded, twanged ;—*n.* a sound, a twang.

କ୍ୱାଥ, *n.* a decoction, extract.

ଖ.

ଖ, the second consonant; * sky.

ଖଁଖଁ, *n.* a wheezing cough.

ଖଙ୍କାର, *n.* phlegm, a hawking sound.

ଖଇ, *n.* rice parched or fried in the husk.

ଖଇତଣ୍ଡା, *n.* a basket used for husking ଖଇ.

ଖଇଚ୍, *a.* partly done, unfinished.

ଖଇଞ୍ଚ, *n.* a cone-shaped fish-trap.

ଖଇର, *n.* catechu and its tree.

ଖଇଖ, *a.* black and red colour mixed ; rough, not oiled (of the skin).

ଖଇରାତ, ଖଏରାତ, *n.* a gift, grant of land given in charity, a pension (see ଖୈରାତ).

ଖଗ, *n.* a crocodile's tail ; * a bird.

* ଖଗୋଳ, *n.* the celestial sphere.

* ଖଗୋଳବିଦ୍ୟା, *n.* astronomy.

ଖଚ, *n.* backbiting, slander.

ଖଚଡ଼, ଖଚଡ଼ା, *a.* vulgar, scurrilous ; vagrant, loose, wild.

ଖଚର, *n.* a mule, a mongrel ;—*a.* * moving in the sky, ærial.

*ଖଚିତ, *a.* inlaid, set as with jewels.
ଖଚୁଆ, *n.* a slanderer, a backbiter.
ଖଜଣା, *n.* rent, revenue, tribute.
ଖଜବଜ, *a.* restless, unsettled.
ଖଜା, *n.* a kind of sweetmeat.
ଖଜାଞ୍ଚି, *n.* a treasurer, cashkeeper.
ଖଜୁରି, *n.* dates, date-palm.
ଖଞ୍ଜ, *a.* lame, limping ;—*n.* plan, way, means.
ଖଞ୍ଜଖାଞ୍ଜ, *n.* device, scheme, plan.
ଖଞ୍ଜଣୀ, *n.* a tabor, a small drum.
* ଖଞ୍ଜନ, ଖଞ୍ଜଲଟି, *n.* the wagtail.
ଖଞ୍ଜା, *n.* an enclosure ;—*a.* joined.
ଖଞ୍ଜାଖଞ୍ଜି, *n.* arrrangement, adjustment.
ଖଞ୍ଜିବା, *v.* to join, to repair, to arrange, to adjust.
ଖଟ, *n.* a cot, a bedstead.
ଖଟଖଟ, *a.* difficult, intricate.
ଖଟଣୀ, *n.* daily offering fixed for an idol.
ଖଟମଲ, *n.* a bed bug.
ଖଟା, *a.* acid, sour.
ଖଟାଲ, ଖଟେଲ, *n.* anything sour—as tamarind, etc.
ଖଟାଲବା, ଖଟେଲବା, *v.* to tie by the leg ; to apply, to set to work.
ଖଟିଆ, *n.* a small bed or litter.
ଖଟିବା, *v.* to serve; to suit.
ଖଟୀ, *n.* a public-house. [sound.
ଖଡଖଡ, *n.* a rattling or clattering
ଖଡଖଡି, *n.* a closed palanquin.
ଖଡମ, *n.* sandals, pattens, clogs.
ଖଡର, *n.* a currycomb.
ଖଡା, *n.* a kind of spinage.
ଖଡାଉ, *n.* pattens, clogs.
ଖଡାଖଡା, *ad.* with dispatch, hastily.
ଖଢଳା, *n.* long fibres of cocoanut leaves.
ଖଢଳାମୁଠା, *n.* a broom, a brush made from cocoanut fibre.
ଖଡି, *n.* chalk.
ଖଡିମାଟି, *n.* a white kind of earth used as a medicine.
ଖଡୁ, *n.* a bracelet, a bangle.
ଖଡୁମରା, *n.* a stroke or blow with a bracelet.
ଖଡୁର, *n.* a maker of metal bracelets, name of a caste.
ଖଡ୍ଗ, *n.* a sword, a scimitar.
ଖଡ୍ଗହସ୍ତ, *a.* having a sword in the hand ; angry, hostile.
* ଖଡ୍ଗୀ, *n.* a rhinoceros;—*a.* armed.
ଖଣତି, ଖଣତ, *n.* a narrow spade.
ଖଣା, *n.* a hole in the road.
ଖଣି, *n.* a mine ; a pit where paddy is stored.
ଖଣିଜ, *a.* mineral.
ଖଣ୍ଟ, *n.* a swindler, a highwayman.
ଖଣ୍ଡ, *n.* a piece, fragment, part, section ; raw sugar.
ଖଣ୍ଡକ, *n.* a piece, a fragment ; a single one. [piece.
ଖଣ୍ଡଖଣ୍ଡ, *ad.* in pieces, piece by
* ଖଣ୍ଡନ, *n.* refuting, cutting to pieces.

* ଖଣ୍ଡନୀୟ, *a.* confutable, frangible.

ଖଣ୍ଡପ୍ରଳୟ, *n.* a catastrophe, a cataclysm ; a great quarrel.

ଖଣ୍ଡା, *n.* a sword, a scimitar.

ଖଣ୍ଡାଇତ, ଖଣ୍ଡାୟତ, *n.* an Oriya yeoman ; the name of a caste.

ଖଣ୍ଡିତ, *a.* broken; maimed, defective.

ଖଣ୍ଡିଏ, ଖଣ୍ଡିକ, ଖଣ୍ଡେ, *n.* a piece, one, a single one.

ଖଣ୍ଡୁଆ, *n.* a kind of shawl or upper [garment.

ଖତ, *n.* dung, manure.

ଖତକୁଡ଼, ଖତକୁଢ଼, *n.* a place where rubbish is thrown, a manure heap.

ଖତଆ, *a.* worm-eaten, old, decayed.

ଖତ୍ୟାନ୍, *n.* the paper or form in which the rents and lands of a ryot are recorded in total.

ଖତେଇହେବା, *v.* to grin, to grimace.

ଖତ୍, *n.* a bond, a record, a writing.

ଖଦଡ଼, ଖଦଡ଼ା, *n.* refuse, scum ; coarse leavings, remnants (of grain, flour, etc.).

ଖଦ, ଖଦା, *n.* a small lower garment, [a dhoti.

ଖଦିର, *n.* catechu.

* ଖଦ୍ୟୋତ, *n.* a firefly.

* ଖନକ, *n.* a digger, a burrower.

* ଖନନ, *n.* a digging, mining.

ଖନା, *n.* a man who speaks through his nose, a stammerer.

* ଖନିତ୍ର, *n.* a special kind of spade.

ଖନୀ, *n.* the *fem.* of ଖନା.

ଖନ୍ଦକ, *n.* a ditch, a trench.

ଖନ୍ଦା, *n.* a long fire-place.

ଖପର, *n.* antimony ; roofing tiles ; * a large piece of broken earthen vessel.

ଖପରା, *n*, a potsherd ; roofing tiles.

ଖପରେଲ୍, *a.* tiled.

ଖପା, *n.* anger, passion;—*a.* angry, passionate.

ଖପୁରି, *n.* a skull, crown of the [head.

ଖପ୍ପେ, *a.* scurrilous; erratic, restless; loose.

* ଖପୁଷ୍ପ, *n.* an absurdity, impossibility.

ଖବର, *n.* news, intelligence, infor- [mation.

ଖବରକାଗଜ, *n.* a newspaper.

ଖବରଦାର୍, *a.* careful, active, vigi- [lant.

ଖମା, *n.* a hollow in a road.

ଖମାର, ଖମାରଘର, *n.* a storehouse, a [barn.

ଖମୀର, *n.* leaven, yeast.

ଖମ୍ବ, *n.* a post, a pillar, a stake.

ଖମ୍ବାଳୁ, *n.* the long yam.

ଖର, *n.* tickling; * an ass;–*a.* quick, [swift.

ଖରକିବା, *v.* to sweep.

ଖରଖର, *a.* excited from anger or [pride.

ଖରଚ, ଖର୍ଚ୍ଚ, *n.* expenditure, expense.

ଖରଚପତ୍ର, *n.* family expenses, expenses, expenditure, a bill of expenses.

ଖରଚ୍, ଖର୍ଚ୍ଚା, *n.* expense ; costs of a [suit.

ଖରଚୁଆ, ଖର୍ଚ୍ଚୀ, *a.* expensive, extravagant.

ଖରଡ଼ା, *a.* slightly parched or roast- [ed.

ଖରଜାପତି, *n.* the extra income of a zemindar beyond the ordinary rents.

ଖରଢବା, *v.* to fry, to parch.

ଖରଖର, *a.* very sharp, very keen; —*ad.* very quickly.

ଖରନଶ୍ୱାସ, *n.* quick respiration, puffing and blowing.

ଖରବୁଜ, ଖର୍ବୁଜ, *n.* the musk melon.

ଖରଭଜା, *a.* over-fried.

ଖରମସ (ଘିଅ), *a.* over-boiled (ghee).

ଖରା, *n.* heat or glare of the sun, sunshine.

ଖରାପ, ଖରାପ୍, *a.* bad, evil, spoiled, rotten.

ଖରିଦ, *n.* a purchase.

ଖରିଦଦାର, *n.* a purchaser, a buyer.

* ଖର୍ପର, *n.* a beggar's dish; the skull, crown; a potsherd.

ଖର୍ବ, *a.* dwarfish, pigmy; ten thousand millions, 10,000,000,000.

ଖଳ, *a.* deceitful, crafty, wicked.

ଖଳତା, *n.* deceitfulness, craftiness.

ଖଳା, *n.* a threshing-floor.

ଖଳି, *n.* starch.

ଖଲ, *n.* a mortar.

ଖଲାସ, *n.* deliverance, freedom; —*a.* delivered; released.

ଖଲାସୀ, *n.* a sailor; a servant in charge of tents, baggage, &c.

ଖଲି, *n.* a dish made of leaves sewn together.

ଖଞ୍ଜ, *a.* lame.

ଖଲିଫା, *n.* a tailor; a Muhammadan ruler.

ଖଳିବା, *v.* to pound, to grind (with a pestle), to strain through a cloth or strainer.

ଖସ୍‌ଖସ୍, *n.* a rustling noise; poppy seed; *khaskhas* (root of *bena* grass).

ଖସଖସିଆ, *a.* rough (surface), not smooth.

ଖସଡା, *a.* slippery; muddy, slubby, clayey; —*n.* a rough copy

ଖସା, *n.* sesamum seed; a mole, freckle.

ଖସାଇବା, *v.* to cause to drop, to slip down.

ଖସି, ଖାସି, *n.* a goat (castrated).

ଖସିପଡିବା, *v.* to fall, to drop down, to loosen and fall.

ଖସିବା, *v.* to drop, to slip down, to fall off.

ଖସିଯିବା, *v.* to slip off.

ଖାଇ, *n.* a ditch, trench; a cotton cleaner.

ଖାଇବା, *v.* to eat; —*n.* the act of eating.

ଖାଉଟି, *n.* one who buys for himself.

ଖାଉଟିଆ, *a.* gluttonous, greedy.

ଖାଉନ୍ଦ, *n.* a master, lord, owner.

ଖାଉନ୍ଦାଣୀ, *n.* mistress.

ଖାଜାଞ୍ଚି, *n.* cashier, treasurer.

ଖାଦଣ, *n.* gunny bag, wallet.

ଖାଣ୍ଡି, *n.* part of a broken pot (only found in Puri).

ଖାଣ୍ଟି, *a.* pure, unadulterated, upright; orthodox.

ଖାତ, *n.* a pit, ditch, moat, pond.

ଖାତକ, *n.* a debtor, borrower of money.

ଖାତିର୍, ଖାତର୍, *n.* care, regard; [security.

ଖାତା, *n.* an account-book, ledger, a book, a file for papers. [alloy.

ଖାଦ, *n.* refuse, dross of metal,

ଖାଦକ, *n.* an eater, a consumer.

ଖାଦ୍ୟ, *n.* food ;—*a.* eatable, fit for food.

ଖାନକୀ, *n.* a whore.

ଖାନସାମା, *n.* a table servant.

ଖାନା, *n.* a meal, a dinner.

ଖାନାବାଡ଼ି, *n.* the grounds surrounding a dwelling-house, a compound.

ଖାନଖରାବ୍, ଖିନ୍‌ଖରାବ୍, *a.* ruined, spoiled.

ଖାପ, *n.* a scabbard, sheath, a groove ;—*a.* thick, close woven (applied to cloth).

ଖାବଡ଼ାଖୁବଡ଼ା, *a.* uneven, rough, up and down.

ଖାବଡ଼ା, *a.* uneven, rough.

ଖାବଳ, *n.* a mortise hole, a groove.

ଖାର, *n.* an impure potash used by *dhobas*, ashes.

ଖାରଜ, *n.* alienation, dismisssal of a case (in law). [measure.

ଖାଣ୍ଟ, *a.* upright, honest ;—*n.* exact

ଖାଣ୍ଡଅ, *a.* insipid, watery.

ଖାଣ୍ଡିବା, *v.* to operate (as in surgery).

ଖାଣ୍ଡି, *n.* a measure.

ଖାଣ୍ଡିତ, *a.* excluded, dismissed.

ଖାଣ୍ଡୁଆ, *n.* a coarse red cloth.

ଖାଲୋଇ, *n.* a fisherman's basket.

ଖାଲ, *n.* a hollow, low land, a creek, inlet, bay. [surface.

ଖାଲଢିପ, *n.* up and down, a rough

ଖାଲି, *a.* vacant, empty, void ;—*ad.* merely.

ଖାସ୍, *a.* peculiar, own ; belonging to or forfeited to Government; —*ad.* merely, singly.

ଖାସ୍-ଅପିଲ, *n.* special appeal.

ଖାସକାମରା, *n.* a private apartment.

ଖାସ୍‌ମହାଲ୍, *n.* Government land.

ଖାସା, *a.* good, superior, excellent.

ଖାସି, *n.* a castrated animal ;—*a.* castrated.

ଖିଆଲ, *n.* whim, idiosyncrasy.

ଖିଙ୍କାରି-ହେବା, *v.* to speak sharply or angrily.

ଖିଖି, *n.* sound of laughing; a fox.

ଖିଟିଖିଟିଆ, *a.* fretful, peevish, snappish.

ଖିଡ଼କି, *n.* a window, a private door.

*ଖିଦ୍ୟମାନ, *a.* distressed, grieving.

*ଖିନ୍ନ, *a.* dejected, fatigued ; sorrowful, grieved.

ଖିଲ, *n.* a peg, wedge, bolt, pin ; a small packet or bundle.

ଖିଲ୍‌କାଟ, ଖିଲିକାଟ, *n.* instrument for cutting betel nuts.

ଖିଲି, *n.* a tunnel; a small packet or bundle. [bundle.

ଖିଲିଏ, ଖିଲେ, *n.* one packet or small

ଖିଲାତ, *n.* an honorary dress.

ଖିଲ୍ଣ, ଖିଲ୍ଲଣ, *n.* an arch, vault, dome.

ଖୁଅ, *n.* a churning stick; upper part of the arm.

ଖୁଆଇବା, ଖୋଆଇବା, *v.* to feed.

ଖୁଆଇଦେବା, ଖୋଆଇଦେବା, *v.* to place food in another's mouth.

ଖୁଆଡ଼, *n.* a shed or fold.

ଖୁଆଖୋଇ, *n.* a fighting or quarrelling with one another; a mutual feeding.

ଖୁଙ୍କି, *n.* a small oblong basket.

ଖୁଞ୍ଚା, *n.* a projecting nail or spike.

ଖୁଞ୍ଚାଦେବା, *v.* to repair a thatched roof, &c.

ଖୁଜୁଳି, *n.* the itch.

ଖୁଡ଼ୀ, *n.* the wife of a father's younger brother, an aunt.

ଖୁଡ଼ା, ଖୁଡ଼ୁଡ଼ା, *n.* father's younger brother.

ଖୁନ, *n.* blood from a wound.

ଖୁଣ, *n.* a defect.

ଖୁନି, ଖୁନ୍, *n.* a wound; murder.

ଖୁଣ୍ଟ, *n.* a stake, pillar, post.

ଖୁଣ୍ଟା, *n.* a peg, pin; an abusive simile.

ଖୁଣ୍ଟି, *n.* a small peg or pin.

ଖୁଣ୍ଟିବା, *v.* to pick up.

ଖୁଣ୍ଟେଣୀ, *n.* a small net tied to the end of a bamboo in which to gather fruit.

ଖୁଦ, *n.* broken rice.

ଖୁଦର, *a.* small, diminutive.

ଖୁଦୁଡ଼ା, *n,* broken rice with refuse.

ଖୁଦୁରୁକୁଣୀ, *n.* a festival among unmarried girls.

ଖୁନ୍ଦା, *n.* a punch in the face.

ଖୁନ୍ଦାଖୁନ୍ଦି, *n.* excessive squeezing or pushing. [push.

ଖୁନ୍ଦିବା, *v.* to thrust, to press, to

ଖୁମ୍ବ, *n.* a post, a pillar.

ଖୁର, *n.* a razor; an animal's hoof.

ଖୁରା, *n.* a hoof; the foot or base of anything.

ଖୁରସୁ, *n.* a kind of fish; a kind of small deer.

ଖୁରଖାଇବା, *v.* to stamp and tear and toss up the ground in anger—as a bull does. [cup.

ଖୁରି, *n.* a small earthen vessel or

ଖୁରୁମ, ଖୁରୁଡ଼, *n.* dried cocoanut.

ଖୁର୍ପା, ଖୁର୍ପୀ, *n.* a small spade to dig up grass.

ଖୁର୍ମା, *n.* dried date-fruit, a kind of sweetmeat.

*ଖୁଲ୍ଲ, *a.* youngest, least.

*ଖୁଲ୍ଲତାତ, *n.* father's younger brother.

ଖୁସାମୋଦ, *n.* flattery, praise.

ଖୁସି, *n.* joy, pleasure; option, as you please.

ଖେଙ୍କଶିଆଳ, *n.* a fox.

ଖେଚଡ଼, ଖେଚଡ଼ା, *a.* vulgar, scurrilous; vagrant; loose, wild.

ଖେଚଡ଼ି, ଖିଚୁଡ଼ି, *n.* a medley; a dish made of rice, *dál*, *ghee* and spices.

ଖେଚର, *a.* ærial, moving in the air; —*n.* a bird.

ଖେଞ୍ଚବା, ଖେଁଚିବା, *v.* to poke at.

ଖେଣ୍ଟା, *n.* a peg, plug, pin, spike.

ଖେଣ୍ଟାଣୀ, ଖେଣ୍ଟେଣୀ, *n.* a procuress, a bawd.

ଖେଦ, *n.* grief, sorrow, regret.

ଖେଦା, *n.* a herd, a flock; a stockade to catch elephants.

ଖେଦାଖେଦା, *ad.* in parties, in companies.

ଖେଦଦେବା, *v.* to drive off.

ଖେଦବା, *v.* to run after.

ଖେଦଷିବା, *v.* to run after; to prevail, to pervade, to spread about.

ଖେପ, *n.* once ; one load.

ଖେପା, *n.* a jump.

ଖେପାଜାଲ, *n.* a kind of net.

ଖେଳ, ଖେଳା, *n.* play, sport.

ଖେଳନା, *n.* a toy, a plaything.

ଖେଳାଡ଼ି, ଖେଳୁଅଡ଼, ଖେଳାଳୀ, ଖେଳୁଅଳ, *a.* playful, sportive.

ଖେଳିବା, *v.* to play.

ଖେସାରତ, *n.* loss, damage.

ଖେସାରି, *n.* a species of pulse.

ଖୈରାତ୍, *n.* a pension, a gift, (see ଖଇରାତ).

ଖୋଇ, *n.* habit, nature, disposition.

ଖୋଜ, *n.* a footmark ; search, inquiry, a trace.

ଖୋଜାଖୋଜି, *n.* a general search.

ଖୋଜିବା, *v.* to search, to seek.

ଖୋଡ଼, *n.* leprosy.

ଖୋଡ଼ଆ, *a.* malicious, quarrelsome ;—*n.* a leper.

ଖୋଦ୍, *pron.* own, ownself.

ଖୋଦା, *n.* God.

ଖୋଦିତ, *a.* engraved, marked, dug.

ଖୋଦିବା, *v.* to engrave, to carve.

ଖୋପା, *n.* a knot of hair tied on the head.

ଖୋରାକ୍, ଖୋରାକି, *n.* maintenance.

ଖୋଳ, *n.* a sheath; shell of a fruit.

ଖୋଳପା, *n.* bark of a tree, rind, peel.

ଖୋଳିବା, *v.* to dig, open, expose ; to engrave, to carve.

ଖୋଲ, *n.* cave, cavern, opening.

ଖୋଲା, *a.* open, loose; easy, simple.

ଖୋଲାସା, *n.* an abstract of a document.

ଖୋଲିବା, *v.* to open ; to untie.

ଖୋଷା, ଖୋସା *n.* a knot of hair tied on the head; the edible part of the jack-fruit.

ଖୋସଣୀ, *n.* a tuck, a dhoti tucked together on the loins.

ଖୋସା, *n.* a shell, pod, husk.

ଖୋସାମୋଦ, *n.* flattery, praise.

ଖୋସିବା, *v.* to tuck in, to put in.

ଖ୍ୟାତ, *a.* famed, renowned, called.

ଖ୍ୟାତାପନ୍ନ, *a.* famous, illustrious.

ଖ୍ୟାତି, *n.* fame, character, a nickname.

ଖ୍ରୀଷ୍ଟ, *n.* Christ.

ଖ୍ରୀଷ୍ଟିୟାନ, *n.* Christian, a follower of Jesus Christ.

ଗ.

ଗ, the third consonant.

ଗଇଁଠି, *n.* pain from severe flogging, an old pain.

ଗଇଁଠିଆ, *a.* hardened by flogging.

ଗଇଁଠିମାଡ଼, *n.* severe flogging.

ଗଇଁଠିମାରୁ, *n.* a deceitful person.

ଗଇଁଣ୍ଠା, *n.* a small unsweetened rice-cake.

ଗଇଣ୍ଠାଇବା, *v.* to tie in a knot.

ଗଇଣ୍ଠାଳ, *n.* the act of tying the wedding garments of the bride and bridegroom together on the dais.

ଗଇତି, *n.* a pick-axe.

ଗଇଣ୍ଡ, *n.* a species of plant and its flower.

ଗଇଁଡ଼ି, *n.* pride, haughtiness.

ଗଉଡ଼, *n.* a cowherd, a milkman, a bearer.

ଗଉଡ଼ୁଣୀ, *n.* a dairywoman, a female cowkeeper.

ଗଉଣୀ, *n.* a corn measure varying in different districts.

ଗଗନ, *n.* the sky, firmament.

ଗଗନମଣ୍ଡଳ, *n.* the whole firmament.

ଗଗରା, *n.* a large brass water vessel.

ଗଙ୍ଗା, *n.* the river Ganges, *Gangá.*

ଗଙ୍ଗାପ୍ରାପ୍ତି, *n.* the arrival on the shore of the Ganges to die there, the casting of a corpse into the Ganges—hence death.

ଗଙ୍ଗାସାଗର, *n.* the estuary of the Ganges; an island of that name.

ଗଛ, *n.* a tree.

ଗଚ୍ଛିତ, *a.* deposited, pledged.

ଗଜ, *n.* a yard measure; *an elephant.

* ଗଜଗାମିନୀ, *n.* a graceful woman; *lit.* one who walks like an elephant.

ଗଜଗଜ, *n.* the noise caused by water falling or being poured, a gurgling noise.

* ଗଜଦନ୍ତ, *n.* elephant's tusk, ivory.

ଗଜପିପ୍ପଳୀ, *n.* the fruit of a climbing plant used in medicine.

ଗଜବ, *n.* an accident, misfortune.

ଗଜମୁକ୍ତା, *n.* a pearl said to be found in the elephant's head or hump.

ଗଜମୂର୍ଖ, *n.* an illiterate, a very stupid fellow, a great ass.

ଗଜରାଜ, *n. fig.* a great personage.

ଗଜା, *n.* a sprout, bud; name of a sweetmeat.

ଗଜାଗଛ, *n.* a young tree, a sapling.

ଗଜାବୟସ, *n.* youth, youthfulness.

ଗଜାମରୁଡ଼, *n.* the withering of vegetation on account of drought.

ଗଞା, *n.* a nit.

ଗଞ୍ଜ, *n.* a mart, place for trade.

ଗଞ୍ଜଡ଼, ଗଞ୍ଜଲ, *a.* addicted to *ganjá.*

ଗଞ୍ଜଣା, *n.* reproachful language.

ଗଞ୍ଜା, *n. ganjá,* hemp; a cock; a tavern, a distillery.

ଗଞ୍ଜାଇ, *n. ganjá,* hemp, the intoxicating drug of that name.

ଗଞ୍ଜାଖୋର, ଗଞ୍ଜେଡ଼ି, *n.* one addicted to hemp smoking;—*a.* addicted to hemp smoking.

ଗଠନ, *n.* shape, make, form.

ଗଠିତ, *a.* made, framed, moulded.

ଗଡ଼, *n.* a fort, a stronghold.

ଗଡ଼ଖାଇ, *n.* a ditch or moat round a fortification.

ଗଡ଼ଜାତ, *n.* the tributary hilly states of Orissa. [the *Gurjats.*

ଗଡ଼ଜାତିଆ, ଗଡ଼ଜାତୀ, *a.* belonging to

ଗଡ଼ନ୍ତ, ଗଡ଼ନ୍ତିଆ, *n.* a declivity, a slope;—*a.* sloping.

ଗଡ଼ବଡ଼, ଗଡ଼ବଡ଼ି, *n.* noise, tumult, an uproar, a quarrel, excitement.

ଗଡ଼ପ୍, *a.* hidden.

ଗଡ଼ପଡ଼, *n.* a tossing in bed; a short slumber.

ଗଡ଼ାଇବା, *v.* to cause to roll; to make into pieces.

ଗଡ଼ାଗଡ଼ି, *n.* a rolling on the ground.

ଗଡ଼ାଣିଆ, *a.* sloping.

ଗଡ଼ିଆ, *n.* a small pond, a tank.

ଗଡ଼ିପଡ଼ିବା, *v.* to roll down.

ଗଡ଼ିବା, *v.* to roll.

ଗଡ଼ିଶା, *n.* a kind of fish.

ଗଡ଼ୁ, *n.* a drinking vessel; * goitre, * a wen.

ଗଢ଼ଣ, *n.* shape, form.

ଗଢ଼ା, *a.* made, formed, fabricated.

ଗଢ଼ାଇବା, *v.* to cause to be made or moulded.

ଗଢ଼ାଗଢ଼ି, *n.* moulding into shape.

ଗଢ଼ିବା, *v.* to make, form, fabricate.

ଗଣ, *n.* generally joined to another noun to indicate a crowd, a class, party, flock, tribe.

ଗଣକ, *n.* an astrologer, a calculator of nativities; an astronomer.

ଗଣକତା, *n.* the astrological profession. [sound.

ଗଣଗଣ, *n.* speaking with a nasal

ଗଣନ, *n.* calculation, enumeration.

ଗଣନ, ଗଣନା, *n.* a counting, a reckoning, calculation.

* ଗଣପତି, *n.* *Ganesh*; ring-leader.

ଗଣା, *a.* counted, calculated.

ଗଣାଗଣି, *n.* counting.

ଗଣାଳି, *n.* one who counts or enumerates.

ଗଣିତ, *n.* mathematics;—*a.* counted, enumerated.

ଗଣିତଜ୍ଞ, *a.* versed in mathematics.

ଗଣିବା, *v.* to count, to reckon, to calculate. [dom.

ଗଣେଶ, *n.* *Ganesh*—the god of wis-

ଗଣ୍ଡେଳା, *n.* a village law-suit.

ଗଣ୍ଠି, *n.* a joint, knot, hinge.

ଗଣ୍ଠିଆ, *a.* miserly, close-fisted;—*n.* a kind of ear-ornament.

ଗଣ୍ଠିଧନ, *n.* one's most precious and valuable treasure. [joints.

ଗଣ୍ଠିବାତ, *n.* rheumatism in the

ଗଣ୍ଠିଲି, *n.* luggage, package.

ଗଣ୍ଠିଲିକଟା, *n.* a pick-pocket, a luggage thief.

ଗଣ୍ଡ, *n.* deep water; name of a jungly tribe; *the cheek; *temples of an elephant;—*a.* very dull.

ଗଣ୍ଡଗୋଳ, *n.* a tumult, uproar.

* ଗଣ୍ଡଦେଶ, ଗଣ୍ଡସ୍ଥଳ, *n.* the cheek.

ଗଣ୍ଡବୁଦ୍ଧି, *a.* very ignorant, stupid.

ଗଣ୍ଡମାଳା, *n.* the mumps, king's-evil.

ଗଣ୍ଡମୂର୍ଖ, *a.* extremely ignorant.

* ଗଣ୍ଡଶୈଳ, *n.* a huge rock thrown down by an earthquake or storm.

ଗଣ୍ଡା, *n.* four units; a rhinoceros.

ଗଣ୍ଡାଏ, *n.* one bunch or heap of four.

ଗଣ୍ଡାକିଆ, *a.* worth four cowries.

* ଗଣ୍ଡାର, *n.* a rhinoceros.

ଗଣ୍ଡି, *n.* trunk of the body, trunk of a tree; log of wood.

ଗଣ୍ଠିଲ, *n.* a bundle (for the back).

* ଗଣ୍ଡୁଷ, *n.* a handful of water.

ଗଣ୍ୟ, *a.* calculable; notable.

ଗତ, *a.* gone, past, last.

ଗତାଗତ, *n.* a going and coming.

* ଗତାନୁଗତିକ, *a.* following precedents, customary.

* ଗତାନୁଶୋଚନା, *n.* after-thought; repentance.

ଗତାୟାତ, *n.* intercourse, coming and going,

* ଗତାୟୁଃ, *a.* dying, at the point of death.

ଗତି, *n.* motion, gait, conduct, course; fate.

ଗତିବିଧି, *n.* a man's movements or character.

ଗତିଶକ୍ତି, *n.* the power of motion.

ଗତ୍ୟନ୍ତର, *n.* an alternative course.

* ଗତ୍ୱର, *a.* movable, locomotive.

ଗଦ, *n.* a medicine; * sickness, a disease.

ଗଦା, *n.* a heap; * a club, bludgeon.

ଗଦାଇବା, ଗଦାଇଦେବା, *v.* to heap up.

ଗଦାଏ, *n.* a collection of things in one place, a heap.

ଗଦି, *n.* a cushion, a mattress; a seat, a throne.

ଗଦିନସୀନ୍, *a.* enthroned.

ଗଦ୍‌ଗଦ୍, *a.* overcome with joy or grief, inarticulate because of deep emotion, panting.

ଗଦ୍ୟ, *n.* prose.

ଗଧ, *n.* an ass.

ଗଧିଆ, *a.* asinine, lazy;–*n.* a hyena.

ଗନ୍ତବ୍ୟ, *a.* passable, accessible.

ଗନ୍ତାଇତ, *n.* head steward.

ଗନ୍ତାଘର, *n.* a wardrobe, a store-house.

ଗନ୍ଧ, *n.* smell, (in common use indicates an unpleasant smell).

ଗନ୍ଧ, *n.* when used as a prefix to nouns indicates scented, perfumed.

ଗନ୍ଧକ, *n.* sulphur, brimstone.

ଗନ୍ଧବଣିକ, *n.* a dealer in drugs; name of a caste.

* ଗନ୍ଧବହ, *n.* wind, air.

ଗନ୍ଧବିରୋଜା, *n.* a medicinal resin.

ଗନ୍ଧବେଣା, *n.* the lemon grass.

ଗନ୍ଧମାର୍ଜାର, *n.* a wild cat, an otter.

ଗନ୍ଧରସ, *n.* myrrh, scented ointment.

ଗନ୍ଧରାଜ, *n.* a shrub and flower of that name.

ଗନ୍ଧର୍ବ, *n.* celestial choristers.

* ଗନ୍ଧର୍ବବିଦ୍ୟା, *n.* the polite arts—music, &c.

* ଗନ୍ଧର୍ବବିବାହ, *n.* a marriage by mutual consent only.

ଗନ୍ଧଶୁଣ୍ଠି, *n.* a medicinal root.

* ଗନ୍ଧସାର, *n.* sandalwood.

ଗନ୍ଧାଇବା, *v.* to emit a bad smell.

ଗନ୍ଧିଆ, *n.* a stink, a bad smell;—*a.* evil-smelling.

ଗପ, *n.* chitchat, tattle, gossip.

ଗପଡ଼, *a.* talkative;—*n.* chatterer.

ଗବ, *n.* castor oil seed, castor oil plant.

* ଗବାକ୍ଷ, *n.* a small window.

* ଗବ୍ୟ, *a.* pertaining to the cow, (as milk and butter, &c.).

ଗଭ, *n.* hair tied in a bunch.

ଗଭୀର, *a.* deep, profound, grave.

ଗଭୂରପକାଇବା, *v.* to bring forth prematurely.

ଗମନ, *n.* a going, motion.

ଗମନାଗମନ, *n.* going and coming, free intercourse.

ଗମସ, *a.* rotten, gone bad.

ଗମାଗମ, *n.* going and coming.

ଗମାର, *a.* stupid, nonsensical.

ଗମିବା, *v.* to walk; to conceive, to understand.

ଗମିଷିବା, *v.* to be fermented, to go bad.

ଗମ୍ଭାରୀ, *n.* name of a tree.

ଗମ୍ଭୀର, *a.* profound, grave, deep.

ଗମ୍ଭୀରା, *n.* an inner room.

* ଗମ୍ଭୀରସାମନ୍ତ, *n.* prince.

* ଗମ୍ୟ, *a.* accessible, practicable.

ଗୟଳ, *n.* species of wild ox; wild buffalo; timber.

ଗୟାଳୁ, *n.* a species of yam.

ଗର, *n.* a log of wood; * poison.

ଗରଗଡ଼, *n.* a plant bearing white seeds and growing among rice plants.

ଗରଗର, *n.* a log cut in short pieces; —*a.* trembling with anger.

ଗରଜ, *n.* necessity, occasion for.

ଗରଜୀ, *a.* necessitous, needy.

ଗରଦ, *n.* a kind of silk cloth.

ଗରମ, *a.* hot, warm; passionate.

ଗରମି, *n.* heat; syphilis.

ଗରଳ, *n.* poison, venom, virus.

ଗରହାଜର, *a.* absent, not present.

ଗରା, *n.* a large brass water vessel.

ଗରିବ, *a.* poor, indigent, humble.

ଗରିମା, *n.* self-importance, pride.

ଗରିଷ୍ଠ, *a.* difficult of digestion; highly important.

* ଗରୁଡ, *n.* a fabulous bird, *Garuda.*

ଗର୍ଗର, *a.* trembling with anger.

ଗର୍ଜ୍ଜନ, *ଗର୍ଜିତ, *n.* a roaring, growling; rage.

ଗର୍ତ୍ତ, *n.* a hole in the ground, a cave, an excavation.

ଗର୍ଦ୍ଦଭ, *n.* an ass, a donkey.
ଗର୍ଦ୍ଦଭୀ, *n.* a she-ass, a jenny-ass.
ଗର୍ବ, *n.* pride, arrogance, scorn.
ଗର୍ବିତ, ଗର୍ବୀ, *a.* proud, arrogant, haughty.
ଗର୍ଭ, *n.* the womb; pregnancy; an embryo, a fœtus.
ଗର୍ଭକେଶର, *n.* the pistils in the flower of a plant.
ଗର୍ଭକୋଷ, *n.* the uterus. [birth.
ଗର୍ଭଚ୍ୟୁତ, *a.* abortive;—*n.* untimely
ଗର୍ଭଣା, *n.* the name of the first solar day of the month of *Kartik.*
ଗର୍ଭଧାରଣ, *n.* conception, pregnancy.
ଗର୍ଭଧାରଣୀ, *a.* pregnant;—*n.* a mother. [abortion.
ଗର୍ଭପାତ, ଗର୍ଭସ୍ରାବ, *n.* miscarriage,
ଗର୍ଭବତୀ, ଗର୍ଭିଣୀ, *a.* pregnant. [nal.
ଗର୍ଭସ୍ଥ, *a.* being in the womb; inter-
* ଗର୍ହଣା, *n.* scurrility, blame, reproach. [graced.
ଗର୍ହିତ, *a.* reviled, despised, dis-
* ଗର୍ହ୍ୟ, *a.* censurable, reproachable.
* ଗଳ, *n.* the neck, throat.
ଗଳକମ୍ବଳ, *n.* the dewlap. [chocele.
ଗଳଗଣ୍ଡ, *n.* a goitre, wen, bron-
ଗଳଦେଶ, *n.* the neck.
* ଗଳନ, *n.* the melting of metals, the dissolution of salt, &c.
ଗଳବସ୍ତ୍ର, *a.* having a cloth round the neck in token of humble submission.

* ଗଳଭଙ୍ଗ, *n.* hoarseness, roughness of voice. [son.
ଗଳହସ୍ତ, *n.* the throttling of a per-
ଗଳା, *n.* the neck, throat. [a hole.
ଗଳାଇବା, *v.* to cause to pass through
ଗଳାଖଙ୍କାର, *n.* sound of clearing of the throat.
ଗଳାଖଙ୍କାରଦେବା, ଗଳାଖଙ୍କାରିମାରିବା, *v.* to make above sound in order to give warning.
ଗଳାଖଙ୍କାରିବା, *v.* to clear the throat.
ଗଳାଚିପିବା, ଗଳାଟିପିବା, *v.* to kill by strangling.
ଗଳାବନ୍ଧ, *n.* a neckcloth, a cravat.
ଗଳି, *n.* a lane, an alley.
ଗଳିପଡିବା, *v.* to run out, to leak.
ଗଳିବା, ଗଳିଯିବା, *v.* to pass or enter through a narrow opening.
* ଗଳିତ, *a.* dissolved, melted, decomposed.
ଗଲ୍‌ଗଲ୍, *ad.* in a state of itchiness.
ଗଲ୍‌ସଟା, ଗଲ୍‌ହଟା, *a.* dirty;—*n.* confusion.
ଗତ, *a.* gone, past, elapsed.
ଗତଦିନ, *n.* yesterday.
ଗଲିଜ୍, *n.* filth, mud, dirt.
ଗଲ୍ଲ, *n.* a scratching sensation.
ଗଳ୍ପ, *n.* chitchat, idle talk; a story.
ଗସ୍ତ, *n.* touring, a walking about, sauntering.
ଗହଣା, *n.* an ornament, a trinket.
ଗହନ, *a.* impervious;—*n.* a thicket.
ଗହମ, *n.* wheat.

ଗହଳ, *n.* a crowd, a dense crowd.

ଗହୀର, *a.* deep ;—*n.* a deep place ; a large rice plain.

ଗହ୍ୱର, *n.* a ravine, hole, cave, den.

ଗହ୍ମାପୂର୍ଣ୍ଣିମା, *n.* full moon in *Shraban.*

ଗାଁ, *n.* a village, hamlet.

ଗାଅଣ, *n.* a singer.

ଗାଇବା, *v.* to sing.

ଗାଈ, *n.* a cow.

ଗାଈପଣିଆ, *n.* giving milk, fecundity of a cow.

ଗାଉଣା, *n.* singing.

ଗାଁଉଲି, ଗାଁଉଲ, *a.* rustic.

ଗାଜର, *n.* a carrot.

ଗାଞ୍ଜିଆ, *n.* a net purse attached to the girdle.

ଗାଡ଼, *n.* a hole, cave, deep place.

ଗାଡ଼ିଆ, *n.* a small pond, (see ଗଡ଼ିଆ).

ଗାଡ଼ି, ଗାଡ଼ୀ, *n.* a cart, hackery, carriage.

ଗାଡ଼ିଆଳ, *n.* a driver, a cartman, a coachman.

ଗାଢ଼, *a.* excessive ; strong ; thick ; close.

ଗାଢ଼ା, *a.* thick, thickened.

ଗାଣ୍ଡି, *n.* the anus, the vent.

ଗାଣ୍ଡୁଆ, *n.* a shallow basket.

ଗାତ, *n.* a hole, pit, cave.

ଗାତୁଆ, *a.* burrowing (insects or animals).

* ଗାତ୍ର, *n.* the body.

* ଗାତ୍ରମାର୍ଜ୍ଜନା, *n.* a towel.

* ଗାତ୍ରୋତ୍ଥାନ, *n.* getting up from sleep or bed, rising.

* ଗାଥା, *n.* a verse, stanza, poem.

ଗାଦ, *n.* lees, dregs, sediment.

ଗାଦି, *n.* throne, seat.

ଗାଧୁଆ, *n.* a bathing, a bath ;—*a.* bathed.

ଗାଧୋଇବା, *v.* to bathe.

ଗାନ, *n.* singing ; a song, vocal music.

ଗାନ୍ଥିବା, *v.* to build, to lay in rows ; to arrange.

ଗାନ୍ଥଣା, ଗାନ୍ଥୁଣା, *n.* the workmanship of a building, bricklaying.

ଗାଫିଲ, *a.* negligent, idle, inattentive.

ଗାଭିଲ, *a.* with young (of animals only).

* ଗାଭୀ, *n.* a cow.

ଗାମୁଛା, *n.* a cloth used as a towel.

* ଗାମ୍ଭୀର୍ଯ୍ୟ, *n.* solemnity, gravity.

ଗାୟକ, *n.* a singer, chanter.

ଗାୟତ୍ରୀ, *n.* a sacred stanza of the *Rigveda.*

ଗାୟନ, *n.* singing; a song.

ଗାର, *n.* a line, a mark.

ଗାରଡ଼, *n.* a horned sheep, a ram.

ଗାରିମା, *n.* pride, arrogancy.

* ଗାର୍ହସ୍ଥ୍ୟ, ଗାର୍ହସ୍ଥ, *a.* pertaining to a householder.

ଗାଲଗଳ୍ପ, *n.* useless talk.

ଗାଳି, * ଗାଳୀ, *n.* abusive language, scurrility.

ଗାଳିଖାଇବା, *v.* to be rebuked, to receive abuse.

ଗାଳିଦେବା, *v.* to rebuke, to abuse.

ଗାଲ, *n.* the cheek.

ଗାଲକଢ଼ିବା, *v.* to speak falsely.

ଗାଲ୍ସି, ଗାଲସି, *n.* the gills; lower part of the cheek.

ଗାଲୁଆ, *n.* a boaster, an exaggerator; mumps.

ଗାଲେଲି, *n.* a lying or boastful woman.

ଗିନା, *n.* a small metal cup.

* ଗିର, *n.* (poetical) a word, speech, saying.

ଗିରହ, *n.* a mark; a measure of $\frac{1}{16}$ of a yard.

* ଗିରି, *n.* a mountain, hill, rock.

* ଗିରିଜା, *n.* a name of *Doorgá.*

ଗିରିବାଟ, *n.* a mountain pass.

* ଗିରୀନ୍ଦ୍ର, ଗିରୀଶ, *n.* the Himalaya mountains; *Siva.*

ଗିର୍ଜା, *n.* a church, a place of worship; worship.

ଗିଳା, *n.* a glutton, a voracious eater.

ଗିଳାଇବା, *v.* to cause to eat much or frequently, to cause to swallow.

ଗିଳିବା, *v.* to swallow, to eat.

ଗିଲି, *n.* a small wild fruit like a bean.

ଗିଲ, *n.* pain of mind; —*a.* damp.

ଗୀତ, *n.* a song, a hymn, an ode.

ଗୀତଗୋବିନ୍ଦ, *n.* a Hindu sacred book.

ଗୀତା, *n.* name of a section of the *Mahábhárat.*

ଗୁଁ, *n.* an imitative sound, like the humming bee.

ଗୁଁଆର, *n.* a fool, a stupid fellow.

ଗୁଆଁଖୁରି, *n.* a small edible bean.

ଗୁଆ, *n.* the betel nut.

* ଗୁଆଳୀ, *n.* a milk-woman.

ଗୁଗୁଚିଆ, *n.* spear-grass (love-thorn).

ଗୁଗ୍ଗୁଳ, ଗୁଗ୍ଗୁଲ, ଗୁଗୁଲ, *n.* a perfume; the lignum aloes.

ଗୁଚ୍ଛ, *n.* a cluster of blossoms; a bunch of flowers; a bundle.

ଗୁଜରାଣ, ଗୁଜୁରାଣ, *n.* a living, support; need; —*a.* spent, gone.

ଗୁଜୁରାତ, *n.* small cardamom.

* ଗୁଞ୍ଜନ, ଗୁଞ୍ଜର, *n.* a humming noise.

* ଗୁଞ୍ଜା, *n.* a small red seed used by goldsmiths.

ଗୁଞ୍ଜାଗୁଞ୍ଜି, *n.* the act of forcing or thrusting in quickly.

ଗୁଞ୍ଜିବା, *v.* to thrust in; to secrete.

ଗୁଡ଼, *n.* raw sugar, treacle, molasses.

ଗୁଡ଼ତ୍ୱକ, *n.* cassia bark, cinnamon.

ଗୁଡ଼ା, ଗୁଡ଼ାଏ, ଗୁଡ଼ାକ, (in *Gram.*) are plural endings (these words are used only in an inferior way or attached to such words as ଲୋକ *i.e.*, ଲୋକଗୁଡ଼ାକ, etc.).

ଗୁଡ଼ାଇବା, *v.* to roll up, to furl, to pack up.

ଗୁଡ଼ାଖୁ, *n.* tobacco mixed with molasses.

ଗୁଡ଼ି, *n.* a paper kite.

ଗୁଡ଼ି, ଗୁଡ଼ିଏ, ଗୁଡ଼ିକ, (in *Gram.*) are plural endings (these indicate respect or affection).

ଗୁଡ଼ିଆ, *n.* a sugar-boiler; a confectioner; *fem.* ଗୁଡ଼ିଆଣୀ ।

ଗୁଡ଼ୁଚି, ଗୁଳୁଚି, *n.* a kind of medicinal creeper.

ଗୁଣ, *n.* a quality, attribute, virtue; sense, gumption; fold (as two-fold, etc.); merit; a bow-string.

ଗୁଣକ, *n.* a multiplier.

ଗୁଣକାରକ, ଗୁଣକାରୀ, *a.* effectual; beneficial, profitable, advantageous. [gyric.

ଗୁଣଗାନ, *ଗୁଣକଥନ, *n.* eulogy, pane-

ଗୁଣଗ୍ରାହକ, ଗୁଣଗ୍ରାହୀ, *a.* appreciative of merit.

ଗୁଣଜ୍ଞ, *a.* able to discern or discriminate qualities.

ଗୁଣନ, *n.* (in *Arith.*) multiplication.

ଗୁଣନୀୟକ, *n.* (in *Arith.*) measure.

ଗୁଣନଫଳ, ଗୁଣଫଳ, *n.* (in *Arith.*) product. [ingenious.

ଗୁଣବନ୍ତ, *a.* talented, distinguished,

ଗୁଣବାଚକ, *a.* expressive of a quality or attribute.

ଗୁଣବାଦୀ, *a.* eulogising, grateful.

ଗୁଣବାନ୍, *a.* talented, distinguished.

ଗୁଣହୀନ, *a.* ignorant, stupid, destitute of knowledge.

ଗୁଣା, *n.* an ornament for the nose; fold, (as two-fold, three-fold, etc.). [ence.

*ଗୁଣାକର, *a.* possessing all excell-

ଗୁଣାଗୁଣ, *n.* virtues and defects.

*ଗୁଣାନ୍ୱିତ, *a.* endowed with virtues (see ଗୁଣବନ୍ତ). [sorcerer.

ଗୁଣିଆ, *n.* a snake-charmer, a

ଗୁଣିତକ, *n.* (in *Arith.*) multiple.

ଗୁଣିବା, *v.* to multiply.

ଗୁଣୀ, *a.* virtuous, accomplished; —*n.* a magician, a snake-charmer.

ଗୁଣ୍ଠ, *n.* a land-measure, $\frac{1}{25}$ of a *mán.*

ଗୁଣ୍ଡ, *n.* powder, dust.

ଗୁଣ୍ଡା, *n.* dust, particles; a morsel of boiled rice.

ଗୁଣ୍ଡି, *n.* particles, dust; tobacco powder mixed with coriander seed, etc.

ଗୁଣ୍ଡିଚା, *n.* the car-festival.

ଗୁଣ୍ଡିମୁଷା, *n.* the grey squirrel.

ଗୁଣ୍ୟ, *n.* (in *Arith.*) multiplicand.

*ଗୁଦାମ, ଗୋଦାମ, *n.* a dock-yard.

ଗୁନ୍ଥା, *a.* strung together.

ଗୁନ୍ଥାଇବା, *v.* to cause to be strung together.

ଗୁନ୍ଥାଗୁନ୍ଥି, *n.* the act of stringing together (as flowers, beads, etc.).

ଗୁନ୍ଥିବା, *v.* to string together.

ଗୁପଚୁପ୍, *ad.* silently, secretly.

ଗୁପ୍ତ, *a.* hidden, secret, concealed, private.

ଗୁପ୍ତଚର, *n.* a spy, a secret messenger.

ଗୁପ୍ତବେଶ, *n.* disguise.

ଗୁପ୍ତପ୍ରେମ, *n.* secrecy; concealed or secret love. [secretly.

ଗୁପ୍ତଭାବରେ, ଗୁପ୍ତରେ, *ad.* privately,

ଗୁପ୍ତି, *n.* a sword-stick.

*ଗୁବାକ, *n.* the betel or areca nut.

ଗୁମ୍, *a.* speechless (through anxiety); concealed, hidden.

ଗୁମର, *n.* haughtiness; a secret, secrecy.

ଗୁମାନ, *n.* arrogance, sulkiness.

ଗୁମାସା, *a.* sulky or sullen.
ଗୁମାସ୍ତା, *n.* an agent, a factor.
ଗୁମ୍ଫା, *n.* a den, cave, cavern.
ଗୁମ୍ବଜ, *n.* a tower, a dome, a vault.
ଗୁରୁ, *n.* a spiritual guide, a teacher; —*a.* heavy; grave.
ଗୁରୁଜନ, *n.* elders, guardians.
ଗୁରୁତର, *a.* important; heavier; higher (in station of life).
ଗୁରୁଦକ୍ଷିଣା, *n.* a fee to a *guru.*
ଗୁରୁଦେବ, *n.* a spiritual guide; a parent. [and feet.
ଗୁରୁଣ୍ଡିବା, *v.* to crawl on the hands
ଗୁରୁପାକ, *a.* solid (food), indigestible. [offence.
ଗୁରୁପାପ, *n.* a great crime, heinous
ଗୁରୁବାର, *n.* Thursday. [round.
ଗୁଳା, *n.* a ball, anything small and
ଗୁଳି, *n.* a pellet, a ball, a pill.
ଗୁଳଘଟି, *n.* a place where opium pills are prepared.
ଗୁଳିଖିଆ, ଗୁଳିଖୋର, *n.* one addicted to eating opium pills.
ଗୁଳିବାଣ୍ଟ, *n.* a casting of lots, a lottery.
* ଗୁଲ୍ଫ, *n.* the ankle, the heel.
ଗୁଳ୍ମ, *n.* a bushy shrub; induration of the mesenteric glands, enlargement of the spleen.
ଗୁହା, *n.* a cave, cavern, dell, defile.
ଗୁହାରି, ଗୁହାରୁ, *n.* a petition, plaint,
ଗୁହାରିଆ, *n.* a petitioner. [suit.
ଗୁହାଳ, *n.* a cow-shed, a cow-pen.

* ଗୁହ୍ୟ, *a.* concealable, secret;—*n.* the anus.
ଗୂଢ, *a.* hidden, concealed, abstruse.
ଗୂଢତା, *n.* secrecy, abstruseness.
* ଗୂଢପୁରୁଷ, *n.* a scout, a spy.
* ଗୃଧ୍ନୁ, *a.* covetous, greedy.
* ଗୃଧ୍ର, *n.* a vulture.
ଗୃହ, *n.* a house, habitation. [house.
ଗୃହକର୍ତ୍ତା, *n.* master or builder of a
ଗୃହଛିଦ୍ର, *n.* domestic quarrel, family disgrace, dissension in a family.
ଗୃହଜାତ, * ଗୃହଜ, *a.* house-born, produced in the house.
ଗୃହଦାହ, *n.* burning of a house.
ଗୃହସ୍ଥ, *n.* a householder, house-dweller;—*a.* residing or situated in a house.
ଗୃହସ୍ଥାଶ୍ରମ, *n.* living in a house; a stage in a Brahmin's life.
ଗୃହାଗତ, *n.* a guest, a stranger;—*a.* arrived at home.
* ଗୃହାଧିପ, *n.* master of the house.
ଗୃହାଶ୍ରମ, *n.* residence, house, abode.
ଗୃହିଣୀ, *n.* mistress of a house, a wife.
ଗୃହ୍ୟ, *a.* domestic, worldly.
ଗୃହୀତ, *a.* accepted, taken, received.
ଗେଙ୍ଗୁଟି, *n.* lime stone.
ଘେଞ୍ଚ, *n.* a crowding; a narrow passage, an alley.
ଘେଞ୍ଚାଘେଞ୍ଚି, *n.* a general crowding or pressing.
ଘେଞ୍ଚିବା, *v.* to pierce, to push, to thrust in, (see ଗୁଞ୍ଜିବା).

ଗେଡ଼, ଗେଡ଼ା, *a.* short, fat; squabby; *em.* ଗେଡ଼ୁ.

ଗେଣ୍ଡା, *n.* a snail.

ଗେଣ୍ଡାଳିଆ, *n.* a snail-eater, a grey crane.

ଗେଣ୍ଡୁ, *n.* the marigold ; * a toy.

ଗେମଣା, *a.* stunted.

ଗେରସ୍ତ, *n.* husband, master.

ଗେରୁ, *n.* red ochre, ruddle.

ଗେରୁଆ, *a.* (cloth) coloured in red ochre.

ଗେର୍ଦ, *n.* a circle, a boundary.

ଗେଲ, *n.* a gibe, joke, mirth, pleasantry.

ଗେହ୍ଲା, *a.* favourite, much loved.

ଗେଁ, *n.* pain from severe flogging; an old pain, (see ଗଣ୍ଠି).

ଗୈଣ୍ଠା, *n.* a kind of unsweetened rice-cake or pasty, (see ଗଣ୍ଠା).

ଗୈଣ୍ଠାଳ, *n.* the act of tying the wedding garments of the bride and bridegroom together on the dais (see ଗଣ୍ଠାଳ).

* ଗୈରିକ, *n.* ruddle, red ochre ;—*a.* (cloth) coloured in red ochre.

ଗୋ, *n.* a feminine vocative; * a cow, an ox, etc.

ଗୋଆର, *n.* a cow-dealer.

ଗୋଇଠା, *n.* a kick.

ଗୋଇଠି, *n.* heel.

ଗୋଇନ୍ଦା, ଗୋଏନ୍ଦା, *n.* a spy, an informer.

ଗୋକ୍ଷେତ, *a.* short of pasture land.

* ଗୋକୁଳ, *n.* a herd of cows.

ଗୋଖର, *n.* a species of cobra.

ଗୋଖରୁ, *n.* a medicinal plant.

ଗୋଖା, *n.* a class of fishermen.

ଗୋଘୃତ, *n.* clarified butter, *ghee* (of cow's milk).

ଗୋଚର, *a.* known, perceptible ;—*n.* pasture land.

ଗୋଛ, *n.* a bunch, a sheaf.

ଗୋଜ, *n.* a peg, pin, stake.

ଗୋଜଣା, *n.* a poker.

ଗୋଜିଆ, *a.* (anything) pointed.

ଗୋଟମା, *n.* a small undeveloped cocoanut.

ଗୋଟା, *a.* one ; whole, entire, unbroken.

ଗୋଟାଇବା, *v.* to pick up, to collect.

ଗୋଟାଏ, *n.* one, a single one, one only.

ଗୋଟାକେତେ, *a.* few, a few.

ଗୋଟାଳି, *n.* a small round piece of chalk.

ଗୋଟି, ଗୁଟି, *n.* a small ball ; a small earthen vessel; a cocoon.

ଗୋଟିଗୋଟି, *ad.* one by one, separately.

ଗୋଟିପୋକ, *n.* a silk-worm.

ଗୋଠ, *n.* a herd, flock, drove; an ornament for the waist.

ଗୋଡ, *n.* the foot; pedestal, base of anything.

ଗୋଡଭଣ୍ଡା, *n.* the calf of the leg.

ଗୋଡାଇବା, *v.* to pursue, to chase.

ଗୋଡି, *n.* gravel, broken bits of pots.

ଗୋଡିଖିଲ, *n.* an iron spike pointed at both ends for joining planks.

ଗୋଗେଗୋଗେ, *ad.* hastily, on the run.

ଗୋତମ, ଗୌତମ, *n.* name of Buddha.

ଗୋତ୍ର, *n.* founder of a family; lineage, race, pedigree.

ଗୋତ୍ରଜ, *a.* lineally descended.

* ଗୋଦ, *n.* elephantiasis.

ଗୋଦଡ଼ି, ଗୁଦଡ଼ି, *n.* a quilt or covering made of rags.

ଗୋଦର, *n.* elephantiasis.

ଗୋଦରା, *n.* one afflicted with elephantiasis. [of arsenic.

ଗୋଦନ୍ତ, *n.* a cow's tooth; sulphate

ଗୋଦାନ, *n.* a gift of cows.

ଗୋଦାମ, ଗୁଦାମ, *n.* godown, a storehouse, a warehouse.

ଗୋଦୋହନ, *n.* the milking of cows.

ଗୋଧନ, *n.* cows regarded as wealth.

* ଗୋଧା, *n.* fence for an archer's arm; the guana.

ଗୋଧି, *n.* the guana;—*a.* lazy.

* ଗୋଧୂମ, *n.* wheat.

ଗୋଧୂଳି, *n.* evening, twilight.

ଗୋନ୍ଦ, *n.* gum, gum-arabic.

* ଗୋପ, *n.* a cowkeeper, milkman.

ଗୋପ, *n.* a kind of gold necklace.

ଗୋପନ, *n.* secrecy, concealment.

ଗୋପନୀୟ, *a.* concealable, secret.

* ଗୋପାଙ୍ଗନା, *n.* a dairy-woman.

ଗୋପାଳ, *n.* a dairy-man; *Krushna.*

* ଗୋପୀ, ଗୋପିକା, *n.* a dairy-woman.

ଗୋପୀମାଟୀ, *n.* a yellowish earth, yellow ochre.

ଗୋବର, *n.* cow-dung, manure.

* ଗୋବାଘ, *n.* a hyena.

ଗୋବିନ୍ଦ, *n.* a name of *Krushna.*

* ଗୋମୟ, *n.* cow-dung.

* ଗୋମାୟୁ, *n.* a jackal.

ଗୋମାଂସ, *n.* cow's flesh, beef.

ଗୋମୁଖୀ, *n.* a bag in which to count the rosary; source of the Ganges.

ଗୋମୂତ୍ର, *n.* cow's urine.

ଗୋମେଧ, *n.* sacrifice of a cow.

ଗୋହଳା, *n.* a pen for cattle. [etc.

ଗୋରସ, *n.* milk, whey, butter-milk,

ଗୋରା, *a.* white, fair;—*n.* a European.

ଗୋରୀ, *n.* a fair woman.

ଗୋରୁ, *n.* a cow, an ox.

ଗୋରୋଚନା, ଗୋଚିନା, *n.* a yellow pigment produced from cows or oxen.

ଗୋଳ, ଗୋଳମାଳ, *n.* a noise, a disturbance, a row, a quarrel.

ଗୋଳା, *n.* a ball, a cannon ball;—*a.* muddy; mixed.

ଗୋଳାଇବା, *v.* to mix ingredients together, to stir up.

ଗୋଳିଆ, ଗୁଳିଆ, *a.* muddy; mixed; thick (as liquids).

ଗୋଲ୍, *n.* a noise, clamour.

ଗୋଲ, *a.* round.

ଗୋଲଆଳୁ, *n.* a potato.

ଗୋଲକ, *n.* a globe; a ball; *a widow's bastard.

ଗୋଲମରିଚ, *n.* black pepper.

ଗୋଲା, *n.* a place where wood, etc., is sold; a bullet.

ଗୋଲାପ, ଗୋଲାବ, *n.* a rose, a rose-tree.

ଗୋଲାମ୍, ଗୁଲାମ୍, *n.* a slave, a servant.

ଗୋଲି, *n.* a ball, cannon ball, bullet.

ଗୋଲୋକ, *n.* *Krushna's* paradise.

ଗୋଶାଳା, *n.* a cow-house.

* ଗୋଷ୍ଠ, *n.* a cow-pen; a flock, a herd.

ଗୋଷ୍ଠୀ, *n.* lineage, family; pedigree.

* ଗୋଷ୍ପଦ, *n.* a cow's footmarks.

ଗୌଡ଼, *n.* a cowkeeper, a palanquin bearer (see ଗଉଡ଼).

* ଗୌଣ, *a.* inferior, subordinate, indirect.

ଗୌଣୀ, *n.* a corn measure (see ଗଉଣୀ).

ଗୌର, *a.* of fair complexion, pale yellow.

ଗୌରଚନ୍ଦ୍ର, *n.* a name of *Chaitanya.*

ଗୌରବ, *n.* honour, glory, greatness.

ଗୌରାଙ୍ଗ, *a.* white-bodied, fair, white;—*n.* a name of *Chaitanya.*

* ଗ୍ରଥିତ, *a.* arranged; strung together, built.

ଗ୍ରନ୍ଥ, *n.* a book, volume; writing.

ଗ୍ରନ୍ଥକାର, *n.* a writer, an author.

* ଗ୍ରନ୍ଥି, *n.* a knot, joint, knuckle.

ଗ୍ରସ୍ତ, ଗ୍ରସିତ, *a.* seized, involved in; swallowed.

ଗ୍ରହ, *n.* a planet.

ଗ୍ରହଣ, *n.* acceptance; an eclipse.

ଗ୍ରହଣକରିବା, *v.* to accept, to receive.

ଗ୍ରହଣୀ, *n.* dysentery, diarrhœa, flux.

ଗ୍ରହଣୀୟ, *a.* acceptable.

* ଗ୍ରହପତି, ଗ୍ରହରାଜ, *n.* the sun.

ଗ୍ରହପୀଡ଼ା, *n.* evil influence of a planet.

* ଗ୍ରହୀତା, *n.* recipient, receiver.

ଗ୍ରାମ, *n.* a village, a hamlet.

ଗ୍ରାମଦେବୀ, *n.* a village idol of a goddess.

ଗ୍ରାମଯାଜକ, *n.* a village priest.

ଗ୍ରାମସ୍ଥ, *a.* situated or residing in a village.

ଗ୍ରାମାନ୍ତ, *n.* end or outskirt of a village.

ଗ୍ରାମାନ୍ତର, *n.* the other village.

ଗ୍ରାମ୍ୟ, *a.* domesticated, rustic.

ଗ୍ରାସ, *n.* eating, a swallowing; food, a full meal.

ଗ୍ରାସାଚ୍ଛାଦନ, *n.* food and raiment.

ଗ୍ରାସୀ, *a.* greedy, gluttonous.

ଗ୍ରାହକ, *n.* a purchaser, a taker, a receiver.

ଗ୍ରାହ୍ୟ, *a.* acceptable, worthy of being received.

ଗ୍ରୀଜା, *n.* church, worship (see ଗିର୍ଜା).

* ଗ୍ରୀବା, *n.* the neck.

ଗ୍ରୀଷ୍ମ, *n.* heat, sultry weather.

ଗ୍ରୀଷ୍ମକାଳ, *n.* the hot season, summer.

ଗ୍ରୀଷ୍ମଛୁଟି, *n.* summer vacation.

ଗ୍ରୀଷ୍ମନିବାସ, *n.* summer resort.

ଗ୍ରୀଷ୍ମମଣ୍ଡଳ, *n.* torrid-zone.

ଗ୍ରେପ୍ତାର, *n.* arrest.

ଗ୍ରେପ୍ତାରୀ, *n.* attachment of goods, arrest.

ଗ୍ଲାନି, *n.* languor lassitude; a slander, backbiting.

ଘ.

ଘ, the fourth consonant.
ଘଇତା, *n.* (a vulgar word) a husband, lord, master.
ଘଉଡାଇବା, ଘଉଡାଇଦେବା, *v.* to drive out, to turn out.
* ଘଟ, *n.* a pitcher, waterpot; the body.
ଘଟକ, *n.* a negotiator of marriages.
ଘଟନ, *n.* a happening, an occurring.
ଘଟନା, ଘଟଣା, *n.* an occurrence, an event, an accident.
* ଘଟନୀୟ, *a.* liable to happen, probable.
ଘଟା, *n.* pomp, parade, a crowd;—*a.* dirty.
ଘଟାଇବା, *v.* to occasion, to cause.
ଘଟାଟୋପ, *n.* an awning.
* ଘଟିକା, *n.* an hour of 45 minutes according to Indian calculation.
* ଘଟିତ, *a.* happened, occurred.
ଘଟିବା, *v.* to happen, to occur.
ଘଡଘଡ, *n.* sound of carriages and clouds; rattling in the throat.
ଘଡଘଡି, *n.* rumbling sound of thunder.
ଘଡିଆଲ, *n.* an alligator.
ଘଡି, *n.* a watch, a clock; an hour; a small earthen pitcher.
ଘଣା, *n.* a country oil-mill.
ଘଣ୍ଟ, ଘଣ୍ଟା, *n.* a bell, a gong.
ଘଣ୍ଟା, *n.* a bell, a gong; a clock; an hour.
ଘଣ୍ଟାଘଣ୍ଟି, ଘଣ୍ଟାଉକଟା, *n.* a keen search.
ଘଣ୍ଟିକା, *n.* the epiglottis, uvula.
ଘଣ୍ଟୀ, *n.* a small bell.
ଘଡ, ଘଡପାଡ, *n.* device, skill, cleverness.
ଘଗା, *a.* skilful, clever.
ଘନ, *a.* thick, dense; cubic, solid;—*n.* * a cloud.
* ଘନକାଳ, *n.* rainy season, cloudy weather.
ଘନଘଟା, ଘନଘଟ୍ଟା, *n.* splendour of the clouds.
ଘନଘନ, *ad.* incessantly, rapidly.
* ଘନଘୋଷ, *n.* roaring of the clouds, thunder.
ଘନଫଳ, *n.* (in *Geom.*) the contents of a solid.
ଘନମୂଳ, *n.* the cube root.
ଘନକ୍ଷେତ୍ର, *n.* (in *Geom.*) a cube.
ଘନିଷ୍ଠ, *a.* close, very near.
ଘନୀଭୂତ, *a.* inspissated, become thick.
ଘମ, *n.* an earthen jar for storing grain.
ଘମାଘୋଟ, *n.* great display, great rejoicings.
ଘମିର, *n.* the prickly heat.
ଘର, *n.* a house, a dwelling.
ଘରକରଣା, *n.* household business.
ଘରଚଟିଆ, *n.* a sparrow.
ଘରଛୁଆ, *n.* thatching a house.
ଘରଣାଘର, *n.* an old and prosperous family.
ଘରଣୀ, *n.* a wife, a housewife.
ଘରତଲାସ୍ *n.* enquiry or search in a house on suspicion.

ଘରଖଣାଳି, *n.* enquiry or search in a house on suspicion, officiousness, prying into family affairs.

ଘର, *n.* a receptacle, a drawer, a passage.

ଘରୁଆ, ଘରେଇ, ଘରେଲି, *a.* domestic; home-made.

ଘର୍ଘର, *n.* the rattling of wheels.

* ଘର୍ମ, *n.* perspiration, sweat.

* ଘର୍ମଜନକ, *a.* sudorific, causing perspiration.

ଘର୍ଷଣ, *n.* rubbing, grinding, friction.

ଘଷର, ଘଷିଆ, *a.* (coins, etc.) worn smooth.

ଘଷା, *a.* rubbed, filed, polished.

ଘଷି, *n.* dried cow-dung.

ଘଷିଆ, *a.* too familiar; worn smooth.

ଘଷିବା, *v.* to rub; to massage.

ଘା, *n.* cut, gash, sore.

ଘାଇ, *n.* a small river or rivulet.

ଘାଇଲା, ଘାଉଆ, ଘାଉଲା, *a.* injured, wounded, bruised.

ଘାଉଡ, *n.* the bite of a snake or other venomous creature.

ଘାଘର, *n.* a kind of petticoat, an apron.

ଘାଗୁଡ଼ି, *n.* a small bell.

ଘାଟ, *n.* a quay, wharf, landing-place, a ferry.

ଘାଟି, *n.* a mountain pass.

ଘାଟିଆ, *n.* a collector of ferry dues; a ferryman.

ଘାଣ୍ଟ, ଘାଣ୍ଟିଆ, *n.* a mixed vegetable curry;—*a.* mixed (curry).

ଘାଣ୍ଟିବା, *v.* to stir up, to churn.

* ଘାତ, *n.* a knock, a blow; wound.

ଘାତସହ, *a.* malleable.

ଘାତକ, ଘାତୁକ, *n.* a murderer; a striker;—*a.* destructive, murderous, cruel.

ଘାବର *a.* confused.

ଘାରିବା, *v.* to render senseless.

ଘାଲୁପଡିବା, ଘାଲେଇବା, ଘାଲେଇ ହୋଇବା, *v.* to feign sleep.

ଘାସ, *n.* grass.

ଘାସକଟା, ଘାସିଆ, ଘାସୀ, *n.* a grass-cutter or dealer.

ଘିଅ, *n.* clarified butter, *ghee*.

ଘିକୁଆଁରି, *n.* a medicinal shrub.

ଘିନିବା, *v.* to wear; to take, to accept.

ଘିନ୍, ଘିନ୍‌ଘିନ୍, *n.* disgust, an expression of disgust.

ଘିମିରି, ଘିମିରି, *n.* the prickly heat (see ଘମିରି).

ଘୁଘୁ, *n.* a dove, a wood-pigeon.

ଘୁଙ୍ଗା, *a.* dumb.

ଘୁଙ୍ଗୁଡ଼ି, *n.* a snare.

ଘୁଙ୍ଗୁରୁ, *n.* small bells, a string of small bells.

ଘୁଞ୍ଚାଇବା, *v.* to remove.

ଘୁଞ୍ଚାଘୁଞ୍ଚି, *n.* moving hither and thither.

ଘୁଞ୍ଚିବା, *v.* to move.

ଘୁଡ଼ି, *n.* a paper kite (see ଗୁଡ଼ି).

ଘୁଣ, *n.* an insect that destroys wood, bamboo, etc., the book-worm. weevil

* ଘୁଣାକ୍ଷର, *n.* the shape of a letter accidentally formed by the boring of an insect, hence—anything done unintentionally.

ଘୁଣ୍ଟି, *n.* a cloth button.

ଘୁମ, *n.* sleep, drowsiness; a large earthen jar for storing grain (see ଘମ).

ଘୁମାଇବା, *v.* to doze, to be drowsy, to nod in sleep.

ଘୁମୁରିବା, *v.* to coo (as a pigeon or dove).

ଘୁମୁଟା, *n.* a veil, the cloth brought over the face.

ଘୁରାଇବା, *v.* to swing round, to cause to revolve.

ଘୁରିବା, *v.* to turn round, to revolve.

ଘୁରୁଘୁରୁ, *n.* the mole-cricket.

ଘୁଷା, *n.* a blow with the fist.

ଘୁଷୁରି, ଘୁଷୁଡ଼ି, *n.* a pig.

ଘୁଷୁରିଆ, *n.* a swineherd.

ଘୁଷୁରିବା, *v.* to roll about (in dust or mud).

ଘୁଷ, *n.* a bribe.

ଘୁଷଖୋର, *n.* one who takes bribes.

ଘୂରଣ, *n.* a revolving, a turning round, a whirling.

ଘୂର୍ଣ୍ଣନ, * ଘୂର୍ଣ୍ଣି, *n.* moving in circles.

* ଘୂର୍ଣ୍ଣାୟମାନ, *a.* turning, revolving, whirling.

* ଘୂର୍ଣ୍ଣିତ, *a.* whirling about.

ଘୂର୍ଣ୍ଣିବାୟୁ, *n.* a whirlwind.

ଘୃଣା, *n.* hate, contempt, disgust, dislike, abhorrence.

ଘୃଣାସ୍ପଦ, * ଘୃଣାର୍ହ, *a.* hateful, disgusting, detestable.

ଘୃଣିତ, *a.* abhorred, hated.

ଘୃଣ୍ୟ, *a.* abominable; disgusting.

* ଘୃତ, *n.* clarified butter, *ghee* (see ଘିଅ).

* ଘୃତକୁମାରୀ, *n.* a medicinal shrub, aloe perfoliata (see ଘିକୁଆଁରି).

ଘେନା, *a.* accepted.

ଘେନାଇଦେବା, *v.* to cause to wear or put on.

ଘେନାଇବା, *v.* to persuade.

ଘେନା କରିବା, *v.* to accept.

ଘେନିବା, *v.* to wear, to put on; to take; to accept.

ଘେନି ଯିବା, *v.* to take away.

ଘେର, ଘେରା, *n.* circumference, boundary enclosure.

ଘେରାଇବା, *v.* to enclose, to fence around.

ଘେରିବା, *v.* to surround, to encompass, to enclose.

ଘୋଷା, *n.* a loud noise, a crying out.

* ଘୋଟକ, *n.* a horse.

* ଘୋଟକୀ, *n.* a mare.

ଘୋଟିବା, *v.* to stir up; to spread, to overspread.

ଘୋଡଣା, *n.* a covering, a veil.

ଘୋଡଣୀ, *n.* a cover; a lid.

ଘୋଡସୱାର, *n.* a rider, a horse-breaker.

ଘୋଡା, *n.* a horse.

ଘୋଡାଇବା, *v.* to cover up, to hide, to secrete.

ଘୋଡାଘୋଡି, *n.* hastily covering up.

ଘୋଡାଶାଳ, *n.* a stable.
ଘୋଡି, *n.* a mare.
ଘୋମଟା, *n.* a veil for the face.
ଘୋର, *a.* dreadful, terrific, gloomy.
ଘୋରରୂପ, * ଘୋରଦର୍ଶନ, *a.* terrific, of horrible or frightful appearance.
ଘୋରଘୋର, *n.* a scraping, a rubbing.
ଘୋରାଇବା, *v.* to cause to stir up or rub up; to cause to wear away by rubbing.
ଘୋରିବା, *v.* to agitate, to stir up, to rub up; to wear away by rubbing.
ଘୋରିହେବା, *v.* to be worn away by rubbing.
ଘୋଳ, *a.* overripe.
ଘୋଳଦହି, *n.* buttermilk.
ଘୋଳାବଙ୍କା, *n.* aching of the limbs.
ଘୋଳିବା, *v.* to ripen overmuch.
ଘୋଳି ହେବା, *v.* to ache.
*ଘୋଷ, *n.* a sound.
ଘୋଷଡା, ଘୋଷର, *a.* lazy, slothful; —*n.* a dragging on the ground, a trailing; a sloping road or incline.
ଘୋଷଣା, *n.* a proclamation; proclaiming, preaching; a sermon.
ଘୋଷଣାପତ୍ର, *n.* a written proclamation or declaration.
ଘୋଷା, *n.* chorus of a stanza; anger, rage, passion;—*a.* angry; learned by heart.
ଘୋଷାଇବା, *v.* to cause to repeat or learn by heart.
ଘୋଷାଘୋଷି, *n.* a repeating.
ଘୋଷାଡିବା, ଘୋଷାରିବା, *v.* to drag on the ground, to trail.
ଘ୍ନ, *a.* (used as a *suffix*) destructive, ruinous.
*ଘୋଷିତ, *a.* proclaimed, declared, preached.
ଘୋଷିବା, *v.* to repeat, to learn by heart.
*ଘ୍ରାଣ, *n.* the act of smelling; the nose.
ଘ୍ରାଣେନ୍ଦ୍ରିୟ, *n.* the sense of smell, the nose.

ଙ.

ଙ, the fifth consonant, never used except when compounded.

ଚ.

ଚ, the sixth consonant.
ଚଁଉର, *n.* the beard of Indian corn; a fly-brush, the yak's tail used as a fan in temples, etc.
ଚଣ୍ଡୁଲ, *n.* bunches of string made of hair for binding up the hair of women.
ଚହାଁଚହିଁ, *n.* a mutual staring, looking at each other.
ଚଇତ, ଚୈତ୍ର, *n.* the month *Choitra.*
ଚଇନ, *n.* ease, relief, tranquility.
ଚଉକ, *n.* a market-place or square.

ଚଉକା, *n.* a fire-place.

ଚଉକି, *n.* a chair; watching; a policeman's beat.

ଚଉଠ, ଚଉଥ, *a.* and *n.* one-fourth, a quarter, ¼. [form.

ଚଉତରା, *n.* a raised out-door plat-

ଚଉଦ, *a.* and *n.* fourteen; 14, XIV.

ଚଉଦିଗ, *n.* four quarters, four sides, all round.

ଚଉପିଠିଆ, *a.* having four sides; of wide and varied knowledge, of all-round experience. [LIV.

ଚଉବନ, *a.* and *n.* fifty-four; 54,

ଚଉବିଶ, ଚବିଶ, *a.* and *n.* twenty-four; 24, XXIV.

ଚଉରସ, *a.* level, smooth. [plant.

ଚଉରା, *n.* a platform for a *tulsi*

ଚଉରାଅଶୀ, ଚଉରାଶୀ, *a.* and *n.* eighty-four, 84, LXXXIV. [XLIV.

ଚଉରାଳିଶ, *a.* and *n.* forty-four; 44,

ଚଉଷଠି, *a.* and *n.* sixty-four; 64, LXIV.

ଚଉପର, ଚଉପାର, *n.* dice. [LXXIV.

ଚଉସ୍ତରି, *a.* and *n.* seventy-four; 74,

ଚଉହଦୀ, *n.* a boundary.

ଚକ, *n.* wheel of a cart, a potter's wheel; a division of land.

ଚକଟା, ଚକ୍ଟା, *n.* a kneading, a crushing;—*a.* kneaded.

ଚକଟାଚକଟି, ଚକ୍ଟାଚକ୍ଟି, *n.* a trampling or mixing, a kneading.

ଚକଟିବା, *v.* to knead, to crush; to trample down.

ଚକବନ୍ଦି, ଚକବନ୍ଦୀ, *n.* specification of land.

ଚକଲା, ଚକଳା, *n.* a part of a district or province or locality; a jurisdiction; a compound.

ଚକା, *a.* circular, round;—*n.* turf.

ଚକାଗୁଉଣା, *n.* laying of turf, turfing.

ଚକାମାଉଳି, *n.* sitting with the legs as in a knot; twirling round on the feet. [stone.

ଚକି, *n.* a millstone, a grinding-

ଚକିତ, *a.* wonder-struck, surprised, alarmed.

ଚକୁଆ, *n.* a large wild duck having reddish-brown feathers (*fem.* ଚକୁଇ).

ଚକୁଳି, *n.* a kind of cake.

ଚକୁଳିଆପଣ୍ଡା, *n.* a low-class brahman who begs only in the month of *Kartik.* [sparkling.

ଚକ୍ଚକ୍, ଚକ୍ମକ୍, *a.* glittering, bright,

ଚକ୍ମକପଥର, *n.* a flint.

ଚକ୍ମକି, *n.* flint and steel for striking fire. [racing.

ଚକ୍କର, *a.* a circular course for

ଚକ୍ତି, *n.* a leather or iron washer, anything flat and round.

ଚକ୍ର, *n.* a wheel, discus, circle; revolution.

*ଚକ୍ରପାଣି, *n.* *Vishnu.*

ଚକ୍ରବର୍ତ୍ତୀ, *n.* an emperor; a king.

ଚକ୍ରବାକ, *n.* (see ଚକୁଆ).

* ଚକ୍ରବାଢ଼, ଚକ୍ରବାଳ, *n.* horizon, a mythical range of mountains supposed to encircle the orb of the earth like a wall and to be the limit of light and darkness.

ଚକ୍ରବୃଦ୍ଧି, *n.* compound interest.

ଚକ୍ରାକାର, *a.* circular, round.

ଚକ୍ରାନ୍ତ, *n.* a conspiracy, a plot.

ଚକ୍ରାନ୍ତକାରୀ, *n.* a conspirator.

ଚଖା, *n.* a tasting; a taster.

ଚଖାଇବା, *v.* to cause to taste.

ଚଖାଚଖି, *n.* a tasting, a smacking of the lips in tasting.

ଚଗଲ, *a.* unsettled, erratic, vagrant.

ଚଗଚଗିଆ, *a.* sly or slippery (character), shifting, uneasy.

ଚଗ୍ର, *n.* a father's younger brother.

ଚଞ୍ଚଳ, *a.* quick in movement, fickle, capricious, unsteady.

* ଚଞ୍ଚଳା, *n.* lightning, the fickle goddess of fortune—*Lakshmee.*

* ଚଞ୍ଚୁ, *n.* the bill of a bird, a beak.

ଚଟ, *n.* a mat; sackcloth, canvass.

ଚଟକ, *n.* addiction to a habit; a sparrow; jugglery, a show.

ଚଟକଣା, *n.* a slap, a box on the ear.

ଚଟକା, *a.* flat;—*n.* * a hen-sparrow.

ଚଟଣୀ, ଚଟ୍‌ଣି, ଚଟ୍‌ଣୀ, *n.* *chutnee*, a pungent sauce.

ଚଟ୍‌, ଚଟ୍‌ପଟ୍‌, *ad.* quickly, speedily.

ଚଟ୍‌ଚଟିଆ, *a.* sticky, glutinous.

ଚଟ୍‌ପଟିଆ, *a.* active, quick.

ଚଟାଇ, ଚଟେଇ, *n.* a mat.

ଚଟାଇବା, *v.* to cause to lick up with the tongue.

ଚଟାଚଟି, *n.* a tasting, a licking; mutual licking;—*a.* mutually angry.

ଚଟାଣ, *n.* a *pucca* floor; a shore.

ଚଟି, ଚଟୀ, *n.* a resting place, end of a stage, bazaar-house; slipper.

ଚଟିଉଠିବା, ଚଟିବା, *v.* to become angry.

ଚଟୁ, *n.* a ladle, a stick to stir up boiling rice.

ଚଡ଼କ, *n.* a thunder-bolt.

ଚଡ଼ଚଡ଼, *n.* a cracking sound.

ଚଡ଼କିବା, *v.* to split, to crack.

ଚଡ଼ା, *n.* an island, a shallow, a shoal.

ଚଡ଼ାଇ, ଚଡ଼େଇ, ଚଢ଼େଇ, *n.* a bird.

ଚଡୁ, ଚଲୁ, *n.* cauterization; burning.

ଚଡୁକାଠି, ଚଲୁକାଠି, *n.* a searing-iron.

ଚଡୁଦେବା, ଚଲୁଦେବା, *v.* to cauterize; to burn.

ଚଢ଼, *n.* an increase.

ଚଢ଼ାଉ, *n.* an attack, aggression, onset.

ଚଢ଼ିବା, *v.* to ascend, mount, climb.

ଚଣା, * ଚଣକ, *n.* gram, a sort of pulse or pea.

ଚଣ୍ଡ, *a.* furious, violent, enraged.

ଚଣ୍ଡାଳ, ଷଣ୍ଡାଳ, *n.* the lowest caste;—*a.* wicked, vile, cruel (*fem.* ଚଣ୍ଡାଳୁଣୀ).

ଚଣ୍ଡୀ, * ଚଣ୍ଡିକା, *n.* *Durgá*; a furious woman.

ଚତୁର, *a.* clever, artful, crafty, cunning, dexterous.

*ଚତୁରଙ୍ଗ, *a.* (an army) composed of four parts, complete.

*ଚତୁରଙ୍ଗୁଳ, *n.* four fingers wide.

ଚତୁରତା, *n.* dexterity, artfulness.

ଚତୁରସ୍ର, *a.* (in *Geom.*) quadrangular; square.

ଚତୁରାଳି, *n.* craftiness, dexterity, acuteness.

*ଚତୁରାନନ, *a.* four-faced;—*n.* *Brahmá.*

ଚତୁରୀ, *n.* an active or clever woman.

ଚତୁର୍ଗୁଣ, *a.* four-fold; quadruple.

ଚତୁର୍ଥ, *a.* fourth, 4th.

ଚତୁର୍ଥାଂଶ, *n.* the fourth part, a quarter (see ଚଉଥ).

ଚତୁର୍ଥୀ, *n.* the fourth day of a fortnight.

*ଚତୁର୍ଦ୍ଦଶ, *a.* and *n.* fourteenth, fourteen.

ଚତୁର୍ଦ୍ଦଶୀ, *n.* the fourteenth day of a fortnight.

ଚତୁର୍ଦ୍ଦିଗ, *ad.* on all (four) sides;—*n.* the four quarters.

*ଚତୁର୍ଦ୍ଦୋଳ, *n.* a litter, *duli.*

*ଚତୁର୍ଦ୍ଧା, *a.* four-fold; of four sorts.

ଚତୁର୍ବର୍ଗ, *n.* the four objects of human pursuit, *viz.*, love, riches, religion, beatitude.

ଚତୁର୍ବର୍ଣ୍ଣ, *n.* the four castes of the Hindus; *four chief colours.

ଚତୁର୍ବିଧ, *a.* of four sorts.

ଚତୁର୍ବେଦ, *n.* the four *Vedas.*

ଚତୁର୍ଭୁଜ, *a.* four-armed;—*n.* *Vishnu.*

ଚତୁର୍ମାସ୍ୟା, *n.* the four rainy months, the rainy season.

*ଚତୁର୍ମୁଖ, *a.* four-faced;—*n.* *Brahmá.*

*ଚତୁର୍ଯୁଗ, *n.* the four ages or *joogs.*

*ଚତୁର୍ବିଂଶ, *a.* twenty-four.

*ଚତୁଷ୍ଟୟ, *a.* four (collectively).

*ଚତୁଷ୍ପଥ, *n.* four cross roads.

ଚତୁଷ୍ପଦ, *a.* four-footed;—*n.* a quadruped.

*ଚତୁଷ୍ପାଠୀ, *n.* a college, an academy.

*ଚତୁସ୍ତ୍ରିଂଶତ୍, *a.* thirty-four.

*ଚତ୍ୱର, *n.* a courtyard.

*ଚତ୍ୱାରିଂଶତ୍, *a.* forty.

ଚଦବା, ଚଢବା, *v.* to scold, to reprimand.

ଚନ୍ଦନ, *n.* sandal-wood.

ଚନ୍ଦନପେଷା, *n.* a stone on which to pound sandal-wood.

ଚନ୍ଦନବୋଡା, *n.* name of a poisonous speckled snake.

ଚନ୍ଦନଯାତ୍ରା, *n.* the sandal-wood festival.

ଚନ୍ଦନା, *n.* a species of parrot.

ଚନ୍ଦା, ଚନ୍ଧା, *n.* a bald spot on the head;—*a.* bald-headed.

ଚନ୍ଦାମୁଣ୍ଡିଆ, ଚନ୍ଧାମୁଣ୍ଡିଆ, *a.* bald-headed.

ଚନ୍ଦ୍ର, *n.* the moon.

ଚନ୍ଦ୍ରଉଦୟ, *n.* a kind of fireworks.

*ଚନ୍ଦ୍ରକ, *n.* the eye in a peacock's feather.

ଚନ୍ଦ୍ରକାନ୍ତ, *n.* a precious stone, a jasper.

ଚନ୍ଦ୍ରଗ୍ରହଣ, *n.* an eclipse of the moon.

*ଚନ୍ଦ୍ରଚୂଡ, *a.* crescent-crested;—*n.* *Shiva.*

ଚନ୍ଦ୍ରବଦନ, *a.* moon-faced, handsome as the moon;—*n.* a handsome face.

ଚନ୍ଦ୍ରବିନ୍ଦୁ, *n.* the sign ‘ଁ’

ଚନ୍ଦ୍ରମଣି, *n.* a moonstone. [moon.

ଚନ୍ଦ୍ରମଣ୍ଡଳ, *n.* the lunar orb, the

* ଚନ୍ଦ୍ରମଲ୍ଲିକା, *n.* a species of chrysanthemum.

ଚନ୍ଦ୍ରମା, *n.* the moon.

ଚନ୍ଦ୍ରମୁଖୀ, *a.* moon-faced;—*n.* a handsome woman. [*n. Shiva.*

* ଚନ୍ଦ୍ରଶେଖର, *a.* crescent-crested ;—

ଚନ୍ଦ୍ରହାର, *n.* a gold or silver girdle or belt worn by women.

* ଚନ୍ଦ୍ରାତପ, *n.* an awning, a canopy.

* ଚନ୍ଦ୍ରାନନ, *a.* moon-faced.

ଚନ୍ଦ୍ରିକା, *n.* moonlight, moon's rays; the eyes in a peacock's feather.

ଚନ୍ଦ୍ରୋଦୟ, *n.* the rising of the moon.

ଚପଟ, *n.* jeopardy, risk, a pressure of trouble.

ଚପରଚପର, *a.* slobby, sloppy ;—*n.* noise of dropping water.

ଚପଚ, *a.* marshy, muddy.

ଚପ୍‌ରାସ୍, *n.* a breastplate, a badge.

ଚପ୍‌ରାସୀ, *n.* a peon, one wearing a badge.

ଚପଳ, *a.* fickle, unsteady.

ଚପଳା, *a.* unsteady;—*n. Lakshmee*; lightning.

ଚପ୍‌କନ୍, *n.* a long coat worn by men.

ଚପ୍‌ଚପ୍, *n.* a splashing sound.

* ଚପେଟ, *n.* a slap, the flat palm.

ଚବିଶ, *a.* and *n.* twenty-four; 24, XXIV.

ଚମ, *n.* skin, leather, a hide.

ଚମକ, *n.* panic; a flash, glance.

ଚମକାଇବା, *v.* to startle, to frighten.

ଚମକିବା, *v.* to start, to shudder ; to flash, to glitter.

ଚମକିତ, *a.* affrighted, alarmed.

ଚମଚ, ଚାମଚ, *n.* a spoon, a ladle.

ଚମଡ଼ା, *n.* leather, skin, hide (see ଚମ). [amazement.

ଚମତ୍କାର, *n.* surprise, astonishment,

ଚମତ୍କୃତ, *a.* surprised, amazed.

ଚମଦଳା, *n.* a skin disease.

ଚମରୀ, *n.* the *Yak* or Tibetan ox.

ଚମାର, *n.* a *tatty* maker, a basket maker, etc.

* ଚମୂ, *n.* a complete army.

* ଚମ୍ପକ, *n.* a fragrant yellow flower, the *champa.*

* ଚମ୍ପକରମ୍ଭା, *n.* the *champa* plantain.

ଚମ୍ପଟ, *n.* fleeing, withdrawing, a departing suddenly.

ଚମ୍ପା, *n.* the *champa* flower.

ଚମ୍ପାକଦଳୀ, *n.* see ଚମ୍ପକରମ୍ଭା ।

ଚମ୍ପେଇଶେଉଳ, *n.* the ground lizard.

ଚମ୍ପୂ, *n.* the name of a poetical composition.

ଚମ୍ରା, *a.* smart, brisk, clever.

ଚୟ, *n.* (used as a *suffix*) a multitude, an assemblage.

* ଚୟନ, *n.* the collecting or culling (of flowers).

ଚର, *n.* a spy, an emissary.
ଚରକ, *n.* the name of one of the famous writers of *Ayurveda* and also of his book.
ଚରଖା, ଚର୍ଖା, *n.* a spinning-wheel.
ଚରଖି, ଚଖ, *n.* anything of the reel or wheel kind.
ଚରଣ, *n.* the foot; in poetry a certain number of syllables forming a distinct part of a verse.
ଚରଣସେବା, *n.* humble service.
ଚରଣାମୃତ, ଚରଣୋଦକ, *n.* water presented to a brahmin in which he dips his toe, holy water.
ଚରବସ୍ତୁ, *n.* alluvial deposit.
* ଚରମ, *a.* last, final; outermost; western; posterior;—*n.* the back.
ଚରମକାଳ, *n.* the hour of death.
ଚରସ, *n.* an intoxicating drug produced from *ganja* or hemp.
ଚରା, *n.* pasturage for cattle.
ଚରାଇବା, *v.* to pasture.
ଚରାଚର, *a.* movable and immovable; —*n.* the whole world.
ଚରାଣୀ, *n.* a pasture, a meadow for cattle.
ଚରିତ, *n.* a history, memoir, narrative, adventures.
ଚରିତାର୍ଥ, *a.* prosperous, successful; satisfied.
ଚରିତ୍ର, *n.* conduct, behaviour.
ଚରିବା, *v.* to graze, to pasture.
ଚରୁ, *n.* a food offering to the gods (milk or vegetable).

ଚର୍ଚ୍ଚା, *n.* casting a reflection upon others; *concentration of mind; an anointing.
ଚର୍ବଣ, *n.* a chewing, masticating.
* ଚର୍ବିତ, *a.* chewed, masticated.
ଚର୍ବି, *n.* fat, suet, tallow.
* ଚର୍ବ୍ୟ, *a.* fit for mastication.
ଚର୍ମ, *n.* skin, leather, a hide.
* ଚର୍ମକାର, *n.* a tanner; shoemaker.
* ଚର୍ମଦଣ୍ଡ, *n.* a whip, a scourge.
ଚର୍ମପାଦୁକା, *n.* a leather shoe.
* ଚର୍ଯ୍ୟା, *n.* practice, habit; nursing, serving.
* ଚଳ, ଚଳନ୍ତ, *a.* moving, active.
* ଚଳନ, *n.* walking, going; habit, conduct.
ଚଳଣସୁ, *a.* passable, fit to pass.
ଚଳନ୍ତି, *a.* current, in general use; movable.
ଚଳାଇବା, *v.* to drive, to drive forward; to conduct business, to manage.
ଚଳାଚଳ, *n.* livelihood;—*a.* fast and loose, stead-fast and wavering.
ଚଳିତ, *a.* current; customary; *sent.
ଚଳିବା, *v.* to move, to pass, to go on.
* ଚଳିଷ୍ଣୁ, *a.* movable, unsteady.
ଚଳେ, *a.* a handful of anything liquid.
ଚଞ୍ଚାଇବା, *v.* to sift; to cause to go, to cause to walk on foot.
ଚଞ୍ଚଲ, ଚଞ୍ଚଳ, *a.* clever, active, smart.
ଚଞ୍ଚଳତା, ଚଞ୍ଚଳତା, *n.* activity, smartness.

ଚଲଚଲ୍, *n.* the act of setting in motion.

ଚଲବୁଲ, *n.* turning and veering.

ଚଲାନ୍, ଚଲାଣ, *n.* sending up of a case or prisoner to the magistrate; a permit; an invoice.

ଚଷମା, *n.* eyeglass, a pair of spectacles.

* ଚଷକ, *n.* a drinking vessel.

ଚଷା, *n.* a farmer, a husbandman.

ଚଷାଟିଆ, *n.* clownish, boorish.

ଚଷାପୁଅ, *n.* a peasant, son of a peasant; a kind of bird.

ଚଷିବା, *v.* to cultivate or plough.

ଚଷୁ, *n.* paddy chaff.

ଚହଟ, *n.* fragrant perfumes; exposure; beauty.

ଚହଳ, *n.* sound of human voices, a buzzing.

ଚହଲ, *a.* disturbed.

ଚହଲିପଡ଼ିବା, *v.* to spill, to overflow.

ଚହଲିବା, *v.* to spring up, to bubble up, to disturb.

ଚକ୍ଷୁ, *n.* the eye.

ଚକ୍ଷୁଗୋଚର, *a.* present to the eye.

* ଚକ୍ଷୁଷ୍ମାନ୍, *a.* having good eyesight.

ଚା, ଚାହା, *n.* tea.

ଚାଁଉବାଠ, *n.* a medicinal wood.

ଚାଁଉପଖାଳ, *n.* boiled rice mixed with water just before it reaches a condition of fermentation.

ଚାଉଳ, *n.* uncooked rice.

ଚାଉଳିଆ, *a.* half-boiled (rice);—*n.* a rice-dealer, a rice-merchant.

ଚାକଚକ୍ୟ, *n.* brilliance, brightness.

ଚାକର, *n.* a servant.

ଚାକିରି, ଚାକରି, *n.* service.

ଚାକରାଣୀ, ଚାକରାଣୀ, *n.* a woman servant.

ଚାକୁ, *n.* a clasp-knife.

ଚାକୁଣ୍ଡା, *n.* name of a tree, *cassiatora.*

ଚାଗଣ୍ଡ, *n.* a span.

ଚାଖ, *n.* pride.

ଚାଖିବା, *v.* to taste.

ଚାଙ୍ଗଡ଼ା, *n.* a basket, a fancy basket.

ଚାଙ୍ଗୁଡ଼, *n.* a small fancy basket.

ଚାଚେର, *n.* the *dol jatra.*

ଚାଞ୍ଚର, ଚାଞ୍ଚିର, *n.* a bamboo or rush mat.

ଚାଞ୍ଚଲ୍ୟ, *n.* fickleness, instability, unsteadiness.

ଚାଞ୍ଛିବା, *v.* to scrape, to pare off the surface.

ଚାଟ, *n.* a student, a reader.

ଚାଟଅକ୍ଷର, *n.* large plain letters.

ଚାଟପିଲା, ଚାଟପୁଅ, *n.* a school-boy.

ଚାଟଶାଳୀ, *n.* a school-room, a place where a school is held.

ଚାଟିବା, *v.* to lick or taste.

ଚାଟୀ, *n.* a small basket.

ଚାଟୁ, ଚାଟୁବାଦ, *n.* soft words, flattery.

ଚାଟୁକାର, ଚାଟୁବାଦୀ, ଚାଟୁଭାଷୀ, *n.* a flatterer, a sycophant.

ଚାଟୂକ୍ତି, *n.* flattery, adulation.

ଚାଟୋଳ, *a.* restless during illness.

ଚାଣକ୍ୟ, *n.* pundit *chanakya*; his book of wise sayings.

ଚାଣ୍ଡାଳ, *n.* a low caste Hindu.

ଚାଣ୍ଡାଳୀ, ଚାଣ୍ଡାଳୁଣୀ, *n. fem.* of above.

ଚାଣ୍ଡେ, *ad.* soon, quickly.

ଚାତକ, *n.* a fabled bird.

ଚଉର, *n.* boastfulness, pride.

ଚତୁରି, *n.* craftiness, roguery.

ଚତୁରାଳି, *n.* craft, cunning.

ଚଁଦର, *n.* a sheet, a wrapper.

ଚନ୍ଦ, *n.* the moon ;—*a.* lunar.

ଚନ୍ଦନୀ, *n.* moonlight ; a raised outdoor platform.

ଚନ୍ଦା, *n.* a collection (of money), a subscription.

ଚନ୍ଦି, ଚନ୍ଦୀ, *n.* pure and good silver.

ଚନ୍ଦୁଆ, *a.* having a white spot on the forehead (applied to animals).

ଚନ୍ଦ୍ରାତପ, *n.* an awning. [month.

ଚାନ୍ଦ୍ରମାସ, ଚାନ୍ଦ୍ରମାସ, *n.* a lunar

ଚାନ୍ଦ୍ରାୟଣ, *n.* an expiatory observance.

ଚପ, *n.* a ferry-boat; *a bow.

ଚପଣ, *n.* a cleaver.

ଚପଟ, ଚପଟା, ଚପୁଟା, *n.* a slap; the flat palm.

ଚପଳତା, *n.* fickleness, unsteadiness.

ଚପିବା, *v.* to press down.

ଚପୁଆ, ଚପୁଆଣି, *n.* a compress; a vice used by carpenters, etc., anything that tightens or squeezes.

ଚାବି, ଚାବୀ, *n.* a key.

ଚାବୁକ, *n.* a whip, a scourge.

ଚାମଚ, ଚାମଚ, *n.* a spoon, a ladle.

ଚାମର, *n.* the *Yak's* tail, a fly brush (see ଚାମର).

ଚର, *n.* a spy, a pryer into secrets; a scafolding. [couch.

ଚାରପାଇ, ଚାରପାଇଁ, *n.* a bedstead, a

ଚାରା, *n.* a plant, a seedling ; an expedient, a help.

ଚାରି, *a.* and *n.* four; 4, IV.

ଚାରିଗୁଣ, *a.* four-fold.

ଚାରିଟା, *a.* four, a *gandá.*

ଚାରିଦିଗ, *n.* the four quarters.

ଚାରିପାୟା, *a.* four-legged;—*n.* a bedstead (see ଚାରପାଇ).

* ଚାରୁ, *a.* beautiful, elegant.

* ଚାରୁଫଳା, *n.* the grape, raisin.

* ଚାର୍ବାକ, *n.* a sophist, a sceptic, an unbeliever.

ଚାଳ, *n.* a thatched roof.

ଚାଳକ, *n.* a driver, a leader; a superintendent.

ଚାଳନ, ଚାଳନା, *n.* the causing a thing to move.

ଚାଳିଶ, *a.* and *n.* forty; 40, XL.

ଚାଳିଶା, *n.* dim sight.

ଚାଲି, *n.* manner, custom.

ଚାଲାକ, *a.* clever, skilful.

ଚାଲାକୀ, *n.* activity, cleverness.

ଚାଲ, *n.* manner of walking.

ଚାଲିବା, *v.* to walk on foot, to go, to move, to pass.

ଚାଲୁଣୀ, *n.* a sieve, colander.

ଚାଷ, *n.* husbandry, agriculture.

ଚାଷୀ, *n.* a ploughman, a farmer.

ଚାଷୁଣୀ, *n.* a woman of the cultivator caste.

ଚାହାଁଣି, *n.* seeing, looking ; manner of looking at. [*shalá.*

ଚାଟଶାଳୀ, *n.* a village school, *path-*

ଚହିଁବା, *v.* to look, to see ; to look wistfully, to desire.

* ଚାକ୍ଷୁଷ, *a.* evident, plainly visible.

ଚିଁଅ, *n.* the mark of a burn.

ଚିଁଆଇବା, *v.* to awaken, to stir up, to arouse.

ଚିକ, *n.* a sort of lattice made of bamboos split very thin and used as a blind to windows or doors ; a kind of ornament worn round the neck by women.

ଚିକଟା, *a.* clayey.

ଚିକିତ୍ସକ, *n.* a physician; a doctor.

ଚିକିତ୍ସା, *n.* practice of medicine; treatment.

ଚିକିତ୍ସିତ, *a.* treated medically, medicated.

* ଚିକୁର, *n.* the hair of the head.

ଚିକ୍କଣ, ଚିକଣ, *a.* smooth, polished, oily, unctuous, glossy.

ଚିକିଚିକ, *a.* glittering, bright, sparkling (see ଚକ ଚକ).

ଚିଙ୍ଗୁଡ଼ି, *n.* a shrimp, a prawn.

ଚିଜ, *n.* thing, article, goods, property.

ଚିଜବସ୍ତୁ, *n.* (*pl.*) baggage, furniture, equipment.

ଚିଠାଉ, *n.* a letter, an epistle.

ଚିଠି, ଚିଟି, *n.* a letter, a note, a *chit.*

ଚିଟା, *n.* a draft (rough copy).

ଚିଡ଼ଚିଡ଼, *n.* vexatiousness, annoyance;—*a.* fretful, snappish.

ଚିଡ଼ଚିଡ଼ିଆ, *a.* snappish, cross.

ଚିଡ଼ାଳୁ, *a.* irritable, easily provoked.

ଚିଡ଼ାଇବା, *v.* to vex, to annoy.

ଚିଡ଼ିଆ, *n.* a bird.

ଚିଡ଼ିଆଖାନା, *n.* zoological garden.

ଚିଡ଼ିବା, *v.* to be angry or displeased

ଚିତଉ, *n.* a kind of cake made of *biri* and rice-flour.

ଚିତା, *n.* a mark or dot, *telak* ; a funeral pile.

ଚିତାବାଘ, *n.* a leopard.

* ଚିତାଭସ୍ମ, *n.* ashes of the funeral pile.

*ଚିତାଭୂମି, *n.* a place where the dead are burned.

ଚିତାସାପ, *n.* a spotted snake.

ଚିତୋଉ, *n.* see ଚିତଉ ।

ଚିତ୍, *a.* lying on the back, supine.

ଚିତ୍କାର, ଚିହ୍କାର, *n.* a cry, a scream.

ଚିତ୍ତ, *n.* the heart, the affections.

ଚିତ୍ତଚୋର, *n.* one who steals the affections.

ଚିତ୍ତଭ୍ରମ, *n.* derangement of mind.

ଚିତ୍ତସ୍ଥ, *a.* situated in the heart.

ଚିତ୍ପଟାଙ୍ଗ, *a.* lying or falling with the face up-turned.

ଚିତ୍ର, *n.* a picture ;—*a.* painted ; variegated, spotted; wonderful.

* ଚିତ୍ରକଣ୍ଠ, *n.* a pigeon, a dove.

* ଚିତ୍ରକମ୍ବଳ, *n.* a variegated carpet or rug.

ଚିତ୍ରକର, ଚିତ୍ରକାର, *n.* a painter, an artist.

ଚିତ୍ରକର୍ମ, *n.* painting, embroidering.

ଚିତ୍ରକାବ୍ୟ, *n.* an acrostic.

ଚିତ୍ରଗୁପ୍ତ, *n.* the registrar of *Jama.*

ଚିତ୍ରପଟ, *n.* a picture; a cloth or paper upon which a picture is drawn.

* ଚିତ୍ରଫଳକ, *n.* that upon which a picture is drawn.

ଚିତ୍ରବିଚିତ୍ର, *a.* variegated, spotted.

ଚିତ୍ରା, *n.* a star in the spike of Virgo;—*a.* spotted.

ଚିତ୍ରାଙ୍ଗ, *a.* spotted, pie-bald.

ଚିତ୍ରିତ, *a.* variegated, spotted, figured, painted.

* ଚିଦାତ୍ମା, *n.* the intellectual soul, the spirit.

ଚିଦାଭାସ, *n.* a semblance of intellect.

ଚିଦ୍ରୂପ, *n.* intelligence; amiability.

ଚିନା, *n.* bird-seed; one 320th part of a tola of gold.

ଚିନାବାଦାମ, *n.* ground-nut, peanut, monkey-nut. (*Arachis*).

ଚିନି, *n.* sugar.

* ଚିନ୍ତକ, *a.* anxious, thoughtful;—*n.* one who thinks.

* ଚିନ୍ତନ, *n.* thinking, pondering, cogitating.

ଚିନ୍ତନୀୟ, *a.* requiring thought, deserving care or reflection.

ଚିନ୍ତା, *n.* anxiety, care, thought.

ଚିନ୍ତାକୁଳ, *a.* anxious, thoughtful.

ଚିନ୍ତାମଣି, *n.* a fabulous gem; *Vishnu.*

ଚିନ୍ତାର୍ତ୍ତ, *a.* anxious, thoughtful, pensive.

ଚିନ୍ତିତ, *a.* troubled, anxious; thought on.

* ଚିନ୍ତ୍ୟ, *a.* worthy of consideration.

ଚିପ, *n.* a cork, a stopper.

ଚିପା, *n.* squeezing, expressing;—*a.* miserly.

ଚିପାଚିପି, *n.* continued pinching or squeezing.

ଚିପିବା, *v.* to press, to squeeze.

* ଚିପିଟକ, *n.* rice soaked, parched and flattened, *chudá.*

ଚିପୁଡ଼ା, *a.* wrung out, squeezed.

ଚିପୁଡ଼ିବା, *v.* to wring, to squeeze, to strain out.

ଚିପୁଲି, ଚେପୁଲି, *n.* a kind of sandal made of a piece of leather fastened to the foot with a string.

ଚିବୁକ, *n.* the lips, the chin.

ଚିମୁଟା, *n.* tongs, pincers, forceps; pinching.

ଚିମୁଟିବା, *v.* to pinch, to pinch with the thumb and finger nails.

ଚିମୁଣି, *n.* a bat.

ଚିମୁଳା, *n.* a pad; a pillow.

ଚିର, *a.* long, lasting a long time; —*n.* a long time.

ଚିରକାଳ, *n.* a long time.

ଚିରକାଳୀନ, *a.* old, ancient; chronic.

ଚିରଘୁଣା, *a.* witch.

ଚିରଜୀବୀ, ଚିରଞ୍ଜୀବୀ, *n.* one who lives a long time;—*a.* long-lived.

ଚିରୁଣି, ଚିରୁଣୀ, *n.* a comb.

ଚିରରୋଗ, *n.* a chronic disease.
ଚିରରୋଗୀ, *a.* of a sickly constitution, long-diseased.
ଚିରନ୍ତନ, *a.* of old, ancient, chronic.
ଚିରସ୍ଥାୟୀ, *a.* durable, of long continuance.
ଚିର, *n.* a rent, fissure, tear;—*a.* torn, rent. [*cheráitá.*
ଚିରଇତା, ଚିରେତା, *n.* a bitter herb,
ଚିରାଗତ, *a.* from time immemorial.
ଚିରାୟୁ, *a.* long-lived;—*n.* a long [life.
* ଚଂଗଳ, *n.* a flag, a banner.
ଚିରିବା, *v.* to tear, to rend, to split; to saw.
ଚିଲୁଆଣୀ, *n.* will o' the wisp, *ignis fatuus*; a witch.
ଚିଁକିବା, *v.* to dirty one's self.
ଚିଁଚିଆଇବା, *v.* to cry out in alarm or distress.
ଚିଲ, ଚିଲ୍ଲ, *n.* a kite, the kite species.
ଚିଲମ, *n.* the bowl of a *hooká.*
ଚିଲମଚି, *n.* a washhand basin.
ଚିଲାଆଖି, *n.* grey or whitish eyes.
ଚିଲୁକା, *n.* a wide expanse of water, a mere, a lake; *Chilka.*
ଚିହୁଁକିବା, *v.* to startle, shock, alarm.
ଚିହ୍ନ, *n.* a mark, a sign, a badge.
ଚିହ୍ନା, *a.* known, recognized.
ଚିହ୍ନାଚିହ୍ନି, *n.* a mutual recognition.
ଚିହ୍ନାପରିଚୟ, *n.* mutual acquaintance.
ଚିହ୍ନିତ, *a.* marked, denoted.
ଚିହ୍ନିବା, *v.* to perceive, to recognize.

ଚୀନା, *n.* bird-seed; a Chinese.
* ଚୀର, *n.* torn clothes, rags; bark used as clothes. [mouse.
ଚୁଆ, *n.* a sweet-scented oil; *a
ଚୁଆଇବା, *v.* to ooze, to cause to ooze or to leak.
ଚୁଆଡ, ଚୁହାଡ, *n.* a term of abuse; a mountain tribe.
ଚୁକାଇବା, *v.* to settle an affair.
ଚୁକ୍ତି, *n.* a bargain, contract, agreement.
ଚୁଗୁଲି, *n.* backbiting, slandering.
ଚୁଗୁଲିଖୋର, *n.* backbiter, slanderer.
ଚୁଙ୍ଗା, ଚୁଙ୍ଗୀ, *n.* a socket, a cup, a tube, a pipe. [ଚିଙ୍ଗୁଡ଼ି).
ଚୁଙ୍ଗୁଡ଼ି, *n.* a shrimp, a prawn, (see
ଚୁଁଚି, *n.* (vulgar) the nipple, paps.
ଚୁଚୁନ୍ଦ୍ରା, *n.* a musk-rat.
ଚୁଚୁମିବା, *v.* to suck.
* ଚୁଚୁକ, *v.* the nipple, teat.
ଚୁଟ୍‌କିଆ, *a.* small, little, trifling.
ଚୁଟ୍‌କା, *n.* noise of snapping the finger and thumb.
ଚୁଟି, *n.* a lock of hair hanging from the crown of the head.
ଚୁଟିଆମୂଷା, *n.* the common mouse.
ଚୁଡ଼ା, *n.* flattened rice, *chudá.*
ଚୁଡ଼ି, *n.* a bracelet.
ଚୁପ, *n.* silence; hush;—*a.* silent.
ଚୁମା, *n.* a kiss.
ଚୁମ୍ବ, ଚୁମ୍ବନ, *n.* a kiss, a kissing.

ଚୁମ୍ବକ, *n.* a magnet; index, abstract.
ଚୁମ୍ବନକରିବା, ଚୁମ୍ବିବା, *v.* to kiss.
ଚୁଲ୍ଲି, ଚୁଲ୍ଲି, ଚୁଲ୍ଲୀ, *n.* a fireplace.
ଚୁଷୁମା, *n.* a rubber teat, a child's comforter.
ଚୁଷିବା, *v.* to suck, to imbibe.
ଚୁସ୍ତ, *a.* tight, tied.
ଚୂଡ଼ା, *n.* a peak, top, topknot, crest.
ଚୂଡ଼ାନ୍ତ, *n.* a decision, result, issue; —*a.* fixed, decided.
ଚୂଡ଼ାମଣି, *n.* a crest-jewel;—*a.* eminent.
*ଚୂତ, *n.* the mango tree and fruit.
ଚୂନ, *n.* lime, *chunam.*
ଚୂନା, *n.* anything pulverized.
ଚୂନାକରିବା, *v.* to cut into small pieces.
ଚୂନୀ, *a.* powdered, fine;—*n.* *a ruby.
ଚୂରିବା, *v.* to pulverize, to powder.
ଚୂର୍ଣ୍ଣ, *a.* pulverized, pounded; destroyed;—*n.* powder, dust; * lime.
ଚୂର୍ଣ୍ଣକ, *n.* powder, dust.
* ଚୂର୍ଣ୍ଣକାର, *n.* a seller of lime, a lime-burner.
ଚୂର୍ଣ୍ଣକୁନ୍ତଳ, *n.* curls or ringlets of hair.
ଚୂର୍ଣ୍ଣିତ, *a.* pulverized, powdered; destroyed.
ଚୂର୍ଣ୍ଣୀଭୂତ, *a.* reduced to dust or powder.
ଚୂଳ, *n.* hair, a lock of hair.
ଚେଇଁବା, *v.i.* to watch.
ଚେକା, *n.* a sod;—*a.* round.
ଚେକାଛୁଆଣି, *n.* turfing, covering with turf or sods.

ଚେକଚେକ, *a.* round (*e.g.*, ଏଲ୍ ଚେକଚେକ କରି କାଟ, etc.).
ଚେଙ୍ଗ, ଚେଙ୍ଗା, *n.* trouble or difficulty caused by deceit or cheating.
ଚେଙ୍ଗିବା, *v.* to be put to trouble through deceit or cheating.
ଚେଙ୍ଗ, *n.* a kind of fish.
ଚେଙ୍ଗା, *a.* in restored health; bearing one's self proudly or smartly.
*ଚେଟୀ, *n.* a female servant or slave.
* ଚେତଃ, *n.* the mind, intellect, reasoning faculty.
ଚେତନ, *a.* conscious, animate, living, sentient.
ଚେତନା, ଚେତା, *n.* sense, consciousness, intelligence, understanding.
ଚେତାଇବା, *v.* to caution; to awake to effort, to stir up.
ଚେତିବା, *v.* to gain experience, to be cautious; to remember; to know.
ଚେପା, ଚେପ୍ସା, *a.* compressed, flattened, flat.
ଚେରସ୍ତ, *a.* vexatious, teazing.
ଚେମଡ଼, ଚେମଡ଼ା, *a.* tough, pliant.
ଚେମଣିଆ, *n.* a bat.
ଚେର, *n.* the root, roots; teats of a cow.
ଚେରୁଆ, *a.* stringy, (as some mangoes).
* ଚେଲ, *n.* cloth, clothes, garment

ଚେଲା, *n.* a child or pupil adopted by a religious mendicant or devotee; a disciple.

* ଚେଷ୍ଟକ, *n.* one engaged in any undertaking;—*a.* persevering.

ଚେଷ୍ଟା, *n.* endeavour, search after, effort.

ଚେଷ୍ଟିତ, *a.* endeavoured;—*n.* endeavour.

ଚେହେରା, *n.* the countenance; general appearance.

ଚୈତନ୍ୟ, *n.* consciousness, spirit; *Chaitanya.*

* ଚୈତ୍ୟ, *n.* the sacred village tree.

ଚୈତ୍ର, *n.* a Hindu month, part of March and April.

ଚୋଖା, *a.* fresh, good, excellent.

ଚୋଗା, *n.* an overcoat.

ଚୋଟ, *n.* a hurt, blow, contusion.

ଚୋଟାଇବା, ଚୋଟେଇବା, *v.* to strike or wound.

ଚୋଟେଟ, *n.* a blow with a weapon.

ଚୋପ, *n.* a document, deed; a drum.

ଚୋପା, *n.* rind, skin.

ଚୋବା, *a.* chewed, masticated.

ଚୋବାଇବା, *v.* to chew, to munch.

ଚୋବାଚୋବି, *n.* the act of chewing or munching.

ଚୋର, *n.* a thief; *fem.* ଚୋରୁଣୀ.

ଚୋରଖାତ, *n.* a peep-hole; a hole made by thieves.

ଚୋରା, *a.* clandestine, stolen, hidden.

ଚୋରାଇବା, *v.* to steal.

ଚୋରାଦ୍ରବ୍ୟ, *n.* stolen property.

ଚୋରାବାଟ, *n.* a crevice, a peep-hole.

ଚୋରାବାଲି, *n.* a quicksand.

ଚୋରାମାଲ, ଚୋରମାଲ, *n.* (see ଚୋରାଦ୍ରବ୍ୟ).

ଚୋରି, *n.* theft, robbery, thieving.

* ଚୋଷଣ, *n.* sucking, imbibing by the mouth.

ଚୋଷିବା, *v.* to suck.

ଚୌ, *a.* four, four-fold.

ଚୌକ, *n.* a square; four *puns* marked thus (।).

ଚୌକା, *a.* four-cornered;—*n.* cooking-place.

ଚୌକାଠ, *n.* a door-frame.

ଚୌକି, *n.* a chair; watching.

ଚୌକିଆ, ଚୌକିଦାର, *n.* a watchman, a sentinel.

ଚୌକିଦାରୀ, *n.* the office of a watchman.

ଚୌଖୁଣ୍ଟ, *n.* square on all sides.

ଚୌଠ, *n.* one-fourth, a quarter.

ଚୌଠୀ, *n.* the fourth day after the marriage ceremony.

ଚୌଡ଼ା, *a.* wide, broad.

ଚୌଦୋଳ, *n.* a vehicle, a kind of litter.

ଚୌତିଶ, *a.* and *n.* thirty-four; 34, XXXIV.

ଚୌଥ, *n.* (see ଚୌଠ).

ଚୌଦ, *a.* and *n.* fourteen; 14, XIV.

ଚୌଦିଗ, *n.* the four quarters.

ଚୌଧୁରୀ, *n.* a title.

ଚୌପଟ, *a.* fourfold;—*n.* dice.

ଚୌପାଢ଼ି, ଚୌପାଢ଼ୀ, *n.* a village school.

ଚୌପାୟା, *a.* four-footed or four-legged ;—*n.* a string cot with four legs.

ଚୌପାଲ, *n.* a *palki*, a litter.

ଚୌପାଶ, *n.* four sides ;—*ad.* on all sides.

ଚୌବିଠିଆ, *a.* having four sides ; clever in all directions, thoroughly qualified, (see ଚଉବିଠିଆ).

ଚୌବଚ୍ଚା, *n.* a cess-pool, a pit, a vat.

ଚୌବନ, *a.* and *n.* fifty-four; 54, LIV.

ଚୌବିଶ, *a.* and *n.* twenty-four; 24, [XXIV.

* ଚୌର, *n.* a thief, a robber.

ଚୌରସ, *a.* smooth, even, level, plain.

ଚୌରା, *n.* a square platform for the *tulsi* plant.

ଚୌରନବେ, *a.* and *n.* ninety-four; 94, XCIV.

ଚୌରାଳିଶ, *a.* and *n.* forty-four; 44, XLIV.

ଚୌରାଶୀ, *a.* and *n.* eighty-four; 84, LXXXIV.

* ଚୌର୍ଯ୍ୟବୃତ୍ତି, *n.* theft, robbery.

ଚୌଷଠି, *a.* and *n.* sixty-four; 64, LXIV.

ଚୌସାର, *n.* dice, play at dice.

ଚୌସ୍ତରି, *a.* and *n.* seventy-four; 74, LXXIV.

* ଚ୍ୟୁତ, *a.* fallen from, dismissed.

* ଚ୍ୟୁତି, *n.* dismissal, release, freedom.

ଛ.

ଛ, the seventh consonant.

ଛ, ଛଅ, *a.* and *n.* six; 6, VI.

ଛଉର, *n.* shaving the face. [LXVI.

ଛଅଷଠି, *a.* and *n.* sixty-six; 66,

ଛଅସ୍ତରି, *a.* and *n.* seventy-six; 76, LXXVI.

ଛଇ, *n.* buffoonery; the roof of a boat; a heap.

ଛଇଳ, ଛଇଳା, *a.* beautiful, humorous, witty, jocose.

ଛଉ, *n.* a skin disease.

ଛଉଆ, *a.* having the above disease; *n.* a person having ଛଉ.

ଛଉକା, *a.* cunning.

ଛକ, *n.* a square, four crossways.

ଛକ, ଛକି, *n.* sign of a cross (†).

ଛକାଛକ, ଛକାପଞ୍ଝା, *n.* an ambush, lying in wait, secret watching.

ଛକିବା, *v.* to watch, to lie in ambush.

ଛଣା, *a.* strained;—*n.* straining or draining water, etc.; a strainer.

ଛଞ୍ଚାଣ, *n.* a bird of prey.

ଛଞ୍ଚିବା, *v.* to save, to collect or gather.

ଛଟକ, *n.* beauty; quickness.

ଛଟଛଟ, *a.* struggling in agony, greatly excited with pain, distressed.

ଛଟପଟ, *a.* restless, turning and tossing; greatly excited with pain or fear.

ଛଟପଟିଆ, *a.* troublesome, perplexing.

ଛଟା, *n.* an excuse, pretence; beauty, lustre, splendour.

ଛଟାଛଟି, *n.* the act of throwing or splashing against; pruning of a tree.

ଛଟାଙ୍କି, *n.* sixteenth part of a seer.

ଛଡ଼, *n.* a spear, a flagstaff.

ଛଡ଼ା, *n.* a heifer;—*a.* left;—*ad.* except, besides, without, apart from.

ଛଡ଼ାଇବା, *v.* to free, to extricate, to wrest from.

ଛଡ଼ାଛଡ଼ି, *n.* a snatching; scattering; separating.

ଛଡ଼ି, *n.* a switch, twig, thin stick.

ଛଡ଼ିଦାର, *n. piádá*, an inferior police officer.

ଛଣ, *n. bená* grass, thatching grass.

ଛଣପଟ, *n.* flax, tow.

ଛଣା, *a.* sifted, strained.

ଛଣି, *n.* flax; a small purse.

ଛତରଖିଆ, *n.* a beggar.

ଛତର, *a.* scattered about; broken, flattened.

ଛତା, *n.* an umbrella.

ଛତାଉର, *n.* name of a medicinal plant.

ଛତଣ, *n.* foulness of the teeth or gums; mould or mill-dew.

ଛତିଶ, *n.* and *a.* thirty-six; 36, XXXVI.

ଛତିଶା, *a.* illegitimate.

ଛତୁ, *n.* mushrooms; a fungus; pulverized matter.

ଛତୁ, ଛତୁଆ, *n.* pulverized matter.

ଛତ୍ର, *n.* a place where alms are bestowed; *an umbrella.

*ଛତ୍ରଧାରୀ, *a.* holding an umbrella;—*n.* a king.

ଛତ୍ରପତି, *n.* a king, a *raja*.

ଛତ୍ରଭଙ୍ଗ, *n.* anarchy.

ଛତ୍ରାକାର, *a.* round, umbrella-shaped.

*ଛତ୍ତିଶ, *a.* and *n.* thirty-six; 36, XXXVI.

ଛତ୍ରୀ, *n.* an awning;—*a.* *holding an umbrella.

ଛଦ୍ମ, *n.* a pretext, a fraud.

ଛଦ୍ମବେଶ, *n.* a disguise;—*a. incog.*

ଛଦ୍ମବେଶୀ, *a.* appearing in disguise.

ଛନକା, *n.* surprise, alarm.

ଛନଛନ, *a.* unsteady, agitated, anxious.

ଛନ୍ଦ, *n.* hypocrisy; a verse, metre, cadence; coma.

ଛନ୍ଦା, *a.* rope twisted or crossed, knotted.

ଛନ୍ଦାଛନ୍ଦି, *a.* entangled, in a ravel, fastened together by fetters.

*ଛନ୍ନ, *a.* covered, concealed.

ଛପନ, *a.* and *n.* fifty-six; 56, LVI.

ଛପର, *n.* thatched roof.

ଛପରବନ୍ଦ, *n.* thatching a house.

ଛପା, *a.* printed; hidden.

ଛପାଇବା, *v.* to cause to be printed; to cause to be concealed.

ଛପାଖାନା, ଛାପାଖାନା, *n.* a printing-office.

ଛବି, *n.* a drawing, picture; splendour, complexion, beauty.

ଛବିଲ, *a.* sportive, jocose.

ଛବଶ, *a.* and *n.* twenty-six; 26, XXVI.

*ଛର୍ଦ୍ଦି, *n.* a vomiting, a belching.

ଛୟାନବେ, *a.* and *n.* ninety-six; 96, XCVI. [XLVI.

ଛୟାଳିଶ, *a.* and *n.* forty-six; 46,

ଛୟାଶୀ, *a.* and *n.* eighty-six; 86, LXXXVI.

ଛରୁସ, ଛେରୁସ, *n.* shot, pe'lets. [fice.

ଛଳ, *n.* contrivance, pretext, arti-

ଛଳନା, *n.* imposing upon, defrauding. [house.

ଛପଣି, *n.* the act of thatching a

ଛାୟା, *n.* shadow, shade, a reflected image.

ଛାଇବା, *v.* to thatch.

ଛାଉଣି, *n.* an encampment, a tent; soldiers (encamped); thatching a house.

ଛାଉଣିଆ, *n.* a thatcher.

ଛାଗଳ, * ଛାଗ, *n.* a he-goat.

ଛାଗଳଯୋନିଆ, *a.* goatish, lecherous.

* ଛାଗୀ, *n.* a she-goat.

ଛାଣିବା, *v.* to strain, to sift, to filter.

ଛାଞ୍ଚ, *n.* a mould; a model, a likeness.

ଛାଞ୍ଚ, *n.* eaves of a house.

ଛାଞ୍ଚପାନ, *n.* a kind of *pán.*

ଛାଞ୍ଚୁଣି, *n.* a broom made of date-palm branches.

ଛାଟ, *n.* a switch.

ଛାଟିଆ, *n.* one holding a switch or stick; a small switch or stick.

ଛାଟିବା, *v.* to splash;—*n.* splashing of rain or mud and water against a wall, etc.

ଛାଟେଣି, *n.* a sling. [in *Kartic.*

ଛାଡପାଣ, *n.* day after the full moon

ଛାଡଚିଠି, *n.* a permit, a pass, a clearance for goods.

ଛାଡପତ୍ର, *n.* a bill of divorce. [tion.

ଛାଡଭଡ, *n.* a going ahead of; separa-

ଛାଡିବା, *v.* to release, relinquish, to leave.

ଛାଣିବା, *v.* to sift, to strain, to filter.

ଛାଣ୍ଟିବା, ଛାଟିବା, *v.* to cut, trim, prune.

ଛାତ, *n.* flat roof of a house, a ceiling-cloth. [courage.

ଛାତି, *n.* the chest, the breast, bosom;

ଛାତିଦମ୍ଭ, *a.* bold, brave.

ଛାତ୍ର, *n.* a scholar, pupil, student.

ଛାତ୍ରବୃତ୍ତି, *n.* scholarship. [school.

*ଛାତ୍ରାବାସ, *n.* hostel; boarding

ଛାନିଆ, *a.* alarmed, excited;—*n.* fear.

ଛାନ୍ଦ, *n.* a chapter or division in a poem, poetry.

ଛାପ, *n.* a die, a stamp; spittle.

ଛାପମୁଦ୍ରା, *n.* a signet-ring.

ଛାପା, *a.* printed, stamped;—*n.* printing. [machine.

ଛାପାକଳ, *n.* a printing press or

ଛାପାଖାନା, *n.* a printing office or works (see ଛପାଖାନା).

ଛାପିବା, ଛାପିଦେବା, *v.* to print, to emboss or stamp.

ଛାମୁ, *n.* presence.

ଛାମୁକରଣ, *n.* a clerk of a raja or zemindar, a steward.

ଛାମୁଚିଠାଉ, *n.* a letter from or to a [raja.

ଛାମୁଣ୍ଡିଆ, ଛାମୁଡିଆ, *n.* an awning made of branches.

ଛାୟା, *n.* shade, shadow, covert, refuge, an apparition, reflection.

ଛାୟାପଥ, *n* milky-way; a shady path.

ଛାୟାମଣ୍ଡପ, *n.* a place under an awning.

ଛାର, *a.* mean, despicable, vile.

ଛାରଖାର, *a.* ruined, reduced to [ashes.

ଛାରପୋକ, *n.* a bed-bug

ଛାଲ, *n.* bark, rind, peel, skin.

ଛାଲିବା, *v.* to bark a tree, to peel, to skin.

ଛିଃ, ଛି, ଛିଛି, *interj.* fie! for shame!

ଛିଚର, *a.* contemptible.

ଛିଙ୍କ, *n.* a sneezing.

ଛିଙ୍କିବା, *v.* to sneeze.

ଛିଟଣା, *a.* sprinkled, scattered.

ଛିଞ୍ଚାଡ଼ିବା, *v.* to sprinkle, to strew, to scatter, to spatter.

ଛିଞ୍ଚିବା, *v.* to sprinkle. [exchange.

ଛିଟ, *n.* chintz; a balance given in

ଛିଟା, *n.* a drop; atom, particle.

ଛିଟାଇବା, *v.* to cause to sprinkle or scatter.

ଛିଟାଗୁଳି, *n.* pellet, shot.

ଛିଟାଣ, *n.* a sprinkling.

ଛିଟାଣମଣ୍ଡଳୀ *n.* a church in which baptism by sprinkling is practised.

ଛିଟିକନ, *n.* a sling, a pellet-bow; *chitkin.*

ଛିଟିକିବା, *v.* to jerk, to scatter or to be thrown with a jerk.

ଛିଡାହେବା, *v.* to stand, to stand upright.

ଛିଡିବା, *v.* to split, tear; to be unfriendly, to be annoyed or displeased; to be settled up.

ଛିଣ୍ଡା *a.* torn, split, cracked.

ଛିଣ୍ଡାଇବା, *v.* to divide, to split; to settle a dispute or account.

ଛିଣ୍ଡାଛିଣ୍ଡି, *n.* a cracking and splitting; settlement of an account or dispute. [abuse).

ଛିଣ୍ଡାଳ, ଛିଣ୍ଡାଳୀ, *n.* adulteress (vulgar

ଛିଣ୍ଡିବା. ଛିଣ୍ଡିଯିବା, see ଛିଡିବା,

ଛିଦ୍ର, *n.* a hole, crack; defect, flaw.

ଛିଦ୍ରାନୁସନ୍ଧାନ, *n.* seeking a blemish.

* ଛିନ୍ନ, *a.* cut asunder, severed, torn.

ଛିନ୍ନଭିନ୍ନ *a.* severed, scattered.

* ଛିଦ୍ରାନ୍ୱେଷଣ, *n.* fault-finding, picking holes in character.

* ଛିଦ୍ରାନ୍ୱେଷୀ, *a.* looking out for faults; —*n.* fault-finder, searcher of faults.

ଛିଲ୍ଲା, *n.* bark, rind, peel; a chip.

ଛୁଁଆ, *a.* unclean; menstruous.

ଛୁଁଆଇବା, *v.* to cause to touch.

ଛୁଁଆଛୁଁଇ, *n.* mutual touch; a touching.

ଛୁଁଇ, *n.* pods (of pulse, peas, &c.).

ଛୁଁଇବା, *v.* to touch, to come in contact.

ଛୁଆ, *n.* a child, the young of an animal.

ଛୁଆର. ଛୁହାର, *n.* dried dates.

ଛୁଞ୍ଚା, *n.* a musk-rat.

ଛୁଞ୍ଚି, *n.* a needle. [leisure.

ଛୁଟି, *n.* dismissal; leave of absence;

ଛୁଟିବା, *v.* to run, to rush, to escape.

ଛୁଡ, *n.* urine.

ଛୁରୀ, * ଛୁରିକା, *n.* a knife, a penknife.

ଛେଉଣ୍ଡ, ଛେଉଣ୍ଡା, *n.* an orphan; —*a.* fatherless, forlorn. [feast.

ଛେକ, *ad.* one time;—*n.* food, a

ଛେକକୁ ଛେକ, *ad.* again and again, time after time.

ଛେଚ. ଛେଚ୍. ଛେଚ୍‌କୁଟା, *n.* the act of pounding beating or pulverizing; a beating or flogging.

ଛେଚ୍, ଛେଚ୍‌କୁଟା, *a.* beaten and pounded.

ଛେଚିବା, *v.* to beat, to pound.

ଛେଣୀ, *n.* a hardened or cold chisel. a punch.

ଛେଦ, *n.* a cut ; a hole. [off.

ଛେଦନ, *n.* cutting asunder, cutting

ଛେଦଭେଦ, *n.* bickerings, family divisions.

ଛେଦା, *n.* cloth without coloured border; curds and whey.

ଛେଦିତ, *a.* cut, divided, severed; separated.

ଛେଦଲ, *a.* penurious (woman).

ଛେନା, *n.* cream, curds.

ଛେପ, *n.* spittle, saliva.

ଛେର. ଛେରା, *n.* watery stools.

ଛେରିବା, *v.* to evacuate watery stools; to suffer from watery stools.

ଛେରୁଆ, ଛେରୁକୁଲ, ଛେରୁକୁଲା, *n.* a coward or one who dirties himself through fear;—*a.* fearful, timid, cowardly.

ଛେଳି, *n.* a goat.

ଛେଳିଗୋଡ଼ିଆ, *n.* an incestuous. person (see ଝିଅଲ ଗୋଡ଼ିଆ).

ଛେଲ, *n.* gunny; a chip.

ଛେଲୁ, *n.* bark of trees.

ଛେଲୁଣ, *n.* a broken pot. [ous.

ଛୈଳଭ, *a.* tall and robust, vigour-

ଛୋକରା, *n.* a lad, a boy.

ଛୋକାର, *n.* low language; a vagabond who lives upon the wages of prostitutes ; the name of a low caste ;—*a.* low, vile.

ଛୋଟ, *a.* small, little, petty, mean.

ଛୋଟଲାଟ, *n.* Lieutenant-Governor.

ଛୋଟା, *a.* lame;—*n.* a lame man; *fem.* ଛୋଟୀ.

ଛୋଟାଇବା, ଛୋଟେଇବା, *v.* to limp; to make smaller. [smaller.

ଛୋଟାଇଦେବା, ଛୋଟେଇଦେବା, *v.* to make

ଛୋଟିଆ, *a.* very small, insignificant.

ଛୋପରା, *a.* ashamed, pretending shyness; making fun, witty.

ଛୋ́ରା, *n.* a large knife, a dagger.

ଛୋଲ, *n.* gram for horses.
ଛିଃ, *interj.* fie ! for shame !

ଜ.

ଜ, the eighth consonant; in *Comp.* it signifies born, produced.

ଜଉ, *n.* lac, sealing-wax.

ଜଉମୁଦ, *n.* a wax seal.

ଜକଜକ, *a.* flashing glaring.

ଜକାଇବା, ଜକେଇବା, *v.* to become damp.

ଜକ.ଜକ, *a.* crowded, pressing upon one another.

ଜଖ, *n.* a term applied to gold buried for a very long time in the earth which is supposed to have become a living creature and moves about.

ଜଖମ, *n.* a wound, hurt, an ulcer.

ଜଖମୀ, *a.* wounded, full of ulcers.

ଜଗତ୍, *n.* world, the universe.

ଜଗତ୍କର୍ତ୍ତା, *n.* the Creator or Governor of the world.

* ଜଗଚ୍ଚକ୍ଷୁ, *n.* the sun.

ଜଗତ୍ତ୍ରାତା, *n.* the Saviour of the world.

* ଜଗତ୍ପ୍ରାଣ, *n.* name of the wind.

* ଜଗତୀ, *n.* the earth.

ଜଗଦୀଶ, ଜଗଦୀଶ୍ୱର, *n.* the Lord or Governor of the world, an appellative of *Vishnu* and *Shiva.*

ଜଗଦୀଶ୍ୱରୀ, *n.* *Doorgá*, queen of the world.

ଜଗନ୍ନାଥ, *n.* *Jagannáth*, one of the names of *Vishnu*, the Lord of the world.

* ଜଗନ୍ମୋହନ, *a.* fascinating the world;—*n.* *Vishnu.*

ଜଗାଇବା, *v.* to cause to watch.

ଜଗାଜଗି, *n.* a watching; the act of watching one another.

ଜଗାରଖା, *n.* a watching and protecting.

ଜଗିବା, *v.* to watch, to be on the alert.

ଜଗୁଆଳ, ଜଗୁଆଳି, *n.* one set to watch; a watchman.

* ଜଙ୍ଗମ, *a.* movable;—*n.* the animal creation.

ଜଙ୍ଗଲ୍, *n.* jungle, a forest, wilderness, thicket.

ଜଙ୍ଗଲୁଡ଼, *a.* wild, desert, uncultivated.

ଜଙ୍ଗଲି, ଜଙ୍ଗଲୁଆ, *a.* wild, sylvan.

* ଜଘନ, *n.* the hip and loins.

ଜଘନ୍ୟ. *a.* low, vile.

ଜଙ୍ଘ, *n.* the thighs, the hips.

ଜଙ୍ଘା, *n.* the calf of the leg.

ଜଙ୍ଘିଆ, *n.* short breeches.

ଜଙ୍ଘିବୁଡ଼ଭା, *n.* a small astringent fruit.

ଜଚ୍‌ଜଚି, *n.* offering or presenting to one another;—*a.* very cheap.

ଜଜବଜ, *a.* abundant, plentiful.

ଜଞ୍ଜାଳ, *n.* trouble, disorder, misfortune.

ଜଞ୍ଜାଳିଆ, *a.* troublesome or mischievous;—*n.* a troublesome or mischievous person.

ଜଞ୍ଜାଳୀ, *a.* troublesome (woman).

ଜଞ୍ଜିର, *n.* a chain.
ଜଟ, ଜଟା, *n.* matted or clotted hair.
ଜଟାଇବା, *v.* to cheat, to palm off.
ଜଟାଜଟି, *n.* a cheating, a palming off.
* ଜଟାଧର, *a.* wearing clotted hair;—*n.* a devotee; a name of *Siva.*
ଜଟାମାଂସୀ, *n.* Indian spikenard.
ଜଟାୟୁ, *n.* name of a fabnlous bird.
ଜଟିଆ, *n.* a wearer of clotted hair.
ଜଟିଳ, *a.* complicated.
ଜଟିଳଭଗ୍ନାଂଶ, *n.* (*in Arith.*) a compound fraction.
* ଜଠର, *n.* the belly, the womb.
* ଜଠରଜ୍ୱାଳା, *n.* extreme hunger; pain in the bowels, colic.
* ଜଠରାନଳ, *n.* inward heat.
ଜଡ, *n.* a root, origin;—*a.* inanimate; stupid; cold, torpid.
ଜଡତା, *n.* stupidity; indistinct utterance.
ଜଡପଦାର୍ଥ, *n.* an inanimate object.
ଜଡଭରତ, *n.* a stupid person; an idiot.
ଜଡସଡ, *a.* overcome with shame; contracted, benumbed; damp, wet.
ଜଡା, *n.* the castor oil tree and its seed;—*a.* dumb.
ଜଡାଉ, *a.* overlaid, plated.
ଜଡାଜଡି, *n.* an embracing, a uniting.
ଜଡାତେଲ, *n.* castor oil.
ଜଡି, *n.* a medicinal root.
ଜଡିତ, *a.* studded, set with.
ଜଡିବା, *v.i.* to mix up, to unite.
ଜଡିବୁଟି, *n.* medicinal roots.
* ଜଡିମା, *n.* stupefaction, numbness.
ଜଡୀଭୂତ, *a.* frozen, congealed; benumbed.
ଜଣ, *n.* a person, an individual.
ଜଣକେତେ, *n.* a small company of people.
ଜଣା, *a.* known, acquainted with.
ଜଣାଇବା, *v.* to make known.
ଜଣାଜଣି, *n.* mutual acquaintance.
ଜଣାଣ, *n.* making known, a supplication.
ଜଣାଶୁଣା, *a.* known and heard, well [known.
ଜଣେ, *n.* one person, an individual.
ଜଣେଜଣେ, *ad.* individually.
* ଜତୁ, *n.* shellac, sealing-wax (see [ଜଉ).
ଜଦାଜଦ, *n.* the act of testing the weight.
ଜଦବା, *v.* to take dimensions of, to measure.
ଜନ, *n.* a person, a man.
ଜନକ, *n.* a father; the name of a king;–*a.* producing, begetting.
* ଜନକତନୟା, *n.* *Sitá*, daughter of ଜନକ.
ଜନତା, *n.* a multitude, a crowd.
ଜନନୀ, *n.* a mother.
ଜନନେନ୍ଦ୍ରିୟ, *n.* the male organ of generation, the *penis.*
ଜନପଦ, *n.* any inhabited country.
ଜନପ୍ରବାଦ, *n.* popular report, rumour.

ଜନପ୍ରିୟ, *a.* popular, generally esteemed. [port.

ଜନରବ, *n.* a rumour, common re-

* ଜନଲୋକ, *n.* one of the seven heavens of Hindus.

* ଜନଶ୍ରୁତି, *n.* a rumour, town-talk.

ଜନସମ୍ମର୍ଦ୍ଦ, *n.* a crowd, a multitude.

ଜନସାଧାରଣ, *n.* common people.

ଜନାନା, *n.* a seraglio; a woman.

ଜନାପବାଦ, *n.* popular reproach, slander.

* ଜନାର୍ଦ୍ଦନ, *n.* a name of *Krushna.*

* ଜନାନ୍ତିକ, *n.* speaking aside, secret communication.

ଜନାଶ୍ରୟ, *n.* a place of shelter.

ଜନିତ, *a.* in *Comp.* it signifies born, produced, caused.

ଜନ୍ତା, *n.* a spout, a watercourse.

ଜନ୍ତାଜନ୍ତି, *n.* people crowding or pressing.

ଜନ୍ତୁ, *n.* an animal.

ଜନ୍ମ, *n.* birth, production.

ଜନ୍ମଗତ, *a.* natural, hereditary.

ଜନ୍ମଦିନ, *n.* a birthday.

ଜନ୍ମପତ୍ରିକା, *n.* a horoscope, a nativity.

ଜନ୍ମଭୂମି, *n.* a birthplace; mother-country. [produce.

ଜନ୍ମାଇବା, *v.* to beget, to bring forth,

ଜନ୍ମାନ୍ତର, *n.* a future birth, another birth.

* ଜନ୍ମାନ୍ତରୀଣ, *a.* belonging to another state of existence.

ଜନ୍ମାନ୍ଧ, *a.* born blind.

ଜନ୍ମାଷ୍ଟମୀ, *n.* *Krushna's* birthday.

ଜନ୍ମିବା, *v.* to come into being, to grow.

ଜନ୍ଦା, *n.* the large black ant. [nally.

ଜପ, *n.* muttering, repeating inter-

* ଜପବଟୀ, *n.* prayer-beads.

ଜପମାଳା, ଜପାମାଳା, *n.* a rosary, a *málá.*

ଜପିବା, *v.* to mutter, to repeat silently.

ଜବତ, ଜବ୍ତ, *a.* confiscate, forfeit.

ଜବର, *a.* powerful, strong.

ଜବରଦସ୍ତ, *a.* forcible, powerful, supreme, predominating.

ଜବରଦସ୍ତି, *n.* force, compulsion;—*ad.* forcibly, powerfully.

ଜବାନ୍, *n.* the tongue, speech.

ଜବାନବନ୍ଦି, *n.* a written deposition.

ଜବାନୀ, *a.* oral.

ଜବାବ, *n.* an answer, a reply.

ଜବାବ୍‌ଦେହୀ, *n.* responsibility.

ଜମିବା, ଜମିଯିବା, *v.* to congeal, to coagulate; to be gathered together.

ଜମା, *n.* a total, collection; a capital sum, a fund;—*a.* collected.

ଜମାଇବା, *v.* to collect; to freeze.

ଜମାଖର୍ଚ୍ଚ, *n.* income and expenditure.

ଜମାଟ, *n.* a crowd; coagulation, cement.

ଜମାଦାର, *n.* a head constable; a conservancy overseer.

ଜମାବନ୍ଦି, *n.* a settlement or account of the revenues of a district, rent of a farm.

ଜମି, *n.* land.

ଜମିଦାର, *n.* a landlord, a landholder.

ଜମିଦାରି, *n.* an estate.

* ଜମ୍ବାଲ, *n.* mud, sludge, clay.

* ଜମ୍ବୀର, ଜମ୍ବୀର, *n.* a lime or lemon.

* ଜମ୍ବୁ, *n.* the rose-apple; Hindusthan.

* ଜମ୍ବୁକ, ଜମ୍ବୂକ, *n.* a jackal.

* ଜମ୍ବୁଦ୍ୱୀପ, *n.* central division of the earth; India. [hail !

ଜୟ, *n.* conquest, victory ;—*interj.*

ଜୟଜୟକାର, *n.* the act of cheering on account of victory, etc.

ଜୟଢକ୍କା, *n.* a kind of drum beaten as a sign of victory.

* ଜୟତ୍ରୀ, *n.* mace (spice).

ଜୟଧ୍ୱନି, *n.* a shout or cry of victory.

ଜୟନ୍ତୀ, *n.* name of a tree; * *Doorgá.*

ଜୟପତାକା, *n.* the flag of victory.

ଜୟପାଲ, *n.* the croton tree.

ଜୟମଙ୍ଗଳ *n.* a fever medicine.

* ଜୟା, *n.* *Doorgá, Parbáti.*

ଜୟୀ, *a.* victorious;—*n.* victor.

ଜର, *n.* fever.

* ଜରତୀ, *n.* a decrepit old woman.

* ଜରଦ୍ଗବ *n.* an old bull or bullock.

ଜରଗଣ୍ଡା, *n.* a kind of sore on the lips caused by fever.

ଜରା, *n.* old age, infirmity, decay.

ଜରାଗ୍ରସ୍ତ, ଜରାଜୀର୍ଣ୍ଣ, *a.* decayed, debilitated, worn out.

ଜରାଗ୍ରସ୍ତା, *n.* decrepitude.

ଜରାତୁର, *a.* decrepit, old, infirm.

ଜରାୟୁ, *n.* the womb, uterus.

ଜରାୟୁଜ, *a.* born from the womb, viviparous.

ଜରିପାଗ, *n.* a turban ornamented with tinsel.

ଜରି, *n.* tinsel; the name of a tree.

ଜରିପ, *n.* the measuring of land, land-surveying.

ଜରିମାନା, *n.* a fine, damage.

ଜରୁର, *a.* urgent, important.

ଜରୁରି, *n.* urgency, importance.

ଜର୍ଜର, *a.* perforated, shaken, shattered; decrepit.

ଜର୍ଜରିତ, *a.* shattered, shaken, rent, torn, tattered, cracked.

ଜଲ, *n.* water.

ଜଲକର, *n.* water-rent, irrigation revenue. [water.

ଜଲକଷ୍ଟ, *n.* drought, scarcity of

ଜଲକା, *a.* not clear-sighted.

* ଜଲକାକ, *n.* the water-crow, a diver.

ଜଲକ୍ରୀଡ଼ା, *n.* playing in water.

ଜଲଖିଆ, *n.* light refreshment, luncheon. [bog.

ଜଲଗଣ୍ଡ, *n.* a swamp, marsh, fen,

ଜଲଚର, *ଜଲଚ୍ଚର, *a.* aquatic (animal).

ଜଲଛତ୍ର, *n.* a place where water is given to drink.

ଜଳଜ, *a.* produced in or from water;—*n.* the lotus.

ଜଳଜନ୍ତୁ, *n.* an aquatic animal.

ଜଳଜଳ, *a.* bright, glistening.

ଜଳଜଳା, *a.* shameless, immodest.

ଜଳତରଙ୍ଗ, *n.* a wave.

* ଜଳଦ, *n.* a cloud;—*a.* giving water.

* ଜଳଦାଗମ, *n.* the rainy season.

* ଜଳଧର, *n.* a cloud; the sea.

* ଜଳଧି, ଜଳନିଧି, *n.* the ocean.

ଜଳନିର୍ଗମ, ଜଳନାଳୀ, *n.* a watercourse or drain.

ଜଳପଥ, *n.* a way by water; an outlet for water.

ଜଳପାତ୍ର, *n.* a water-vessel.

ଜଳପାନ, *n.* refreshment; drinking of water.

ଜଳପ୍ରପାତ, *n.* a cataract, a waterfall.

ଜଳପ୍ଲାବନ, *n.* a deluge, an inundation.

ଜଳପ୍ଲାବିତ, *a.* inundated, flooded.

ଜଳବତ୍, *a.* liquid; limpid.

* ଜଳବାୟସ, *n.* the water-crow (see ଜଳକାକ).

ଜଳବାୟୁ, *n.* climate.

ଜଳବିନ୍ଦୁ, *n.* drop of water.

ଜଳବୁଦ୍‌ବୁଦ, *n.* a bubble.

* ଜଳବେଣୀ, *n.* a stream, current, torrent.

ଜଳମଗ୍ନ, *a.* immersed in water; drowned.

ଜଳମୟ, *a.* watery, full of water.

* ଜଳମାର୍ଜାର, *n.* an otter.

ଜଳଯନ୍ତ୍ର, *n.* stone vessels containing water and placed under the feet of almirahs to keep ants out; a machine for raising water, a water-mill.

* ଜଳଯାନ, *n.* a ship, a steamer.

ଜଳଯୋଗ, *n.* a slight repast, refreshment (see ଜଳଖିଆ).

* ଜଳସ୍ତମ୍ଭ, *n.* waterspout.

ଜଳା, *a.* watery, marshy;—*n.* burning.

ଜଳାଦବାଟୀ, *n.* a window.

ଜଳାଙ୍ଗ, *n.* (in *Geog.*) watershed.

ଜଳାଞ୍ଜଳି, *n.* an oblation of water.

ଜଳାଞ୍ଜଳିଦେବା, *v.* to give up, to relinquish; to offer oblation of water to gods or ancestors.

ଜଳାଧାର, *n.* a pond, a receptacle for water.

ଜଳାପୋଡ଼ା, *n.* a burning or smarting pain.

* ଜଳାବର୍ତ୍ତ, *n.* an eddy, a whirlpool.

ଜଳାମୁହଁ, *n.* a spout or drain.

* ଜଳାର୍ଦ୍ର, *a.* wet, moist.

ଜଳାର୍ଣ୍ଣବ, *n.* a wide expanse of water caused by rain or flood.

ଜଳାଶୟ, *n.* a reservoir of water.

ଜଳିବା, *v.* to burn.

ଜଲିବୋଟ୍, *n.* a jolly-boat.

ଜଳୋଚ୍ଛ୍ୱାସ, *n.* overflow, flood, wave, excess of water.

ଜଳୋଦର, *n.* the dropsy.

ଜଳୋଦରସ୍ତ, *a.* dropsical;—*n.* the dropsy.

*ଜଲୌକା, *n.* a leech.
ଜଲ୍ଦ, *ad.* quickly, soon, hastily.
* ଜଲ୍ପ, ଜଳ୍ପନା, *n.* chat, gossip, wrangling.
ଜହର, *n.* poison, venom.
ଜହରମହୁର, ଜହରମହୁରା, *n.* bezoar, an antidote to poison.
ଜହୁରୀ, ଜେହୁରୀ, *n.* a dealer in precious stones, a jeweller.
ଜହ୍ନ, *n.* moonlight, moonbeams.
ଜହ୍ନିପୋକ, *n.* a firefly, glow-worm.
ଜହ୍ନୀ, *n.* name of a vegetable.
ଜା, *n.* a husband's brother's wife.
ଜାଅଳ, *n.* fish spawn, young fish.
ଜାଇ, *n.* split pulse; a kind of flower.
ଜାଇଫୀ, *n.* mace (spice).
ଜାଇଫଳ, *n.* the nutmeg.
ଜାଇଫୁଲ, *n.* a kind of small white sweet-smelling flower.
ଜାଉ, *n.* rice overboiled, gruel.
ଜାକଜମକ, *n.* pomp, parade.
ଜାଁତି, *n.* a betel-nut cutter.
ଜାକ, *n.* a crowd; a tightening;—*a.* narrow.
ଜାକିବା, *v.* to crowd, to press, to tighten.
ଜାକୁଅ, *a.* tight, fast; crowded; narrow.
ଜାଗର, *n.* a night festival in honour of *Shiva.*
ଜାଗରଣ, *n.* the circumstance of waking.
ଜାଗରୂକ, *a.* wakeful, vigilant.
ଜାଗରୁକ, *a.* keeping awake, wakeful.

ଜାଗା, *n.* a place, room; land.
ଜାଗିବା, *v.* to awake, to keep guard.
ଜାଗିର, *n.* a grant of land for special service.
ଜାଗିରଦାର, *n.* a person who holds a ଜାଗିର.
ଜାଗ୍ରତ, *a.* awake, roused, alert.
* ଜାଙ୍ଗଲିକ, ଜାଙ୍ଗୁଳିକ, *n.* a snake-charmer.
ଜାଜ୍ଜ୍ୱଲ୍ୟମାନ, *a.* refulgent, shining, prosperous.
ଜାଡ, *n.* cold, frost, cold season, the winter.
* ଜାଡ୍ୟ, *n.* apathy, stupidity, folly.
ଜାଣପଶୁ, *n.* a knowing or intelligent animal.
ଜାଣିବା, *v.* to know, to be informed of.
ଜାତ, *a.* born, produced, begotten.
ଜାତକ, *n.* a horoscope.
ଜାତକର୍ମ *n.* a ceremony at the birth of a child.
* ଜାତାନ୍ଧ, *a.* born blind (see ଜନ୍ମାନ୍ଧ).
* ଜାତାପତ୍ୟା, *n.* a mother.
ଜାତି, *n.* a nation, tribe, caste; kind.
ଜାତିଆ, *a.* of good caste, noble, well-born; kindred.
ଜାତିଚାର, *n.* a caste ceremony.
ଜାତିଚ୍ୟୁତ, *a.* fallen from caste, outcasted.
ଜାତିଧର୍ମ, *n.* the duties of caste.
ଜାତିଧ୍ୱଂସ, *n.* destruction of caste.
ଜାତିପାଂକ୍ତ, *n.* all of one caste.
ଜାତିଭାଇ, ଜାତିଭାଇ, *n.* one belonging to the same caste, a kinsman.

* ଜାଇ, *n.* mace; the *málti* flower.

* ଜାଇଫଳ, *n.* the nutmeg (see ଜାଠିଫଳ).

ଜାତୀୟ, *a.* pertaining to caste, national, racial.

ଜାଦୁ, *n.* ringworm; sorcery, magic.

ଜାଦୁଗର, *n.* a magician, sorcerer.

ଜାଦୁଆ, *n.* one having ringworm ; —*a.* having ringworm.

ଜାଦୁଗିରି, *n.* the arts of sorcery, magic.

ଜାନ୍, *n.* life, soul.

* ଜାନକୀ, *n.* *Sita* the wife of *Rama.*

ଜାନୁ, *n.* the knee.

ଜାବୁଡ଼ିବା, *v.* to clasp, to embrace, to hug.

ଜାଫ୍ରାନ୍, ଜାଫ୍ରାନ୍‌କେଶର, *n.* saffron.

ଜାବତା, *n.* discipline, control.

ଜାବୁଡ଼ା, *n.* a box on the ear, a slap.

ଜାମଦାନ୍, *n.* a figured cloth.

ଜାମା, *n.* a frock, coat, gown.

ଜାମାତା, *n.* a son-in-law.

ଜାମିନ୍, *n.* bail, security.

ଜାମିନ୍‌ଦାର, *n.* a surety.

ଜାମିନ୍‌ନାମା, *n.* the paper on which a surety is written and signed.

ଜାମିନ୍‌ଭତା, *n.* allowance to a surety.

ଜାମୁ, *n.* name of a tree and its fruit.

ଜାୟ, ଜାୟଦାଦ, *n.* goods, chattels, assets.

* ଜାୟା, *n* a wife.

* ଜାୟାପତି, *n.* a man and wife.

* ଜାର, *n.* a paramour, a gallant.

* ଜାରକ, *a.* dissolving; digestive.

ଜାରଜ, *a.* illegitimate;—*n.* a bastard.

ଜାରଣ, *n.* a dissolving or digesting.

ଜାରମଣ୍ଡପ, *n.* see ଜରମଣ୍ଡପ.

ଜାରିବା, *v.* to calcine drugs.

ଜାରି, *a.* put in force.

ଜାଳ, *n.* firewood.

ଜାଳା, *n.* trouble, disorder; inflamation.

ଜାଳିବା, *v.* to kindle, to light a lamp, etc.

ଜାଲ୍, *n.* forgery.

ଜାଲ୍‌ଖତ, *n.* a forged letter or bond.

ଜାଲ, *n.* a net, a web, a snare.

ଜାଲଜାଲିଆ, *a.* dim, dim-sighted; net-like.

ଜାଲପାଦ, *a.* web-footed.

ଜାଲସାଜି, *n.* forgery.

ଜାଲିଆ, *n.* a fisherman.

ଜାଲି, ଜାଲିକାମ, *n.* a fringe, network.

ଜାଲିଚଟୁ, *n.* a perforated iron ladle (for straining and lifting up sweetmeats from the boiling *ghee*).

ଜାହାଜ, *n.* a ship, a sailing vessel.

ଜାହାଜିଆ, ଜାହାଜୀ, *n.* a sailor.

ଜାହାଜୀ, *a.* pertaining to a ship ;—*n.* a sailor.

ଜାହାଲ, *n.* a large water vessel, a large jar.

* ଜାହ୍ନବୀ, *n.* the Ganges personified.

ଝପଲ, *n.* a small live fish used as bait; an iron staple on a plough through which the share passes.

ଜିଆ, *n.* a worm, earthworm.

ଜିଆଦା, *a.* more, more than enough, excessive.

ଜିକଜିକ, *a.* shining, sparkling.

ଜିଗର. *n.* teasing, importunity.

ଜିଗରଦାର, *n.* a teaser, a tormentor.

* ଜିଗୀଷା, *n.* emulation, rivalry, envy.

* ଜିଗୀଷୁ, *a.* desirous of c^nquest.

* ଜିଘାଂସା, *n.* malice, revenge, rancour.

* ଜିଘାଂସୁ, *a.* revengeful, malicious.

ଜିଜ୍ୟା, *n.* a capitation tax levied by Muhammadans on non-Muhammadans.

ଜିଜ୍ଞାସା, *n.* a question, query, an enquiry.

ଜିଜ୍ଞାସିତ, *a.* asked, enquired after.

* ଜିଜ୍ଞାସୁ, *a.* inquisitive, desirous to know.

ଜିଜ୍ଞାସ୍ୟ, *a.* worthy of enquiry. .

ଜିଞ୍ଜୀର, *n.* a chain, fetters (see ଜଞ୍ଜୀର).

ଜିଣନ୍ତା, *a.* victorious, conquering.

ଜିଣିବା, *v.* to conquer, to subdue, to win.

* ଜିତ, *a.* conquered, subdued.

* ଜିତାହାର, *a.* of subdued appetite.

ଜିତିବା, *v.* to win, to conquer (see ଜିଣିବା).

ଜିତେନ୍ଦ୍ରିୟ, *a.* of subdued passions.

ଜିଦ୍, *n.* pertinacity, obstinacy, vexation.

ଜିଦ୍‌କରିବା, *v.* to insist, to persist.

ଜିଦ୍‌ମାରିବା, *v.* to make a bet, to stake.

ଜିଦାଜିଦ୍, *n.* rivalry, emulation, strife, betting.

ଜିନ୍, ଜୀନ୍, *n.* a saddle.

ଜିନ, *n.* a *Jain* sage.

ଜିନିଷ, *n.* a thing; goods.

ଜିଭି, *n.* a tongue-scraper.

ଜିଭ, *n.* the tongue.

ଜିଭଛେଲା, ଜିଭି, *n.* see ଜିଭି.

ଜିମା, *n.* custody, charge, care.

ଜିଲଦ୍, *n.* the cover of a book.

ଜିଲା, ଜିଲ୍ଲା, *n.* a district, a province.

ଜିଲାଦାର, *n.* zilladar.

ଜିଲାବନ୍ଦୀ, *n.* a settlement of the revenue and expenditure of a district.

ଜିଲେପି, *n.* a kind of sweetmeat.

* ଜିହ୍ୱା, *n.* the tongue.

ଜିହ୍ୱାମୂଳୀୟ, *a.* (in *Gram.*) guttural (see କଣ୍ଠ୍ୟ).

ଜୀଅନ୍ତା, *a.* living, being alive.

ଜୀଆଇବା, *v.* to animate, to revive, to give life.

ଜୀଇବା, *v.* to live, to be alive.

ଜୀବ, *n.* life, soul; a living being.

ଜୀବଜନ୍ତୁ, *n. pl.* living creatures.

ଜୀବନ୍ତ, *a.* living, alive, extant.

ଜୀବଦଶା, *n.* lifetime, season of life.

ଜୀବଧନ, *n.* an object of affection.

ଜୀବନ, *n.* life, existence, living; * water.

ଜୀବନଯାତ୍ରା, *n.* livelihood.

ଜୀବନାବଧି, *ad.* during life.

ଜୀବନୋପାୟ, *n.* livelihood, mode of subsistence, method of preserving life.

ଜୀବନ୍ୟାସ, *n.* a giving of life to an idol.

ଜୀବନ୍ତ, *a.* alive, living.

ଜୀବନ୍ମୁକ୍ତ, *a.* having obtained final liberation while yet alive.

ଜୀବନ୍ମୃତ, *a.* dead while living.

ଜୀବଲୋକ, *n.* men; land of the living.

ଜୀବହତ୍ୟା, *n.* the taking of life, murder.

ଜୀବହୀନ, *a.* without life, dead.

* ଜୀବାତୁ, *n.* a livelihood.

ଜୀବାତ୍ମା, *n.* living principle, the soul.

* ଜୀବାନ୍ତକ, *n.* *Jama*, destroyer of life.

ଜୀବିକା, ଜୀବିକାନିର୍ବାହ, *n.* a livelihood, maintenance.

ଜୀବିତ, *a.* living, alive;—*n.* * life.

ଜୀବିତକାଳ, *n.* the period of life.

* ଜୀବିତେଶ, ଜୀବେଶ, *n.* husband, lord of life.

ଜୀବୀ, *a.* living (only in *Comp.*)

* ଜୀମୂତ, *n.* a cloud, clouds.

ଜୀର. * ଜୀରକ, *n.* an aromatic seed used in curry and medicine, cummin seed.

ଜୀର୍ଣ୍ଣ, *a.* digested; worn out, decayed, old.

ଜୀର୍ଣ୍ଣବସ୍ତ୍ର, *n.* worn-out clothes.

* ଜୀର୍ଣ୍ଣସଂସ୍କାର, *n.* the repairing of a decayed thing, mending.

* ଜୀର୍ଣ୍ଣୋଦ୍ଧାର, *n.* repairing, renewal.

ଜୁଅଁର, *n.* a son-in-law.

ଜୁଆ, *n.* gambling.

ଜୁଆଙ୍ଗ, *n.* name of a jungle tribe.

ଜୁଆଚୋର, *n.* a cheat, a sharper, a knave.

ଜୁଆଚୋରି, *n.* the practice of cheating, knavery.

ଜୁଆଣୀ, *n.* a small spice-seed.

ଜୁଆର, *n.* the flood-tide.

ଜୁଆରିଆ, *a.* tidal, brought in by the tide.

ଜୁଆଡ଼ି, *n.* a gambler.

ଜୁଆଳି, *n.* a yoke (for bullock's neck.)

ଜୁଈ, *n.* a jasmine.

* ଜୁଗୁପ୍ସା, *n.* a reproach, vituperation.

ଜୁଡ଼ା, *n.* the hair tied in a knot.

ଜୁଣ, *n.* a kind of rush.

ଜୋତା, *n.* a shoe, slipper, boot.

ଜୁଳୁଜୁଳିପୋକ, *n.* a fire-fly.

ଜୁଳୁଜୁଳୁ, *n.* sorrowful peeps or glances.

ଜୁଲମ୍. *n.* violence, tyranny, fierceness.

ଜୁଲାବ, *n.* any aperient medicine.

ଜୁହାର, *n.* salutation (joining the two hands).

ଜୁହାରିବା, *v.* to salute (by joining the two hands).

ଜୁଟାଇବା, ଜୁଟେଇବା, *v.* to cause to reach, meet or arrive.

ଜୁଟିବା, *v.* to reach, to meet, to arrive.

ଜର, *a.* spoiled, destroyed, ruined.

ଜୁଦା, *a.* separate, distinct.

* ଜୃମ୍ଭା, *n.* a yawn, gaping.

ଜେଝୁଟ, *n.* an edible fruit used in curry.
ଜେଠପା, ଜେଠା, ଜେଠୁଭା, *n.* father's elder brother.
ଜେଠାଈ, *n.* wife of father's elder brother.
ଜେଭଶୁର, ଦେଭଶୁର, *n.* husband's elder brother.
ଜେଉଭାଶୁର, ଜେଠାଶୁର, *n.* kusband's father's elder brother.
* ଜେତା, *n.* a conqueror.
ଜେନା, *n.* title of a caste.
ଜେନାମଣି, *n.* a king's son, a prince.
ଜେବ୍, *n.* a pocket. [daughter.
ଜେମା, ଜେମାଦେଈ, *n.* a king's
* ଜେୟ, *a.* conquerable.
ଜେର, *n.* cross-examination.
ଜେଲ୍, ଜେଲ୍‌ଖାନା, *n.* a prison, jail.
ଜେଲ୍ ଘଟିବା, *v.* to suffer imprison-
ଜେଲ୍ ଦାରୋଗା, *n.* a jailer. [ment.
* ଜୈତ୍ର, *a.* victorious, leading to victory. [ଜାଇଫଳ).
* ଜୈତ୍ରୀ, *n.* an aromatic spice (see
ଜୈନ, *n.* one of the *Jain* sect.
ଜୈପାଳ, *n.* the croton tree.
ଜୋକ, *n.* a leech.
ଜୋଖିବା, *v.* to join, to unite; to yoke.
ଜୋଗାଡ଼, *n.* endeavour, attempt, arrangement; preparation of food. [cooking.
ଜୋଗାଡ଼ିବା, *v.* to prepare food for
ଜୋତା, *n.* shoes, sandals (see ଜୁତା).
ଜୋର, *n.* force, compulsion.

ଜୋର, ଜୋଡ଼, *n.* a small stream.
* ଜୋଷା, *n.* a woman.
ଜୌ, *n.* lac, gum-lac.
ଜ୍ଞ, a *suffix* indicating knowing, perceiving.
ଜ୍ଞାତ, *a.* aware, informed, known.
ଜ୍ଞାତବ୍ୟ, *a.* knowable.
ଜ୍ଞାତସାରରେ, ଜ୍ଞାତସାରେ, *ad.* knowingly, intentionally.
* ଜ୍ଞାତା, *n.* one who knows.
ଜ୍ଞାତି, *n.* a relative, a kinsman.
ଜ୍ଞାନ, *n.* knowledge, wisdom.
ଜ୍ଞାନକୃତ, *a.* done knowingly or intentionally.
* ଜ୍ଞାନତଃ, *ad.* knowingly. [ally.
ଜ୍ଞାନପୂର୍ବକ, *ad.* knowingly, intention-
ଜ୍ଞାନବାନ୍, ଜ୍ଞାନୀ, *a.* wise, intelligent.
ଜ୍ଞାନେନ୍ଦ୍ରିୟ, *n.* organs of perception.
ଜ୍ଞାନୋଦୟ, *n.* the rise of knowledge.
ଜ୍ଞାପକ, *n.* one who makes known; —*a.* making known, informing.
* ଜ୍ଞାପନ, *n.* the making known.
ଜ୍ଞାପିତ, *a.* notified, revealed, discovered.
* ଜ୍ଞେୟ, *a.* knowable, cognizable.
ଜ୍ୟା, *n.* the cord of an arc, *a bow-string.
ଜ୍ୟାମିତି, *n.* geometry.
ଜ୍ୟାମିତିକ, *a.* geometric, geometrical.
ଜ୍ୟେଷ୍ଠ, *a.* elder, eldest, firstborn; chief; name of a month—the part of May and June.

* ଜ୍ୟେଷ୍ଠତାତ, *n.* father's elder brother.

ଜ୍ୟେଷ୍ଠତ୍ୱ, *n.* primogeniture, seniority.

* ଜ୍ୟେଷ୍ଠମାତା, *n.* wife of father's elder brother.

ଜ୍ୟେଷ୍ଠା, *n.* the 18th stellar mansion.

ଜ୍ୟେଷ୍ଠାଂଶ, ଜ୍ୟେଷ୍ଠା, *n.* the right of the eldest brother to a larger share of the patrimonial property.

ଜ୍ୟୋତିଃ, *n.* light, a luminous body.

ଜ୍ୟୋତିଃଶାସ୍ତ୍ର, ଜ୍ୟୋତିର୍ବିଦ୍ୟା, *n.* the science of astronomy or astrology.

*ଜ୍ୟୋତିର୍ବିଦ୍, ଜ୍ୟୋତିର୍ବେତ୍ତା, *n.* an astronomer, an astrologer.

ଜ୍ୟୋତିର୍ମୟ, *a.* luminous, bright; consisting of stars, starry.

* ଜ୍ୟୋତିଶ୍ଚକ୍ର, *n.* the zodiac.

ଜ୍ୟୋତିଷ, *n.* astronomy, astrology.

ଜ୍ୟୋତିଷ, * ଜ୍ୟୋତିଷିକ, * ଜ୍ୟୌତିଷିକ, *n.* an astronomer, an astrologer.

*ଜ୍ୟୋତିଷିକ, *a.* astronomical, astrological.

*ଜ୍ୟୋତିଷ୍କ, *n.* the planetary or heavenly bodies.

ଜ୍ୟୋତ୍ସ୍ନା, *n.* moonlight.

ଜ୍ୱର, *n.* fever.

ଜ୍ୱରଘ୍ନ, ଜ୍ୱରନାଶକ, *a.* febrifuge, mitigating fever, anti-febrile.

ଜ୍ୱରାତିସାର, *n.* a fever and flux.

* ଜ୍ୱଳନ, *n.* burning, smarting; shining, being lighted.

ଜ୍ୱଳନୀୟ, *a.* combustible, inflammable.

ଜ୍ୱଳନ୍ତ, *a.* burning, inflamed, on fire.

ଜ୍ୱାଳା, *n.* inflammation, burning.

*ଜ୍ୱାଳିତ *a.* inflamed, burnt; vexed.

ଝ.

ଝ, the ninth consonant.

ଝକଝକ, ଝକଝକିଆ, *a.* luminous, shining.

ଝକମକ, ଝକମକ ପଥର, *n.* a flint (see ଚକମକ).

ଝକ୍ମାରିବା, *v.* to acknowledge fault; to suffer or get into trouble.

ଝଗଡ଼ା, ଝଗଡ଼, *n.* a quarrel, squabble.

ଝଙ୍କା, ଝଙ୍କାଝଙ୍କା, *a.* extended, widely spread.

ଝଙ୍କାଲୋର, *a.* laden (as trees with fruit or blossom); dead drunk.

ଝଙ୍କାର, *n.* a low murmuring sound, buzzing.

ଝଞ୍ଜଟ, ଝଞ୍ଝଟ, *n.* perplexity, vexation.

ଝଞ୍ଜା, ଝଞ୍ଝା, *n.* hot winds; a storm, tempest.

ଝଟ, ଝଟ୍‌ପଟ, *ad.* quickly, speedily.

ଝଟକ, *n.* beauty, brilliancy.

ଝଟକବିଜୁଳି, *n.* forked lightning.

ଝଟକିବା, *v.* to shine, to dazzle, to look bright.

ଝଟଝଟ, *a.* dazzling as lightning; —*ad.* more rapidly.

ଝଟଝଟିଆ, *n.* the early morning.

ଝଟା, *n.* dead or dried branch of a tree; a broom.

ଝଟାପଟା, ଝଟାପଟି, *n.* grappling, struggling, quarrelling.

ଝଟିକା, *n.* fog; strong wind, tempest.

ଝଟିତ, *ad.* quickly, speedily, apace (see ଝଟ୍).

ଝଡ, ଝଡ଼, *n.* continuous rain; a storm, a tempest.

ଝଡା, *n.* sweeping, cleansing; shaking, dusting;—*a.* swept, cleansed; dropped down (from a tree, etc.).

ଝଡପୋକ, ଝଡ଼ପୋକ, *n.* flying white [ants.

ଝଡିବା, *v.* to fall, to drop down.

ଝଣ୍ଝାର, *n.* clanking of chains or metals.

ଝଣଝଣ, *n.* a clanking sound.

ଝଟ୍, ଝଟ୍‌ଝଟ୍, *ad.* speedily, hastily.

ଝପଟ, *n.* running, scampering.

ଝପଟାଝପଟି, *n.* a general running or scampering.

ଝମ୍ପ, ଝ ମ୍ପ, *n.* a jump, leap, spring.

ଝର, ଝରଣା, *n.* a cascade, a waterfall, a springing of water.

ଝରକା, *n.* a window.

ଝରଝର, ଝର୍ଝର, *n.* a dropping sound.

* ଝର୍ଝରୀ, *n.* a cymbal.

ଝଲ, *n.* a gold or silver tassel.

ଝଲାଇବା, *v.* to cause to drip, ooze or fall.

ଝର, *n.* a kind of brass water vessel.

ଝରିବା, *v.* to drip, ooze, fall.

ଝଲକମାରିବା, *v.* to dazzle the sight.

ଝଲକିବା, *v.* to glisten; to spring up, to bubble up.

ଝଲଝଲ, *a.* dangling, flapping.

ଝଲମଲ, *a.* pellucid, glistening.

* ଝଷ, *n.* fish, a fish.

* ଝଷକେତନ, *n.* cupid.

ଝାଁଉ, *a.* burnt to a cinder.

ଝାଉଁ, *n.* a species of pine tree (*tamarix indicus*).

ଝାଉଁଳିବା, *v.* to languish or droop.

ଝାଙ୍କ, *n.* a flock (of birds), a swarm (of fish).

ଝାଙ୍କିବା, *v.* to peep.

ଝାଞ୍ଜ, *n.* cymbals.

ଝାଞ୍ଜି, ଝାଞ୍ଜୀ, *n.* hot winds.

ଝାଞ୍ଜିରି, *n.* an iron grating for fire-place.

ଝାଟି, *n.* brushwood, peasticks (see [ଝଟା).

ଝାଟୁଅ, *n.* sweepings ; a broom, a brush.

ଝାଟେଇବା, *v.* to sweep.

ଝାଡ, *n.* a chandelier; a tree, a shrub.

ଝାଡଣ, *n.* a duster, a towel.

ଝାଡା, *n.* evacuation of the bowels, stool, diarrhœa.

ଝାଡାବଉ, ଝାଡାବାନ୍ତି, *n.* cholera (evacuating and vomiting).

ଝାଡିବା, *v.* to dust; shake; sweep; to exorcise.

ଝାଡି, *n.* a thicket, low jungle.

ଝାଡୁ, *n.* a broom, besom.

ଝାଡୁବରଦାର, *n.* a sweeper, a *mehtar*.

ଝାପ୍ସା, *n.* a film on the eye, dimness.

ଝାମ୍ପ, *n.* a leap, a swoop down.

ଝାଞ୍ଜି, *n.* a palm-leaf hat worn by field workers. [down.
ଝାମ୍ପିବା, *v.* to jump, to swoop
ଝାଳ, *n.* sweat, perspiration.
ଝାଲ, ଝାଲୁଆ, *a.* pungent, hot.
ଝାଲର, *n.* a fringe, edging, frill.
ଝାସ, *n.* a plunge into fire or water with the object of taking or sacrificing one's life.
ଝିଅ, *n.* a daughter.
ଝିଅଣ୍ଡ, *n.* a niece.
ଝିଙ୍କ, *n.* a noisy kind of cricket.
ଝିକର, *n.* tiles; pieces of broken pots, etc. [a fire-place.
ଝିକା, *n.* the knobs or elevations on
ଝିକାଓଟରା, *n.* a pulling and snatch-
ଝିଙ୍କାରି, *n.* a noisy cricket. [ing.
ଝିଙ୍କିବା, *v.* to snatch, to jerk, to haul.
ଝିଞ୍ଜାଇବା, *v.* to spoil by tearing or boring (used only of insects).
ଝିଟିପିଟି, *n.* the house lizard.
ଝିଣ୍ଟିକା. *n.* a grasshopper.
ଝିଣଝିଣ, *n.* sound of metals.
ଝିପିଝିପି, *n.* flying showers. [limb.
ଝିମିଝିମି, *n.* a tingling sensation in a
ଝିପିଟ, *n.* a moment, a short time.
ଝିଲ, *n.* a shallow lake, a swamp, a jheel.
ଝିଲିମିଲି, *n.* venetians; vivid light.
ଝିଲ୍ଲୀ, *n.* a noisy shrill grasshopper; a membrane.
ଝୁଅ, *n.* a daughter.

ଝୁଙ୍କ, *n.* intoxication; drunkenness; whim. [ing.
ଝୁଙ୍କାଝୁଙ୍କି, *n.* a staggering or totter-
ଝୁଙ୍କିବା *v.* to drop the head forward as in dosing, to lean; to be intoxicated.
ଝୁଙ୍କା, *a.* whimsical;—*n.* responsibility, liability. [*sál* tree.
ଝୁଣା, *n.* resin obtained from the
ଝୁଣିବା, *v.* to devour, to bite, to gnaw.
ଝୁଣ୍ଟା *n.* a mode of prohibition during an appeal to higher autho-
ଝୁଣ୍ଟିଆ, *n.* a ring for the toes. [rity.
ଝୁଣ୍ଟିବା, *v.* to stumble, to trip.
ଝୁଟ, *a.* false.
ଝୁଠା, *n.* a lie; a liar; orts, refuse.
ଝୁପୁଡ଼ି, *n.* cabin, hut, shed.
ଝୁମ୍କା, *n.* a kind of ear ornament.
ଝୁମୁଝୁମୁ, ଝମଝମ, *n.* a jingling sound.
ଝୁମ୍ପା, *n.* tassels.
ଝୁର, *n.* a crumb, a morsel; the forepart of a bullock-cart.
ଝୁରିବା, *v.* to weep, to lament.
ଝୁଲି, ଝୋଲି, *n.* a spark of fire; soot.
ଝୁଲଣ, *n.* swinging, oscillating.
ଝୁଲଣଯାତ୍ରା, *n.* swinging festival.
ଝୁଲଣା, *n.* a swinging, a hanging pendant; a valuable coloured cloth used for adorning elephants.
ଝୁଲାଇବା, *v.* to cause to swing.

ଝୁଲି *n.* a bag, wallet, satchel.
ଝୁଲିବା, *v.* to swing.
ଝୋଟ, *n.* jute. [vessel.
ଝୋବା, *n.* a small earthen water
ଝୋଳ, *n.* broth, soup.
ଝୋଳିଆ, *n.* juicy or savoury food.
ଝୋଲି, ଝୋଲଣା, *n.* a valuable coloured cloth used for adorning ele- [phants.
ଝୋଲି, ଝୋଲୁ, *n.* see ଝୁଲି.
ଝୋଳମାରିବା, *v.* to fall into a fainting fit, to become unconscious.

ଞ.

ଞ, the tenth consonant: not used as an initial.

ଟ.

ଟ, the eleventh consonant.
ଟକ, *a.* acid, sour;—*n.* acidity.
ଟକଟକ, *n.* a rapping;—*a.* or *ad.* strongly desiring (equal to the English idiom "it made my mouth water".)
ଟକଟକା, ଟକଲା, *n.* a gourmand, a glutton;—*a.* gluttonous, epicurean.
ଟକର, *n.* emulation; a rap, knock.
ଟଙ୍କଶାଳ, *n.* the mint.
ଟଙ୍କା, *n.* a rupee.
ଟଙ୍କାର, *n.* twang of a bowstring.
ଟଙ୍କି, *n.* quit-rent.
ଟଙ୍କିଲ, *a.* stony (ground).
ଟଙ୍ଗାଇବା, *v.* to cause to be hanged or be suspended.
ଟଟ୍ଟୁ, *n.* a small pony.
ଟଣଟଣ, *n.* a throbbing sensation.
ଟଣାଟଣି, *n.* a jerking or pulling.
ଟସଟସ, ଟସଟାସୁ, *ad.* sharply (a thorn or other sharp point piercing the finger, etc.)
ଟପଟପ, ଟପରଟପର, *ad.* with a pattering sound (of rain).
ଟପ୍ପା, *n.* a solo, a glee, a short merry song. [overleap.
ଟପିବା, ଟପିଯିବା, *v.* to transgress, to
ଟଭା, *n.* a kind of lemon.
* ଟମକ, *n.* making known by beat of drum. [ing.
ଟଳଟଳ, ଟଳମଳ, *a.* staggering, reel-
ଟଳାଟଳି, *n.* putting off, temporizing.
ଟଳିବା, *v.* to stagger, to reel, to vacillate. [lating.
ଟହଲ, *n.* walking about, perambu-
ଟହଲିଆ, *n.* one who waits upon another.
ଟହଲିବା, *v.* to wander, perambulate.
ଟା, an *enclitic particle* expressive of superiority or inferiority.
ଟାଣ, *a.* hard, firm, tough.
ଟାଇଲ୍, ଟାଇଲି, *n.* flooring tiles.
ଟାଉଏଲ୍, *n.* a towel (erroneously pronounced ଟୌଲିଆ).
ଟାଉଟାଉ, *ad.* quickly, swiftly, with haste.

ଟାହିର, *n.* a knock on the head with the knuckles.

ଟାହକ, *n.* a sound made by quickly withdrawing the tongue from the palate.

ଟାକିବା, *v.* to watch, to tend, to look out for.

ଟାକୁଆ, *n.* seed-stone of a mango.

ଟାଙ୍କ, ଟାଙ୍କା, *n.* a stitch, stitching, sewing.

ଟାକ, ଟାକୁ, *n.* baldness, loss of hair.

ଟାଙ୍କିବା, *v.* to stitch, to tack together.

ଟାକୁରିବା, *v.* to have one's hair stand on end.

ଟାଙ୍କେ, *n.* one stitch.

ଟାଙ୍ଗଣ, *n.* a hill pony.

ଟାଙ୍ଗଣା, *n.* an article used to polish gold, etc.

ଟାଙ୍ଗର, *n.* rocky ground;—*a.* bald (head).

ଟାଙ୍ଗସ. *n.* baldness; a bald-headed man;—*a.* bald.

ଟାଙ୍ଗିଆ, *n.* a small hatchet.

ଟାଙ୍ଗିବା, *n.* to hang up, to suspend.

ଟାଙ୍ଗୀ, ଟାଙ୍ଗିଆ, *n.* a battle-axe, halberd.

ଟାଟକା, *a.* fresh, new, not stale.

ଟାଟି, *n.* a screen; a privy.

ଟାଣ, *a.* tough, hard, strong.

ଟାଣିବା, *v.* to drag, to pull, to draw.

ଟାଣୁଆ, *a.* strong, tough, astringent.

ଟାପସ, *n.* a gibe, sneer, mockery.

ଟାପୁ. *n.* an island, an isle.

ଟାଳ, *n.* procrastination; dilly-dallying.

ଟାଳଟୁଳ, ଟାଳମଟାଳ, *n.* temporizing, procrastinating.

ଟାଳଦେବା, ଟାଳଆରିବା, ଟାଳିବା, *v.* to put off, to make excuses.

ଟାହୁଲି, *n.* a gibe, a laugh, a sneer.

ଟିଆ; *n.* a species of parrot.

ଟିକର, *n.* a sandbank, an elevation, high-ground.

ଟିକା, *n.* inoculation, vaccination.

ଟିକାୟତ. ଟିକାଏତ, *n.* a prince, king's son.

ଟିକିଆ, *n.* charcoal-dust cakes used to kindle a hooka, etc.

ଟିକିଏ, *a.* little, very little.

ଟିକିଟିକି. *a.* very small, tiny;—*ad.* little by little;—*n.* a house-lizard.

ଟିକିଲି, *n.* a wafer (often worn between eye-brows by women); a postage stamp, etc., a label.

ଟିଙ୍କ, *n.* a tick or small bug.

ଟିଟିଭ, ଟିଟ୍ଟିଭ, *n.* lapwing, peewit.

ଟିଣା, *a.* angry, peevish;—*n.* tin metal, a tin can.

ଟିଣିଟିଣି, *n.* sound of a bell.

ଟିଣ, *n.* tin metal.

ଟିପ, *n.* tips of the fingers.

ଟିପା, ଟିପାଟିପି, *n.* a note or memorandum to help the memory.

ଟିପାଇ, *n.* a teapoy; a forked stick used to prop up a bullock-cart.

ଟିପାଟିପି, *n.* a pinching, a squeezing.
ଟିପ୍ପଣୀ, *n.* a comment.
ଟିପିବା, *v.* to make a note of; to pinch, to press.
ଟିପେ, *n.* a pinch (of sugar, salt, etc.), a very small space.
ଟିସା, *a.* short and thick, dumpy.
ଟୀକା, *n.* a comment, an annotation.
ଟୀକାକାର, *n.* a commentator. [etc.
ଟୁଁଇବା, *v.* to lance boils or blisters,
ଟୁକୁଡ଼ା, *n.* a bit, piece, fragment.
ଟୁଙ୍ଗା, *n.* an edible jungle root.
ଟୁଙ୍ଗି, ଟୁଙ୍ଗା, *n.* a hut, a shed.
ଟୁଣା, *n.* magic, enchantment.
ଟୁଣୁଟୁଣୁ, *n.* a throbbing; sound of bells.
ଟୁଳୁଟୁଳୁ, *a.* sleepy; weak, emaciated.
ଟେକ, *n.* glory, honour.
ଟେକା, *n.* a clod, clump of earth.
ଟେକାଟେକି, *n.* the act of lifting or raising up anything; flattery.
ଟେକିବା, *v.* to raise, to lift up.
ଟେର, *n.* a trace or indication.
ଟେରା, *a.* cross-eyed; *fem.* ଟେରୀ.
ଟେରାଟାଟି, *n.* a screen or curtain used to hide *purdah* ladies from the public gaze.
ଟେଳା, *n.* a clod of earth; (see ଟେକା).
ଟେହୁଡ଼ିବା, ଟେହୁଡ଼େଇବା, *v.* to excite, to give encouragement to (used mainly with regard to quarrels or fights).

ଟୋକୀଟା, *n.* a girl, a lass (abusive).
ଟୋକା, *n.* a boy, a lad; *fem.* ଟୋକୀ.
ଟୋକାଇ, *n.* a basket.
ଟୋକାଏ, *n.* (*pl.*) boys, lads.
ଟୋକିବା, *v.* to peck; to reprove.
ଟୋପର, *n.* a crown, a hat, a helmet.
ଟୋପା, *n.* a drop (of liquid).
ଟୋପାଟୋପା, *ad.* drop by drop.
ଟୋପାଏ, *n.* a single drop.
ଟୋପି, ଟୋପୀ, *n.* a hat, cap, bonnet.
ଟୋପିଟୋପି, *ad.* (falling) by drops.
ଟୋଲ, *n.* a Sanskrit college.
ଟୋଲି, *n.* a dent, a bruise. [ed.
ଟୋଲା, *a.* indented, flattened, bruis-

ଠ.

ଠ, the twelfth consonant. [ledge.
ଠଉର, *n.* certainty, certain know-
ଠଉରାଇବା, *v.* to notice, to guess, to ascertain.
ଠଉରିବା, *v.* to stand, to wait, to be sustained.
ଠକ, ଠଗ, *n.* a rogue, sharper, swindler.
ଠକଠକ, *n.* imitative sound.
ଠକାଠକି, *n.* defrauding.
ଠକାମି, ଠଗାମି, *n.* fraud, extortion.
ଠକିବା, *v.* to cheat, to extort.
ଠକୁଣୀ, *n.* a female swindler.
ଠଣଠଣ, *n.* the clang of a bell.
ଠଣା, *n.* a recess in a wall; a blow with the fist.

ଠସଠର, *n.* a nodding or winking at one another.

ଠସା, *n.* a mould.

ଠା, *n.* a place, spot; place for eating.

ଠାକୁର, *n.* a god, lord; sir, master.

ଠାକୁରଘର, ଠାକୁରବାଡ଼ି, *n.* an idol temple.

ଠାକୁରାଣୀ, *n.* a goddess; lady; wife of a spiritual guide.

ଠାଣି, ଠାଣ, ଠାଣିମାଣି, *n.* attitude, manner, etiquette.

ଠାଧୁଆ, *a.* lazy, dilatory; *fem.* ଠାଧୋଇ.

ଠାବ. *n.* a place, dwelling-place.

ଠାବକରିବା, *v.* to know the address or abode of a person.

ଠାର, *n.* a signal, hint, inuendo.

ଠାରିବା, *v.* to intimate by signs.

ଠାରୁ, *prep.* ablative ending = from.

ଠାରେ, *prep.* locative ending = in.

ଠାଉ, *n.* signal, nod, wink.

ଠିଆ, *a.* erect, upright.

ଠିଆକରିବା-ହେବା, *v.* to make to stand; to stand.

ଟିପଟିଆ, *ad* hastily, quickly, (see ଟପ ଟେପୋଟେ).

ଠିକ, ଠିକଠାକ, *a.* accurate, exact.

ଠିକ, *n.* a sum, a total.

ଠିକଣା, *n.* certainty; residence, the place where any person or thing is to be found, address.

ଠିକା, *a.* hired; temporary;—*n.* job-work, piece work.

ଠକିବା, *v.* to be hindered; to be cheated.

ଠିକେଠିକେ, *ଠିକେ, *ad.* briefly; mainly.

ଠୁକଠୁକ, *n.* a rapping or tapping.

ଠୁକର, *n.* a tap, a knock; a stumble.

ଠୁଣ୍ଟା, *a.* short and thick, stout; *fem.* ଠୁଣ୍ଟୀ.

ଠୁଙ୍ଗ, *a.* dwarfish;—*n.* a dwarf; *fem.* ଠୁଙ୍ଗୀ.

ଠୁଳ, *a.* gathered together; total.

ଠୁଳାଇବା, ଠୁଳେଇବା, *v.* to heap. to gather together.

ଠେକ, *n.* a prop, support, stay.

ଠେକା, *n.* a turban or head-dress.

ଠେକି, *n.* a small earthen vessel.

ଠେକୁଆ, *n.* a hare, a rabbit.

ଠେଙ୍ଗ, *n.* high ground; the leg.

ଠେଙ୍ଗା, *n.* a staff, bludgeon, club.

ଠେଙ୍ଗାଇବା, *v.* to beat with a club.

ଠେଙ୍ଗିଣି, *n.* *a* part of the leg, *i.e.*, from knee to ankle.

ଠେଲ, *n.* a push, a shove; crowding.

ଠେଲାଠେଲି, *n.* a press of people, a jostling; pushing one another.

ଠେଲିବା, *v.* to push, to jostle.

ଠେସ, *n.* reliance, support, a prop.

ଠୋକର, *n.* a tap, knock; a stumble.

ଠୋଠା, *n.* an imitative sound, a loud report (as of fireworks or guns).

ଠୋଠୋ, *n.* sound of laughter.

ଠୋଙ୍ଗା, *n.* a cup made of a leaf.

ଠୋସ୍, ଠୋଷ୍, *n.* hard or rough language; loud voice, clear voice.

ଠୌର, *n.* certainty; a sight, a guess.

ଡ.

ଡ, the thirteenth consonant.

ଡଉଁରଥ, ଡେଉଁରଥ, *n.* a metal charm.

ଡଉଲ, *n.* manner, attitude, form, fashion;—*a.* pretty, handsome, nice.

ଡକ୍ଡବା, *n.* marvel teller, an exaggerator.

ଡକା, *n.* a cry; a call.

ଡକାଇତ, ଡକାଏତ, *n.* a robber, highwayman, bandit.

ଡକାଇତି, ଡକାଏତି, *n.* robbery, burglary.

ଡକାଇବା, *v.* to send for, to call for, to summon; to cause to call.

ଡକାବୋବାଳି, *n.* a cry of distress, a wail.

ଡଗର, *n.* a messenger; a spy.

ଡଗସ, *n.* a herald.

ଡଙ୍କ, *n.* tendrils of climbing plants.

ଡଙ୍କା, *n.* a ladle made of a cocoanut shell or wood; a large drum.

ଡଙ୍କାର, *n.* a medicinal plant.

ଡଙ୍କି, *n.* a small metal spoon.

ଡଙ୍କଣା, *n.* a sorcerer, a wizard.

ଡଙ୍କଣୀ, *n.* a sorceress, a witch.

ଡଟଡଟ, *ad.* hastily.

ଡଙ୍ଗା, ଡଙ୍ଗୀ, *n.* a canoe, a dug-out, a small boat.

ଡବଡବ, *n.* a dull sound.

ଡବଡବା, *n.* an exaggerator; a bully.

ଡବା, *n.* a small metal case; a railway carriage or wagon.

ଡଲ୍ଲ, *a.* large, thick (bamboo).

ଡମ, ଡୋମ, *n.* a low caste; basket or mat makers; *fem.* ଡମୁଣୀ.

ଡମଣି, ଡମଣିକବ୍ଜା, *n.* a special kind of hinge used on gates.

ଡମରୁ, *n.* a small drum.

ଡମାଡୋଳ, *n.* destruction of property, desolation.

ଡମ୍ଫା, *n.* a teller of improbabilities, one who "draws the long bow;" —*a.* boastful.

ଡର, *n.* fear, terror, alarm.

ଡରକୁସ, ଡରକୁଳା, *a.* fearful, timid.

ଡରାଇବା, *v.* to alarm, to put in fear.

ଡରିବା, *v.* to be afraid or alarmed.

ଡରୁଆ, *a.* timorous, fearful.

ଡହକ, *n.* heat; inflamation;—*a.* hot.

ଡହଡହ, *a.* very hot.

ଡହସ, *a.* ravenous, never satisfied; unable to keep a secret.

ଡହଳବିକଳ, *a.* having a longing or yearning.

ଡାଁଆଣା, *n.* a wizard, a sorcerer.

ଡାଁଆଣୀ, ଡାଇଣୀ, *n.* a witch, a sorceress.

ଡାଁଆସ, *n.* a gadfly.

ଡାକ, *n.* a call, a shout; the post, courier.

ଡାକଘର, *n.* post-office.

ଡାକରା, *n.* a call, summons.

ଡାକହାକ, *n.* a shouting and calling.
ଡାକୁ, *n.* a robber.
ଡାକୁଆ, *n.* a caller, a shouter.
ଡାଉର, *n.* a louse.
ଡାଙ୍ଗ, *n.* a stick, a switch.
ଡାଙ୍କଣ, *n.* a packing-needle.
ଡାବ, *n.* a green cocoanut; a medical prescription.
ଡାମର, *n.* a large crow, a raven.
ଡାଳ, *n.* a bough, branch of a tree.
ଡାଳଚିନି, *n.* cinnamon.
ଡାଳିଆ, *n.* a small branch.
ଡାଳିମ୍ବ, ଡାଳିମ, *n.* the pomegranate.
ଡାଳୁଅ, *n.* late paddy sown in swampy soil.
ଡାଲା. *n.* a tray; a tray of vegetables, fruit or sweetmeats as a present; cover, lid.
ଡାଲି, *n.* split pulse; a tray of vegetables, fruit, or sweetmeats as a present.
ଡାଲିଆ, *n.* a small tray.
ଡାହା, *n.* heat of the body.
ଡାହାଣ, *a.* right (in opposition to left).
ଡାଳୁ, *n.* see ଡାଳ.
ଡାହୁକ, *n.* a species of moor-hen.
ଡିଆଁ, *n.* a jump, leap, bound; a stile.
ଡିଆଁଡେଇଁ, *n.* a bounding along.
ଡିଙ୍ଗା, *n.* a small boat, a skiff.
ଡିଣ୍ଡିମ, *n.* a tabour, a small drum.
ଡିବା, *n.* a small metal case; a small measure.

ଡିବଡିବ, *n.* a sound made by beating a small drum.
ଡିମିର, ଡିମ୍ବୁର, ଡିମ୍ବୁରୁ, *n.* a fig, a fig tree.
ଡିମ୍ବ, *n.* an egg, spawn, chrysalis.
* ଡିମ୍ବଜ, *a.* oviparous.
ଡିହ, *n.* high ground; a dwelling-place; a blow with the end of a stick.
ଡୁବକ, *n.* one who immerses; a baptizer, a Baptist.
ଡୁବନ, *n.* immersion, baptism.
ଡୁବିତ, *a.* immersed, baptized; sunk.
ଡୁବିବା, ଡୁବିଯିବା, *v.* to be immersed, to be plunged into water; to be drowned.
ଡୁବୁର, *n.* one who can remain long under water.
ଡୁବୁରି, *n.* a diver.
ଡେଇଁବା, *v.* to jump, to leap.
ଡେକ୍‌ଚି, *n.* a metal cooking vessel.
ଡେଙ୍ଗା, *a.* long, tall, lank, (*fem.* ଡେଙ୍ଗୀ).
ଡେଙ୍ଗୁରା, *n.* proclamation by beat of drum.
ଡେଣା, *n.* a wing, pinion, fin.
ଡେଲୁଆ, *n.* a small stone.
ଡେଣ୍ଡ, *n.* the stem of anything.
ଡେବର *a.* left (in opposition to right).
ଡେବରିଆ, *a.* left-handed.
ଡେରା, *n.* a tent.
ଡେରିବା, *v.* to lean.
ଡୋର, ଡୋରି, *n.* a line, string, twine, rope, cord.

ଢୋରଅ, *a.* striped, corded, ribbed.

ଢୋଳା, *n.* the pupil of the eye.

ଢୋଲ, **ଢୋଲ୍**, *n.* a wicker basket for storing grain.

ଢୋଲା, **ଢୋଲ୍ଲା**, *n.* a covered litter, a [palki.

ଢୌଁରିଅ, *n.* a small metal tube worn as a charm (see ଜଉଁରିଅ).

ଢୌଲ, *n.* form, attitude, mien, gait; —*a.* pretty, handsome, (see ଜଉଲ).

ଢ.

ଢ, the fourteenth consonant.

ଢକ, *n.* weights (for scales).

ଢକଢକ, *n.* noise made in drinking.

ଢକ୍କା, *n.* a drum, a large drum.

ଢକ୍କାର, **ଢକାର**, *n.* belching; flatulency.

ଢକା, *a.* closed, covered.

ଢଗ, *n.* a sarcastic or dry allusion; a squib or gibe in rhyme; a proverb.

ଢଙ୍ଗ, **ଢଙ୍ଗଢାଙ୍ଗ**, *n.* manners, gait, appearance.

ଢଙ୍ଗଢଙ୍ଗ, *n.* sound of jostling of handies.

ଢପ, *n.* shape, form, mien, gait.

ଢମ, *n.* boasting, vainglory.

ଢମା, *n.* a basket or trough from which cattle are fed; a boaster.

ଢମାଲି, *n.* a jeer, gibe, witticism.

ଢଳଢଳ, *a.* tremulous; pellucid.

ଢଳଢଳିଅ, *a.* sparkling; waving, fluid-like.

ଢଳା, *a.* poured out; made of melted metal.

ଢଳାଢଳି, *n.* a pouring out.

ଢଳିବା, *v.* to stumble, to totter.

ଢାଉ, *n.* butting of a goat or ram.

ଢାଁଉଢାଁଉ, *n.* sound of a drum.

ଢାଉ, *n.* red stone, ruddle.

ଢାଉକ, *n.* a sort of moor-hen.

ଢାଙ୍କିବା, *v.* to cover or conceal.

ଢାଙ୍କୁଣୀ, *n.* a cover, lid, top.

ଢାଗା, *n.* single-stitch.

ଢାଞ୍ଚା, *n.* a pattern.

ଢାମଣା, *n.* a species of non-poisonous snake which sometimes drinks milk from the cow. It grows to about 6 ft. long and has yellow and black markings.

ଢାଙ୍ପିବା, *v.* to cover or conceal (see ଢାଙ୍କିବା).

ଢାଳ, *n.* a brass water vessel, a *lotá.*

ଢାଳିବା, *v.* to pour out, to spill.

ଢାଲ, *n.* a shield.

ଢାଲୁ, *a.* slanting, sloping.

ଢିଙ୍କି, **ଢେଙ୍କି**, **ଢେଙ୍କୀ**, *n.* pedal arrangement for cleaning or pounding rice, lime, etc., a *dhenki.*

ଢିପ, *n.* a hillock, heap.

ଢିବର, *n.* an iron nut; a small tin [lamp.

ଢିଗ, *n.* a holder, a support, a prop.

ଢିଲା, *a.* dilatory, slow; slack, lax; —*n.* slackness, negligence.

ଢୁଲୁ, *n.* report of a gun.
ଢୁଲାଇବା, ଢୋଲାଇବା, *v.* to nod with sleep.
ଢୁଲୁଢୁଲୁ, *a.* sleepy, drowsy.
ଢେଉ, *n.* a wave, a billow.
ଢେଣ୍ଡରା, ଢେଣ୍ଡୁରା, *n.* proclamation by beat of drum, (see ଢେଣ୍ଡୁରା).
ଢେମଣା, *a.* illegitimate ;—*n.* a gallant, a paramour; a bastard.
ଢେମଣୀ, *n.* an adulteress ; a concubine.
ଢେର, *a.* much, many, plenty.
ଢେଲା, *n.* a clod of earth, a stone.
ଢୋକିବା, *v.* to drink, to gulp.
ଢୋକେ, *n.* a draught, a gulp.
ଢୋଳ, *n.* drowsiness, sleepiness.
ଢୋଲ, *n.* a drum.
ଢୋଆଣ, *n.* carrying or carting burdens; hire for the same.
ଢୋଲିଆ, *n.* a drummer.

ଣ.

ଣ, the fifteenth consonant: not used as an initial.

ତ.

ତ, the sixteenth consonant.
ତଁଅର, *n.* red border or selvedge, red cotton thread.
ତଁଉର, *n.* a kind of cloth.
ତଁବ, *n.* a kind of snake.
ତକ, a *particle* signifying to, unto, till, until.
ତକରାର, *n.* a dispute, an altercation.
ତକସୀର, *n.* a fault, offence, error.
ତକିଆ, *n.* a pillow, a bolster.
ତଖ୍ତ, *n.* a throne, chair of state.
ତଖ୍ତପୋଷ, *n.* a kind of bedstead, a table.
ତଖ୍ତା, *n.* a board, a plank.
* ତକ୍ର, *n.* diluted buttermilk.
ତଗାର, *n.* a small earthen vessel used to carry mortar in.
ତଜବିଜ, *n.* judgment, investigation, scrutiny.
ତଞ୍ଚକ, *n.* a deceiver, imposter, cheat.
* ତଟ, *n.* a shore, bank, strand.
ତଟକା, *a.* new, fresh, good.
ତଟସ୍ଥ, *a.* surprised; on the shore.
* ତଟିନୀ, *n.* a river.
ତଡବଡ, *ad.* all of a bustle, in haste.
ତଡା, ତଡ, *n.* a shore, strand, coast.
* ତଡାଗ, *n.* a large pond.
ତଡାବଡ, ତଡବଡ, *ad.* hastily, in a bustle.
ତଡିତ୍, *n.* lightning; electricity.
ତଡିବା, *v.* to expel, to drive out.
ତଣ୍ଟା, *n.* trouble, risk, responsibility.
ତଣ୍ଟି, *n.* the neck, throat, gullet.
ତଣ୍ଟିଆ, *n.* a seizing by the throat.
ତଣ୍ଡ, *n.* loss, unjustifiable fines or payments; money paid for a security.
ତଣ୍ଡକାର, * ତଣ୍ଡକ, *n.* a receiver of the above.
ତଣ୍ଡାଇବା, ତଣ୍ଡିବା, *v.* to enforce a fine or security.
ତଣ୍ଡି, *n.* a long grass used for thatching.

ତଣ୍ଡିନେବା, *v.* to take a fine by force.

* ତଣ୍ଡୁଲ, *n.* rice, husked rice.

* ତତଃ, *ad.* from that, afterwards.

ତତଲ, *a.* hot, warm; heated.

ତତାଇବା, *v.* to heat, to boil, to warm.

* ତତ୍, *pron.* it, that, he.

ତତ୍କାଳ, *n.* that time, that instant; —*ad.* quickly.

ତତ୍କାଳିକ, ତତ୍କାଳୀନ, *a.* of that time, relating to any particular time.

* ତତ୍କୃତ, *a.* done by him, her, or that.

* ତତ୍କ୍ରମେ, *ad.* in that order or degree.

ତତ୍ତୁଲ୍ୟ, *a.* like that, similar.

ତତ୍ପର, *a.* closely intent on, eagerly engaged in, diligent.

ତତ୍ପରେ, *ad.* after that, afterwards.

ତତ୍ପୁରୁଷ, *n.* (in *Gram.*) the name of a class of compounds.

ତତ୍କ୍ଷଣାତ୍, *ad.* thenceforth, immediately.

ତତ୍ତ୍ୱ, *n.* essence, reality; scrutiny.

* ତତ୍ତ୍ୱଚାରକ, *n.* one who investigates, a philosopher, a scrutinizer.

* ତତ୍ତ୍ୱଜ୍ଞ, *a.* knowing the fundamental truth.

ତତ୍ତ୍ୱଜ୍ଞାନ, *n.* knowledge of any fundamental truth.

ତତ୍ତ୍ୱବାଦୀ, *a.* speaking philosophically.

ତତ୍ତ୍ୱାବଧାରକ, *n.* superintendent.

ତତ୍ତ୍ୱାବଧାରଣ, *n.* superintendence.

ତତ୍ର, *ad.* there, in that place.

* ତତ୍ରତ୍ୟ, *a.* of that place, being there.

ତଥାପି, *ad.* nevertheless, still, even.

ତଥା, *ad.* thus, so, as before.

ତଥାଚ, ତଥାପି, *conj.* even thus, nevertheless, yet, still.

* ତଥାସ୍ତୁ, *interj.* so be it, amen.

* ତଥି, *ad.* there (poetical).

ତଥ୍ୟ, *a.* true, real;—*n.* truth, reality.

ତଦନନ୍ତର, *ad.* afterwards, after that.

ତଦନୁରୂପ, *a.* like that, thus, so.

ତଦନୁସାରେ, *ad.* according to that, so.

ତଦନ୍ତ, *n.* enquiry, investigation; object, aim.

ତଦନ୍ତର, *ad.* after that, beside that.

ତଦବଧି, *ad.* thenceforth, till then.

* ତଦବସ୍ଥ, *a.* thus conditioned, thus situated, placed in such circumstances.

* ତଦା, ତଦାନୀଂ, *ad.* then, at that time.

ତଦାନୀନ୍ତନ, *a.* of that time, contemporaneous.

ତଦାରକ, ତଦାରଖ, *n.* investigation.

* ତଦୀୟ, *a.* of that, relating to that person or thing.

ତଦୁତ୍ତରେ, *ad.* after that.

ତଦୁପରି, *ad.* thereupon, upon that, him, or her.

ତଦ୍ଦଣ୍ଡ, *ad.* immediately, at once.

ତଦ୍ଧିତ, *n.* (in *Gram.*) a derivative noun.

ତଦ୍ବତ୍, *ad.* like that, resembling.

ତଦ୍ଭିନ୍ନ, *ad.* beside that.

ତଦ୍ରୂପ, *a.* such.

* ତନୟ, *n.* a son.

* ତନୟା, *n.* a daughter.
* ତନୁ, *n.* the body;—*a.* small, little; thin, slender.
* ତନୁଜ, *n.* a son.
* ତନୁଜା, *n.* a daughter.
ତନଖା, *n.* pay, salary, wages.
ତନ୍ତ, *n.* a weaver's loom; catgut, a leather string.
ତନ୍ତି, *n.* a weaver.
* ତନ୍ତୁ, *n.* a thread; a wire; catgut, a leather string.
* ତନ୍ତୁବାୟ, *n.* a weaver.
ତନ୍ତ୍ର, *n.* books teaching mystical formularies for the attainment of super-human power; Government, administration; a loom; a thread; catgut; *a charm;—*a.* subject to, dependent.
* ତନ୍ତ୍ରୀ, *n.* the musical instrument *biná*; a professor of the *Tantras.*
ତନ୍ଦୁର, *n.* an oven.
ତନ୍ଦ୍ରା, *n.* drowsiness, lassitude; hurry.
ତନ୍ଦ୍ରାଳୁ, * ତନ୍ଦ୍ରିତ, *a.* weary, drowsy, sleepy. [ly.
ତନ୍ନତନ୍ନ, *ad.* not so not so; minute-
* ତନ୍ମୟ, *a.* wholly absorbed in that, become one with that.
ତପ, ତପଃ, *n.* austerity, penance.
* ତପନ, *n.* the sun.
ତପସ୍ୟା, *n.* see ତପ ।

ତପସ୍ୱୀ, *a.* practising penance, devout;—*n.* an ascetic, a devotee, *fem.* ତପସ୍ୱିନୀ ।
* ତପୋଧନ, *n.* a devotee;—*a.* rich in religious penance, pious.
* ତପୋବନ, *n.* a place in the forest where ascetics practise penance.
* ତପ୍ତ, *a.* heated, hot.
ତପ୍ତି, *n.* heat, glare, warmth.
ତଫସୀଲ୍, ତଫସିଲ୍, *n.* a detail, an explanation, analysis.
ତଫାତ୍, *a.* distant; separate, unlike;—*n.* distance; difference.
ତବ, *pron.* relating to you, your (poetical).
ତତଲ, *n.* hot rice. [drum.
ତବଲା, *n.* a kettle-drum, a small
ତମଃ, ତମ, ତମସ, *n.* darkness, gloom; delusion; pride.
ତମ, *n.* darkness; (in *Gram.*) an affix of the superlative degree.
ତମସୁକ, *n.* a bond, a written agreement.
ତମାଖୁ, *n.* tobacco. [barred.
ତମାଦି, *a.* time-expired, statute-
ତମାମ୍, *a.* all, the whole.
* ତମିସ୍ର, *n.* darkness.
* ତମି, ତମୀ, *n.* night.
ତମୋଗୁଣ, *n.* one of the three primeval qualities of matter.
* ତମୋମୟ, *a.* full of darkness.
* ତମୋନୁଦ, *n.* the sun; the moon.

ତମ୍ପ, *n.* see ଚମ୍ପ ।
ତମ୍ବା, *n.* copper.
ତମ୍ବି, *n.* admonition, reproof.
ତମ୍ବୁ, *n.* a tent, a marquee.
ତମ୍ବୁର, *n.* a three-stringed lute.
ତର, *n.* leisure; (in *Gram.*) an affix of the comparative degree.
ତରକ, *n.* reasoning ; quickness, (poetical form of ତର୍କ).
ତରକା, *a.* vigilant; fleeing in alarm.
ତରକାରି, *n.* curry.
ତରକିବା, *v.* to be vigilant, to flee away with alarm.
* ତରଙ୍ଗ, *n.* a wave, a billow.
* ତରଙ୍ଗିଣୀ, *n.* a river.
ତରଜମା, *n.* a translation.
ତରଭା, *n.* name of an edible fruit.
* ତରଣ, *n.* crossing over, getting over a difficulty.
* ତରଣି, ତରଣୀ, *n.* a boat, a raft.
ତରତର, *a.* quick, hasty ;—*ad.* quickly, hastily.
ତରତରିଆ, *a.* quick, capricious.
ତରଫ, *n.* a side, a party.
ତରବାର, ତରବାରି, *n.* a sword, scimitar.
ତରଭୁଜ, ତରବୁଜ, *n.* a water-melon.
ତରଳ, *a.* fluid, liquid; tremulous.
ତରଳାଇବା, *v.* to melt, to liquefy.
ତରଳିତ, *a.* liquefied.
ତରଳିବା, *v.* to become liquid.
ତରବର, *a.* quick, swift.
ତରା, *n.* a star, a constellation.
ତରାଜୁ, *n.* a pair of scales.
ତରାଟ, *n.* name of a flower.
ତରାଟି ଚାହିଁବା, *v.* to look upon angrily.
* ତରି, ତରୀ, *n.* a boat, a raft.
ତରିବା, *v.* to be saved, to cross over.
* ତରୁ, *n.* a tree, shrub, plant.
* ତରୁଣ, *n.* a young man ;-*a.* young, fresh, new.
* ତରୁଣୀ, *n.* a young woman.
ତର୍କ, *n.* reasoning; logic.
ତର୍କଣା, *n.* reasoning out a point.
ତର୍କବିଦ୍ୟା, ତର୍କଶାସ୍ତ୍ର, *n.* the science of logic or reasoning, a treatise on logic.
ତର୍କାରି, *n.* curry, see ତରକାରି.
ତର୍କିଳ, *n.* growling, scolding, railing.
* ତର୍ଜନୀ, *n.* the forefinger.
ତର୍ଜମା, *n.* translation, see ତରଜମା.
* ତର୍ପଣ, *n.* satisfying ; a libation of water to the dead.
ତଲ, *n.* bottom, under part, base ; surface, floor.
ତଲ-ମହଲ, *n.* lower storey of a house.
ତଳାତଳ, *n.* a division of hell.
ତଳି, *a.* lying at the bottom, below; —*n.* bottom, under part, base ; plants for transplanting.
ତଳିତଳିଆ, *a.* rejected, falling at the bottom ;—*n.* refuse, dregs.
ତଳିପା, *n.* sole of the foot.
ତଳିପେଟ, *n.* the abdomen, belly.
ତଳେ, *ad.* at the bottom, below.
* ତଳ୍ପ, *n.* a bed.
ତଲବ, *n.* a summons ; wages.

ତଲ୍‌ବାର, *n.* a sword, a scimitar.
ତଲେଇ, *n.* bamboo mat or sail.
ତଲ୍ଲସ, ତଲ୍ଲାସ, *n.* a search.
ତସଲା, *n.* a brass vessel.
ତସଦକ୍, *n.* verification of a signature; trouble, vexation, distress.
ତସର, ଟସର, *n.* a coarse kind of silk, [tussore.
ତସରୁଫ୍, *n.* embezzlement.
ତସା, *n.* a husbandman.
ତଷୁ, *n.* husk or chaff of rice.
* ତସ୍କର, *n.* a thief, a robber.
ତହ, *n.* a layer, a fold, a pleat.
ତହକରିବା, *v.* to pleat, to gather.
ତହବିଲ୍, *n.* fund, treasury, treasure, cash.
ତହସିଲ, *n.* collection of revenue.
ତହସିଲଦାର, *n.* one who collects revenue, *tahsildar*.
ତହିଁ, *ad.* there, (*poetical*).
ତହୁଁ, *ad.* thence, from this, afterwards, then.
ତକ୍ଷକ, *n.* a fabled serpent.
ତା, *pron.* that;–*n.* sitting on eggs.
ତାଉବା, ତାଇବା, *v.* to work bellows; to enrage, to excite.
ତାକ, ତାଖ, *n.* a recess in a wall.
ତାକତ୍, *n.* strength, power, force.
ତାଗିଦ୍, *n.* a warning, a reminding.
ତାଙ୍କୁ, *pron.* him, to him.
ତାକୁଆ, *n.* the iron pin in a spinning wheel.
ତାଗ, *n.* a thread.
ତାଗିବା, *v.* to sew (with thick thread.)
ତାଚ୍ଛଲ୍ୟ, *n.* disregard, contempt, [distrust.
ତାଜମହଲ, *n.* the mausoleum at Agra built by Shah Jehan in honour of his wife Mumtaj Mahal.
ତାଜା, *a.* fresh, green, new, active.
ତାଜିଆ, *n.* model of a mausoleum or tomb carried at the time of *Mohorrum*.
ତାଜୁବ୍, *a.* wonderful, surprising.
ତାଟ, *n.* a coarse kind of curtain.
ତାଟକା, *a.* fresh, new; surprising.
* ତାଟଙ୍କ, *n.* an ornament for the ear.
ତାଟକା, ତାଟଙ୍କା, *a.* fearful, timid.
ତାଟି, *n.* a palm-leaf screen or door.
ତାଟିଆ, *n.* a small brass basin.
ତାଡ, *n.* an ornament for the arm; a vessel in which seeds are sown.
ତାଡନ, *n.* driving away; persecuting.
ତାଡନା, *n.* persecution.
* ତାଡଣି, *n.* a horsewhip, riding-whip.
ତାଡା, *n.* bundle, packet.
ତାଡି, ତାଳି, *n.* toddy, juice of the palm.
ତାଡିଆ, *n.* a large earthen cooking pot.
ତାଡିତ, *a.* driven away; beaten, chastised, persecuted;–*n.* electricity.
ତାଡିତ, ତାଡିତକ, *a.* electric.

ତାଡବା, *v.* to uproot.

* ତାଣ୍ଡବ, *n.* frantic dancing.

ତାତ, *n.* * heat; father.

ତାତି, *n.* heat, warmth, glare.

ତାତିବା, *v.* to become hot.

ତାତ୍କାଳିକ, *a.* of the same time, happening at the same time.

ତାତ୍ପର୍ଯ୍ୟ, *n.* meaning, import, object.

* ତାଦୃକ୍, ତାଦୃଶ, *a.* such, so, like that.

ତାନ, *n.* the raising and lowering of the voice in singing; angry voice.

* ତାନ୍ତବ, *a.* made of threads or wires; ductile.

ତାନ୍ତବତା, *n.* ductility.

ତାନ୍ତ୍ରିକ, *a.* versed in the *Tantras.*

ତାପ, *n.* heat; pain, sorrow, distress.

ତାପମାନଯନ୍ତ୍ର, *n.* thermometer.

* ତାପସ, *a.* practising austerities; —*n.* a devotee.

ତାପିତ, *a.* distressed, afflicted; [heated.

ତାପିବା, *v.* to cause to blaze; to make the perpetual sacred fires of ascetics burn or blaze.

ତାବତ୍, *ad.* so long;—*pron.* all, the whole.

ତାବିଜ, *n.* a charm, an amulet.

ତାବେ, *n.* subjection.

ତାବେଦାର, *a.* subject to, under control.

* ତାମରସ, *n.* a lotus.

ତାମଲୀ, *n.* name of pan-seller caste.

ତାମାସା, ତାମସା, *n.* fun, show, sport.

* ତାମସ, *a.* dark, consisting of darkness, ignorant; vicious.

* ତାମସୀ, *n.* night; gloom, stupidity.

ତାମ୍ବୁ, *n.* a tent, a pavilion.

ତାମ୍ବୁର, ତାନପୁର, *n.* a three-stringed guitar.

ତାମ୍ବୁଲ, *n.* *pán*, betel-leaf.

ତାମ୍ବୁଲୀ, *n.* see ତାମଲୀ.

* ତାମ୍ର, *n.* copper.

* ତାମ୍ରକାର, *n.* a coppersmith, [brazier.

* ତାମ୍ରକୁଟ, *n.* the tobacco leaf.

ତାର, *n.* a wire; * a star;—*pron.* his, her, hers, its.

ତାରକ, *n.* a saviour, a pilot.

* ତାରକ *n.* a star; pupil of the eye.

ତାରକସ, *n.* a wire-drawer.

ତାରକସୀ, *a.* filigreed.

ତାରକା, *n.* a star.

ତାରକିତ, *a.* starry (sky).

ତାରଣ, *n.* a crossing over, saving; * a raft.

ତାରତମ୍ୟ, *n.* greater or less degree, difference.

* ତାରଲ୍ୟ, *n.* fluidity; fickleness.

ତାରା, *n.* a star; pupil of the eye.

* ତାରାପତି, *n.* the moon.

ତାରାମଣ୍ଡଳ, *n.* the starry sky; * eye-[ball.

ତାରିଖ, *n.* date, day of the month.

ତାରିଫ୍, *n.* praise, applause;—*a.* excellent.

ତାରିବା, *v.* to save, to deliver.

* ତାରୁଣ୍ୟ, *n.* youth, youthfulness.

* ତାର୍କିକ, *n.* a logician, a sophist.

ତାଳ, *n.* the fan-palm tree and its fruit, the palmyra; beating time.

* ତାଳକ, *n.* a lock, bolt.

* ତାଳଚଞ୍ଚୁ, *n.* the common swallow.

ତାଳପତ୍ର, *n.* leaf of the fan-palm (palmyra).

* ତାଳବୃନ୍ତ, *n.* a palm-leaf fan.

ତାଳଶଜ, *n.* fruit (soft seed) of the palmyra palm.

* ତାଳାନ୍ତ, *n.* a rest (in music).

ତାଳି, ତାଳୀ, *n.* clapping hands; a patch.

ତାଳି ପକାଇବା, ତାଳି ଦେବା, *v.* to patch (a garment).

ତାଳି ମାରିବା, ତାଳି ଦେବା, *v.* to clap one's hands.

ତାଳୁ, *n.* the roof of the mouth; the top of the head. [palate.

ତାଳୁଅ, *n.* the palm; sole; crown;

ତାଳବ୍ୟ, *a.* palatal, from the palate.

ତାଲା, *n.* a lock; storey of a building.

ତାଲା ଦେବା, ତାଲା ପକାଇବା, *v.* to lock a door, to lock.

ତାଲିକା, *n.* a list, a catalogue.

ତାଲିମ୍, *a.* trained; learned, clever; disciplined.

ତାଲୁକ୍, *n.* a manor, an estate.

ତାଲୁକ୍‌ଦାର୍, *n.* the owner of an estate.

ତାଲେବର, ତାଲବର, *a.* rich.

ତାସ୍, *n.* a playing-card.

ତାଷ, *n.* husbandry.

ତାଷଣ, *n.* preparing of the warp for weaving.

ତାଷୁଣୀ, *n.* a woman of the farmer [caste.

ତାହା, *pron.* that, it.

ତିଅଣ, ତିଉଣ, *n.* curry.

ତିଅର, *n.* a class of fishermen.

ତିଆର କରିବା, ତିଆର କରିବା, *v.* to prepare, to make, to build, to make ready; to manufacture.

ତିଆର, ତୟାର, *a.* ready, prepared, complete; at hand.

ତିଆର ମାଲ୍, *n.* ready made goods or [articles.

* ତିକ୍ତ, *a.* bitter.

* ତିକ୍ତତା, *n.* bitterness.

ତିତାଲା, *a.* three-storied.

* ତିତିକ୍ଷା, *n.* patience, forbearance.

* ତିତିକ୍ଷୁ, *a.* patient, forbearing, resigned.

ତିତିର, ତିତର, *n.* a partridge.

ତିଥି, *n.* day of a lunar change

ତିନି, *a.* and *n.* three, 3: III.

ତିନିକାଳ, *n.* three periods—past, present, future; or childhood, youth, maturity.

ତିନ୍ତା, *a.* wet, damp, moist.

ତିନ୍ତାଇବା, *v.* to wet, to moisten.

* ତିନ୍ତିଡ଼ୀ, *n.* tamarind tree and fruit.

ତିନ୍ତିବା, *v.* to be wet.

ତିନ୍ତୁଳି, ତେନ୍ତୁଳି, *n.* tamarind tree and its fruit.

ତିଘଟ, *a.* thrice, three times.

ତିମି, *n.* a large fish; a whale.

ତିମିଙ୍ଗିଳ, *n.* a fabulous sea monster (swallowing even the whale).

*ତିମିର, *n.* darkness, obscurity.

ତିରସ୍କାର, *a.* insult, reproach, censure.

ତିରସ୍କୃତ, *a.* scolded, reproached, insulted.

*ତିରୋଧାନ, *n.* disappearance, concealment.

ତିରୋଭାବ, *n.* disappearance, vanishing away.

ତିରୋହିତ, *a.* disappeared, removed from sight.

*ତିର୍ଯ୍ୟକ୍, *a.* crooked.

*ତିଳ, *n.* sesamum seed; a moment; a mole, a freckle.

ତିଳକ, *n.* a mark on the forehead; —*a.* *chief, principal.

ତିସି, *n.* linseed.

ତୀଖ, ତିଖ, *a.* sloping, steep.

*ତୀବ୍ର, *a.* sharp, severe, pungent.

*ତୀବ୍ରତା, *n.* sharpness, keenness.

ତୀର, *n.* arrow; a shore, bank.

ତୀରନ୍ଦାଜ, *n.* an archer.

ତୀର୍ଥ, *n.* a place of pilgrimage.

ତୀର୍ଥଗାମୀ, *n.* a pilgrim.

ତୀର୍ଥଯାତ୍ରା, *n.* pilgrimage to a sacred place.

ତୀକ୍ଷ୍ଣ, *a.* sharp, acute, keen.

*ତୀକ୍ଷ୍ଣତା, *n.* sharpness.

ତୀକ୍ଷ୍ଣବୁଦ୍ଧି, *n.* wit, acuteness;—*a.* witty, sagacious.

*ତୀକ୍ଷ୍ଣାଗ୍ର, *a.* sharp-pointed.

ତୁ, *pron.* thou, you, (inferior, or familiar).

ତୁଏତୁଏ, ତୁଏକ୍ତୁଏ, *ad.* from time to time, again and again.

*ତୁଙ୍ଗ, *a.* lofty, elevated, tall.

ତୁଚ୍ଛ, *a.* despised, despicable, mean; worthless.

ତୁଚ୍ଛ କରିବା, *v.* to despise, to contemn, to disregard.

ତୁଚ୍ଛଜ୍ଞାନ, *n.* contempt.

ତୁଚ୍ଛତା, *n.* insignificance, *hollowness, emptiness.

ତୁଚ୍ଛବୋଧ, *n.* contempt.

ତୁଚ୍ଛା, *a.* empty;—*ad.* merely.

ତୁଟା, *a.* broken, defective, injured.

ତୁଟି, ତୁଟ, *n.* loss, detriment, injury.

ତୁଟିବା, *v.* to break; to call abusive names.

ତୁଠ, *n.* a bathing or landing-place.

ତୁଣ, ତୂଣ, *n.* see ତରକାଷ.

ତୁଣ୍ଡ, *n.* the tongue, the mouth.

ତୁଣ୍ଡପତ୍ର, *n.* tobacco leaf.

ତୁଣ୍ଡପୋଡା, *n.* a pungent (mouth burning) shrub.

ତୁଣ୍ଡି, *n.* a muzzle.

ତୁଣ୍ଡୁଆ, *n.* a brawler, noisy talker.

ତୁଣ୍ଡେଇ, *n.* a noisy brawling woman.

ତୁତକୋଳି, *n.* a mulberry.

ତୁତ୍ଥା, *n.* blue vitriol, sulphate of copper.

ତୁନି, *a.* silent, quiet, grave.

*ତୁନ୍ଦିଳ, *a.* big-bellied.

ତୁଫାନ, *n.* a storm, hurricane.

ତୁମ୍ବଡ, ତୁମ୍ବା, *n.* a snake-catcher's pipe.

*ତୁମୁଳ, *a.* tumultuous; fierce;—*n.* tumult, uproar.

ତୁମ୍ବା, ତୁମ୍ବି, ତୁମ୍ବା, *n.* dried gourd used as a waterpot.

ତୁମ୍ଭେ, *pron.* you, thou.

* ତୁରଙ୍ଗ, ତୁରଙ୍ଗମ, ତୁରଗ, *n.* a horse.

* ତୁରଙ୍ଗୀ, *n.* a mare.

ତୁରନ୍ତ, ତୁରତ, *ad.* quickly, speedily.

ତୁରୁକ୍, *n.* a Turk.

ତୁରୁତୁରିଆ, *a.* hasty, impatient.

ତୁଲ, *n.* balances, scales; weight; sign *libra.*

ତୁଲନା, *n.* likeness, equality, comparison.

ତୁଳସୀ, *n.* the basil tree.

* ତୁଳା, *n.* scales; sign *libra.*

ତୁଳାଇବା, *v.* to cause to be weighed.

ତୁଳିଥୁଣ୍ଟ, *n.* a centre prop or post.

* ତୁଳିତ, *a.* weighed; raised up.

ତୁଳିବା, *v.* to weigh.

ତୁଲ, *n.* likeness, resemblance, similarity.

ତୁଲାଇବା, *v.* to manage, to discharge (a work).

ତୁଲ୍ୟ, *a.* alike, equal, resembling.

ତୁଷ, *n.* chaff, husk of grain.

* ତୁଷାର, *n.* fog, rime, hoar-frost.

ତୁଷ୍ଟ, *a.* pleased, glad, gratified.

ତୁଷ୍ଟି, *n.* pleasure, gratification.

ତୁହି, *pron.* thou, you.

* ତୂଣ, ତୂଣୀ, ତୂଣୀର, *n.* a quiver, case for arrows.

ତୂରୀ, *n.* a trumpet.

* ତୂର୍ଣ୍ଣ, *a.* swift, quick, hastily.

ତୂଳା, *n.* picked cotton.

ତୂଳାଧୁଣା, *n.* a caste of cotton cleaners; the act of cleaning cotton.

ତୂଳୀ, ତୂଳିକା, *n.* a painter's brush or pencil.

* ତୃଣ, *n.* grass, straw, herbage.

ତୃଣଜୀବୀ, *a.* subsisting on grass, graminivorous.

* ତୃଣଧାନ୍ୟ, *n.* wild grain, tares, etc.

* ତୃଣରାଜ, *n.* the fan-palm.

ତୃତୀୟ, *a.* third, 3rd.

ତୃତୀୟା, *n.* the third lunar day.

ତୃପ୍ତ, *a.* satisfied, pleased, filled.

ତୃପ୍ତି, *n.* satisfaction, gratification.

ତୃଷା, *n.* thirst; desire, appetite.

ତୃଷାର୍ତ୍ତ, ତୃଷିତ, *a.* athirst, thirsty; desirous.

ତୃଷ୍ଣା, *n.* see ତୃଷା.

ତେଇଶ, *a.* and *n.* twenty-three, 23, XXIII.

ତେଜଃ, ତେଜ, *n.* lustre; vitality, vigour, ardour.

ତେଜପତ୍ର, *n.* cassia leaves.

ତେଜସ୍କର, *a.* illuminating, irradiating, invigorating.

ତେଜସ୍ୱୀ, *a.* shining; energetic, ardent.

ତେଜାରତ୍, ତେଜାରତି, *n.* trade, commerce.

ତେଜାରତୀ, *a.* belonging to trade.

ତେଜାଲ, *n.* a portable earthen oven.

ତେଜାଲି, *a.* energetic, shining, ardent.

ତେଜୀୟାନ୍, *a.* splendid, very powerful or vigorous.

ତେଜୋମୟ, *a.* luminous, brilliant, bright.

ତେଢ଼ା, *a.* crooked, awry; cock-eyed.

ତେଣିକି, *ad.* there, in that direction.

ତେଣୁ, ତେଣୁକରି, *ad.* therefore.
ତେଣେ, *ad.* in that place, there.
ତେଣ୍ଟା, *n.* fishing-tackle.
ତେଣ୍ଟେଲି, *n.* an obstinate woman.
ତେଣ୍ଟୋଲି, *n.* a kind of bird.
ତେଣ୍ଡା, *n.* an appliance for raising water for irrigating.
ତେଣ୍ଡିବା, *a.* to irrigate; to gulp [down.
ତେଢାଙ୍ଗ, *a.* see ତିଢାଙ୍ଗ.
ତେତକ, *a.* thus much, so much; so [far.
ତେତକବେଳେ, ତେତେବେଳେ, *ad.* at that time, then.
ତେତିଶ, *a.* and *n.* thirty-three, 33, [XXXIII.
ତେତେ, *a.* so much, so many, so long.
ତେନ୍ତର, *n.* the two pieces of wood on the axle of a bullock-cart to support the body of the cart.
ତେନ୍ତୁଳୀ, ତେନ୍ତୁଳି, *n.* tamarind tree and fruit.
ତେପଟ, *a.* see ତିପଟ.
ତେପନ, *a.* and *n.* fifty-three, 53, [LIII.
ତେପାୟା, *a.* three-legged.
ତେବେ, *ad.* then.
ତେବେହେଁ, *ad.* even then.
ତେମନ୍ତ, *a.* and *ad.* like that, such, so, in that manner.
ତେୟାଅଶୀ, *a.* and *n.* eighty-three, 83, LXXXIII.
ତେୟାନବେ, *a.* and *n.* ninety-three, [93, XCIII.
ତେୟାଳିଶ, *a.* and *n.* forty-three, 43, XLIII.
ତେର, *a.* and *n.* thirteen, 13, XIII.

ତେଲ, *n.* oil.
ତେଲଙ୍ଗା, *n.* *Telanga*, Telugu.
ତେଲଙ୍ଗା, *a.* belonging to Telugu country or caste.
ତେଲଚଟା, *n.* a cockroach.
ତେଲ୍ଲଭଣି, *n.* a concave earthen pan.
ତେଲିଆ, *a.* oiled, smeared with oil.
ତେଲି, *n.* an oilman, oil-grinder; name of the caste; *fem.* ତେଲୁଣୀ.
ତେସନ, ତେସେ, *ad.* likewise, in that manner, so (poetical).
* ତୈଜସ, *a.* metallic.
ତୈୟାର, *a.* see ତିଆର.
ତୈଳ, *n.* oil, unctuous matter.
* ତୈଳକାର, *n.* see ତେଲି.
* ତୈଳଯନ୍ତ୍ର, *n.* an oil-mill.
ତୈଲଙ୍ଗ, *n.* the *Telanga* or Telugu [country.
ତୋଟା, *n.* a grove, a garden, a *tope* of trees.
ତୋଣ୍ଟି, *n.* throat.
ତୋଡ, *n.* the violence of a stream; [anger.
ତୋଡା, *n.* a purse, bag of money.
ତୋରାଣି, ତୋରଣି, *n.* rice water.
ତୋଢ, *n.* a kind of fish.
ତୋତଲ, *a.* stammering.
ତୋତା, *n.* a parrot, parrakeet.
ତୋପ, *n.* a big gun, cannon, artillery.
ତୋଫା, *a.* bright, pure, good.
ତୋଫାନ, *n.* tempest, cyclone, hurricane.
* ତୋୟ, *n.* water.
* ତୋୟଦ, *n.* a cloud.

ତୋର, ତୋହର, ତୋହୋର, *pron.* thy, thine, your, yours, (inferior or familiar).

* ତୋରଣ, *n.* a portal, porch, verandah.

ତୋଫା, *a.* pretty, fine, beautiful.

ତୋଲା, *n.* a rupee's weight.

ତୋଳାଇବା, *v.* to cause to be gathered or plucked ; to cause to be built.

ତୋଳିବା, *v.* to pluck; to build; to lift up, to raise.

ତୋଷ, *n.* pleasure, gratification.

ତୋଷକ, *n.* a cotton bed, mattress.

* ତୋଷଣ, *n.* the gratifying of a person.

ତୋଷାମୋଦ, *n.* flattery, undue praise.

ତୋଷିବା, *v.* to gratify, to please, to satisfy.

ତୌଲ, *n.* the act of weighing; weight.

ତୌଲିବା, *v.* to weigh.

ତ୍ୟକ୍ତ, *a.* left, forsaken, forlorn.

ତ୍ୟାଗ, *n.* forsaking, letting go.

* ତ୍ୟାଗପତ୍ର, *n.* a bill of divorcement.

* ତ୍ୟାଗଶୀଳ, *a.* generous, liberal.

* ତ୍ୟାଗଶୀଳତା, *n.* generosity.

* ତ୍ୟାଗୀ, *a.* relinquishing.

* ତ୍ୟାଜ୍ୟ, *a.* liable to be forsaken.

* ତ୍ରପା, *n.* shame, modesty, shyness.

* ତ୍ରୟ, *a.* three together.

* ତ୍ରୟୋଦଶ, *a.* thirteen.

ତ୍ରୟୋଦଶୀ, *a.* the thirteenth day of the moon (applies to the first and second half of the moon).

* ତ୍ରସରେଣୁ, *n.* a mote in a sun-beam.

ତ୍ରସ୍ତ, *a.* frightened, alarmed.

ତ୍ରାଣ, *n.* salvation, preservation.

ତ୍ରାଣକର୍ତ୍ତା, *n.* a saviour, a deliverer.

ତ୍ରାତା, *n.* a saviour, redeemer.

ତ୍ରାସ, *n.* fear, dread, alarm.

ତ୍ରାହି, *v.* save ! deliver !

* ତ୍ରି, *a.* three.

* ତ୍ରିଂଶ, *a.* thirtieth.

* ତ୍ରିଂଶତ୍, *a.* thirty.

ତ୍ରିକଟୁ, *n.* the three spices, *viz.*, ginger, long pepper, black pepper.

ତ୍ରିକାଳ, *n.* past, present, future.

* ତ୍ରିକୂଟ, *a.* three-peaked.

ତ୍ରିକୋଣ, *a.* triangular ;—*n.* a triangle.

ତ୍ରିକୋଣମଣ୍ଡଳ, ତ୍ରିକୋଣଭୂମି, *n.* (in *Geog.*) a delta.

ତ୍ରିକୋଣମିତି, *n.* Trigonometry.

ତ୍ରିଗୁଣ, *n.* the three primeval qualities of matter—*viz.* existence (ସତ୍ତ୍ୱ), activity (ରଜଃ), inertness (ତମଃ);—*a.* consisting of three threads or cords; threefold.

ତ୍ରିଜଗତ, *n.* three worlds.

* ତ୍ରିତଳ, *a.* three-storied.

* ତ୍ରିଦଶ, *n.* a god.

* ତ୍ରିଦଶାରି, *n.* enemy of the gods.

* ତ୍ରିଦଶାଳୟ, *n.* heaven of the gods.

* ତ୍ରିଦିବ, *n.* heaven, sky, atmosphere.

ତ୍ରିଦୋଷ, *n.* a vitiated state of the three humours, *viz.* bile, wind, phlegm.

ତ୍ରିଧା, *a.* threefold; of three kinds; —*ad.* in three parts.

* ତ୍ରିପଥଗା, *n.* the river Ganges.

ତ୍ରିପଣ୍ଡ, *a.* excessively (black).

* ତ୍ରିପଦୀ, *n.* a tripod, a teapoy.

ତ୍ରିଫଳା, *n.* three medicinal fruits.

* ତ୍ରିବର୍ଗ, *n.* three objects of pursuit, *viz.* love, duty, wealth.

* ତ୍ରିବର୍ଣ୍ଣ, *n.* the three great castes.

* ତ୍ରିବଳି, ତ୍ରିବଳୀ, *n.* the three wrinkles of skin above the navel.

ତ୍ରିବିଧ, *a.* of three kinds.

* ତ୍ରିବେଣୀ, *n.* confluence of three streams.

ତ୍ରିଭୁଜ, *n.* three-sided figure, triangle;—*a.* having three arms.

ତ୍ରିଭୁବନ, ତ୍ରିଲୋକ, *n.* the three worlds.

* ତ୍ରିଲୋକେଶ, *n.* the sun.

ତ୍ରିଶୂଳ, *n.* a trident.

* ତ୍ରିସନ୍ଧ୍ୟା, *n.* dawn, noon, evening.

ତ୍ରୁଟି, ତ୍ରୁଟୀ, *n.* defect, flaw, fault; loss.

ତ୍ରେତା, *n.* the second *yúg.*

ତ୍ରୈମାସିକ, *a.* quarterly.

ତ୍ରୈରାଶିକ, *n.* the rule of three.

* ତ୍ରୈଲୋକ୍ୟ, *n.* the three worlds together.

* ତ୍ର୍ୟାହିକ, *a.* of every third day, tertian.

* ତ୍ୱକ୍, *n.* skin, bark, rind.

* ତ୍ୱକ୍‌ଛେଦ, *n.* circumcision.

* ତ୍ୱକ୍‌ପତ୍ର, *n.* the cassia leaf.

* ତ୍ୱଦୀୟ, *pron.* thy, thine.

* ତ୍ୱରା, *n.* quickness, haste, hurry.

ତ୍ୱରିତ, *ad.* soon, rapidly, quickly.

* ତ୍ୱିଷାମ୍ପତି, *n.* the sun.

ଥ.

ଥ, the seventeenth consonant.

ଥକା, *a.* fagged, wearied.

ଥକାମରା, *a.* weary, fatigued; suspicious.

ଥକିବା, *v.* to become weary.

ଥଙ୍ଗଥଙ୍ଗ, *a.* slow to proceed, suspicious.

ଥଙ୍ଗେଇହେବା, *v.* to pause, to be in suspense.

ଥଟା, ଥଟ୍ଟା, *n.* mockery, jest, ridicule.

ଥଟାରି, *n.* a brazier, brass-founder, (*fem.* ଥଟାରୁଣୀ).

ଥଣ୍ଟ, *n.* a beak.

ଥଣ୍ଟିଆ, *n.* a kind of alligator.

ଥଣ୍ଡା, *a.* cold; tranquil, mild.

* ଥନ, *n.* the bosom, breast, nipple.

ଥନଥନ, *a.* full of tears, ready to weep.

ଥନଦୁଷ, *n.* a disease in the breast of a woman.

ଥଣ୍ଡୁସ, *a.* blunt, dull-edged.

ଥନ୍ଦୁଲ, *a.* corpulent, abdominous.

ଥପଥପ, *n.* sound of liquids dripping.

* ଥବିର, *a.* old, aged.

ଥମାଇବା, *v.* to cause to stop, to appease, to cool down.

ଥମିବା, ଥମିଥିବା, ଥମ୍ବିବା, *v.* to stop, to cease.

ଥସ୍, *a.* calm, serene.

ଥର, *n.* times (as ଏକଥର once, ଦୁଇ-ଥର twice, etc.)

ଥରକୁଥର, *ad.* time after time.

ଥରଥର, *a.* shivering, palpitating.

ଥରିବା, *v.* to tremble, to shiver.

ଥରେ, *ad.* once

ଥରେଥରେ, *ad.* sometimes; time after time.

ଥଳ, *n.* a ford, ground; a bottom.

ଥଳପଦ୍ମ, *n.* a flowering shrub, lily of the valley.

ଥଳୀ, ଥଳି, ଥଳିଆ, *n.* a string bag, a sack, a pouch.

ଥାକ, *n.* layer; a recess in a wall.

ଥାକୁଲ, *a.* very stout.

ଥାକୁଲି, *a.* very stout (woman).

ଥାଟ, *n.* framework of a roof, a bamboo framework for decoration purposes; an army.

ଥାତ, *n.* a deposit of money.

ଥାନ, *n.* a place, room; piece of cloth; a sheet of gold, silver or copper; a utensil for holding anything.

*ଥାନମୁଦ୍ରା, *n.* the temples.

ଥାନା, *n.* a police station, watch-house.

ଥାନି, *n.* resident.

ଥାନିପଟ୍ଟା, *n.* lease given to a resident ryot.

ଥାନେ, *ad.* in one place;—*n.* a whole length (of cloth).

ଥାପିବା, *v.* to plant, to establish.

ଥାଳ, *n.* a bowl or similar article made from the rind of a gourd, etc.; a plate.

ଥାଳିଆ, *n.* a small plate.

ଥିବା, *v.* to be, to remain.

ଥିର, *a.* settled, steadfast, grave, not moving.

ଥୁ, ଥୁକ, ଥୁଡ଼, *n.* spittle, saliva;—*inter.* fye!

ଥୁଆଥୋଇ, *n.* a putting; marriage of a widow.

ଥୁଣ୍ଟା, *a.* maimed, lopped; bereft.

ଥେଣ୍ଟା, *a.* disobedient, *fem.* ଥେଣ୍ଟୀ.

ଥୈଲା, ଥୈଲି, *n.* a bag, sack, purse.

ଥୋଇବା, *v.* to put down, to place.

ଥୋକେ, ଥୋକାଏ, *a.* some, a few, certain.

ଥୋଡ, *n.* green ear of corn, the spathe of a plantain tree.

ଥୋଡା, *a.* few, a little.

ଥୋଡିଆ, ଥୋଇଆ, *a.* (bullock) carrying a burden on the back.

ଥୋପ, *n.* a bait for fish.

ଥୋପା, *n.* a bunch, cluster, tassel.

ଥୋମଣି, ଥୋମ୍ବଣା, *n.* the lips of cattle.

ଥୋର, ଥୋରପାଡ଼ାର, *n.* an elephant's trunk.

ଥୋବର, *a.* wearied; shameless.

ଦ.

ଦ, the eighteenth consonant.

*ଦଂଶ, *n.* tooth, sting; bite; a gadfly.

*ଦଂଶକ, *n.* a gadfly.

ଦଂଶନ, *n.* a biting, a stinging.

*ଦଂଶିତ, *a.* bitten, stung.

*ଦଂଷ୍ଟ୍ରା, *n.* a tooth, fang, sting.

ଦଉଡ଼, ଦଉଡ଼ା, ଦଉଡ଼ି, *n.* string, rope.

ଦଉରି, *n.* the sessions.

ଦକ, ଦକା, *n.* fear, anxiety.

ଦକଦକ, *a.* fearful, anxious.

ଦଖଲ, *n.* possession; mud.

ଦଖଲ୍ କରିବା, *v.* to take possession of, to occupy.

ଦଖଲକାର, *n.* one who has possession, possessor.

ଦଖଲନାମା, *n.* deed of occupancy right.

ଦଖଲି, *a.* muddy.

ଦଗା, *n.* deceit, imposture, treachery.

ଦଗାଦିଆ, ଦଗାବାଜ୍, ଦଗାଦାର, *n.* a cheat, a traitor, an impostor; —*a.* deceitful, treacherous.

ଦଗାବାଜି, *n.* cheating, treachery.

ଦଗ୍ଧ, *a.* burnt, consumed.

ଦଙ୍ଗା, *n.* tumult, uproar, a row.

ଦଙ୍ଗାବାଜ୍, *a.* riotous, rowdy, quarrelsome.

ଦଢ଼, *a.* uninjured, firm, stiff, hard.

ଦଣ୍ଡ, *n.* punishment; a stick; sceptre; a division of time equal to 24 minutes.

ଦଣ୍ଡକରେ, ଦଣ୍ଡକେ, *ad.* in an instant.

ଦଣ୍ଡଦାତା, *n.* one who punishes.

*ଦଣ୍ଡଧର, ଦଣ୍ଡଧାରୀ, *n.* a king.

ଦଣ୍ଡନୀୟ, *a.* punishable.

*ଦଣ୍ଡପାଳ, *n.* a doorkeeper, *durwan.*

ଦଣ୍ଡବତ୍, *n.* prostration;—*a.* like a staff.

ଦଣ୍ଡବିଧି, *n.* criminal law.

ଦଣ୍ଡା, *n.* side-pieces of a bullock-cart; a village path.

*ଦଣ୍ଡାଘାତ, *n.* a blow with a staff.

ଦଣ୍ଡାୟମାନ, *a.* standing, standing erect.

ଦଣ୍ଡାଜ୍ଞା, *n.* judicial sentence of condemnation.

*ଦଣ୍ଡାର୍ହ, *a.* deserving of punishment.

*ଦଣ୍ଡିତ, *a.* punished, sentenced, fined.

ଦଣ୍ଡି, *n.* an ornament for the nose.

ଦଣ୍ଡିଦାର, ଦଣ୍ଡିଆ, *n.* a middle-man, a weigher of grain.

ଦଣ୍ଡିବା, *v.* to punish.

ଦଣ୍ଡିଲ, *a.* wicked, mischievous.

*ଦଣ୍ଡୀ, *n.* an ascetic, a mendicant.

*ଦଣ୍ଡ୍ୟ, *a.* punishable; worthy of punishment.

ଦଣ୍ଡୁଆରି, *n.* a watchman; pincers.

ଦତ୍ତ, *a.* given, bestowed, given away.

*ଦତ୍ତକପୁତ୍ର, *n.* an adopted son.

*ଦତ୍ତା, *a.* betrothed (maid).

ଦତ୍ତାପହାରୀ, *n.* one who gives and then takes away.

ଦଦରା, *a.* shattered, cracked, shaky.

* ଦଦ୍ରୁ, ଦଦ୍ରୂ, *n.* ringworm.

ଦଧି, *n.* curds, curdled milk.

ଦନା, *n.* a cup made of a leaf.

ଦନ୍ତ, *n.* a tooth, fang, tusk.

* ଦନ୍ତଧାବନ, *n.* cleansing the teeth.

ଦନ୍ତଶୂଳ, *n*, the toothache.

* ଦନ୍ତଶୋଧନୀ, *n.* a tooth-pick.

ଦନ୍ତହୀନ, *a.* toothless.

ଦନ୍ତା, *a.* having prominent teeth; —*n.* a male elephant.

* ଦନ୍ତାବଳ, *n.* an elephant.

ଦନ୍ତାଳୋକ, *n.* a competent or all-round man.

* ଦନ୍ତୀ, *a.* tusked ;—*n.* a male elephant ; a medicinal plant.

* ଦନ୍ତୁର, *a.* uneven, thickly studded with.

ଦନ୍ତ୍ୟ, *a.* dental.

ଦପ୍ତର, ଦଫତର, *n.* a book, a journal.

ଦପ୍ତର ଖାନା, ଦଫତର ଖାନା, *n.* a counting house ; an office ; a book-binding room.

ଦପ୍ତରି, ଦଫ୍ତରି, *n.* a book-binder.

ଦଫା, *n.* an instalment ; a section, division ; paragraph ; item ; time, once.

ଦଫାକୁ ଦଫା, ଦଫାଦଫା, *ad.* repeatedly, time after time, by instalments.

ଦଫାଦାର, *n.* an officer at the head of a small number of watchmen or chaukidars, *dafadar*.

ଦଫାଦାରି, *n.* duties of a *dafadar*.

ଦଫେ, *ad.* once, at one time, again.

ଦବ୍‌କ, *n.* fear, alarm, dread.

ଦବ୍‌କିବା, *v.* to startle, to draw back.

ଦବଦବ, *n.* cholera.

ଦବାଇ, ଦବେଇ, *n.* medicine.

ଦବାଇବା, ଦବେଇବା, *v.* to cause to sink or yield ; to cause to over-awe.

ଦବିବା, ଦବିଯିବା, *v.* to sink, to be over-awed, to be cowed.

ଦମ୍, *n.* breath; life; false hope.

ଦମ୍‌ଦେବା, *v.* to wind (a clock) ; to give false hope to, to deceive.

ଦମ୍‌ନେବା, *v.* to take rest, to rest.

* ଦମ, *n.* self-restraint.

ଦମକଳ, *n.* a pump ; a fire engine ; a screw-jack, a crane.

ଦମନ, *n.* subduing, keeping in order.

ଦମା, *n.* panting, asthma.

* ଦମ୍ପତି, *n.* husband and wife.

ଦମ୍ଭ, *n.* bragging, arrogance.

ଦମ୍ଭିଷ୍ଟ, *a.* strong, stiff.

ଦମ୍ଭୀ, *a.* proud, arrogant.

* ଦମ୍ୟ, ଦମନୀୟ, *a.* subduable.

ଦୟା, *a.* pity, compassion, mercy.

ଦୟାପାତ୍ର, ଦୟାଭାଜନ, *n.* an object of compassion.

ଦୟାନିଧି, *n.* an ocean of pity.

ଦୟାବାନ୍, ଦୟାମୟ, *a.* merciful, compassionate.

ଦୟାଳୁ, *a.* kind, merciful, compassionate.

* ଦୟିତ, *a.* favoured, beloved;—*n.* a husband.

* ଦୟିତା, *n.* a beloved wife.
ଦର, *n.* rate, price, value; * fear.
ଦରକାର, *n.* need, want, necessity.
ଦରକାରୀ, *a.* necessary, important.
ଦରଖାସ୍ତ, *n.* a petition, a request.
ଦରଖିଆ, *a.* having eaten only a portion of one's meal.
ଦରଗାଧୁଆ, *a.* partly bathed.
ଦରଜି, ଦରଜୀ, *n.* a tailor.
ଦରଦ, ଦରଜ, *n.* pain;—*a.* painful.
ଦରପାଚିଲା, *a.* half-ripe.
ଦରପେଶ, *n.* bringing into view.
ଦରପୋଡା, *a.* half-burnt.
ଦରବାର, ଦର୍ବାର, *n.* a court, *durbar*, hall of audience.
ଦରବୁଢା, *a.* a little old.
ଦରଭଙ୍ଗା, *a.* partly broken.
ଦରମରା, *a.* half-dead.
ଦରମା, ଦରମାହା, *n.* salary, monthly wages.
ଦରସିଝା, *a.* partly boiled or cooked.
ଦରହସା, *a.* smiling (sneeringly).
ଦରାଜ, *n.* drawers (of a desk, table, etc.)
ଦରାଣ୍ଡିବା, *v.* to search, to grope in darkness.
ଦରିଆ, *n.* sea.
ଦରିଦ୍ର, *a.* very poor, indigent.
ଦରିଦ୍ରତା, *n.* poverty, indigence.
ଦରୀ, ଦରି, *n.* a carpet, *durrie*; * a mountain cleft, a cave.
ଦରେଡି, *a.* half-boiled.
ଦରେଡି କଥା, *n.* baby-talk.
ଦରୋଆନ, *n.* a doorkeeper, a porter, *durwan.*
ଦରୋଜା, ଦରଜା, *n.* door, gate.
ଦର୍ଗା, ଦରଗା, *n.* the tomb of some reputed Muhammadan saint.
ଦର୍ପ, *n.* boasting, vanity, pride.
* ଦର୍ପକ, *n.* a boaster; cupid.
ଦର୍ପଣ, *n.* a mirror, looking-glass.
ଦର୍ପୀ, *a.* proud, arrogant.
ଦର୍ଶକ, *n.* a spectator.
ଦର୍ଶନ, *n.* seeing, a sight, view; philosophical books of the Hindus.
ଦର୍ଶନୀ, *n.* a present on meeting.
* ଦର୍ଶନୀୟ, *a.* visible; beautiful, agreeable to the sight.
ଦର୍ଶାଇବା, *v.* to point out, to show.
* ଦର୍ଶିତ, *a.* seen, viewed ; shewn, exhibited ; manifested.
* ଦର୍ଶୀ, *n.* seeing, beholding, viewing (*e.g.* ସର୍ବଦର୍ଶୀ, ଦୂରଦର୍ଶୀ).
ଦଳ, *n.* an aquatic grass; a party, detachment; * a leaf.
* ଦଳନ, *n.* treading, kneading, pressing.
ଦଳପତି, *n.* the leader of a party.
ଦଳାଦଳି, *n.* a trampling, kneading or squeezing.
* ଦଳିତ, *a.* trodden down, ground (to powder).
ଦଳିବା, *v.* to tread down, to crush, to knead.
ଦଳୁଆ, *a.* weedy, full of weeds (water).
ଦଲ୍‌ଦଲ୍, *a.* tremulous, shaking.
ଦଲସ, *n.* materials for building, &c.

ଦଲାଲ, *n.* a broker.
ଦଲାଲି, *n.* brokerage ; percentage.
ଦଲିଲ, ଦଲୀଲ, *n.* written proof, document, voucher.
ଦଶ, *a.* and *n.* ten, 10, x.
ଦଶକ, *n.* tens.
ଦଶକର୍ମ, *n.* the ten actions or rules necessary to *Brahmins.*
*ଦଶନ, *n.* a tooth, tusk, fang.
ଦଶମ, *a.* tenth.
ଦଶମିକ, *a.* decimal.
ଦଶମୀ, *n.* the tenth lunar day (applied to first and second half of the moon).
ଦଶମୂଳ, *n.* ten medicinal roots.
ଦଶହରା, *n.* a festival held on the tenth day of the moon in *Ashwina.*
ଦଶା, *n.* state, condition. [*Vishnu.*
ଦଶାବତାର, *n.* ten incarnations of
ଦଶି, ଦଶୀ, *n.* a hem or border ; coarse thread.
ଦଶିଆ, *n.* a coarse kind of cloth.
ଦସ୍ତ, *n.* the hand; stool.
ଦସ୍ତକ, *n.* a summons, pass, permit.
ଦସ୍ତଖତ, *n.* a signature.
ଦସ୍ତା, *n.* pewter, zinc.
ଦସ୍ତାନା, *n.* a glove. [voucher.
ଦସ୍ତାବିଜ, ଦସ୍ତାବେଜ, *n.* a document,
ଦସ୍ତି, *n.* land measurement rod.
ଦସ୍ତୁର, *n.* a custom, fashion, mode, rule. [*dasturi.*
ଦସ୍ତୁରି, ଦସ୍ତୁରୀ, *n.* custom; percentage,

*ଦସ୍ୟୁ, *n.* a plunderer, a robber.
*ଦସ୍ୟୁତା, *n.* robbery, plunder.
ଦହ, *n.* an abyss, chasm ;—*a.* muddy, slobby.
*ଦହନ, *n.* burning, conflagration.
*ଦହନୀୟ, *a.* combustible.
ଦହଲ, *n.* mud, sludge.
ଦହି, *n.* curds. [to burn.
ଦହିବା, *v.* to cause intense anxiety;
ଦହିହେବା, *v.* to be burnt, to be in great anxiety. [ing.
*ଦହ୍ୟ, *a.* combustible, fit for burn-
*ଦକ୍ଷ, *a.* clever, expert, able.
ଦକ୍ଷିଣ, *n.* south, the right hand side. [southern.
ଦକ୍ଷିଣା, *n.* a religious fee ;—*a.*
*ଦକ୍ଷିଣାପଥ, *n.* southern country; Deccan.
*ଦକ୍ଷିଣାବର୍ତ୍ତ, *a.* turning to the right, turned towards the south.
*ଦକ୍ଷିଣାୟନ, *n.* south declension of the sun. [corn.
ଦକ୍ଷିଣାୟନାନ୍ତବୃତ୍ତ, *n.* tropic of capri-
ଦା, ଦାଆ, *n.* a sickle, a bill-hook.
ଦାଉଶ, *n.* a small sickle for weed-
ଦାଈ, *n.* a midwife, a nurse. [ing.
ଦାଉ, *n.* revenge, retaliation.
ଦାଉଦା, *n.* a claim;—*a.* revengeful.
ଦାଉଦାଉ, *a.* blazing or flaring up, bright.
ଦାଉଣା, *n.* a rope used to yoke bullocks together while threshing.

ଦାଏର, *a.* filed, instituted, pending, (*e.g.* a suit in court).
ଦାଖଲ୍, *n.* a delivering of.
ଦାଖଲ୍‌ଖାରଜ୍, *a.* transference of property from one person to another, settlement of the division of a joint estate.
ଦାଖିଲା, *n.* a receipt, acquittance.
ଦାଗ, *n.* a stain, a mark, a blot.
ଦାଗିବା, *v.* to mark, to brand, to stain.
ଦାଗୀ, *a.* marked, spotted;—*n.* a convict, a marked man.
* ଦାଡମ୍ବ, *n.* a pomegranate.
ଦାଢ, *n.* a sharp edge.
ଦାଢି, *n.* beard, the chin.
ଦାଢିଆ, *n.* and *a.* a person wearing a beard.
ଦାଢ଼ୁଆ, *a.* sharpened, whetted.
ଦାଣ୍ଡିବା, *v.* to check, to restrain.
ଦାଣ୍ଡ, *n.* a road, way, path, high road.
ଦାଣ୍ଡି, *n.* by-road, path.
ଦାତବ୍ୟ, *a.* suitable to be given.
ଦାତା, *n.* a giver, a liberal or generous man.
* ଦାତୃତ୍ୱ, *n.* generosity, charitableness.
* ଦାତ୍ର, *n.* a sickle, a bill-hook.
ଦାଦନ, *n.* money advanced, earnest money.
ଦାଦା, *n.* an uncle (paternal); elder brother.
ଦାଦ, *n.* an uncle (paternal).
ଦାଦୁ, *n.* ringworm.

ଦାନ, *n.* a donation, gift; giving.
ଦାନପତ୍ର, *n.* deed of gift, a will.
ଦାନପାତ୍ର, *n.* recipient of a gift.
* ଦାନବ, *n.* a demon, fiend, giant.
ଦାନଶୀଳ, *a.* liberal, charitable.
* ଦାନଶୌଣ୍ଡ, *a.* generous, munificent.
ଦାନା, *n.* food; seed or grain.
ଦାନାଦାର, *a.* liberal, bountiful.
ଦାନାପାଣି, *n.* food and drink, maintenance.
ଦାନୀ, *a.* liberal, generous, openhanded.
ଦାନ୍ତ, *n.* a tooth;—*a.* * tamed, subjected; self-controlled.
ଦାନ୍ତକାଠି, *n.* a (stick) toothbrush.
ଦାନ୍ତଖୁଣ୍ଟା, *n.* a toothpick.
ଦାନ୍ତଘଷା, *n.* cleaning the teeth;—*a.* tooth-cleaning (powder, etc.).
ଦାନ୍ତପାଟି, *n.* a full set of teeth—upper and lower.
ଦାନ୍ତୁଆ, ଦାନ୍ତୁରା, *a.* having large teeth; *fem.* ଦାନ୍ତୁଈ, or ଦାନ୍ତୁରୀ.
ଦାନ୍ତେଉଠବା, *v.* to teethe.
* ଦାବାଗ୍ନି, ଦାବାନଳ, *n.* a forest-fire.
ଦାବି, ଦାବୀ, *n.* a claim, demand, accusation.
ଦାବିଦାର, *n.* a plaintiff, accuser.
ଦାମ୍, *n.* price, rate, value.
* ଦାମନୀ, *n.* a tethering rope.
ଦାମିକା, ଦାମୀ, *a.* valuable, expensive.
ଦାମୁଡ, *n.* a young bullock.
ଦାମ୍ପତ୍ୟ, *a.* conjugal.
ଦାମ୍ଭିକ, *a.* haughty, boasting, proud.
ଦାୟ, *n.* jeopardy; patrimony.

ଦାୟକ, an *affix* indicating that which gives.

ଦାୟଗ୍ରସ୍ତ, *a.* involved in trouble, overwhelmed with trouble, responsible.

ଦାୟଭାଗ, *n.* name of a book which treats of the laws of inheritance; * division of the inheritance.

* ଦାୟାଦ, *n.* a son, heir; claimant.

ଦାୟିତ୍ୱ, *n.* liability, responsibility.

ଦାୟୀ, *a.* responsible; liable; in debt.

* ଦାରଗ୍ରହଣ, *n.* taking a wife.

* ଦାର, *n.* a wife, married woman.

* ଦାରିଦ୍ର୍ୟ, ଦାରିଦ୍ର, *n.* see ଦରିଦ୍ରତା.

ଦାରୀ, *n.* a whore, an adulteress.

ଦାରୁ, *n.* wood, timber; a kind of wine.

ଦାରୁଚିନି, *n.* cinnamon.

ଦାରୁଣ, *a.* awful, cruel, intolerable.

ଦାରୁମୟ, *a.* wooden, made of wood.

ଦାରୋଗା, *n.* inspector of police; jailer; tax-collector.

* ଦାର୍ଢ୍ୟ, *n.* firmness, hardness, [strength.

ଦାର୍ଶନିକ, *n.* a philosopher;—*a.* philosophical.

ଦାଳୁଅ, *n.* late sown rice or paddy.

ଦାଶ, *n.* a surname of a Brahman.

ଦାଶରଥି, *n.* *Rama Chandra.*

* ଦାଶେରକ, ଦାସେର, ଦାସେରକ, *n.* a camel.

ଦାସ, *n.* a servant, slave, serf; a [surname.

ଦାସତ୍ୱ, *n.* servitude, slavery, bondage.

ଦାସୀ, *n.* a female servant or slave.

* ଦାସ୍ୟ, *n.* slavery, servitude;—*a.* slavish.

* ଦାହ, *n.* a burning, conflagration.

* ଦାହକ, *n.* one who burns, an incendiary; *fem.* ଦାହକା.

* ଦାହନ, *n.* burning, inflaming.

* ଦାହସ୍ଥଳ, *n.* a place to burn corpses.

ଦାହିକାଶକ୍ତି, *n.* a power of burning.

* ଦାହ୍ୟ, *a.* combustible, fit to be burnt.

ଦାକ୍ଷିଣାତ୍ୟ, *a.* coming from, belonging to or living in the south;—*n.* the Deccan country.

* ଦାକ୍ଷିଣ୍ୟ, *n.* courtesy, kindness; talent, cleverness.

ଦିଅ, *n.* a divinity;—*v. imp.* of to give.

ଦିଅର, *n.* a husband's younger [brother.

ଦିଆଉଦେବା, *v.* to cause to give; to cause to be given.

ଦିଆନ୍, ଦେୱାନ୍, *n.* political adviser of a Raja, *Dewan.*

ଦିକ୍, *n.* trouble, vexation; * a point of the compass.

ଦିକଦାର୍, ଦିକ୍‌ସିକ୍, *a.* displeased, vexed, out of humour.

* ଦିକ୍‌ପତି, ଦିକ୍‌ପାଳ, *n.* a ruler of the [quarters.

ଦିଗ, *n.* a quarter (as the east, the west, etc.).

* ଦିଗନ୍ତ, *n.* extreme distance, the horizon.

* ଦିଗମ୍ବର, *a.* naked, unclothed;—*n.* [*Shiva.*

* ଦିଗ୍‌ଦର୍ଶନ, *n.* a look on all sides.
ଦିଗ୍‌ଦର୍ଶନଯନ୍ତ୍ର, *n.* the compass.
ଦିଗ୍‌ବିଜୟ, *n.* universal conquest.
ଦିଗ୍‌ବିଜୟୀ, *a.* conquering the universe.
* ଦିଙ୍ମଣ୍ଡଳ, *n.* the circle of the heavens.
ଦିଦି, *n.* sister.
ଦିନ, *n.* day, daytime.
ଦିନେକ, *n.* one day.
ଦିନକର, *n.* of a day's duration; * the sun.
ଦିନକୁଦିନ, ଦିନପରଦିନ, ଦିନୁଦିନ, *ad.* day by day, daily.
ଦିନତମାମ୍, ଦିନମାନ, ଦିନସାର, ଦିନସାରା, *ad.* the whole day.
ଦିନପାତ, *n.* spending one's days.
* ଦିନମଣି, *n.* the sun.
ଦିନରାତି, *n.* and *ad.* day and night.
ଦିନାକେତେ, *ad.* for a few days, for some days.
ଦିନାତି, *ad.* every day;—*n.* an almanac.
* ଦିନାନ୍ତ, ଦିନାବସାନ, *n.* the evening.
ଦିନିଆ, used as an *affix* meaning consisting of a day or days (as ଏକଦିନିଆ, ଦୁଇଦିନିଆ, ଦଶଦିନିଆ, etc.).
ଦିନିକିଆ, *a.* for one day or time, not customary, unusual, occasional, not common.
ଦିନୁଦିନ, *ad.* from day to day.
ଦିବସ, *n.* a day, daytime.
* ଦିବା, *n.* a day, daytime.
* ଦିବାକର, *n.* the sun.
ଦିବାରାତ୍ର, *n.* and *ad.* see ଦିନରାତି.

ଦିବ୍ୟ, *a.* excellent; divine.
ଦିଲାସା, *n.* encouragement, hope.
* ଦିଶାହରା, *n.* lost, bewildered.
ଦିଶିବା, *v.* to come into sight, to appear.
ଦିସ୍ତ, *a.* a little, a few, some.
ଦିସ୍ତା, *n.* a quire of paper.
ଦିସ୍ତାପଡିବା, *v.* to become thin (of cloth).
ଦିସ୍ତାପଟ, *n.* corrugated iron sheet.
ଦିହୁଡି, *n.* a torch.
ଦୀଅଲି, *n.* a festival of illuminations held in the month of *Kartica.*
ଦୀଅଶଲିଆ, *n.* a lucifer match.
ଦୀଘୀ, *n.* an oblong pond.
ଦୀନ, *a.* poor, indigent, destitute.
ଦୀନନାଥ, ଦୀନବନ୍ଧୁ, *n.* God.
ଦୀପ, *n.* a light, lamp, candle.
* ଦୀପକ, *a.* illuminating, irradiating.
ଦୀପ-ଦଣ୍ଡି, *n.* pagoda built in the centre of a tank.
ଦୀପରଖା, ଦୀପରୁଖା, *n.* a lamp stand.
ଦୀପାବଳୀ, ଦୀପମାଳା, *n.* a row of lamps.
* ଦୀପିକା, *n.* a lamp, a light.
ଦୀପ୍ତି, *n.* light, brilliancy, beauty, splendour.
* ଦୀପ୍ତିମାନ୍, *a.* luminous, glorious, effulgent, radiant.
ଦୀର୍ଘ, *a.* long, tall, high.
ଦୀର୍ଘଜୀବୀ, *a.* long-lived, living long.
ଦୀର୍ଘନିଦ୍ରା, *n.* a long sleep; * death.
ଦୀର୍ଘନିଶ୍ୱାସ, ଦୀର୍ଘଶ୍ୱାସ, *n.* a deep-drawn sigh, a deep breath.

* ଦୀର୍ଘସୂତ୍ରିତା, ଦୀର୍ଘସୂତ୍ରତା, *n.* dilatoriness.
* ଦୀର୍ଘସୂତ୍ରୀ, *a.* dilatory, slow.
ଦୀର୍ଘସ୍ୱର, *n.* a long voice; (in *Gram.*) long vowel.
ଦୀର୍ଘାକାର, *a.* oblong, tall.
ଦୀର୍ଘାୟୁଃ, *a.* long-lived.
* ଦୀର୍ଘିକା, *n.* see ଦୀଘୀ.
ଦୀକ୍ଷା, *n.* religious services; initiation into a sacred mystery.
ଦୀକ୍ଷାଗୁରୁ, *n.* a teacher who initiates into sacred mysteries.
* ଦୀକ୍ଷିତ, *a.* initiated, engaged in religious service.
ଦୁଅ, *n.* a layer of a mud wall; a blessing.
ଦୁଅଏ, *n.* one layer of a mud wall.
ଦୁଅତ, *n.* an inkstand.
ଦୁଅର, *n.* a doorway, gateway, opening.
ଦୁଅଳିଅ, *a.* bankrupt.
ଦୁଇ, *a.* and *n.* two; 2; II.
ଦୁଇଏକ, *a.* one or two.
ଦୁଇଟା, *a.* two (single and entire).
ଦୁଇପହର, *n.* twelve o'clock, midday.
ଦୁଃଖ, *n.* affliction, trouble, want.
ଦୁଃଖକର, *a.* painful, afflicting, troublesome.
ଦୁଃଖଦାୟକ, * ଦୁଃଖଦ, *a.* afflictive, troublous.
ଦୁଃଖଧନ୍ଦା, *n.* labour, toil.
ଦୁଃଖସ୍ତା, *a.* unhappy.
ଦୁଃଖାର୍ତ୍ତ, *a.* afflicted, distressed.
ଦୁଃଖିତ, *a.* sad, morose.
ଦୁଃଖୀ, *a.* poor, distressed, miserable.
* ଦୁଃଶୀଳ, *a.* ill-natured, evil-disposed.
* ଦୁଃସହ, *a.* insupportable, intolerable.
ଦୁଃସାଧ୍ୟ, *a.* difficult to accomplish.
ଦୁଃସାହସ, *n.* temerity, audacity.
* ଦୁଃସ୍ଥ, *a.* badly off, indigent, poor.
ଦୁଃସ୍ୱପ୍ନ, *n.* a bad dream, nightmare.
ଦୁଃସ୍ୱଭାବ, *n.* an evil inclination, a wicked propensity, evil nature.
ଦୁରୁଦୁରୁ, *a.* trembling with fear.
ଦୁରୁଦୁରୁ, *n.* palpitation.
* ଦୁକୂଳ, *n.* a silk cloth.
ଦୁଗ୍ଧ, *n.* milk.
ଦୁଗ୍ଧପାନ, *n.* the act of sucking or drinking milk.
* ଦୁଗ୍ଧପୋଷ୍ୟ, *a.* feeding on milk;—*n.* a babe.
* ଦୁଗ୍ଧବତୀ, *a.* in milk, milch.
ଦୁଦୁର, *n.* name of a tree.
ଦୁଧ, *n.* milk.
ଦୁଧୁଆଳୀ, *a.* giving milk, milch.
ଦୁନିଆ, *n.* the earth, the world.
* ଦୁନ୍ଦୁଭି, *n.* a trumpet, kettle-drum.
ଦୁବ, *n.* *duba* grass.
ଦୁମ, *n.* a tail.
ଦୁମ୍ଚି, *n.* a crupper.
ଦୁରଦୃଷ୍ଟ, *n.* ill-fate, misfortune.
* ଦୁରନ୍ତ, *a.* unruly, malicious, cruel.
ଦୁରବସ୍ଥା, *n.* sad condition, misfortune.
* ଦୁରଭିସନ୍ଧି, *n.* evil intent.
* ଦୁରାକାଙ୍କ୍ଷା, *n.* inordinate ambition.

ଦୁରାଚାର, *n.* wickedness, profligacy; —*a.* wicked, profligate.

ଦୁରାଚାରୀ. *a.* wicked, profligate.

ଦୁରାତ୍ମା, *a.* evil-minded, tyrannical, wicked.

* ଦୁରାରୋହ, *a.* difficult of ascent, very high.

* ଦୁରାଳାପ, *n.* scurrilous language.

* ଦୁରାଶୟ, *a.* evil-minded, wicked, malicious.

ଦୁରାଶା, *n.* a bad or wicked desire.

* ଦୁରିତ, *n.* evil, sin.

* ଦୁରୂହ, *a.* hard to comprehend, abstruse, difficult.

ଦୁର୍ଗ, *n.* a fort.

ଦୁର୍ଗତି, *n.* distress, poverty, wretchedness.

ଦୁର୍ଗନ୍ଧ, *n.* a bad smell ;—*a.* stinking.

ଦୁର୍ଗମ, *a.* difficult of access.

ଦୁର୍ଗା, *n.* the goddess *Durgá.*

ଦୁର୍ଗାପୂଜା, *n.* the worship of *Durgá.*

* ଦୁର୍ଘଟ, *a.* hard to accomplish ;—*n.* a calamity.

ଦୁର୍ଘଟଣା, *n.* calamity.

ଦୁର୍ଜନ, *a.* wicked; hardhearted;—*n.* a tyrant.

ଦୁର୍ଜୟ, *a.* hard to be conquered.

ଦୁର୍ଦ୍ଦମ, *a.* fierce, invincible.

* ଦୁର୍ଦ୍ଦର୍ଶ, *a.* hardly visible, indistinct.

ଦୁର୍ଦ୍ଦଶା, *n.* a hard or sad condition.

ଦୁର୍ଦ୍ଦିନ, *n.* a cloudy day; adverse time.

ଦୁର୍ଦ୍ଦୈବ, *n.* ill luck, misfortune.

ଦୁର୍ନୟ, *n.* bad conduct, injustice.

ଦୁର୍ନାମ, *n.* a bad name, obloquy.

* ଦୁର୍ନିବାର, *a.* irresistible.

* ଦୁର୍ନୀତି, *n.* injustice, bad morals.

ଦୁର୍ବଳ, *a.* weak, feeble, impotent.

* ଦୁର୍ବହ, *a.* unbearable.

ଦୁର୍ବାକ୍ୟ, *n.* scurrility, obscene language.

* ଦୁର୍ବାର, *a.* irresistible.

ଦୁର୍ବିନୀତ, *a.* ill-mannered, ill-behaved, wicked.

ଦୁର୍ବୁଦ୍ଧି, *n.* stupidity, wickedness; a rogue;—*a.* stupid, wicked.

* ଦୁର୍ବୃତ୍ତ, *a.* unmanageable, unruly.

* ଦୁର୍ଭଗା, *n.* a wife not beloved;—*a.* hated.

ଦୁର୍ଭାଗା, *a.* unfortunate.

ଦୁର୍ଭାଗ୍ୟ, *n.* ill fortune, misfortune.

ଦୁର୍ଭାବନା, *n.* evil thought, malevolence.

ଦୁର୍ଭିକ୍ଷ, *n.* a famine, dearth, scarcity.

* ଦୁର୍ମତି, *a.* obstinate, ill-natured.

ଦୁର୍ମନା, *a.* dejected, low-spirited, sad.

* ଦୁର୍ମୁଖ, *a.* foul-mouthed, scurrilous.

ଦୁର୍ମୂଲ୍ୟ, *n.* dearness;—*a.* dear, high-priced.

ଦୁର୍ଯୋଗ, *n.* unfavourable conjuncture.

ଦୁର୍ଲଭ, *a.* difficult to get, scarce, rare.

ଦୁର୍ଲକ୍ଷଣ, *n.* bad sign, ill omen.

ଦୁଲିଚା, *n.* a kind of carpet.

ଦୁଲେଇ, *n.* a thin quilt.

ଦୁଶ୍ଚରିତ, *a.* evil-disposed, vicious.

* ଦୁଶ୍ଚିକିତ୍ସ୍ୟ, *a.* incapable of being medically treated, incurable.

ଦୁଶ୍ଚିନ୍ତା, *n.* evil thought, malevolence.
ଦୁଷ୍କର, *a.* difficult.
ଦୁଷ୍କର୍ମ, *n.* an evil deed, a crime.
* ଦୁଷ୍କର୍ମୀ, *a.* wicked, criminal, profligate.
ଦୁଷ୍କୃତ, *n.* an evil deed;–*a.* * wicked.
ଦୁଷ୍କୃତି, ଦୁଷ୍କୃତ, *n.* sin, evil deed.
ଦୁଷ୍ଟ, *a.* wicked, depraved, vicious.
ଦୁଷ୍ଟତା, *n.* wickedness, depravity.
ଦୁଷ୍ଟାମି, *n.* wickedness, turpitude.
ଦୁଷ୍ପ୍ରାପ୍ୟ, *a.* difficult to obtain, scarce.
* ଦୁଷ୍ପୁତ୍ର, *n.* a bad son, a wicked son.
ଦୁସ୍ତର, *a.* difficult, hard to get over.
ଦୁହାଁଳ, ଦୁହାଁଳିଆ, *a.* milch (cow).
ଦୁହିବା, *v.* to milk.
* ଦୁହିତା, *n.* a daughter.
ଦୂତ, *n.* a messenger, spy, an angel.
ଦୂତୀ, ଦୂତି, * ଦୂତିକା, *n.* a female messenger; a procuress.
ଦୂର, *a.* far, afar, distant, remote; —*n.* distance.
ଦୂରଦର୍ଶୀ, *a.* far-seeing, sagacious.
ଦୂରବର୍ତ୍ତୀ, *a.* remote.
ଦୂରବୀକ୍ଷଣ, ଦୂରବୀଣ, *n.* a telescope, spy-glass.
* ଦୂରୀକୃତ, *a.* removed, dismissed.
ଦୂଷଣ, *n.* blame; guilt.
* ଦୂଷଣୀୟ, *a.* blameworthy, condemnable.
* ଦୃକ୍, *n.* an eye, sight, seeing.
ଦୃକ୍‌ପାତ, *n.* a glance, look, notice.
ଦୃଢ, *a.* firm, hard, tough, fast.
* ଦୃଢପ୍ରତିଜ୍ଞ, *a.* firm to a promise, faithful to an agreement.
* ଦୃଢବାକ୍ୟ, *n.* one true to his word.
ଦୃଢବୋଧ, *n.* firm conviction, presumptive evidence.
ଦୃଶ୍ୟ, *n.* scenery;—*a.* visible, fit to be seen.
* ଦୃଷ୍ଟ, *a.* seen, apparent, evident.
ଦୃଷ୍ଟାନ୍ତ, *n.* a parable, simile, illustration.
ଦୃଷ୍ଟି, *n.* a view, look, sight, seeing.
ଦୃଷ୍ଟିଗୋଚର, *a.* in sight, in view.
ଦୃଷ୍ଟିପାତ, *n.* looking, regarding.
ଦେଉଳ, *n.* a temple, an idol temple.
ଦେଉଳିଆ, *n.* a class of brahmans; a bankrupt.
ଦେଖ, *inter.* behold! see!
ଦେଖଣାହାରି, *n.* spectators.
ଦେଖା, *n.* meeting;—*a.* seen.
ଦେଖାଇବା, *v.* to show, exhibit, point out.
ଦେଖାଦେଖି, *ad.* face to face; the act of looking into; searching.
ଦେଖିବା, *v.* to see, to look, to observe.
ଦେଖୁଁ ଦେଖୁଁ, *ad.* instantly, without delay.
ଦେଢଶୁର, ଦେଢଶ୍ୱୁର, *n.* a husband's elder brother.
ଦେଢ, *a.* one-and-a-half.
ଦେଢିଆ, *a.* aslant, leaning; one-and-a-half.
ଦେଢୀ, *n.* fifty per cent interest;—*a.* one-and-a-half.
ଦେଣ, ଦେଣା, *n.* a debt.
ଦେଣଦାର, ଦେଣାଦାର, *n.* a debtor;—*a.* having debts.
ଦେଦାର, *a.* plentiful, abundant.

* ଦେଦୀପ୍ୟମାନ, *a.* intensely bright, refulgent.

* ଦେବ, *n.* a god, a lord, a king.

ଦେବକୀ, *n.* mother of *Krushna*.

* ଦେବକୁସୁମ, *n.* a clove.

ଦେବତା, *n.* a deity, a god.

ଦେବତ୍ୱ, *n.* divinity, godhead.

ଦେବତ୍ର, *n.* lands endowed for the support of a temple.

ଦେବଦାରୁ, *n.* name of a tree, *Deodar*.

ଦେବନାଗର, ଦେବନାଗରୀ, *n.* a kind of character in which the Sanskrit is usually written and printed.

ଦେବପୁରୀ, *n.* heaven of the gods.

ଦେବପୂଜକ, *n.* an idolater, image-worshipper.

ଦେବପୂଜା, *n.* idolatry.

ଦେବବାଣୀ, *n.* oracle, a word from heaven.

* ଦେବର, *n.* a husband's younger brother.

* ଦେବରାଜ, *n.* *Indra* the king of the gods.

ଦେବର୍ଷି, *n.* a divine sage.

ଦେବଲୋକ, *n.* the abode of the gods.

ଦେବସ୍ୱ, *n.* property of the gods.

ଦେବହିଂସକ, *n.* an enemy of the gods.

ଦେବା, *v.* to give, to bestow.

ଦେବାଳୟ, *n.* a temple, a pagoda.

ଦେବୀ, *n.* a goddess ; a queen.

ଦେବୋତ୍ତର, *n.* see ଦେବତ୍ର.

ଦେୟ, *a.* due, fit to be given.

ଦେରି, *n.* lateness, delay.

ଦେଶ, *n.* a country, province; region or part of the body (in *Comp.*).

ଦେଶଜ, *a.* of genuine descent, indigenous.

ଦେଶଭାଷା, *n.* language of the country, vernacular.

ଦେଶାଚାର, *n.* customs or habits of a country.

* ଦେଶାନ୍ତ, *n.* a frontier.

ଦେଶାନ୍ତର, *n.* a foreign country.

ଦେଶୀ, ଦେଶୀୟ, *a.* of a country, home-made.

ଦେହ, *n.* the body.

* ଦେହତ୍ୟାଗ, ଦେହାନ୍ତର, *n.* death.

* ଦେହୀ, *a.* corporeal, embodied.

ଦେହୁଡ଼ି, *n.* a big door or gate.

* ଦୈତ୍ୟ, *n.* a demon, fiend, evil genius.

* ଦୈତ୍ୟାରି, *n.* a god, foe of demons.

* ଦୈନନ୍ଦିନ, *a.* happening daily.

ଦୈନିକ, *a.* daily.

* ଦୈନ୍ୟ, *n.* destitution, meanness.

ଦୈବ, *n.* providence;—*a.* providential, accidental.

ଦୈବଘଟଣା, *n.* an accident.

ଦୈବବାଣୀ, *n.* an oracle.

* ଦୈବଜ୍ଞ, *n.* an astrologer, fortune-teller.

ଦୈବଯୋଗ, *n.* an impulse, divine interposition.

ଦୈବଯୋଗେ, ଦୈବାତ୍, *ad.* accidentally, providentially, unexpectedly.

ଦୈବାଧୀନ, *a.* subject to providence.

ଦୈବୀ, *a.* providential, accidental or sudden.

* ଦୈହିକ, *a.* relating to the body.
* ଦୈର୍ଘ୍ୟ, *n.* length, longitude.
ଦୋଅଣା, *n.* an eighth, a two-anna bit.
ଦୋଅଢ଼, *n.* see ଦୁଅଢ଼.
ଦୋଓଳ, ଦୋଓର, *a.* twice, second time (of cultivation).
ଦୋଓଳା, *n.* second meal, lunch.
ଦୋଓଡ଼ାଇବା, *v.* to fold double; to go over twice.
ଦୋକତା, *n.* dried tobacco leaves.
ଦୋହର, *a.* double, twice.
ଦୋହାଠିଆ, *n.* pegs in the wall for holding articles.
ଦୋକାନ, *n.* a shop, a store.
ଦୋକାନଦାର, ଦୋକାନୀ, *n.* a shop or storekeeper.
ଦୋସ୍ଥ, *a.* occupying two places.
ଦୋଘାଢ଼, *n.* the crossing of two streams; contention or disputation between two parties.
ଦୋତାଲ, *a.* two-storied;—*n.* the upper storey.
* ଦୋଦୁଲ୍ୟମାନ, *a.* swinging backwards and forwards.
ଦୋନାକଡ଼ା, *a.* two-faced, deceitful.
ଦୋପଟ, *a.* twofold, twice.
ଦୋପରତା, *a.* with two thicknesses.
ଦୋଫସଲ, ଦୋଫଳୀ, *a.* (ground) producing two crops in the year.
ଦୋଭାଷୀ, *a.* bi-lingual.
ଦୋମହଲ, *a.* and *n.* see ଦୋତାଲ ।
ଦୋମାସୀ, *n.* an intercalary month.
ଦୋମୁଣ୍ଡିଆ, ଦୋମୁଁହା, *n.* a small worm-like snake said (erroneously) to have two heads.
ଦୋମୁହାଁଲୋକ, *n.* a two-faced man, a deceitful man.
ଦୋରସ୍ତ, *a.* whole, all.
ଦୋରୁପ, *n.* juice; juice of the sugarcane.
ଦୋରୁଆ, *a.* twice transplanted.
ଦୋଳ, ଦୋଳନ, *n.* swinging, oscillating.
ଦୋଳ, ଦୋଳଯାତ୍ରା, *n.* a swinging festival held in *Falguna.*
ଦୋଳା, *n.* a swing; litter, palkey.
ଦୋଳିବା, *v.* to swing, to oscillate.
ଦୋଷ, *n.* fault, defect, guilt, crime.
ଦୋଷଗୁଣ, *n.* defects and merits.
ଦୋଷଯୁକ୍ତ, *a.* guilty, full of evil.
ଦୋଷଗ୍ରାହୀ, *a.* malicious, malignant.
*ଦୋଷଜ୍ଞ, *a.* understanding faults or defects;—*n.* one who understands faults or defects.
ଦୋଷମନ୍, *n.* an enemy; enmity.
ଦୋଷାଦୋଷ, *n.* defects and merits, evil and good.
ଦୋଷାବହ, *a.* accusatory.
ଦୋଷୀ, *a.* guilty, in fault, culpable.
ଦୋସର, *n.* a second, a co-operator.
ଦୋସରା, *a.* another, second.
ଦୋସୂର, *a.* two-stringed, double-stringed.
ଦୋସନ୍ଧି, *n.* space between two boundaries.
ଦୋସ୍ତ, *n.* a friend, a companion.

ଦୋସ୍ତି, *n.* friendship.

* ଦୋହନ, *n.* milking, drawing out.

ଦୋହର, *a.* two-fold, double.

ଦୋହରା, *n.* see ଦୋଓଡ଼ା ।

ଦୋହରା. ଦୋହରି, *a.* double, twofold.

ଦୋହରାଇବା, *v.* to double, to fold.

ଦୋହଲାଇବା, *v.* to rock, to move to and fro.

ଦୋହଲିବା, *v.i.* to be ro^ked, to be moved backwards and forwards.

ଦୋହା, *n.* a couplet, a sort of verse.

ଦୋହାଁଳ, *a.* milch.

ଦୋହି, ଦୋହାଇ, *n.* an oath, appeal to God for justice. [ning.

ଦୌଡ଼, ଦୌଡ଼ା, *n.* a run, race, run-

ଦୌଡ଼ାଇବା, *v.* to cause to run.

ଦୌଡ଼ାଦୌଡ଼ି, *n.* running about, a general running.

ଦୌଡ଼ିବା, *v.* to run. [atrocity.

ଦୌରାତ୍ମ୍ୟ, *n.* violence, outrage,

* ଦୌର୍ଜନ୍ୟ, *n.* unprincipled conduct.

ଦୌର୍ବଲ୍ୟ, *n.* weakness.

ଦୌଲତ, *n.* riches, wealth, treasure.

* ଦୌହିତ୍ର, *n.* a daughter's son, grandson.

* ଦ୍ୟୁତି, *n.* light, splendour, lustre.

* ଦ୍ୟୁଲୋକ, *n.* celestial world, heaven.

* ଦ୍ୟୂତ, *n.* dice, gambling with dice.

* ଦ୍ରବ, *a.* watery;—*n.* fusion.

* ଦ୍ରବୀକୃତ, *a.* liquefied, made fluid.

* ଦ୍ରବୀଭୂତ, *a.* become fluid or liquid.

ଦ୍ରବ୍ୟ, *n.* substance, thing, material.

ଦ୍ରବ୍ୟବନ୍ତ, *a.* possessed of property.

ଦ୍ରଷ୍ଟବ୍ୟ, *a.* worth looking at.

* ଦ୍ରଷ୍ଟା, *n.* observer.

ଦ୍ରାଘିମା, *n.* longitude, length.

* ଦ୍ରାବକ, *a.* solvent, liquefying;—*n.* a solvent, flux for metals.

ଦ୍ରାକ୍ଷା, *n.* a grape, a raisin.

ଦ୍ରାକ୍ଷାଲତା, *n.* a vine. [grape.

ଦ୍ରାକ୍ଷାରସ, *n.* wine, the juice of the

ଦ୍ରୁତ, *a.* swift, fleet, quick, speedy.

* ଦ୍ରୁମ, *n.* a tree.

ଦ୍ରୋହ, *n.* malice, injury, spite.

ଦ୍ରୋହୀ, *a.* malignant, rebellious.

* ଦ୍ୱନ୍ଦ୍ୱ, *n.* a couple of opposites; strife; (in *Gram.*) name of a compound.

* ଦ୍ୱୟ, *n.* a couple, two, a pair.

* ଦ୍ୱାଦଶ, *a.* twelve.

ଦ୍ୱାଦଶୀ, *n.* the twelfth day of the lunar fortnight.

ଦ୍ୱାପର, *n.* third *Yuga*.

* ଦ୍ୱାବିଂଶ, *a.* twenty-two.

* ଦ୍ୱାବିଂଶତ, *a.* twenty-second.

ଦ୍ୱାର, ଦ୍ୱାରଦେଶ, *n.* a door-way, passage, entrance.

* ଦ୍ୱାରପାଳ, *n.* a porter, doorkeeper.

ଦ୍ୱାରା, *ad.* by, through, by means of.

ଦ୍ୱାରୀ, *n.* doorkeeper, porter.

ଦ୍ୱିଗୁଣ, *a.* twofold, double.

ଦ୍ୱିଜ, -*n.* a brahman. [ous.

* ଦ୍ୱିଜ, ଦ୍ୱିଜାତ, *a.* twice-born, ovipar-

* ଦ୍ୱିତଳ, *a.* and *n.* see ଦୋତାଲା.

ଦ୍ୱିତୀୟ, *a.* second;—*n.* the second.
ଦ୍ୱିତୀୟତଃ, *ad.* secondly.
ଦ୍ୱିତୀୟା, *n.* the second day of the lunar fortnight.
ଦ୍ୱିତ୍ୱ, *n.* duality; the dual; reduplication.
ଦ୍ୱିଧା, *n.* a dilemma;—*ad.* * in two parts, in two ways.
* ଦ୍ୱିରଦ, *n.* an elephant.
ଦ୍ୱିବିଧ, *a.* of two kinds.
ଦ୍ୱିରୁକ୍ତି, *n.* repetition, tautology.
* ଦ୍ୱିରେଫ, *n.* a humble-bee.
ଦ୍ୱିବଚନ, *n.* the dual number.
ଦ୍ୱୀପ, *n.* an island.
ଦ୍ୱୀପାନ୍ତରପ୍ରେରଣ, *n.* transportation.
ଦ୍ୱେଷ, *n.* malice, hatred, envy.
* ଦ୍ୱେଷୀ, *a.* envious, malicious, spiteful.
* ଦ୍ୱୈତ, *n.* duality, dualism in philosophy.
ଦ୍ୱୈତଜ୍ଞାନ, *n.* an idea of dualism.
ଦ୍ୱୈତବାଦ, *n.* the doctrine of dualism.
ଦ୍ୱୈତବାଦୀ, *n.* a dualist.
* ଦ୍ୱୈଧ, *n.* an ambiguity, a dilemma.
ଦ୍ୱୈପାୟନ, *n.* *Byásadeba* the compiler of the *Puranas.*
* ଦ୍ୱ୍ୟର୍ଥ, *a.* ambiguous;—*n.* a quibble, a pun.
* ଦ୍ୱ୍ୟାହିକ, *a.* occurring every other day.

ଧ.

ଧ, the nineteenth consonant.
ଧଁଇ, *n.* a cough, asthma.
ଧଇଁଆ, ଧଁସ୍ୱା, *a.* asthmatic.
ଧଁଇଧଁଇହେବା, *v.* to pant for breath.
ଧକଧକ, *n.* aching pain (as in tooth-ache, etc.).
ଧକାଇବା, *v.* to pant, to palpitate.
ଧକ୍କା, *n.* a push, shove, squeeze, a collision.
ଧକ୍କାଧକ୍କି, *n.* a crowding or pushing.
ଧକ୍କାମାରିବା, *v.* to push, to shove.
ଧଡ, *n.* the body, trunk, an emaciated body.
ଧଡଧଡ, *n.* a rumbling sound;—*a.* very infirm.
ଧଡସଡ, *ad.* quickly, hastily.
ଧଡସ୍ତ, *a.* very infirm, much shattered.
ଧଡା, *n.* a scale-beam; scales.
ଧଡଆ, *a.* emaciated, feeble, thin.
ଧଡି, *n.* border, edge, brink.
ଧଡିଦାର, *a.* having a hem or border (used of cloth).
ଧଣ୍ଡ, *n.* a water-snake.
ଧଣ୍ଡା, *n.* a necklace of flowers; an ensign.
ଧନ, (1) *n.* property, wealth, riches.
ଧନ, (2) *n.* an object of affection.
ଧନବାନ୍, ଧନବନ୍ତ, *a.* wealthy, rich, opulent.
ଧନାଢ୍ୟ, *a.* wealthy, very rich.
* ଧନାଧ୍ୟକ୍ଷ, *n.* a treasurer; *Kubera.*
ଧନାର୍ଜ୍ଜନ, *n.* acquisition of wealth.
ଧନସ୍ଥ, *n.* the Indian flax plant.
ଧନଆ, ଧନିଆ, *n.* coriander seed.
ଧନିଷ୍ଠା, *n.* 23rd stellar mansion.
ଧନୀ, *a.* see ଧନବାନ୍.
ଧନୁଃ, ଧନୁ, *n.* a bow; sign *Saggitarious.*

ଧନୁର୍ଗୁଣ, *n.* a bowstring.
ଧନୁର୍ଦ୍ଧର, *n.* an archer, a bow-man.
ଧନୁର୍ବିଦ୍ୟା, * ଧନୁର୍ବେଦ, *n.* archery.
ଧନୁଷ୍ଟଙ୍କାର, *n.* spasm; twang of a bowstring.
* ଧନୁଷ୍ପାଣି, *a.* armed with a bow.
ଧନ୍ଦଳ, *a.* dim-sighted.
ଧନ୍ଦା, *n.* work, the engagements and worry of life.
ଧନ୍ଦାଳିହେବା, *v.* to be in confusion, to be searching anxiously (as in the case of anything misplaced or lost).
ଧନ୍ଦହେବା, *v.* to be unsettled, to be in confusion; to be busy.
ଧନ୍ୟ, *a.* fortunate, happy, blessed.
ଧନ୍ୟବାଦ, *n.* thanksgiving, ascription of praise.
ଧନ୍ୱନ୍ତରି, *n.* physician of the gods.
ଧପା, *n.* swindling, deception, gambling. [swindle.
ଧପାଇବା, ଧପେଇବା, *v* to deceive, to
ଧପାବାଜ, ଧପାବାଜ୍, *n.* a deceiver, a swindler.
* ଧବ, *n.* a husband.
* ଧବଳ, *a.* white.
ଧବଳକୁଷ୍ଠ, *n.* white leprosy.
ଧମକ, ଧମକାଣ, *n.* reproof, scolding, threat.
ଧମକାଇବା, *v.* to reprove or threaten.
ଧମକାଧମକ, *n.* a scolding, a brawling.
ଧମନୀ, *n.* artery.
ଧରଣ, *n.* form, style, fashion; rate.
ଧରଣା ଦେବା, ଧାରଣା ଦେବା, *n.* to dun, to sit at a person's door with a threat of starving in order to recover a debt.
ଧରଣା ପଡିବା, ଧାରଣା ପଡିବା, *v.* to remain fasting before an idol under a declaration of not leaving without a boon (as recovery from sickness, etc.).
ଧରଣୀ, ଧରଣୀତଳ, *n.* the earth.
ଧର, *n.* a seizing, catching, holding; * the earth. [or hold.
ଧରାଇବା, *v.* to cause to seize, catch
ଧରାତଳ, *n.* surface of the earth, surface.
ଧରାଧରି, *n.* a clasping, wrestling.
ଧରାଟ, *a.* settled, adjusted.
* ଧରିତ୍ରୀ, *n.* the earth. [to arrest.
ଧରିବା, *v.* to catch, to hold; to seize,
ଧର୍ତ୍ତବ୍ୟ, *a.* apprehensible.
ଧର୍ମ, *n.* religion, piety; inherent virtue, nature, temper, character.
ଧର୍ମକର୍ମ, *n.* a religious action.
* ଧର୍ମତଃ, *ad.* according to law or rule; religiously.
ଧର୍ମଭ୍ରଷ୍ଟ, *n.* an apostate.
* ଧର୍ମପତ୍ନୀ, *n.* a lawful wife.
ଧର୍ମପଥ, *n.* way of religion or virtue.
ଧର୍ମପରାୟଣ, *a.* pious, religious.
ଧର୍ମପୁତ୍ର, *n.* an adopted son; *Yudhisthira.*
ଧର୍ମପୁସ୍ତକ, *n.* the Bible, the holy book.

ଧର୍ମବନ୍ତ, *a.* righteous, just, good.

* ଧର୍ମରାଜ, *n.* *Jama* the regent of death; *Yudhisthira.*

ଧର୍ମଶାଳା, *n.* an almshouse, hospital.

ଧର୍ମଶାସ୍ତ୍ର, *n.* a religious book, scriptures, the Bible.

ଧର୍ମଶିକ୍ଷା, *n.* religious teaching.

ଧର୍ମଶୀଳ, *a.* virtuous, religious.

ଧର୍ମସଭା, *n.* a holy convocation; a religious meeting; a court of justice.

ଧର୍ମାତ୍ମା, *n.* the Holy Spirit;—*a.* pious, holy.

ଧର୍ମାଧର୍ମ, *n.* religion and irreligion, virtue and vice. [judge.

* ଧର୍ମାଧିକରଣ, *n.* a court of law; a

ଧର୍ମାଧିକାରୀ, *n.* a sheriff;—*a.* having to adminster the law.

* ଧର୍ମାଧ୍ୟକ୍ଷ, *n.* a spiritual teacher.

ଧର୍ମାବତାର, *n.* a term of address used in petitions; an incarnation of justice or virtue. [nal.

* ଧର୍ମାସନ, *n.* judgment-seat, tribu-

ଧର୍ମୋପଦେଶ, *n.* a religious address or sermon, religious instruction.

ଧର୍ମୋପଦେଶକ, *n.* a preacher of religion.

ଧର୍ମିଷ୍ଠ, ଧର୍ମନିଷ୍ଠ, *a.* religious, pious, virtuous, just.

ଧଳା, *a.* white, fair.

ଧାଁଇବା, *v.* to run quickly. [wife.

ଧାଇ, *n.* a nurse, wetnurse, mid-

ଧାଉଡ଼ିଆ, *n.* a runner, an express.

ଧାଉଁଥିବା, *v.* to come constantly.

ଧାଡ଼ି, *n.* a row, a line, a range.

ଧାଡ଼ିକିଧାଡ଼ି, *ad.* in each row, in rows.

ଧାଡ଼ିଧାଡ଼ି, *ad.* in rows, in lines.

ଧାତକୀ, *n.* name of a tree and the medicine obtained from it.

* ଧାତା, *n.* providence; a nourisher.

ଧାତୁ, *n.* metal ore; a verbal root; semen, virile; an element; humour of the body (as phlegm, wind, bile).

ଧାତୁଭଙ୍ଗ, *n.* gleet, gonorrhœa.

ଧାତୁପୁଷ୍ଟି, *n.* nourishment, nutrition.

ଧାତୁପୁଷ୍ଟିକର, *a.* nourishing, nutritious.

ଧାତୁମୟ, *a.* made of metal, metallic.

ଧାତୁକ୍ଷୟ, *n.* gonorrhœa, decay of vital functions.

* ଧାତ୍ରୀ, *n.* a wet-nurse, midwife.

ଧାତ୍ରୀବିଦ୍ୟା, *n.* obstetric science, midwifery.

ଧାନ, ଧାନ୍ୟ, *n.* unhusked rice, paddy.

ଧାନୁଆ, *a.* mixed (rice with paddy); very small.

ଧାନୁଆମରିଚ, *n.* small chillies.

ଧାନେ, *n.* $\frac{1}{320}$ part of a *tola* of gold; a minute quantity.

ଧାପ, *n.* step in a staircase or ladder.

* ଧାବକ, *n.* a runner, messenger.

* ଧାବନ, *n.* a running.

* ଧାବମାନ, *a.* in the act of running.

* ଧାବିତ, *a.* running towards, going quickly.

ଧାମ, *n.* a sacred place; a dwelling place, a spot; a house; * the body.

ଧାର, *n.* a margin, edge; a loan, debt; a channel, water-course.

ଧାରକ, *a.* astringent;—*n.* *a holder.

*ଧାରଣ, *n.* holding, wearing.

ଧାରଣା, *n.* memory, a retentive memory; belief.

ଧାରା, *n.* a rule, a method, custom, habit; a channel, water-course.

ଧାରାକ୍ରମେ, *ad.* according to custom.

ଧାରାବାହିକ, ଧାରାବାହୀ, *a.* serial, according to custom, customary.

ଧାରୀ, *a.* having, holding (used in *Comp.*).

ଧାରୁଆ, *a.* in debt; sharpened, whetted.

ଧାରେଧାରେ, *ad.* along the side of.

ଧାର୍ମିକ, *a.* religious, pious, just, righteous.

ଧାର୍ଯ୍ୟ, *a.* fit to be retained; settled.

ଧାସ, *n.* glare, heat.

ଧିକ୍, *interj.* fie on it! out upon it!

ଧିକ୍କାର, *n.* contempt, reproach.

ଧିଠ, *a.* shameless, immodest.

ଧିମା, *a.* slow, deliberate; pacified.

*ଧୀ, *n.* understanding, knowledge (used in *Comp.*).

*ଧୀବର, *n.* a fisherman.

*ଧୀମାନ୍, *a.* intelligent, sensible, wise.

ଧୀର, *a.* intelligent, cautious; slow.

ଧୀରତା, *n.* patience, steadiness, deliberateness.

ଧୀରା, *a.* slow, *intelligent or docile (woman).

ଧୀରେ, ଧୀରେଧୀରେ, *ad.* slowly, calmly, gradually.

*ଧୀଶକ୍ତି, *n.* intelligence, understanding.

ଧୁଆ, *a.* washed, cleansed.

ଧୁଆଧୋଇ, *n.* the act of washing.

ଧୁକୁଧୁକୁ, *n.* palpitating, panting.

ଧୁଣ୍ଡା, *n.* a fat or corpulent man.

ଧୁଣ୍ଡିବା, ଧୁନ୍ଦିବା, *v.* to seek, to search.

ଧୁଣ୍ଡୀ, *n.* a fat woman.

ଧୁତୁରା, *n.* the thorn apple, *dhaturá*.

ଧୁନି, *n.* an ascetic's fire-heap.

ଧୁମଧାମ, ଧୁମାଧୁମି, *n.* much-a-do, hubbub, tumult.

ଧୁରନ୍ଧର, *a.* capable.

ଧୁରା, *n.* the fore part of a bullock-cart.

ଧୁଲେଇ, *n.* washing;—*a.* washed.

ଧୁଆଁ, *n.* smoke, steam, vapour.

ଧୁଆଁକଳ, *n.* steam-engine.

ଧୁଆଁକଳଜାହାଜ, *n.* a steamship.

ଧୁଆଁଟିଆ, *a.* smoky.

ଧୁଆଁପତ୍ର, *n.* tobacco, tobacco leaf.

*ଧୁନା, *n.* resin, incense.

ଧୁପ, *n.* incense.

ଧୁପାଟି, *n.* a censer, incense-pot.

*ଧୂମ, *n.* smoke, steam, vapour.

*ଧୂମକେତୁ, *n.* a comet.

ଧୂମାଳ, *a.* smoky;—*n.* a whirlwind, a wind storm.

ଧୂମ୍ର, *a.* purple, smoke-coloured;—*n.* smoke.

ଧୂର୍ତ୍ତ, *a.* crafty, subtle, knavish.

*ଧୂର୍ତ୍ତତା, *n.* craftiness, waggishness.

ଧୂଳି, *n*. dust; pollen.
ଧୂଳିଆ, *a*. dusty.
ଧୂଳିଆଘର, ଧୂଳିଆ, *n*. a house with wooden roofing. [dust.
ଧୂଳିଧୂସର, *a*. grey as dust, grey with
ଧୂସ, *n*. refuse or dust of corn.
ଧୂସା, *n*. flannel, woollen stuff.
ଧୂସର, *a*. grey.
* ଧୁସ୍ତୁର, *n*. see ଧାତୁର.
* ଧୃତ, *a*. caught, seized, arrested; held, taken.
* ଧୃତି, *n*. patience; tenacity.
* ଧୃଷ୍ଟ, *a*. bold, shameless, insolent.
ଧେଡ଼, *n*. a low-caste; *fem*. ଧେଡ଼ୁଆଣୀ.
ଧେଣ୍ଡୁର, *n*. drum, the beat of a drum.
* ଧେନୁ, *n*. a milch cow.
ଧୈର୍ଯ୍ୟ, *n*. patience, steadiness, forbearance, composure.
ଧୈର୍ଯ୍ୟବନ୍ତ, ଧୈର୍ଯ୍ୟବାନ, *a*. patient, forbearing, steady.
ଧୈର୍ଯ୍ୟଶୀଳ, *a*. forbearing, continent.
ଧୋଇ, *n*. inundation. [dation.
ଧୋଇଆ, *a*. (land) liable to inun-
ଧୋଇବା, *v*. to wash, to clean. [tion.
ଧୋକା, *n*. doubt, illusion, decep-
ଧୋତି, ଧୂତି, *n*. a small lower cloth.
ଧୋବ, *a*. white, glistening.
ଧୋବା, *n*. a washerman.
ଧୋବଣୀ, *n*. a washerwoman.
* ଧୌତ, *a*. washed, purified. [plate.
ଧ୍ୟାଇବା, *a*. to meditate, contem-
ଧ୍ୟାନ, *n*. meditation, contemplation.
* ଧ୍ୟାନଯୋଗ, *n*. religious abstraction. [*Yogi*.
* ଧ୍ୟାନୀ, *a*. contemplative ;—*n*. a
* ଧ୍ୟେୟ, *a*. to be meditated upon; —*n*. the object of meditation.
* ଧ୍ରୁବ, *a*. fixed, certain, permanent,
ଧ୍ରୁବତାରା, *n*. the polar star. [eternal.
ଧ୍ରୁବରେଖା, *n*. the equator.
* ଧ୍ରୁବଲୋକ, *n*. heaven.
ଧ୍ୱଂସ, *n*. destruction, ruin, loss.
* ଧ୍ୱଂସକ, *a*. destructive, ruinous.
ଧ୍ୱଂସନ, *n*. see ଧ୍ୱଂସ । [organ.
* ଧ୍ୱଜ, *n*. a flag, a standard; male
ଧ୍ୱଜଭଙ୍ଗ, *n*. impotency. [ner.
ଧ୍ୱଜା, *n*. a flag, a standard, a ban-
ଧ୍ୱଜାଧାରୀ, *n*. a standard bearer.
ଧ୍ୱନି, *n*. a noise, sound.
* ଧ୍ୱନିତ, *a*. sounded.
* ଧ୍ୱସ୍ତ, *a*. ruined, depraved, fallen.
* ଧ୍ୱାନ୍ତ, *n*. darkness, gloom. [moon.
* ଧ୍ୱାନ୍ତହାରୀ, ଧ୍ୱାନ୍ତାରି, *n*. the sun, the

ନ.

ନ, the twentieth consonant; a negative, no, not ;—*a*. an *n*. nine, 9, IX. [ments.
ନଅର, *n*. a palace ; inner apart-
ନଇଁବା, *v*. to bend, to incline.
ନଳ, ଲଳ, *n*. split cane, or fibres used for tying.
ନଈ, *n*. a river.
ନବେ, *a*. and *n*. ninety, 90, XC.

ନଉଡ, ଲଉଡ, *n.* a staff, cane, stick.
ନଉଡ, *n.* a large earthen pot, a large *handi.* [the nails.
ନଉରୁଣି, ନହୁରୁଣି, *n.* a tool for pairing
ନକଲ, *n.* a transcript, a copy; sport, mimicry.
ନକଲନବିସ୍, *n.* a copyist. [copying.
ନକଲିଆ, *a.* mimicking, imitating,
ନକ୍ସା, ନକ୍ଶା, *n.* picture, sketch, imitation. [(rice).
ନକାଉ, ନକେଉ, *a.* soft or over boiled
* ନକୁଳ, *n.* a mongoose, ichnuman.
* ନକ୍ର, *n.* a crocodile, an alligator.
ନଖ, * ନଖର, *n.* a finger or toe nail, a claw;—*a.* having nails, claws, or talons.
ନଖକଟା, *n.* paring of the nails.
ନଖଚିହ୍ନ, *n.* nail marks.
* ନଖଆୟୁଧ, ନଖାୟୁଧ, *a.* having nails or claws;—*n.* a lion; a tiger.
* ନଖଶୂଳ, *n.* a whitlow.
ନଖାଇବା, *v.* to scratch, to claw.
* ନଗ, *n.* an immovable object, a mountain.
ନଗଣ୍ୟ, *a.* mean, contemptible.
ନଗଦ, *a.* ready, in hand.
ନଗର, ନଗରୀ, *n.* a city, a town.
ନଗରବାସୀ, *n.* a citizen.
* ନଗରପାଳ, *n.* guardian or protector of the town, watchman.
ନଗରପ୍ରାନ୍ତ, *n.* the outskirts of a city.
ନଗରସ୍ଥ, *a.* urban, town-bred, city-bred.

ନଗାମ, ଲଗାମ, *n.* bridle.
ନଙ୍ଗି, *n.* a hooked pole.
* ନଗ୍ନ, ନଗ୍ନକ, *a.* naked.
* ନଗେନ୍ଦ୍ର, *n.* the chief mountains.
ନଚାଇବା, *v.* to cause to dance; to sift.
ନଚେତ୍, *ad.* if not; otherwise, else.
ନଜର, *n.* a view, sight; a present.
ନଜରବନ୍ଦ, *a.* guarded, imprisoned, watched.
ନଜରବନ୍ଦି, *n.* imprisonment.
ନଜିକ, *a.* near.
ନଜିର, *n.* parable, example, specimen; law.
ନଟ, *n.* intricacy; trouble; * a dancer, actor.
ନଟଖଟ, ନଟପଟ, *n.* an intricate affair; —*a.* troublesome, vexatious.
ନଟଖଟିଆ, *a.* difficult or intricate.
ନଟପଟ, ଲଟପଟ, *n.* a struggling, rolling in the mud. [adorned.
ନଟବର, *n.* one very beautifully
ନଟା, ଲଟା, *n.* a creeper, climbing plant; a forest.
ନଟାଇବା, ଲଟାଇବା, *v.* to climb (applied to creeping plants). [pet.
* ନଟୀ, *n.* a dancing girl; a strum-
ନଡନଡ, *a.* oscillating, loose, shaking.
ନଡା, *n.* rice straw.
ନଡିଆ, *n.* a cocoanut.
ନଡୁ, ଲଡୁ, *n.* a kind of sweetmeat.
ନଢ଼ାଇ, ଲଢ଼ାଇ, *n.* war, fighting.

ନଢାନଢି, ଲଢାଲଢି, *n.* wrestling, scuffling, disputation.

ନଢିବା, ଲଢିବା, *v.* to fight, to wrestle.

ନଣନ୍ଦ, *n.* a husband's sister.

ନଣନ୍ଦେଇ, ନଣନ୍ଦୋଇ, *n.* masculine of ନଣନ୍ଦ ।

ନଣ୍ଡା, ଲଣ୍ଡା, *a.* without a top-knot, having the hair cropped; *fem.* ନାଣ୍ଡୀ, ଲଣ୍ଡୀ ।

* ନତ, *a.* bowed down, humbled.

ନତନତ, *a.* soft and puffy.

* ନତନାସିକ, *a.* having a depressed nose.

ନତୁବା, *ad.* if not, otherwise, else.

ନଥ, ନୋଥ, *n.* a woman's nose-ring.

ନଥି, *n.* a file of official papers.

ନଥିସାମିଲ *a.* filed with official records.

ନଦ, *n.* a river bearing a masculine name, a river flowing towards the west.

ନଦନ, ଲଦନ, *n.* a loading, load; a pack-saddle.

ନଦାନଦ, ଲଦାଲଦ, *n.* a general loading.

ନଦିବା, ଲଦିବା, *v.* to load, to pack.

ନଦୀ, *n.* river, a river bearing a feminine name.

ନଦୀମାତୃକ, *a.* irrigated by the water of rivers, watered by rivers.

ନନା, *n.* eldest brother; father; brother-in-law (used differently in different places).

* ନନ୍ଦନ, *n.* son;—*a.* gladdening.

ନନ୍ଦଘ, *n.* a large earthen vessel.

ନନ୍ଦିଘୋଷ, *n.* the name of the car of *Jagannath.*

* ନନ୍ଦିନୀ, *n.* a daughter.

ନପୁଂସକ, *n.* neuter; a eunuch.

* ନପ୍ତା, *n.* a grandson; *fem.* ନପ୍ତ୍ରୀ ।

ନଫର, *n.* a servant.

ନଫା, ଲଫା, *n.* profit, gain.

* ନବ, *a.* nine.

* ନବ, ନବ୍ୟ, *a.* new, fresh, young.

ନବଗ୍ରହ, *n.* the nine planets.

* ନବଦଳ, *n.* young leaves, new grass.

* ନବଦ୍ୱାର, *n.* nine outlets of the body.

* ନବନୀତ, *n.* butter, fresh butter.

* ନବବଧୂ, *n.* a bride, a newly married woman.

ନବମ, *a.* the ninth, 9th.

ନବମୀ, *n.* the ninth lunar day.

ନବଯୌବନ, *n.* opening into youth.

ନବଯୌବନା, *n.* a young woman, a maiden;—*a.* (a girl) blooming with fresh youth.

ନବର, *n.* see ନଫର.

ନବରଙ୍ଗ, *n.* a round-about way of speaking or acting; a trick; a fashion; gesture; play, fun, frolic; gaiety.

ନବରଙ୍ଗିଆ, *a.* frolicsome, gay; witty.

ନବରତ୍ନ, *n.* the nine gems.

ନବରସ, *n.* (*pl.*) the nine sentiments in literature.

ନବିସନ୍ଦା ନବିସନ୍ଦା, *n.* a writer of a document.

* ନବପ୍ରସୂତା, *n.* a woman newly delivered of a child.

ନବାତ, *n.* sugar.

ନବାନ୍ନ, *n.* new rice; a harvest festival.

ନବାବ, *n.* a *Nawab.*

ନବାବୀ, *a.* princely, befitting a *Nawab.*

* ନବୀକରଣ, *n.* renewal; revival.

ନବୀନ, *a.* new, fresh, young.

ନବେ, *a.* and *n.* ninety, ୯୦; xc.

* ନବୋଢା, *a.* newly married (woman);—*n.* a bride.

ନବ୍ୟସଭ୍ୟ, *a.* new-fashioned, new-fangled.

* ନଭ, *n.* the sky, atmosphere.

* ନଭଶ୍ଚର, *a.* moving in the sky;—*n.* a bird.

* ନଭସ୍ଥଳ, *n.* the sky.

* ନଭୋମଣି, *n.* the sun.

* ନଭୋମଣ୍ଡଳ, *n.* sky, the atmosphere.

* ନମନ, *n.* bending, stooping, bowing down.

* ନମନୀୟ, ନମ୍ର, *a.* flexible.

ନମସ୍କାର, * ନମଃ, *n.* a bow, salutation, obeisance.

ନମୁନା, ନମୁଣା, *n.* a pattern, a sample.

ନମ୍ର, *a.* humble, lowly, bent.

ନମ୍ରତା, *n.* humility, lowliness.

ନମ୍ରସ୍ୱଭାବ, *n.* humble nature;—*a.* of a humble nature.

* ନୟନ, *n.* the eye.

ନୟନଯୋଡ, ନୟନଯୋଉ, *n.* small pits along canal or road sides made by taking earth for roads or embankments.

ନର, *n.* a man, a male.

ନରକ, *n.* the infernal region, hell.

ନରକକୁଣ୍ଡ, *n.* hell-fire, Gehenna.

* ନରଦେବ, *n.* a sovereign; a Brahman.

ନରପତି, *n.* a sovereign, a governor.

* ନରପ୍ରିୟ, *a.* philanthropic.

ନରବଳି, *n.* human sacrifice.

* ନରଭକ୍ଷ, *n.* a cannibal.

ନରମ, *a.* soft, tender, gentle, mild.

ନରଲୋକ, *n.* the earth, habitation of man.

* ନରସିଂହ, *n.* the fourth incarnation of *Vishnu.*

ନରାଧମ, *n.* a vile man, worst of men.

* ନରାଧିପ, *n.* a sovereign, a king.

* ନରେନ୍ଦ୍ର, *n.* a king.

* ନରେଶ, ନରେଶ୍ୱର, *n.* a king.

* ନର୍ତ୍ତକ, *n.* a dancer, an actor.

* ନର୍ତ୍ତଶାଳା, *n.* a ball-room, theatre.

* ନର୍ତ୍ତକୀ, *n.* a dancing-girl, actress.

* ନର୍ତ୍ତନ, *n.* act of dancing, acting.

ନର୍ଦ୍ଦମା, *n.* a gutter, drain, ditch.

ନଳ, *n.* a reed, tube; measuring-rod.

ନଳା, *n.* a drain, a ditch, a channel.

ନଳିତା, *n.* the jute plant and its leaves.

* ନଳିନ, *n.* a water-lily, lotus.

* ନଳିନୀ, *n.* a lotus; a group of lotus flowers.

ନଳୀ, *n.* a tube, gun-barrel;—*a.* cylindrical (bone), thin, slender.

ନଶମ, *n.* a cold, cough.
ନଶ୍ୱର, *a.* perishable, transitory.
ନଷ୍ଟ, *a.* destroyed, ruined, spoiled.
ନଷ୍ଟା, *n.* a strumpet, debauched woman.
ନଷ୍ଟି, *n.* loss.
ନସୀବ୍, *n.* fate, destiny, fortune.
*ନସ୍ୟ, *n.* snuff.
ନହୁଡା, *a.* flexible, not erect, bent.
ନହୁଲା, *n.* a wave.
ନହୁରପହୁର, *n.* a going and coming.
ନହୁ. ଲହୁ, *n.* blood.
ନହୁଣି, ଲହୁଣି, *n.* fresh butter.
ନହୁରୁଣୀ, *n.* an instrument for paring nails, a manicure instrument.
ନକ୍ଷତ୍ର, *n.* a star, a constellation.
*ନକ୍ଷତ୍ରପତି, *n.* the moon.
*ନକ୍ଷତ୍ରମଣ୍ଡଳ, *n.* the starry region, [sky.
ନା, *ad.* no, not; or;—*n.* name.
ନା, ନାଆ, *n.* a boat.
ନାଉ, *n.* a gourd, bottle-gourd.
ନାଉରି, ନାଉରିଆ, *n.* a boatman.
ନାକ, *n.* the nose; *heaven, sky.
ନାକଘଷା, *n.* rubbing the nose on the ground as a punishment.
ନାକଚଣା, *n.* a nose ornament.
ନାକଟା, *a.* noseless; flat-nosed.
ନାକଲା, *n.* a polypus of the nose.
ନାକଦଣ୍ଡା, ନାକଦଣ୍ଡି, *n.* the bridge of the nose.
ନାକପୁଡା, *n.* the nostrils.
ନାକଫୋଡା, *a.* having the nose bored.
ନାକମୋଡା, *n.* pulling the nose as a punishment.
ନାକଚ, *a.* bad, fit for nothing.
ନାକା, *a.* large-nosed.
ନାକୁଆସୀ, *n.* nippers to pluck hairs from the nose.
ନାକେଦମ୍, *ad.* in great trouble, at the last gasp.
ନାଖିବା, *v.* tc adhere to, to stick.
ନାଗ, *n.* a snake, serpent; *an elephant.
*ନାଗକେଶର, *n.* see ନାଗେଶର ।
*ନାଗଦନ୍ତ, ନାଗଦନ୍ତକ, *n.* a peg in a wall.
*ନାଗପାଶ, *n.* a deadly (serpent) noose; a lasso.
ନାଗଫେଣିଆ, *n.* the prickly-pear, [cactus.
*ନାଗବଲ୍ଲୀ, *n.* pán, betel plant and its leaf.
ନାଗର, *n.* a smartly dressed man; a rake; a citizen; a wag; the *Nágcri* character.
*ନାଗରଙ୍ଗ, *n.* an orange.
ନାଗରା, *n.* a kind of drum.
*ନାଗରାଜ, *n.* king of serpents, [*Básuki.*
ନାଗାକ୍ଷର, *n.* see ଦେବନାଗର ।
ନାଗରିକ, *a.* urban ;—*n.* a citizen.
ନାଗରୀ, *n.* an intriguing woman; the *Nágari* character.
*ନାଗଲୋକ, *n.* the lower regions.
ନାଗହାନ, *ad.* in vain.
ନାଗା, *a.* unclothed;—*n.* a hermit.
ନାଗୁଣୀ, *n.* a female serpent.

ନାଗେଶ୍ୱର, *n.* name of a flowering tree and its flower, *Mesua ferrea.*

ନାଚ, *n.* a dance, gesticulation.

ନାଚଘର, *n.* ball-room; dancing.

ନାଚାର, *a.* poor, helpless, nonplussed.

ନାଚିବା, *v.* to dance.

ନାଟ, *n.* a dance, a pantomime.

ନାଟକ, *n.* a drama, *a dancer, actor.

* ନାଟକୀୟ, *a.* dramatic.

ନାଟବନ, *n.* the due date of paying Government revenue.

ନାଡ଼ିକା, *n.* the pulse of the hand or foot; intestines; *a short comedy.

ନାଟୁଆ, *n.* a dancing boy.

* ନାଟ୍ୟ, *n.* the act of dancing.

ନାଟ୍ୟଶାଳା, *n.* a theatre, a ball-room.

ନାଡ଼, *n.* a nerve, pulse; umbilical cord; the root or stem of a water plant; the stem of a flower, fruit or leaf.

ନାଡ଼ି, ନାଡ଼ୀ, *n.* the pulse; intestines, navel string.

* ନାଡ଼ୀବ୍ରଣ, *n.* an ulcer, running sore.

ନାଡ଼ୀମନ୍ଦ, *a.* without appetite.

* ନାଡ଼ୀମଣ୍ଡଳ, *n.* the equator.

ନାତ, *n.* a kick.

ନାତମାରିବା, *v.* to kick.

ନାତି, *n.* a grandson.

ନାତୁଆ, *a.* kicking;—*n.* a kicker.

ନାତୁଣୀ, *n.* a grand-daughter.

ନାତେ, *n.* one kick.

* ନାଥ, *n.* a lord, protector; husband.

* ନାଦ, *n.* a sound, roar.

ନାଦାନ୍, *a.* poor, indigent; ignorant.

ନାଦାବୀ, *a.* unclaimed;—*n.* a writing saying there is no claim.

ନାନା, *a.* various, diverse.

* ନାନାର୍ଥ, *a.* having various meanings.

ନାନାବିଧ, ନାନାପ୍ରକାର, *a.* of various kinds.

ନାନୀ, *n.* an older sister.

ନାପସନ୍ଦ, *a.* not approved.

* ନାପିତ, *n.* a barber.

ନାବ, *n.* a boat.

ନାବାଳକ, ନାବାଳିଗ, *n.* a minor, under age.

ନାବିକ, *n.* a boatman, a sailor.

ନାବ୍ୟ, *a.* navigable; marine.

ନାଭି, ନାଭିଦେଶ, ନାଭିମଣ୍ଡଳ, ନାଭିସ୍ଥଳ, *n.* the navel; hub of a wheel.

ନାମ, *n.* a name, appellation; (in *Gram.*) noun.

ନାମକରଣ, *n.* naming a child.

ନାମଞ୍ଜୁର, *a.* not granted, not sanctioned, refused.

ନାମଞ୍ଜୁରି, *n.* dissent, refusal.

ନାମଧାରୀ, *a.* named, titular.

* ନାମଧେୟ, *n.* see ନାମ ।

ନାମଜାଦା, *a.* illustrious, renowned.

ନାମର୍ଦା, *a.* effeminate, unmanly.

* ନାମବାର, *a.* titular.

ନାମାବଳୀ, *n.* a garment stamped with the names of the gods.

ନାୟକ, *n.* the name of a caste; a surname; the hero of a story; leader, guide; a lover.

ନାୟିକା, *n. fem.* of ନାୟକ; a wife, a mistress.

ନାରକୀ, *a.* sinful, hellish, infernal.

ନାରଖାର, *a.* see ଛାରଖାର ।

ନାରଙ୍ଗ, ନାରଙ୍ଗୀ, *n.* an orange.

ନାରଦ, *n.* name of a sage.

* ନାରାଚ, ନାରାଜ, *n.* an iron arrow.

ନାରାଜ, *a.* not pleased, unwilling.

ନାରାଜି, *n.* unwillingness.

ନାରାୟଣ, *n.* a name of *Vishnu.*

* ନାରିକେଳ, *n.* a cocoanut.

ନାରୀ, *n.* a woman, a female.

ନାଳ, ନାଳୀ, *n.* a rivulet; * a tubular stalk.

ନାଳ, *n.* saliva; a canal.

ନାଲିଆ, *n.* a large grain basket.

ନାଲୁଆ, *a.* salival.

ନାଲି. *a.* red ;—*s.* a horseshoe.

ନାଲବନ୍ଧ, *n.* a farrier, shoeing-smith.

ନାଲାଏକ. *a.* unfit;—*n.* land unfit for tillage.

ନାଲିଶ, *n.* sueing; plaint, a complaint.

ନାଶ, *n.* destruction, spoliation.

ନାଶକାରୀ, * ନାଶକ, *n.* a destroyer.

* ନାଶନ, *n.* the act of destroying.

* ନାଶ୍ୟ, *a.* perishable, destructible.

ନାସ, *n.* snuff.

ନାସଡବା, ନାସଦାନ, *n.* snuff-box.

* ନାସା, ନାସିକା, *n.* the nose.

ନାସ୍ତି, *n.* denial, refusal.

ନାସ୍ତିକ, *n.* atheist, infidel, an unbeliever.

ନାସ୍ତିକତା, *n.* atheism, infidelity.

ନାହକ, *a.* useless, causeless.

ନାହାକ, *n.* *Naik*, schoolmaster.

ନାହିଁ, *ad.* no, not, certainly not.

ନାଭି, *n.* the navel.

ନାଭିଆ, *n.* the hub of a wheel.

ନାହୁଡ, *n.* a sting.

ନିଃଶଙ୍କ, *a.* fearless.

ନିଃଶବ୍ଦ, *a.* silent, noiseless, mute.

ନିଃଶେଷ, *a.* entire, without remainder.

* ନିଃଶ୍ରେଣୀ, *n.* a ladder, flight of steps.

ନିଃଶ୍ୱାସ, *n.* breathing, respiration.

ନିଃଶ୍ୱାସପ୍ରଶ୍ୱାସ, *n.* exhaling and inhaling.

ନିଃସଂଶୟ, *a.* undoubted, certain.

* ନିଃସଙ୍ଗ, *a.* solitary, alone.

ନିଃସନ୍ତାନ, *a.* childless.

ନିଃସନ୍ଦେହ, *a.* doubtless, certain.

ନିଃସମ୍ପର୍କ. *a.* without connection.

* ନିଃସମ୍ବଳ, *a.* poor, helpless.

ନିଃସହାୟ, *a.* companionless, helpless.

* ନିଃସାର, *a.* pithless, sapless, spiritless.

* ନିଃସାରଣ, *n.* expelling of a thing; oozing; expressing the juice of fruits, etc.

* ନିଃସୃତ, *a.* extracted, exuded, issued.

* ନିଃସ୍ପୃହ, *a.* without desire, apathetic.

* ନିଃସ୍ରବ, *n.* flowing out, exudation.

ନିଃସ୍ୱ, *a.* poor, indigent, destitute.

ନିଁଅ, *n.* a foundation.

ନିଅଂଶା, *a.* having no posterity or successors.

ନିଅଣ୍ଟ, *a.* not enough, insufficient.

ନିଆଁ, *n.* fire. [or boaster.

ନିଆଁଚିଲା, *n.* a liar, an insolent liar

ନିଆର, *a.* distinct, different.

ନିଆଳି, *n.* the double jasmine.

ନିଆଶା, *a.* hopeless, despairing.

ନିକ, *a.* good, fine (only used of rice). [near.

ନିକଟ, *n.* proximity, nearness ;—*a.*

ନିକଟବର୍ତ୍ତୀ, ନିକଟସ୍ଥ, *a.* near; neighbouring. [sure.

* ନିକର, *n.* a multitude, many ;—*a.*

ନିକମା, ନିକମ୍ମା, *a.* without employment; unable to work.

ନିକଲ୍, *interj.* get out ! get away !

* ନିକଷ, ନିକସ, *n.* touchstone.

ନିକା, *n.* widow marriage among Muhammadans.

ନିକାଳିବା, *n.* to drive away.

ନିକାଶ, ନିକାଶି, *n.* clearing an account; the finish. [mean.

ନିକଟା, *a.* shameless, persistent,

ନିକୁଛ, ନିକୁଛିଆ, *a.* low, improper, mean.

* ନିକୁଞ୍ଜ, *n.* an arbour, a bower.

ନିକୃଷ୍ଟ, *a.* debased, low, despised.

ନିକେଇବା, *v.* to sweep, to clean up.

* ନିକେତନ, *n.* a house, a habitation.

ନିକ୍ତି, ନିକତି, *n.* a small pair of scales.

ନିଖ, *n.* a nit, a louse. [lent.

ନିଖଟୁ, *a.* unworthy, unable, indo-

ନିଖର୍ବ, *n.* ten billions, 10,000,000,000;—*a.* dwarfish.

* ନିଖିଳ, *a.* all, whole, entire.

ନିଖୁଣ, ନିଖୁଣ୍ଟ, *a.* faultless, without flaw, whole.

ନିଘେ, *a.* little, very little.

* ନିଗଡ, *n.* iron fetters, shackles.

* ନିଗମ, *n.* the *Veda*.

ନିଗାଡିବା, *v.* to pour off, to express juice, etc. [to drip.

ନିଗିଡିବା, *v.i.* to drop or ooze out,

ନିଗୂଢ, *a.* mysterious, abstruse, hidden.

* ନିଗୃହୀତ, *a.* persecuted, treated with severity. [vour.

ନିଗ୍ରହ, *n.* harsh treatment, disfa-

* ନିଗ୍ରାହକ, *a.* disfavouring, ill-treating. [tion.

ନିଘା, *n.* care, supervision; atten-

* ନିଚୟ, *n.* a collection, heap, batch.

ନିଛାଟିଆ, ନିଛାଟ, *a.* lonely, solitary.

ନିଜ, *pro.* own, one's own.

ନିଜ୍‌ଯୋଗ, *n.* land cultivated by the zemindar.

ନିଜଞ୍ଜାଳ, *a.* tranquil, at ease, quiet.

ନିଜାମ୍, *n.* the title of the ruler of Hyderabad, *Nizam*. [accord.

ନିଜେ, *pro.* by one's self, of own

ନିଟ, *a.* certain, true, exact.

ନିଠୁର, ନିଷ୍ଠୁର, *a.* merciless, cruel, harsh. [minutely.

ନିଠେଇ, *ad.* slowly, dilatorily;

ନିଠେଇବା, *v.* to do a thing deliberately and repeatedly.

* ନିତମ୍ବ, *n.* the buttocks. [quite.

ନିତାନ୍ତ, *ad.* downright, entirely,

ନିତ, *ad.* daily.
ନିତେନିତ, *ad.* perpetually, day by day.
ନିତ୍ୟ, *a.* continuous, perpetual, eternal;—*ad.* daily. [duties.
ନିତ୍ୟକର୍ମ, ନିତ୍ୟକ୍ରିୟା, *n.* every-day
ନିତ୍ୟାନନ୍ଦ, *n.* perpetual happiness; a title of *Vishnu*;—*a.* perpetually happy.
ନିତ୍ୟାନି, *a.* and *ad.* daily, every day.
ନିଦ, *n.* sleep, slumber.
ନିଦକୁଳା, ନିଦକୁଆ, *a.* sleepy, drowsy.
ନିଦର୍ଶନ, *n.* illustration, proof, sign.
ନିଦର୍ଶପତ୍ର, *n.* security for money.
ନିଦା, *a.* solid, not hollow.
* ନିଦାଘ, *n.* the hot season, heat.
ନିଦାସମୂର୍ଖ, *n.* a regular fool. [death.
ନିଦାନ, *n.* a first-cause; time of
ନିଦାନୁଆ, *a.* worthless (gift); useless; stingy.
ନିଦାରୁଣ, *a.* harsh, cruel, severe.
* ନିଦେଶ, *n.* a direction, command.
ନିଦ୍ରା, *n.* sleep, drowsiness, sloth.
ନିଦ୍ରାକର୍ଷଣ, *n.* the being seized with sleep, sleepiness.
ନିଦ୍ରାଭଙ୍ଗ, *n.* awaking from sleep.
ନିଦ୍ରାଳୁ, *a.* sleepy, drowsy, lethargic.
ନିଦ୍ରିତ, *a.* asleep. [verty.
* ନିଧନ, *n.* death, destruction; po-
ନିର୍ଧନ, *a.* poor, needy, indigent.
* ନିଧାନ, *n.* receptacle (used only when joined to another word).
ନିଧି, *n.* a gem, treasure; * receptacle.
* ନିନାଦ, *n.* a sound, roar, bellow.
* ନିନାଦିତ, *a.* sounded.
ନିନ୍ଦକ, *a.* calumnious, abusive.
ନିନ୍ଦା, *s.* blame, slander, abuse.
ନିନ୍ଦିତ, *a.* reproached, villified.
ନିନ୍ଦନୀୟ, ନିନ୍ଦ୍ୟ, *a.* blamable, reprehensible.
ନିନ୍ଦିତ, *a.* hated, reviled, reproached.
ନିପଟ, ନିପଟି, *ad.* really; completely, entirely.
* ନିପତିତ, *a.* fallen down.
ନିପାତ, *n.* death, ruin, falling.
ନିପାତନ, *n.* (in *Gram.*) exception.
* ନିପୀଡିତ, *a.* pressed; oppressed; embraced.
ନିପୁଣ, *a.* clever, expert, skilful.
ନିପୁଣତା, *n.* cleverness, skilfulness.
ନିବୃତ୍ତ, *a.* ceased, restrained
ନିବର୍ତ୍ତିତ, *a.* stopped, ceased. [from.
ନିବର୍ତ୍ତିବା, *v.* to cease, to restrain
* ନିବଦ୍ଧ, *a.* composed, bound, worn, fastened. [confining.
* ନିବନ୍ଧନ, *n.* a cause, a binding or
ନିବହ, an *affix.* implying plurality.
ନିବାଡ଼, *a.* strong.
* ନିବାତ, *a.* calm, close, sultry.
* ନିବାରକ, *a.* preventing, hindering.
ନିବାରଣ, *n.* the act of stopping or preventing.
ନିବାରଣୀୟ, ନିବାର୍ଯ୍ୟ, *a.* restrainable, preventible. [obstructed.
* ନିବାରିତ, *a.* resisted, prevented,
ନିବାସ, *n.* a habitation, house.

ନିବାସୀ, *n.* an inhabitant;—*a.* dwelling, residing.

ନିବିଡ଼, *a.* dense, impenetrable, close.

ନିବିଷ୍ଟ, *a.* engaged with, occupied in. [ed.

ନିବୃତ୍ତ, *a.* stopped, checked, appeas-

ନିବୃତ୍ତି, *n.* a ceasing, stopping, desisting.

ନିବେଦନ, *n.* request, representation.

ନିବେଦନପତ୍ର, *n.* written application.

ନିବେଦିତ, *a.* made known, represented. [upon.

* ନିବେଶ, *n.* attention to, entrance

* ନିବେଶିତ, *a.* placed, entered into.

ନିଭାଇବା, *v.* to extinguish; to complete or carry on.

ନିଭିବା, ନିଭିଯିବା, *v.* to go out (as a light); to gain a subsistence.

* ନିଭୃତ, *a.* concealed, secluded, private, solitary.

ନିମ, *n.* the *nimb* tree.

ନିମକ୍, *n.* salt.

ନିମକ୍‌ଦାନ୍, *n.* a salt-cellar.

ନିମକ୍‌ହଲଲ୍, ନିମକ୍‌ହଲା, *a.* faithful, grateful. [ful.

ନିମକ୍‌ହାରାମ୍, *a.* unfaithful, ungrate-

ନିମକ୍‌ହାରାମି, *n.* ingratitude, unfaithfulness.

ନିମଗ୍ନ, *a.* dipped, immersed, sunk.

* ନିମଜ୍ଜନ, *n.* dipping, immersion, bathing.

ନିମନ୍ତେ, *prep.* for, because of.

ନିମନ୍ତ୍ରଣ, *n.* an invitation, a call.

ନିମନ୍ତ୍ରଣପତ୍ର, *n.* a letter or card of invitation.

ନିମନ୍ତ୍ରିତ, *a.* invited, called.

ନିମାଜ୍, *n.* Muhammadan prayer.

ନିମିକମାହାଲ, *n.* salt department.

ନିମିତ୍ତ, *n.* adequate cause, motive; —*prep.* for. [twinkle.

ନିମିଷ, ନିମେଷ, *n.* a moment, a

* ନିମୀଳନ, *n.* the closing of the eyes.

* ନିମୀଳିତ, *a.* closed, shut up.

ନିମ୍ନ, *a.* low, depressed, deep, sunk.

* ନିମ୍ନଗା, *n.* a river;—*a.* descending, flowing. [mentioned.

ନିମ୍ନଲିଖିତ, *a.* written below, under-

ନିମ୍ନାଙ୍କିତ, *a.* drawn or written below.

ନିମ୍ନୋଦ୍ଧୃତ, *a.* quoted below.

ନିମ୍ବ, *n.* see ନିମ ।

* ନିୟତ, *a.* constant, regular.

* ନିୟତି, *n.* destiny, fate, fortune.

ନିୟନ୍ତା, *n.* a leader, a guide; a ruler, regulator. [subdued.

* ନିୟନ୍ତ୍ରିତ, *a.* checked; governed,

ନିୟମ, *n.* stipulation, covenant, rule. [government.

ନିୟମତନ୍ତ୍ର, *n.* constitutiona form of

ନିୟମପତ୍ର, *n.* a written agreement.

ନିୟମଭଙ୍ଗ, *n.* the making of a rule void. [fixed.

ନିୟମିତ, *a.* regulated, stipulated,

* ନିୟାମକ, *a.* regulating; governing, checking;—*n.* a ruler, a legislator, lawgiver.

ନିଯୁକ୍ତ, *a.* appointed, constituted, engaged.

ନିଯୁତ, ନିଯୁତ, *a.* a million, 1,000,000.

* ନିଯୋକ୍ତା, *n.* he who appoints.

ନିଯୋଗ, *n.* arrangement, appointment; an order, a command.

ନିଯୋଗପତ୍ର, *n.* appointment letter.

* ନିଯୋଗୀ, *n.* one appointed.

* ନିଯୋଜିତ, *a.* appointed; ordered; employed.

* ନିରଂଶ, *a.* having no share.

ନିରକ୍ତିଆ, ନିରକ୍ତ, *a.* bloodless, sallow.

ନିରଖ, *n.* authorized rate, price current.

* ନିରଙ୍କୁଶ, *a.* unrestrained, self-willed.

ନିରଞ୍ଜନ, *a.* pure, free from stain;—*n.* God.

ନିରତ, *ad.* incessantly;—*a.* * enraptured with.

ନିରତିଶୟ, *a.* exceeding, too much.

ନିରତେ, *ad.* incessantly (poetical).

ନିରନ୍ତର, *ad.* incessantly, continuously.

ନିରନ୍ନ, *a.* destitute of food, very poor.

* ନିରପତ୍ୟ, *a.* childless, without issue.

ନିରପରାଧ, *a.* not guilty, innocent.

ନିରପେକ୍ଷ, *a.* independent; impartial.

ନିରପେକ୍ଷତା, *n.* independence; impartiality.

ନିରବଧି, *ad.* always.

* ନିରବୟବ, *a.* formless, incorporeal, inorganic

ନିରବଲମ୍ବନ, *a.* having nothing to depend on.

* ନିରମ୍ବୁ, *a.* destitute of water, dry.

* ନିରୟ, *n.* see ନରକ ।

ନିରର୍ଥକ, *a.* without an object, vain.

* ନିରଳସ, *a.* not idle; diligent.

ନିରସା, *a.* inferior, not good.

ନିରସ୍ତ, *a.* desisted, restrained, appeased.

ନିରସ୍ତ୍ର, *a.* weaponless, unarmed.

ନିରକ୍ଷ, *n.* orphan;—*a.* without protection.

ନିରକ୍ଷବୃତ୍ତ, ନିରକ୍ଷରେଖା, *n.* equator.

ନିରକ୍ଷାନ୍ତର, *n.* (in *Geog.*) latitude.

ନିରାକରଣ, *n.* preventing, setting aside, expelling.

ନିରାକାର, *a.* without form, shapeless; —*n.* the universal spirit—God.

ନିରାଟ, *a.* solid, not hollow, sound.

ନିରାଣ, *a.* helpless, without protection.

* ନିରାତଙ୍କ, *a.* fearless, safe.

ନିରାନନ୍ଦ, *a.* sad, joyless.

ନିରାପଦ, *a.* free from misfortune, secure.

* ନିରାମୟ, *a.* free from disease or defect

ନିରାମିଷ, *a.* without animal food.

ନିରାଲମ୍ବ, *a.* not depending on, self-supported.

ନିରାଶ, *a.* hopeless, disappointed.

ନିରାଶା, *n.* despair, disappointment.

ନିରାଶ୍ରୟ, *a.* destitute, without refuge.

ନିରାହାର, *a.* fasting, abstaining from food;—*n.* abstinence.

* ନିରୀଶ୍ୱର, *a.* atheistic.

* ନିରୀଶ୍ୱରବାଦୀ, *n.* an atheist.

ନିରୀହ, *a.* innocent, quiet, inoffensive.

ନିରୀକ୍ଷଣ, *n.* eyeing, looking at.

ନିରୁତ୍ତର, *a.* without answer.

* ନିରୁଦ୍ଧ, *a.* blocked up, beseiged.

ନିରୁପମ, *a.* incomparable, unequalled.

ନିରୁପାୟ, *a.* left without resource; without expedients.

ନିରୂପଣ, *n.* planning, settling, fixing.

ନିରୂପିତ, *a.* ascertained, determined; appointed, selected.

ନିରେଶ, *a.* without protection, forlorn.

ନିରେଖିବା, *v.* to look at a thing steadily (poetical).

ନିରୋଧ, *n.* obstruction, blocking up.

ନିରୋଳ, *a.* solitary, lonely, alone.

ନିର୍ଗତ, *a.* gone forth, expelled, issued.

ନିର୍ଗମନ, ନିର୍ଗମ, *n.* going out, proceeding.

ନିର୍ଗନ୍ଧ, *a.* scentless, without smell.

ନିର୍ଗୁଣ, *a.* without qualities, useless.

ନିର୍ଘଣ୍ଟ, *n.* table of contents, index.

ନିର୍ଘାତ, *n.* a thunderstroke; a severe blow.

* ନିର୍ଘୋଷ, *n.* a sound, report.

ନିର୍ଜନ, *a.* uninhabited, solitary, secluded.

* ନିର୍ଜର, *a.* free from infirmities of age;—*n.* a god.

ନିର୍ଜଳ, *a.* destitute of water.

ନିର୍ଜୀବ, *a.* lifeless, inanimate, languid.

ନିର୍ଝର, *n.* a fountain, spring, cascade.

ନିର୍ଝରଣୀ, *n.* a torrent, a river.

ନିର୍ଣ୍ଣୟ, *n.* ascertaining, determining.

* ନିର୍ଣ୍ଣାୟକ, *a.* decisive, deciding, ascertaining.

* ନିର୍ଣ୍ଣେୟ, *a.* to be ascertained.

ନିର୍ଣ୍ଣୀତ, *a.* ascertained, confirmed.

ନିର୍ଦ୍ଦୟ, *a.* merciless, cruel, unfeeling.

ନିର୍ଦ୍ଦିଷ୍ଟ, *a.* fixed upon, appointed.

* ନିର୍ଦ୍ଦେଶ, *n.* appointment, mandate.

ନିର୍ଦ୍ଦୋଷ, *a.* without fault, blameless.

ନିର୍ଦ୍ଦ୍ୱନ୍ଦ୍ୱ, *a.* free from trouble or jealousy; indifferent.

ନିର୍ଦ୍ଧନ, *a.* poor, indigent, penniless.

ନିର୍ଦ୍ଧାରଣ, *n.* deciding, determining, an agreement.

ନିର୍ଦ୍ଧାରିତ, *a.* ascertained, determined, confirmed, ratified, settled, decided.

ନିର୍ଦ୍ଧାର୍ଯ୍ୟ, *a.* certain, confirmed.

ନିର୍ବଂଶ, *a.* without progeny.

ନିର୍ବନ୍ଧ, *n.* obligation, an engagement.

ନିର୍ବଳ, *a.* weak, powerless, helpless.

ନିର୍ବାଚନ, *n.* selection, choice, election.

ନିର୍ବାଚିତ, *a.* selected, chosen.

* ନିର୍ବାଣ, *n.* extinguishing;—*a.* extinct.

* ନିର୍ବାତ, *a.* calm, close, sultry.

* ନିର୍ବାପିତ, *a.* extinguished, put out.

* ନିର୍ବାସନ, *a.* transportation, banishment, expulsion.

ନିର୍ବାସିତ, *a.* transported, banished, expelled.

ନିର୍ବାହ, *n.* management, livelihood.

ନିର୍ବାହକ, ନିର୍ବାହକା, *a.* providing for, managing;—*n.* a manager.

ନିର୍ବାହିତ, *a.* provided for, accomplished, done.

* ନିର୍ବିକାର, *a.* immutable, uniform.

ନିର୍ବିଘ୍ନ, *a.* without obstacle ; safe.

ନିର୍ବିବେକ, *a.* foolish, without discrimination.

* ନିର୍ବିଶେଷ, *a.* same, like, indiscriminating.

* ନିର୍ବୃତ, *a.* easy, tranquil, happy.

* ନିର୍ବୃତ୍ତ, *a.* finished, accomplished, done.

* ନିର୍ବୃତି, *n.* tranquility, ease, safety.

* ନିର୍ବୃତ୍ତି, *n.* satisfaction, the accomplishing of a work.

ନିର୍ବୋଧ, ନିର୍ବୁଦ୍ଧି, *a.* foolish, stupid, silly.

ନିର୍ବୁଦ୍ଧିତା, *n.* silliness, foolishness, dulness.

ନିର୍ଭୟ, *a.* free from fear, safe, secure.

ନିର୍ଭର, *n.* resting, dependence, reliance.

ନିର୍ଭରସା, *n.* despair, hopelessness.

ନିର୍ଭ୍ରଗତ. *n.* obtaining a maintenance.

ନିର୍ଭୀକ, *a.* fearless, bold.

* ନିର୍ମମ. *a.* without affection or regard for one's own things; not appropriated, not caring for; cruel.

* ନିର୍ମର୍ଯ୍ୟାଦ, *a.* disrespectful, irreverent.

ନିର୍ମଳ, *a.* free from filth, pure, clear.

ନିର୍ମାଣ, *n.* making, forming, modeling.

* ନିର୍ମାତା, *n.* a maker, fabricator.

ନିର୍ମାଲ୍ୟ, *n.* food or flowers that have been presented before an idol; * stainlessness.

ନିର୍ମିତ. *a.* made, moulded, built.

ନିର୍ମୁକ୍ତ, *a.* liberated, set free.

ନିର୍ମୂଳ, *a.* rootless; eradicated, extirpated; ended.

ନିର୍ମୂଳୀ, *n.* the name of a rootless medicinal climbing plant.

* ନିର୍ମୋକ, *n.* the cast skin of a snake.

* ନିର୍ଯ୍ୟାତନ, *n.* revenge, retaliation; killing, slaughter.

ନିର୍ଯ୍ୟାସ, *n.* decoction; gum.

ନିର୍ଲଜ୍ଜ. *a.* shameless, impudent.

ନିର୍ଲୋଭ, *a.* uncovetous;—*n.* contentment.

* ନିଲୟ, *n.* a house, habitation, abode.

ନିଲାମ, *n.* auction.

ନିଶ, *n.* moustache.

ନିଶା, *n.* intoxicating drugs; night.

* ନିଶାକର, ନିଶାମଣି, *n.* the moon.

* ନିଶାଚର, *n.* a night prowler, a goblin, demon.

ନିଶାଣ, ନିଶାଣି, *n.* a flag, sign, mark, badge.

ନିଶାଦଳ, *n.* ammonia, smelling salts.

ନିଶାପ. ନିସାପ, *n.* a judgment.

* ନିଶି, *n.* night.

* ନିଶିତ, *a.* sharpened, whetted, set.

*ନିଶୀଥ. *n.* midnight.

*ନିଶୀଥିନୀ, *n.* night.

ନିଶୁଆ, *a.* having a moustache.

ନିଶୁଣୀ, *n.* a ladder.

ନିଶ୍ଚୟ, *n.* certainty, positiveness, a clear knowledge of a thing.

ନିଶ୍ଚଳ, *a.* immovable, fixed.

*ନିଶ୍ଚାୟକ, *a.* ascertaining, deciding.

ନିଶ୍ଚିତ, *a.* ascertained, certain, sure.

ନିଶ୍ଚିନ୍ତ, *a.* careless, without anxiety.

ନିଶ୍ଚେ, *ad.* certainly, truly.

ନିଶ୍ଚେଷ୍ଟ, *a.* without exertion, listless.

*ନିଶ୍ୱସିତ. *a.* breathing;—*n.* breath.

ନିଶ୍ୱାସ, ନିଶ୍ୱାସ ପ୍ରଶ୍ୱାସ, *n.* breath, respiration.

*ନିଷଙ୍ଗ, *n.* a quiver, case for arrows.

*ନିଷଣ୍ଣ, *a.* placed, established.

*ନିଷାଦ, *n.* a hunter of low caste; ame of an aboriginal Indian tribe; a note in music.

ନିଷିଦ୍ଧ, *a.* forbidden, prohibited.

ନିଷେଧ, *n.* forbidding, prohibition.

*ନିଷେଧକ, *a.* preventing, prohibiting, forbidding. [forbidding.

ନିଷେଧୁଆ. *a.* preventing, prohibiting,

*ନିଷେବିତ, *a.* served, observed; enjoyed.

ନିଷ୍କଣ୍ଟକ, *a.* without a thorn, without enemies; at ease.

*ନିଷ୍କମ୍ପ, *a.* not shaking, not moving, still, calm.

ନିଷ୍କର୍ମୀ, *a.* unemployed, idle.

ନିଷ୍କର, *a.* free from taxes.

ନିଷ୍କଳଙ୍କ, *a.* without a stain or fault.

*ନିଷ୍କାମ, ନିଷ୍କାମା, *a.* free from lust or irregular desire; unselfish.

*ନିଷ୍କାସନ, *n.* expulsion.

*ନିଷ୍କାସିତ, *a.* expelled, turned out.

ନିଷ୍କୃତି, *n.* acquittal, pardon, clearance.

*ନିଷ୍କୋଷ, ନିଷ୍କୋଷିତ. *a.* forced or drawn out, pulled out, (as a sword from its case). [ed.

*ନିଷ୍କ୍ରାନ୍ତ, *a.* expelled, gone, depart-

*ନିଷ୍କ୍ରିୟ, *a.* idle, unoccupied, abstaining from ceremonial rites.

ନିଷ୍ଠା, *n.* stability (especially of faith).

ନିଷ୍ଠୁର, *a.* merciless, cruel, harsh.

ନିଷ୍ପତ୍ତି, *n.* final settlement, decision; ratio.

ନିଷ୍ପନ୍ନ. *a.* accomplished, settled.

*ନିଷ୍ପାଦନ, *n.* completing, finishing.

ନିଷ୍ପାପ, ନିଷ୍ପାପୀ, *a.* without sin, pure.

ନିଷ୍ପୀଡ଼ନ, *n.* squeezing or pressing out, extraction.

*ନିଷ୍ପେଷଣ, *n.* grinding to powder.

*ନିଷ୍ପ୍ରଭ, *a.* gloomy, without light.

ନିଷ୍ପ୍ରୟୋଜନ, *a.* unnecessary, useless.

ନିଷ୍ଫଳ, *a.* fruitless, useless.

*ନିସର୍ଗ, *n.* natural state; rejection.

ନିସାପ, *n.* a decision, an award.

ନିସ୍ତବ୍ଧ, *a.* stopped, paralized, silent.

ନିସ୍ତରିବା, *v.i.* to be saved, to be rescued. [verance.

ନିସ୍ତାର, ନିସ୍ତାରଣ, *n.* salvation, deli-

* ନିସ୍ତାରକ, *n.* a deliverer, saviour.
ନିସ୍ତାରପର୍ବ, *n.* the feast of passover.
ନିସ୍ତାରିବା, *v.* to save, to rescue.
ନିସ୍ତେଜ, *a.* without lustre or vigour.
* ନିସ୍ପନ୍ଦ, ନିଷ୍ପନ୍ଦ, *a.* motionless, still.
* ନିସ୍ପୃହ, *a.* see ନିଃସ୍ପୃହ.
ନିସ୍ୱନ, *n.* sound, noise.
ନିହତ, *a.* killed, smitten.
ନିହାଇ, *n.* an anvil.
ନିହାଣ, *n.* a carpenter's iron chisel.
ନିହାତି, *ad.* too, too much, very.
ନିହାଲ, *a.* successful, fortunate.
* ନିହିତ, *a.* placed, deposited with.
ନିକ୍ଷେପ, *n.* throwing, casting away.
ନୀଚ, *a.* low, deep, vile, mean.
ନୀଚତା, *n.* lowness, baseness, inferiority, depravity.
* ନୀଚଗା, *n.* a river.
ନୀଚଜାତି, *a.* of low caste or origin.
ନୀଚଭାଷା, *n.* low or rustic language.
ନୀଚାଶୟ, *a.* low-minded, grovelling.
ନୀଚୁ, ଲିଚୁ, *n.* a kind of fruit.
* ନୀଡ, *n.* a bird's nest.
* ନୀଡଜ, *a.* born in a nest;—*n.* a bird.
* ନୀତ, *a.* taken, received, obtained.
ନୀତି, *n.* guidance, morality, virtue.
ନୀତିକଥା, *n.* a moral sentence, a fable.
* ନୀତିଜ୍ଞ, *a.* aquainted with the rules of morality.
ନୀତିବିଦ୍ୟା, *n.* science of morals, ethics.
* ନୀତିବିରୁଦ୍ଧ, *a.* opposed to justice, contrary to good morals.
ନୀତିଶାସ୍ତ୍ର, *n.* the science of ethics.

* ନୀପ, *n.* the *kadamba* tree.
* ନୀବାର, *n.* rice growing wild or without cultivation.
* ନୀର, *n.* water, juice.
* ନୀରଜ, *n.* the water-lily, *padma.*
* ନୀରଦ, *n.* a cloud.
ନୀରବ, *a.* speechless, silent, mute.
ନୀରସ, *a.* without moisture, dry; uninteresting, inferior.
ନୀରୋଗ, ନୀରୋଗୀ, *a.* free from disease.
ନୀଳ, *a.* blue ;—*n.* indigo.
ନୀଳତ୍ୱ, * ନୀଳିମା, *n.* blueness.
* ନୀଳକଣ୍ଠ, *a.* blue-throated;—*n.* a peacock, jay; name of *Shiva.*
* ନୀଳକମଳ, *n.* the blue waterlily.
ନୀଳକାନ୍ତମଣି, *n.* a sapphire.
ନୀଳପଦ୍ମ, *n.* the blue waterlily.
ନୀଳବଟି, *n.* ball or cake of indigo.
ନୀଳବର୍ଣ୍ଣ, *a.* blue, blue-coloured;—*n.* blue-colour.
* ନୀଳା, *n.* a precious stone.
ନୀଳାଚଳ, *n.* a blue mountain which is said to have been the site of the temple of *Jagannath.*
* ନୀଳାମ୍ବୁ, *n.* the sea, the ocean.
ନୀଳୀ, *n.* the indigo plant, indigo.
* ନୀଳୋତ୍ପଳ, *n.* the blue waterlily.
ନୀଲାମ, *n.* an auction sale.
* ନୀହାର, *n.* frost, hoar frost, dew.
ନୁଆଁଇବା, *v.* to bend.
ନୁଆଁଣିଆ, *a.* bent, crooked, stooping.
ନୁଖୁରୁଣା, *a.* sulky; unfortunate, luckless.

ନୁଖୁର, *a.* not oiled, not glossy.
ନୁଗୁର, *a.* pilfering;—*n.* a lewd person, an adulterer.
ନୁଗୁଏ, *a.* many, great many.
ନୁଣ, ଲୁଣ, *n.* salt.
ନୁଣିଆ, ଲୁଣିଆ, *a.* saltish;—*n.* a salt-dealer.
ନୁଡ଼ା, *n.* a wisp of straw to light a fire.
ନୁଡ଼ି, *n.* preparation of the warp for weaving.
ନୁଣ୍ଡା, *a.* maimed in the hand.
ନୂଆ, ନୂତନ, *a.* new, recent, novel.
ନୂଆଖିଆ, *n.* eating of new rice.
ନୂପୁର, *n.* a tinkling anklet.
ନୃତ୍ୟ, *n.* dancing, acting.
* ନୃପ, ନୃପତି, *n.* a king.
* ନୃଶଂସ, *a.* malignant, murderous.
ନୃସିଂହ, *n.* the fourth incarnation—man-lion.
ନେଉଟାଇବା, *v.* to cause to return, to turn over.
ନେଉଟିଆ, *n.* a kind of spinach.
ନେଉଟିବା, *v.* to turn, to turn back.
ନେଉଳ, *n.* a mongoose.
ନେକଡ଼ା, *n.* a rag, a shred of cloth; a wolf.
ନେକଡ଼ିଆ, *n.* a hyena, a wolf.
ନେକ୍‌ନାମ, *n.* fame, reputation, good name.
ନେଙ୍ଗଡ଼ା, *a.* lame, limping, hobbling.
ନେଝର, *a.* unswept, scattered about;—*n.* rubbish, sweepings; the mucus of the eye.
ନେଟା, *a.* left-handed.

ନେଡ଼, *n.* the wrist.
ନେତ, *n.* banner, flag.
ନେତା, *n.* a leader, regulator.
ନେତୃତ୍ୱ, *n.* leadership, guidance.
* ନେତ୍ର, *n.* the eye.
* ନେତ୍ରାମ୍ବୁ, *n.* tears.
ନେତ୍ରୋତ୍ସବ, *n.* a ceremony held on the day before the car-festival.
* ନେପଥ୍ୟ, *n.* a dressing-room.
* ନେମପାଦା, *a.* web-footed, palmiped.
ନେପାଳି, *n.* a hyena.
ନେପାଳୀ, *a.* inhabiting in or belonging to Nepal;—*n.* Nepalese, native of Nepal.
ନେପୁର, *n.* an ornament for the feet.
ନେଫଡ଼ା, *a.* grinning;—*n.* a silly laugh.
ନେବା, *v.* to take or receive.
* ନେମି, ନେମୀ, *n.* circumference of a wheel.
ନେମ୍ବୁ, *n.* a lime, lemon, orange.
ନେଳିଆ, *a.* blue.
ନେଳୀ, *n.* blue colour, indigo.
ନେସିବା, *v.* to smear. to besmear.
ନେହାଇ, *n.* an anvil.
ନେହାଲ, *a.* successful, fortunate.
ନେହି, *n.* paste; an anvil.
ନେହୁର, *n.* a humble request.
* ନୈକଟ୍ୟ, *n.* nearness, proximity.
* ନୈପୁଣ୍ୟ, *n.* cleverness, expertness.
ନୈବେଦ୍ୟ, *n.* anything to be offered to a god.
* ନୈମିତ୍ତିକ, *a.* casual;–*n.* producing, causing.

ନୈୟାୟିକ, *n.* a logician.
ନୈରାଶ୍ୟ, *n.* despair, disappointment.
ନୈଋତ, *n.* the south-west point.
* ନୈଶ, *a.* nocturnal.
* ନୈସର୍ଗିକ, *a.* arising from nature.
ନୋକ୍‌ସାନ, *n.* loss, detriment.
ନୋଚ, *a.* crumpled, rumpled; adulterous.
ନୋଚୁଡ଼ିବା, *v.* to shrink as if afraid.
ନୋଟା, *n.* a brass water vessel.
ନୋଟି, *n.* an apparatus made of wood or cane on which thread is wound.
ନୋଥ, *n.* a nose ornament.
ନୋଳି, *n.* an ear ornament.
ନୋଳିଆ, *n.* name of a fisherman caste (found largely in Puri).
ନୋହିଲେ, *conj.* if not, otherwise.
ନୌକା, * ନୌ, *n.* a boat.
ନୌକାଦଣ୍ଡ, *n.* an oar.
ନୋଡ଼, *n.* a large *handy*; a measure for grain.
* ନୌବିଦ୍ୟା, *n.* the science of navigation.
* ନୌଯାନ, *n.* navigation.
* ନୌଷାଦର, *n.* sal-ammoniac.
* ନ୍ୟସ୍ତ, *a.* deposited, placed, cast aside.
ନ୍ୟାୟ, *n.* justice, equity; logic;—*a.* like.
ନ୍ୟାୟବନ୍ତ, * ନ୍ୟାୟପର, *a.* just, righteous.
ନ୍ୟାୟଶାସ୍ତ୍ର, *n.* the system of logic.
ନ୍ୟାୟସଙ୍ଗତ, *a.* reasonable.
* ନ୍ୟାଯ୍ୟ, *a.* rational, right, just.
ନ୍ୟାଯ୍ୟ, *a.* doing right, doing justice, litigable.
* ନ୍ୟାସ, *n.* a deposit, a pledge.
* ନ୍ୟୁବ୍ଜ, *a.* convex; bent downwards.
ନ୍ୟୂନ, *a.* less, deficient.
ନ୍ୟୂନତା, *n.* a deficit, deficiency.
ନ୍ୟୂନାଧିକ, *a.* less or more, about.

ପ.

ପ, the twenty-first consonant.
ପଁଛଣ, ପଛଣ, *n.* a broom made of the fibres of the cocoanut leaf; sweeping, clearing;—*a.* swept.
ପଁଇଚ, ପଇଚ, *n.* a kind of bracelet.
ପଇଁଚାଳିଶ, *a.* and *n.* forty-five, 45; XLV.
ପଇଁତିରିଶ, *a.* and *n.* thirty-five, 35; XXXV.
ପଇକାର, *n.* a hawker, a small retail trader or shopkeeper.
ପଇଖାନା, *n.* a privy.
ପଇଟ, *a.* learned by heart.
ପଇଟକରିବା, *v.* to learn by heart.
ପଇଠ, *n.* a payment; delivering.
ପଇଡ, *n.* a green cocoanut, dáb.
ପଇତା, *n.* the *poita* or sacred thread.
ପଇସା, *n.* a pice, one-fourth of an anna; money; one-fourth of a *chattáck* in weight.
ପକାଇବା, *v.* to throw or cast down.
ପକ୍କା, *a.* thorough, (applied to things well done) solid, substantial, permanent, *pukká.*

ପକ୍ୱ, *a.* ripe, mature; cooked.

ପକ୍ୱାନ୍ନ, *n.* baked meats, a sort of sweet cake.

ପଙ୍କ, *n.* mud, mire.

* ପଙ୍କଜ, *n.* the waterlily.

* ପଙ୍କିଳ, *a.* miry, muddy, plashy.

ପଖା, *n.* a wing; knob on a *chulli.*

ପଖାଉଜ, *n.* a kind of musical instrument, an Indian drum.

ପଖାଳ, *n.* stale rice, rice soaked in water.

ପଖାଳିବା, *v.* to mix water with boiled rice; * to wash.

ପଗିଆ, *n.* an arrangement made from the leaves of the palmyra palm and worn suspended from the head and covering the back as a protection from rain.

ପଗଡ଼, *n.* a turban, *pugree.*

ପଗାର, ପଘାର, *n.* a raised ridge of earth marking the boundary of a piece of land.

* ପଙ୍କ୍ତି, ପଂକ୍ତି, *n.* row, line, rank.

ପଙ୍ଗତ, *n.* eating seated in a row.

ପଙ୍ଗପାଳ, *n.* a grasshopper, locust.

ପଙ୍ଗାଲୁଣ, *n.* salt prepared by boiling.

ପଙ୍ଗୁ, *a.* lame, halt, crippled.

ପଘା, *n.* a sort of halter to tie up cattle.

ପଚରା, *a.* rotten, bad, putrid; asked; —*n.* asking.

ପଚରାଉଚରା, *n.* interrogating, asking one another.

ପଚ, *a.* rotten, putrid, decayed.

ପଚାଇବା, *v.* to cause a thing to rot or ripen.

ପଚାରିବା, *v.* to ask, to enquire.

ପଚାଶ, *a.* and *n.* fifty, 50; L.

ପଚିଶ, *a.* and *n.* twenty-five, 25; XXV.

ପଛ, *n.* back, behind.

ପଛୁଆ, *n.* backwardness.

ପଛେ, *ad.* after, afterwards.

ପଛେଇବା, *v.* to be late, to be behindhand.

ପଛେ, *ad.* following or going after.

ପଞ୍ଚ, *n.* a *panchayat*; a body of arbitrators;—*a.* five.

ପଞ୍ଚକ, *n.* the last five days of the lunar month of *Kartika*; a group of five.

* ପଞ୍ଚଗବ୍ୟ, *n.* five productions of the cow.

ପଞ୍ଚତିଂଶ, *a.* and *n.* thirty-five, 35; XXXV.

* ପଞ୍ଚତ୍ୱ, *n.* elementary state, death.

* ପଞ୍ଚଦଶ, *a.* fifteen.

* ପଞ୍ଚପ୍ରାଣ, *n.* the five vital airs.

* ପଞ୍ଚବିଂଶ, *a.* twenty-five.

ପଞ୍ଚକୋଣ, *a.* (in *Geom.*) pentagonal.

* ପଞ୍ଚଭୂତ *n.* the five primary elements.

* ପଞ୍ଚଭୂତାତ୍ମ, *n.* a being composed of five elements; a living individual.

ପଞ୍ଚମ, *a.* the fifth, 5th.

ପଞ୍ଚମୀ, *n.* the fifth day of the lunar fortnight.

ପଞ୍ଚମୀ ବିଭକ୍ତି, *n.* (in *Gram.*) the ablative case.

ପଞ୍ଚରତ୍ନ, *n.* the five precious things, (viz. gold, silver, pearls, crystal, and copper).

* ପଞ୍ଚଶର, *n.* a name of cupid.

ପଞ୍ଚଷଠି, *a.* and *n.* sixty-five, 65; LXV.

ପଞ୍ଚସ୍ତରି, ପଚସ୍ତରି, *a.* and *n.* seventy-five, 75; LXXV.

ପଞ୍ଚାନବେ, *a.* and *n.* ninety-five, 95; [XCV.

ପଞ୍ଚାବନ, *a.* and *n.* fifty-five, 55; LV.

ପଞ୍ଚାୟତ, *n.* a committee for arbitration, *panchayat.*

ପଞ୍ଚାମୃତ, *n.* sugar, milk, curds, ghee and honey all mixed together.

ପଞ୍ଚାଶ, * ପଞ୍ଚାଶତ୍, *a.* fifty.

ପଞ୍ଚାଶୀ, *a.* and *n.* eighty-five, 85; [LXXXV.

* ପଞ୍ଚାସ୍ର, *n.* a pentagon;—*a.* pentagonal.

ପଞ୍ଚୁଆତ, *n.* a ceremony observed on the 5th day after a child's birth.

* ପଞ୍ଚେନ୍ଦ୍ରିୟ, *n.* the five senses.

ପଜାଇବା, *v.* to sharpen, to whet.

ପଞ୍ଜସ, ପଞ୍ଜର, *n.* a rib, the side.

ପଞ୍ଜାବୀ, *a.* inhabiting in or belonging to the Punjab.

ପଞ୍ଜିକା, * ପଞ୍ଜୀ, *n.* an almanac.

ପଞ୍ଜିକାକାର, * ପଞ୍ଜୀକାର, *n.* an almanac-maker, an astronomer.

ପଞ୍ଜୁର, *n.* a bird-cage.

ପଗୁଳେଇବା, *v.* to chew the cud.

ପଞ୍ଝା, *n.* a group, party, flock.

ପଞ୍ଝାଏ, *n.* one group, one party, one flock.

ପଟ, *n.* canvas or ground of a picture; a screen or curtain; bark or root used for tying.

* ପଟବାସ, *n.* a tent.

ପଟଣା, *n.* a village.

ପଟଳ, *n.* a film on the eyes; * roof or thatch of a house.

* ପଟହ, *n.* a kettle-drum.

ପଟା, *n.* a plank; a lease for land.

ପଟାନ୍ତର, *n.* similitude, comparison.

ପଟି, *n.* a bandage, a plaster, palm leaves for weaving, &c.

ପଟୁ, *n.* alluvial deposit;—*a.* clever, vigorous, expert, able.

ପଟୁଆ, *n.* a small boat; fibres of the bark of the plantain tree.

ପଟୁଆର, *n.* a government land surveyor.

ପଟୁକା, *n.* a girdle, belt, sash.

* ପଟୁତା, *n.* cleverness, expertness, skill.

ପଟେ, *n.* one of a pair.

ପଟୋଳ, *n.* the *potal*, a vegetable used particularly in curries.

* ପଟ୍ଟ, *n.* silk, tassar; cloth; curtain.

* ପଟ୍ଟଗୃହ, *n.* a tent.

* ପଟ୍ଟବସ୍ତ୍ର, *n.* silk cloth.

ପଟ୍ଟଦେଈ, * ପଟ୍ଟମହିଷୀ, *n.* a raja's chief queen.

ପଟ୍ଟା, *n.* a lease.

ପଟ୍ଟାଦାର, *n.* a lease-holder.

ପଟ୍ଟାସଲାମି, *n.* money given to a landlord on executing a lease.

ପଠନ, *n.* reading, reciting.

* ପଠନୀୟ, *a.* legible, fit to be read.

ପଠା, *n.* a river island; a boil on the back, a carbuncle.

ପଠାଇବା, *v.* to send, to despatch.

ପଠାଣ, *n.* a Mussalman.

ପଠାଣୁଣୀ, *n. fem.* of above.

* ପଠିତ, *a.* read, studied.

ପଡା, *n.* a village, a hamlet.

ପଡ, *n.* a regular offering of food.

ପଡିଆ, *n.* uncultivated or fallow land, a field.

ପଡିଆଣ, *n.* the woof of cloth.

ପଡଦାତା, *n.* a bestower of food.

ପଡିବା, *v.* to fall.

ପଡିଶା, ପଡୋଶୀ, *n.* a neighbour.

ପଡିହାରି, *n.* doorkeeper, an assistant at temples.

ପଢା, *n.* lesson;—*a.* read, studied.

ପଢ଼ାଇବା, *v.* to cause to read; to teach.

ପଢାପଢି, *n.* reading, study.

ପଢିବା, *v.* to read.

ପଢ଼ଁଆ, *a.* first, eldest, (used of a child).

ପଢ଼ୁଆ, *n.* a pupil, a scholar.

ପଣ, *n.* 80 cowries or 80 of anything; a wager, pledge: * price, value.

ପଣକିଆ, *n.* multiplication tables.

ପଣତ, *n.* a border on a cloth (*sari*) worn by women.

ପଣସ, *n.* the ják fruit.

ପଣା, *n.* a sweet drink.

ପଣାସଂକ୍ରାନ୍ତି, *n.* the first day of the month of Baishakha or the first day of the Hindu year.

ପଣିବା, *v.* to push paddy, lime etc., under the head of the dhenki.

* ପଣ୍ଡ, *a.* futile, fruitless;—*n.* a eunuch.

ପଣ୍ଡଶ୍ରମ, *n.* useless labour.

ପଣ୍ଡା, *n.* a surname of Brahman caste; a bull-buffalo; * learning, philosophy.

ପଣ୍ଡିତ, *n.* a learned man;—*a.* learned.

* ପଣ୍ୟ, *a.* marketable, fit for sale.

* ପଣ୍ୟଜୀବୀ, *n.* one who lives by trading.

* ପଣ୍ୟବୀଥିକା, ପଣ୍ୟବୀଥୀ, *n.* a market, a [*hát*.

* ପଣ୍ୟଶାଳା, *n.* a market-place.

ପତଙ୍ଗ, * ପତଙ୍ଗମ, *n.* a grasshopper; a paper kite.

ପତନ, *n.* falling, dropping down.

ପତର, *n.* a leaf; a flat piece of any metal.

ପତରସବରୁଣୀ, *n.* women of an aboriginal tribe who wear twigs and leaves instead of clothes.

ପତା, *n.* the eye-lid.

ପତାକା, *n.* a flag, ensign, standard.

ପତି, *n.* leaves of the ganja plant; a master, a husband.

ପତିଆର, *n.* faith, confidence, trust.

ପତିତ, *a.* fallen, degraded, sinful.

ପତିତପାବନ, *n.* a purifier of the fallen, God.

* ପତିପ୍ରାଣା, *n.* a devoted wife.

ପତିବ୍ରତା, *a.* chaste;—*n.* a chaste wife.

* ପତିମ୍ବରା, *a.* choosing her own husband.

ପତ୍ତନ, *n.* foundation; a town.

ପତ୍ତା, *n.* trace, token, clue.

ପତ୍ନୀ, *n.* a wife, proprietress.

ପତ୍ର, *n.* a leaf, sheet; a letter.

ପତ୍ରକୁଟୀର, *n.* a hut of leaves.

ପତ୍ରାଙ୍କ, *n.* paging of a book.

ପତ୍ରିକା, *n.* leaf for writing on; letter, note; magazine.

ପଥ, *n.* a road, way, path, route.

ପଥ କଢାଇବା, *v.* to lead, to guide.

ପଥକର, *n.* road cess.

ପଥଦର୍ଶକ, *n.* a guide, a conductor.

ପଥର, *n.* a stone.

ପଥ୍ୟ, *n.* diet, regimen.

ପଥିକ, *n.* a traveller, passer-by.

* ପଥିକଶାଳା, *n.* a *serái*, resting place.

ପଥୁଆ, *n.* a traveller.

ପଥୁରି, *n.* a stone cup or dish.

ପଥୁରିଆ, *n.* a stonecutter, a stone-mason.

ପଥ୍ୟ, *a.* wholesome;—*n.* diet, regimen.

ପଦ, *n.* a foot; a verse, a word; position in life.

ପଦକ, *n.* a medal.

ପଦକ, ପଦଏ, ପଦେକ, *n.* one word, one verse, a small sentence.

ପଦଚିହ୍ନ, *n.* a footstep, a footmark.

ପଦଚ୍ୟୁତ, *a.* dismissed from office.

ପଦତଳ, *n.* sole of the foot.

ପଦବୀ, *n.* a surname, title; * road.

ପଦବ୍ରଜରେ, *ad.* on foot, walking.

ପଦବୃଦ୍ଧି, *n.* advancement in rank or office.

ପଦସ୍ଥ, *a.* employed, official.

ପଦା, *n.* an open place, a plain, a valley.

ପଦାଘାତ, *n.* a kick.

* ପଦାଙ୍କ, *n.* a footmark, footprint.

ପଦାଙ୍ଗୁଳି, *n.* a toe.

ପଦାତି, *n.* infantry, a footman.

ପଦାର୍ଥ, *n.* thing, material object.

ପଦାର୍ଥବିଦ୍ୟା, *n.* natural philosophy.

ପଦାର୍ପଣ, *n.* setting foot on; * induction of a person into office.

* ପଦାସନ, *n.* a footstool.

ପଦିକା, *n.* a land-measuring rod.

ପଦେ, *n.* one word; one step.

ପଦେପଦେ, *ad.* step by step, at every step; word by word.

ପଦ୍ଧତି, *n.* a surname; * a road, a way; a liturgy.

ପଦ୍ମ, *n.* a lotus; ten thousand billions.

ପଦ୍ମନାଭ, *n.* a name of *Vishnu.*

* ପଦ୍ମଯୋନି, *n.* *Brahmá.*

ପଦ୍ମରାଗ, *n.* a ruby,

* ପଦ୍ମିନୀ, *n.* a cluster of lotus flowers; a fine woman.

ପଦ୍ୟ, *n.* verse, metre.

ପଧାନ, *n.* head man of a village; a surname.

* ପଦସ୍ତ, *n.* see ପଣସ୍ତ ।
ପନ, ପନ୍ନା, *n.* tin-foil, tin.
ପନୀର, *n.* cheese.
ପନ୍ତାରିଆଖୁ, *n.* sugarcane produced on the seashore or sandy land.
ପନ୍ଥା, *n.* a way (teaching or doctrine), means, a path.
* ପନ୍ଥୀ, *n.* a follower, a votary.
* ପନ୍ନଗ, *n.* a serpent, snake, reptile.
ପପୟା, *n.* the papaya fruit.
ପବ, *n.* a section from one joint to another.
ପବନ, * ପବମାନ, *n.* the wind; god of wind.
* ପବି, *n.* thunder.
ପବିତ୍ର, *a.* holy, sacred, pure, clean.
ପବିତ୍ରାତ୍ମା, *n.* the Holy Spirit.
* ପୟଃ, *n.* milk; water.
* ପୟର, *n.* the foot.
* ପୟସ୍, ପୟଃ, *n.* milk; water.
* ପୟସ୍ୱିନୀ, *a.* milch, giving milk.
ପୟାର, ପୟର, *n.* a piece of poetry with a poetical translation appearing verse by verse.
* ପୟୋଧର, *n.* a teat, udder, a woman's breast; a cloud.
* ପୟୋଧି, *n.* the sea, the ocean.
ପର, *n.* a stranger; a feather;—*ad.* after, next.
ପରକାଳ, *n.* another world, future state.
* ପରକୀୟ, *a.* belonging to another.
ପରଖ, *n.* trial, test, ordeal.
ପରଖିଆ, *a.* living upon another.
ପରଖିବା, *v.* to examine, to test.
ପରଗଣା, *n.* a district or division of country.
ପରଚ, *n.* an aquaintance.
ପରଚର୍ଚ୍ଚା, *n.* meddling in the affairs of others.
ପରଚ୍ଛ, ପାର୍ଚ୍ଚା, *n.* record of right, title-deed.
ପରଛଡ, *n.* eaves of a house; a wall.
ପରଛିଦ୍ର, *n.* another's faults.
ପରଜାତି, *n.* another caste or nation, foreigner, Gentile.
ପରତ, *n.* a fold, a crease.
ପରତନ୍ତ୍ର, *a.* subject to another, dependent.
ପରତାଲ, *n.* revision of land survey; review.
ପରଦା, *n.* a screen, a *purdah.*
ପରଦାନଶିନ୍, *n.* see ପର୍ଦାନଶିନ୍ ।
ପରଦାର, *n.* adultery.
ପରଦେଶ, *n.* a foreign land.
* ପରଦ୍ୱେଷୀ, *n.* an envious person.
* ପରନ୍ତପ, *n.* a conqueror;—*a.* subduing an enemy.
ପରନ୍ତୁ, *conj.* moreover, but.
ପରପୁରୁଷଗାମିନୀ, *n.* an unfaithful wife, a jilt.
* ପରପୂର୍ବା *n.* a twice-married woman.
ପରବଶ, *a.* subject, subservient.
ପରବ୍ରହ୍ମ, *n.* the supreme deity.
ପରଭାଗ୍ୟୋପଜୀବୀ, *a.* living upon another's wealth.
* ପରଭୃତ, *n.* the black cuckoo.
ପରମ, *a.* supreme, principal, chief, excellent.

ପରମପୁରୁଷ, *n.* God, the most excellent Spirit.

ପରମଙ୍ଗଳ, *n.* happiness, consolation, contentment.

ପରମହଂସ, *n.* an ascetic.

ପରମାଣୁ, *n.* an atom, a particle

ପରମାତ୍ମା, *n.* the supreme Spirit.

* ପରମାନ୍ନ, *n.* sweetened rice-milk.

ପରମାୟୁ, *n.* life, duration of life.

ପରମାର୍ଥ, *n.* the chief good.

ପରମେଶ୍ୱର, *n.* the supreme God.

* ପରମେଷ୍ଠୀ, *n.* *Brahmá.*

ପରମ୍ପରା, *n.* successive order, rotation, lineage.

ପରମ୍ପରାଗତ, *a.* descended by tradition.

ପରଳ, *n.* a disease of the eye.

ପରଲୋକ, *n.* the other world, future state.

ପରଶପଥର, *n.* the philosopher's stone.

* ପରଶୁ, *n.* a kind of battle-axe.

ପରଶ୍ରୀକାତର, *a.* envious, malicious.

ପରସ୍ତ, *a.* single-fold.

ପରସ୍ପର, *a.* each other, mutual.

ପରହସ୍ତଗତ, *a.* transferred from one to another; betrayed.

ପରା, a *prefix*; also a particle conveying a slight reproach or remonstrance.

* ପରାକାଷ୍ଠା, *n.* end; the uttermost point.

ପରାକ୍ରମ, *n.* strength, power, prowess.

ପରାକ୍ରମୀ, *a.* powerful, brave, strong.

* ପରାକ୍ରାନ୍ତ, *a.* powerful, dignified.

ପରାଗ, *n.* eclipse of the sun; pollen.

ପରାଙ୍ମୁଖ, *a.* averse, turning from.

ପରାଜୟ, *n.* defeat, overthrow.

ପରାଜିତ, *a.* defeated, overcome.

* ପରାତ୍ପର, *n.* God, the Most High.

ପରାଧିକାରଚର୍ଚ୍ଚା, *n.* interference with another's concerns.

ପରାଧୀନ, *a.* dependent on another.

* ପରାନ୍ନ, *n.* food belonging to another.

* ପରାବୃତ୍ତ, *a.* returned, reverted to.

ପରାଭବ, *n.* defeat, discomfiture.

ପରାଭୂତ, *a.* defeated, overcome.

ପରାମର୍ଶ, *n.* advice, suggestion, counsel.

ପରାୟଣ, *a.* devoted to (usually affixed to a noun).

ପରାଶ୍ରିତ, *a.* dependent;—*n.* a dependant; a parasite.

ପରାସ୍ତ, *a.* defeated, vanquished.

ପରାହତ, *a.* struck down; repulsed.

ପରାହ୍ନ, *n.* afternoon.

ପରି, a *prefix* implying entireness; —*a.* like, resembling.

* ପରିକର, *n.* girdle; retinue, a dependant.

* ପରିକ୍ରମ, *n.* walking for pleasure.

ପରିଖା, *n.* a ditch, moat, trench.

ପରିଗଣିତ, *a.* reckoned, counted.

* ପରିଗୃହୀତ, *a.* accepted.

* ପରିଗ୍ରହ, *n.* accepting, assenting; a wife.

ପରିଚୟ, *n.* acquaintance, introduction to a person.

* ପରିଚର୍ଯ୍ୟା, *n.* service, attendance.

* ପରିଚାୟକ, *a.* causing to know;—*n.* one who introduces another.

* ପରିଚାରକ, *n.* a servant, attendant.

* ପରିଚାରିକା, *n.* a female servant.

ପରିଚିତ, *a.* acquainted with, known.

* ପରିଚ୍ଛଦ, *n.* clothing, a garment.

ପରିଚ୍ଛନ୍ନ, *a.* cleansed; well-dressed, covered.

ପରିଛା, *n.* a superintendent of a temple.

ପରିଚ୍ଛେଦ, *n.* a limit, section, division.

ପରିଜନ, *n.* one of the household; attendant.

* ପରିଜ୍ଞାନ, *n.* complete idea, conviction.

ପରିଣତ, *a.* changed, altered; ripe, bent down.

ପରିଣୟ, *n.* marriage, nuptials.

ପରିଣାମ, *n.* a change, transmutation.

ପରିଣାମଦର୍ଶୀ, *a.* using foresight, prudent.

ପରିଣୀତା, *a. fem.* married.

ପରିତାପ, *n.* great heat, anguish.

ପରିତୁଷ୍ଟ, *a.* satisfied, contented.

ପରିତୋଷ, *n.* satisfaction, joy.

ପରିତ୍ୟକ୍ତ, *a.* forsaken, deserted.

ପରିତ୍ୟାଗ, *n.* forsaking, desertion.

ପରିତ୍ରାଣ, *n.* salvation, deliverance.

ପରିତ୍ରାତା, *n.* a saviour, deliverer.

ପରିତୃପ୍ତ, *a.* fully satisfied, filled.

ପରିଦିନ, *n.* the day before yesterday; the day after to-morrow.

* ପରିଧାନ, *n.* putting on; dress.

* ପରିଧାପନ, *n.* clothing, causing to dress.

ପରିଧି, *n.* a circumference, a disk.

ପରିଧେୟ, *a.* wearable, fit to be worn;—*n.* dress, robe.

ପରିପକ୍ୱ, *a.* fully ripe or cooked.

* ପରିପନ୍ଥୀ, *n.* an enemy, antagonist.

ପରିପପ, *a.* self-important, self-opinionated.

ପରିପାକ, *n.* perfect cooking; ripeness, digestion.

ପରିପାଟୀ, *n.* order, method; elegance.

ପରିପାଳନ, *n.* observing; nourishing.

ପରିପାଳିତ, *a.* nourished, maintained, supported.

ପରିପୂର୍ଣ୍ଣ, *a.* filled, fulfilled, complete.

* ପରିପ୍ଲବ, *a.* movable, changeable, fickle, inconstant.

* ପରିପ୍ଲୁତ, *a.* immersed, bathed; overwhelmed.

* ପରିବର୍ଜ୍ଜନ, *n.* abandoning, shunning.

* ପରିବର୍ତ୍ତ, *n.* turn, stead, exchange.

ପରିବର୍ତ୍ତନ, *n.* changing, requiting, change.

ପରିବର୍ତ୍ତିତ, *a.* changed, exchanged.

ପରିବର୍ତ୍ତେ, *ad.* instead of, in lieu of.

ପରିବର୍ଦ୍ଧିତ, *a.* increased, augmented.

ପରିବା, *n.* uncooked vegetables.

* ପରିବାଦ, *n.* accusation, slander.

* ପରିବାଦୀ, *n.* an accuser, slanderer.

ପରିବାର, *n.* household, family; relatives.

* ପରିବେଶ, *n.* disk, circumference.

ପରିବେଷଣ, *n.* serving out of food.

ପରିବେଷ୍ଟନ, *n.* surrounding, fencing.

ପରିବେଷ୍ଟିତ, *a.* surrounded, enclosed.
* ପରିବ୍ରାଜକ, *n.* a traveller, a pilgrim, a religious mendicant; *fem.* ପରିବ୍ରାଜିକା ।
ପରିବୃତ, *a.* surrounded, attended by.
* ପରିଭବ, *n.* defeat; disrespect.
ପରିଭାଷା, *n.* technical terms; * discourse; preface.
* ପରିଭୋଗ, *n.* enjoyment of anything.
ପରିଭ୍ରମଣ, *n.* wandering, roving about.
* ପରିଭ୍ରଷ୍ଟ, *a.* corrupted, quite spoiled.
* ପରିଭ୍ରମକ, *n.* a wanderer, mendicant.
* ପରିମଳ, *n.* perfume, scent.
ପରିମାଣ, *n.* measure, weighing, size.
ପରିମାଣଫଳ, *n.* result of measurement, area.
ପରିମିତ, *a.* measured; moderate.
ପରିମିତାଚାର, *n.* moderate living, temperate conduct, economy.
ପରିମିତାହାର, ପରିମିତଭୋଜନ, *n.* moderate eating.
ପରିମିତି, *n.* mensuration; * measure.
* ପରିମେୟ, *a.* measurable, finite.
* ପରିରମ୍ଭ, *n.* an embrace, a hug.
ପରିଶିଷ୍ଟ, *n.* a supplement, an appendix;—*a.* * left, remaining.
* ପରିଶୀଳନ, *n.* intercourse, study.
ପରିଶୁଦ୍ଧ, *a.* cleansed, cleared off.
ପରିଶୁଷ୍କ, *a.* properly dry.
ପରିଶେଷ, *n.* a complete end, limit.
ପରିଶୋଧ, *n.* liquidation, retaliation.
ପରିଶ୍ରମ, *n.* exertion, industry, labour.
ପରିଶ୍ରମୀ, *a.* laborious, industrious.
ପରିଶ୍ରାନ୍ତ, *a.* wearied, fatigued, tired.
* ପରିଶ୍ରାନ୍ତି, *n.* toil, fatigue, labour.
* ପରିଷଦ୍, *n.* assembly, audience; council.
ପରିଷ୍କାର, *n.* tidiness, cleanliness.
* ପରିଷ୍କାରକ, *a* cleansing, purifying, clearing up.
ପରିଷ୍କୃତ, *a.* cleansed, cleared, purified.
* ପରିସର, *n.* width, dimension.
* ପରିସୀମା, *n.* extreme boundary; upshot.
* ପରିହରଣ, *n.* confuting, repelling.
ପରିହାର, *n.* abandonment; confutation, disregard, disesteem.
* ପରିହାର୍ଯ୍ୟ, *a.* fit to be abandoned; confutable, despicable.
ପରିହାସ, *n.* ridicule, raillery, jesting.
ପରିହାସ୍ୟ, *a.* laughable, ridiculous.
ପରିହାସକ, *n.* a jester, a buffoon.
* ପରିହିତ, *a.* clad, clothed, put round.
ପରୀ, *n.* a fairy, an elf.
ପରୀକ୍ଷକ, *n.* an examiner, a tempter.
ପରୀକ୍ଷା, *n.* an examination, a test, trial, temptation.
* ପରୀକ୍ଷିତ, *a.* examined, tried, put to the test, tempted.
ପରୁୱାନା, *n.* an official order, *perwana*, a letter of appointment.

* ପରୁଷ, *a.* severe, unkind, scurrilous.

ପରେ, *ad.* afterwards, after.

ପରେଡ଼, (ପରେଡ୍), *n.* parade, military procession or display.

ପରୋପକାର, *n.* assistance to another, charity, benevolence, aid.

ପରୋପକାରୀ, *a.* benevolent; charitaable, good to others, beneficent.

ପରୋକ୍ଷ, *a.* not under one's own eyes, absent.

* ପର୍ଣ୍ଣ, *n.* a leaf, betel leaf. [bour.

* ପର୍ଣ୍ଣଶାଳା, *n.* a hermitage; an ar-

ପର୍ଦ୍ଦା, *n.* a screen, curtain, *purdah.*

ପର୍ଦ୍ଦାନସିନ୍, *a.* *purdanasheen*, *purdah* (woman). [joint.

ପର୍ବ, *n.* a festival; a chapter; * a

ପର୍ବତ, *n.* a mountain, a rock.

* ପର୍ବସନ୍ଧି, *n.* a joint; full and change of the moon.

* ପର୍ବାହ, *n.* a festival day.

* ପର୍ଯ୍ୟଙ୍କ, *n.* a bedstead, a bed.

* ପର୍ଯ୍ୟଟକ, *n.* a traveller.

ପର୍ଯ୍ୟଟନ, *n.* perambulating, roving.

ପର୍ଯ୍ୟନ୍ତ, *ad.* as far as, until, unto.

* ପର୍ଯ୍ୟବସାନ, *n.* end, termination.

ପର୍ଯ୍ୟବେକ୍ଷଣ, *n.* observation.

ପର୍ଯ୍ୟାପ୍ତ, *a.* enough, abundant; obtained, gained.

* ପର୍ଯ୍ୟାପ୍ତି, *n.* satisfaction, repletion, fulness.

* ପର୍ଯ୍ୟାୟ, *n.* regular order, succession.

* ପର୍ଯ୍ୟାଲୋଚନା, *n.* looking attentively, deliberating, consideration.

* ପର୍ଯ୍ୟୁଷିତ, *a.* stale, a day old.

* ପର୍ଶୁ, *n.* a hatchet, tomahawk.

ପଳ, *n.* an eighteenth of a Cuttack seer, or fourteenth of a Balasore seer; * a minute.

ପଳସା, *n.* that part of timber gone soft through exposure to the weather.

ପଳା, *n.* an oil ladle.

ପଳାଇବା, *v.* to run away, to escape.

ପଳାତକ, *n.* a fugitive, a runaway.

ପଳାୟନ, *n.* flight, escape, absconding. [ed.

* ପଳାୟିତ, *a.* fled, absconded, escap-

ପଳାଶ, ପଳଶ, *n.* name of a tree—*Butea frondosa.* [hair).

* ପଳିତ, *a.* grey, hoary, (of the

ପଳିତା, *n.* a wick, wick of a lamp.

ପଳେ, *n.* one ପଳ (see above).

ପଲ, *n.* a flock, a herd. [eyelid.

ପଲକ, *n.* a wink, twinkling, of the

ପଲଙ୍କ, *n.* a bed, bedstead. [corps.

ପଲ୍ଟନ, ପଲ୍ଟଣ, *n.* a regiment, a

ପଲପଲ, *ad.* in flocks, herds, or companies. [or dish.

ପଲମ, *a.* a concave earthen cover

ପଲସ୍ତର, *n.* plastering.

ପଲ୍ଲ, *n.* a hut; a *machan*, a high platform erected on bamboos from which to watch for wild animals.

ପଲଣ, *n.* a packsaddle for a bullock.
* ପଲଣ୍ଡୁ, *n.* onions.
ପଲେ, *n.* one flock;—*a.* in a flock.
* ପଲ୍ୱଳ, *n.* a small pond, a pool.
ପଲ୍ଲବ, *n.* a twig, sprout, shoot.
* ପଲ୍ଲବଗ୍ରାହୀ, *a.* catching at trifling objections, carping.
ପଲ୍ଲବିତ, *a.* covered with twigs.
ପଲ୍ଲୀ, *n.* a hamlet, district, canton.
ପଲ୍ଲୀଗ୍ରାମ, *n.* a country village, hamlet.
ପଶମ, *n.* wool, fur.
ପଶମୀ, *a.* woollen, made of wool.
ପଶା, *n.* dice.
ପଶିବା, *v.* to enter; to take refuge.
ପଶୁ, *n.* an animal, a beast.
ପଶୁପାଳକ, * ପଶୁପାଳ, *n.* one who keeps or feeds cattle. [lion.
* ପଶୁରାଜ, *n.* the king of beasts, a
ପଶ୍ଚାତ୍, *ad.* back part, behind, after.
* ପଶ୍ଚାତ୍ତାପ, *n.* after regret, remorse.
ପଶ୍ଚାଦ୍ଗାମୀ, *n.* a follower.—*a.* following. [hind.
ପଶ୍ଚାଦ୍ବର୍ତ୍ତୀ, *a.* following, situated be-
ପଶ୍ଚିମ, *n.* the west;—*a.* posterior.
ପଶ୍ଚିମା, *a.* western;—*n.* an inhabitant of western India. [bation.
ପସନ୍ଦ, *n.* choice, preference, appro-
ପସରା, *n.* vegetables and fruit being hawked for sale.
ପସାରି, *n.* a green-grocer, a hawker.
ପସାରୁଣୀ, *n.* a creeping plant.
ପସୁରି, *n.* five seers.

ପସ୍ତାଇବା, *v.* to regret, to repent with remorse.
ପହଣ୍ଡ, *n.* a footprint, footstep.
ପହଣ୍ଡି, *n.* slow walk. [the day.
ପହର, *n.* a watch, fourth part of
ପହରା, *n.* the act of watching or guarding. [guard.
ପହରାବାଲା, ପହରୀ, *n.* a watchman, a
ପହେଳି, *n.* a riddle, a puzzle, an enigma; doggrel poetry.
ପହଁରା, *n.* a broomstick; swimming.
ପହଁରିବା, *v.* to swim; to sweep.
ପହଞ୍ଚାଇବା, ପହୁଞ୍ଚାଇବା, *v.* to cause to arrive, to deliver.
ପହଞ୍ଚିବା, ପହୁଞ୍ଚିବା, *v.* to arrive.
ପହି, *n.* a ridge of earth round a field.
ପହିଆ, *n.* the wheel of a cart.
ପହିଲା, *a.* first;—*n.* first day of the month, the first.
* ପହୁଡ଼, *n.* the seclusion of idols.
ପହୁଡ଼ିବା, *v.* to retire, to repose (used of kings or idols).
ପହେଲ୍ୱାନ୍, ପହଲମାନ୍, *n.* wrestler.
ପହ୍ନା, *n.* the udder of a cow, &c.
ପହ୍ନାଇବା, ପହ୍ନେଇବା, *v.* to allow the milk contained in the udder to enter the dugs or nipples (applied to cows, goats, etc.).
ପକ୍ଷ, *n.* a wing, side, party; fortnight. [lusion.
ପକ୍ଷପାତ, ପକ୍ଷପାତିତା, *n.* partiality, col-
ପକ୍ଷପାତୀ, *a.* partial;—*n.* a partisan.

ପକ୍ଷାଘାତ, *n.* palsy, paralysis.

ପକ୍ଷାଘାତୀ, *a.* paralytic.

*ପକ୍ଷାନ୍ତ, *n.* end of a lunar fortnight; end of a plea.

ପକ୍ଷାନ୍ତରେ, *ad.* otherwise, on the other hand.

*ପକ୍ଷିଣୀ, *n.* a female bird.

*ପକ୍ଷିରାଜ, *n.* *Garuda*, regent of birds; a peacock.

ପକ୍ଷୀ, *n.* a bird, fowl.

*ପକ୍ଷ୍ମ, *n.* eyelashes. [foot, leg.

ପା, *n.* one-fourth of a seer; the

ପାଇ, *n.* the twelfth of an anna, a *paulá*. [watchman.

ପାଇକ, *n.* an armed footman, a

ପାଇକ କାହାଣୀ, *n.* incredible tales.

ପାଇକସ୍ତ, *n.* a non-resident tenant.

ପାଇକାଳି, *a.* (land) awarded to a *Paik.*

ପାଇଖାନା, *n.* latrine, privy.

ପାଇଜାମା, *n.* see ପାଜାମା ।

ପାଇଟି, *n.* work, household work.

ପାଇବା, *v.* to receive, to get, to obtain, to find.

ପାଇଲ୍, *n.* a sail, an awning.

ପାଉଁଶ, *n.* ashes.

ପାଉଁଶିଆ, *a.* ashy, grey;—*n.* a devotee smeared with ashes.

ପାଉଣା, *n.* a claim, due.

ପାଉତି, *n.* a receipt for rent.

ପାଉଧଅ, ପାଜି, *n.* a cheat, a rogue.

ପାଏ, *n.* fourth part of a seer, a quarter.

*ପାଂଶୁଳ, *a.* covered with dust, polluted; defiling, disgracing; —*n.* a profligate, a libertine.

*ପାଂଶୁଳା, *n.* a lewd woman.

ପାକ, *n.* cooking of food; digestion.

ପାକଳ, *a.* of full growth but still green. [ing.

ପାକଳାପାକଳି, *n.* wheedling, cajol-

ପାକ୍ୱ, *a.* ripe, mature; grey.

*ପାକଶାଳା, *n.* a kitchen, cook-room.

ପାକସ୍ଥଳୀ, *n.* the stomach.

ପାକୁଆ, *a.* toothless, *fem.* ପାକୋଇ ।

ପାକୁଳି, *n.* the act of chewing the cud.

ପାଖ, *n.* nearness, vicinity;—*a.* at hand, near-by.

ପାଖଣ୍ଡ, *a.* immodest, shameless.

ପାଖୁଡ଼ା, *n.* the petals of flowers.

ପାଖେଇବା, *v.* to move on one side.

ପାଖେପାଖେ, *ad.* side by side.

ପାଗ, *n.* a turban; weather. [man.

ପାଗଳ, *a.* mad, insane;—*n.* a mad-

ପାଗଲଖାନା, ପାଗଳଗାରଦ, *n.* a lunatic asylum.

ପାଗଲାଣୀ, ପାଗଳୀ, *n.* a mad woman.

ପାଗା, *n.* livery stables.

ପାଗିବା, *v.i.* (earth) to become fit for sowing seeds.

ପାଚକ, *n.* a cook;—*a.* digestive.

ପାଚନ, *n.* a medicinal decoction.

ପାଚିଆ, *n.* a small basket made of split bamboos. [to fester.

ପାଚିବା, *v.* to ripen; to become grey;

ପାଚିଲା, ପାଚଲା, *a.* ripe; grey.

ପାଚେରି, *n.* a boundary wall.

ପାଛୁଡା, *a.* winnowed;—*n.* an upper garment.

ପାଛୁଡିବା, *v.* to winnow grain.

ପାଛୋଟିଆଣିବା, *v.* to welcome, to receive and bring with honour.

ପାଜାମା, *n.* pair of drawers, trousers, sleeping suit.

ପାଜି, *a.* low, base, mean, slavish.

ପାଞ୍ଚ, *a.* and *n.* five, 5; ୫;—*n.* thought, consideration.

ପାଞ୍ଚଣ, *n.* a switch, a stick. [der.

ପାଞ୍ଚିବା, *v.* to think, imagine, consi-

ପାଞ୍ଜି, *n.* an almanac, a calendar.

ପାଟ, *n.* silk, *tassár*; a plain, swamp.

ପାଟକ, *n.* race, class, rank, caste.

ପାଟଣା, *n.* a village.

ପାଟସୂଲି, *n.* red tassels to tie a woman's hair.

ପାଟମହାଦେଈ, *n.* a queen, chief wife of a raja.

ପାଟର, *n.* name of a caste; makers of coloured silk and cotton thread.

ପାଟରଣୀ, *n.* a raja's chief wife; a woman of the *Patara* caste.

ପାଟଲ, *n.* a pink colour.

ପାଟହାତୀ, ପାଟହସ୍ତୀ, *n.* a raja's favourite elephant. [noise.

ପାଟି, *n.* the mouth; loud talk, loud

ପାଟୀଗଣିତ, *n.* arithmetic. [festival.

ପାଟୁଆ, *n.* dancers at the swinging

ପାଠ, *n.* a lesson, reading, study.

ପାଠକ, *n.* a reader, a student.

ପାଠଗୁରୁ, *n.* a schoolmaster, tutor.

ପାଠଶାଳା, *n.* an elementary school

ପାଠୁଆ, *n.* a scholar, pupil, learner.

* ପାଠ୍ୟ, *a.* worth reading; legible.

ପାଦ, *n.* the breaking of wind.

ପାଡୁଆ, ପାଡୁ, *n.* a debtor who refuses to pay.

ପାଣ, *n.* a low caste, a *Pán*.

* ପାଣି, *n.* the hand.

ପାଣି, ପାଣୀ, *n.* water, liquid.

ପାଣିଆ, *a.* watery, saturated with water, diluted.

ପାଣିକଖାରୁ, *n.* a species of grey-coloured pumpkin.

ପାଣିକୁଆ, *n.* the water-crow, a diving bird.

* ପାଣିଗ୍ରହଣ, *n.* marrying, marriage.

ପାଣିଗ୍ରାହୀ, *n.* a surname peculiar to the Brahman caste; * a husband. [tasteless.

ପାଣିଚ, ପାଣିଚିଆ, *a.* watery, insipid,

ପାଣିଛତ୍ର, *n.* a place where water is given to travellers.

ପାଣିପାଟିଆ, *n.* the lowest bamboo lath on a thatched roof.

ପାଣିପାଣ୍ଡେ, *n.* a railway servant who supplies the railway passengers with water.

ପାଣିଫୋଟକା, *n.* a water-bubble.

ପାଣିଶିଉଳା, *n.* a creeping water-plant.

ପାଣ୍ଠା, ପାଣ୍ଠୀ, *n.* a she-goat.
ପାଣ୍ଠି, *n.* capital (sum).
ପାଣ୍ଡା, *n.* a surname of Brahman caste in north-west India.
ପାଣ୍ଡବ, *n.* a descendant of *Pándu.*
* ପାଣ୍ଡର, *a.* pale, or yellowish white.
ପାଣ୍ଡିତ୍ୟ, *n.* scholarship, learning.
ପାଣ୍ଡୁ, *n.* jaundice.
ପାଣ୍ଡୁସ, ପାଣ୍ଡୁର, ପାଣ୍ଡୁ, *a.* pale, or yellowish white.
ପାଣ୍ଡୁଲିପି, * ପାଣ୍ଡୁଲେଖ୍ୟ, *n.* rough draft.
ପାନ୍ତୋଇ, *n.* slippers, shoes, sandals.
ପାନ୍ତୋଇଖିଆ, *a.* liable to be beaten with slippers (abusive).
ପାତକ, *n.* guilt, sin; cause of fall.
ପାତକୀ, *a.* sinful, guilty, criminal.
ପାତଳ, *a.* thin, lean, fine, slender.
ପାତାଳ, *n.* the infernal region.
ପାତି, *a.* diminutive, little.
ପାତିଆ, *n.* thin leaf of gold, silver or copper, etc.; bamboo laths.
ପାତିଚୋର, *n.* a pilferer, petty thief.
* ପାତିତ, *a.* thrown, cast, shed, dropped.
ପାତିମାଙ୍କଡ, *n.* the small red monkey.
ପାତିଶିଆଳ, *n.* a fox.
ପାତିହଂସ, *n.* a duck, a drake.
ପାତ୍ର, *n.* a vessel, receptacle; a bridegroom; a minister, a counsellor.
* ପାତ୍ରୀ, *n.* a bride; a copper oblation-vessel.
* ପାଥେୟ, *n.* requisites for travelling.
ପାଦ, *n.* a foot, leg; one line of a stanza.
* ପାଦପ, *n.* a tree.
ପାଦପଦ୍ମ, *n.* lotus-foot; a term of flattery.
ପାଦପୀଠ, *n.* a footstool.
ପାଦପୂରଣ, *n.* completing a stanza.
* ପାଦପ୍ରକ୍ଷାଳନ, *n.* the washing of the feet.
ପାଦସେବା, *n.* obsequious attendance.
ପାଦାଘାତ, *n.* a kick.
ପାଦାତି, *n.* infantry.
* ପାଦାର୍ପଣ, *n.* setting foot, stepping.
ପାଦୁକ, ପାଦୋଦକ, *n.* water in which a Brahman has dipped his toe or foot.
ପାଦୁକା, *n.* sandals, shoes.
ପାନ, *n.* drinking; *pán.*
* ପାନପାତ୍ର, *n.* a drinking-vessel.
ପାନପିକ, *n.* saliva induced by chewing *pán.*
ପାନବଟା, *n.* a case or box to hold *pán.*
ପାନବଟିଆ, *n.* a roll of *pán* leaves.
* ପାନାର୍ଥୀ, *a.* thirsty.
ପାନାସକ୍ତ, *a.* fond of drink or spirits.
ପାନିଆ, *n.* a comb, a weaver's comb.
ପାନୀୟ, *a.* drinkable;—*n.* * water.
ପାନେ, *n.* a single dose of medicine.
ପାନେଉ, *n.* a seller of *pán.*
* ପାନ୍ଥ, *n.* a traveller, a passer-by.
* ପାନ୍ଥନିବାସ, ପାନ୍ଥଶାଳା, *n.* an inn.
ପାପ, *n.* sin, crime.
ପାପକର୍ମ, *n.* a sinful action, a crime.

* ପାପକର୍ମୀ, *a.* guilty of sin, criminal.

ପାପଗ୍ରହ, *n.* unlucky planet, ill-luck.

ପାପମୋଚନ, *n.* forgiveness of sin.

ପାପଡ଼, *a.* rotten, old; worm-eaten.

ପାପାତ୍ମ, *a.* sinful, wicked.

ପାପିଷ୍ଠ, *a.* sinful, wicked, guilty.

ପାପିନୀ, * ପାପୀୟସୀ, *fem. a.* sinful, wicked.

ପାପୀ, *n.* a sinner, a rascal.

ପାପୁଲି, *n.* palm of the hand.

* ପାବକ, *n.* fire ;—*a.* cleansing, purifying.

* ପାବଚ୍ଛ, *n.* steps, stairs, a ladder.

* ପାବନ, *a.* purifying, cleansing.

ପାଲୁଅ, *n.* the part under the eaves.

* ପାମ, *n.* eruption, itch, ringworm.

ପାମର, *a.* base, mean, silly, wicked.

ପାମ୍ନା, *n.* a disease occasioning baldness.

ପାୟଜାମା, *n.* see ପାଜାମା ।

ପାୟସ, *n.* sweetened rice-milk.

ପାୟା, *n.* a table-leg; a pillar; position, dignity.

* ପାୟୁ, *n.* the anus.

ପାର, *n.* the opposite shore.

ପାରକ, ପାରଗ, *a.* able, capable, clever.

ପାରକରିବା, *v.* to transport over a river, to take across, to ferry.

ପାରଣା, *n.* first meal after fasting.

* ପାରତ୍ରିକ, *a.* relating to another world.

* ପାରଦ, *n.* quicksilver.

* ପାରଦର୍ଶୀ, *n.* far-seeing, skilful.

* ପାରଦାରିକ, *a.* adulterous;—*n.* an adulterer.

ପାରମାର୍ଥିକ, *a.* spiritual, excellent.

* ପାରମ୍ପର୍ଯ୍ୟ, *a.* traditional; successional.

* ପାରଲୌକିକ, *a.* of another world.

ପାରସୀ, *n.* Persian language or people.

ପାରହେବା, *v.i.* to cross over, to get over.

ପାରା, *n.* quicksilver; pigeon.

* ପାରାବତ, *n.* a dove, a pigeon.

* ପାରାବାର, *n.* the sea, the ocean.

* ପାରାୟଣ, *n.* study, reading of the *Puranas.*

ପାରି, *n.* the opposite shore.

ପାରି କରିବା, *v.* see ପାର କରିବା ।

ପାରିତୋଷିକ, *n.* a reward, gratuity.

ପାରିଧ, *n.* hunting, shooting.

ପାରିପାଟ୍ୟ, *n.* regular order, neatness.

ପାରିବା, *v.* to be able, to grow up.

ପାରିଭାଷିକ, *a.* technical, not common.

* ପାରିଷଦ, *n.* a member of a board, council, etc.; an attendant.

ପାରି ହେବା, *v.* see ପାର ହେବା ।

ପାର୍ଥକ୍ୟ, *n.* difference; separation.

* ପାର୍ଥିବ, *a.* referring to the earth, earthly;—*n.* a king.

ପାର୍ବଣ, *n.* a festival day, Durga Pujah festival.

ପାର୍ବତୀ, *n.* *Durgá.*

* ପାର୍ବତୀୟ, *a.* mountainous.

ପାର୍ଶ୍ୱ, *n.* side, margin, edge.

ପାର୍ଶ୍ୱବର୍ତ୍ତୀ, *a.* adjacent. [side.
ପାର୍ଶ୍ୱଶୂଳ, *n.* pleurisy, pain in the
ପାଳ, *n.* folder for cattle consisting of treaded-out straw. [pastor.
ପାଳକ, *n.* a nourisher, keeper, a
ପାଳକପୁତ୍ର, *n.* an adopted son.
ପାଳକୁଟା, *n.* fodder, treaded-out straw.
ପାଳଙ୍ଗ, *n.* beetroot.
ପାଳଧୁଅ, *n.* name of a thorny tree.
ପାଳନ, *n.* nourishing, feeding, keeping.
ପାଳନୀୟ, *a.* fit to be nourished.
ପାଳି, ପାଳୀ, *n.* a turn, a turn in succession, rotation.
ପାଳିଜ୍ୱର, *n.* intermittent fever.
ପାଳିତ, *a.* nourished, supported, adopted.
ପାଳିବା, *v.* to keep, to observe; to nourish, support; to obey.
ପାଳୁଅ, *n.* a sort of wild arrow-root. [tent.
ପାଲ, *n.* a sail, sailcloth, a sort of
ପାଲଙ୍କି, *n.* a palanquin, palkey.
ପାଲଟ, *n.* exchange, barter.
ପାଲଟା, *a.* changed (clothes).
ପାଲଟିବା, *v.* to be changed; to change (a dress).
ପାଲା, *n.* the worship of *Satyanarain.*
ପାଣୁଣୀ, *n.* a woman of the *Pán* caste.
ପାଶ, *n.* noose, snare, a rope; a side.
* ପାଶକ, *n.* a die, dice.
* ପାଶକ୍ରୀଡା, *n.* play at dice.
* ପାଶୀ, *n.* a fowler; *Varuna.*
ପାଶ୍ଚାତ୍ୟ, *a.* western.
ପାଷଣ୍ଡ, *a.* heretical, impious, blasphemous;—*n.* a heretic.
* ପାଷଣ୍ଡତା, *n.* blasphemy, impiety.
ପାଷାଣ, *n.* a rock, a stone.
ପାସୋର, *n.* forgetfulness, oblivion.
ପାସୋରିହେବା, *v.i.* to be forgotten.
ପାସୋରିବା, *v.* to forget.
ପାହାଚ, *n.* steps, stairs, a ladder.
ପାହାଡ, *n.* a mountain, a hill. [god.
ପାହାଡା, *n.* offering of cloth to a
ପାହାଡିଆ, *n.* a mountaineer;—*a.* of a mountain, hilly.
ପାହାନ୍ତା, ପାହାନ୍ତି, *n.* break of day.
ପାହାର, *n.* beating.
ପାହୁ, *n.* a fourth part of an anna; one-third of a pice.
ପାଜୁ, *n.* a cheat, a traitor.
ପାହୁଡ, *n.* an ornament for the feet.
ପାହୁସଣି, *n.* the hammer of the *dhenki.* [the foot.
ପାହୁଲ, *n.* the foot, the length of
ପାହୁଲା, *n.* one-third of a pice.
ପିଆଇବା, *v.* to cause to drink.
ପିଆଜ, *n.* onions.
ପିଅଦା, *n.* a messenger, a peon.
ପିଆଲା, *n.* a cup. [wood.
ପେଅଶାଳ, *n.* a kind of tree and its
ପିଇବା, *v.* to drink. [husband.
ପିଉସା, *n.* an uncle, father's sister's
ପିଉସୀ, *n.* an aunt, father's sister.

ପିକ, *n.* *pán* spittle; *the black cuckoo.

ପିକଦାନି, *n.* a spittoon.

ପିକା, ପିକ୍କା, *n.* a cigar, cheroot.

ପିଙ୍ଗଳ, *a.* tawny.

ପିଚୁ, *n.* the buttocks, hinder part.

ପିଚିକାରି, *n.* a syringe, an enema.

ପିଚ୍, *n.* a peach.

ପିଛୁପଡ଼ିବା, *v.* to follow or depend on a person.

*ପିଞ୍ଛ, *n.* a peacock's tail.

ପିଛା, *n.* a following after, a resorting to.

ପିଛାଡ଼, *n.* the back part; horse's heel-rope.

*ପିଚ୍ଛିଳ, *a.* slippery; wet, damp.

ପିଞ୍ଜୁଡ଼ା, ପିଞ୍ଜଡ଼ା, *n.* a blinking of the eyelids.

ପିଞ୍ଜରା, ପିଞ୍ଜର, *n.* a cage.

ପିଞ୍ଜିବା, *v.* to clean cotton.

ପିଟଣା, *n.* a rammer, a mallet.

ପିଟା, *a.* beaten, hammered out;—*n.* flogging, beating.

ପିଟାଇବା, *v.* to cause to be beaten or hammered.

ପିଟାପିଟି, *n.* a beating, a hammering.

ପିଟିବା, *v.* to beat, to hammer.

ପିଠା, *n*, a pastry cake.

ପିଠାଉ, *n.* ground rice, pulse, &c., for making the above.

ପିଠି, *n.* the back.

ପିଠିଆ, *n.* one constantly flogged.

ପିଡ଼ଙ୍ଗ, *n.* a kind of greens.

ପିଢ଼ା, *n.* a low wooden stool; the thatch of a house.

ପିଣ୍ଡ, *n.* funeral cake; the body; a lump, ball, clod.

ପିଣ୍ଡଦାତା, *ପିଣ୍ଡଦ, *n.* one whose right it is to make the funeral offering.

ପିଣ୍ଡଦାନ, *n.* a funeral offering.

ପିଣ୍ଡା, *n*, a raised veranda to a house.

ପିତା, *n.* a father;—*a.* bitter.

ପିତାକରଲା, *n.* fruit of a climbing plant.

ପିତାକଳିତା, *n.* leaves of the jute plant used as a vegetable, and as a medicine.

*ପିତାମହ, *n.* a paternal grandfather.

*ପିତାମହୀ, *n.* a paternal grandmother.

ପିତାଶୁଣୀ, ପିତ୍ଶୁଣୀ, *n.* a sort of witch.

ପିତୁଳା, *n.* an image, an idol.

ପିତୃ, *n.* a father;—*a.* paternal.

ପିତୃକର୍ମ, *n.* funeral obsequies.

ପିତୃତର୍ପଣ, *n.* offering of water to the dead.

ପିତୃଧନ, *n.* paternal property.

ପିତୃପକ୍ଷ, *n.* the dark fortnight of the month of *Aswina*; paternal relations.

ପିତୃପୁରୁଷ, *n.* paternal ancestors.

*ପିତୃବ୍ୟ, *n.* paternal uncle.

ପିତୃଭକ୍ତି, *n.* filial duty to a father.

ପିତୃଲୋକ, *n.* ancestors, forefathers.

*ପିତୃଘ୍ନ, *n.* a parricide.

ପିତ୍ତ, *n.* gall, bile.

*ପିତ୍ତଘ୍ନ, *a.* antibilious.

ପିତ୍ତଜ୍ୱର, *n.* bilious fever.
ପିତ୍ତଳ, *n.* brass.
ପିତ୍ତ, *a.* bitter.
ପିଜୁଳ, ପିଜୁଳି, *n.* a guava.
ପିନ୍ଧାଇବା, *v.* to cause to put on or wear clothes.
ପିନ୍ଧାପାଛୁଡ଼ା, *n.* upper and lower [garments.
ପିନ୍ଧିବା, *v.* to put on clothes, to dress, to wear.
ପିପାସା, *n.* thirst.
*ପିପାସିତ, *a.* thirsty, athirst.
*ପିପାସୁ, *a.* desirous of drinking, thirsty.
*ପିପୀଲିକା. *n.* an ant.
ପିପ୍ପଳ, *n.* the *pepul* or poplar tree.
ପିପ୍ପଳୀ, *n.* long pepper.
ପିମ୍ପା, *n.* a barrel, a cask.
ପିମ୍ପୁଡ଼, *n.* an ant.
ପିଆଲା, *n.* a cup.
ପିର, *n.* a Muhammadan saint or spiritual guide.
ପିଲା, *n.* a child, a boy, the young.
ପିଲାପିଲି, *n.* boys and girls, children.
ପିଲସୋଜ, *n.* a candlestick, lampstand.
ପିଲପାୟା, *n.* a pillar (of masonry).
ପିଶାଚ, *n.* a fiend, a fiendish man.
ପିଶାଚୀ, *n. fem.* of the above.
*ପିଶୁନ, *a.* base, mean, cruel.
*ପିଷ୍ଟକ, *n.* baked meats, a cake (loaf).
ପିହ୍ଳୋଇ, *n.* the spleen.
ପୀଠ, *n.* a raised platform or seat, an altar, a stool.

*ପୀଡକ, *a.* giving pain, hurtful.
ପୀଡା, *n.* pain, illness, distress.
ପୀଡିତ, *a.* sick, pained, afflicted.
*ପୀତ, *a.* yellow.
ପୀତମଣି, *n.* a topaz.
*ପୀନ, *a.* fat, fleshy; large, thick.
ପୀନସ, *n.* a disease of the nose.
*ପୀବର, *a.* fat, corpulent, stout, strong.
*ପୀୟୂଷ, *n.* nectar.
ପୁଂ, *a.* (in *Gram.*) masculine.
*ପୁଂବତ୍, *a.* man-like, masculine.
ପୁଂଲିଙ୍ଗ, *n.* masculine gender.
*ପୁଂସ୍ତ୍ୱ, *n.* manhood, virility.
ପୁଅ, *n.* a son.
ପୁଆ, *n.* a young plantain or bamboo plant; screw of the cotton cleaning machine.
ପୁଆଣି, *n.* a bride's going to the house of her father-in-law to join her husband.
*ପୁଙ୍ଖାନୁପୁଙ୍ଖ, *a.* minute, thorough.
ପୁଙ୍ଗା, *n.* a gipsy's pipe or flute made of a bottle-gourd.
ପୁଚ୍ଛ, *n.* the tail.
ପୁଚ୍ଛିବା, *v.* to ask (used only in poetry).
ପୁଜ, *n.* pus, matter.
*ପୁଞ୍ଜ, *n.* a group, a bundle, heap.
ପୁଞ୍ଜାଏ, *a.* four together.
ପୁଞ୍ଜି, *n.* wealth, capital, stock.
ପୁଟ, *n.* a solvent, a flux; *a fold.
ପୁଟୁଳି, *n.* a packet, small parcel.

ପୁଡା, *n.* as ପୁଡଲି; leaf of a book; the nostrils. [moreover.

ପୁଣି, *ad.* and *conj.* again, and,

ପୁଣ୍ୟ, *n.* righteousness, merit.

ପୁଣ୍ୟକର୍ମ, *n.* meritorious or religious actions. [genii.

* ପୁଣ୍ୟଜନ, *n.* designation of certain

ପୁଣ୍ୟବାନ୍, *a.* righteous, meritorious.

ପୁଣ୍ୟଭୂମି, *n.* a holy place, holy ground.

ପୁଣ୍ୟଶୀଳ, *a.* righteous, meritorious.

ପୁଣ୍ୟାତ୍ମା, *a.* holy, religious, virtuous.

* ପୁତ, *n.* a son.

ପୁତୁର, *n.* a nephew. [an idol.

ପୁତ୍ତଳି, ପୁତ୍ତଳୀ, ପୁତ୍ତଳିକା, *n.* an image,

ପୁତ୍ର, ପୁତ୍ତ୍ର, *n.* a son.

ପୁତ୍ରବତୀ, *a. fem.* having a son.

ପୁତ୍ରବନ୍ତ, ପୁତ୍ରବାନ୍, *a.* having a son.

* ପୁତ୍ରବଧୂ, *n.* a son's wife.

* ପୁତ୍ରୀ, *n.* a daughter.

ପୁଦିନା, *n.* mint.

* ପୁନଃ, *ad.* again, once more.

ପୁନଃପୁନଃ, *ad.* again and again.

ପୁନରପି, *ad.* once more, again.

* ପୁନରାଗମନ, *n.* returning, coming back.

ପୁନର୍ବାର, *ad.* again.

ପୁନରୁକ୍ତି, *n.* repetition, tautology.

ପୁନରୁତ୍ଥାନ, *n.* resurrection.

ପୁନରୁତ୍ଥିତ, *a.* risen again, resurrected.

ପୁନର୍ଜନ୍ମ, *n.* second birth, regeneration. [again.

* ପୁନର୍ଜାତ, *a.* regenerated, born

ପୁନର୍ବସୁ, *n.* seventh stellar mansion.

* ପୁନର୍ବିବାହ, *n.* a second marriage.

ପୁନଶ୍ଚ, *ad.* again, once more.

ପୁନାଗ, * ପୁନ୍ନାଗ, *n.* a tree from the fruit of which oil is expressed.

ପୁର, *n.* a village; residence; * a a city, town (generally used as a termination as ରାଜପୁର).

* ପୁରଃସର, *a.* preceding, going before.

* ପୁରଜନ, *n.* a citizen.

* ପୁରଦ୍ୱାର, *n.* a city gate. [gods.

* ପୁରନ୍ଦର, *n.* *Indra*, king of the

ପୁରସ୍କାର, *n.* prize, reward, present, gratuity.

ପୁରସ୍କୃତ, *a.* rewarded, honoured.

* ପୁରସ୍ତ୍ରୀ, *n.* a housewife.

* ପୁରା, *ad.* formerly.

ପୁରାକାଳ, *n.* ancient time. [* old.

ପୁରାଣ, *n.* a legendary *shástra*;—*a.*

ପୁରାତନ, *a.* old, ancient, antique.

* ପୁରାବୃତ୍ତ, *n.* history, tradition, legend.

* ପୁରାବିତ୍, *n.* historian;—*a.* knowing, acquainted with the past.

ପୁରି, *n.* a sweet *chapáti* fried in ghee or butter.

* ପୁରୀ, *n.* a residence, a town, city.

* ପୁରୀଷ, *n.* ordure, excrement.

ପୁରୁଖା, *a.* old, experienced.

ପୁରୁଣା, *a.* old.

ପୁରୁଣି, *n.* name of an edible plant.

ପୁରୁଷ, *n.* a man, a male.

ପୁରୁଷତ୍ୱ, *n.* manliness, manhood.

ପୁରୁଷପରମ୍ପର, *n.* succession of generations.

ପୁରୁଷସିଂହ, *n.* a most eminent man, a man-lion.

ପୁରୁଷାଧମ, *n.* a vile or base man.

ପୁରୁଷାର୍ଥ, *n.* manliness, courage.

ପୁରୁଷୋତ୍ତମ, *n.* one of the names of Puri; * an excellent man.

* ପୁରୋଗାମୀ, *a.* preceding, chief.

* ପୁରୋବର୍ତ୍ତୀ, *a.* situated in front.

ପୁରୋହିତ, *n.* a family priest.

ପୁଳାଏ, *a.* a handful, as much as can be grasped.

ପୁଳି, *n.* a kind of cake.

* ପୁଲକ, *n.* horripilation, thrill of joy.

ପୁଲକିତ, *a.* thrilled with joy, delighted.

ପୁଡ଼ିଆ, *n.* a parcel, bundle, package.

ପୁଷ, *n.* month of *Pusa.*

* ପୁଷ୍କର, *n.* lotus; water.

ପୁଷ୍କରିଣୀ, *n.* a pond, a tank.

* ପୁଷ୍କଳ, *a.* much, many.

ପୁଷ୍ଟ, *a.* well-fed, fat, plump, well-off.

* ପୁଷ୍ଟି, *n.* nourishment, support, aid, good condition.

ପୁଷ୍ଟିକର, *a.* nourishing.

ପୁଷ୍ପ, *n.* a flower, blossom; menses.

ପୁଷ୍ପବତୀ. *n.* a menstruous woman.

* ପୁଷ୍ପବାଟିକା, ପୁଷ୍ପବାଟୀ, *n.* flower garden.

* ପୁଷ୍ପମୟ, *a.* flowery.

* ପୁଷ୍ପରସ, *n.* the honey in flowers.

ପୁଷ୍ପରେଣୁ, *n.* pollen of flowers.

* ପୁଷ୍ପସମୟ, *n.* spring, spring-time.

ପୁଷ୍ପାଞ୍ଜଳି, *n.* a handful of flowers.

* ପୁଷ୍ପିତ, *a.* in flower, prime, blooming.

ପୁଷ୍ୟା, *n.* the eighth stellar mansion.

ପୁସ୍ତକ, * ପୁସ୍ତିକା, *n.* a book, a volume.

ପୁସ୍ତକାଳୟ, * ପୁସ୍ତକାଗାର, *n.* library.

ପୂଜକ, *n.* a worshipper.

* ପୂଜନ, *n.* worshipping, showing respect.

ପୂଜନୀୟ, ପୂଜ୍ୟ, *a.* worthy of veneration.

ପୂଜା, *n.* worship, adoration.

ପୂଜାହାରୀ, *n.* a temple worshipper; a cook.

* ପୂଜିତ, *a.* worshipped, honoured, venerated.

* ପୂତ, *a.* pure, clean, holy.

ପୂନେଇ, *n.* the day of full moon.

* ପୂତିଗନ୍ଧ, *n.* stench, putrid odour.

* ପୂପ, *n.* a baked cake, loaf.

ପୂର, *n.* inside of tarts, &c.

* ପୂରକ, *n.* a multiplier.

ପୂରଣ, *n.* filling, completing, multiplying.

ପୂରା, *a.* complete, full, copious.

ପୂରଇବା, *v.* to fill, to fill up.

ପୂର୍ଣ୍ଣ, *a.* filled, full, complete, whole.

ପୂର୍ଣ୍ଣକୁମ୍ଭ, *n.* a full water vessel.

ପୂର୍ଣ୍ଣିମା, * ପୂର୍ଣ୍ଣିମାସୀ, *n.* the day of full moon.

* ପୂର୍ତ୍ତ, *n.* an act of public utility—such as digging a tank, sinking a well.

ପୂର୍ତ୍ତବିଭାଗ, *n.* Public Works Department, P.W.D.

ପୂର୍ବ, *a.* former, preceding;—*n.* the east.

ପୂର୍ବକ, an *affix*, implying with, by means of.

ପୂର୍ବକାଳ, *n.* former time, past.

ପୂର୍ବକାଳୀନ, *a.* ancient, belonging to former times

* ପୂର୍ବଜ, *a.* elder, eldest.

ପୂର୍ବତନ, *a.* former.

ପୂର୍ବଦିଗ, *n.* the east quarter.

* ପୂର୍ବପକ୍ଷ, *n.* the opening statement of a plaintiff, the major proposition in a syllogism, a thesis; a plaintiff, a suitor.

ପୂର୍ବପୁରୁଷ, *n.* ancestor, forefather.

ପୂର୍ବଫାଲ୍‌ଗୁନୀ, *n.* the eleventh stellar mansion.

ପୂର୍ବବତ୍, *ad.* as formerly, as before.

ପୂର୍ବଭାଦ୍ରପଦ, *n.* the 25th stellar mansion.

* ପୂର୍ବରାତ୍ର, *n.* the first part of the night.

ପୂର୍ବଲକ୍ଷଣ, ପୂର୍ବରୂପ, *n.* indication of some approaching change, symptoms of disease.

ପୂର୍ବାପର, *a.* in regular order; chronic.

ପୂର୍ବାବଧି, *ad.* from a former time.

ପୂର୍ବାଷାଢା, *n.* the 20th stellar mansion.

ପୂର୍ବାହ୍ନ, *n.* the forenoon, morning.

ପୂର୍ବେ, *ad.* before, previously.

ପୂର୍ବୋକ୍ତ, *a.* aforesaid, aforementioned.

ପୃଥକ୍, *a.* apart, distinct, separate.

* ପୃଥକ୍‌କରଣ, *n.* the making of a separation.

ପୃଥକ୍‌ପୃଥକ୍, *ad.* separately.

* ପୃଥଗ୍‌ବିଧ, *a.* of different kinds, multiform.

ପୃଥିବୀ, *a.* the earth.

* ପୃଥିବୀପତି, *n.* a sovereign, king.

* ପୃଥୁ, *a.* large, extended.

* ପୃଥୁକ, *n.* flattened rice, *chudá*; a young one.

ପୃଥୁଳ, *a.* stout, thick, large.

* ପୃଥ୍ୱୀ, *n.* the earth.

* ପୃଷ୍ଟ, *p.a.* asked, interrogated.

ପୃଷ୍ଠ, *n.* the back, a surface.

ପୃଷ୍ଠଭଙ୍ଗ, *n.* defeat and flight.

ପୃଷ୍ଠା, *n.* page (of a book).

ପେଁଚ, ପେଚ, *n.* a screw; a fix; perplexity.

ପେଚକା, ପେଚିଲି, *n.* excuse, pretence.

ପେଗୁ, *n.* a Pegu pony.

ପେଚକସ, *n.* a screw-driver.

ପେଚା, * ପେଚକ, *n.* an owl.

ପେଚାମୁହାଁ, *a.* owl-faced, flat-faced.

ପେଚାମୁହିଁ, ପେଚି, *n. fem.* of above.

ପେଜ, *n.* rice-water.

ପେଜଭାତ, *n.* rice and rice-water.

ପେଟ, *n.* the belly, stomach, womb; pregnancy.

ପେଟଖସା, ପେଟଭଙ୍ଗା, *n.* miscarriage, abortion.

ପେଟଚଲା, *n.* diarrhœa.

ପେଟଜାଳା, ପେଟଜ୍ୱାଳା, *n.* hunger; inward heat.

ପେଟଟଣା, *n.* pain in the bowels, stomach-ache. [tion.
ପେଟପୂର, ପେଟଭର, *a.* filled to reple-
ପେଟବିନ୍ଧା, ପେଟମର, *n.* colic pain.
ପେଟରେ ହେବା, *v.* to be pregnant.
ପେଟର, *n.* a wicker basket, a tin box used in travelling.
ପେଟା, *a.* abdominous, corpulent; greedy.
ପେଟାଳିବା, ପେଟେଟଳିବା, *v.* to crawl like an infant on its stomach.
ପେଟାର୍ଥୀ, ପେଟୁ, ପେଟୁକ, *a.* gluttonous, greedy.
* ପେଟିକା, *n.* see ପେଡ଼ି ।
ପେଟୁଆ, *a.* corpulent.
ପେଟୁଲି, *n.* a pregnant woman.
ପେଡ଼ା, *n.* a kind of sweetmeat.
ପେଡ଼ି, *n.* a wicker or cane basket, a box.
ପେଢବା, *v.* to squeeze.
ପେଣ୍ଠ, *n.* a mart.
ପେଣ୍ଠା, *a.* short, squatty, dwarfish.
ପେଣ୍ଠୀ, *n.* a short and sturdy woman.
ପେଣ୍ଡା, *n.* a cluster or bunch of fruit.
ପେଣ୍ଡୁ, *n.* a ball.
* ପେୟ, *a.* drinkable;—*n.* a drink.
ପେରୁ, *n.* a turkey.
ପେଲପେଲ, *n.* a pushing or shoving.
ପେଲିବା, *v.* to push, to shove.
ପେଶ୍‌କସ, *n.* tribute.
ପେଶକାର, *n.* a *Peshkar*, one whose duty it is to produce records before a judge or magistrate.

ପେଶା, *n.* a profession, trade.
ପେଶୀ, *n.* muscle.
ପେଷଣ, *n.* grinding of corn, &c.
* ପେଷଣୀ, *n.* millstones, rollers.
ପେଷା, *n.* grinding.
ପେଷିବା, *v.* to grind; to send (used in poetry).
ପୈଁଠ, *n.* payment by instalments.
ପୈଡ଼, *n.* an unripe cocoanut, a *dáb*.
ପୈତକପୋଡ଼ା, *n.* burning sensation in the urinary tract.
ପୈତା, *n.* see ପଇତା ।
ପୈତାପକାଇବା, *v.i.* to wear a sacred thread, to be invested with the sacred thread.
ପୈତୃକ, *a.* paternal, ancestral.
* ପୈତ୍ତିକ, *a.* bilious.
* ପୈଶାଚ, ପୈଶାଚିକ, *a.* demoniacal, infernal. [slander.
* ପୈଶୁନ୍ୟ, *n.* malignity, spite,
ପୈସା, ପୈଶା, *n.* a copper coin value one-quarter anna.
ପୈସାଖାଇବା, *v.* to take money.
ପୈସାବଙ୍କାଇବା, *v.* to exchange copper money for rupees.
ପୈସାଭଙ୍ଗାଇବା, *v.* to exchange rupees for copper money.
ପୈଁଇବା, ଷୁଁଇବା, *v.* to warm oneself.
ପୋଇ, *n.* a kind of greens, *ság*.
ପୋଇଲ, *n.* a slave, a servant.
ପୋଇଲି, *n.* a female slave, maid-servant.
ପୋକ, *n.* an insect, a worm.

ପୋକଉ, ପୋକା, *a.* worm-eaten.

ପୋଙ୍ଗାଳ, *n.* making of salt by evaporation.

ପୋଖତ, *a.* ripe, mature; expert.

ପୋଖଳ, *n.* a newly-delivered woman.

ପୋଖରୀ, *n.* a tank, a pond.

* ପୋଗଣ୍ଡ, *n.* a boy between the age of five and sixteen.

ପୋଚ, *n.* a painter's brush, a white-washer's brush.

ପୋଛପୋଛ, *n.* a wiping, a dusting.

ପୋଛିବା, *v.* to wipe, to dust.

ପୋଟଳ, *n.* a vegetable creeper and its fruit.

ପୋଡ଼ା, *a.* burnt, scorched.

ପୋଡ଼ାଇବା, *v.* to cause to be burnt. to inflame.

ପୋଡ଼ାକପାଳ, *n.* ill-fortune, bad luck.

ପୋଡ଼ିବା, *v.* to burn, to set fire to.

ପୋଡ଼ୁଅ, *n.* a bull buffalo.

ପୋଢ଼ୁଅଁ, *a.* first-born (child).

* ପୋତ, *n.* a ship, a boat.

ପୋତକ, *n.* a flying insect, the mango fly.

* ପୋତବଣିକ, *n.* a sea merchant.

* ପୋତବାହକ, ପୋତବାହ, *n.* a sailor, boatman.

ପୋତା, *n.* buried, hid in the earth.

ପୋତାଧନ, *a.* hidden or buried treasure.

* ପୋତାଧ୍ୟକ୍ଷ, *n.* owner or captain of a ship.

* ପୋତାଶ୍ରୟ, *n.* a harbour.

ପୋତିବା, *v.* to bury; to plant, to fix.

ପୋଥି, *n.* a palm-leaf book, a book, a *shastra.*

ପୋଦନା, ପୋଦିନା, *n.* mint (herb).

ପୋଦ୍ଦାର, *n.* money-changer, cashier, banker.

ପୋପଉ, *a.* worm-eaten.

ପୋବଡ଼ା, *n.* a kind of fish.

ପୋରଟ, *a.* old, decayed.

ପୋଲ, *a.* hollow;—*n.* a bridge

ପୋଲା, *a.* hollow; gratuitous, gratis; unregistered (document).

ପୋଲାଫିଟ, *n.* a vagrant, a pauper.

ପୋଷ, *n.* the palm formed into a cup.

ପୋଷକ, *n.* nourisher, supporter;—*a.* nourishing, maintaining.

ପୋଷଣ, *n.* feeding, keeping, support.

ପୋଷଣକାରୀ, *n.* a supporter, a nourisher.

ପୋଷା, *a.* tame, domesticated, adopted.

ପୋଷାକ, *n.* clothing, dress.

ପୋଷାପୁଅ, *n.* an adopted son.

ପୋଷିବା, *v.* to support, to maintain, to tame.

ପୋଷେ, *a.* a handful.

* ପୋଷ୍ୟ, *a.* worthy of support.

* ପୋଷ୍ୟବର୍ଗ, *n.* a household, dependents.

ପୋସ୍ତଦାନା, ପୋସ୍ତ, *n.* seed of the opium fruit used as spice.

ପୋହଳା. *n.* coral.

ପୋହଳାମାଛ, ପୋହଳା, *n.* a kind of fish.

ପୋହୁଁପ, *n.* a kind of fish-trap.

* ପୌଗଣ୍ଡ, *a.* boyish;—*n.* boyhood.

* ପୌତ୍ତଳିକ, *a.* idolatrous.

ପୌତ୍ତଳିକତା, *n.* idolatry.

* ପୌତ୍ର, *n.* a grandson, son's son.

ପୌତ୍ରୀ, *n.* a granddaughter, son's daughter.

ପୌନଃପୁନିକ, *n.* (in *Arith*) a recurring number or point;—*a.* * recurring again and again.

* ପୌର, *a.* relating to a city.

* ପୌରୁଷ, *n.* manliness, virility, vigour.

ପୌରାଣିକ, *a.* versed in the *Puránas.*

* ପୌରୋହିତ୍ୟ, *n.* family priesthood.

* ପୌର୍ଣ୍ଣମାସୀ, *n.* the day of the full [moon.

ପୌଷ, *n.* month of *Pousa.*

ପ୍ରକଟ, *a.* manifest, plain, notorious.

ପ୍ରକଟିତ, *a.* laid open, apparent.

* ପ୍ରକମ୍ପ, ପ୍ରକମ୍ପନ, *n.* trembling, shaking, tremor.

* ପ୍ରକରଣ, *n.* a chapter, section of a book, subject of a treatise.

* ପ୍ରକର୍ଷ, *n.* excellence, superiority.

ପ୍ରକାଣ୍ଡ, *a.* vast, gigantic, lofty, stout, strong.

ପ୍ରକାର, *n.* sort, kind, manner, mode.

ପ୍ରକାରାନ୍ତର, *n.* another kind or method.

ପ୍ରକାଶ, * ପ୍ରକାଶନ, *n.* opening out, disclosing, coming to light.

ପ୍ରକାଶକ, *n.* publisher, displayer;—*a.* displaying, shining.

ପ୍ରକାଶିତ, *a.* manifested, made public; full-blown.

ପ୍ରକାଶ୍ୟ, *a.* suitable for publication or mention in public.

ପ୍ରକୃତ, *a.* real, true, veritable, genuine.

ପ୍ରକୃତତା, *n.* rectitude, veracity, reality, propriety.

ପ୍ରକୃତରୂପେ, *ad.* truly, rightly, pro- [perly.

ପ୍ରକୃତାର୍ଥ, *n.* real meaning.

ପ୍ରକୃତି, *n.* original and unformed matter; nature.

* ପ୍ରକୃତିସିଦ୍ଧ, *a.* natural, effected by nature, in-born, innate.

* ପ୍ରକୃତିସ୍ଥ, *a.* being in the natural state or condition, natural, genuine.

ପ୍ରକୃଷ୍ଟ, *a.* good, excellent, superior.

ପ୍ରକୋପ, *n.* irritation, provocation.

ପ୍ରକୋପିତ, *a.* angry, vexed.

ପ୍ରକୋଷ୍ଠ, *n.* a room, an apartment; * the forearm.

ପ୍ରକ୍ରିୟା, *n.* process.

ପ୍ରଖର, *a.* strong, keen, pungent, acute, acrid.

ପ୍ରଖରବୁଦ୍ଧି, *n.* acuteness, penetration;—*a.* acute.

ପ୍ରଖ୍ୟାତ, *a.* celebrated, famous.

ପ୍ରଗଳ୍ଭ, *a.* bold; pompous, impudent.

ପ୍ରଗାଢ, *a.* firm, strong, profound; [difficult.

ପ୍ରଚଣ୍ଡ, *a.* furious, fiery, violent; powerful, bold. [vity.

ପ୍ରଚଳନ, *n.* currency; usage; acti-

ପ୍ରଚଳିତ, *a.* moved; having obtained currency.

ପ୍ରଚକ୍ଷୁ, *n.* spectacles. [publishing.

ପ୍ରଚାର, *n.* preaching, proclaiming,

ପ୍ରଚାରକ, *n.* a preacher, proclaimer, publisher; *fem.* ପ୍ରଚାରିକା ।

ପ୍ରଚାରିତ, *a.* preached, proclaimed, published.

ପ୍ରଚୁର, *a.* plentiful, abundant, much.

ପ୍ରଚୁରତା, *n.* abundance, plenty.

ପ୍ରଚ୍ଛନ୍ନ, *a.* covered, concealed.

ପ୍ରଜା, *n.* a subject, a ryot; offspring.

ପ୍ରଜାତନ୍ତ୍ର, *n.* a republic.

ପ୍ରଜାପତି, *n.* butterfly; the lord of creation—*Brahmá.* [subjects.

ପ୍ରଜାପାଳନ, *n.* preservation of the

ପ୍ରଜାପୀଡ଼କ, *a.* tyrannical;—*n.* a tyrant.

* ପ୍ରଜେଶ୍ୱର, *n.* a king, a sovereign.

* ପ୍ରଜ୍ୱଳନ, *n.* a blazing up.

ପ୍ରଜ୍ୱଳିତ, *a.* enkindled. [wise.

* ପ୍ରଜ୍ଞ, *a.* learned, well-informed,

* ପ୍ରଜ୍ଞା, *n.* sense, understanding.

* ପ୍ରଣତ, *a.* humble, lowly, prostrate.

* ପ୍ରଣତି, *n.* obeisance, prostration.

ପ୍ରଣବ, *n.* the mystic syllable *Om.*

ପ୍ରଣୟ, *n.* friendly feeling, affection.

* ପ୍ରଣୟନ, *n.* composition, a writing.

* ପ୍ରଣୟିନୀ, *n* a loving wife;—*a.* loving.

* ପ୍ରଣୟୀ, *a.* intimate, friendly, affectionate;—*n.* a lover.

ପ୍ରଣାମ, *n.* bowing, salutation.

ପ୍ରଣାଳୀ, *n.* a series, a water-course, straits (in *Geog.*).

* ପ୍ରଣିଧାନ, *n.* attention, regard, stress.

* ପ୍ରଣିଧି, *n.* a spy; a request.

ପ୍ରଣିପାତ, *n.* obeisance, prostration.

ପ୍ରଣୀତ, *a.* composed, written by.

* ପ୍ରଣେତା, *n.* an author, a composer.

* ପ୍ରଣୋଦିତ, *a.* incited, moved, directed.

ପ୍ରତାପ, *n.* splendour, dignity, ardour, influence.

ପ୍ରତାପୀ, *a.* influential; brilliant.

ପ୍ରତାପାନ୍ୱିତ, *a.* glorious, powerful, influential, ardent.

ପ୍ରତାରକ, *n.* a deceiver, cheat, rogue.

ପ୍ରତାରଣା, * ପ୍ରତାରଣ, *n.* deception, deceit, fraud.

ପ୍ରତାରଣାପୂର୍ବକ, *ad.* fraudulently.

ପ୍ରତାଳ, *n.* revision, comparison.

ପ୍ରତି, *a.* every, each;—*prep.* to, towards;—used as a *prefix* implying all, opposite, a reflected or reiterated action, &c.

ପ୍ରତିକାର, ପ୍ରତୀକାର, *n.* a preventative, a remedy; a return.

* ପ୍ରତିକାର୍ଯ୍ୟ, *a.* remediable. [trary.

ପ୍ରତିକୂଳ, *a.* adverse, opposite, con-

ପ୍ରତିକୃତି, *n.* a reflected image, a picture. [spittoon.

* ପ୍ରତିଗ୍ରହ, *n.* receiving, accepting; a

ପ୍ରତିଘାତ, *n.* a blow in return, resistance.

* ପ୍ରତିଚକ୍ଷୁ, *n.* spectacles.

* ପ୍ରତିଚ୍ଛାୟା, *n.* a shadow, reflected image.

ପ୍ରତିଜ୍ଞା, *n.* a promise, agreement, a proposition in geometry.

ପ୍ରତିଜ୍ଞାତ, *a.* promised, declared.

ପ୍ରତିଜ୍ଞାପତ୍ର, *n.* a written promise.

* ପ୍ରତିଦାନ, *n.* giving back, recompense.

ପ୍ରତିଦିନ, *ad.* every day, daily.

ପ୍ରତିଦ୍ୱନ୍ଦ୍ୱୀ, *a.* hostile;—*n.* a rival.

ପ୍ରତିଧ୍ୱନି, *n.* an echo, reverberation.

ପ୍ରତିନିଧି, *n.* a representative, deputy.

ପ୍ରତିପଦ୍, *n.* the first day of the moon's increase or wane.

* ପ୍ରତିପତ୍ତି, *n.* success; ascendency.

* ପ୍ରତିପନ୍ନ, *a.* effected, demonstrated.

ପ୍ରତିପକ୍ଷ, *n.* an enemy, an opponent.

* ପ୍ରତିପାଦନ, *n.* demonstrating; signifying, treating of, accomplishing.

* ପ୍ରତିପାଦିତ, *a.* ascertained, demonstrated.

ପ୍ରତିପାଳକ, *n.* a supporter, maintainer.

ପ୍ରତିପାଳନ, *n.* keeping, maintaining.

ପ୍ରତିପୋଷକ, *n.* a protector, benefactor.

ପ୍ରତିପୋଷଣ, *n.* support, maintenance.

ପ୍ରତିଫଳ, *n.* retribution, recompense.

* ପ୍ରତିଫଳିତ, *a.* reflected.

ପ୍ରତିବନ୍ଧ, ପ୍ରତିବନ୍ଧକ, *n.* impediment, obstacle.

ପ୍ରତିବନ୍ଧକ, *n.* an opposer, gainsayer.

ପ୍ରତିବର୍ଷ, *ad.* yearly.

ପ୍ରତିବାଦ, *n.* a reply, a pleading in reply.

ପ୍ରତିବାଦୀ, *n.* opponent, respondent;—*a.* replying, rejoining.

ପ୍ରତିବାସୀ, ପ୍ରତିବେଶୀ, *n.* a neighbour.

ପ୍ରତିବିଧାନ, *n.* counteraction, precaution, remedy.

ପ୍ରତିବିମ୍ବ, *n.* a reflected image.

* ପ୍ରତିଭା, *n.* understanding, presence of mind, energy; a reflected light.

* ପ୍ରତିଭାଶାଳୀ, *a.* possessed of genius, quick-witted, intelligent.

* ପ୍ରତିଭୂ, *n.* delegate, representative, security, surety, bail.

ପ୍ରତିମା, *n.* an image, idol, picture.

ପ୍ରତିମାସ, *ad.* every month, monthly.

ପ୍ରତିମୂର୍ତ୍ତି, *n.* an image, likeness.

ପ୍ରତିଯୋଗୀ, *a.* of equal power, opposing, impeding;—*n.* an opponent, a rival.

ପ୍ରତିଯୋଗିତା, *n.* rivalry, competition; coadjutorship.

* ପ୍ରତିରବ, *n.* echo, reverberation.

ପ୍ରତିରୁପ, *n.* see ପ୍ରତିରୂପ ।

ପ୍ରତିରୋଧ, *n.* opposition, prohibition; besieging.

ପ୍ରତିରୂପ, *n.* a copy.

ପ୍ରତିଶବ୍ଦ, *n.* a synonym; an echo.

ପ୍ରତିଶୋଧ, *n.* revenge, retaliation.

ପ୍ରତିଶ୍ରୁତ, *a.* assented to, promised.

* ପ୍ରତିଷେଧ, *n.* prohibition, denial.

* ପ୍ରତିଷେଧକ, *a.* denying, pohibiting, hindering.

ପ୍ରତିଷ୍ଠା, *n.* fame, renown; consecration, dedication.

ପ୍ରତିଷ୍ଠିତ, *a.* celebrated, famed; consecrated, dedicated.

ପ୍ରତିହତ, *a.* smitten in return, resisted; killed, destroyed. [man.

* ପ୍ରତିହାରୀ, *n.* a doorkeeper, watch-

ପ୍ରତିହିଂସା, *n.* revenge, retaliation.

ପ୍ରତିକ୍ଷଣ, *ad.* always, every moment.

* ପ୍ରତୀଚୀ, *n.* the west quarter.

ପ୍ରତୀତି, *n.* conviction, belief; knowledge. [retrograde.

* ପ୍ରତୀପ, *a.* opposite, contradictory,

* ପ୍ରତୀୟମାନ, *a.* visible, inferable.

* ପ୍ରତୀକ୍ଷା, *n.* expectation, waiting.

* ପ୍ରତ୍ନତତ୍ତ୍ୱ, *n.* antiquity.

* ପ୍ରତ୍ନତତ୍ତ୍ୱବିତ୍, *a.* and *n.* versed in antiquities; antiquarian.

ପ୍ରତ୍ୟଙ୍ଗ, *n.* every limb, extremities of the body.

* ପ୍ରତ୍ୟନ୍ତ, *a.* contiguous, bordering.

ପ୍ରତ୍ୟବାୟ, *n.* an obstacle; sin, crime.

ପ୍ରତ୍ୟୟ, *n.* faith, trust, confidence.

ପ୍ରତ୍ୟୟୀ, *a.* trustworthy;–*n.* believer.

ପ୍ରତ୍ୟର୍ପଣ, *n.* delivering back, restoring.

ପ୍ରତ୍ୟହ, *ad.* daily, every day.

ପ୍ରତ୍ୟକ୍ଷ, *a.* manifest, plain, obvious.

* ପ୍ରତ୍ୟାକର୍ଷଣ, *n.* drawing back or pulling in a contrary direction.

* ପ୍ରତ୍ୟାଖ୍ୟାନ, *n.* rejection, refutation, a denial.

ପ୍ରତ୍ୟାଗତ, *a.* returned.

ପ୍ରତ୍ୟାଗମନ, *n.* returning, return.

* ପ୍ରତ୍ୟାଦିଷ୍ଟ, *a.* warned; spoken as an oracle.

* ପ୍ରତ୍ୟାଦେଶ, *n.* supernatural warning, a revelation. [back.

ପ୍ରତ୍ୟାବର୍ତ୍ତନ, *n.* returning, coming

* ପ୍ରତ୍ୟାବୃତ୍ତ, *a.* returned, come back.

* ପ୍ରତ୍ୟାରମ୍ଭ, *n.* a second commencement.

ପ୍ରତ୍ୟାଶା, *n.* hope, expectation.

ପ୍ରତ୍ୟାଶୀ, *a.* hoping, waiting for.

* ପ୍ରତ୍ୟାସନ୍ନ, *a.* near, nigh, contiguous.

* ପ୍ରତ୍ୟୁତ, *ad.* on the contrary, rather.

ପ୍ରତ୍ୟୁତ୍ତର, ପ୍ରତ୍ୟୁକ୍ତି, *n.* a reply, rejoinder.

* ପ୍ରତ୍ୟୁତ୍ପନ୍ନ, *a.* ready, prompt.

ପ୍ରତ୍ୟୁତ୍ପନ୍ନମତି, *n.* presence of mind;—*a.* quick-minded.

ପ୍ରତ୍ୟୁପକାର, *n.* a return of kindness.

* ପ୍ରତ୍ୟୂଷ, *n.* morning dawn, morning.

* ପ୍ରତ୍ୟୂହ, *n.* obstacle, impediment.

ପ୍ରତ୍ୟେକ, *a.* each, every;—*n.* each one, everybody.

ପ୍ରଥମ, *a.* first, previous, chief.

ପ୍ରଥମାବିଭକ୍ତି, *n.* (in *Gram.*) nominative case. [firstborn.

ପ୍ରଥମାଷ୍ଟମୀ, *n.* a ceremonial day for

ପ୍ରଥମେ, ପ୍ରଥମତଃ, *ad.* in the first place, firstly.

ପ୍ରଥା, *n.* custom, usage.

* ପ୍ରଥିତ, *a.* famous, illustrious.

ପ୍ରଦତ୍ତ, *a.* given, bestowed, conferred.

ପ୍ରଦର, *n.* menorrhagia, a disease of women.

ପ୍ରଦର୍ଶକ, *a.* shewing, producing the sight;—*n.* a person who shows.

ପ୍ରଦର୍ଶନ, *n.* showing, pointing out.

ପ୍ରଦର୍ଶିତ, *a.* shown, mentioned.

ପ୍ରଦକ୍ଷିଣ, *n.* walking or going round.

ପ୍ରଦାନ, *n.* giving, presenting, gift.

ପ୍ରଦୀପ, *n.* a lamp, a light.

ପ୍ରଦେଶ, *n.* a district, a province.

ପ୍ରଦେଶୀୟ, *a.* provincial.

* ପ୍ରଦୋଷ, *n.* evening, dusk, twilight.

ପ୍ରଧାନ, *a.* chief, principal, prime.

ପ୍ରଧାନତା, *n.* pre-eminence.

ପ୍ରଧାନଯାଜକ, *n.* high priest.

ପ୍ରପଞ୍ଚ, *n.* delusion; the world.

* ପ୍ରପନ୍ନ, *a.* obtained; taking refuge with; poor, needy.

* ପ୍ରପା, *n.* water-place for travellers.

ପ୍ରପାତ, *n.* a cascade or waterfall, a precipice.

ପ୍ରପିତାମହ, *n.* father's grandfather.

ପ୍ରପିତାମହୀ, *n.* father's grandmother.

* ପ୍ରପୌତ୍ର, *a.* a great-grandson.

ପ୍ରଫୁଲ୍ଲ, *a.* smiling, gay; expanded.

ପ୍ରଫୁଲ୍ଲତା, *n.* cheerfulness, gladness.

ପ୍ରଫୁଲ୍ଲଚିତ୍ତ, *a.* glad-hearted, joyful.

ପ୍ରଫୁଲ୍ଲବଦନ, *n.* cheerful or smiling countenance.

* ପ୍ରବକ୍ତା, *n.* a speaker, orator;—*a.* eloquent.

ପ୍ରବଞ୍ଚକ, *n.* a deceiver, a cheat.

ପ୍ରବଞ୍ଚନା, *n.* deception, fraud.

ପ୍ରବଣ, *a.* inclined, prone, disposed to (in this sense used only at the end of a noun).

ପ୍ରବନ୍ଧ, *n.* an essay, an address, a treatise, narrative.

* ପ୍ରବର, *n.* line of ancestors; chief.

ପ୍ରବର୍ତ୍ତକ, *n.* an instigator, inciter, stimulus;—*a.* exciting, stimulating.

ପ୍ରବର୍ତ୍ତନା, *n.* persuasion.

ପ୍ରବର୍ତ୍ତାଇବା, *v.* to influence or incite, to persuade.

ପ୍ରବର୍ତ୍ତିବା, *v.i.* to engage in, to enter upon.

ପ୍ରବଳ, *a.* strong, powerful, cogent.

ପ୍ରବାଦ, *n.* rumour, report.

* ପ୍ରବାଳ, *n.* coral.

ପ୍ରବାସ, *n.* temporary residence.

ପ୍ରବାସୀ, *n.* a sojourner, lodger.

ପ୍ରବାହ, *n.* stream, current; train of events.

ପ୍ରବିଷ୍ଟ, *n.* entered, engaged in.

ପ୍ରବୀଣ, *a.* clever, accomplished.

* ପ୍ରବୀର, *n.* a chief warrior, chief.

* ପ୍ରବୁଦ୍ଧ, *n.* awakened, roused, wary.

ପ୍ରବୃତ୍ତ, *a.* engaged (in work), setting about, ready, eager. [for.

ପ୍ରବୃତ୍ତି, *n.* an inclination; a turn

ପ୍ରବେଶ, *n.* entering, introduction.

ପ୍ରବେଶିକା, *n.* entrance (standard); introduction.

ପ୍ରବୋଧ, *n.* conviction, vigilance, a soothing; intellect.

* ପ୍ରବୋଧକ, *n.* one who convinces or consoles. [soled.

ପ୍ରବୋଧିତ, *a.* convinced, roused, con-

* ପ୍ରଭଞ୍ଜନ, *n.* air, wind.

* ପ୍ରଭବ, *n.* origin, production; the generative cause.

ପ୍ରଭା, *n.* splendour, lustre, light.

ପ୍ରଭାକର, *n.* a proper name, * the sun, a luminary.

ପ୍ରଭାତ, *n.* dawn, daybreak, morning.

ପ୍ରଭାତତାରା, *n.* morning star.

ପ୍ରଭାବ, *n.* majesty, dignity, power.

ପ୍ରଭୁ, *n.* lord, a master, owner.

ପ୍ରଭୁତା, ପ୍ରଭୁତ୍ୱ, *n.* lordship, sovereignty.

ପ୍ରଭୁଭକ୍ତ, *a.* devoted to a lord or master, loyal.

ପ୍ରଭୁଭକ୍ତି, *n.* devotedness to one's master, loyalty.

* ପ୍ରଭୂତ, *a.* much, many, sufficient.

ପ୍ରଭୃତି, *n,* and the like, etcetera.

ପ୍ରଭେଦ, *n.* difference, distinction.

ପ୍ରମତ୍ତ, *a.* elated, intoxicated, rash.

ପ୍ରମାଣ, *n.* evidence, proof; instance.

ପ୍ରମାଣପତ୍ର, *n.* a voucher, affidavit.

ପ୍ରମାତାମହ, *n.* a mother's grandfather. [mother.

ପ୍ରମାତାମହୀ, *n.* a mother's grand-

ପ୍ରମାଦ, *n.* error, inadvertence, an accident, a mishap, calamity, danger.

* ପ୍ରମାଦୀ, *a.* careless, inattentive, negligent.

ପ୍ରମୁଖ, *a.* foremost, chief, principal, (used as an *affix*).

* ପ୍ରମୁଖାତ୍, *ad.* from the lips, orally.

* ପ୍ରମୁଦିତ, *a.* overjoyed, elated.

* ପ୍ରମେୟ, *a.* measurable, capable of proof, provable.

ପ୍ରମେହ, *n.* gleet, gonorrhœa.

* ପ୍ରମୋଚନ, *n.* liberating, setting free, delivering. [ture.

ପ୍ରମୋଦ, *n.* great joy, delight, rap-

ପ୍ରଯତ୍ନ, *n.* great exertion, effort.

* ପ୍ରୟାଣ, *n.* a going, departure, exit.

* ପ୍ରୟାସ, *n.* inclination, desire, bias.

ପ୍ରୟାସୀ, *a.* diligent, persevering.

ପ୍ରଯୁକ୍ତ, *a.* in consequence of, owing to.

ପ୍ରୟୋଗ, *n.* application, exertion, effort, attempt.

ପ୍ରୟୋଜକ, *n.* an exciting cause;—*a.* exciting, causing, stirring up, stimulating.

ପ୍ରୟୋଜନ, *n.* need, necessity, occasion, motive.

ପ୍ରୟୋଜନୀୟ, *a.* necessary, suited to.

* ପ୍ରୟୋଜ୍ୟ, *a.* applicable; excitable, susceptible.

* ପ୍ରରୋଚନା, *n.* exciting, stimulating.

ପ୍ରଳୟ, *n.* universal dissolution.

ପ୍ରଳାପ, *n.* random talk, delirious talk.

* ପ୍ରଳାପୀ, *n.* a random or raving talker.

ପ୍ରଲେପ, *n.* plaster, salve, ointment.

ପ୍ରଲୋଭ, *n.* covetousness ; a desire.

ପ୍ରଲୋଭନ, *n.* allurement, inducement, attraction, temptation.

ପ୍ରଲୋଭିତ, *a.* allured, enticed, induced, tempted.

ପ୍ରଶଂସନୀୟ, *a.* praiseworthy, laudable.

ପ୍ରଶଂସା, *n.* praise, commendation.

ପ୍ରଶଂସାପତ୍ର, *n.* letter of recommendation.

ପ୍ରଶଂସିତ, *a.* praised, applauded.

* ପ୍ରଶମନ, *n.* assuaging, appeasing, mitigating, soothing.

* ପ୍ରଶମିତ, *a.* pacified, appeased.

ପ୍ରଶସ୍ତ, *a.* wide, roomy ; * praised, right.

* ପ୍ରଶସ୍ତତା, *n.* width; goodness, excellence.

ପ୍ରଶାନ୍ତ, *a.* pacific, smooth, calm.

ପ୍ରଶାନ୍ତମହାସାଗର, *n.* Pacific Ocean.

ପ୍ରଶ୍ନ, *n.* a question, inquiry.

ପ୍ରଶ୍ନଚିହ୍ନ, *n.* a query mark (?).

* ପ୍ରଶ୍ନବାଚକ, *a.* interrogative.

ପ୍ରଶ୍ୱାସ, *n.* breathing, respiration.

ପ୍ରଶ୍ରୟ, *n.* love, affection, fondness, indulgence.

* ପ୍ରଷ୍ଟବ୍ୟ, *a.* questionable.

* ପ୍ରସକ୍ତ, *a.* fond of; treated of; eternal.

* ପ୍ରସକ୍ତି, *n.* fondness; a topic, theme.

ପ୍ରସଙ୍ଗ, *n.* a topic, subject, treatise.

ପ୍ରସନ୍ନ, *a.* gracious, propitious, pleased, cheerful.

ପ୍ରସନ୍ନତା, *n.* propitiousness, graciousness, kindness.

ପ୍ରସବ, *n.* giving birth, parturition.

ପ୍ରସବଗୃହ, *n.* a lying-in room.

ପ୍ରସବିବା, *v.* to bring forth, to give birth to.

* ପ୍ରସର, *n.* dimension, extent, width.

ପ୍ରସାଦ, *n.* favour, grace; the remnants of food offered to a god or to a superior, orts.

* ପ୍ରସାଧନୀ, *n.* a comb.

ପ୍ରସାର, *n.* extent, dimension, size.

ପ୍ରସାରଣ, *n.* extension, expanding.

ପ୍ରସାରିତ, *a.* widened, extended, enlarged.

ପ୍ରସିଦ୍ଧ, *a.* celebrated, famous, renowned.

ପ୍ରସୂତ, *a.* born, brought forth.

ପ୍ରସୂତି, * ପ୍ରସୂତା, *n.* a woman recently delivered of a child.

ପ୍ରସ୍ତର, *n.* a stone, a gem.

ପ୍ରସ୍ତାବ, *n.* a proposition, proposal; a discourse; a topic, theme.

* ପ୍ରସ୍ତାବନା, *n.* introduction, preface, foreword.

ପ୍ରସ୍ତାବିତ, *a.* proposed, related, mentioned, told.

ପ୍ରସ୍ତୁତ, *a.* prepared, ready, prompt.

ପ୍ରସ୍ଥ, *n.* width.

ପ୍ରସ୍ଥାନ, *n.* departure, setting off.

* ପ୍ରସ୍ଥାପନ, *n.* despatching, sending.

ପ୍ରସ୍ଫୁଟିତ, ପ୍ରସ୍ଫୁଟ, *a.* blown, expanded.

ପ୍ରସ୍ରବଣ, *n.* a spring; * leaking, oozing.

ପ୍ରସ୍ରାବ, *n.* urine; making water.

ପ୍ରହର, *n.* a watch of three hours.

ପ୍ରହରୀ, *n.* a watchman, sentry, sentinel.

ପ୍ରହସନ, *n.* a farce, a comedy.

ପ୍ରହାର, *n.* a blow with a stick.

* ପ୍ରହାରକ, *n.* a striker, smiter.

* ପ୍ରହାରିତ, *a.* smitten, struck.

* ପ୍ରହୃଷ୍ଟ, *a.* glad, gratified, happy.

ପ୍ରହେଳିକା, * ପ୍ରହେଳୀ, *n.* a riddle, enigma, puzzle.

ପ୍ରକ୍ଷାଳନ, *n.* a washing, cleansing.

ପ୍ରକ୍ଷାଳିତ, *a.* washed, cleansed, expiated.

* ପ୍ରକ୍ଷିପ୍ତ, *a.* thrown, cast, projected.

* ପ୍ରକ୍ଷେପ *n.* a throwing, propulsion.

* ପ୍ରାକାର, *n.* enclosure, wall, rampart.

ପ୍ରାକୃତ, *a.* common, vulgar, plebeian.

ପ୍ରାକୃତିକ, *a.* belonging to nature, natural, physical;—ପ୍ରାକୃତିକ ଭୂଗୋଳ, physical geography;—ପ୍ରାକୃତିକ ଇତିହାସ, ପ୍ରାକୃତିକ ଇତିବୃତ୍ତ, natural history;—ପ୍ରାକୃତିକ ବିଜ୍ଞାନ, natural science.

* ପ୍ରାକ୍, *ad.* before, previously.

* ପ୍ରାକ୍କାଳ, *n.* olden time; a crisis.

ପ୍ରାକ୍ତନ, *n.* destiny, fate, luck.

* ପ୍ରାଖର୍ଯ୍ୟ, *n.* acuteness.

* ପ୍ରାଗଲ୍ଭ୍ୟ, *n.* pomposity.

* ପ୍ରାଙ୍ଗଣ, *n.* a court-yard, enclosure.

* ପ୍ରାଙ୍ମୁଖ, *a.* facing eastwards.

ପ୍ରାଚୀ, *n.* the east; name of a river.

ପ୍ରାଚୀନ, *a.* old, ancient, antique, aged.

ପ୍ରାଚୀର, *n.* a wall, enclosure, fence.

* ପ୍ରାଚୁର୍ଯ୍ୟ, *n.* abundance, plenty.

* ପ୍ରାଚ୍ୟ, *a.* eastern.

* ପ୍ରାଜ୍ଞ, *a.* learned, sensible, clever.

* ପ୍ରାଞ୍ଜଳ, *a.* straight forward, simple, candid, easy.

* ପ୍ରାଞ୍ଜଳି, *a.* having the hands joined like a cup.

ପ୍ରାଣ, *n.* life, soul, spirit, breath.

ପ୍ରାଣଘାତକ, *a* murderous, fatal, deadly.

ପ୍ରାଣତ୍ୟାଗ, *n.* dying, death.

ପ୍ରାଣଦଣ୍ଡ, *n.* a death-sentence.

ପ୍ରାଣଧାରଣ, *n.* living, sustenance, supporting life.

* ପ୍ରାଣନାଥ, *n.* a husband; a beloved.

ପ୍ରାଣପଣ, *n.* great exertion, risking life.

* ପ୍ରାଣପ୍ରତିମ, *a.* dear as life, beloved.

ପ୍ରାଣପ୍ରିୟ, *a.* beloved of one's soul, as dear as life;—*n.* a lover, husband; *fem.* ପ୍ରାଣପ୍ରିୟା ।

ପ୍ରାଣବିୟୋଗ, *n.* separation from life, death.

ପ୍ରାଣସମ, *a.* equal to or as dear as life;—*n.* a lover, husband; *fem.* ପ୍ରାଣସମା ।

ପ୍ରାଣହନ୍ତା, * ପ୍ରାଣହା, *n.* a murderer.

ପ୍ରାଣହିଂସା, *n.* injury to life, murder.

* ପ୍ରାଣାଧାର, *n.* the body.

ପ୍ରାଣାଧିକ, *a.* dearer than life;—*n.* a son.

ପ୍ରାଣାନ୍ତ, *n.* the close of life, death.

* ପ୍ରାଣାୟାମ, *n.* holding the breath.

ପ୍ରାଣିତତ୍ତ୍ୱ, ପ୍ରାଣିବିଦ୍ୟା, *n.* zoology.

ପ୍ରାଣ, *n.* a living creature; the soul.
ପ୍ରାଣେଶ୍ୱର, ପ୍ରାଣେଶ, *n.* a husband, lord of life.
ପ୍ରାତଃ, *n.* the dawn.
*ପ୍ରାତଃକର୍ମ, *n.* morning duties.
ପ୍ରାତଃକାଳ, *n.* morning.
ପ୍ରାତଃକୃତ୍ୟ, *n.* morning religious observances or duties.
ପ୍ରାତଃସ୍ନାନ, *n.* the morning ablution.
ପ୍ରାଥମିକ, *a.* primary, entitled to priority, first.
ପ୍ରାଦୁର୍ଭାବ, *n.* manifestation, displaying, showing off. [rife.
*ପ୍ରାଦୁର୍ଭୂତ, *a.* manifest, exhibited,
ପ୍ରାଦେଶିକ, *a.* provincial, local.
ପ୍ରାଧାନ୍ୟ, *n.* superiority.
ପ୍ରାନ୍ତ, *n.* limit, extremity, outskirts.
ପ୍ରାନ୍ତର, *n.* an open plain, prairie.
ପ୍ରାପ୍ତ, *a.* obtained, received.
ପ୍ରାପ୍ତଯୌବନ, *a.* young, youthful.
ପ୍ରାପ୍ତି, *n.* an obtaining, gain, profit.
ପ୍ରାପ୍ୟ, *n.* that which is due;—*a.* attainable, obtainable.
*ପ୍ରାବରଣ, *n.* an outer garment, screen.
*ପ୍ରାବଲ୍ୟ, *n.* power, predominancy.
*ପ୍ରାବୃଟ୍, *n.* rainy season.
*ପ୍ରାମାଣିକ, *a.* credible, authentic.
ପ୍ରାୟ, *ad.* almost, about, nearly.
ପ୍ରାୟଶ୍ଚିତ୍ତ, *n.* expiation, atonement.
ପ୍ରାରବ୍ଧ, *n.* destiny, fate;—*a.* * predestined; begun. [ment.
ପ୍ରାରମ୍ଭ, *n.* beginning, commence-
*ପ୍ରାର୍ଥକ, *n.* one who requests, a suitor.
ପ୍ରାର୍ଥନା, *n.* prayer, request, petition.
ପ୍ରାର୍ଥିତ, *a.* prayed for, asked for.
ପ୍ରାର୍ଥୀ, *a.* wishing, desiring;—*n.* a candidate, a petitioner, a suitor.
ପ୍ରାଲବ୍ଧ, *n.* luck, fortune.
*ପ୍ରାଶନ, *n.* eating, a meal, food.
*ପ୍ରାଶସ୍ତ୍ୟ, *n.* largeness, excellence.
ପ୍ରାସ, *n.* pain, ache, smart.
*ପ୍ରାସଙ୍ଗିକ, *a.* connected with an introduced topic. [temple.
*ପ୍ରାସାଦ, *n.* an edifice, palace;
ପ୍ରିୟ, *a.* beloved, dear, pleasing.
*ପ୍ରିୟକର, *a.* pleasing, amiable.
ପ୍ରିୟତମ, *a.* most amiable, dearly beloved; *fem.* ପ୍ରିୟତମା ।
ପ୍ରିୟତା, *n.* amiableness, fondness.
ପ୍ରିୟପାତ୍ର, *n.* an object of love or favour.
ପ୍ରିୟବାଦୀ, *n.* one who speaks kindly.
ପ୍ରିୟଭାଷୀ, *a.* speaking agreeable things.
*ପ୍ରିୟମ୍ବଦ, *a.* of pleasing address; *fem.* ପ୍ରିୟମ୍ବଦା ।
ପ୍ରିୟା, *n.* a beloved wife; a mistress.
ପ୍ରୀତ, *a.* pleased, satisfied; beloved.
ପ୍ରୀତି, *n.* love, fondness, regard.
ପ୍ରୀତିକର, *a.* giving satisfaction to, pleasing.
ପ୍ରେକ୍, *n.* a nail, peg, pin. [ceased.
ପ୍ରେତ, *n.* a ghost, apparition; de-
*ପ୍ରେତକାର୍ଯ୍ୟ, *n.* funeral obsequies.

*ପ୍ରେତଗୃହ, *n.* a place where the dead are burned.

*ପ୍ରେତପତି, *n.* *Yama*—regent of death.

ପ୍ରେମ, *n.* love, affection, tenderness.

ପ୍ରେମଡୋରି, *n.* cords of love.

ପ୍ରେମିକ, *a.* loving.

ପ୍ରେମୀ, *a.* loving, affectionate.

ପ୍ରେୟସୀ, *a. fem.* dear, best beloved.

ପ୍ରେରକ, *n.* one who sends or despatches.

ପ୍ରେରଣ, *n.* sending, despatching.

ପ୍ରେରିତ, *a.* sent, despatched;—*n.* an apostle.

*ପ୍ରେଷ୍ୟ, *n.* a messenger.

ପ୍ରୋକ୍ତ, *a.* uttered, mentioned.

*ପ୍ରୋତ୍ଫୁଲ୍ଲ, *a.* expanded; cheerful, gay.

*ପ୍ରୋଥିତ *a.* buried, interred; planted.

*ପ୍ରୋଷିତ, *a.* sojourning abroad.

*ପ୍ରୋକ୍ଷଣ, *n.* purifying by sprinkling of water.

ପ୍ରୌଢ, *a.* married, full grown, old.

ପ୍ରୌଢା, *a. fem.* married; a woman from the age of 30 to 55.

*ପ୍ରୌଢି, *n.* controversy, zeal, enterprise.

*ପ୍ଲବଙ୍ଗମ, ପ୍ଲବଗ, *n.* whatever goes by leaps.

*ପ୍ଲାବନ, *n.* overflowing, inundating; a flood.

*ପ୍ଲାବିତ, *a.* overflowed, flooded, inundated.

ପ୍ଲୀହା, ପ୍ଲିହା, *n.* the spleen; enlargement of the spleen.

ଫ.

ଫ, the 22nd consonant.

ଫଁଫଁ, *n.* hissing of a snake.

ଫଉଜ, *n.* an army.

ଫକତ୍, *ad.* only merely, simply.

ଫକା, ଫକ୍କା, ଫିକା, *a.* pale, light-coloured.

ଫକାସା. *n.* breath of life.

*ଫକ୍କିକା, *n.* deception; a sophism.

ଫକୀର, *n.* a Mussalman beggar.

ଫଗୁ, *n.* the red *hori* powder, *abir.*

ଫଗୁଣ, *n.* a mouth of that name, part of Feb. and March.

ଫଜିହତ, *n.* abuse, reproach.

ଫଟକା, *n.* sound of a cracker or squib; fireworks.

ଫଟଫଟ୍, *n.* a popping sound.

ଫଟା, *a.* cracked, burst, split, torn.

ଫଟାଇବା, *v.* to split or crack; to ask with persistence.

ଫଡଫଡ, *n.* a 'noise of flapping or tearing

ଫଡା, *n.* a piece of split wood;—*a.* split.

ଫଡାଏ, ଫଡାକ, *n.* one piece of anything such as split wood.

ଫଢଅ, ଫଡଅ, *n.* a leg, upper part of the thigh.

ଫଡଙ୍ଗ, *n.* a grasshopper, a locust.

ଫଣଫଣା, *n.* name of a tree.

ଫଣା, *n.* the expanded hood of the cobra.

*ଫଣୀ, *n.* a snake; the cobra;—*a.* hooded.

* ଫଣୀନ୍ଦ୍ର, *n.* king of serpents.
ଫତେ, *n.* victory;—*a.* accomplished.
ଫନ୍ଦ, *n.* a rim or brim; a contrivance, a trick.
ଫନ୍ଦା, *n.* shelter, support, means of livelihood; a trick, a contrivance.
ଫନ୍ଦୀ, *a.* tricky, contriving, scheming.
ଫମ୍ପା, *a.* hollow, puffy spongy.
ଫମ୍ପାଇବା, *v.* to blow up, to inflate; to cause fermentation.
ଫୟସଲା, *n.* decree of a court, a decision.
ଫରକ୍, *a.* separate, distinct;—*n.* difference.
ଫର୍ଫର, *n.* vain show, bragging;—*ad.* excessively.
ଫରମାସ୍, *n.* an order for any article, order.
ଫଇଲଉ, *a.* spread out, expanded.
ଫରିଆଦୀ, *n.* a plaintiff, complainant
ଫରୁଆ, *n.* a small box, a gallipot.
ଫରେବ, *n.* trick, fraud, roguery.
ଫର୍ଚ୍ଚା, *a.* expanded, stretched, opened.
ଫର୍ଚ୍ଛା, *a.* clear, transparent, open.
ଫର୍ଦ୍ଦ, *n.* a sheet of paper, a flat piece (of anything); a list, catalogue.
ଫର୍ଫନ୍ଦ, *n.* a contrivance, shuffle, trick.
ଫର୍ମାସି, ଫର୍ମାଇସି, *a.* made as per order.
ଫଳ, *n.* fruit; effect, result, profit, reward.
* ଫଳକ, *n.* a shield, a plank.
ଫଳଭାଗୀ, *n.* receiver of fruit or consequences of an action.
* ଫଳତଃ, *ad.* in reality, indeed.
ଫଳନ୍ତା, ଫଳନ୍ତି, ଫଳବନ୍ତ, *a.* fruitful.
ଫଳପ୍ରଦ, *a.* yielding fruit, productive.
ଫଳମୁହାଁ, *a.* in blossom.
ଫଳା, *n.* a part of a compound letter as ୍ (ଯ-ଫଳା) etc.
ଫଳାଇବା, *v.* to render fruitful or advantageous.
ଫଳାଫଳ, *n.* good or ill results.
ଫଳାହାର, *n.* act of eating fruit.
ଫଳାହାରୀ, *a.* living on fruit;—*n.* a fruitarian, vegetarian.
ଫଳି, *n.* staves of a ladder or hackery; a kind of fish; an arrow-head.
ଫଳିତ ଜ୍ୟୋତିଷ, *n.* astrology.
ଫଲଣା, ଫଲଣେଇ, *a.* certain, such (not specifically named).
ଫସ୍କା, *a.* slack, loose, flaccid, lax, useless, not heavy.
ଫସଲ, *n.* a crop, a harvest.
ଫାଜୁ, *n.* overplus, surplus; borrowing and not returning.
ଫାଉଡ଼ା, *n.* a digging hoe.
ଫାଙ୍କ, *n.* a cavity, a hole, a crack.
ଫାଙ୍କୁ, *a.* separate, distinct.
ଫାଁକି, *n.* trick, deceit; a powder.
ଫାଙ୍କି, *n.* breath, life-breath.
ଫାଜିଲ, ଫାଜଲ, *a.* clever;—*n.* an overplus.

ଫାଟ, *n.* a crack, burst, split. [jail.
ଫାଟକ, *n.* an outer door or gate; a
ଫାଟିବା, *v.* to crack, burst, break.
ଫାଟୁଆ, *n.* a foot disease of cattle.
ଫାଡିବା, *v.* to cleave, split, divide, to tear.
ଫାଣ୍ଡି, *n.* a watchhouse, a branch police station.
ଫାନ୍ଦ, *n.* a trap, snare, noose.
ଫାନୁସ, *n.* a lamp-shade.
ଫାମ୍ପିବା, *v.i.* to swell, to distend.
ଫାର୍ଶା, *n.* a weapon, small battle-axe.
ଫାର୍ସୀ, *n.* a Persian.
ଫାଳ, *n.* a ploughshare; the halves of that which has been cut into two.
ଫାଳିଆ, *n.* a chip, slice, cutting.
ଫାଳେ, *n.* one half of any thing cut in two.
ଫାଲ୍ଗୁନ, *n.* see ଫଗୁଣ ।
ଫାସ, *n.* a noose, slip-knot.
ଫାସୀ, *n.* hanging to death.
ଫାସିଆ, *n.* an earring.
ଫାଶିକାଠ, *n.* the gallows.
ଫିକର, *n.* a contrivance, scheme.
ଫିକରବାଜ, *n.* a cunning contriver.
ଫିକା, *a.* pale, light-coloured, vapid.
ଫିଙ୍ଗିବା, *v.* to throw, to cast away.
ଫିଟାଇବା, *v.* to unloose, to untie, to open. [untying.
ଫିଟାଫିଟି, *n.* repeated opening or
ଫିଟିବା, *v.i.* to be loosened or untied, to open.
ଫିତା, *n.* tape, ribbon, a lace.
ଫିରଙ୍ଗୀ, ଫିରିଙ୍ଗୀ, *n.* European, foreigner.
ଫିସିଫିସ, *n.* dropping of water, a fine drizzle; an ear ornament.
ଫୁଃ, *interj.* poh! pugh! oh! foolish!
ଫୁଙ୍କ, *n.* a blowing with the mouth.
ଫୁଙ୍କିବା, *v.* to blow with the mouth; to whisper the *mantra* in the ear; to perform charms.
ଫୁଟ, *n.* a foot or twelve inches; a division of a cotton pod.
ଫୁଟା, *a.* burst, torn, split, expanded.
ଫୁଟାଇବା, *v.* to cause a thing to burst or boil up in bubbles.
ଫୁଟି, *n.* a kind of melon.
ଫୁଟିବା, *v.* to boil, bubble, burst.
ଫୁଟକ, *n.* snapping of the fingers.
ଫୁଟେ, *n.* a foot, one foot in length.
*ଫୁତ୍କାର, *n.* blowing with the mouth.
ଫୁରୁସତ, *n.* leisure, time,
ଫୁଲ, *n.* a flower, blossom; the placenta; menstrual flux; a cataract.
ଫୁଲଖଡି, *n.* chalk.
ଫୁଲଗନ୍ଧକ, *n.* flowers of sulphur.
ଫୁଲଗୁଣା, *n.* a kind of nose ornament. [ling.
ଫୁଲଫୁଲିଆ, *a.* gaudy, foppish; swel-
ଫୁଲା, *n.* a swelling; cataract of the eye. [swell.
ଫୁଲାଇବା, *v.* to distend, to cause to

ଫୁଲିବା, *v.* to swell, to expand.

ଫୁଲ୍ଲି, *n.* a kind of nose ornament; a string with tassels worn by women round the hair knot.

ଫୁଲ୍କା, *n.* a fish's gills; a spark;—*a.* swollen.

ଫୁଲ୍କାମୁହାଁ, *a.* having a swollen face.

* ଫୁଲ୍ଲ, *a.* expanded, blown, opened.

ଫୁସଫୁସ୍, *n.* whispering; the lungs.

ଫୁସଲାଇବା, *v.* to coax, to persuade, to cajole.

ଫୁସଲାଫୁସଲି, *n.* wheedling, cajoling coaxing.

ଫେରାଇବା, *v.* to cause to turn back.

ଫେଡାଙ୍କ, ଫେଡାଣ, *n.* subtraction.

ଫେଡାମିଶା, ଫେଡମିଶା, *n.* subtraction and addition.

ଫେଣ, *n.* foam, froth, scum; hood of a snake.

ଫେଣା, *n.* a kind of sweetmeat; hood of a snake.

ଫେଣିବା, *v.* to foam or froth.

* ଫେନ, *n.* foam, froth.

* ଫେନିଲ, *a.* foamy, frothy.

ଫେନିଲ୍, *n.* a disinfectant liquid, phenyle.

ଫେର୍, *ad.* again.

ଫେରଣ, *n.* turning, reversion.

ଫେରଣ୍ଡା, *n.* a he-jackal.

ଫେରନ୍ତ, *ad.* (give or take) back again.

ଫେରନ୍ତା, *a.* returning.

ଫେରଫାର, *n.* transposition, change; confusion; sale.

ଫେରସ୍ତ, *n.* a list, a duplicate copy.

ଫେରାଇବା, *v.* to return, to restore, to change.

ଫେରାଦ, *n.* plaint or suit, a complaint.

ଫେରାଫେର, *n.* receiving and returning anything.

ଫେରିବା, *v.* to turn, to come back, to change.

ଫୋଟକା, *n.* a bubble, bladder, blister; fireworks.

ଫୋଡ, *n.* a small aperture, a hole.

ଫୋଡଣା, *n.* an instrument for boring or piercing, an awl, gimlet, auger.

ଫୋଡିବା, *v.* to pierce, to bore, to perforate.

ଫୋପଡ, *n.* a stick for throwing at anything.

ଫୋପଡାଫୋପଡି, *n.* a throwing or scattering about.

ଫୋପର, *a.* decayed, worm-eaten.

ଫୋପାଡିବା, *v.* to throw, to cast, to throw away.

ଫୋପ୍ସା, *n.* the lungs.

ଫୌଜ, *n.* an army.

ଫୌଜଦାରୀ, *a.* criminal, opposed to civil.

ବ.

ବ, the 23rd consonant.

ବଇନା, *n.* money in advance, earnest money.

ବଉନି, *n.* the first sale of the day.

ବଇଁଶୀ, *n.* a flute, fife, a piccolo, a long whistle made of tin, brass or other metals.

ବଉଳ, *n.* blossom, bloom, a bud.

ବଉଳିବା, *v.* to bloom, to blossom.

ବଏବାକୁ, *n.* a loan, expenditure; foreclosure.

ବଂଶ, *n.* race, lineage, family; * a bamboo.

* ବଂଶଜ, *a.* born of a certain race or family.

ବଂଶଧର, *n.* perpetuating a family.

* ବଂଶଯାବ୍, *n.* grain of the bamboo.

ବଂଶପରମ୍ପରା, *n.* lineage, descent.

ବଂଶବୃଦ୍ଧି, *n.* increase of a race or family.

ବଂଶଲୋଚନା, *n.* manna (pith) of the bamboo.

ବଂଶହୀନ, *a.* without progeny.

ବଂଶାନୁଚରିତ, *n.* the history of a family.

ବଂଶାବଳୀ, *n.* genealogy.

ବଂଶୀ, *n.* see ବଇଁଶୀ ।

ବଂଶୀଧର, ବଂଶୀଧାରୀ, *n.* a flute player, *Krushna.*

ବକ, *n.* a heron, paddy-bird, crane.

ବକଟେ, *a.* a little, some.

ବକଡା, *n.* the fruit of the cotton plant.

ବକବକ, *n.* chatter, idle talk.

ବକମ, *n.* logwood; duckweed.

ବକ-ଯନ୍ତ୍ର, *n.* a long-necked apparatus used for distilling.

ବକର, *n.* a he-goat; ବକରୀ, *n.* a she-goat.

ବକଲ, *n.* bark or rind of trees; a scab.

ବକଲମ, *n.* guiding the hand of an illiterate in writing his signature.

ବକା, *a.* talkative, garrulous.

ବକାବକି, *n.* a mutual or general talking.

ବକିବା, *v.* to talk, to chatter.

ବକୁଆ, *a.* talkative, loquacious.

* ବକୁଳ, *n.* name of a tree and its flower.

ବକେୟା, ବକୟା, *a.* and *n.* remaining; arrears.

ବକ୍ତବ୍ୟ, *a.* fit to be spoken.

ବକ୍ତା, *n.* a speaker, lecturer, orator, talker.

ବକ୍ତୃତା, *n.* a speech, a lecture.

* ବକ୍ର, *a.* curved, crooked, tortuous.

* ବକ୍ରଦୃଷ୍ଟି, *a.* squint-eyed;—*n.* a side-glance.

* ବକ୍ରୋକ୍ତି, *n.* evasion, pun, irony.

ବକସିସ, *n.* a reward, gift, present.

ବଖତ, *n.* time, season; time of taking food; a meal.

ବଖତେ, *n.* one meal;—*ad.* once.

ବଖରା, *n.* a room in a house, an apartment; a share, portion.

ବଖରାଦାର, *n.* a sharer, a partner.

ବଖାଣିବା, *v.* to describe, to narrate.

ବଖିଆ, *n.* backstitching.

ବଗ, *n.* a paddy-bird, heron, crane.

ବଗଡ, *n.* a bastard, a mule, a cross-breed.

ବଗଡା, *a.* coarse, rough.

ବଗଲ, *n.* the armpit, the side.

ବଗିଚ୍ଛ, *n.* a garden, a grove.

ବଗୀ, *n.* a buggy.

ବଙ୍କା, *a.* crooked, curved, bent, winding.

ବଙ୍ଗ, *n.* Bengal; a kind of ashes, calx of tin.

ବଙ୍ଗଳା, *a.* belonging to Bengal;—*n.* Bengali language.

ବଙ୍ଗଲ, ବଙ୍ଗଳା, *n.* a bungalow.

ବଙ୍ଗାଳୀ, *n.* inhabitant or Bengal, a Bengali.

ବଚ, *n.* the orris root.

ବଚନ, *n.* a saying, sentence, word; (in *Gram.*) number.

* ବଚନୀୟ, *a.* utterable, proper to be spoken.

ବଚସା, *n.* wrangling, altercation.

ବଚ୍ଛୁର, *a.* obedient, subordinate.

ବଛଉବା, *v.* to cause to weed rice fields, &c.

ବଛବଛି, *n.* picking and choosing; the act of weeding.

ବଛାଳି, *n.* one who weeds; one who selects.

ବଜ୍‌ବଜ୍, *n.* fermentation;—*a.* frothy.

ବଜରା, *n.* a barge.

ବଜାଇବା, *v.* to sound, beat, ring, play.

ବଜାୟ, *a.* vindicated, upheld.

ବଜାର, *n.* a bazaar, shops.

ବଜାରୁ, *n.* bazaar people;—*a.* low.

ବଜାରୁଣୀ, *n.* *fem.* of above.

ବଜ୍ଜାତ, *a.* baseborn (abusive).

ବଜ୍ର, *n.* a thunderbolt; * a diamond.

ବଜ୍ରପାତ, *n.* fall of a thunderbolt.

ବଞ୍ଚକ, *a.* deceitful, crafty;—*n.* a deceiver, rogue; * a jackal.

ବଞ୍ଚନା, *n.* deceit, fraud, imposition.

ବଞ୍ଚାଇବା, *v.* to save, spare, preserve, defend or sustain

ବଞ୍ଚିବା, *v.* to live.

* ବଟ, *n.* the banyan tree.

ବଟଖରା, *n.* weights for weighing.

ବଟା, *n.* the price of exchange, discount on defective coin; a case or box for *pán* leaves;—*a.* pulverized.

ବଟାବଟି, *n.* grinding or pulverizing.

ବଟାଳି, *n.* a carpenter's chisel.

ବଟିକା, *n.* a pill or bolus.

ବଟୁଆ, *n.* *pán*-bag, a purse, money-bag.

ବଡ଼, *a.* great, large, big;—*ad.* greatly, very.

ବଡ଼ବଡ଼, *n.* a grumbling, a murmuring.

ବଡ଼ବଡ଼ିଆ, *a.* grumbling, murmuring.

ବଡ଼ବାନଳ, *n.* submarine fire.

ବଡ଼ବାପ, *n.* grandfather.

ବଡ଼ଭାଇ, *n.* an older brother.

ବଡ଼ି, *n.* kind of cake; a scalp disease.

ବଡ଼ାଇ, *n.* vaunting, boasting, pride.

ବଡ଼ାଇଖୋର, *n.* a pompous or vain man;—*a.* pompous, boastful.

ବଡ଼ିଆ, *n.* a wisp of straw twisted tightly so that it may smoulder slowly when lighted.

ବଡ଼ା, *n.* little balls made of ground pulse; a pill, bolus.

ବଢା, *n.* a kind of earthen vessel.
ବଢାଇ, ବଢେଇ, *n.* a carpenter.
ବଢାଇବା, *v.* to cause to increase, enlarge or stretch forth.
ବଢଣି, *n.* a brush, broom.
ବଢିବା, *v.* to increase, to prosper; to grow up, to thrive.
ବଢି, *n.* a flood, an inundation.
ବଣ, *n.* jungle, thicket, forest.
ବଣବିରାଡି, *n.* a wild or jungle cat.
ବଣା, *a.* bewildered, lost;—*n.* a vessel to hold molasses.
ବଣାକରିବା, *v.* to make a mistake, to err. [be in error.
ବଣାହେବା, *v.i.* to be mistaken, to
ବଣି, *n.* a bird, the *myná.*
ବଣିଆ, *n.* goldsmith; trader.
ବଣିକ, *n.* trader, merchant.
ବଣିଜ, *n.* trade, merchandise. [ise.
*ବଣିଜାର, *n.* a dealer in merchand-
ବଣୁଆ, *a.* sylvan, wild.
ବଣ୍ଟନ, *n.* distributing, sharing out.
ବଣ୍ଟା, *n.* a share, an assigned lot.
ବଣ୍ଟାବଣ୍ଟି, *n.* a sharing out.
ବତ୍, a termination meaning *like.*
ବତକ, *n.* a duck.
ବତର, *a.* soaked (grain); menstruous (animals). [boo.
ବତା, *n.* bamboo lath, split bam-
ବତାଇବା, *v.* to direct, to instruct.
ବତାସ, *n.* wind, a hurricane.
ବତାସା, *n.* white frosted sweetmeats or sugar-cakes.

ବତି, ବତୀ, *n.* a candle, wick of a lamp.
ବତିଘର, *n.* a lighthouse. [xxxii.
ବତିଶ, *a.* and *n.* thirty-two, 32;
ବତୁର, *a.* damp, moistened, soft.
ବତୁରାଇବା, *v.* to damp, to moisten.
ବତୁରିବା, *v.i.* to soften, to moisten.
ବତ୍ସ, *n.* a young animal; a calf; an affectionate vocative, as *O child.*
*ବତ୍ସତର, *n.* a steer, bull-calf.
*ବତ୍ସତରୀ, *n.* a heifer, cow-calf.
*ବତ୍ସର, *n.* a year, a twelvemonth.
ବତ୍ସଳ, *a.* fond, affectionate, kind.
ବଥ, *n.* a boil.
ବଥା, *n.* pain, ache.
ବଥାଇବା, *v.* to ache, to give pain or anguish.
ବଥୁଆ, *n.* a kind of *sag* or greens.
ବଦ୍, *a.* bad, evil, vile.
ବଦ୍‌ଖୋ, ବଦ୍‌ଖୋଇ, *n.* bad habit.
ବଦ୍‌ଚଲ୍ଲ, *n.* bad character.
ବଦ୍‌ଜାତ, *a.* see ବଜ୍ଜାତ (abusive).
*ବଦନ, *n.* the face, countenance.
ବଦନାମ, *n.* defamation, a bad name.
ବଦଳ, *n.* exchange, barter.
ବଦଳ, ବଦଳୀ, *n.* a substitute, successor; a thing given in exchange.
ବଦଳାଇବା, *v.* to exchange, to barter, to change. [ing.
ବଦଳାବଦଳି, *n.* a barter, an exchang-
ବଦଳିବା, *v.i.* to be changed.
ବଦଳେ, *ad.* instead of.

* ବଦାନ୍ୟ, *a.* munificent, liberal.

ବଦ, *n.* defamation, slander.

ବଧ, *n.* murder, killing, slaughter.

* ବଧକ, *n.* a slayer, a murderer.

ବଧଦଣ୍ଡ, *n.* capital punishment, death-sentence.

* ବଧାର୍ଥ, ବଧେଥ, *n.* a present, remuneration.

ବଧିର, *a.* deaf.

* ବଧୂ, *n.* a daughter-in-law; a newly married woman, a wife.

* ବଧ୍ୟ, *a.* deserving death.

* ବଦ୍ଧ, *a.* shut, closed, tied, bound.

* ବଦ୍ଧପରିକର *a.* girded; resolved, determined.

ବଦ୍ଧମୂଳ, *a.* firmly rooted.

ବନ, *n.* forest, wood, thicket.

ବନଚର, *a.* living in the forest.

ବନଜାତ. * ବନଜ, *a.* produced in a wood; wild.

ବନବାସୀ, *a.* living in a forest;—*n.* a hermit.

ବନଭୋଜ, * ବନଭୋଜନ, *n.* a picnic, the eating a social meal in a forest or garden.

* ବନମଲ୍ଲିକା, *n.* the wild jasmine.

* ବନମକ୍ଷିକା, *n.* the gadfly.

ବନମନୁଷ୍ୟ, *n.* the orang-outang or gorilla.

* ବନରାଜ, *n.* the lion, king of the forest.

ବନସ୍ତ, *n.* a wilderness, forest, thicket.

* ବନସ୍ପତି, *n.* a large tree, a tree yielding fruit without apparent blossoms.

ବନା, *n.* spelling, combination of vowels and consonats;–*a.* made.

ବନାଇବା, *v.* to make, to fabricate, to construct.

ବନାତ, *n.* woollen cloth, broadcloth.

ବନାନ, *n.* spelling, orthography, combining vowels with consonants.

* ବନିତା, *n.* a wife; a woman.

ବନିବା, *v.* to spell, to combine vowels with consonants;—*v.i.* to become ready to ripen.

ବନ୍ସୀ, *n.* fishing tackle.

ବନ୍ତଲକଦଲୀ, *n.* vegetable plantains.

ବନ୍ଥଡା, *a.* blunt, dull-edged.

ବନ୍ଦ, *n.* custody, confinement.

ବନ୍ଦନ, ବନ୍ଦନା, *n.* prayer with praise, a salutation, bow; invocation.

* ବନ୍ଦନୀୟ, *a.* worthy of homage, praiseworthy, adorable.

ବନ୍ଦର, *n.* a port, a harbour; an emporium.

ବନ୍ଦଶାଳା, ବନ୍ଦିଶାଳା, *n.* a jail.

ବନ୍ଦୀ, *n.* a captive, a prisoner; a panegyrist.

ବନ୍ଦେଜ, *n.* elegancy;—*a.* fixed in order.

ବନ୍ଦୋବସ୍ତ, *n.* a contract, settlement, bargain; a betrothal.

ବନ୍ଦ୍ୟ, *a.* worthy of homage.

ବନ୍ଧ, *n.* an embankment, a bridge.

ବନ୍ଧକ, *n.* a pledge, a mortgage.

ବନ୍ଧକନାମା, *n.* a deed of mortgage.

ବନ୍ଧକୀ ତମସୁକ, *n.* a bond by which property is pledged, a mortgage.

ବନ୍ଧନ, *n.* a binding; a tie; a bond.

ବନ୍ଧନୀ, *n.* a bracket,–as ( ), { }, [ ].

ବନ୍ଧୁ, *n.* a friend, a kinsman.

ବନ୍ଧୁକ, *n.* a musket, a gun, a rifle.

ବନ୍ଧୁତା, *n.* friendship, intimacy.

* ବନ୍ଧୁର, ବନ୍ଧୂର, *a.* uneven, undulated.

* ବନ୍ଧ୍ୟ, *a.* unproductive, unfruitful (tree).

ବନ୍ଧ୍ୟା, *n.* a barren woman.

ବନ୍ୟ, *a.* of a forest, wild, sylvan.

* ବନ୍ୟା, *n.* flood, deluge.

* ବପନ, *n.* sowing of seed.

* ବପୁଃ, *n.* the body.

ବବ୍ଲିଆ, ବବୁଲିଆ, *a.* bold, false;—*n.* a cheat.

* ବମନ, *n.* vomiting, retching.

ବମା, ବୋମା, *n.* a bomb.

* ବୟଃ, *n.* age (attained).

ବୟଃକ୍ରମ, *n.* age; the allotted period of life.

ବୟଃପ୍ରାପ୍ତ, *a.* grown up, of age, adult.

ବୟସ, *n.* age, time of life.

* ବୟସ୍ଥ, *a.* youthful, of age;—*n.* a friend.

* ବୟସ୍ଥା, *n.* a young woman, a female companion.

* ବୟସ୍ୟ, *a.* of the same age, co-eval; —*n.* a companion (usually of the same age); *fem.* ବୟସ୍ୟା ।

ବୟାନ, *n.* a narration, explanation.

ବୟାର, *n.* a strong wind, a gale.

ବର, *n.* bridegroom; a gift, boon; —*a.* * chief.

ବରଂ, ବରଂଚ, ବରଞ୍ଚ, *ad.* rather, in preference.

ବରକତ, *n.* a blessing, benediction.

ବରକନ୍ୟା, *n.* bridegroom and bride.

ବରକନ୍ଦାଜ, *n.* a petty police officer.

ବରକୋଳି, *n.* a kind of eatable plum.

ବରଖାସ୍ତ, *a.* removed from office, dismissed.

ବରଗଛ, ବର, *n.* the banyan tree.

ବରଗା, *n.* a rafter.

* ବରଗିବା, *v.* to send, to despatch.

ବରଜ, *n.* a *pán* plantation.

ବରଜୀ, *n.* an owner of a *pán* plantation.

ବରଡା, *n.* a palm branch.

ବରଢଅ, *a.* and *n.* a milch cow long since calved.

ବରଣ, *n.* welcome to a bridegroom, a welcome.

* ବରଦ, *a.* propitious, giving boons.

ବରଦାସ୍ତ, *n.* a bearing or enduring.

ବରଫ, *n.* ice, snow.

ବରଯାତ୍ରୀ, *n.* attendant of a bridegroom.

ବରଷ, *n.* a year, twelve months.

ବରଷା, *n.* rain, rainy weather.

ବରଷିବା, *v.* to rain

* ବରାକ, *a.* poor, pitiable; low, vile.

* ବରାଟକ, ବରାଟିକା, ବରାଟ, *n.* cowrie-shell.

ବରାତ, *n.* a commission, warrant, assignment; a cheque.

ବରାବର, *a.* abreast, even, level, like, uniform, equal;—*ad.* straight on, up to.

ବରାମଦ, *n.* recovery of stolen property.

ବରାହ, *n.* a wild boar, a boar.

ବରୁଣ, *n.* name of the Indian Neptune.

* ବରେଣ୍ୟ, *a.* excellent, pre-eminent.

ବର୍ଗ, *n.* a class, the totality; a square number.

ବର୍ଗଘନ, *n.* the square of a cube.

ବର୍ଗମୂଳ, *n.* the square root.

ବର୍ଗକ୍ଷେତ୍ର, *n.* (in *Geom.*) a square.

* ବର୍ଗୀକୃତ, *a.* classified, arranged.

* ବର୍ଗୀୟ, ବର୍ଗ୍ୟ, *a.* belonging to a class.

ବର୍ଛା, ବର୍ଛି, *n.* a spear, pike, lance.

* ବର୍ଜନ, *n.* abandoning, excepting.

* ବର୍ଜିତ, *a.* excepted, left out, rejected.

ବର୍ଣ୍ଣ, *n.* colour; caste; a letter of the alphabet.

ବର୍ଣ୍ଣନ, *n.* a describing, delineating.

ବର୍ଣ୍ଣନା, *n.* a description, eulogium.

ବର୍ଣ୍ଣନାପତ୍ର, *n.* a plaint, petition.

ବର୍ଣ୍ଣବୋଧକ, ବର୍ଣ୍ଣବୋଧ, *n.* spelling book, alphabetical primer.

ବର୍ଣ୍ଣମାଳା, *n.* the alphabet.

* ବର୍ଣ୍ଣଯୋଜକ, *n.* a compositor.

ବର୍ଣ୍ଣସଙ୍କର, *a.* of mixed blood, mongrel.

ବର୍ଣ୍ଣାଶୁଦ୍ଧି, *n.* a mistake in spelling.

ବର୍ଣ୍ଣିତ, *a.* described, narrated, eulogized

ବର୍ତ୍ତନ, *n.* wages, pay, salary.

ବର୍ତ୍ତମାନ, *ad.* now, at present;—*a.* present, extant, existing.

* ବର୍ତ୍ତି, *n.* see ବତି ।

ବର୍ତ୍ତୁଳ, *a.* circular, round;—*n.* a circle, ball.

* ବର୍ତ୍ମ, *n.* a road, way, path.

* ବର୍ଦ୍ଧକ, *a.* promoting growth.

* ବର୍ଦ୍ଧକି, *n.* a carpenter.

* ବର୍ଦ୍ଧନ, *n.* increase, growth; thriving.

ବର୍ଦ୍ଧନଶୀଳ, *a.* increasing, growing.

* ବର୍ଦ୍ଧମାନ, *a.* growing, prospering.

ବର୍ଦ୍ଧିତ, *a.* increased, grown.

* ବର୍ଦ୍ଧିଷ୍ଣୁ, *a.* growing, prospering.

ବର୍ବର, *n.* barbarian, blockhead.

* ବର୍ମ୍ମ, *n.* armour, coat of mail.

ବର୍ଷ, *n.* a year.

* ବର୍ଷଣ, *n.* raining, showering.

ବର୍ଷବୃଦ୍ଧି, *n.* a birthday, anniversary.

ବର୍ଷା, *n.* rain; rainy season.

ବର୍ଷାତି, *n.* a mackintosh, an apron to a buggy or carriage; a disease in horses' feet.

* ବର୍ହ, *n.* a peacock's tail or crest.

* ବର୍ହୀ, *n.* a peacock.

ବଳ, *n.* strength, force, energy; an army.

ବଳକା, *a.* surplus;—*n.* that which is left.

ବଳକିବା, *v.* to be more than enough.

ବଳଦ, *n.* an ox, a bullock.

ବଳଦେବ, *n.* *Balbhudra, Balaram.*

ବଳବନ୍ତ, *a.* in force, powerful, strong.

ବଳବାନ୍, ବଳବନ୍ତ, *a.* strong, powerful, vigorous.

* ବଳୟ, *n.* a bracelet.

ବଳହୀନ, *a.* weak, without strength.

ବଳା, *n.* a wrist ornament; * a son.

ବଳାଇବା, *v.* to force, to compel;—*v.i.* to be in excess.

ବଳାତ୍କାର, *n.* violence, force, rape.

ବଳାବଳ, *n.* strength, power; fitness or unfitness.

ବଳି, *n.* a sacrifice, victim; * a wrinkle.

ବଳିଆ, *n.* a wild dog.

ବଳିତା, *n.* wick of a lamp, a rag rolled into a wick.

ବଳିଦାନ, *n.* the act of offering a victim.

ବଳିବା, *v.* to knead, to make into a ball or roll, to twist (as in making rope).

ବଳିବା, ବଳିପଡିବା, *v.* to remain over, to be in excess.

ବଳିଷ୍ଠ, *a.* powerful, very strong.

* ବଳୀ, *a.* strong, powerful. [able.

* ବଳୀବର୍ଦ୍ଦ, *n.* an ox, a bullock.

ବଳୀୟାନ୍, *a.* see ବଳିଷ୍ଠ ।

ବଳୁଆ, *a.* strong.

* ବଲ୍କଳ, ବଲ୍କ, *n.* bark of a tree.

* ବଲ୍ଗା, *n.* the bit of a bridle, a rein.

ବଲ୍ଗାହରିଣ, ବଲ୍ଗା, *n.* reindeer.

* ବଲ୍ମୀକ, *n.* a white-ant; ant-hill.

ବଲମ, *n.* a spear, a lance.

ବଲୁର, *n.* a wasp.

ବଲ୍ଲଭ, *a.* beloved, desired, dear;—*n.* dear one; *fem.* ବଲ୍ଲଭା ।

* ବଲ୍ଲୀ, *n.* a creeper, a climbing plant.

ବଶ, *a.* subject to, influenced by, under the control of;—*n.* submission, control, subjection.

ବଶତଃ, *ad.* by force of, on account of, owing to.

ବଶତା, *n.* subjection, control.

ବଶବର୍ତ୍ତୀ, *a.* obsequious, servile, compliant.

ବଶମ୍ବଦ, *a.* acknowledging obedience or subjection, submissive.

ବଶୀଭୂତ, *a.* subjected, subdued.

* ବଶ୍ୟ, *a.* docile, manageable, tame.

ବଶ୍ୟତା, *n.* subjection, submission, subjugation.

ବସଣି, *n.* an ornament for the nose; an addition to the rent of land, etc.

ବସତି, *n.* an abode, a dwelling, a house.

ବସନ, *n.* clothes, a garment. [pox.

ବସନ୍ତ, *n.* spring-time; the small-

ବସନ୍ତମୁହାଁ, *a.* pock-marked, pock-pitted.

ବସା, *n.* a lodging, temporary dwelling; * fat, marrow.

ବସାଇବା, *v.* to cause to sit, to cause to settle.

ବସିବା, *v.* to sit, to take a seat.

ବସିସିବା, ବସିବା, *v.* to coagulate, to thicken.

ବସାଦହି, *n.* coagulated curds.

ବସିବା, ବାସିବା, *n.* an inhabitant, a dweller.

* ବସୁ, *n.* wealth, a gem; demigod.

ବସୁଦେବ, *n.* the father of *Krushna.*

ବସୁଧା, ବସୁନ୍ଧରା, * ବସୁମତୀ, *n.* the earth.

ବସ୍ତା, *n.* a bale, package, bundle.

ବସ୍ତି, *n.* village; the abdomen, pelvis.

ବସ୍ତାନି, *n.* a satchel or piece of cloth for holding books and papers.

* ବସ୍ତୁ, *n.* a thing, material object.

ବସ୍ତୁତଃ, *ad.* in reality, in fact.

ବସ୍ତ୍ର, *n.* a garment, cloth, clothing.

* ବସ୍ତ୍ରଗୃହ, *n.* a tent.

* ବସ୍ତ୍ରାଗାର, *n.* a room in which clothing is kept.

ବହନ, *n.* carrying; bearing; blowing; flowing;—*ad.* speedily, quickly (in poetry only).

ବହନି, *n.* the first sale of the day (see ବଉନି).

* ବହନୀୟ, *a.* portable, light; flowing.

ବହଳ, *a.* thick, dense.

ବହିଃସ୍ଥ, *a.* external, outer.

ବହି, *n.* a book.

ବହିରା, *a.* deaf;—*n.* a deaf man.

ବହିର୍ଗତ, *a.* gone forth, gone out.

ବହିର୍ଦ୍ୱାର, *n.* a gate, outer door.

ବହିର୍ଦେଶ, *n.* outskirts; a privy.

ବହିର୍ଭୂତ, *a.* out of; expelled.

ବହୁ, *a.* much, many, very; exceeding.

ବହୁକାଳୀନ, *a.* of long standing, chronic.

ବହୁତ, *a.* much, many, abundant.

ବହୁଦର୍ଶୀ, *a.* observant, wise, experienced.

* ବହୁଧା, *a.* in various ways; manifol

ବହୁବଚନ, *n.* (in *Gram.*) the plural number.

ବହୁବିଧ, *a.* in various ways; of various sorts.

ବହୁବ୍ରୀହି, *n.* (in *Gram.*) a compound adjective.

* ବହୁଭାଷୀ, *a.* talkative, garrulous.

ବହୁମୂତ୍ର, *n.* diabetes.

ବହୁମୂଲ୍ୟ, *a.* of great value, valuable, costly, expensive.

ବହୁରୂପା, *n.* a chameleon; a man assuming many shapes or forms.

ବହୁରୂପୀ, *a.* assuming many forms.

ବହୁଳ, *a.* many, much.

* ବହ୍ନି, *n.* fire, the god of fire.

* ବକ୍ଷ, *n.* the breast, chest, bosom.

* ବକ୍ଷୋଜ, *n.* a woman's breast.

ବା, *conj.* or, either;—*n.* the wind.

ବାଁ, *n.* left (in opposition to right).

ବାଁହାତ, *n.* the left hand.

ବାଅନ, *a.* and *n.* fifty-two; 52; LII.

ବାଉ, *n.* wind, flatulency; a dancing girl, a prostitute; a term of respect attached to female names, Lady, Madam.

ବାଇଗଣ, *n.* fruit of the egg-plant, brinjal. [colour.

ବାଇଗଣିଆ, *a.* purple;—*n.* purple

ବାଇଗବା, *n.* a juicy plant of which hedges are made.

ବାଇଡଙ୍କ, *n.* name of a pod-bearing creeper, cowhage. [XXII.

ବାଇଶ, *a.* and *n.* twenty-two; 22;

ବାଇଶୀବୃକ୍ଷ, *n.* the weeping willow.

ବାଇହେବା, *v.* to be attached to, mad after, or fond of. [caste.

ବାଉରଣୀ, *n.* a woman of the Bauri

ବାଉରି, *n.* name of a low caste.

ବାଉଳା, *a.* insane, idiotic, mad.

ବାଉଁଶ, *n.* a bamboo.

ବାଉଁଶିଆ, *n.* a small bamboo basket.

ବାକ୍, *n.* word, utterance, speech, (used as a *prefix*).

ବାକ୍‌ଗୁମ୍ଫ, *n.* joke, sally, witticism.

ବାକ୍‌ପଟୁ, *a.* eloquent, fluent, voluble.

* ବାକ୍‌ପତି, *n.* *Bruhaspati*; an orator.

ବାକୁଲି, *n.* a peg fixed in each end of the yoke used with a bullock cart. [cramp.

ବାକୁଲିଉଠିବା, *v.i.* to be seized with

ବାକି, ବାକୀ, *n.* remainder, residue.

ବାକ୍ୟ, *n.* a word, expression, sentence. pression.

* ବାକ୍ୟାର୍ଥ, *n.* the meaning of an ex-

ବାଙ୍କ, *n.* a bend, a crook; an iron vice;—*a.* bent, crooked.

ବାଗର, *n.* a kind of spice.

ବାଗ, *n.* a garden; rein of a bridle.

ବାଗଡୋର, *n.* a bridle or halter.

ବାଗାଡମ୍ବର, *n.* verbosity, bombast.

* ବାଗୀଶ, *n.* an orator, an eloquent man.

ବାଗୁଡ଼, *n.* a boy's game.

* ବାଗୁରା, *n.* a net for catching deer.

* ବାଗୁରିକ, *n.* a deer-catcher, hunter.

ବାଗୁଲି, *n.* the betel-bearer of a king.

ବାଗ୍‌ଦଣ୍ଡ, *n.* a reproof, an admonition (by word).

ବଗ୍‌ଦତ୍ତ, *a.* betrothed, affianced.

ବାଗ୍‌ଦାନ, *n.* betrothal, betrothing; verbal promise.

ବାଗ୍‌ଦେବୀ, * ବାଗୀଶ୍ୱରୀ, *n.* the goddess of speech, *Saraswati.*

ବାଗ୍‌ବ୍ୟୟ, *n.* waste of words, talkativeness.

* ବାଗ୍ମୀ, *a.* fluent, talkative, loquacious. [words.

ବାଗ୍‌ଯୁଦ୍ଧ, *n.* disputation, strife of

ବାଙ୍ଗରୁ, *a.* short, stumpy, dwarfish.

ବାଙ୍ଗିସି, *n.* a short dwarfish woman.

ବାଘ, *n.* a tiger.

ବାଘି, *n.* a bubo.

ବାଘୁଣୀ, *n.* a tigress.

* ବାଚ୍ଚୁସ୍, *a.* wordy, verbose.

* ବାଚ୍ଚଲ, *n.* abusive language

* ବାଚକ, *a.* expressive;—*n.* a speaker.

ବାଚନିକ, *a.* verbal.

* ବାଚସ୍ପତି, *n.* a master of language; *Bruhaspati.* [box.

ବାଚାଳ, *a.* talkative;—*n.* a chatter-

ବାଛୁଡ଼, *n.* a colt; teething sickness.

ବାଞ୍ଛିବା, *v.* to choose, select, pick; to weed.

ବାଛୁରି, *n.* a calf

ବାଞ୍ଛନୀୟ, *a.* desirable

ବାଞ୍ଛା, *n.* a wish, longing, desire, [will.

ବାଞ୍ଛିତ, *a.* desired, wished for;—*n.* desired object.

ବାଜ, *n.* a hawk.

ବାଜଣା, *n.* music, a musical instrument (see ବାଜା).

ବାଜକାର, *n.* a musician.

ବାଜରା, *n.* a kind of grain; a market basket.

ବାଜା, *n.* music; a musical instrument, (see ବାଜଣା).

ବାଜାଦାର, *n.* a drummer.

ବାଜି, *n.* a stake, wager; legerde- [main.

ବାଜିକର, *n.* a magician, a conjurer.

ବାଜିବା, *v.* to sound, to ring; to hit, to strike.

*ବାଜିପାଳ, *n.* a horsekeeper, a [groom.

*ବାଜିଶାଳା, *n.* a stable.

*ବାଜୀ, *n.* a horse; a bird.

ବାଜୁ, ବାଜୁବନ୍ଧ, *n.* a kind of ornament for the arm; side-post of a door.

ବାଜେ, *a.* incidental, certain, sundry.

ବାଜେଖର୍ଚ୍ଚ, *n.* incidental expenses.

ବାଜେଣି, *n.* tinkling ornaments; a twinkling.

ବାଜେୟାପ୍ତ, *a.* escheated, resumed.

ବାଞ୍ଝ, *a.* barren, sterile, unfruitful.

ବାଟ, *n.* a road, a way, a path.

ବାଟମାର, *n.* a highwayman, a robber.

ବାଟି, *n.* a stone, or metal cup; a marble.

ବାଟିଆ, *n.* fault, guilt.

*ବାଟିକା, ବାଟୀ, *n.* a small garden.

ବାଟିବା, *v.* to pulverize, to pound.

ବାଟୀ, *n.* twenty *máns* of land; a large or fine residence; a marble.

ବାଟୁଆ, *n.* a traveller, one on the [road.

ବାଟୁଳି, *n.* a pellet.

ବାଟୁଳିଧନୁ, *n.* a bow for shooting [pellets.

ବାଟୋଇ, *n.* see ବାଟୁଆ।

ବାଡ, *n.* a hedge, a fence.

*ବାଡବ, *n.* submarine fire.

ବାଡି, *n.* a homestead, garden; a stick, staff.

ବାଡିବାନ୍ତି, *n.* cholera.

ବାଡୁଅ, *a.* unmarried;—*n.* a bache- [lor.

ବାଡେଇବା, *v.* to beat with a stick, to flog.

ବାଡୋଇ, *n.* a spinster.

ବାଢିବା, *v.* to deal out cooked rice, vegetables, &c., for eating, to serve out food.

ବାଣ, *n.* fireworks; a dart, an ar- [row.

ବାଣି, *n.* strings on which mats or chicks are woven.

ବାଣିଜ୍ୟ, *n.* trade, traffic, commerce.

ବାଣୀ, *n.* a voice, saying, sentence.

ବାଣୁଆ, *n.* an archer, a hunter; a maker of fireworks.

ବାଣ୍ଟ, *n.* a share, a portion.

ବାତ, *n.* rheumatism; air, flatulency.

ବାତଜ୍ୱର, *n.* rheumatic fever.
ବାତରୋଗୀ, *n.* rheumatic or gouty person.
ବାତଶୂଳ, *n.* colic from flatulency.
ବାତାଜୀର୍ଣ୍ଣ, *n.* hypochondria, flatulency.
ବାତାବିଲେମ୍ବୁ, *n.* the *pumelo*, shaddock.
* ବାତାୟନ, *n.* a window or shutter.
ବାତାସା *n.* a sweetmeat.
ବାତୁଆ, *a.* afflicted with rheumatism.
ବାତୁଳ, *a.* crazy, insane, deranged.
* ବାତ୍ୟା, *n.* strong wind, gale, a great tempest.
ବାତ୍ସଲ୍ୟ, *n.* affection, fondness, love (for children).
ବାଦ୍, *ad.* after;—*n.* a deduction.
ବାଦ, *n.* malice, envy, emulation; * a word, dispute.
* ବାଦକ, *n.* a speaker; a musician.
* ବାଦନ, *n.* playing on an instrument.
ବାଦଲ, *n.* a cloud, continued rain.
ବାଦ୍ସା, ବାଦସାହ, *n.* a king, a sovereign.
ବାଦାନୁବାଦ, *n.* dispute, a controversy.
ବାଦାମ, *n.* an almond.
ବାଦାମୀ, *a.* brown.
ବାଦୀ, *n.* plaintiff, suitor; * a speaker.
ବାଦୁଆ, *a.* emulative, argumentative;—*n.* emulator; *fem.* ବାଦୋଇ ।
ବାଦୁଡ଼ା, ବାଦୁଡ଼, *n.* a large bat, flying-fox.
ବାଦ୍ୟ, *n.* musical instrument, music.
ବାଦ୍ୟକର, *n.* a musician.
* ବାଧକ, *a.* obstructive;—*n.* obstructor.
ବାଧା, *n.* hindrance, objection, obstacle, obstruction, impediment, interruption.
ବାଧିତ, *a.* obliged; hindered, obstructed.
ବାଧ୍ୟ, *a.* obedient, docile, restrainable.
* ବାନପ୍ରସ୍ଥ, *n.* a hermitage, hermit's cell.
ବାନର, *n.* a monkey.
ବାନା, *n.* a flag, a banner.
ବାନ୍ତି, *n.* vomiting, disgorging.
ବାନ୍ଧବ, *n.* kinsman, a relation.
ବାନ୍ଧିବା, *v.* to bind, confine, tie.
ବାନ୍ଧୁଣି, *n.* a piece of string for fastening anything.
ବାପ, ବାପା, *n.* a father.
* ବାପକ, *n.* a sower.
ବାପରେ, *inter.* an exclamation, Oh father!
* ବାପୀ, *n.* a stone well or tank.
ବାବଦ, *n.* an item, affair, article;—*ad.* on account of.
* ବାବଦୂକ, *a.* talkative, loquacious.
ବାବା, *n.* father.
ବାବାଜି, *n.* a title given to a *bairági* or devotee.
ବାବୁ, *n.* gentleman, Sire, Sir, a Babu.
ବାବୁଗିରି, *n.* the attitude or fashion of a Babu.
ବାବୁରି, *n.* hair uncut or unshaven.
ବାମ, *a.* left (hand); contrary, opposed.
ବାମନ, *n.* a dwarf; * the fifth incarnation.
* ବାମା, *n.* a woman.

* ବାମେତର, *a.* right (opposite to left).

ବାଷ୍ପ, *n.* steam, vapour.

ବାପୀ, *n.* a stone well.

* ବାୟସ, *n.* a crow.

ବାୟା, *a.* insane, mad;—*n.* an idiot.

ବାୟାଚଢ଼ାଇ, ବାୟାଚଢ଼େଇ, *n.* the tailor bird, gross-beak.

ବାୟୁ, *n.* wind, air.

ବାୟୁକୋଣ, *n.* the north-west point.

ବାୟୁଗ୍ରସ୍ତ, *a.* inflated; hypochondriac.

ବାୟୁମାନଯନ୍ତ୍ର, *n.* a barometer.

ବାୟୁଶୂଳ, *n.* colic.

ବାର, *n.* a day; occasion; turn, time.

ବାର, *a.* and *n.* twelve; 12; XII.

ବାରଣ, *n.* preventing, forbidding; * an elephant.

* ବାରବଧୂ, *n.* a prostitute.

ବାରବାର, ବାରମ୍ବାର, *ad.* repeatedly, again and again.

ବାରବୁଲା, *n.* a wanderer. [day.

ବାରବେଳା, *n.* unlucky parts of the

ବାରାଣସୀ, *n.* Benares. [more.

ବାରନ୍ତରେ, *ad.* next time, again, once

* ବାରି, *n.* water. [ber.

ବାରିକ, *n.* the barber caste; a bar-

ବାରିକ୍, *a.* thin, fine. [water.

* ବାରିଜ, *n.* a lotus;—*a.* born in

* ବାରିଦ, *n.* a cloud. [rain.

* ବାରିଧାର, *n.* drops or streams of

* ବାରିଧି, *n.* the sea, ocean.

* ବାରିନିଧି, *n.* the sea, ocean. [tanks.

ବାରିପର୍ଣ୍ଣୀ, *n.* a grass growing in

ବାଛିବା, *v.* to guess, to pick and choose.

* ବାରିବାହ, *n.* a cloud.

ବାଇଷି, ବାଷିଁ, *n.* a carpenter's adze.

ବାରୁଣୀ, *n.* a bathing festival on 13th of Chaitra; * the west.

ବାରୁଦ, *n.* gunpowder.

ବାରେ, ବାରେକ, *ad.* once, one time.

ବାରେବାରେ, *ad.* once and again.

ବାର୍ତ୍ତା, *n.* news, information, report.

* ବାର୍ତ୍ତାକୁ, *n.* fruit of the egg-plant.

* ବାର୍ତ୍ତାବହ, *n.* one carrying news.

ବାର୍ଦ୍ଧକ୍ୟ, *n.* old age, senility.

ବାର୍ଷିକ, *a.* yearly, annual.

ବାଳ, *n.* a child; hair.

ବାଳକ, *n.* a boy, child, infant.

* ବାଲକୃମି, *n.* a head louse.

* ବାଲଗର୍ଭିଣୀ, *a.* pregnant for the first time.

ବାଲା, ବାଲିକା, *n.* a lass, a girl.

ବାଲିଆ, *n.* a kind of fish, the pike.

* ବାଲେନ୍ଦୁ, *n.* a new moon, crescent.

ବାଲି, ବାଲୁକା, *n.* sand. [sand.

ବାଲିଗରଡା, *n.* little pebbles found in

ବାଲିସ, *n.* a pillow.

ବାଲୁକାଯନ୍ତ୍ର, *n.* a sand hour-glass.

ବାଲ୍ୟ, ବାଲ୍ୟକାଳ, *n.* infancy, childhood.

ବାଲ୍ମୀକି, ବାଲ୍ମୀକ, *n.* author of the *Rámáyan.* [LXII.

ବାଷଠି, *a.* and *n.* sixty-two; 62;

ବାସ, *n.* a dwelling, abode, house; scent, odour; * clothing, cloth.

ବାସଙ୍ଗ, *n.* name of a plant.
ବାସନ, *n.* a plate, a dish.
ବାସନା, *n.* scent, odour; * desire, wish, will, choice. [* vernal.
ବାସନ୍ତୀ, *n.* goddess of spring;—*a.*
* ବାସବ, *n.* *Indra.*
* ବାସର, *n.* day.
ବାସି, *a.* stale, old; clean, washed.
ବାସିତ, *a.* perfumed, scented.
ବାସିଧୋବ, *a.* well washed (cloth).
ବାସିନ୍ଦା, *n.* a resident, an inhabitant.
ବାସୁକି, *n.* king of serpents.
ବାସୁଙ୍ଗା, *n.* rind of the plantain tree.
* ବାସୁଦେବ, *n.* a name of *Krushna.*
ବାସ୍ତବ, ବାସ୍ତବିକ, *a.* real, genuine, true.
ବାସ୍ତବିକ, *ad.* really, in truth, in reality. [LXXII.
ବାସ୍ତରି, *a.* and *n.* seventy-two; 72;
ବାସ୍ତୁଘ, *n.* an indigent person, a spendthrift, a bankrupt.
ବାଷ୍ପ, *n.* steam, vapour; * a tear.
ବାଷ୍ପୀୟ, *a.* relating to steam.
ବାହକ, *n.* a porter, one who carries burdens.
ବାହନ, *n.* an animal (*lit.* one that carries or bears burdens), a vehicle or conveyance of any kind.
ବାହା, *n.* the arms; marriage.
ବାହାଦୁର, *n.* a title; a hero, a knight.
ବାହାନା, *n.* an excuse, pretence.
ବାହାପିଆ, *n.* a liar, a boaster.
ବାହାର, *n.* the outside; beauty.
ବାହାରିବା, *v.* to exude, to proceed from.
ବାହାଲ୍, *a.* reinstated; upheld.
* ବାହିନୀ, *n.* an army, a legion.
ବାହିବା, *v.* to transport by rowing, to row.
ବାହୁ, *n.* the arms; * a fathom.
ବାହୁଙ୍ଗା, *n.* a branch of any kind of a palm tree. [ing burdens.
ବାହୁଙ୍ଗି, *n.* a bamboo yoke for carry-
ବାହୁଟିଆ, *n.* a species of deer.
ବାହୁଡା, *n.* turning back, returning.
ବାହୁଡିବା, *v.* to return, turn back.
ବାହୁମୂଳ, *n.* the shoulder-blade.
ବାହୁଯୁଦ୍ଧ, *n.* wrestling, pugilism.
ବାହୁଲ୍ୟ, *n.* abundance, superfluity.
ବାହ୍ୟ, *a.* external, outward; * portable.
ବାହ୍ୟକ୍ରିୟା, *n.* evacuation, going to stool. [&c.
ବାହ୍ୟେନ୍ଦ୍ରିୟ, *n.* the eyes, nose, tongue,
ବାଁହାତ, *n.* the left hand.
ବି, a *prefix*, signifying away, off; reversion, etc.
ବିଂଶତି, ବିଂଶ, *a.* twenty.
ବିଆଜ, *n.* usury, interest on money.
ବିଆଣ, *n.* birth, bringing forth.
ବିଆଳି, *n.* the early rice.
ବିଉଷ୍ଣ, *n.* a skin disease.
* ବିକଚ, *a.* expanded, opened out.
ବିକଟ, *a.* frightful, hideous, horrid.
ବିକଳ, *a.* distressed, perplexed.
ବିକଳାଙ୍ଗ, *n.* a cripple;—*a.* deformed.

* ବିକଳ୍ପ, *n.* alternative, option; doubt.

ବିକଶିତ, *a.* expanded (as a flower).

ବିକା, *n.* selling;—*a.* sold.

ବିକାକିଣା, *n.* selling and buying.

ବିକାର, *n.* change of natural state, change for the worse.

ବିକାଶ, *n.* display; opening, expansion.

ବିକିବା, *v.* to sell.

* ବିକୀର୍ଣ୍ଣ, *a.* scattered, spread about.

ବିକୃତ, *a.* altered, distorted, spoiled.

ବିକ୍ରମ, *n.* power, valour, prowess.

ବିକ୍ରମୀ, *a.* powerful, daring, valiant.

ବିକ୍ରୟ, *n.* selling, sale.

ବିକ୍ରେତା, * ବିକ୍ରୟୀ, *n.* a seller, salesman, vendor.

ବିକ୍ରି, *n.* selling, sale.

* ବିକ୍ରେୟ, *a.* saleable, fit for sale.

ବିଖ୍ୟାତ, *a.* renowned, celebrated.

ବିଗଡ଼, *n.* deterioration, depravity.

ବିଗାଡ଼ିବା, *v.* to deteriorate, to spoil, to destroy.

ବିଗିଡ଼ିବା, *v.i.* to alter, change; to apostatise.

ବିଗତ, *a.* past, gone, extinct.

ବିଗର୍ହିତ, *a.* censured, vilified, abused.

* ବିଗଳିତ, *a.* fallen, slipped or oozed out.

ବିଗୁଣ, *a.* worthless, injurious, evil.

* ବିଗ୍ରହ, *n.* war; an idol; the body.

ବିଘଟନ, *n.* an unfortunate event, a calamity.

* ବିଘଟିତ, *a.* happened, occurred.

ବିଘା, *n.* a *bighá* nearly ⅓ of an acre.

* ବିଘାତ, *n.* obstacle, detriment.

ବିଘ୍ନ, *n.* obstacle; repulse, danger.

ବିଚର୍ଚ୍ଚିକା, *n.* an eruption on the foot, scab.

ବିଚଳିତ, *a.* unsteady, slipped.

ବିଚକ୍ଷଣ, *a.* learned, clever, skilful.

ବିଚାର, *n.* judgment, thought, consideration, investigation.

ବିଚାରକର୍ତ୍ତା, ବିଚାରକ, *n.* a judge, investigator.

ବିଚାରଣା, *n.* judging, investigating.

ବିଚାରିତ, *a.* judged, examined.

* ବିଚାର୍ଯ୍ୟ, *a.* worthy of investigation or of discussion.

ବିଚରା, *a.* destitute, helpless, poor; *fem.* ବିଚରୀ ।

ବିଚୁଳି, *n.* rice straw, litter.

ବିଚିତ୍ର, *a.* variegated, gaudy, beautiful; surprising.

ବିଚିତ୍ରାଙ୍ଗ, *n.* the peacock, tiger, &c.

ବିଛଣା, *n.* bedding, a bed, a mat.

ବିଛା, *n.* centipede, scorpion; the sign scorpio.

ବିଛାଇବା, *n.* to spread out, to lay down.

ବିଛୁଆତି, *n.* a creeping plant and fruit the touch of which causes great irritation to the skin.

ବିଚ୍ଛିନ୍ନ, *a.* divided, cut, separate, cleft.

ବିଚ୍ଛେଦ, *n.* separation, severing.

ବିଜନ, *a.* solitary, lonely, private.

ବିଜନ୍ମା, *n.* a bastard;—*a.* illegitimate.

ବିଜୟ, *n.* victory, triumph.

ବିଜୟୀ, *a.* victorious;—*n.* conqueror.

ବିଜାତ, *a.* base-born;—*n.* bastard.

ବିଜାତୀୟ, *a.* of other caste, unnatural.

ବିଜିତ, *a.* vanquished, defeated.

ବିଜୁଳି, *n.* lightning.

ବିଜେ, *n.* a going; march of a raja and the gods, etc.

ବିଜେତା, *n.* a conqueror, victor.

ବିଜ୍ଞ, *a.* clever, learned, intelligent.

ବିଜ୍ଞତମ, *a.* (one) well-informed.

ବିଜ୍ଞତା, *n.* cleverness, wisdom.

ବିଜ୍ଞାନ, *n.* science; * practical knowledge.

ବିଜ୍ଞାପନ, *n.* a notice, an advertisement, publishing.

ବିଞ୍ଚଣା, *n.* a fan, a *punkhá.*

ବିଞ୍ଚିବା, *v.* to fan.

* ବିଟପ, *n.* a young shoot; a profligate.

ବିଟପୀ, *n.* a fornicatress; * a tree.

* ବିଟଘୁଲୁଷ, *n.* a lecher, fornicator.

ବିଟଲବଣ, *n.* black salt

ବିଟାଳ, *n.* a villain, a varlet.

ବିଟୋଳ, *a.* wicked, vile, lecherous.

ବିଡଙ୍ଗ, *n.* a plant used as a vermifuge.

ବିଡମ୍ବନ, ବିଡମ୍ବନା, *n.* deception, a tantalizing; an imitation; ridiculousness, a matter for laughter.

* ବିଡମ୍ବିତ, *a.* deceived, frustrated; mocked, ridiculed.

ବିଡା, *n.* a sheaf, bundle.

ବିଡାଳ, *n.* a cat, tom-cat.

ବିଡିଆ, *n.* a packet, bundle; quid of *pán.*

ବିଢ଼ିବା, *v.* to test, to act deceitfully.

ବିଢପ, *a.* deformed, distorted, ugly.

ବିଣ୍ଡା, ବିଣ୍ଡିଆ, *n.* a plug, anything used to stuff in a hole.

ବିତଣ୍ଡା, *n.* discussion, refutation.

ବିତରଣ, *n.* giving, distributing.

ବିତର୍କ, *n.* doubt, inquiry, reasoning.

* ବିତସ୍ତି, *n.* a span.

ବିତାଇବା, *v.* to pass the time.

ବିତିବା, *v.* to be spent.

* ବିତୃଷ୍ଣ, *a.* displeased, dissatisfied.

ବିତ୍ତ, *n.* wealth, property, substance.

ବିଦ୍, a *particle* used as an *affix,* signifying knowing, versed in.

ବିଦ, *n.* an arm ornament for the arm.

* ବିଦଗ୍ଧ, *a.* clever, sagacious; amorous;—*n.* a humorous person.

ବିଦା, *n.* a harrow, a garden rake.

ବିଦାଗି, *n.* dismissal with a present.

ବିଦାବଦ, *n.* dismissal.

ବିଦାୟ, *n.* dismissal, leave to depart.

ବିଦାରକ, *n.* who or that which rends or tears;—*a.* rending, tearing.

ବିଦାରଣ, *n.* tearing, lacerating.

ବିଦାରିବା, *v.* to tear, to lacerate, to pierce.

ବିଦିତ, *a.* known, acquainted with.

ବିଦୀର୍ଣ୍ଣ, *a.* torn, lacerated, split, cleft.

* ବିଦୁଷୀ, *n.* a learned or wise woman.

ବିଦୂଷକ, *n.* a comedian, a detractor; —*a.* censorious.

ବିଦେଶ, *n.* a foreign land.

ବିଦେଶୀ, *n.* a foreigner, a stranger; —*a.* foreign, strange, of another country.

ବିଦ୍ୟମାନ, *a.* present, existing, extant.

ବିଦ୍ୟା, *n.* science, art, literature, knowledge, learning.

ବିଦ୍ୟାଗୁରୁ, ବିଦ୍ୟାଦାତା, *n.* a teacher, an instructor.

ବିଦ୍ୟାଧନ, *n.* learning (regarded as wealth).

ବିଦ୍ୟାବନ୍ତ, ବିଦ୍ୟାବାନ୍, *a.* learned, erudite, educated.

ବିଦ୍ୟାଭ୍ୟାସ, *n.* gaining knowledge.

ବିଦ୍ୟାର୍ଥୀ, *a.* studious;—*n.* a student.

ବିଦ୍ୟାଳୟ, *n.* a school, academy, college.

ବିଦ୍ୟାର୍ଜନ, *n.* acquisition of learning.

ବିଦ୍ୟାସାଗର, *n.* a sea of learning, a title given to a highly learned man.

ବିଦ୍ୟୁତ୍, *n.* lightning.

* ବିଦ୍ୟୁଚ୍ଛଟା, *n.* forked lightning, zigzag flashing.

* ବିଦ୍ରୁମ, *n.* coral; a fabulous tree.

ବିଦ୍ରୂପ, *n.* a jeer, mockery.

ବିଦ୍ରୋହ, *n.* malevolence, malice; rebellion.

ବିଦ୍ରୋହୀ, *a.* malicious, malignant; rebellious.

ବିଦ୍ୱାନ୍, *a.* learned, intelligent.

ବିଦ୍ୱେଷ, *n.* enmity, malice, hatred.

ବିଦ୍ୱେଷୀ, *a.* inimical, hostile.

ବିଧ, *n.* a kind (used as an *affix*).

ବିଧବା, *n.* a widow.

ବିଧର୍ମ, *n.* heterodoxy, apostacy, irregularity.

ବିଧର୍ମୀ, *a.* heterodox, apostate.

ବିଧା, *n.* a blow with the fist, a punch.

ବିଧାତା, *n.* God, the God of providence.

ବିଧାନ, *n.* rule, regular form, law.

ବିଧାଣ, *n.* bad habit, bad conduct.

* ବିଧାୟକ, *n.* a legislator, prescriber.

ବିଧି, *n.* a statute, law, decree, rule.

ବିଧିପୂର୍ବକ, *ad.* according to rule.

ବିଧିବଦ୍ଧ, *a.* legalized, becoming law, authorized.

ବିଧିବିଧାନ, *n.* rules and regulations, precepts.

ବିଧିମତ, ବିଧିମତେ, *ad.* according to law or precept.

* ବିଧୁ, *n.* the moon; camphor.

* ବିଧୁନ୍ତୁଦ, *n.* *Ráhu*, the mythological demon who causes eclipses, the ascending node (in *Astron.*).

* ବିଧୁର, *a.* destitute, distressed.

ବିଧେୟ, *a.* proper, just.

ବିଧ୍ୱଂସ, *n.* destruction, utter ruin.

ବିଧ୍ୱଂସୀ, *a.* destructive, malevolent, ruinous.

ବିନତ, *a.* humble, bowed down.

ବିନତି, ବିନୟ, *n.* humility, entreaty.

ବିନୟୀ, *a.* humble, modest, affable.

ବିନଷ୍ଟ, *a.* destroyed, damaged.

* ବିନଶ୍ୱର, *a.* perishable.

ବିନା, *prep.* except, without, beside.

ବିନାଶ, *n.* destruction, ruin, loss.

ବିନାଶକ, *a.* destructive;—*n.* a destroyer.
ବିନାଶ୍ୟ, *a.* destructible, perishable.
*ବିନିଦ୍ର, *a.* sleepless.
ବିନିମୟ, *n.* barter, exchange; *requital.
ବିନୀତ, *a.* humble, unassuming.
ବିନୁ, *prep.* without, except, besides.
ବିନୋଦ, *n.* joy, happiness, sport.
ବିନ୍ଦୁ, *n.* a drop, dot, point, spot.
ବିନ୍ଧ, *n.* a hole, perforation, chink.
ବିନ୍ଧା, *a.* bored, pierced, perforated.
ବିନ୍ଧାଳି, *n.* a mechanic, a borer.
ବିନ୍ଧାବିନ୍ଧି, *n.* piercing, stabbing.
ବିନ୍ଧିବା, *v.* to bore, to perforate, to spear, to stab.
*ବିନ୍ୟାସ, *n.* array, orderly arrangement; dressing the hair, etc.
*ବିପଣି, ବିପଣୀ, *n.* a shop, a market, bazaar.
ବିପତ୍ତି, *n.* adversity, misfortune.
ବିପତ୍ତିକାଳ, *n.* time of adversity.
ବିପଥ, *n.* a by-road, wrong way; evil course.
ବିପଥଗାମୀ, *a.* perverse, going in an evil way.
ବିପଦ, *n.* sad condition, misfortune.
ବିପଦଗ୍ରସ୍ତ, ବିପନ୍ନ, *a.* fallen into adversity.
ବିପରୀତ, *a.* opposed, contrary, reverse.
ବିପକ୍ଷ, *a.* hostile;—*n.* an enemy.
ବିପକ୍ଷତା, *n.* enmity, hostility.
ବିପକ୍ଷତ୍ୱ, *ବୈପରୀତ୍ୟ, *n.* contrariety, repugnance, averseness.

ବିପାକ, *n.* maturity; consequence, result of actions; adverse turn of fate.
*ବିପିନ, *n.* a wood, forest, thicket.
*ବିପୁଳ, *a.* abundant, much, plentiful.
*ବିପ୍ର, *n.* a Brahman.
*ବିପ୍ରକୃଷ୍ଟ, *a.* distant, remote.
*ବିପ୍ରଳାପ, *n.* idle talk, speaking adversely, a dispute, wrangling.
ବିପ୍ଳବ, *n.* great desolation, a plague, revolution, confusion.
ବିଫଳ, *a.* vain, fruitless.
ବିବର, *n.* a hole, a cave.
ବିବରଣ, *n.* description, narrative.
ବିବର୍ଜନ, *n.* relinquishing, deserting, quitting.
ବିବର୍ଣ୍ଣ, *a.* discoloured, blushing, pale.
ବିବଶ, *a.* not under control; weak.
*ବିବସନ, ବିବସ୍ତ୍ର, *a.* naked, unclothed.
*ବିବକ୍ଷିତ, *a.* intended to be said or spoken.
ବେବାକ, *ad.* wholly, without remainder.
ବିବାଦ, *n.* dispute, controversy.
*ବିବାଦକ, *n.* a disputant, wrangler.
ବିବାଦୀ, *n.* a disputant;—*a.* quarrelsome, disputatious.
ବିବାହ, *n.* a wedding, marriage.
ବିବାହିତ, *a.* married, wedded; *fem.* ବିବାହିତା ।
ବିବି, *n.* a lady, a mistress.
ବିବିଧ, *a.* various, diverse, sundry.

* ବିବୁଧ, *n.* a god, a deity, a philosopher. [played.

ବିବୃତ, *a.* narrated, expressed; dis-

ବିବେକ, *n.* conscience, discrimination, knowledge of good and evil.

ବିବେକୀ, *a.* conscious, discriminating, distinguishing one thing from another.

ବିବେଚକ, *a.* thoughtful, judicious.

ବିବେଚନା, *n.* consideration, reflection.

ବିବେଚନୀୟ, ବିବେଚ୍ୟ, *a.* capable of being discriminated or examined. [rated.

ବିବେଚିତ, *a.* discriminated, delibe-

ବିଭକ୍ତ, *a.* divided, allotted.

ବିଭକ୍ତି, *n.* division; (in *Gram.*) termination. [wealth.

ବିଭବ, *n.* eminence, grandeur,

ବିଭବବନ୍ତ, ବିଭବଶାଳୀ, *a.* stately, wealthy. [lustre.

ବିଭା, *n.* marriage; * brilliancy,

* ବିଭାକର, *n.* the sun, fire.

ବିଭାଗ, *n.* a part, share; a department; division, distribution.

ବିଭାଗୀ, *n.* a sharer, partner.

* ବିଭାଜକ, *n.* a divider.

* ବିଭାଜ୍ୟ, *a.* divisible.

ବିଭାଜ୍ୟତା, *n.* divisibility.

* ବିଭାବରୀ, *n.* night.

ବିଭିନ୍ନ, *a.* different, divided, separated.

ବିଭିନ୍ନତା, *n.* difference, separation, distinction.

ବିଭୀଷଣ, *n.* brother of *Rábana*;—*a.* frightful, terrific.

ବିଭୀଷିକା, *n.* terror; a means of terrifying, a scare.

ବିଭୁ, *n.* God the omnipresent.

ବିଭୂତି, *n.* glory; affluence, property; ashes. [coration.

ବିଭୂଷଣ, * ବିଭୂଷା, *n.* ornament, de-

ବିଭୂଷିତ, *a.* ornamented, decorated.

ବିଭେଦ, *n.* separation, distinction.

ବିଭୋଳ, *a.* foolish, demented, crazy.

ବିଭ୍ରମ, *n.* an error, blunder; * whirling.

ବିଭ୍ରାଟ, *n.* an emergency.

* ବିଭ୍ରାନ୍ତ, *a.* mistaken.

ବିମନାଃ, * ବିମନସ୍କ, *a.* absent-minded, perplexed.

ବିମର୍ଦ୍ଦନ, *n.* grinding, triturating, rubbing. [like.

ବିମର୍ଷ, *n.* regret, repentance; dis-

ବିମଳ, *a.* clean, pure, transparent.

ବିମଳା, *n.* name of a goddess.

ବିମା, *n.* insurance.

ବିମାତା, *n.* a stepmother. [gods.

ବିମାନ, *n.* a car, a vehicle of the

ବିମାର୍ଗ, *n.* a wrong road, evil course.

ବିମୁକ୍ତ, *n.* liberated, emancipated.

ବିମୁକ୍ତି, *n.* liberation, emancipation.

ବିମୁଖ, *a.* averse, turning away from.

ବିମୁଗ୍ଧ, *a.* absorbed, bewildered, charmed.

* ବିମୂଢ଼, *a.* confounded, bewildered; tempted, beguiled; stupid.

ବିମୋଚନ, *n.* releasing, liberating; pardon.

* ବିମୋହନ, *a.* fascinating, alluring.

ବିମୋହିତ, *a.* fascinated, tempted.

ବିମ୍ବ, *n.* a reflected object; * a planet's disc.

ବିମ୍ବାକାର, *a.* convex, discoid.

ବିମ୍ବାଫଳ, *n.* red fruit of a creeping plant.

ବିମ୍ବାଧର, ବିମ୍ବୋଷ୍ଠ, *n.* red lips like the *bimbá* fruit.

ବିମ୍ବିତ, *a.* reflected, shadowed out.

ବିଯୁକ୍ତ, *a.* separated, disunited, minus.

ବିଯୋଗ, *n.* disjunction, separation; subtraction; death.

* ବିଯୋଗୀ, *a.* separated.

ବିଯୋଡ଼, *a.* ill-matched, uneven.

ବିରକ୍ତ, *a.* displeased, annoyed, averse.

ବିରକ୍ତି, *n.* aversion, displeasure, dislike.

ବିରଚିତ, *a.* composed, compiled, made.

ବିରତ, *a.* ceased, desisted, stopped.

ବିରତି, *n.* cessation, a stopping.

ବିରଳ, *a.* rare, scarce; not thick or compact.

ବିରସ, *a.* insipid, vapid, ill-flavoured.

ବିରହ, *n.* separation, painful absence.

ବିରହିଣୀ, *a. fem.* separated or absent from; bereft of;—*n.* a woman separated from her lover or husband.

ବିରହୀ, *a.* lonely, bereft; love-sick, lustful.

ବିରାଗ, *n.* indifference, disgust, dislike.

ବିରାଜମାନ, *a.* brilliant, conspicuous.

ବିରାଜମାନ ହେବା, *v.* to appear with glory or brilliance.

ବିରାଜିତ, *a.* manifested, displayed.

ବିରାଟ, *a.* gigantic, enormous.

ବିରାମ, *n.* rest, repose, leisure.

ବିରାମ ଚିହ୍ନ, *n.* punctuation marks.

ବିରୁଡ଼, *n.* a wasp, a hornet.

ବିରୁଦ୍ଧ, *a.* contrary, opposed, absurd.

ବିରୂପ, *a.* deformed, ill-shaped.

ବିରେଚକ, *a.* purgative, cathartic.

* ବିରେଚନ, *n.* operating by stool, purging.

ବିରୋଧ, *n.* dissension, quarrel, strife.

ବିରୋଧୀ, *a.* quarrelsome, disputatious;—*n.* an enemy, an opponent.

* ବିଳ, *n.* a hole, a cave.

ବିଳମ୍ବ, *n.* delay, procrastination, a long time.

ବିଳାପ, *n.* lamentation, mourning.

ବିଳାପୀ, *a.* lamenting, bewailing.

ବିଳାସ, *n.* merry enjoyment, sport; dalliance.

ବିଳାସିନୀ, *n.* a coquettish woman; a prostitute.

ବିଳାସୀ, *a.* merry, sportive, wanton.

ବିଳିବିଳେଇବା, *v.* to talk in sleep.

* ବିଳେଶୟ, *n.* a snake.

ବିଲକୁଲ୍, *ad.* wholly, entirely.

ବିଲ, *n.* a field, a plain.

* ବିଲଗ୍ନ, *a.* unconnected, irrelevant.

ବିଲୟ, *n.* destruction, dissolution.

ବିଲକ୍ଷଣ, *a.* conspicuous; excellent.

ବିଲାତ, *n.* England.

ବିଲାତି, *a.* English, pertaining to England.

ବିଲାତିଆଳୁ, *n.* the common potato.

* ବିଲୀନ, *a.* disappeared, vanished; dead, perished: united or blended with.

ବିଲୁଅ, *n.* a jackal.

ବିଲୁପ୍ତ, *a.* effaced, destroyed.

ବିଲେଇ, ବିଲାଇ, *n.* a cat.

* ବିଲେପନ, *n.* anointing, smearing the body with sandal-wood, etc.

* ବିଲୋକନ, *n.* viewing, inspection.

* ବିଲୋଡ଼ନ, *n.* stirring up, churning.

ବିଲୋପ, *n.* destruction; disappearance.

ବିଲୋମ, *n.* reverse order, inversion; —*a.* opposite, contrary.

* ବିଲ୍ୱ, *n.* the wood-apple or *bél.*

ବିଂଶ, *a.* twenty.

* ବିଶଙ୍କ, *a.* bold, fearless, secure.

ବିଶଲ୍ୟକରଣୀ, *n.* the name of a medicinal plant.

ବିଶା, *n.* a one-scaled weighing balance; 18 or 20 *pals* weight.

ବିଶାଖା, *n.* the sixteenth stellar mansion.

* ବିଶାରଦ, *a.* learned, eminent, clever.

ବିଶାଳ, *a.* great, large, extensive.

* ବିଶିଖ, *n.* an arrow.

ବିଶିଷ୍ଟ, *a.* invested with, possessed of, having; genteel; excellent.

ବିଶିଷ୍ଟତା, *n.* superiority, gentility.

ବିଶୁଆଳ, *n.* a surname of the cultivator caste.

ବିଶୁଦ୍ଧ, *a.* cleansed, rectified.

ବିଶୁଦ୍ଧି, *n.* purity, holiness, correction.

ବିଶୃଙ୍ଖଳ, *a.* disorderly, irregular.

ବିଶେଷ, *n.* peculiarity, difference; a particular;—*a.* peculiar, special, different, particular.

* ବିଶେଷକ, *a.* particularizing, distinguishing.

ବିଶେଷଣ, *n.* attribute; an adjective.

ବିଶେଷତଃ, *ad.* especially, particularly.

ବିଶେଷ୍ୟ, *a.* distinguishable;—*n.* a noun.

ବିଶୋଇବା, *v.* to take rest.

* ବିଶୋକ, *a.* free from grief or sorrow.

ବିଶୋଧନ, *n.* purifying, cleansing, correcting; a receipt in full.

* ବିଶ୍ରାନ୍ତ, *a.* rested, refreshed, recovered.

ବିଶ୍ରାମ, *n.* rest, repose, cessation.

ବିଶ୍ରାମବାର, *n.* the Sabbath, Sunday.

ବିଶ୍ରୀ, *a.* deformed, ugly.

* ବିଶ୍ଳେଷ, *n.* a separation, disunion.

* ବିଶ୍ୱ, *n.* the universe;—*a.* all, entire.

* ବିଶ୍ୱକର୍ମା, *n.* architect of the gods.

* ବିଶ୍ୱଜନୀନ, *a.* good for all men, beneficial to all men.

ବିଶ୍ୱନାଥ, ବିଶ୍ୱେଶ୍ୱର, *n.* a name of *Siva.*

ବିଶ୍ୱବିଦ୍ୟାଳୟ, *n.* a university.

ବିଶ୍ୱବ୍ୟାପକ, ବିଶ୍ୱବ୍ୟାପୀ, *a.* pervading the universe.

* ବିଶ୍ୱବଞ୍ଚ, *a.* all-deceptive.

* ବିଶ୍ୱମ୍ଭର, *n.* preserver of the world; God.

* ବିଶ୍ୱମ୍ଭରା, *n.* the earth.

* ବିଶ୍ୱରୂପ, *a.* assuming all forms.

* ବିଶ୍ୱସନୀୟ, *a.* trustworthy, trusty.

* ବିଶ୍ୱସିତ, *a.* trusted, confided in.

ବିଶ୍ୱସ୍ତ, *a.* faithful, believed, trusted.

ବିଶ୍ୱସ୍ତତା, *n.* faithfulness, honesty.

ବିଶ୍ୱା, *n.* a land measure, $=\frac{1}{100}$ of an acre.

ବିଶ୍ୱାସ, *n.* belief, trust, faith.

ବିଶ୍ୱାସଘାତକ, *a.* treacherous;—*n.* a traitor.

ବିଶ୍ୱାସୀ, *a.* faithful, trustworthy;—*n.* a believer.

* ବିଶ୍ୱାସ୍ୟ, *a.* worthy of confidence.

ବିଷ, *n.* venom, poison, virus.

ବିଷଘ୍ନ, *n.* an antidote (to poison).

ବିଷଣ୍ଣ, *a.* dejected, sad, pensive.

ବିଷଣ୍ଣତା, *n.* dejection, sadness.

ବିଷଦନ୍ତ, ବିଷଦାନ୍ତ, *n.* the fang of a serpent.

* ବିଷଧର, *n.* a snake;—*a.* venomous.

ବିଷବୈଦ୍ୟ, *n.* a charmer of snake-bites; a doctor who administers poison.

ବିଷମ, *a.* uneven, unequal; distressing, intolerable, difficult;—ବିଷମଜ୍ୱର, *n.* a violent intermittent fever;—ବିଷମବିଭୁଜ, *n.* (in *Geom.*) a scalene triangle;—ବିଷମରାଶି, *n.* (in *Arith.*) an odd number;—ବିଷମସାହସ, *n.* temerity, rashness.

ବିଷୟ, *n.* matter, object, thing, wealth.

ବିଷୟକର୍ମ, *n.* worldly business, secular affairs.

ବିଷୟୀ, *a.* worldly-wise; secular.

ବିଷୟେ, *ad.* in reference to, about.

ବିଷାକ୍ତ, *a.* poisoned, mixed with poison.

* ବିଷାଣ, *n.* a horn, tusk, ivory;—*a.* poisonous.

ବିଷାଦ, *n.* dejection, sadness, regret.

ବିଷୁବ, *n.* the equinox.

ବିଷୁବରେଖା, *n.* the equator.

ବିଷ୍ଠା, *n.* dung, ordure, excrement.

ବିଷ୍ଣୁ, *n.* the Preserver—*Vishnu.*

* ବିସମ୍ବାଦ, *n.* a dispute, contention, quarrel.

ବିସର୍ଗ, *n.* the letter (ः); *a gift.

ବିସର୍ଜନ, *n.* relinquishing, casting off.

* ବିସର୍ପଣ, *n.* moving, extending, spreading.

ବିସଙ୍ଗ, *n.* a rake, a libertine, a fop.

ବିସୂଚିକା, *n.* spasmodic cholera.

ବିସ୍ତର, *a.* much, ample.

ବିସ୍ତାର, *n.* width, extent, diameter.

ବିସ୍ତାରଣ, *n.* spreading out, enlarging, dilating

ବିସ୍ତାରିତ, ବିସ୍ତୃତ, *a.* extended, spun out.

ବିସ୍ତୀର୍ଣ୍ଣ, ବିସ୍ତାରିତ, ବିସ୍ତୃତ, *a.* spread out, expanded.

ବିସ୍ତୃତି, *n.* expansion, width.

* ବିସ୍ପଷ୍ଟ, *a.* manifest, evident, clear.

* ବିସ୍ଫାରିତ, *a.* dilated, expanded.

ବିସ୍ଫୋଟକ, *n.* a boil, an abscess.

ବିସ୍ମୟ, *n.* astonishment, surprise.

ବିସ୍ମୟାପନ୍ନ, *a.* filled with surprise, wonder-struck.

ବିସ୍ମିତ, *a.* astonished, surprised.

ବିସ୍ମରଣ, *n.* forgetting, oblivion.

ବିସ୍ମୃତ, *a.* having forgotten, forgetful; forgotten.

ବିସ୍ମୃତି, *n.* forgetting, oblivion.

ବିସ୍ୱାଦ, *n.* insipidity, ill-flavour.

ବିହଙ୍ଗ, ବିହଙ୍ଗମ, * ବିହଗ, *n.* a bird.

ବିହନ, *n.* seed corn; fish roe, spawn.

* ବିହରଣ, *n.* taking an airing, strolling about.

ବିହାର, *n.* motion, exercise, pastime.

ବିହି, *n.* providence, *Brahmá.*

ବିହିତ, *a.* legitimate, lawful, fit, proper.

ବିହୀନ, *a.* destitute of, without.

ବିହ୍ୱଳ, *a.* bewildered, delirious.

ବିକ୍ଷିପ୍ତ, *a.* scattered, thrown about.

* ବିକ୍ଷେପ, *n.* throwing, propelling, scattering.

ବିକ୍ଷୋଭିତ, *a.* agitated, moved.

* ବୀଚି, *n.* a ripple, wave, billow.

ବୀଜ, *n.* a seed, grain, kernel; source, origin; semen;–ବୀଜକୋଷ, *n.* the pericarpium, seed vessel; —ବୀଜଗଣିତ, *n.* algebra;—* ବୀଜବପନ, *n.* sowing of seed;—* ବୀଜବାପକ, *n.* one who sows seeds, a sower.

* ବୀଟିକା, *n.* a leaf of *pán*, spices, etc., rolled up ready for chewing.

ବୀଣା, *n.* the Indian lute, guitar.

ବୀଣାବାଦକ, *n.* a player of the lute.

* ବୀତ, *a.* gone, past.

* ବୀଥି, ବୀଥିକା, *n.* a road, range, an avenue, a row; terrace, shop.

ବୀବର, *n.* a beaver.

ବୀଭତ୍ସ, *a.* cruel, disgusting.

ବୀର, *n.* a hero, a warrior.

ବୀରତ୍ୱ, *n.* prowess, valour, heroism.

* ବୀରାସନ, *n.* a kneeling posture.

ବୀର୍ଯ୍ୟ, *n.* valour, might; semen.

ବୀର୍ଯ୍ୟବାନ୍, *a.* heroic, energetic, robust.

ବୁକ, *n.* the breast, chest, bosom.

ବୁକ୍‌ନା, *n.* powder of anything.

ବୁଜାଇବା, *v.* to cause to close, shut, fill up; to extinguish.

ବୁଜିବା, *v.* to shut, fill up, put out.

ବୁଝାଇବା, *v.* to explain, to make to understand.

ବୁଝାବୁଝି, *n.* an explanation or understanding.

ବୁଝିବା, *v.* to understand, comprehend.

ବୁଟ, ବୁଟ୍ଟ, *n.* a kind of pea, gram.

ବୁଟା, *n.* small spots or flowers on cloth.

ବୁଟାଦାର, *a.* flowered or figured [(cloth).

ବୁଡ, *n.* immersion.

ବୁଡିବା, *v.* to dip, to sink in water.

ବୁଢା, *n.* an old man;—*a.* old, aged.

ବୁଢାଅଙ୍ଗୁଠି, *n.* the thumb, great toe.

ବୁଢୀ, *n.* an old woman.

ବୁଢୀଆଣି, *n.* a spider.

ବୁଢୀଆଣିଜାଲ, *n.* a spider's web.

ବୁଣା, *n.* sown, scattered; woven; knitted.

ବୁଣାଣ, *n.* texture of cloth; lacing or tying of a bamboo roof.

ବୁଣାଳୀ, *n.* a sower of grain; a weaver; a cane-worker.

ବୁଣିବା, *v.* to sow seed; to weave; to knit; to cane chairs, etc.

ବୁଦା, *n.* a bush, thorny bush. [ing.

ବୁଦ୍ଧ, *n.* *Buddha*;—*a.* wise, know-

ବୁଦ୍ଧି, *n.* sense, cleverness, sagacity.

ବୁଦ୍ଧିଗମ୍ୟ, *a.* rational, intellectual.

ବୁଦ୍ଧିମାନ୍, ବୁଦ୍ଧିମନ୍ତ, *a.* sensible, intelligent.

* ବୁଦ୍ଧୀନ୍ଦ୍ରିୟ, *n.* organs of sense.

ବୁଦ୍ବୁଦ, *n.* a bubble.

ବୁଧ, *n.* the planet Mercury.

ବୁଧବାର, *n.* Wednesday.

ବୁନିଆଦ, *n.* foundation; origin, ground of.

* ବୁଭୁକ୍ଷା, *n.* appetite, hunger.

* ବୁଭୁକ୍ଷିତ, *a.* hungry, desirous of food.

ବୁରୁଲ, *n.* an inch.

ବୁଲା, *a.* turning, wandering;—*n.* a rambler, wanderer.

ବୁଲାଇବା, *v.* to cause to walk or go round; to whirl; to cause to revolve. [ing road.

ବୁଲାଣି, *n.* a circuitous route, wind-

ବୁଲିବା, *v.* to walk, to go round, to wander, to roam.

* ବୃଜନ, *n.* sin, wickedness.

ବୃତ୍ତ, *n.* custom; metre; a circle.

ବୃତ୍ତଖଣ୍ଡ, *n.* (in *Geom.*) a segment of a circle.

ବୃତ୍ତସୂଚ୍ୟଗ୍ର, *n.* (in *Geom.*) a cone.

ବୃତ୍ତାନ୍ତ, *n.* an account, narrative, tale, history.

ବୃତ୍ତାଭାସ, *n.* (in *Geom.*) an oval shaped figure.

ବୃତ୍ତି, *n.* pay, allowance, stipend, pension; occupation, profession.

ବୃତ୍ତିଭୋଗୀ, *a.* living upon pension.

ବୃଥା, *ad.* in vain;—*a.* useless, futile.

ବୃଦ୍ଧ, *a.* old, increased, grown.

ବୃଦ୍ଧକାଳ, *n.* old age, senility.

* ବୃଦ୍ଧପ୍ରପିତାମହ, *n.* paternal great grandfather.

* ବୃଦ୍ଧପ୍ରମାତାମହୀ *n.* maternal great grandmother.

* ବୃଦ୍ଧାଙ୍ଗୁଷ୍ଠ, *n.* the thumb, great toe.

ବୃଦ୍ଧି, *n.* growth, increase, prosperity.

*ବୃଦ୍ଧିଜୀବୀ, *n.* a usurer, money-lender. [ple.

* ବୃନ୍ତ, *n.* a stalk, footstalk; a nipple.

ବୃନ୍ଦ, *n.* a multitude, heap; one thousand millions.

ବୃନ୍ଦାବତୀ, *n.* the basil or *tulsi* plant.

* ବୃଶ୍ଚିକ, *n.* a centipede; sign Scorpio.

ବୃଷ, *n.* sign Taurus; *a bull.

ବୃଷଭ, *n.* a bull.

ବୃଷ୍ଟି, *n.* rain, a shower.

ବୃଷ୍ଟିମାନଯନ୍ତ୍ର, *n.* a rain-gauge, a pluviameter. [mense.

ବୃହତ୍, *a.* large, great, huge, immense.

ବୃହତ୍କାୟ, *a.* gigantic, large-bodied.

ବୃହସ୍ପତି, *n.* the planet Jupiter.

ବୃକ୍ଷ, *n.* a tree.

* ବୃକ୍ଷବାଟିକା, *n.* a grove, a park.

ବେ, *n.* a Hindustani *prefix* equal in Oriya to ଅ ।

ବେଅଦାଜ, *a.* immoderate, profuse.

ବେଆଇନୀ, *a.* illegal.

ବେଅଦବ, *a.* unmannerly, impolite.

ବେଇଜ୍ଜତ, *a.* void of honour or respect, disrespectful.

ବେଇମାନ, *a.* irreligious, unconscionable, ungrateful.

ବେଉଣ୍ଟିବା, *v.* to divide, to distribute.

ବେୱା, *n.* a widow.

ବେଓାରସ, ବେଓାରିସ, *a.* without a master or owner.

ବେଓରା, *n.* a report; details or particulars, narration.

ବେଉଷଣ, *n.* the second ploughing of the paddy fields when the plants are about 6 inches high.

ବେଉଷିବା, *v.* to revisit; to plough the second time.

ବେଉସା, *n.* a trade, a calling, a business, a profession, an occupation.

ବେଓଜର, *a.* without excuse, inexcusable.

ବେକ, *n.* the neck.

ବେକସୁର, *a.* faultless, innocent.

ବେଢା, *n.* a handful of grass or straw, etc.

ବେଢାଏ, ବେଢଏ, *n.* one handful.

ବେକୁବ, *a.* foolish.

ବେଖରଚ, *a.* without expense.

ବେଗ, *n.* speed, haste, impulse, eagerness. [ous.

ବେଗବାନ, *a.* rapid, swift, impetuous.

ବେଗର, *ad.* without, except, beside.

ବେଗାର, *n.* a person impressed into service or compelled to work gratis. [service.

ବେଗାରୁ, *n.* the act of pressing into service.

ବେଗେ, *ad.* with speed, in haste; quickly.

ବେଙ୍ଗ, *n.* a frog.

ବେଙ୍ଗଳା, *n.* treading out corn.

ବେଙ୍ଗା, *n.* a disease; fœtid smell.

ବେଚଇନ, *a.* uneasy, unsteady, unsettled, fickle.

ବେଚଲ୍ଲ, *n.* a bad habit or practice; —*a.* not proper.

ବେଜାଏ, *a.* unjust, improper.

ବେଜାର, *a.* angry, displeased, out of humour.

ବେଠି, *n.* impressed labour.

ବେଠିଆ, *n.* an impressed labourer.

ବେଠିକ, *a.* erroneous, inaccurate.

ବେଠିକତା, *n.* uncertainty, inaccuracy.

ବେଠୌର, *a.* unsteady, not sure.

ବେଡ଼, *n.* fetters, shackles.

ବେଡୌଲ, *a.* ill-shaped, ugly.

ବେଢଣ, *n.* a small *sari*; fencing in.

ବେଢା, *n.* an enclosure, a fence, wall.

ବେଢିବା, *v.* to enclose, surround.

ବେଡ଼ି, *n.* fetters, shackles; tongs.

ବେଣା, *n.* thatching grass.

ବେଣୀ, *n.* a braid of hair; branch of a river.

* ବେଣୁ, *n.* a flute, pipe; a bamboo.

*ବେଣୁଯବ, *n.* grain of the bamboo.

ବେଣ୍ଟ, *n.* handle of a tool or weapon.

ବେଣ୍ଟି, *n.* the short hair round the topknot of Hindus.

ବେତ, *n.* a cane, rattan.

ବେତନ, *n.* wages, salary, pay.

ବେତା, *n.* a large split-cane basket.

ବେତାଳ, *n.* a demon, fiend, goblin.

* ବେତ୍ତା, *a.* versed in, acquainted with.

* ବେତ୍ର, *n.* a cane, rattan, (see ବେତ).

ବେତ୍ରାଘାତ, *n.* beating with a cane.

ବେଦ, *n.* the *Veda*; science.

ବେଦଖଲ, *a.* dispossessed, not possessing, not subject to.

ବେଦଜ୍ଞ, *a.* versed in the *Vedas*.

ବେଦନା, *n.* pain, ache, distress.

ବେଦନିନ୍ଦକ, *n.* an infidel, an opposer of the *Vedas*.

ବେଦବ୍ୟାସ, *n.* the sage *Vyása*.

ବେଦମ୍, *a.* breathless; out of breath.

ବେଦର୍ଦ୍ଦୀ, *a.* unfeeling, cruel.

ବେଦସ୍ତୁର, *a.* not customary, unusual.

ବେଦାଙ୍ଗ, *n.* the six sciences appendant on the *Vedas*, viz., the formation and arrangement of ideas, logic, grammar, a knowledge of technical terms, astronomy, and prosody.

ବେଦାନ୍ତ, *n.* one of the six schools of philosophy, usually called the *Darshanas*.

ବେଦାନ୍ତୀ, *a.* professing the *Vedanta* [philosophy.

ବେଦି, ବେଦୀ, *ବେଦିକା, *n.* an altar, mound, seat.

ବେଦୋକ୍ତ, *a.* mentioned in the *Vedas*.

* ବେଦ୍ୟ, *a.* capable of being known.

ବେଧ, *a.* born of adultery;—*n.* thickness, * perforation.

* ବେଧନ, *n.* boring, perforating.

ବେଧପିଣ୍ଡ, *n.* illegitimate child.

ବେଧାଗ, *a.* not according to rule, contrary.

ବେଧୂଆ, *a.* illegitimate, base-born.

ବେଯୋଇ, *n.* an adulteress; a destroyer of her bastard offspring.

ବେନାମା, *a.* anonymous;—*n.* a false or assumed name.

ବେନି, *a.* two, a couple; both.

* ବେପଥୁ, *n.* shaking, quaking.

ବେପର୍ଦା, *a.* unscreened, exposed; immodest.

ବେପସନ୍ଦ, *a.* unapproved, without choice.

ବେପାର, *n.* trade, business, calling.

ବେପାରୀ, *n.* a trader, tradesman.

ବେଫାଇଦା, *a.* profitless, useless, disadvantageous; vain.

ବେଫିକର, *a.* unconcerned, thoughtless, careless.

ବେବର୍ତ୍ତ, *n.* a chief, ruler, manager.

ବେବାକ, *ad.* wholly, without remainder.

ବେଭାର, *n.* trading; conduct; sending of presents to friends.

ବେଭାରୀ, *n.* a tradesman or merchant.

ବେମାର, *a.* sick.

ବେମାରି, *n.* sickness, disease.

ବେମାଲୁମ, *a.* unknown, not evident.

ବେମିଆଦ, *a.* not confined to a stipulated time.

ବେମୁନାସିବ, *a.* improper, unfit.

ବେରୋଜଗାର, ବେରୋଜଗାରୀ, *a.* without employment or support.

ବେଳ, ବେଳା, *n.* time, daytime.

ବେଳସୁଁ, ବେଳକୁଁ, *ad.* beforehand, from aforetime.

* ବେଳାଭୂମି, ବେଳା, *n.* the sea-coast, sea-shore.

ବେଲ, *n.* the *bél* fruit.

ବେଲଣା, *n.* a paste-pin, rolling-pin.

ବେଲ୍ଲ, *n.* a bowl made of mixed metals.

ବେଶ, *a.* preferable, good, superior, capital;—*ad.* well, all right.

ବେଶ, *n.* dress, garb, guise, habit.

ବେଶଭୂଷା, *n.* embellishment, decoration.

ବେଶର, *n.* pounded mustard-seed; an ornament for the nose.

ବେଶରମ, *a.* shameless, immodest.

ବେଶି, *a.* surplus, more than enough.

ବେଶ୍ୟା, *n.* a prostitute, bad woman.

ବେଶ୍ୟାଳୟ, *n.* house of a prostitute; a bawdy-house.

ବେଷ୍ଟନ, *n.* surrounding, encircling.

ବେଷ୍ଟିତ, *a.* surrounded, encompassed

ବେସନ, *n.* gram flour, flour.

ବେସବୁର, ବେସବର, *a.* impatient.

ବେସୁମାର, *a.* countless, numberless, much.

ବେସାତ, *n.* worth, value, a stock, capital.

ବେହକ, *a.* wrong, not right, unjust.

ବେହଦ, *a.* boundless, unlimited.

ବେହୟା, *a.* shameless, impudent.

ବେହାଲ, *a.* thin, emaciated, wretched.

ବେହୁଦା, *a.* having no office or post, without rank.

ବେହୁକୁମ, *a.* without or contrary to orders.

ବେହୁରମତ, *a.* void of honour or virtue.

ବେହୁଶିଆର, *a.* inattentive, careless.

ବେହେରା, *n.* a bearer, headman, applied to the *Gowála*, *Chamár*, and *Keuta* castes.

ବେହେଲା, *n.* a violin, a fiddle

ବେହୋସ୍, *a.* senseless, stupid; intoxicated.

*ବୈକଲ୍ୟ, *n.* discomposure, agitation.

ବୈକୁଣ୍ଠ, *n.* *Vishnu's* paradise.

ବୈଗୁଣ୍ୟ, *n.* absence of good qualities, a defect, a fault.

ବୈଚିତ୍ର୍ୟ, *n.* variety, diversity; a wonder.

*ବୈଜୟନ୍ତୀ, *n.* a banner; a kind of garland.

ବୈଜ୍ଞାନିକ, *a.* scientific;—*n.* scientist.

ବୈଠକ, ବୈଠିକ, *n.* an assembly, a conference.

ବୈଠା, *n.* a lampstand; a light.

*ବୈତନିକ, *n.* a hired labourer, a hireling.

ବୈତରଣୀ, *n.* the Hindu styx; name of a river near Jajpur.

ବୈଦିକ, *a.* relating to the *Vedas*;—*n.* a learned man.

ବୈଦୂର୍ଯ୍ୟ, *n.* a mineral of beautiful ultramarine colour.

*ବୈଦେଶିକ, *n.* a foreigner;—*a.* foreign.

ବୈଦେହୀ, *n.* *Sita, Janaki.*

ବୈଦ୍ୟ, *n.* a physican, a doctor.

ବୈଦ୍ୟଶାସ୍ତ୍ର, *n.* the science of medicine.

ବୈଦ୍ୟୁତିକ, *ବୈଦ୍ୟୁତ, *a.* electrical.

ବୈଧବ୍ୟ, *n.* widowhood.

*ବୈଧର୍ମ୍ୟ, *n.* heterodoxy, atheism.

*ବୈପରୀତ୍ୟ, *n.* contrariety, hostility.

*ବୈବାହିକ, *a.* nuptial.

*ବୈଭବ, *n.* eminence, grandeur, wealth.

ବୈମାତ୍ରେୟ, *ବୈମାତ୍ର, *a.* (brother or sister) born of a step-mother.

*ବୈମୁଖ୍ୟ, *n.* aversion, turning from.

*ବୈୟାକରଣ, *n.* a grammarian.

*ବୈର, *n.* enmity, hostility; emulation.

*ବୈରକ୍ତ୍ୟ, *n.* aversion, displeasure.

*ବୈର-ନିର୍ଯାତନ, *n.* revenge, retaliation.

ବୈରାଗୀ, *a.* free from worldly attachments;—*n.* a mendicant, an ascetic.

ବୈରାଗ୍ୟ, *n.* stoicism, freedom from passion.

*ବୈରତା, *n.* enmity, hostility, hatred.

ବୈରୀ, *n.* an enemy, a foe, adversary.

*ବୈଲକ୍ଷଣ୍ୟ, *n.* variation, disparity.

ବୈଶାଖ, *n.* the first Hindu month, part of April and May.

ବୈଶ୍ୟ, *n.* the third or merchant caste of Hindus.

ବୈଷମ୍ୟ, *n.* inequality.

* ବୈଷୟିକ, *n.* a sensualist, one occupied with worldly objects or interests;—*a.* relating to worldly objects; sensual.

ବୈଷ୍ଣବ, *n.* a votary of *Vishnu.*

*ବୈସାଦୃଶ୍ୟ, *n.* inequality, disparity.

ବୋ, ବୋଉ, *n.* a stench, bad smell.

ବୋଇତ, *n.* a ship, barge, large boat.

ବୋଇତାଳୁ, ବୋଇତକଖାରୁ, *n.* a pumpkin.

ବୋକ, *n.* a kiss; kissing.

ବୋକା, *n.* a blockhead, numskull.

ବୋଚକ୍, *n.* a bundle or parcel carried on the back.

ବୋଝ, ବୋଝା, *n.* a burden, package, load.

ବୋଝାଇ, *n.* a cargo, lading, burden, load.

ବୋଝିଆ, *n.* a cooley, one who carries burdens.

ବୋଡ଼ା, *n.* a species of snake, the boa constrictor.

ବୋଡ଼ି, *n.* five *gandás*, or 20 *kadás.*

ବୋଡ଼, *n.* the empty shell or husk of grain.

ବୋଡ଼ଅ, *n.* stench from animals.

ବୋଦା, *n.* a living victim for sacrifice; a he-goat.

ବୋଧ, *n.* idea, mental impression, opinion.

ବୋଧକ, *a.* knowing, comprehending.

ବୋଧଗମ୍ୟ *a.* comprehensible.

* ବୋଧ୍ୟ, *a.* knowable, perceivable, perceptible.

ବୋଦ୍ଧା, *a.* sagacious, wise.

ବୋବା, *a.* dumb, speechless.

ବୋବାଉବା, ବୋବେଉବା, *v.* to cry (used only of animals and birds).

ବୋବାଳି, *n.* a cry or call in distress.

ବୋରଝାଙ୍କି, *n.* water-weeds.

ବୋସ୍, *a.* bad, evil;–*n.* a sack, bag.

ବୋଳ, *n.* a kind of glaze; saliva induced by éating *pán.*

ବୋଳିବା, *v.* to smear, to plaster; to dye; to apply.

ବୋଲ୍, ବୋଲି, *n.* speech; a saying, dialect.

ବୋଲଣା, *n.* abuse.

ବୋଲ, *n.* singing.

ବୋଲବୋଲି, *n.* chanting, singing; excited talk or conversation.

ବୋଲିବା, *v.* to recite, to sing; to speak.

ବୋହିବା, *v.* to carry, to bear.

ବୋହୂ, *n.* a son's wife; the bride.

ବୌଦ୍ଧ, *n.* a Buddhist, an atheist.

* ବ୍ୟକ୍ତ, *a.* manifest, evident, distinct.

ବ୍ୟକ୍ତି, *n.* a person, individual.

ବ୍ୟକ୍ତିତ୍ୱ, *n.* individuality.

ବ୍ୟଗ୍ର, *a.* eager, zealous, ardent.

ବ୍ୟଗ୍ରତା, *n.* zeal, eagerness, ardour, agitation.

* ବ୍ୟଙ୍ଗ୍ୟ, *n.* a sneer, sarcasm, pun.

ବ୍ୟଙ୍ଗୋକ୍ତି, *n.* a witty saying, sarcasm.

* ବ୍ୟଜନ, *n.* a fan, a winnow.

*ବ୍ୟଞ୍ଜକ, *a.* expressing passion or feeling, indicating, distinguishing, making plain.

ବ୍ୟଞ୍ଜନ, *n.* consonant; a mark; curry.

ବ୍ୟଞ୍ଜନବର୍ଣ୍ଣ, *n.* a consonant. [viation.

ବ୍ୟତିକ୍ରମ, *n.* inversion, variation, de-

ବ୍ୟତିରିକ୍ତ, *a.* excepted, withdrawn.

ବ୍ୟତିରେକ, *n.* exception, separation, withdrawal. [sides.

ବ୍ୟତିରେକେ, *ad.* without, except, be-

ବ୍ୟତିବ୍ୟସ୍ତ, *a.* disgusted, agitated, alarmed.

ବ୍ୟତୀତ, *a.* past, gone; excepted;—*ad.* without.

ବ୍ୟଥା, *n.* pain, ache, smart, distress.

ବ୍ୟଥିତ, *a.* pained, distressed, hurt.

ବ୍ୟବକଳନ, *n.* (in *Arith.*) subtraction. [ces.

*ବ୍ୟବଚ୍ଛିନ୍ନ, *a.* divided, cut into pie-

*ବ୍ୟବଚ୍ଛେଦ, *n.* dividing, cutting up, anatomy. [tomy.

ବ୍ୟବଚ୍ଛେଦବିଦ୍ୟା, *n.* the science of ana-

ବ୍ୟବଧାନ, *n.* a partition, interval.

ବ୍ୟବସାୟ, *a.* occupation, trade, business. [calling.

ବ୍ୟବସାୟୀ, *a.* professing a trade or

ବ୍ୟବସ୍ଥା, *n.* a law, statute, rule.

ବ୍ୟବସ୍ଥାପକ, *n.* a legislator, judge; lawyer;–*a.* legislative; settling, arranging.

ବ୍ୟବସ୍ଥାପକସଭା, *n.* legislative council.

ବ୍ୟବସ୍ଥାପନ, *n.* proper adjustment; settling, deciding.

*ବ୍ୟବସ୍ଥାପିତ, *a.* legislated, enacted.

*ବ୍ୟବସ୍ଥିତ, *a.* ordered, arranged, regulated, decreed. [tice.

ବ୍ୟବହାର, *n.* usage, conduct, prac-

*ବ୍ୟବହାରଜୀବ, *n.* one who earns his livelihood by the profession of law, a lawyer, a solicitor, atorney, judge, magistrate, etc.

*ବ୍ୟବହାରିକ, *a.* designed or calculated for practical use.

*ବ୍ୟବହାରୀ, *n.* one who acts according to custom or usage;—*a.* acting customarily.

ବ୍ୟବହାର୍ଯ୍ୟ, *a.* fit for use, customary, practicable.

ବ୍ୟବହୃତ, *a.* usual, in practice, used.

ବ୍ୟଭିଚାର, *n.* fornication, adultery; straying.

ବ୍ୟଭିଚାରିଣୀ, *n.* an adulteress; a jilt.

ବ୍ୟଭିଚାରୀ, *a.* adulterous, whorish; —*n.* an adulterer.

ବ୍ୟୟ, *n.* outlay, expenditure.

ବ୍ୟୟକାତର, *ବ୍ୟୟକୁଣ୍ଠ, *a.* parsimonious, niggardly; stingy.

ବ୍ୟୟଶୀଳ, *a.* extravagant, lavish.

ବ୍ୟୟିତ, *a.* expended, spent, consumed.

*ବ୍ୟୟୀ, *a.* expensive, extravagant.

ବ୍ୟର୍ଥ, *a.* useless, ineffectual, unprofitable, unmeaning.

ବ୍ୟସନ, *n.* trouble, an affliction; a vice. [anxious.

ବ୍ୟସ୍ତ, *n.* busy; distressed, agitated,

ବ୍ୟଗ୍ରତା, *n.* agitation, perplexity.
ବ୍ୟାକରଣ, *n.* grammar.
ବ୍ୟାକୁଳ, *a.* perturbed, distracted.
ବ୍ୟାକୁଳତା, *n.* agitation, perturbation.
ବ୍ୟାକୁଳିତ, *a.* agitated, bewildered.
ବ୍ୟାଖ୍ୟା, *n.* explanation, exposition.
* ବ୍ୟାଖ୍ୟାତ, *a.* stated, explained.
ବ୍ୟାଖ୍ୟାନ, *n.* a narration, an interpretation, a commending, explaining.
ବ୍ୟାଘାତ, *n.* an impediment, obstacle.
* ବ୍ୟାଘ୍ର, *n.* a tiger.
* ବ୍ୟାଜ, *n.* artifice; usury; delay.
* ବ୍ୟାଦାନ, *n.* opening.
ବ୍ୟାଧ, *n.* a fowler, huntsman.
ବ୍ୟାଧି, *n.* disease, malady, sickness.
ବ୍ୟାଧିଗ୍ରସ୍ତ, *a.* seized by disease.
ବ୍ୟାପକ, *a.* pervading, spreading.
ବ୍ୟାପକତା, *n.* prevalence, diffusion.
ବ୍ୟାପାର, *n.* affair, business, trade.
* ବ୍ୟାପାରୀ, *n.* a trader, merchant.
ବ୍ୟାପୀ, *a.* spreading, covering, pervading (used in composition as an *affix*).
ବ୍ୟାପୃତ, *a.* engaged, busy.
ବ୍ୟାପ୍ତ, *a.* pervaded, overrun, filled.
ବ୍ୟାପ୍ତି, *n.* an overspreading, a pervading; a putting into force.
ବ୍ୟାବହାରିକ, *a.* fit to be practised, legal, practical.
ବ୍ୟାୟାମ, *n.* athletic exercise, gymnastics, fatigue, labour.
ବ୍ୟାୟାମଶୀଳ, *a.* active, robust, athletic.
* ବ୍ୟାବର୍ତ୍ତନ, *n.* a rolling back.
* ବ୍ୟାବୃତ, *a.* covered, surrounded.
ବ୍ୟାସ, *n.* a celebrated Hindu author who arranged the *Vedas*; diameter; * extension.
ବ୍ୟାସାର୍ଦ୍ଧ, *n.* (in *Geom.*) a radius.
* ବ୍ୟୁତ୍କ୍ରମ, *n.* inverted order, confusion.
ବ୍ୟୁତ୍ପତ୍ତି, *n.* proficiency; derivation.
* ବ୍ୟୁତ୍ପନ୍ନ, *a.* proficient; derived.
* ବ୍ୟୂହ, *n.* array of troops in various positions; systematizing.
* ବ୍ୟୋମ, *n.* the sky, the firmament.
ବ୍ୟୋମଯାନ, *n.* a balloon.
ବ୍ରଜ, *n.* the district about Agra; * a herd, an assemblage.
ବ୍ରଜାଙ୍ଗନା, *n.* a woman of *Braj*, a cowkeeper's wife.
ବ୍ରଣ, *n.* a boil, pimple, pustule, ulcer.
ବ୍ରତ, *n.* a vow, voluntary penance.
* ବ୍ରତୀ, *a.* making or performing vows.
ବ୍ରହ୍ମ, *n.* *Brahma*,—the first cause.
ବ୍ରହ୍ମଚାରୀ, *n.* a religious student, an ascetic.
ବ୍ରହ୍ମଜ୍ଞାନ, *n.* knowledge of *Brahma*, *Vedantism*.
ବ୍ରହ୍ମଜ୍ଞାନୀ, *a.* having the knowledge of *Brahma*.
ବ୍ରହ୍ମତ୍ୱ, *n.* deity, godhead.
ବ୍ରହ୍ମବାଦୀ, *n.* a *Vedantist*.

ବ୍ରହ୍ମରନ୍ଧ୍ର, *n.* a tiny hole said by Hindus to be in the centre of the crown of the head.
ବ୍ରହ୍ମଲୋକ, *n.* the heaven of *Brahma.*
ବ୍ରହ୍ମସ୍ୱ, *n.* property of *Brahmans.*
ବ୍ରହ୍ମହତ୍ୟା, *n.* murder of a *Brahman.*
ବ୍ରହ୍ମା, *n. Brahma,* first of the Hindu triad.
ବ୍ରହ୍ମାଣ୍ଡ, *n.* the universe, the world.
ବ୍ରାହ୍ମ, *n.* a follower of Ram Mohan Roy's doctrine, a Brahma Samajist; a *Vedantist.*
ବ୍ରାହ୍ମଣ, *n.* a *Brahman.*
* ବ୍ରାହ୍ମଣ୍ୟ, *n. Brahmanship.*
* ବ୍ରୀହି, *n. bihri, kulde,* pulse, vetches.

ଭ.

ଭ, the 24th consonant.
ଭଅଁର, *n.* the humble-bee; an auger, gimlet.
ଭଅଁରମାଛି, *n.* the upas tree.
ଭଉଣୀ, *n.* sister.
ଭଉଁରଆ, *n.* landholder's papers showing the boundaries and measurement of lands.
ଭଉଁରୀ, *n.* a whirlpool, an eddy.
ଭକ୍‌ଭକ୍, *n.* chatter, chattering sound.
ଭକୁଆ, *n.* an ignoramus, a simpleton.
ଭକ୍ତ, *a.* devoted, pious;–*n.* a votary, a follower, a devotee; * boiled rice, food.
ଭକ୍ତବତ୍ସଳ, *a.* kind to adherents.
ଭକ୍ତି, *n.* faith, devotedness, homage, reverence, love, attachment, devotion.
ଭକ୍ତିପରାୟଣ, *a.* devoted, zealous.
ଭକ୍ତିମାନ୍, *a.* devoted, religious, pious.
ଭକ୍ତିମାର୍ଗ, *n.* the way of devotion to God.
* ଭଗ, *n.* glory, fame, excellence, vigour; the vulva.
ଭଗନ୍ଦର, *n.* fistula in ano.
ଭଗବଦ୍‌ଗୀତା, *n.* the popular poem *Bhagabatgita,*—a Hindu religious book teaching of the theological section of the *Mahabharat.*
ଭଗବାନ୍, *n.* God;—*a.* divine, glorious.
ଭଗାରି, *n.* an enemy; *fem.* ଭଗାରୁଣୀ।
ଭଗାରପଣ, ଭଗାରପଣିଆ, *n.* enmity, opposition.
ଭଗିନୀ, ଭଗ୍ନୀ, *n.* a sister (see ଭଉଣୀ)।
ଭଗିଲ, *n.* sarcasm, gibe, sneer.
ଭଗ୍ନ, *a.* broken, fractured; defeated.
ଭଗ୍ନାଂଶ, *n.* a fractional part.
* ଭଗ୍ନାଶ, *a.* disappointed, hopeless.
ଭଙ୍ଗ, *n.* breaking; a breach; a wave; a disease of the mouth.
ଭଙ୍ଗପ୍ରବଣ, *a.* brittle, fragile.
ଭଙ୍ଗା, *a.* broken, cracked.
ଭଙ୍ଗାଇବା, *v.* to cause to break, crack, destroy; to change (money).
ଭଙ୍ଗି, ଭଙ୍ଗୀ, *n.* gesture, attitude; hint, repartee; trick.

* ଭଙ୍ଗିମା, *n.* **gesture, attitude; hint, repartee; trick, deception, irony; a fracture.**

*ଭଙ୍ଗୁର, *a.* brittle; transient, transitory, perishable; changeful, variable; crooked, bent;—*n.* the bend of a river.

ଭଜନ, *n.* a doxology, adoration, worshipping.

ଭଜନା, *n.* religious worship.

ଭଜନାଳୟ, *n.* a temple, a synagogue, place of worship.

ଭଜା, *n.* roasted meat or vegetables;—*a.* fried, parched, baked, roasted.

ଭଜିବା, *v.* to worship, to serve; to practice, to follow; to suffer, to experience; to love, to court, to show love for.

ଭଞ୍ଜନ, *n.* breaking, dissolving, settling.

ଭଟା, *n.* the ebb tide.

ଭଟ୍ଟାଚାର୍ଯ୍ୟ, *n.* a philosopher; a literary title.

ଭଟ୍‌ଭଟ୍, *n.* sound of talking, gibble-gabble.

ଭଡ଼, *n.* a kind of tobacco and *pán* leaf.

ଭଡ଼କ, *n.* fear, confusion; false display.

ଭଡ଼ଙ୍ଗା, *n.* a hooka.

ଭଡ଼କିବା, *v.* to escape or flee through fear.

ଭଡ଼ଙ୍ଗ, *n.* a false display; deception, imposition.

ଭଡ଼ଭଡ଼, *n.* sound of snuffling or snoring, etc.

17

ଭଡ଼ା, *n.* rent of a house, hire, freight, fare, cartage.

ଭଡ଼ାଟିଆ, *n.* a tenant; anything hired.

ଭଡ଼ୁଆ, *n.* a vagabond who lives upon the wages of prostitutes.

ଭଣଜା, *n.* a sister's son, nephew.

ଭଣଭଣ, *n.* a buzzing sound.

ଭଣଭଣାମାଛି, *n.* the blue-bottle fly.

ଭଣିତ, *a.* composed or written by.

ଭଣିତା, *n.* an author, composer.

ଭଣିବା, *v.* to write or compose; to utter, to speak.

ଭଣ୍ଡ, *n.* deceit, swindling; a dissembler; mimic, buffoon.

ଭଣ୍ଡତପସ୍ୱୀ, *n.* a hypocritical ascetic.

ଭଣ୍ଡା, *n.* the blossom-sheath of the plantain: calf of the leg.

ଭଣ୍ଡାଇବା, ଭଣ୍ଡିବା, *v.* to cheat or impose.

ଭଣ୍ଡାଇଣି, *n.* cheating or imposition.

ଭଣ୍ଡାମି, *n.* deceitfulness, imposition.

ଭଣ୍ଡାର, *n.* a treasury, storehouse.

ଭଣ୍ଡାରଘରିଆ, *n.* a steward, master of the wardrobe.

ଭଣ୍ଡାରୀ, *n.* a barber; *fem.* ଭଣ୍ଡାରୁଣୀ।

ଭଣ୍ଡି, *n.* the cob or cone of Indian corn, jack-fruit, &c.

ଭଣ୍ଡୁର, ଭଣ୍ଡୋର, *a.* interrupted, hindered; gone bad;—*n.* interruption, hindrance; failure.

ଭଦଭଦଳିଆ, *n.* the skylark.

ଭଦ୍ର, *a.* good, respectable;—*n.* welfare.

ଭଦ୍ରତା, *n.* goodness, respectability

ଭଦ୍ରାଭଦ୍ର, *n.* good and evil.

*ଭବ, *n.* the world; existence, state of being; welfare, prosperity.

* ଭବଦୀୟ, *pron.* thine, yours.

* ଭବନ, *n.* a house, edifice.

* ଭବାଦୃଶ, *a.* like you (honorific).

ଭବାନୀ, *n.* a name of *Durgá.*

ଭବାବ୍ଧି, ଭବାର୍ଣ୍ଣବ, *n.* the ocean of the world; being.

ଭଭସ, *n.* display, great fuss.

ଭବିଷ୍ୟତ୍, ଭବିଷ୍ୟ, ଭବିତ, *a.* future, about to be.

ଭବିଷ୍ୟତ୍କାଳ, *n.* (in *Gram.*) future tense.

ଭବିଷ୍ୟଦ୍ବକ୍ତା, *n.* a prophet, predictor.

ଭବିଷ୍ୟଦ୍ବାକ୍ୟ, ଭବିଷ୍ୟଦ୍ବାଣୀ, *n.* a prophecy.

* ଭବ୍ୟ, *a.* polite; auspicious; probable.

* ଭବ୍ୟତା, *n.* politeness, urbanity.

ଭୟ, *n.* fear, dread, alarm, terror.

ଭୟଙ୍କର, *a.* causing fear, terrible, dreadful.

ଭୟଜନକ, ଭୟାବହ, *a.* terrifying, fearsome, fearful.

ଭୟଶୀଳ, *a.* timid, fearful, cowardly.

ଭୟାନକ, *a.* formidable, terrific.

ଭୟାନକତା, *n.* awfulness, frightfulness.

ଭୟାଳୁ, *a.* fearful, timid.

ଭୟାବହ, *a.* alarming, terrible.

ଭରଣ, *n.* a measure for grain consisting of 80 *Gaunis*; a full cart-load; * filling up; nourishing.

ଭରଣପୋଷଣ, *n.* food and clothing maintenance.

ଭରଣା, *n.* fulness.

ଭରଣେ, *a.* and *n.* as much as can be loaded on a cart, (as ଭରଣେ ଧାନ) ।

ଭରତ, *n.* brother of *Ráma*; a skylark.

ଭରତପକ୍ଷୀ, ଭରତଏ, *n.* a skylark.

ଭରଦ୍ୱାଜ, *n.* a skylark; name of a sage.

ଭରପୂର, *a.* full, brimful.

ଭରସା, *n.* hope, expectation; courage.

ଭରସାଯୁକ୍ତ, *a.* full of hope.

ଭରା, *a.* full;—*n.* a cargo; charge of a gun.

ଭରାଣ୍ଡି, *n.* the hole in which the *dhinki* works.

ଭରାଭର, *a.* completely full, thronged.

ଭରି, *n.* a rupee weight, ten *mashás.*

ଭରିଦେବା, ଭରାଇଦେବା, *v.* to make up for, to compensate.

ଭରିଦେବା, ଭରିବା, *v.* to fill.

* ଭର୍ଜ୍ଜନ, *n.* frying, parching, baking.

* ଭର୍ଜ୍ଜିତ, *a.* fried, parched, baked, roasted, (see ଭଜା) ।

ଭର୍ତ୍ତା, *n.* husband, a nourisher, protector.

ଭର୍ତ୍ତି, *n.* fulness; a load, cargo; entering.

ଭର୍ତ୍ସନା, *n.* reproach, censure.

ଭର୍ତ୍ସିତ, *a.* reproached, censured.

ଭଲ, *a.* good, excellent;—*ad.* well, splendidly.

ଭଲମନ୍ଦ, *n.* good and evil, well and ill.

ଭଲା, *ad.* well, very well, good.

ଭଲାବୋଲ, *n.* good and ill.

* ଭଲ୍ଲ, *n.* an arrow with a crescent-shaped head.

* ଭଲ୍ଲୁକ, ଭଲ୍ଲୂକ, *n.* a bear.

ଭଳି, *n.* kind, sort;—*ad.* like.

ଭସଭସ, *n.* sound of running water.

ଭସାଇବା, *n.* to set afloat on water.

ଭସ୍ମ, *n.* ashes.

ଭସ୍ମସାତ୍, * ଭସ୍ମୀଭୂତ, *a.* burnt to ashes, reduced to ashes.

ଭକ୍ଷକ, *n.* an eater.

ଭକ୍ଷଣ, *n.* eating.

ଭକ୍ଷଣୀୟ, ଭକ୍ଷ୍ୟ, *a.* eatable, fit for food.

ଭକ୍ଷିତ, *a.* eaten, devoured.

* ଭକ୍ଷ୍ୟ, *n.* anything eatable, food.

ଭାଇ, *n.* brother, cousin; friend.

ଭାଇବୋହୂ, *n.* a younger brother's wife.

ଭାଉ, *n.* rate, price, value.

ଭାଉଜ, *n.* an elder brother's wife.

ଭାଷା, *n.* vernacular language.

ଭାକୁଡ, ଭାକୁର, *n.* a species of fish.

ଭାଗ, *n.* a part, portion, share; division.

ଭାଗଫଳ, *n.* (in *Arith.*) a quotient.

ଭାଗବତ, *a.* devoted to *Vishnu*;—*n.* a Hindu shastra *Bhagabat.*

ଭାଗଶେଷ, *n.* a remainder.

ଭାଗ-ହାର, *n.* (in *Arith.*) the process of division, division.

* ଭାଗିନେୟ, *n.* see ଭଣଜା ।

ଭାଗୀ, *n.* a sharer, partner, an accomplice;—*a.* partaking with.

ଭାଗୀଦାର, *n.* a sharer, co-partner.

ଭାଗୀରଥୀ, *n.* the river Ganges.

ଭାଗ୍ୟ, *n.* good luck, destiny.

ଭାଗ୍ୟବାନ୍, ଭାଗ୍ୟବନ୍ତ, *a.* fortunate, lucky, well off.

ଭାଙ୍ଗ, *n.* hemp, an intoxicating drug.

ଭାଙ୍ଗିବା, *v.* to break, split.

ଭାଜକ, *n.* the divisor in arithmetic.

ଭାଜନ, *a.* worthy, fit, suitable.

ଭାଜିବା, *v.* to fry, to parch.

ଭାଜା, *n.* anything fried or parched.

ଭାଜ୍ୟ, *a.* divisible;—*n.* (in *Arith.*) the dividend.

ଭାଟ, *n.* a panegyrist, a bard; a royal messenger.

ଭାଟୀ, *n.* a furnace, a kiln, a still.

ଭାଟୁଇ, *n.* a quail.

ଭାଡ, *n.* a raised platform for stacking anything upon.

ଭାଣିଜୀ, *n.* sister's daughter.

ଭାଣ୍ଡ, *n.* an earthen vessel; a juggler; buffoon.

ଭାତ, *n.* boiled rice, food.

ଭାଥି, *n.* a blacksmith's bellows.

ଭାତୁଆ, *n.* one who serves for food (used in a derogatory sense).

ଭାତୁଡ, *n.* a kind of boil or pimple.

ଭାଦ୍ରବ, * ଭାଦ୍ରପଦ, ଭାଦ୍ର, *n.* an Indian month, part of Aug. and Sept.

* ଭାନୁ, *n.* the sun; a ray of light.

ଭାପ, ଭାମ୍ପ, *n.* steam, vapour, gas.

ଭାବ, *n.* idea, meaning, sentiment, disposition; drift; love, friendship.

ଭାବନା, *n.* anxiety, care, concern; thought, reflection.

ଭାବାର୍ଥ, *n.* purport, subject matter.

ଭାବିତ, *a.* anxious, apprehensive.

ଭାବୀ, *a.* future, about to be.

ଭାବୁକ, *n.* an appreciator of a sentiment.

ଭାର, *n.* weight, load, burden, a charge; a banghy load; yoke.

ଭାରକେନ୍ଦ୍ର, *n.* centre of gravity.

ଭାରଗ୍ରସ୍ତ, *a.* heavy-laden.

ଭାରତ, *n.* the *Mahabharat.*

ଭାରତ, ଭାରତବର୍ଷ, *n.* India.

* ଭାରତୀ, *n.* *Saraswati*; speech; a quail. [burden.

ଭାରବାହକ, * ଭାରବାହ, *n.* bearer of a

ଭାରା, *n.* a scaffolding.

ଭାରାକ୍ରାନ୍ତ, *a.* loaded, entrusted with.

ଭାରି, ଭାରୀ, *a.* heavy, important, weighty.

ଭାରୁଆ, *n.* a bearer of burdens, a banghy-man.

ଭାର୍ଯ୍ୟା, *n.* a wife. [sider.

ଭାଳିବା, *v.* to think, reflect, con-

* ଭାଳ, *n.* forehead.

ଭାଲୁ, * ଭାଲୁକ, *n.* a bear.

ଭାଷଣ, *n.* talking, speaking, conversing.

ଭାଷା, *n.* language; dialect; style.

ଭାଷାନ୍ତର, *n.* translation, a different language.

ଭାଷାନ୍ତରିତ, *a.* translated.

ଭାଷୀ, *a.* speaking (used as an *affix*). [tion.

* ଭାଷ୍ୟ, *n.* a commentary, exposi-

ଭାସନ୍ତା, ଭାସମାନ, *a.* floating.

ଭାସିବା, *v.* to float; to be borne on the flood.

ଭାସ୍କର, *n.* a sculptor, stone-cutter; * the sun.

* ଭାସ୍ୱର, *a.* shining, bright, radiant.

ଭିଆଇବା, *v.* to bring forth, produce.

ଭିଆଣ, *n.* the originating or proposing of a matter; a record of assessment.

ଭିକ, *n.* alms, begging. [cant.

ଭିକାରି, ଭିକାରୀ, *n.* a beggar, mendi-

ଭିକାରୁଣୀ, *n.* a female beggar.

ଭିଜା, *a.* wet, moist, damp.

ଭିଜାଇବା, ଭିଜେଇବା, *v.* to wet, to moisten, to saturate.

ଭିଡ଼, *n.* a crowd, multitude, mob.

ଭିଡ଼ାଭିଡ଼ି, *n.* a tugging or hugging; a binding or tightening.

ଭିଡ଼ିବା, *v.* to tie, to bind, to tighten, to pull.

ଭିଡ଼ୁଣୀ, *n.* a binder for the hair.

ଭିଣିବା, *v.* to prepare or pick cotton, etc.

ଭିଣୋଇ, *n.* a sister's husband.

ଭିତର, *n.* the inside, interior, centre.

ଭିତରେ, *ad.* in, within, between.

* ଭିତ୍ତି, *n.* a foundation, structure, wall.

ଭିନ୍ନ, *a.* separate, different, distinct; other;—*ad.* besides,

ଭିନ୍ନଭିନ୍ନ, *ad.* separately, distinctly.

ଭିନ୍ନତା, *n.* a distinction, a difference.

ଭିକ୍ଷା, *n.* begging; alms.

ଭିକ୍ଷାପାତ୍ର, *n.* a begging-bowl, an alms-dish.

ଭିକ୍ଷାବୃତ୍ତି, *n.* living by begging.

ଭିକ୍ଷାଶୀ, *a.* living on alms.

ଭିକ୍ଷୁ, *n.* a religious mendicant, a beggar.

ଭିକ୍ଷୁକ, *n.* a beggar, mendicant.

ଭିସ୍ତି, *n.* a water-carrier.

ଭୀତ, *a.* afraid, terrified, alarmed.

ଭୀମ, *n.* one of the five *Pandava* princes;—**a.* dreadful, terrific, awful.

ଭୀରୁ, *a.* timid, afraid, fearful.

ଭୀରୁତା, *n.* fear, timidity, fearfulness.

ଭୀଷଣ, *a.* dreadful, terrific, awful.

ଭୀଷଣତା, *n.* frightfulness, dreadfulness

ଭୁଁଆବୁଲିବା, *v.* to wander having lost the way.

ଭୁଆ, *n.* a tomcat.

ଭୁଆସୁଣୀ, *n.* a newly-wedded wife.

* ଭୁକ୍ତ, *a.* eaten; included, comprised in.

ଭୁକ୍ତଭୋଗୀ, *a.* enjoying and suffering, well-experienced.

* ଭୁକ୍ତାବଶିଷ୍ଟ, ଭୁକ୍ତାବଶେଷ, *n.* leavings of food, orts.

ଭୁଜ, *n.* the arm, the hand.

* ଭୁଜଗ, ଭୁଜଙ୍ଗ, *n.* a serpent, snake.

ଭୁଜା, *n.* parched rice.

ଭୁଞ୍ଜିବା, *v.* to eat, to enjoy.

ଭୁଡ଼ଭୁଡ଼, *n.* a bubbling sound.

ଭୁଡ଼ଙ୍ଗ, *n.* a large trumpet.

ଭୁଣ୍ଡି, *n.* a kind of knot or knob.

ଭୁଣି, *n.* a widow's garment without border.

* ଭୁବନ, *n.* the universe.

ଭୁର, *n.* a kind of sugar.

ଭୁଲ, *n.* a mistake, blunder, error, oversight.

ଭୁଲାଇବା, *v.* to deceive, delude.

ଭୁଲିବା, *v.* to mistake, to forget, to omit.

ଭୁଷିବା, *v.* to thrust, to stab.

ଭୁଷା, ଭୁଷୀ, *n.* bran, husk, chaff.

ଭୁଶୁଡ଼ିବା, ଭୁଶୁଡ଼ିପଡ଼ିବା, *v.* to fall in, to collapse.

ଭୂଇଁ, *n.* land, ground.

ଭୂଇଁକମ୍ପ, ଭୂକମ୍ପ, *n.* an earthquake.

ଭୂଗର୍ଭ, *n.* inside of the earth.

ଭୂଗୋଳ, ଭୂଗୋଳକ, *n.* the globe, earth.

ଭୂଗୋଳ, ଭୂଗୋଳବିଦ୍ୟା, *n.* geography.

ଭୂଚର, *a.* moving on land, terrestrial.

ଭୂତ, *n.* ghost, evil spirit;—*a.* passed, past.

ଭୂତକାଳ, *n.* (in *Gram.*) past tense.

ଭୂତଗ୍ରସ୍ତ, *a.* possessed by a demon.

ଭୂତଭଣ୍ଡା, *n.* a conjurer, exorcist.

ଭୂତପୂର୍ବ, *a.* existed before, former.

ଭୂତଳ, *n.* the earth, its surface.

* ଭୂଦେବ, *n.* a *brahman.*

ଭୂପତି, * ଭୂପ, *n.* a king, sovereign

ଭୂମଣ୍ଡଳ, *n.* the earth; terrestrial globe.

ଭୂମି, *n.* ground, land, earth.

ଭୂମିକମ୍ପ, *n.* an earthquake.

ଭୂମିକା, *n.* a preface, introduction.

ଭୂମିଷ୍ଠ, *a.* flat on the ground; born of.

* ଭୂରି, *a.* plentiful, abundant.

* ଭ୍ରୂ, *n.* an eyebrow.

ଭୂର୍ଲୋକ, *n.* earth, human habitation.

ଭୂଷଣ, *n.* ornament, decoration.

* ଭୂଷା, *n.* an ornament, jewel, dress.

ଭୂଷିତ, *a.* adorned, ornamented.

ଭୂସ୍ୱାମୀ, *n.* a zemindar; a king.

* ଭୃଗୁ, *n.* a precipice, tableland.

* ଭୃଙ୍ଗ, *n.* the large black bee.

ଭୃଙ୍ଗରାଜ, *n.* a medicinal creeping plant.

ଭୃତ୍ୟ, *n.* a servant, dependent.

ଭେକ, *n.* dress, robe; disguise; * a frog.

ଭେକଟା, ଭେକୁଟା, *n.* name of a fish.

ଭେଟ, *n.* an interview, a meeting.

ଭେଟିବା, *v.* to meet.

ଭେଟାଭେଟି, *n.* a mutual interview.

ଭେଟୀ, *n.* a present, gift at meeting; a superior.

ଭେଡା, *n.* a sheep, a ram.

ଭେଣ୍ଡା, *n.* a young man; *fem.* ଭେଣ୍ଡୀ ।

ଭେଣ୍ଡି, *n.* name of a vegetable.

ଭେଦ, *n.* division, distinction; * purging.

ଭେଦକ, *a.* piercing, cathartic;—*n.* one who sows dissension.

ଭେଦଜ୍ଞାନ, *n.* power of discrimination.

* ଭେଦନ, *n.* piercing, rending, splitting.

ଭେଦା, *n.* a collection, contribution.

ଭେଦାଭେଦ, *n.* separation and union.

ଭେଦାଭେଦଜ୍ଞାନ, *n.* discriminating knowledge, discrimination.

ଭେଦିଆ, ଭେଦୁଆ, *n.* a pryer into secrets; one who discriminates.

ଭେଦ୍ୟ, *n.* a purgative medicine;—*a.* * penetrating, separating.

ଭେରଣ୍ଡା, *n.* a male jackal; * the castor-oil plant.

ଭେରି, ଭେରୀ, *n.* a long trumpet.

ଭେଲ୍କି, *n.* magic, sleight of hand.

ଭେଳା, *n.* a raft, a float.

ଭେଳ, *n.* alloy; a trick; a fraud.

* ଭେଷଜ, *n.* a drug, a medicine, medicament.

ଭେଷଣ୍ଡା, *a.* ugly, ill-shaped;—*n.* a foul-mouthed fellow.

ଭେଷଣୀ, *n.* a slattern. [*Siva.*

*ଭୈରବ, *a.* terrible, dreadful;—*n.*

*ଭୈଷଜ୍ୟ, *n.* a medicine, a drug; —*a.* curative. [so ho!

ଭୋ, *n.* a vocative particle, O ho!

ଭୋଇ, *n* a surname of the *Báuri* caste.

ଭୋକ, *n.* hunger.

ଭୋକିଲା, ଭୋକଲା, *a.* hungry.

*ଭୋକ୍ତା, *n.* an eater, a glutton; one who bears (either in enjoyment or suffering). [ing.

ଭୋଗ, *n.* enjoyment; suffering; eat-

ଭୋଗବାନ୍, *a.* enjoying, suffering.

ଭୋଗରାଗ, *n.* offering of food to a god.

ଭୋଗା, *n.* imposture, cheat.

ଭୋଗାଭୋଗ, *n.* enjoyment or non-enjoyment.

ଭୋଗୀ, *a.* sensual, enjoying.

ଭୋଗ୍ୟ, *a.* capable of being enjoyed or suffered.

ଭୋଜ, *n.* a feast, a banquet, a meal.

ଭୋଜନ, *n* eating, taking a meal.

ଭୋଜବାଜି, ଭୋଜବିଦ୍ୟା, *n.* sleight of hand, conjuring, magic.

ଭୋଜ୍ୟ, *n.* anything that can be eaten.

ଭୋଟ, *n.* a blanket from Bhutan, a native of Bhutan.

ଭୋପା, *n.* an attendant on a temple of *Mahádeb.*

ଭୋର, *n.* early dawn, morning.

ଭୋଳ, *a.* forgetful, half-witted;—*n.* escape of water. [witted.

ଭୋଳା, *a.* forgetful, stupid, half-

ଭୌତିକ, *a.* material; relating to evil spirits. [stance.

ଭୌତିକପଦାର୍ଥ, *n.* elementary sub-

*ଭୌମ, *a.* terrestrial;—*n.* the planet Mars.

*ଭୌମିକ, *a.* belonging to land, produced from the ground.

*ଭ୍ରଂଶ, *n.* a fall; depravity, ruin.

ଭ୍ରମ, *n.* error, mistake, delusion.

ଭ୍ରମଣ, *n.* walking, going about or astray.

ଭ୍ରମଣକାରୀ, *n.* a traveller, a wanderer, one who walks.

ଭ୍ରମର, *n.* a large black bee.

*ଭ୍ରମି, *n.* an eddy; a whirlwind.

ଭ୍ରମିବା, *v.* to go or wander about; to whirl or move round; to go astray; to travel.

ଭ୍ରଷ୍ଟ, *a.* fallen from virtue; depraved, corrupted.

ଭ୍ରଷ୍ଟତା, *n.* corruption, depravity.

ଭ୍ରଷ୍ଟା, *n.* an adulteress, a bad woman.

ଭ୍ରଷ୍ଟାଚାର, *n.* depraved conduct.

ଭ୍ରାତା, *n.* a brother.

*ଭ୍ରାତୃପୁତ୍ର, *n.* a brother's son, nephew.

*ଭ୍ରାତୃ-ଜାୟା, *n.* elder brother's wife.

ଭ୍ରାନ୍ତ, *a.* gone astray; mistaken.

ଭ୍ରାନ୍ତି, *n.* mistake, error, straying.

*ଭ୍ରାମକ, *a.* misleading.

* ଭ୍ରୂ, *n.* the eyebrow. [glance.
ଭ୍ରୂକୁଟି, ଭ୍ରୁକୁଟି, *n.* a frown, scowl,
ଭ୍ରୂଣ, *n.* a fœtus, embryo.
ଭ୍ରୂଣହତ୍ୟା, *n.* procuring abortion.
ଭ୍ରୂଭଙ୍ଗ, ଭ୍ରୂଭଙ୍ଗି, ଭ୍ରୂଭଙ୍ଗୀ, *n.* a frown; distortion of the eyebrow.
* ଭ୍ରୂଲତା, *n.* the brow.
ଭ୍ରୂକ୍ଷେପ, *n.* a frown, a glance.

ମ.

ମ, the 25th consonant.
ମଇଳ, *n.* dirt, filth.
ମଇ, *n.* a kind of harrow.
ମଇତ୍ର, *n.* a friend.
ମଇଦା, *n.* flour.
ମଇଦାନ, *n.* a plain, meadow.
ମଇନା, *n.* name of a bird, a *myna.*
ମଇଳା, *a.* dirty, unclean;—*n.* dirt, filth.
ମଇଁଷି, *n.* a buffalo.
ମଇଁଷିପାଳ, *n.* a man who tends a buffalo-herd.
ମଉଡ, ମଉଡ଼, *n.* a crown.
ମଉନ, *a.* silent, speechless.
ମଉରସି, *a.* hereditary.
ମଉରି, *n.* aniseed.
ମଉଳା, ମଉସା, *n.* a maternal uncle.
ମଉଳିବା, *v.* to fade, to droop.
ମକଚିବା, *v.* to wrench, to twist.
ମକଦମ, *n.* a village collector.
ମକଦମୀ, *n.* land rented from a zemindar.
ମକଦମା, ମୋକଦମା, *n.* a law-suit; an affair.
ମକର, *n.* the sign Capricorn; * a marine monster.
ମକରକ୍ରାନ୍ତି, *n.* tropic of Capricorn.
ମକରଧ୍ୱଜ, *n.* name of a medicine; * the Hindu cupid.
ମକରନ୍ଦ, *n.* the honey of a flower.
ମକା, *n.* Indian corn or maize.
ମକୁଟ, *n.* crown, diadem. [silk.
ମକୁଟା, *n.* cloth or *dhoti* made of
ମକୁଫ, *a.* deferred, postponed, left off.
ମକୁଳ, *n.* a bud, blossom-bud.
ମଖନ, *n.* butter.
ମଖମଲ, ମଖ୍ମଲ୍, *n.* velvet.
ମଖାଇବା, *v.* to anoint, to smear (another).
ମଗଜ, *n.* the brains, marrow, pith.
ମଗଜି, *n.* a border, hem, an edging.
ମଗଦୁର, *n.* power, strength, ability.
ମଗଦୁରମତ, *ad.* according to one's power, strength or ability.
ମଗର, *n.* see ମକର ।
ମଗର, *a.* sulky, obstinate, head-strong.
ମଗାମଗି, *n.* asking, begging for.
ମଗାମଗୁ, *n.* asking and offering.
ମଗୁଶିର, *n.* name of a month, part of Nov. and Dec. [ed.
ମଗ୍ନ, *a.* immersed, sunk, overwhelm-
ମଙ୍ଗ, *n.* prow of boat or ship,
ମଙ୍ଗଧର, *n.* helm of a boat or ship.

ମଙ୍ଗଣ, ମଙ୍ଗଳଖାଣ, *n.* the ceremony observed on the day before the marriage.

ମଙ୍ଗଳ, *n.* welfare, prosperity; Mars.

ମଙ୍ଗଳକୃତ୍ୟ, *n.* marriage, a solemn ceremony.

ମଙ୍ଗଳବାର, *n.* Tuesday.

ମଙ୍ଗଳସମାଚାର, *n.* good news, the Gospel.

ମଙ୍ଗଳା, *n.* name of a goddess.

ମଙ୍ଗଳାଚରଣ, *n.* a propitiatory ceremony or prayer.

ମଙ୍ଗାଇବା, *v.* to persuade.

ମଙ୍ଗିବା, *v.* to consent, to acquiesce.

ମଙ୍ଗୁଆଳ, *n.* a helmsman.

ମଘା, *n.* the tenth stellar mansion.

ମଚକବା, *v.* see ମଚକିବା ।

ମଚଳା, *n.* a disease of the scrotum.

* ମତ୍ସ୍ୟ, *n.* fish, fish incarnation.

ମଦୁକ୍ତ, *a.* before-mentioned, aforesaid.

ମଜବୁତ, *n.* strong, firm, tough.

ମଜଗ, *n.* weariness, fatigue.

ମଜଲିସ୍, *n.* an assembly, company.

ମଜା, *n.* a flavour, taste; delight, pleasure, enjoyment;—*a.* rubbed, chafed, cleansed.

ମଜାମଜ, *n.* continued rubbing or chafing.

ମଜୁରା, *n.* payment of what is due.

ମଜୁରୀ, *n.* wages for labour, hire.

* ମଜ୍ଜନ, *n.* immersion, plunging, a sinking in water or distress.

ମଜ୍ଜା, *n.* marrow, pith, sap.

ମଜ୍ଜାଗତ, *a.* affecting the marrow, inward.

ମଝାଲି, ମଝି, *n.* the middle or centre.

ମଝିଆଁ, *a.* middle (son, brother, etc.) *fem.* ମଝିଆଣୀ ।

ମଞ୍ଚ, *n.* the earth; platform, stage; bedstead.

ମଞ୍ଚା, *n.* a stage; watch-tower; *machán.*

ମଞ୍ଜ, *n.* the pith of timber or trees.

* ମଞ୍ଜରି, ମଞ୍ଜରୀ, *n.* an ear of corn; a spike of flowers.

* ମଞ୍ଜରିତ, *a.* budded.

ମଞ୍ଜା, *n.* the pith of a plantain tree.

* ମଞ୍ଜାରୀ, *n.* a cat.

ମଞ୍ଜି, ମଞ୍ଜୀ, *n.* seed; the spawn of fish.

ମଞ୍ଜିଷ୍ଠା, *n.* the Indian madder.

* ମଞ୍ଜୀର, *n.* tinkling ornament for the ankle.

* ମଞ୍ଜୁ, *a.* beautiful, captivating.

ମଞ୍ଜୁଆତ, *n.* name of a tree, the privet.

ମଞ୍ଜୁର, *a.* approved, chosen, admitted.

ମଞ୍ଜୁରି, *n.* approval, sanction.

* ମଞ୍ଜୁଳ, *a.* beautiful, agreeable, pleasing.

* ମଞ୍ଜୁଷ, ମଞ୍ଜୁଷା, *n.* a box, a chest; a wicker or cane basket.

ମଟ୍କା, *a.* apt to break easily, fragile;—*n.* ridge of a thatched roof; the name of an edible jungle fruit.

ମଟ୍ମଟ୍, *n.* staring with distended eyes.

ମଟକାପାଣି, *n.* dropping ot water through a roof.

ମଟର, *n.* a pea, peas.

ମଟାସ, *n.* a T square, a builder's square L; an instrument having right angles.

ମଟାଲ, *n.* clay;—*a.* clayey.

ମଠ, *n.* a monastery, abbey; delay.

ମଠଧାରୀ, *n.* chief of a monastery; —*a.* being in charge of a monastery.

ମଠା, *n.* cloth made of tassar or raw silk.

ମଠୁଆ, *a.* lazy, slothful, dilatory.

ମଡକ, *n.* a pestilence; mortality.

ମଡମଡ, *n.* a crunching sound.

ମଡା, *n.* a corpse, dead body.

ମଡାଇବା, *v.* to cause to set foot on, to trample or tread down; to cause to press; to cause to intertwine or climb.

ମଡାମଡି, *n.* a trampling or treading down.

ମଢ, *n.* a corpse.

ମଢିଆ, *n.* a Brahman who assists at the burning of a body; a hut.

ମଢୁଆ, *n.* the fibres of the *tál* leaf.

ମଣା, ମଣୁଆ, *a.* broken-in, trained.

ମଣାଇବା, *v.* to persuade, to bring over.

ମଣି, *n.* a precious stone, a gem.

* ମଣିକାର, *n.* a lapidary, a jeweller.

ମଣିବନ୍ଧ, *n.* the wrist (medical term).

ମଣିବା, *v.* to regard, acquiesce.

ମଣିମା, *n.* a mode of address to a raja or rani.

ମଣିହାରୁ, *n.* a jeweller, a seller of trinkets.

ମଣୋହି, *n.* the meal of a raja or great person.

ମଣ୍ଡ, *n.* starch, paste.

ମଣ୍ଡନ, *n.* plating, gilding; ornamentation.

ମଣ୍ଡପ, *n.* a house for a god; a hall, a booth, a *pandal.*

ମଣ୍ଡଳ, *n.* a circle, * a district.

ମଣ୍ଡଳାକାର, *a.* circular, round.

ମଣ୍ଡଳୀ, *n.* a church, a society, congregation.

* ମଣ୍ଡଳେଶ୍ୱର, *n.* a raja.

ମଣ୍ଡା, *n.* a cake or pasty.

ମଣ୍ଡିତ, *a.* overlaid, plated, adorned.

ମଣ୍ଡିବା, *v.* to adorn, to decorate, to clothe, to dress.

* ମଣ୍ଡୁକ, *n.* a frog; *fem.* ମଣ୍ଡୁକୀ ।

ମତ, *n.* opinion: mode, manner; doctrine.

* ମତଙ୍ଗଜ, *n.* an elephant.

ମତଲବ, *n.* purpose, intention, wish.

ମତାଇବା, *n.* to persuade, to influence.

ମତାନ୍ତର, *n.* another opinion;—*a.* changed.

ମତାବଲମ୍ବନ, *n.* following an opinion.

ମତାବଲମ୍ବୀ, *n.* a professor of any given doctrine.

ମତାମତ, *n.* approval and disapproval.

ମନ, *n.* mind, inclination, feeling.

ମନଭ୍ରମ, ମନଭ୍ରଂଶ. *n.* loss of sense.

*ମତିମାନ୍, *a.* judicious, reflecting, wise.

ମତୁଆଳା, ମତୁଆଳ, *a.* mad, drunk, drunken.

ମତେ, *ad.* according to, agreeably to;—*pron.* me

ମତ୍ତ, *a.* intoxicated, drunk, mad, insane; ruttish, lustful; excited with joy; proud, arrogant; *fem.* ମତ୍ତା ।

*ମତ୍ସର, *n.* envy, jealousy; hostility;—*a.* envious, grudging.

ମତ୍ସ୍ୟ, *n.* fish.

*ମତ୍ସ୍ୟଜୀବୀ, *n.* a fisherman.

ମତ୍ସ୍ୟଧାରୀ, *n.* a fisherman.

*ମଥନ, *n.* churning, agitating, stirring.

ମଥା, *n.* the head.

ମଥାତେଲ, *n.* oil, lamp oil.

ମଥାନ, *n.* the ridge of a house.

ମଥାମଣି, *n.* ornament for the head.

ମଦ, *n.* spirituous liquor; ardent passion.

ମଦତ, *n.* a narcotic drug prepared from opium; assistance, help.

*ମଦନ, *n.* cupid;—*a.* exhilarating.

ମଦନମୋହନ, *n.* *Krushna*;—*a.* very beautiful.

*ମଦାତଙ୍କ, ମଦାତ୍ୟୟ, *n.* any indisposition (such as head-ache, etc.,) resulting from drunkenness.

ମଦାନ୍ଧ, *a.* blinded by intoxication, dead drunk

ମଦାର, *n.* charge, trust, responsibility.

*ମଦିରା, *n.* strong liquor.

*ମଦୀୟ, *pron.* my, mine.

ମଦୁଆ, *ମଦ୍ୟପ, *n.* a tippler, a sot;—*a.* sottish.

*ମଦୋତ୍କଟ, *a.* intoxicated; lustful; proud, haughty; ruttish;—*n.* a ruttish elephant.

ମଦ୍ୟ, *n.* intoxicating liquor.

*ମଦ୍ୟଜୀବୀ, *n.* a seller of spirits.

*ମଦ୍ୟଶାଳା, *n.* a liquor-shop.

ମଧୁ, *n.* honey, nectar.

*ମଧୁକର, *n.* the humble bee; a bee.

ମଧୁକାଳ, ମଧୁମାସ, *n.* springtime, the spring, the month of *Chaitra*.

*ମଧୁକୋଷ, ମଧୁକ୍ରମ, ମଧୁଚକ୍ର, *n.* a honeycomb, a bee-hive.

*ମଧୁପ, ମଧୁବ୍ରତ, *n.* a bee, black bee.

ମଧୁମୟ, *a.* sweet, pleasant, agreeable, honied.

ମଧୁମକ୍ଷିକା, *n.* the honey bee.

*ମଧୁଯଷ୍ଟିକା, ଯଷ୍ଟିମଧୁ, *n.* liquorice root.

ମଧୁର, *a.* sweet, agreeable, pleasant.

ମଧୁସୂଦନ, *n.* a name of *Krushna.*

ମଧ୍ୟ, *n.* the middle, centre;—*a.* central;—*ad.* also.

*ମଧ୍ୟତଃ, *ad.* in the middle.

*ମଧ୍ୟଦିନ, *n.* noon, the middle of the day. [C. P.

ମଧ୍ୟପ୍ରଦେଶ, *n.* the central province,

ମଧ୍ୟବର୍ତ୍ତୀ, *a.* situated between, inward, internal.

ମଧ୍ୟମ, ମଧ୍ୟବିତ୍ତ, *a.* middling, ordinary.

* ମଧ୍ୟମା, *n.* the middle finger.

ମଧ୍ୟରାତ୍ର, *n.* midnight.

ମଧ୍ୟସ୍ଥ, *a.* in the midst, central, inward;—*n.* a mediator.

ମଧ୍ୟାହ୍ନ, *n.* midday, noon.

ମଧ୍ୟେ, *ad.* in the midst, within.

ମଧ୍ୟେ୨, *ad.* meantime, sometimes.

ମନ, ମନଃ, *n.* the mind, heart, conscience.

ମନଃପୀଡ଼ା, *n.* mental distress, anguish.

ମନଃସ୍ଥ, *a.* situated in the mind;—*n.* determination, purpose.

ମନକୁ, *ad.* by itself.

ମନଦେବା, *v.* to give heed to.

* ମନନ, *n.* thinking, reflecting, minding.

ମନସ୍କାମ, ମନସ୍କାମନା, *n.* mental desire, wish.

ମନସ୍ତାପ, *n.* mental pain, remorse.

ମନସ୍ୱୀ, *a.* intelligent, wise; high-minded; *fem.* ମନସ୍ୱିନୀ ।

ମନା, *n.* a prohibition, prevention.

ମନାସ, *n.* the wish or desire of the mind.

ମନାସିବା, *v.* to wish, to desire.

* ମନୀଷା, *n.* intellect, understanding.

* ମନୀଷୀ, *a.* wise, learned, intelligent.

ମନୁ, *n.* *Manu*—the Hindu legislator.

ମନୁଆ, *a.* whimsical, wilful.

ମନୁଷ୍ୟ, * ମନୁଜ, *n.* a human being.

ମନୁଷ୍ୟଜାତି, *n.* mankind, human race.

ମନୁଷ୍ୟତ୍ୱ, ମନୁଷ୍ୟତା, *n.* manliness, manhood, humanity.

ମନୁଷ୍ୟଭକ୍ଷକ, * ମନୁଷ୍ୟଭୋଜୀ, *a.* feeding on human flesh;—*n.* a cannibal.

ମନେକରିବା, *v.* to remember, to recollect; to think, to reflect.

ମନେହେବା, *v.i.* to be remembered or recollected.

ମନୋଗତ, *a.* situated in the mind, mental.

* ମନୋଜ୍ଞ, *a.* engaging, beautiful.

ମନୋଦୁଃଖ, *n.* mental distress.

ମନୋନିବେଶ, *n.* close attention.

ମନୋନୀତ, *a.* chosen, approved.

ମନୋବାଞ୍ଛା, *n.* a wish of the heart, a desire.

* ମନୋବିକାର, *n.* emotion of the mind.

ମନୋବିଜ୍ଞାନ, *n.* metaphysics.

* ମନୋବୃତ୍ତି, *n.* the operations of the mind.

ମନୋବ୍ୟଥା, *n.* pain of mind, grief.

* ମନୋଭଙ୍ଗ, *n.* distraction, melancholy.

ମନୋମତ, *a.* agreeable to the mind.

ମନୋଯୋଗ, *n.* attention, application.

ମନୋଯୋଗୀ, *a.* attentive, earnest.

ମନୋରଞ୍ଜନ, *n.* gratification of the mind, pleasure.

ମନୋରଥ, *n.* a wish, a desire.

ମନୋରମ, ମନୋରମ୍ୟ, *a.* inviting, pleasant, agreeable.

ମନୋହର, *a.* captivating, winning, beautiful.

ମନ୍ତବ୍ୟ, *n.* remarks, reflection;—*a.* * worthy of regard, fit to be thought upon.

ମନ୍ତ୍ର, *n.* a form of prayer, a mystical charm.

ମନ୍ତ୍ରଜ୍ଞ, *a.* versed in the *mantras.*

ମନ୍ତ୍ରଣା, *n.* counsel, consultation, advice; plot.

ମନ୍ତ୍ରଦାତା, *n.* a preceptor, mentor.

ମନ୍ତ୍ରୀ, *n.* a counsellor, minister of state.

ମନ୍ଥନ, *n.* churning, stirring.

* ମନ୍ଥନଦଣ୍ଡ, *n.* a churning-stick.

* ମନ୍ଥନୀ, *n.* a churn.

* ମନ୍ଥର, *a.* slow, heavy, dilatory.

ମନ୍ଥା, *a.* churned, stirred.

ମନ୍ଦ, *a.* evil, bad, vile; slow, gentle.

* ମନ୍ଦଗତି, *a.* slow, sluggish.

ମନ୍ଦମନ୍ଦ, *ad.* mildly, gently.

ମନ୍ଦହାସ, *n.* a smile, a simper.

ମନ୍ଦା, *n.* a swarm of fish or of insects; a hollow at the root of trees to retain water.

ମନ୍ଦାଏ, *a.* a little (water).

* ମନ୍ଦାକିନୀ, *n.* the galaxy.

ମନ୍ଦାଗ୍ନି, *n.* indigestion, dyspepsia.

* ମନ୍ଦାଦର, *a.* negligent, disrespectful.

ମନ୍ଦାମନ୍ଦା, *ad.* in swarms, in small heaps.

ମନ୍ଦାର, *n.* Hibiscus; a tree of paradise.

ମନ୍ଦିର, *n.* a temple, mansion.

ମନ୍ଦିରା, *n.* small cymbals.

ମନ୍ଦୁରା, *n.* a mat; * a stable.

* ମନ୍ଦୋଷ୍ଣ, *n.* lukewarm.

* ମନ୍ଦ୍ର, *n.* a deep sound, thunder; —*a.* deep, low, rumbling.

* ମନ୍ମଥ, *n.* a name of cupid.

* ମନ୍ୟୁ, *n.* resentment, wrath.

* ମନ୍ୱନ୍ତର, *n.* seventy-one *yugas* or ages.

ମପା, *a.* measured, weighed.

ମପାଇବା, *v.* to cause to measure or weigh; to cause to be measured.

ମପାମପି, *n.* the act of measuring or weighing.

ମଫସଲ, *n.* the rural district, country.

ମବଲଗ, *n.* ready money, cash.

* ମମ, *pron.* my, mine (poetical).

ମମତା, * ମମତ୍ୱ, *n.* sense of ownership; affectionate regard, attachment to, regard for.

ମୟଦାନ, *n.* a meadow, a plain, prairie.

ମୟନା, *n.* a *myna.*

* ମୟୂଖ, *n.* a ray, lustre, a flame.

ମୟୂର, *n.* a peacock.

ମୟୂରପୁଚ୍ଛ, *n.* a peacock's tail.

* ମର, *a.* perishable, mortal.

ମରକ, *n.* a pestilence, mortality.

ମରକଟିଆ, *a.* lean, emaciated; monkey-like.

ମରକତ, *n.* an emerald.

ମରଣ, *n.* dying; death.

ମରାମତି, *n.* repairs, repairing.

ମର. *a.* killed, dead.

ମରଇ, ମରେଇ, *n.* a granary, store for grain.

ମରାମରି, *n.* a mutual beating.

ମରଚ, ମରିଚ, *n.* pepper.

ମରଚ୍‌ଧରିବା, *v.* to rust.

ମରିବା, *v.* to die.

* ମରୀଚି, *n.* a ray of light.

* ମରୀଚିକା, *n.* mirage.

* ମରୁ, *a.* arid, sterile, barren.

ମରୁଆ, *n.* name of a flower.

ମରୁଡ଼ି, *n.* drought; pestilence, mortality.

* ମରୁତ, ମରୁତ୍, *n.* the air, wind; god of wind.

ମରୁଭୂମି, *n.* a desert or barren land.

* ମର୍କଟ, *n.* a monkey.

ମର୍ଜି, ମରଜି, *n.* will, inclination, pleasure.

ମର୍ତ୍ତ୍ୟ, *n.* earth;—*a.* * earthly, mortal.

ମର୍ତ୍ତ୍ୟପୁର, *n.* earth, residence of mortals.

ମର୍ତ୍ତ୍ୟଲୋକ, *n.* the earth, the habitation of mortals.

ମର୍ଦ୍ଦ, *n.* a man.

ମର୍ଦ୍ଦନ, *n.* rubbing, grinding, threshing.

ମର୍ଦ୍ଦଳ, *n.* a kind of drum.

* ମର୍ଦ୍ଦିତ, *a.* bruised, rubbed.

ମର୍ମ୍ମ, *n.* purport; core, quick; a joint.

ମର୍ମ୍ମଜ୍ଞ, *a.* profoundly learned.

ମର୍ମ୍ମଭେଦୀ, *a.* cutting to the quick, piercing, painful.

ମର୍ମ୍ମର, *n.* marble; the rustling of dry leaves.

ମର୍ମ୍ମସ୍ଥାନ, *n.* a vital part, secret part.

ମର୍ମ୍ମସ୍ପର୍ଶୀ, *a.* stinging to the quick, poignant, sharp.

* ମର୍ମ୍ମାନ୍ତିକ, *a.* wounding the vital parts, mortal, deadly.

ମର୍ଯ୍ୟାଦା, *n.* honour, respect; limit.

ମଳ, *n.* excrement, filth; rust; sin.

ମଳା, *n.* a hollow at the root of trees to retain water.

ମଳଙ୍ଗ, *n.* a place where salt is made.

ମଳବନ୍ଧ, *a.* costive;—*n.* constipation.

ମଳମାସ, *n.* an intercalary month.

ମଳୟ, *n.* the name of a mountain range in the south-west of India, the Malaya mountains; Malabar.

ମଳୟଗିରି, ମଳୟପର୍ବତ, ମଳୟାଚଳ, *n.* the Malaya mountains.

* ମଳୟଜ, *n.* sandal-wood.

ମଳୟପବନ, ମଳୟାନିଳ, *n.* the vernal wind blowing from the Malaya mountains; south wind.

ମଳାମଳି, *n.* twisting and twirling, rubbing and squeezing; threshing.

ମଳି, *n.* dirt, filth.

ମଳିଆ, *a.* dirty.

ମଳିକ, *n.* a surname.

ମଳିନ, *a.* dirty, filthy, foul; pale.

ମଳିନତା, *n.* filthiness, dirtiness; paleness.

ମଳିନମୁଖ, *a.* grim-looking;—*n.* pale face.

ମଲୁ, *n.* a patient, invalid, sick man.

ମଲୁଆ, *n.* refuse of flour after being sifted.

ମଲ, *n.* an ornament for the ankle, anklet.

ମଲଙ୍ଗୀ, *n.* a salt-maker.

ମଲମ, *n.* an ointment, salve.

ମଲମଲ, *n.* muslin, book muslin.

ମଲା, *a.* dead.

ମଲ୍ଲୀ, *n.* name of a flower, species of jasmine.

*ମଲ୍ଲ, *n.* a wrestler, a boxer.

ମଲ୍ଲଯୁଦ୍ଧ, *n.* wrestling.

* ମଲ୍ଲଯୋଦ୍ଧା, *n.* a wrestler, pugilist.

ମଲ୍ଲି, ମଲ୍ଲିକା, ମଲ୍ଲୀ, *n.* the Indian jasmine.

ମଶା, *ମଶକ, *n.* a mosquito, a gnat.

ମଶାଣି, *n.* a place where bodies are burnt.

ମଶାରି, ମଶୁରି, *n.* mosquito curtains.

ମଶାଲ, *n.* a torch, link.

ମଶାଲ୍‌ଚି, *n.* a torch-bearer; a dish-washer.

ମଶାଲ୍‌ଦାନ, *n.* an oil vessel to feed a torch.

ମସଲା, *n.* spices, condiments; also used in a general sense of ingredients.

*ମସି, ମସୀ, ମଷି, ମଷୀ, *n.* writing ink.

ମସିଆ, *a.* dirty.

ମସିଣା, *n.* a flag or rush mat.

ମସୁଦା, *n.* advice, counsel; a rough draft.

ମସୁର, ମସୂର, *n.* a kind of pulse.

ମସୂରିକା, *n.* a virulent kind of small-pox.

*ମସୃଣ, *a.* soft, glossy.

ମସ୍ଖରା, *n.* a humourist.

ମସ୍ଖରାମି, *n.* jesting, buffoonery.

ମସ୍ତା, ମସ୍ତକା, *a.* liable to be broken easily, brittle.

ମସ୍ତ, *a.* full of lust, wanton.

ମସ୍ତକ, *n.* the head, top.

ମସ୍ତି, *n.* wantonness; drunkenness.

ମସ୍ତିଷ୍କ, *n.* the brain.

ମହକ, *n.* a perfume, sweet scent.

ମହକିବା, *v.* to exhale agreeable smells, to emit odour, to perfume.

ମହକୁମା, *n.* a tribunal, court of justice; a department in the court.

ମହଣ, *n.* a maund; forty seers; about 80 pounds; in Cuttack district 105 pounds.

ମହତ, *a.* great, noble, excellent; *fem.* ମହତୀ ।

ମହତ୍ତ୍ୱ, *n.* greatness, dignity.

*ମହନୀୟ, *a.* glorious, noble, exalted, worthy of homage.

ମହନ୍ତ, *n.* chief of a *math.*

ମହରମ, *n.* a mussalman festival.

ମହର୍ଘ, *a.* dear, high-priced.

ମହର୍ଷି, *n.* a great sage.

ମହଲ, *n.* a large building, a house, a seraglio, one storey of a building.

ମହଲତ, *n.* postponement; time, opportunity.

ମହଲା, *n.* a storey of a building.'

ମହା, *a.* great, noble, excellent.

ମହାକବି, *n.* a great poet.

ମହାକାବ୍ୟ, *n.* an epic poem, a great or classical poem.

ମହାକାୟ, *a.* big-bodied, bulky, gigantic.

ମହାଘୋର, *a.* very awful.

ମହାଜନ, *n.* a merchant, creditor; a noble man.

ମହାଜନୀ, *n.* commerce, money-lending.

ମହାତ୍ମା, *a.* magnanimous, large-hearted.

ମହାଦେଈ, *n.* a rani or queen.

ମହାଦେବ, *n.* *Siva.*

ମହାଦେଶ, *n.* a continent.

ମହାନ୍, *a.* great, eminent, grand.

ମହାନଦୀ, *n.* the great river, Mahanadi.

* ମହାନିଦ୍ରା, *n.* the great sleep—death.

* ମହାନିଶା, *n.* midnight.

ମହାନୁଭବ, ମହାନୁଭାବ, *a.* generous, magnanimous.

ମହାପାତକ, ମହାପାପ, *n.* a heinous sin.

ମହାପାତକୀ, *a.* guilty of mortal sin.

ମହାପୁରୁଷ, *n.* a saint, a great man.

ମହାପ୍ରଭୁ, *n.* the Supreme Being; applied also to *Jagannath, Siva,* and to great men, etc.

ମହାପ୍ରଳୟ, *n.* universal destruction.

ମହାପ୍ରସାଦ, *n.* food which has been presented to *Jagannath*, and afterwards sold to pilgrims.

ମହାବଳ, *n.* a large tiger;—*a.* very strong.

ମହାବାହୁ, *a.* very powerful, mighty.

ମହାବୀର, *n.* a great hero.

* ମହାଭାଗ, *a.* virtuous in a high degree, pure, holy, eminent.

ମହାଭାରତ, *n.* name of the great Hindu poem—*Mahabharat.*

* ମହାଭୁଜ, *a.* see ମହାବାହୁ ।

ମହାଭୂତ, *n.* the five primary elements.

ମହାମନା, * ମହାମତି, *a.* magnanimous, high-minded.

ମହାମନ୍ତ୍ର, *n.* any sacred text of the *Vedas*; a great or efficacious charm, a powerful spell.

* ମହାମହିମ, *a.* great, majestic, noble.

ମହାମହୋପାଧ୍ୟାୟ, *n.* a title given to learned men and reputed scholars;—*a.* most learned.

* ମହାମାଂସ, *n.* human flesh.

ମହାମାୟା, *n.* illusion; *Durgá.*

ମହାମାରୀ, *n.* plague, pestilence.

ମହାମୁନି, *n.* a great sage; a name of *Vyasa.*

ମହାମୂଲ୍ୟ, *a.* costly, precious.

ମହାଯଶା, *a.* very famous.

ମହାଯାତ୍ରା, *n.* the great pilgrimage—death.

ମହାରଣ୍ୟ, *n.* a dense forest.

* ମହାରଥ, *n.* a great warrior or hero.

ମହାରାଜ, *n.* an emperor; your majesty.

ମହାରାଷ୍ଟ୍ର, *n.* the country of the Mahrattas.

ମହାରାଷ୍ଟ୍ରୀ, *n.* the language of the people of Maharastra.

* ମହାର୍ଘ, *a.* dear, costly, high-priced.

ମହାଳୟା, *n.* name of a particular dark fortnight in the lunar month of *Aswina.*

ମହାଲ, *n.* a district.

ମହାବ୍ୟାଧି, *n.* leprosy.

ମହାଶୟ, *n.* sir, your honour.

ମହାଷ୍ଟମୀ, *n.* eighth day of the moon in *Aswina.*

ମହାସମୁଦ୍ର, ମହାସାଗର, *n.* ocean.

ମହିନା, *n.* wages; month.

ମହିମା, *n.* greatness, majesty, dignity.

ମହିମାସାଗର, *n.* ocean of greatness or glory.

ମହିଳା, *n.* a lady, a woman.

* ମହିଷ, *n.* a buffalo.

* ମହିଷୀ, *n.* a queen; a female buffalo.

ମହୀ, ମହି, *n.* the earth.

* ମହୀପତି, *n.* a king, a sovereign.

* ମହୀୟସୀ, *a. fem.* greater, mightier, stronger.

* ମହୀରୁହ, *n.* a tree.

* ମହୀଲତା, *n.* an earth-worm.

ମହୁ, *n.* honey.

ମହୁଆ, *a.* having the taste or scent of honey.

ମହୁପଣ, ମହୁଫେଣ, *n.* honey-comb.

ମହୁଡ, *n.* a crown, top.

ମହୁଫେଣା, ମହୁବସା, *n.* honey-comb.

ମହୁମାଛି, *n.* a honey bee.

ମହୁର, *n.* a gold mohur; a curry.

ମହୁରା, *n.* name of a poisonous drug.

ମହୁରି, *n.* aniseed; a drain; a trumpet.

ମହୁଲ, *n.* a species of edible flower from which spirit is distilled.

ମହେନ୍ଦ୍ର, *n.* *Indra*; *Vishnu*; a portion of the eastern ghâts from the south of Orissa to the northern Circars.

* ମହେଶ, ମହେଶ୍ୱର, *n.* titles of *Siva.*

ମହୋତ୍ସବ, *n.* great festival, a feast.

* ମହୋଦଧି, *n.* the great ocean.

ମହୋଦୟ, *a.* prosperous, dignified; —*n.* a lord, dignified person.

* ମହୋଦ୍ୟମ, *n.* great effort, energy, exertion.

ମହୌଷଧ, *n.* a specific medicine, a sovereign remedy, a panacea.

* ମକ୍ଷିକା, *n.* a fly, the common fly.

ମା, *n.* mother.

ମାଇକିନିଆଁ, *n.* a woman, a common appellation for woman.

ମାଇପ, *n.* a wife, a married woman.

ମାଇଁ, *n.* a mother's brother's wife.

ମାଈ, *n.* a female, a woman;—*a.* female.

ମାଇଚ୍, ମାଇଚିଆ, ମାଇଚ୍ଛା, *a.* effeminate, woman-like.

ମାଇମୁଁହା, *a.* bashful, womanfaced.

ମାଂସ, *n.* flesh, meat.

ମାଂସିଆ, *a.* fleshy, plump.

ମାଉସୀ, *n.* aunt.

ମାଂସ, *n.* flesh, meat.

ମାଂସଗ୍ରନ୍ଥି, *n.* a gland.

ମାଂସପେଶୀ, *n.* a muscle.

*ମାଂସଳ, *a.* stout, corpulent, lusty.

ମାଂସାଶୀ, *a.* carnivorous.

ମାକଡ଼, ମାଙ୍କଡ଼, *n.* a monkey.

ମାକଡ଼ସା, *n.* a spider.

ମାକୁ, *n.* a weaver's shuttle.

ମାଖଣ, *a.* not oiled, not glossy; worthless.

ମାଖିବା, *v.* to smear, to plaster.

ମାକୁନ୍ଦା, *n.* a beardless youth.

ମାଗଣ, *n.* a contribution, collection.

ମାଗଣା, *a.* and *ad.* for nothing, gratis.

ମାଗନ୍ତା, *a.* asking, begging.

ମାଗିଖିଆ, *n.* a beggar, one who begs and eats.

ମାଗିବା, *v.* to ask, to request.

ମାଗୁଣି, *n.* a request, supplication.

ମାଗୁର, *n.* a kind of fish.

ମାଘ, *n.* the tenth Hindu month, part of Jan. and Feb.

*ମାଙ୍ଗଳିକ, ମାଙ୍ଗଲ୍ୟ, *a.* propitious, auspicious.

ମାଛ, *n.* a fish, fish.

ମାଛମଞ୍ଜି, *n.* fish-roe.

ମାଛରଙ୍କା, *n.* a king-fisher.

ମାଛି, *n.* a fly, the common fly.

ମାଛୁଆ, *n.* fisherman, fishmonger; —*a.* fond of fish.

ମାଜଣା, *n.* scouring, rubbing, polishing.

ମାଜିବା, *v.* to scour, to clean, to polish.

ମାଝି, *n.* a boatman, helmsman.

ମାଞ୍ଚିଆ, ମାଚିଆ, *n.* a chair (this word is used in country districts).

ମାଟି, *n.* earth, soil.

ମାଟିଆ, *a.* earthy, earth-coloured.

ମାଠ, *n.* a coarse cloth; a field, plain.

ମାଠିଆ, *n.* a water-vessel, *kalsi.*

ମାଠିବା, *v.* to polish, to brighten.

ମାଡ଼, *n.* a blow, a stroke.

ମାଡ଼ମାରିବା, *v.* to thrash, to strike, to beat.

ମାଡ଼ିବା, *v.* to press; to intertwine or climb (spoken of creeping or climbing plants); to spread.

ମାଡ଼ୁଆ, *a.* deserving of being thrashed or beaten.

ମାଢ଼, *n.* weight or quantity.

ମାଢ଼ି, *n.* the gums; a double tooth.

ମାଣ, *n.* 25 *gunths* of land, one acre; a small grain measure.

*ମାଣବକ, *n.* a child or boy of Brahman caste; a child, a boy.

ମାଣସାରୁ, *n.* a large species of the *sáru (arum).*

ମାଣିକ୍ୟ, ମାଣିକ, ମାଣିକା, *n.* a ruby.

ମାଣିଖୁଣ୍ଟି, *n.* the stump in a mill-stone.

ମାଣ୍ଡି, *n.* a bolster.

ମାଣ୍ଡିଆ, *n.* a kind of small round grain.

* ମାଣ୍ଡୁ, *n.* fire, hot iron, etc., used in an ordeal.

* ମାତଙ୍ଗ, *n.* an elephant; a savage; *fem.* ମାତଙ୍ଗୀ ।

ମାତବ୍ବର, ମାତବର, *a.* strong, firm; chief, important; well up, well to do.

ମାତା, *n.* mother.

* ମାତାମହ, *n.* a maternal grand- [father.

* ମାତାମହୀ, *n.* a maternal grandmother.

ମାତିବା, *v.* to be infatuated with any object.

* ମାତୁଳ, *n.* a maternal uncle.

* ମାତୁଳାଣୀ, ମାତୁଳୀ, *n.* see ମାଇଁ ।

* ମାତୃ, *n.* a mother, divine mother.

ମାତ୍ର, ମାତ୍ରକ, *ad.* only, merely; least; but.

ମାତ୍ରା, *n.* the marks or symbols placed above or below letters in Oriya composition to represent letters; * quantity.

ମାତ୍ସର୍ଯ୍ୟ, *n.* envy, malice, jealousy.

ମାଦକ, *a.* intoxicating;—*n.* an intoxicant.

ମାଦଳ, *n.* a tabor; a person without hands or feet.

ମାଦା, *a.* female;—*n.* female animal.

* ମାଦୃଶ, *a.* like me; *fem.* ମାଦୃଶୀ ।

ମାଧବ, *n.* a name of *Krushna*; * part of April and May.

ମାଧବୀ, *n.* a large creeper bearing white flowers.

ମାଧୁରୀ, ମାଧୁର୍ଯ୍ୟ, *n.* sweetness, suavity; beauty, agreeableness.

ମାଧ୍ୟାକର୍ଷଣ, *n.* gravitation.

* ମାଧ୍ୟାହ୍ନିକ, *a.* belonging to the middle of the day.

ମାନ, *n.* respectability, hauteur; a measure; standard or class in a school.

ମାନଚିତ୍ର, *n.* a map.

ମାନତ, ମାନସ୍ତ, *n.* a vow.

ମାନଦଣ୍ଡ, *n.* a measuring rod.

ମାନନା, *n.* honouring, showing res- [pect.

ମାନନୀୟ, *a.* worthy of regard;—*n.* a form of respectful address.

ମାନବ, *n.* a man, a mortal.

* ମାନବୀ, *n.* a woman;—*a.* relating to a man, manly.

* ମାନବୀୟ, *a.* manly, human.

ମାନଭଙ୍ଗ, *n.* dishonouring.

ମାନମନ୍ଦିର, *n.* an observatory.

ମାନସ, *a.* mental;—*n.* mind, intention, design.

ମାନସିକ, *a.* mental, imaginary, [ideal.

ମାନହାନି, *n.* wounding a person's honour.

ମାନହୀନ, *a.* disreputable, base.

ମାନିତ, *a.* respected, honoured.

* ମାନିନୀ, *n.* a respectable or a proud woman.

ମାନିବା, *v.* to obey, to mind, to regard, to observe; to confess, to admit

* ମାନୀ, *a.* proud, sulky; honoured.

*ମାନୁଷ, *n.* a man, human being; *fem.* ମାନୁଷୀ ।

*ମାନୁଷିକ, *a.* human.

ମାନ୍ୟ, *a.* honourable, respectable; —*n.* honour, respect.

ମାନ୍ୟବାନ୍, *a.* receiving honours.

ମାନ୍ଦା, *n.* diminution;—*a.* sluggish.

* ମାନ୍ଦ୍ୟ, *n.* badness, slowness, indisposition, stupidity.

ମାପ, *n.* measure, weight; measurement.

*ମାପକ, *n.* one who measures.

ମାପିବା, *n.* to measure, to weigh.

ମାପୁଣି, *n.* who or what measures; measuring.

ମାଫ୍, *a.* forgiven; exempted;—*n.* forgiveness; exemption.

ମାଫି, *n.* exemption.

ମାଫିକ୍, *a.* like to, agreeing with.

ମାମଲତ୍, ମାମଲା, *n.* a lawsuit, an affair, a negotiation.

ମାମା, *n.* mother; a maternal uncle.

ମାମୁଁ, *n.* a maternal uncle.

ମାମୁଲ, ମାମୁଲ, *a.* customary, established;—*n.* custom, practice.

ମାୟା, *n.* illusion, magic, deceit; affection, attachment; *a woman.

ମାୟାଜାଲ, *n.* conjuring, jugglery.

ମାୟାବୀ, *a.* illusive;—*n.* a juggler; a deceiver.

ମାୟାମୟ, *a.* illusive, deceptive.

* ମାୟିକ, *a.* affectionate, clement.

* ମାରକ, *a.* destroying.

ମାରଣ, *n.* smiting, striking, slaying; calcination.

ମାରଣା, *n.* a betrayer, murderer; vicious.

ମାରପିଟ୍, *n.* a general beating or drubbing.

ମାରଫତ୍, *ad.* by means of, through, by.

ମାରାତ୍ମକ, *a.* murderous, deadly, fatal.

ମାରିବା, *v.* to strike, to beat.

ମାରୀ, *n.* a pestilence, plague.

ମାରୁ, *a.* unclean, impure, menstruous; rotten, useless.

* ମାରୁତ, *n.* wind, air.

ମାର୍ଗ, *n.* a road, way, path, passage.

ମାର୍ଗଶିର, * ମାର୍ଗଶୀର୍ଷ, *n.* a month of that name, part of Nov.- and Dec.

ମାର୍ଜନା, * ମାର୍ଜନ, *n.* scouring, cleansing; forgiveness, remission.

*ମାର୍ଜନୀ, *n.* a towel, rubber, duster, a brush.

ମାର୍ଜନୀୟ, *a.* pardonable, purifiable.

* ମାର୍ଜାର, *n.* a cat.

ମାର୍ଜିତ, *a.* pardoned, purified, cleansed; scoured.

* ମାର୍ତ୍ତଣ୍ଡ, *n.* the sun.

ମାଳଭୂମି, ମାଳ, *n.* high ground.

ମାଲ୍, *n.* goods, merchandise, property, luggage, parcel.

ମାଲ, *n.* a wrestler.

ମାଲଖାନା, *n.* a store-house.

ମାଲଗୁଜାର, *n.* the rent of land payable to Government.

ମାଲ୍ଜାମୀନ୍, *n.* a security or surety for property. [mine.
ମାଲତୀ, *n.* the great flowering jas-
ମାଲସା, *n.* oil, lamp oil.
ମାଲବ, *n.* name of a tune; *Malwa.*
ମାଲମାଲ, *ad.* in parties, portions or sections.
ମାଲଶ୍ରୀ, *n.* name of a tune or air.
ମାଳା, * ମାଳିକା, *n.* a wreath, a garland; a necklace.
ମାଳି, *n.* a rosary; a necklace.
ମାଳୀ, * ମାଳାକାର *n.* a florist, flower-seller.
ମାଳୀ, *n.* a gardener; a rosary.
ମାଳୁଣୀ, * ମାଳିନୀ, *n. fem.* of ମାଳୀ ।
ମାଳୁଅ, *n.* a Kond.
ମାଳିନ୍ୟ, *n.* dirtiness, dinginess; gloominess, sadness.
ମାଲିକ, *n.* an owner, master, proprietor. [landholder.
ମାଲିକାନା, *n.* allowance paid to a
ମାଲିସ୍, *n.* rubbing, shampooing.
ମାଲୁମ୍, *a.* known, acquainted with.
ମାଲୋ, an exclamation—O mother!
* ମାଲ୍ୟ, *n.* a wreath, chaplet, neck-
ମାଶୁଲ *n.* tax, duty, excise. [lace
* ମାଷ, *n.* a kind of pulse, *biri.*
ମାସ, *n.* a month.
ମାସାନ୍ତ, *n.* the end of the month.
ମାସିକ, ମାସିକିଆ, ମାସୁଆରି, *a.* monthly.
ମାସେ, ମାସକ, *n.* a month, one month.
ମାସ୍ତୁଲ, *n.* a mast.

ମାହାତ୍ମ୍ୟ, *n.* magnanimity; glory.
ମାହାନ୍ତି, *n.* name of a caste.
ମାହାଫିଜ୍, *n.* assignee; record-keeper.
ମାହାଣ, *n.* a drain, a gully.
ମାହାରୀ, *n.* a temple dancing woman; a prostitute. [a caste.
ମାହାଲ, *n.* name of a tree; name of
ମାହାଳିଆ, *ad.* vainly, for nothing; —*a.* empty, vain.
ମାହିନା, *n.* monthly pay.
ମାହୁନ୍ତ, *n.* an elephant-driver.
ମିଆଁ, *n.* a title among Musalmans, Mr. [agreed upon.
ମିଆଦ, ମିଆଦ, *n.* time allotted or
ମିଆଦୀ, *a.* of agreed or allotted time. [*tanjan.*
ମିଆନା, *n.* a kind of palanquin, a
ମିଛ, *a.* false;—*n.* falsehood, vanity.
ମିଛକଥା, *n.* a lie.
ମିଛୁଆ *n.* and *a.* a liar; *fem.* ମିଛେଇ ।
ମିଜାଜ, *n.* temper, disposition.
ମିଞ୍ଜିମିଞ୍ଜିଆ, *n.* a glimmering, a faint light. [join, to fit in.
ମିଶାଇବା, ମିଶେଇବା, *v.* to unite, to
ମିଟାଇବା, *v.* to terminate (a dispute), to decide.
ମିଟିମିଟି, *n.* twinkling, expiring.
ମିଠା, *a.* sweet;—*n.* sweetness, sweets, suavity. [fectionery.
ମିଠାଇ, ମିଠେଇ, *n.* sweetmeats, con-
ମିଣିଷ, *n.* a man.
ମିତ, *n.* a friend, a namesake;—*a.* moderate, regular, frugal.

ମିତବ୍ୟୟୀ, *a.* economical, frugal.

*ମିତଭାଷୀ, *a.* temperate in language.

ମିତା, *n.* a friend, confidant, crony.

*ମିତାଚାର, *n.* proper behaviour.

*ମିତାହାର, *n.* moderation in eating, abstemiousness;—*a.* sparing in diet.

ମିତାକ୍ଷରା, *n.* a celebrated commentary on the law treatise of *Yajnavalka.*

ମିତ୍ର, *n.* a friend, companion.

ମିତ୍ରତା, ମିତ୍ରତ୍ୱ, *n.* friendship, intimacy.

ମିତ୍ରଲାଭ, *n.* the acquisition of a friend.

ମିତ୍ରାକ୍ଷର, *n.* rhyme in poetry.

ମିଥୁନ, *n.* sign Gemini; *a couple; cohabitation.

ମିଥ୍ୟା, *a.* false;–*n.* falsehood, vanity.

ମିଥ୍ୟାବାଦୀ, *n.* a liar;—*a.* lying.

ମିଥ୍ୟାସ୍ୱୀକୃତ, *n.* perjury.

ମିନତି, *n.* supplication, entreaty.

ମିର୍ଜାଇ, *n.* a kind of jacket.

ମିଳନ, *n.* being reconciled, meeting, agreeing.

ମିଳାଇବା, *v.* to unite, to reconcile, to join; to compare; to be mixed by melting.

ମିଳାଇଯିବା, ମିଳିଯିବା, *v.i.* to be mixed by melting.

ମିଳାପ, *n.* social intercourse, sociality.

ମିଳାପୀ, *a.* social, affable, friendly.

ମିଳିତ, *a.* met, met with, united, mixed.

ମିଳିବା, *v.* to be united; to meet; to be reconciled; to be obtained or received.

ମିଳିମିଳା, *n.* the measles.

ମିଲ୍‌କିୟତ, *n.* proprietary right.

ମିଶା, *a.* mixed, mingled, incorporated.

ମିଶାଇବା, *v.* to mix; to add; to compare.

ମିଶାଣ, *n.* addition.

ମିଶାମିଶି, *a.* mixed up together; *n.* a mixing up.

ମିଶିବା, *v.* to be mixed.

ମିଶ୍ର, *a.* mixed, mingled, combined, compound;—*n.* a surname of Brahman caste.

ମିଶ୍ରଗୁଣନ, *n.* compound-multiplication.

ମିଶ୍ରଣ, *n.* addition; mixture.

ମିଶ୍ରବିୟୋଗ, *n.* compound-subtraction.

ମିଶ୍ରଯୋଗ, *n.* compound-addition.

ମିଶ୍ରହରଣ, *n.* compound-division.

ମିଶ୍ରିତ, *a.* mixed, compounded.

ମିଷ୍ଟ, *a.* sweet, honeyed, nice.

*ମିଷ୍ଟତା, *n.* sweetness, agreeableness.

ମିଷ୍ଟାନ୍ନ, *n.* sweetmeats.

ମିସର, ମିଶର, ମିଶ୍ର, *n.* Egypt.

ମିସଲ, *n.* a seat of justice.

ମିସି, *n.* a black powder for the teeth.

ମିସିରି, ମିଶ୍ରି, *n.* sugar-candy.

ମିହିଁ, *a.* thin, fine, delicate.

*ମିହିର, *n.* the sun.
ମୀନ, *n.* a fish; sign Pisces.
*ମୀନକେତନ, *n.* cupid.
ମୀମାଂସକ, *n.* an arbitrator, umpire.
ମୀମାଂସା, *n.* settling, examination; one of the Hindu philosophical systems.
*ମୀଳିତ, *a.* shut up, closed.
ମୁଁ, *pron.* inferior pronoun I.
ମୁଆଁ, *n.* a kind of sweetmeat.
ମୁକର, *ad.* surely, certainly, positively.
ମୁକା, *n.* a party; flock, herd.
ମୁକାବଲା, *n.* comparing; a meeting, confronting.
ମୁକାମ, *n.* a place of staying or putting up at, a halting place, station, residence.
ମୁକୁଟ, *n.* a crown, crest, tiara.
*ମୁକୁର, *n.* a looking-glass, mirror.
*ମୁକୁଳ, *n.* blossom, a bud.
ମୁକୁଳା, *a.* opened, expanded; free.
ମୁକୁଳାଇବା, *v.* to deliver, to liberate.
*ମୁକୁଳିତ, *a.* half-closed, half-shut; having buds, budded, blossoming.
ମୁକୁଳିବା, *v.* to be set free, to be liberated.
ମୁକ୍ତ, *a.* delivered, liberated, free, open, loose.
ମୁକ୍ତକଣ୍ଠ, *n.* loud voice.
ମୁକ୍ତହସ୍ତ, *a.* open-handed, liberal.
ମୁକ୍ତା, *n.* a pearl.
ମୁକ୍ତି, *n.* salvation, emancipation, freedom,
ମୁକ୍ତିଆର, ମୁକ୍ତାର, *n.* an attorney, an agent.
ମୁକ୍ତିଆରନାମା, ମୁକ୍ତାରନାମା, *n.* a power of attorney.
ମୁକ୍ତିଦାତା, *n.* a saviour, a deliverer.
ମୁକ୍ତିମାର୍ଗ, ମୁକ୍ତିପଥ, *n.* way of salvation.
ମୁଖ, *n.* the mouth, face;—*a.* *foremost.
ମୁଖଚୋରା, *a.* bashful, shy, sheepish.
ମୁଖିଆ, *a.* head (man), chief, principal.
ମୁଖବନ୍ଧ, *n.* a preface.
*ମୁଖବ୍ୟାଦାନ, *n.* the act of gaping.
ମୁଖମଣ୍ଡଳ, *n.* the orb of the face, the face.
*ମୁଖର, *a.* foul-mouthed, scurrilous; *fem.* ମୁଖରା ।
*ମୁଖରିତ, *a.* made noisy or resonant with.
ମୁଖରୋଗ, *n.* a cancer in the mouth.
ମୁଖଶୁଦ୍ଧି, *n.* cleanliness of the mouth.
ମୁଖସ୍ଥ, *a.* in the mouth, oral, learnt by heart.
ମୁଖା, *n.* the face of an image.
ମୁଖାଗ୍ନି, *n.* fire to be put in a corpse's mouth.
ମୁଖାପେକ୍ଷା, *n.* partiality, partial regard.
ମୁଖାମୁଖି, *ad.* face to face, front to front.
ମୁଖି, *n.* a blow in the mouth.
ମୁଖ୍ୟ, *a.* foremost, chief, primary.
ମୁଗ, *n.* a kind of pulse.
ମୁଗୁନି, *n.* a kind of black marble.
ମୁଗୁର, *n.* a mallet, club, bludgeon.
ମୁଗୁଏ, *n.* a cone-shaped fishing trap made of cocoanut fibres.

ମୁଗ୍ଧ, *a.* infatuated, deluded, stupified.

ମୁଛ, ମୋଛ, *n.* moustache.

ମୁଚଲିକା, *n.* recognizance.

ମୁଚି, *n.* a shoemaker, a currier.

ମୁଚୁକୁନ୍ଦ, *n.* a kind of tree and its flower.

ମୁଚୁକିହାସ, *n.* a smile, a simper.

ମୁଚୁଳା, *n.* a small pillow or bolster.

ମୁଜାହିମ, *a.* forbidding, hindering;—*n.* an obstacle, a claimant.

ମୁଠା, *a.* handful;—*n.* the fist; handle.

ମୁଠାଇବା, *v.* to take a handful, to clinch.

ମୁଠି, *n.* a handful, the fist; a barber's tools.

ମୁଠୁଣି, *n.* a measure from the elbow to the joints of the closed fist.

ମୁଢି, *n.* parched rice.

ମୁଣା, ମୁଣି, *n.* a purse or small bag.

ମୁଣୁହିଁ, *ad.* never, not at all.

ମୁଣ୍ଡ, *n.* the head; chief or head person.

*ମୁଣ୍ଡନ, *n.* shaving the entire head.

ମୁଣ୍ଡବଥା, *n.* headache.

ମୁଣ୍ଡବୁଲା, *n.* dizziness of the head, vertigo.

ମୁଣ୍ଡା, *n.* a piece of wood; piece of fish or flesh;—*a.* blunt, dull-edged.

ମୁଣ୍ଡାଇବା, *v.* to take or carry on the head.

ମୁଣ୍ଡି, *n.* the head of a nipple, the head or end of anything; a log of timber.

ମୁଣ୍ଡିଆ, *n.* butting of a goat or ram; a log of timber.

*ମୁଣ୍ଡିତ, *a.* shaven, shorn, lopped.

ମୁଣ୍ଡୁଳା, *n.* a cipher (•); a circle.

ମୁଣ୍ଡୁଳାକାଟିବା, *v.* to draw a circle.

ମୁଣ୍ଡା, *n.* a lopped tree; a man without wife or children.

ମୁତଇନ୍, ମୁତଏନ୍, *a.* appointed.

ମୁତାବକ୍, *ad.* sequentially, in accordance with.

ମୁତିବା, *v.* to make water.

ମୁତୁରା, *n.* one who wets his bed.

ମୁତୋଫତ, *n.* deceased.

ମୁଥ, *n.* the clenched fist;—*ad.* once.

ମୁଥା, *n.* a bulbous-rooted grass.

ମୁଦ, *n.* a stamp, seal, impression; *joy, pleasure.

ମୁଦା, *a.* closed, shut up.

ମୁଦାଲା, *n.* defendant, respondent.

ମୁଦି, *n.* a finger ring; a retail shopkeeper.

ମୁଦିଆ, *n.* a ring, a ring for the toes.

ମୁଦିବା, *v.* to shut up, to close, to stop.

*ମୁଦ୍ଗ, ମୁଗ, *n.* a kind of pulse, (see ମୁଗ) ।

ମୁଦେଇ, ମୁଦ୍ଦେଇ, *n.* complainant, plaintiff, petitioner.

ମୁଦ୍ଗର, *n.* a mallet, club.

ମୁଦ୍ରଣ, ମୁଦ୍ରାଙ୍କନ, *n.* printing.

*ମୁଦ୍ରା, *n.* a coin, seal, stamp.

*ମୁଦ୍ରାଙ୍କିତ, *a.* printed, sealed, stamped.

ମୁଦ୍ରାଯନ୍ତ୍ର, *n.* a printing or stamping press.

* ମୁଦ୍ରିକା, *n.* a ring.

* ମୁଦ୍ରିତ, *a.* sealed, imprest, closed.

ମୁଦ୍ଦତ, *n.* a space of time, a long time.

ମୁନ, *n.* a sharp point.

ମୁନଫା, ମୁନାଫା, *n.* gain, profit, advantage.

ମୁନାସବ, *a.* proper, fit, pertinent.

ମୁନି, *n.* a sage, a philosopher.

ମୁନିଆ, *a.* sharp-pointed.

ମୁନିବ, *n.* a master, patron, lord.

* ମୁନୀନ୍ଦ୍ର, *n.* a chief sage; *Buddha.*

ମୁନସୀ, *n.* a scribe, writer, teacher of languages.

ମୁନସଫ, *n.* a munsiff.

* ମୁମୁକ୍ଷା, *n.* a desire for freedom or liberty.

* ମୁମୁକ୍ଷୁ, *a.* desirous of emancipation.

ମୁମୂର୍ଷୁ, *a.* about to die.

ମୁରଗ, *n.* a cock fowl or bird; *fem.* ମୁରଗୀ।

ମୁରବ୍ବା, *n.* preserve; a confection.

ମୁରବି, *n.* a patron, guardian.

ମୁରଲୀ, *n.* a flute, pipe, whistle.

* ମୁରାରି, *n.* a name of *Vishnu.*

ମୁରୁଜ, ମୁର୍ଜ, *n.* ground rice.

ମୁର୍କୁଟିଆ, *a.* thin, lank.

ମୁର୍ଦ୍ଦାର, *n.* a corpse, dead body.

ମୁଲକ, *n.* a kingdom, a country.

ମୁଲତବି, *a.* delayed, postponed.

ମୁଲାକାତ, *n.* an interview, a meeting.

ମୁଲେଇବା, *v.* to bargain.

ମୁଲାୟମ, ମୁଲମ, *a.* soft, tender.

ମୁସବର, *n.* aloes, a medicinal gum.

ମୁଷଳ, *n.* a pestle, hammer of the *dhinki*; a clublike instrument.

* ମୁଷ୍କ, *n.* the scrotum.

ମୁଷ୍କଗ୍ରନ୍ଥି, *n.* (in *Anat.*) the testes.

* ମୁଷ୍କମୋଚନ, *n.* castration, gelding.

* ମୁଷ୍ଟି, *n.* the fist; a handful.

* ମୁଷ୍ଟିଯୋଗ, *n.* quack medicines.

ମୁସଲମାନ, *n.* a Mussalman.

ମୁସାଫିର, ମୁସାଫେର, *n.* a traveller, passenger, stranger.

ମୁସାବିଦା, *n.* a rough draft or copy.

ମୁସ୍ତକି, *n.* an officer of the court.

ମୁସ୍କିଲ, *a.* difficult, intricate, hard.

ମୁସ୍ତାଜିର, *n.* hereditary landholder.

ମୁହଁ, *n.* the mouth, face, countenance.

ମୁହାଣ, *n.* the conflux of two rivers, the outlet or mouth of a river.

ମୁହାଁଇବା, *v.* to turn away the face; to give water to cattle; to thrust wood into a fireplace.

ମୁହାଁମୁହିଁ, *ad.* face to face.

ମୁହିଁ, *pron.* I (poetical).

ମୁହସିଲ, *n.* a bailiff, a nazir; a dun, a *piada* placed over a defendant in a suit.

ମୁହୁର୍ମୁହୁଃ, *ad.* repeatedly, again and again.

ମୁହୂର୍ତ୍ତ, *n.* a short time; the fifteenth part of a day.

ମୂକ, *n.* a dumb person.

ମୂଢ଼, *a.* stupid, ignorant;—*n.* a dunce.

ମୂତ, * ମୂତ୍ର, *n.* urine.

ମୂତ୍ରକୃଚ୍ଛ୍ର, *n.* strangury (medical).

ମୂତ୍ରଦୋଷ, *n.* gonorrhœa.
ମୂତ୍ରନିଷେଧାସ୍ତ୍ର, *n.* a catheter.
ମୂତ୍ରପଥ, ମୂତ୍ରରନ୍ଧ୍ର, *n.* the urethra.
* ମୂତ୍ରବର୍ଦ୍ଧକ, *a.* diuretic.
ମୂତ୍ରାଶୟ, *n.* the bladder.
ମୂର୍ଖ, *a.* ignorant, illiterate, stupid, clownish.
ମୂର୍ଖତା, *n.* ignorance, stupidity.
ମୂର୍ଖାମି, *n.* ignorance, stupidity.
ମୂର୍ଚ୍ଛା, *n.* syncope, swoon, stupor.
ମୂର୍ଚ୍ଛାଗତ, *a.* fainted, swooned.
* ମୂର୍ଚ୍ଛାପନ୍ନ, *a.* fallen into a swoon, bereft of sensation.
ମୂର୍ଚ୍ଛିବା, *v.* to forsake. [form.
ମୂର୍ତ୍ତି, *n.* an image, a statne, bodily
* ମୂର୍ତ୍ତିମାନ୍, *a.* having a visible form, embodied.
* ମୂର୍ତ୍ତ୍ୟନ୍ତର, *n.* transformation, metamorphosis.
ମୂର୍ଦ୍ଧନ୍ୟ, *a.* (in *Gram.*) cerebral or lingual.
* ମୂର୍ଦ୍ଧା, *n.* the head, cerebellum.
ମୂର୍ବା, *n.* a tree from which bowstrings are obtained.
ମୂଳ, *n.* a root, origin, first cause.
ମୂଳକାରଣ, *n.* radical cause, source.
ମୂଳଭୂମି, *n.* the foundation.
ମୂଳଧନ, *n.* original stock in trade, capital.
ମୂଳଭିତ୍ତି, *n.* foundation, base.
ମୂଳା, *n.* a radish; the 19th stellar mansion. [origin.
ମୂଳୀଭୂତ, *a.* become a source or
ମୂଲ, *n.* price, wages, value of anything. [anything.
ମୂଲଛିଣିବା, *v.* to settle the price of
ମୂଲିଆ, *n.* a day-labourer.
ମୂଲ୍ୟ, *n.* price, value, worth.
ମୂଲ୍ୟବାନ୍, *a.* valuable, precious.
ମୂଷା, * ମୂଷିକ, *n.* a rat, a mouse.
ମୃଗ, *n.* a deer, antelope.
ମୃଗତୃଷ୍ଣା, *n.* a mirage, illusive scene.
* ମୃଗନାଭି, ମୃଗମଦ, *n.* musk. [eyed.
ମୃଗନେତ୍ରା, * ମୃଗାକ୍ଷୀ, *a. fem.* fawn-
ମୃଗୟା, *n.* hunting, the chase.
ମୃଗଶିରଃ, ମୃଗଶୀର୍ଷ, *n.* the fifth stellar
* ମୃଗାଙ୍କ, *n.* the moon. [mansion.
ମୃଗୀ, *n.* a doe; epilepsy.
* ମୃଗେନ୍ଦ୍ର, *n.* a lion.
* ମୃଣାଳ, *n.* stalk of the waterlily.
* ମୃଣାଳିନୀ, *n.* lotus plant.
* ମୃଣ୍ମୟ, *a.* made of earth or clay.
ମୃତ, *a.* dead, deceased, defunct.
ମୃତକ; *n.* ceremonial impurity caused by the death of a relative.
* ମୃତକଳ୍ପ, *a.* dying, almost dead.
* ମୃତଦାର, *n.* a widower.
* ମୃତବତ୍ସା, *a. fem.* having the offspring die at birth;—*n.* a woman whose offspring dies at birth.
ମୃତସଞ୍ଜୀବନୀ, *n.* a charm for reviving the dead.
* ମୃତାଶୌଚ, *n.* see ମୃତକ। [soil.
ମୃତ୍ତିକା, * ମୃଦ୍, *n.* earth, mould, clay,

ମୃତ୍ୟୁ, *n.* death, decease.
ମୃତ୍ୟୁଛାୟା, *n.* the shadow of death.
ମୃତ୍ୟୁଞ୍ଜୟ, *n.* the conqueror of death, applied to *Siva.*
ମୃଦଙ୍ଗ, *n.* a double or egg-shaped [drum.
* ମୃଦଙ୍ଗାର, *n.* coal.
ମୃଦୁ, *a.* gentle, meek, mild, affable.
* ମୃଦୁତା, *n.* gentleness, mildness, tenderness.
* ମୃଦୁଗମନା, *n.* a waddling woman; [a duck.
* ମୃଦୁଳ, *a.* tender, soft, gentle.
ମୃଦୁହାସ୍ୟ, *n.* a smile.
ମେକାପ, *n.* a servant who looks after the wardrobe of a king.
ମେକି, *a.* counterfeit (coin).
ମେଖ, *n.* a pin, stake, tent peg.
* ମେଖଳା, *n.* a woman's girdle.
ମେଘ, *n.* a cloud.
ମେଘଦୂତ, *n.* the name of a celebrated poem written by *Kalidas.*
* ମେଘନାଦ, *n.* thunder.
ମେଘମାଳା, *n.* a collection of clouds.
ମେଘୁଆ, ମେଘଲା, *a.* cloudy, overcast.,
* ମେଘାଗମ, *n.* the rains, the rainy season.
ମେଘାଚ୍ଛନ୍ନ, *a.* overcast, covered with [clouds.
ମେଘାଡମ୍ବର, *n.* a heavy bank of clouds.
ମେଞ୍ଚାଏ, *n.* a handful.
ମେଜ, *n.* a table.
ମେଜିଷ୍ଟର, *n.* the magistrate.
ମେଝିଆ, ମେଝିଆଁ, *n.* a floor.
ମେଢ, *n.* a framework, frame.
ମେଣ୍ଟ, *n.* a crowd, a company.
ମେଣ୍ଟଣ, *n.* removing, taking away; deciding.
ମେଣ୍ଟା, *n.* a small bundle of tobacco.
ମେଣ୍ଟିବା, *v.* to remove; to rescind; to confute; to adjust; to manage, to live.
ମେଣ୍ଢା, *n.* a sheep, a ram.
ମେଣ୍ଢୀ, *n.* an ewe.
ମେଥି, *n.* name of a plant and its seed, fenugreek.
ମେଦ, *n.* fat, marrow; corpulence.
ମେଦା, *a.* dull, sluggish, stupid.
* ମେଦିନୀ, *n.* the earth.
* ମେଦୁର, *a.* smooth, bland.
ମେନ୍ଦୀ, *n.* a shrub, privet.
* ମେଧା, *n.* aptness of comprehension, understanding.
* ମେଧାବାନ୍, ମେଧାବୀ, *a.* apt, of good [abilities.
ମେରିଆ, *n.* a human victim, a sacrifice among the Konds.
ମେରୁ, *n.* a fabulous mountain; axis.
ମେରୁଗ୍ରନ୍ଥି, *n.* the kidneys.
ମେରୁହାଡ, ମେରୁଦଣ୍ଡ, *n.* the spine, backbone; axis.
ମେଳ, *n.* concord, peace, agreement; union, reconciliation; an assembly.
ମେଳକ, *n.* a meeting, a coming together.
ମେଳା, *n.* a fair; an assembly, [a crowd.
ମେଳି, *n.* a riot or rebellion; an unlawful assembly.

ମେଲିଆ, *a.* riotous, rebellious.

ମେଲା, *a.* open, free, unrestrained; —*n.* the front room.

ମେଲାଇବା, *v.* to spread open, to unfold.

ମେଲାଙ୍କ, *n.* (in *Arith.*) a subtrahend.

ମେଲାଣି, *n.* a friendly dismissal.

ମେଲିବା, *v.* to burst open, to expand.

*ମେଷ, *n.* a sheep; the sign Aries.

ମେଷପାଳକ, *n.* a shepherd.

ମେହ, *n.* gleet, gonorrhœa.

*ମେହକର, ମେହବର୍ଦ୍ଧକ, *a.* diuretic.

ମେହନତ, *n.* labour, toil, exertion.

ମେହନତି, *a.* laborious, toilsome; active.

ମେହନ୍ତାନା, *n.* wages, payment for work.

ମେହନ୍ତର, *n.* a low caste man, sweeper; *fem.* ମେହନ୍ତରାଣୀ।

ମେହେନ୍ଦିଆ, *n.* a kind of colour.

ମେହେର, *n.* grace, favour.

ମୈତ୍ର, *n.* a friend, companion; a namesake.

*ମୈତ୍ରୀ, ମୈତ୍ର୍ୟ, *n.* friendship, intimacy.

*ମୈଥୁନ, *n.* copulation, marriage, union.

ମୈଦା, *n.* wheat flour.

ମୈଦାନ, *n.* a plain, a large open space, a meadow; evacuation.

ମୈନା, *n.* name of a bird, *myna.*

ମୈରଭିରଥ, *n.* blue vitriol, sulphate of copper.

ମୈଳା, *a.* dirty, filthy, impure;—*n.* dirt, filth.

ମୋ, *pron.* my.

ମୋକଦ୍ଦମା, *n.* a lawsuit, a law case.

*ମୋକ୍ତା, *n.* a liberator, a saviour.

ମୋକ୍ତାର, ମୋଖ୍ତାର, *n.* an agent, attorney (see ମୁକ୍ତିଆର).

ମୋଗଲ, *n.* the Mogul tribe, a Mogul.

ମୋଗଲବନ୍ଦି, *n.* Government territory in Orissa.

ମୋଚ, ମୋଛ, *n.* moustache.

ମୋଚନ, *n.* a wiping off, forgiving, releasing.

ମୋଚି, *n.* a dealer or worker in leather, a shoemaker.

ମୋଜା, *n.* a stocking, gaiters, etc.

ମୋଟ, *n.* the gross total; a burden, load;—*a.* thick, coarse.

ମୋଟା, *a.* thick, fat; coarse; gross.

ମୋଟାବୁଦ୍ଧି, *a.* thick-headed, stupid.

ମୋଟାମୋଟି, *ad.* in the gross; cursorily, indiscriminately.

ମୋଟିଆ, *n.* a porter, cooly.

ମୋଟୀ, *n.* a corpulent woman; a kind of greens.

ମୋଡ଼, *n.* a twist, bend, crook.

ମୋଡ଼ା, *n.* a footstool; anything twisted;—*a.* twisted.

ମୋଡ଼ାମୋଡ଼ି, *n.* twisting and screwing, squeezing and turning.

ମୋଡ଼ିବା, *v.* to turn, to twist, to screw, to wind.

*ମୋଦ, *n.* pleasure, delight.

ମୋଦକ, *n.* an electuary; a kind of cake;—*a.* exhilarating, gladdening.

ମୋଫତ୍, *a.* and *ad.* gratis, freely, for nothing.

ମୋମ୍, *n.* wax, bee's wax.

ମୋମ୍‌ଜାମା, *n.* wax cloth.

ମୋହ, *n.* stupefaction, fascination.

ମୋହନ, *a.* stupefying, bewildering;—*n.* a stupefying, a fascinating. [meat.

ମୋହନଭୋଗ, *n.* a kina of sweet-

ମୋହବତ୍, *r.* friendship, affection, regard.

ମୋହର, *n.* a coin, seal, stamp.

ମୋହରର, ମୋହରର୍, *n.* a writer, clerk.

ମୋହିତ, *a.* stupefied, infatuated, fascinated, bewildered.

ମୋହିନୀ, *n.* a fascinating woman; —*a.* fascinating.

ମୋହିବା, *v.* to fascinate, enchant.

ମୋକ୍ଷ, *n.* final emancipation.

* ମୋକ୍ଷଣ, *n.* shedding; deliverance, setting at liberty.

ମୌକଲ୍, *n.* a client.

* ମୌକ୍ତିକ, *n.* a pearl. [left off.

ମୌକୁଫ୍, *a.* deferred, postponed,

ମୌଖିକ, *a.* oral, verbal.

ମୌଚକ, *n.* a honey-comb.

ମୌଜ, *n.* enjoyment, delight.

ମୌଜା, *n.* a village, district; a wave; a stocking. [near.

ମୌଜୁଦ, *a.* present, existing, being

ମୌତ *n.* death, decease, demise.

ମୌନ, *n.* silence, taciturnity.

ମୌନୀ, *a.* silent, reserved, taciturn.

ମୌନବ୍ରତ, *n.* a vow of silence.

* ମୌର୍ବୀ, *n* a bowstring.

ମୌରୁଷୀ, *a.* hereditary.

ମୌଲା, *n.* a maternal uncle. [knot.

* ମୌଳି, *n.* the head; diadem, top-

ମୌଳିକ, *a.* fundamental.

ମୌଳିବା, *v.* to fade, wither, droop.

ମୌଲବୀ, *n.* a learned Mussalman, a Muhammadan teacher.

* ମ୍ରକ୍ଷଣ, *n.* smearing, anointing.

* ମ୍ରିୟମାଣ, *a.* dying, expiring.

ମ୍ଳାନ, *a.* faded, pale; dejected, sad.

ମ୍ଳାନବଦନ, *a.* downcast;—*n.* dejected countenance, pale face. [ing.

* ମ୍ଳାନି, *n.* sadness, languor, a fad-

ମ୍ଳେଚ୍ଛ, *n.* a barbarian;—*a.* barbarous.

ଯ.

ଯ, the 26th consonant.

ଯ, ଯବ, *n.* barley.

ଯଉତୁକ, *n.* a dower, a marriage portion.

* ଯକୃତ୍, *n.* the liver. [ping.

* ଯଜନ, *n.* sacrificing, worship-

ଯଜମାନ, *n.* the person who makes an offering, a worshipper.

ଯଜୁର୍ବେଦ, ଯଜୁଃ, *n.* the second *Veda.*

ଯଜୁର୍ବେଦୀ, *n.* pertaining to the *Yajur Veda.*

ଯଜ୍ଞ, *n.* a sacrifice.

ଯଜ୍ଞକୁଣ୍ଡ, *n.* sacrificial pit

ଯଜ୍ଞପଶୁ, *n.* an animal for sacrifice, sacrificial victim.

ଯଜ୍ଞବେଦୀ, *n.* an altar for sacrifice.

*ଯଜ୍ଞସୂତ୍ର, *n.* the Brahmanical thread.

* ଯଜ୍ଞୀୟ, *a.* sacrificial, fit for sacrifice.

ଯତି, *n.* an ascetic, a devotee.

ଯତ୍କିଞ୍ଚିତ୍, *ad.* a little, ever so little.

ଯତ୍ସାମାନ୍ୟ, *a.* little; common, mean.

ଯତ୍ନ, *n.* active endeavour, effort, zeal.

ଯତ୍ନବାନ୍, ଯତ୍ନଶୀଳ, *a.* zealous, active, strenuous.

* ଯତ୍ର, *ad.* where, in which.

ଯତ୍ପରୋନାସ୍ତି, *ad.* utmost, *ne plus ultra.*

ଯଥା, *ad.* as, for instance; *where.

ଯଥାକାଳ, *n.* proper time, due season;—*ad.* according to the time.

* ଯଥାକ୍ରମ, *ad.* in order, successively.

ଯଥାକ୍ରମେ, ଯଥାକ୍ରମରେ, *ad.* respectively, in succession. [way.

ଯଥାତଥା, *ad.* anyhow, in whatever

ଯଥାବତ୍, *ad.* duly, properly.

* ଯଥାଯଥ, *ad.* fitly, properly.

* ଯଥାଯୋଗ୍ୟ, *ad.* according to merit.

ଯଥାର୍ଥ, *a.* real, genuine, correct, just.

ଯଥାର୍ଥତା, *n.* reality, truth, righteousness, genuineness.

ଯଥାଶକ୍ତି, ଯଥାସାଧ୍ୟ, *ad.* according to one's power.

ଯଥେଚ୍ଛାଚାର, *n.* acting as one likes, spontaneous action or conduct.

ଯଥେଚ୍ଛାଚାରତନ୍ତ୍ର, *n.* absolute government by one person, autocracy.

ଯଥେଷ୍ଟ, *a.* enough, abundant. plenty.

ଯଥୋଚିତ, *a.* right, merited, condign;—*ad.* as is proper.

ଯଥୋପଯୁକ୍ତ, *ad.* properly. [while.

ଯଦବଧି, *ad.* since or until (which),

* ଯଦା, *ad.* when, at the time when.

ଯଦି, ଯଦ୍ବା, ଯଦ୍ୟପି, *ad.* if, though.

ଯଦସ୍ୟାତ୍, *ad.* even if, in case.

* ଯଦୃଚ୍ଛା, *n.* self-will, independence.

ଯଦୃଚ୍ଛାକ୍ରମେ, *ad.* voluntarily, spontaneously.

ଯଦ୍ୟପି, *ad.* even if, although.

ଯନ୍ତା, *n.* a trap; millstone.

ଯନ୍ତାଯନ୍ତି, *n.* overcrowding, a throng.

ଯନ୍ତ୍ର, *n.* an engine, machine, instrument. [pain.

ଯନ୍ତ୍ରଣା, *n.* anguish, agony, torture,

ଯନ୍ତ୍ରମନ୍ତ୍ର, *n.* diagrams and cabalistical figures.

* ଯନ୍ତ୍ରିତ, *a.* restrained, controlled, checked, curbed.

* ଯନ୍ତ୍ରୀ, *a.* ingenious, mechanical.

ଯବ, *n.* barley.

* ଯବଗଣ୍ଡ, *n.* a pimple, a wart.

ଯବନ, *n.* western foreigners; Muhammadans.

ଯବନିକା, *n.* a drop-scene, a curtain.

ଯବକ୍ଷାର, *n.* nitre, saltpetre.

ଯବକ୍ଷାରଜ, *a.* nitrous, nitric. [tis.

ଯବକ୍ଷାରଜାମ୍ଳ, *n.* nitric acid, aqua for-

* ଯବାଗୂ, *n.* see ଯାଉ ।

ଯବାନ୍, *a.* young, youthful.
ଯବାନି, *n.* youthfulness.
ଯବ, *n.* length of one barley-corn, ⅓ of an inch.
ଯମ, *n.* *Yama*, regent of death.
ଯମକ, *n.* alliteration, rhyme.
*ଯମଜ, *n.* twin-born, twin.
ଯମଦୂତ, *n.* a messenger of death.
*ଯମଳ, *n.* a pair, a couple.
*ଯମାନୀ, *n.* see ଜୁଆଣି ।
ଯଶଃ, *n.* renown, fame, celebrity.
ଯଶସ୍କର, *a.* conferring glory, glorious.
ଯଶସ୍ୱୀ, *a.* famous, renowned.
*ଯଷ୍ଟି, *n.* a stick, staff, wand, club.
ଯଷ୍ଟିମଧୁ, *n.* liquorice-root.
ଯହିଁ, *ad.* where (poetical).
ଯହିଁରୁ, *ad.* whereof, whence.
ଯକ୍ଷ, *n.* servants of the god of wealth.
ଯକ୍ଷ୍ମା, *n.* pulmonary consumption, phthisis.
ଯା, *n.* a husband's brother's wife.
ଯାଁଅଳା, *n.* twins.
ଯାଉ, *n.* rice-gruel, over-boiled [rice.
ଯାଈଁଲି, *n.* a cloth with anything carried in each end and slung over the shoulder.
ଯାକ, *a.* all, the whole;—*n.* a tightening, a throng.
ଯାକିବା, *v.* to press.
ଯାଗ, *n.* a sacrifice, oblation.
*ଯାଚକ, *n.* a beggar, one who asks.
*ଯାଚନା, ଯାଚ୍ଞା, *n.* prayer, request, suit.
ଯାଚିବା, *v.* to offer.
ଯାଜକ, *n.* a priest, a sacrificer.
*ଯାଜ୍ଞିକ, *n.* a sacrificial priest.
ଯାତ, *n.* a festival.
ଯାତନା, *n.* anguish, pain, agony.
ଯାତାୟାତ, *n.* a going and coming.
ଯାତ୍ରା, *n.* a festival, a fair; a going, journey, pilgrimage, a procession.
ଯାତ୍ରୀ, *ଯାତ୍ରିକ, *n.* a pilgrim, a tra- [veller.
*ଯାଥାର୍ଥିକ, *a.* real, genuine, righteous.
*ଯାଥାର୍ଥିକତା, *n.* righteousness, genuineness, truth.
*ଯାଥାର୍ଥ୍ୟ, *n.* truth, reality, genu- [ineness.
ଯାଦୁ, *n.* sorcery, magic; ringworm.
*ଯାଦୃକ୍, ଯାଦୃଶ, *ad.* as, like as, such as.
*ଯାନ, *n.* a vehicle, carriage, palkey, [horse, etc.
*ଯାନବାହକ, *n.* an animal or person by which a vehicle is drawn or carried.
ଯାପନ, *n.* spending or passing [(time.)
ଯାପିତ, *a.* spent, passed (time).
ଯାବଜ୍ଜୀବନ, *ad.* as long as life; till death.
ଯାବତ୍, *ad.* and *a.* as long as, while; [all.
ଯାବତୀୟ, ଯାବନ୍ତ, *a.* all, entire, whole.
*ଯାମ, *n.* fourth part of a day
*ଯାମଳ, *n.* a pair, a couple.
ଯାମା, *n.* a garment.

*ଯାମାତା, *n.* a son-in-law.

*ଯାମିନୀ, *n.* night.

*ଯାଯାବର, *a.* vagrant, having no fixed abode;—*n.* a vagrant, a mendicant.

ଯୁଅଁର, *n.* a son-in-law.

ଯୁଆଣି, *n.* a small seed (see ଜୁଆଣି) ।

ଯୁଆନ, *a.* young, youthful;—*n.* a youth, an adult.

ଯୁଆଳି, *n.* a yoke.

ଯୁକ୍ତ, *a.* joined, connected with; fit, proper.

ଯୁକ୍ତାକ୍ଷର, *n.* a compound letter.

ଯୁକ୍ତି, *n.* reasoning, inference, advice.

*ଯୁକ୍ତିବିରୁଦ୍ଧ, *a.* contrary to reason.

*ଯୁକ୍ତିସିଦ୍ଧ, *a.* logical, according to reason.

ଯୁଗ, *n.* an age of the world, a dispensation; *a pair; an axle-tree.

ଯୁଗତ, *a.* good, excellent, well.

ଯୁଗଧର୍ମ, *n.* the character of an age.

*ଯୁଗପତ୍, *ad.* at once.

*ଯୁଗଳ, *n.* a pair; a yoke; a mate.

*ଯୁଗ୍ମ, *n.* a couple, a pair, a brace.

ଯୁଗାନ୍ତ, *n.* the end of an age.

ଯୁଝିବା, *v.* to fight.

ଯୁଦ୍ଧ, *n.* a fight, battle, contest, war.

ଯୁଦ୍ଧବିଦ୍ୟା, *n.* science of war.

ଯୁଦ୍ଧଭୂମି, ଯୁଦ୍ଧସ୍ଥଳ, *n.* the battlefield.

ଯୁଦ୍ଧସଜ, ଯୁଦ୍ଧସଜ୍ଜା, *n.* military equipment, weapons of war, armour.

ଯୁବକ, ଯୁବା, *n.* a young man.

ଯୁବତ, ଯୁବତୀ, *n.* a young woman.

*ଯୁବତ୍ୱ, *n.* youthfulness, youth.

ଯୁବରାଜ, *n.* a prince, heir-apparent.

ଯୁବା, *n.* a young man;—*a.* young, youthful.

ଯୁବାକାଳ, *n.* time of youth.

ଯୂର, *n.* plunder, destruction.

ଯୂଈ, *ଯୂଥିକା, *n.* a species of jasmine.

ଯୂଥ, *n.* a flock, drove, swarm, herd.

*ଯୂପ, *n.* a sacrificial post or stake.

ଯେ, *pron.* that which, he who; that.

ଯେଦବଧି, *ad.* from which time.

ଯେଉଁ, *pron.* who, which.

ଯେଉଟ, *n.* see ଜେଉଟ ।

ଯେଉଁଠାରେ, *ad.* wherever, where.

ଯେଉଁପରି, *ad.* in what way, as.

ଯେକେହି, *pron.* whoever, whosoever.

ଯେକିଛି, *pron.* whatever, whichever.

ଯେଭେ, *ad.* whatever, like as.

ଯେଣିକି, *ad.* where, whither.

ଯେତେ, *ad.* as much, as many.

ଯେତେଥର, *ad.* as many times.

ଯେତେବେଳେ, *ad.* when, at what time.

ଯେପର୍ଯ୍ୟନ୍ତ, *ad.* till, until; whilst.

ଯେବେ, *conj.* if;—*ad.* when.

ଯେମନ୍ତ, ଯେମନ୍ତି, ଯେମତ, ଯେମିତ, ଯିମିତ, *ad.* as like, like as.

ଯେରୂପ, *ad.* such as, like as.

ଯେସନ, *ad.* as like as (poetical).

ଯେହୁ, *pron.* who, which (poetical).

ଯେହେତୁ, *conj.* because, for as much as.

ଯେହ୍ନେ, *ad.* as like as (poetical).

ଯେଣେ, *ad.* whenever.

ଯୋକ, ଯୌଁକ, *n.* a leech.

*ଯୋକ୍ତା, *n.* one who unites.

ଯୋଖା, *n.* mental calculation;—*a.* joined, mentally calculated.

ଯୋଖିବା, *v.* to join; to do mental calculation.

ଯୋଗ, *n.* junction, connection, union, addition; abstraction of mind.

ଯୋଗନିଦ୍ରା, *n.* sleep which admits of the full exercise of the mental powers.

ଯୋଗମାୟା, *n.* *Durga*, *Bhagabati*.

ଯୋଗାଇବା, *v.* to supply, to provide.

ଯୋଗାକର୍ଷଣ, *n.* cohesion.

ଯୋଗାଡ, *n.* a preparing of food for cooking; an expedient, means.

*ଯୋଗାରୂଢ, *a.* continuing in a state of abstraction;—**n.** a *yogi*.

*ଯୋଗାସନ, *n.* a posture assisting the mind in profound contemplation.

ଯୋଗିନୀ, *n.* a female ascetic.

ଯୋଗୀ, *n.* an ascetic, a devotee.

ଯୋଗେ, *ad.* through, by means of.

ଯୋଗ୍ୟ, *a.* worthy, fit, suitable.

ଯୋଗ୍ୟତା, *n.* worthiness, fitness, ability.

ଯୋଜକ, *n.* an isthmus; *a negotiator.

ଯୋଜନ, *n.* four koss or eight miles; *uniting.

*ଯୋଜନା, *n.* union, conjuncture, grammatical construction.

ଯୋଡ, *n.* a pair; junction; a small stream.

ଯୋଡା, *a.* joined; suitable;—*n.* a couple, a pair.

ଯୋଡାଇବା, *v.* to cause to unite, to cause to join together.

ଯୋଡାଏ, *n.* a pair, a couple (only).

ଯୋଡିବା, *v.* to join, to unite.

ଯୋତ, *n.* the tie of a yoke; a farm.

ଯୋତା, *n.* shoes, sandals.

ଯୋତିବା, *v.* to yoke (bullock or horse, etc.).

*ଯୋତ୍ର, *n.* wealth, income, capital; the tie of a yoke.

ଯୋଦ୍ଧା, *n.* a warrior, combatant.

*ଯୋନି, *n.* the vulva, the womb.

*ଯୋଷା, ଯୋଷିତ୍, *n.* a woman, a female.

*ଯୌକ୍ତିକ, *a.* founded on reasoning, logical.

*ଯୌଗିକ, *a.* derivative, regularly formed.

ଯୌତୁକ, *n.* a dower, marriage gift.

ଯୌବନ, *ଯୌବ, *n.* youth, youthfulness.

ଯୌବରାଜ୍ୟ, *n.* the rank or rights of an heir-apparent.

ର.

ର. the 27th consonant.

ରଇତ, *n.* a tenant; a peasant.

ରଇତି, *a.* belonging to a tenant.
ରଓଆନା, *n.* a pass for goods; a go- [ing.
ରକବା, *n.* land records; area.
ରକମ୍, *n.* a sort, kind; goods, materials.
ରକା, *n.* a sudden pain or spasm.
ରକ୍ତ, *n.* blood.
ରକ୍ତଚନ୍ଦନ, *n.* red sandal-wood.
ରକ୍ତପଦ୍ମ, *n.* the red lotus.
ରକ୍ତପାତ, *n.* shedding of blood.
*ରକ୍ତପାୟୀ, *a.* bloodsucking.
ରକ୍ତପିତ୍ତ, *n.* a disease; sudden flow of blood from the nose or mouth.
ରକ୍ତବର୍ଣ୍ଣ, *a.* and *n.* red, blood-colour.
ରକ୍ତମୋକ୍ଷଣ, *n.* the act of blood-letting.
ରକ୍ତସ୍ରାବ, *n.* hemorrhage.
ରକ୍ତହୀନ, *a.* bloodless.
*ରକ୍ତାକ୍ତ, *a.* smeared with blood.
ରକ୍ତାଶୟ, *n.* heart.
ରକ୍ତାତିସାର, *n.* bloody-flux.
*ରକ୍ତିମା, *n.* redness.
ରକ୍ତୋତ୍ପଳ, *n.* a red lotus.
ରଖାଇବା, *v.* to cause to remain or stay, to cause to stop.
ରଖାରଖି, *n.* a putting or laying down.
ରଖିବା, *v.* to put, to place, to keep or preserve anything, to take care of anything. [shepherd.
ରଖୁଆଳ, *n.* a hired cowkeeper or
ରଗ, *n.* a sinew; anger.

ରଗଡ଼ା, *a.* rough, gravelly; ground, pulverized;—*n.* grinding or pulverizing.
ରଗଡ଼ିବା, *v.* to rub, to rub out or bruize corn, etc., to grind or pulverize.
ରଗରଗ, *a.* harsh, severe, bitter.
ରଘୁବଂଶ, *n.* the race of *Raghu*; name of a poem.
ରଙ୍କ, *a.* poor, miserly;—*n.* a miser.
ରଙ୍କଣା, *n.* a miser;—*a.* miserly, niggardly; *fem.* ରଙ୍କୁଣୀ ।
ରଙ୍ଗ, *n.* paint, colour; mirth, fun; theatre, dramatic play; tin.
ରଙ୍ଗଢଙ୍ଗ, *n.* wanton antics, wantonness, merriment.
ରଙ୍ଗଣୀ, *n.* name of a flower.
ରଙ୍ଗଭୂମି, *n.* a field of battle; *a stage, a theatre. [fun.
ରଙ୍ଗରସ, *n.* merry-making, sport,
*ରଙ୍ଗଶାଳା, *n.* a ball-room, a theatre.
ରଙ୍ଗା, *a.* red; painted, coloured.
ରଙ୍ଗିଆ, ରଙ୍ଗିଲା, *a.* gaudy, flash, showy, highly-coloured.
ରଚକ, *n.* an author, compiler, maker.
*ରଚନ, *n.* making, forming, composing
ରଚନା, *n.* composition of literary works; an orderly arrangement (of parts), a making, the arraying (of troops).

ରଚୟିତା, *n.* an author, a maker; *fem.* ରଚୟିତ୍ରୀ ।

ରଚିତ, *a.* composed, written, made, put together.

*ରଜଃ, ରଜ, *n.* dust, pollen of flowers; menses; secularity.

ରଜକ, *n.* a washerman; *fem.* ରଜକୀ ।

*ରଜତ, *n.* silver; ivory; white substance.

ରଜନୀ, ରଜନି, *n.* night; *turmeric.

*ରଜନୀମୁଖ, *n.* evening, nightfall.

ରଜସ୍ୱଳା, *a.* menstruous.

*ରଜ୍ଜୁ, *n.* a rope, cable, hawser.

ରଞ୍ଜକ, *a.* jovial, merry, cheering.

ରଞ୍ଜକପଥ, *n.* touch-hole of a gun.

ରଞ୍ଜନ, *n.* an exciting, a pleasing.

ରଞ୍ଜା, *n.* anything for plants to climb on. [rumour, fame.

ରଟନା, *ରଟନ, *n.* report; publicity,

ରଟରଟ, *n.* a sound of breaking.

ରଟିବା, *v.* to utter, to repeat, to announce, to proclaim, to twitter, to shout with joy or sorrow.

ରଡ, *n.* fire without smoke.

ରଡ, *n.* a scream, a loud cry.

ରଡିବା, *v.* to call like crows and other birds.

ରଣ. *n.* conflict, battle, war.

ରଣଜୟୀ, *a.* victorious in war.

ରଣତରୀ, *n.* a war-ship.

ରଣବାଦ୍ୟ, *n.* a military instrument of music.

*ରଣଭଙ୍ଗ, *n.* defeat, discomfiture.

ରଣଭୂମି, *n.* a field of battle.

ରଣଶିଙ୍ଗା, *n.* a war trumpet.

*ରଣସଜ୍ଜା, *n.* military equipment (an inclusive term as applied to all kinds of military equipment—clothes, guns, etc.).

*ରଣସ୍ତମ୍ଭ, *n.* a monument of war, a trophy.

*ରଣାଙ୍ଗନ, *n.* battle-field.

ରଣ୍ଡ, *n.* a widower.

ରଣ୍ଡୀ, *n.* a widow, a woman.

ରଣ୍ଡୀବାଜ, *n.* a whoremonger.

ରତ, *a.* attached, devoted to, given.

ରତରଭ, *n.* sunset, sun's rays at sunset.

ରତା, *n.* a kind of fish; a pallidness of complexion.

ରତି, *n.* a small red seed used as a gold-smith's weight; sensual enjoyment, sexual intercourse; *wife of Cupid.

*ରତିପତି, *n.* Cupid.

ରତିଶକ୍ତି, *n.* virile power.

ରତ୍ନ, *n.* precious stone, jewel, gem.

ରତ୍ନାକର, *n.* the sea; jewel-mine.

ରଥ, *n.* a car, a chariot.

ରଥଯାତ୍ରା, *n.* the car festival of *Jagannath.*

ରଥଯାତ୍ରୀ, *n.* a pilgrim to the car festival.

*ରଥାଙ୍ଗ, *n.* a wheel; a kind of bird (see ଚକ୍ରବାକ).

ରଥୀ, *n.* a charioteer, *coachman.

ରଦ୍, ରଦ, *n.* rejection, refutation; —*a.* rejected, refuted.

*ରଦ, *n.* a tooth, a tusk.

*ରଦଚ୍ଛଦ, ରଦନଚ୍ଛଦ, *n.* the lips.

ରଦା, *n.* a layer, one layer of a wall, etc.

ରଦ୍ଦ, ରଦ୍ଦି, *a.* rejected, (anything) become useless, spoiled.

ରନ୍ଦା, *n.* a carpenter's plane.

ରନ୍ଧନ, *n.* cooking of food.

ରନ୍ଧନଶାଳା, *n.* a cookroom.

ରନ୍ଧ୍ର, *n.* a hole, cavity, fissure.

ରପଟ, *n.* *Eng.* a report or account.

ରପ୍ତାନି, *n.* the export of goods.

ରଫା, *n.* the settlement of a dispute or matter of business, a compromising.

ରଫାନାମା, *n.* a writing or deed of settlement of disputes.

ରଫୁ, *n.* the mending or darning of clothes.

ରବ, *n.* a sound, voice, rumour.

ରବି, *n.* various kinds of pulse; *the sun.

ରବିବାର, *n.* Sunday.

*ରଭସ, *n.* speed, hurry; joy, gladness.

ରମଣ, *n.* sexual enjoyment, coition, sport, dalliance.

ରମଣୀ, *n.* an agreeable woman; a wife.

ରମଣୀୟ, *a.* delightful, charming.

ରମା, *n.* a name of *Lakshmi.*

ରମ୍ପାକୁଣ୍ଡିଆ, *n.* dry itch.

ରମ୍ପାରମ୍ପି, *n.* a scratching.

*ରମ୍ଭା, *n.* the plantain.

*ରମ୍ୟ, *a.* lovely, beautiful, charming.

ରଶୁଣ, *ଲଶୁନ, *n.* garlic.

*ରଶ୍ମି, *n.* a sunbeam, ray of light.

ରସ, *n.* juice, sap; relish; wit, essence (in literature).

ରସକର୍ପୂର, *n.* muriate of mercury.

ରସଗୋଲା, *n.* a kind of round ball sweetmeat.

*ରସଜ୍ଞ, *a.* capable of discerning the beauty of things, witty;—*n.* a man of taste or feeling; a critic; a poet; a physician.

ରସଦ, *n.* provision made for a visitor or touring officer; provision for an army or camp.

ରସନେନ୍ଦ୍ରିୟ, *ରସନା, *n.* the tongue, organ of taste.

ରସବାତ, *n.* rheumatism.

ରସମୟ, *a.* juicy; sentimental.

ରସା, *n.* broth, juice, gravy; a rope; *the earth.

ରସାଇବା, *v.* to excite lustful passions.

ରସାଞ୍ଜନ, *n.* a colouring for the eyes; sulphate of copper.

ରସାଣ, *n.* an article for polishing metals.

ରସାଣିବା, *v.* to make bright by rubbing or cleansing, to polish metals.

ରସାତଳ, *n.* the lower regions.

ରସାୟନ, *n.* compounded medicine; any poison; chemistry.

ରସାଳ, *a.* juicy, savoury;—*n.* *a juicy mango.

ରସାସ୍ୱାଦ, *n.* the taste of a savoury substance.

ରସିକ, *a.* sentimental, witty, droll.

ରସିକତା, *n.* wittiness, humour, jocularity.

ରସିକା, *a. fem.* merry, witty;—*n.* a coquette.

ରସିବା, *v.* to be blinded or subjected by affection or love.

ରସିଦ, ରସିଦ୍, *n. Eng.* a receipt, an acknowledgment.

ରସୀ, *n.* a cord, line, halter.

ରସୁଣିଆ, *n.* an ornament for the arms;—*a.* having the scent of garlic.

ରସୁଣ, *ରସୁନ, ରସୋଣ, *n.* garlic.

ରସୁମ, ରେସମ୍, *n.* duty, tax, toll, postage.

ରହଣି, *n.* a residence.

ରହଣିଗନ୍ଧ, *n.* a bad smell arising from stale *ghee.*

ରହସ୍ୟ, *n.* a secret, mystery; a mystical doctrine; joke, diversion.

ରହିତ, *a.* deprived of, free from, without.

ରହିବା, *v.* to remain, stay, desist.

*ରକ୍ଷଃ, *n.* a demon, fiend, giant.

ରକ୍ଷକ, *n.* a keeper, a protector.

ରକ୍ଷଣ, *n.* protecting, preserving, saving.

ରକ୍ଷଣାବେକ୍ଷଣ, *n.* protecting and supervising.

*ରକ୍ଷଣୀୟ, *a.* preservable.

ରକ୍ଷା, *n.* protection, security, preservation.

ରକ୍ଷାକର୍ତ୍ତା, ରକ୍ଷାକାରୀ, *n.* a protector, preserver.

ରକ୍ଷିତ, *a.* preserved, saved, protected, kept.

*ରକ୍ଷିସୈନ୍ୟ, *n.* guard, sentinel.

ରଇ, *n.* white mustard.

ରଇକା, *n.* a woman's bodice.

ରଇତା, ରଇ, *n.* cooked vegetables mixed with pulverized mustard.

ରଉଟୀ, *n.* a small tent.

ରଉତ, *n.* a surname.

ରଉତରାୟ, *n.* younger brother of a prince or king.

ରଉଳ, *n.* a surname; a *máli.*

ରଗ, *n.* passion, anger, flush; pungency; a tune.

ରଗାନ୍ଧ, *a.* blind with rage or passion.

ରଗାନ୍ୱିତ, *a.* passionate, irritable.

ରଗିଣୀ, *a.* a key-note, tune.

ରଗୀ, *n.* passionate, irritable.

ରଘବ, *n.* *Ráma*; name of a fish.

ରଙ୍ଗା, *a.* red, scarlet;—*n.* solder, spelter.

ରଜ, *n.* a bricklayer, mason.

ରଜକନ୍ୟା, *n.* a princess.

ରଜକର, *n.* tribute, royal revenue.

ରଜକୀୟ, *a.* royal, kingly.

ରାଜକୁମାର, *n.* a prince, king's son.
ରାଜକୁମାରୀ, *n.* a princess.
ରାଜକୁଳ, *n.* a royal family.
*ରାଜକୋଷ, *n.* see ରାଜଭଣ୍ଡାର ।
ରାଜଛତ୍ର, *n.* an umbrella which is the sign of royalty.
ରାଜତ୍ୱ, *n.* royalty, government, empire, reign.
ରାଜଦଣ୍ଡ, *n.* royal sceptre; a punishment imposed by a king or Government.
ରାଜଦାଣ୍ଡ, ରାଜମାର୍ଗ, *n.* the king's highway.
ରାଜଦ୍ରୋହ, *n.* treason, rebellion.
ରାଜଦ୍ରୋହୀ, *a.* seditious, rebellious.
ରାଜଦ୍ୱାର, *n.* a law-court; a king's gate; a levee.
ରାଜଧର୍ମ, *n.* royal duties or virtues.
ରାଜଧାନୀ, *n.* a royal residence, capital.
ରାଜନ, *n.* a king, a sovereign (poetical).
ରାଜନଅର, *n.* a king's palace.
ରାଜନୀତି, *n.* politics, the duties of a king.
*ରାଜନ୍ୟ, *n.* of royal birth, a *kshatriya.*
*ରାଜପତ୍ନୀ, *n.* a queen.
ରାଜପଥ, *n.* see ରାଜଦାଣ୍ଡ ।
ରାଜପୁର, *n.* a king's palace; a royal city.
ରାଜପୁରୁଷ, *n.* a king's servants, authorized Government officers.
ରାଜଭକ୍ତ, *a.* loyal.
ରାଜଭକ୍ତି, *n.* loyalty.
ରାଜଭଣ୍ଡାର, *n.* king's treasury.
ରାଜଭାଷା, *n.* king's language, court language.
ରାଜଯକ୍ଷ୍ମା, ରାଜଜକ୍ଷ୍ମା, *n.* pulmonary consumption.
*ରାଜର୍ଷି, *n.* a royal sage.
ରାଜଲକ୍ଷଣ, *n.* sign or mark of royalty.
ରାଜଲକ୍ଷ୍ମୀ, *n.* the fortune of a king.
*ରାଜସଦନ, *n.* a palace, royal residence.
ରାଜସଭା, *n.* privy council; court of justice.
ରାଜସ୍ୱ, *n.* taxes, tribute; king's due.
ରାଜହଂସ, *n.* a gander, male goose.
ରାଜା, *n.* a king, sovereign.
ରାଜାଜ୍ଞା, *n.* royal edict.
ରାଜାଧିରାଜ, *n.* supreme sovereign.
ରାଜି, ରାଜୀ, *n.* assent, consent; a row, rank;—*a.* consented, agreed.
ରାଜିନାମା, *n.* a deed of adjustment.
*ରାଜୀବ, *n.* a waterlily, lotus.
ରାଜ୍ୟ, *n.* kingdom, empire, realm.
*ରାଜ୍ୟାଙ୍ଗ, *n.* the *personnel* and paraphernalia of government.
ରାଜ୍ଞୀ, *n.* a queen.
ରାଡ଼, *a.* uncivilized, rude, barbarous; cruel, miserly;—*n.* name of a jungle tribe.
ରାଡ଼ି, *n.* a class of fishermen.
ରାଣ, *n.* an oath; *a king.
ରାଣୀ, *n.* a queen.
ରାଣ୍ଡି, *n.* a widow.
ରାତି, *n.* night.
ରାତିକଣା, *a.* suffering from night-blindness;—*n.* night-blindness.

ରାତପିନ୍ଧା, *n.* night-clothes.
ରାତି, ରାତ୍ର, *n.* night.
ରାତିଚର, *n.* a night-prowler; a bat; imp, goblin.
ରାଧା, *n.* the favourite mistress of *Krishna*.
ରାନ୍ଧଣା, *n.* cookery, cooking.
ରାନ୍ଧଣାଘର, *n.* a cook-room, kitchen.
ରାନ୍ଧିବା, *v.* to cook.
ରାନ୍ଧୁଣିଆ, *n.* a male cook; *fem.* ରାନ୍ଧୁଣୀ।
ରାବ, *n.* a sound, noise, shout, yell.
ରାମ, *n.* *Ráma*, hero of the *Rámáyana*.
ରାମଦୂତ, *n.* *Hanumán*.
ରାମନବମୀ, *n.* a festival in honour of *Ráma's* birth.
*ରାମା, *n.* a beautiful woman.
ରାମାୟଣ, *n.* the celebrated epic poem *Rámáyana*.
ରାମ୍ପ, *n.* a scratch.
ରାମ୍ପିବା, ରାମ୍ପୁଡ଼ିବା, *v.* to scratch, to [scrape.
ରାୟ, *n.* a title of honour; an opinion on any matter; a decision.
ରାଳ, *n.* tar.
ରାଶ୍, ରାସ୍, *n.* a bridle.
ରାଶି, *n.* a number; sesamum seed; a heap; a sign of the zodiac; a term of the rule of proportion.
ରାଶିଚକ୍ର, *n.* the zodiac.
ରାଶିତେଲ, *n.* sesamum oil.
ରାଶୀକୃତ, *a.* heaped up, abundant.
ରାଷ୍ଟ୍ର, *n.* country, realm.
ରାଷ୍ଟ୍ରବିପ୍ଳବ, *n.* revolution.
*ରାସ, *n.* play, sport, toying, dalli- [ance.
*ରାସଭ, *n.* an ass.
ରାସଯାତ୍ରା, *n.* a festival of *Krishna* held on the full moon of *Kartic*.
ରାସାୟନିକ, *a.* chemical.
ରାସ୍ତା, *ରାହା, *n.* a road, path, way.
ରାସ୍ନା, *n.* a species of acacia, a drug.
ରାହା, *n.* room; *a road.
ରାହାଗିର, *n.* travelling.
ରାହାମାରା, *n.* robbing or killing on the road.
ରାହୁ, *a.* the ecliptic shadow; the ascending node or dragon's head.
*ରାହୁଗ୍ରସ୍ତ, *a.* eclipsed, seized by [*Ráhu*.
ରାହୁଗ୍ରାସ, *n.* eclipse of the sun or moon.
ରାକ୍ଷସ, *n.* a fabulous cannibal or fiend; *fem.* ରାକ୍ଷସୀ।
*ରିକ୍ତ, *a.* empty, void, destitute.
ରିକ୍ତହସ୍ତ, *a.* empty-handed.
ରିକ୍ତା, *n.* the fourth, ninth, and fourteenth day of the moon.
ରିଠା, *n.* the soap-nut or berry.
*ରିପୁ, *n.* an enemy, a foe.
ରିଷ୍ଟ, *n.* evil, misfortune.
ରୀତି, *n.* manner, habit, rite, custom.
ରୁଆ, *n.* the rafters of a thatched roof.
ରୁଆ, *n.* transplanting of rice, etc.; —*a.* transplanted.
ରୁଆଳି, *n.* a transplanter.

ରୁଇ, *n.* cleaned cotton.

ରୁଖା, *n.* a lampstand;—*a.* dry.

ରୁଗ୍ଣ, *a.* diseased, sick, ill.

ରୁଚି, *n.* inclination, appetite, relish.

ରୁଚିକର, *a.* producing appetite, causing desire.

ରୁଚିବା, *v.* to suit the taste, to be pleasing or agreeable. [nice.

*ରୁଚିର, *a.* engaging, pleasing,

ରୁଟି, ରୋଟି, ରୁଟୀ, ରୋଟୀ, *n.* bread, a

ରୁଟିବାଲା, *n.* a baker. [loaf.

ରୁଣ୍‌ଝୁଣ, *n.* a jingling sound.

ରୁଣ୍ଡ, *a.* assembled, crowded.

ରୁଣ୍ଡାଇବା, *v.* to assemble, to crowd. to gather together. [ed.

*ରୁଦ୍ଧ, *a.* shut, blocked up, hinder-

ରୁଦ୍ର, *n.* *Siva*; *the sun;—*a.* furious.

ରୁଦ୍ରାକ୍ଷ, *n.* a berry used for rosaries,

*ରୁଧିର, *n.* blood. [etc.

ରୁସି, *n.* scurf.

ରୁଦ୍‌ବାସୁ, *n.* an order in the proceeding of an action.

ରୁମ, *n.* hair, wool, fur.

ରୁମାଲ, *n.* a handkerchief.

ରୁଷା, *n.* sullen anger.

ରୁଷିବା, *v.* to be angry and vexed.

*ରୁଷ୍ଟ, *a.* enraged, furious, angry.

*ରୁଷ୍ଟି, *n.* anger, rage, fury.

*ରୂକ୍ଷ, *a.* rude, hard, cruel.

ରୂଢ଼, *n.* short hair which has been or is to be shaved off;—**a.* harsh; produced; sprouted.

*ରୂଢ଼ପଦାର୍ଥ, *n.* elements.

ରୂପ, *n.* form, shape; manner, kind, sort; beauty; (in *Gram.*) a declension of nouns or verbs.

ରୂପକ, *a.* figurative, allegorical.

ରୂପକବାକ୍ୟ, *n.* a figurative or allegorical expression.

ରୂପବତୀ, *ରୂପସୀ, *a.* beautiful or elegant (woman).

ରୂପବାନ୍, *a.* beautiful, elegant.

ରୂପଲାବଣ୍ୟ, *n.* elegance, loveliness.

*ରୂପସୀ, *a. fem.* elegant, beautiful, comely.

ରୂପା, *n.* silver. [of form.

ରୂପାନ୍ତର, *n.* transfiguration, change

ରେ, a vocative particle employed in addressing a person in contempt, "Hear, you."

ରେକଟା, *a.* rough, tough.

ରେକାବ, *n.* a stirrup.

ରେକାବୀ, *n.* a dish, a saucer.

ରେଖା, *n.* a line, streak, stripe, slit.

ରେଖାଗଣିତ, *n.* geometry.

ରେଚକ, *a.* and *n.* a purgative.

ରେଚନ, *n.* purging, oozing, dropping.

ରେଜ୍‌କି, *n.* small silver coin, a four anna or two anna piece, etc., small change.

ରେଜା, *n.* small change, overplus, remnants;—*a.* of small use.

ରେଜାଇ, *n.* a quilt, bed-quilt.

*ରେଣୁ, *n.* dust, pollen, sand; an atom.

*ରେତଃ *n.* the seminal fluid. [(ʻ).
ରେଫ୍, *n.* the letter ର or its symbol
ରେବତୀ, *n.* the 27th stellar mansion.
ରେଲବାଟ, *n.* a railway.
ରେଶମ, *n.* silk.
ରେଶମୀ, *a.* silken, silky.
ରୈଖିକ, *a.* lineal.
ରୋଇବା, *v.* to transplant; to plant.
ରୋକଠୋକ୍, *n.* ready money, cash.
ରୋକଡ଼, *n.* a cash-book, a record.
ରୋକା, *n.* a note. [obstruct.
ରୋକିବା, *v.* to stop, to hinder, to
ରୋଗଶୋଦ୍, *n.* dismissal.
ରୋଗ, *n.* disease, illness, distemper.
ରୋଗଗ୍ରସ୍ତ, *a.* taken ill, diseased.
ରୋଗା, ରୋଗୀ, *a.* ill, sickly, diseased.
ରୋଚକ, *a.* sharpening the appetite; agreeable. [daily.
ରୋଜ୍, *n.* a day; ରୋଜ୍‌ରୋଜ୍;—*ad.*
ରୋଜଗାର, *n.* earning, income; employment, service.
ରୋଜନାମା, *n.* a day-book, diary.
ରୋଜା, *n.* a mussalman fast.
ରୋଟ, *a.* stout, thick, corpulent.
ରୋଟି, ରୋଟୀ, *ରୋଟିକା, *n.* bread, a loaf.
ରୋଦନ, *n.* weeping, wailing, crying.
*ରୋଧ, *n.* obstruction, prohibition.
*ରୋଧକ, *a.* obstructing, prohibitory. [man.
*ରୋପକ, *n.* a planter, sower, seeds-
ରୋପଣ, *n.* planting, fixing, grafting.

ରୋପିତ, *a.* planted, sown. [wool.
ରୋମ, *n.* hair of the body, down,
ରୋମକୂପ, *n.* pores of the skin.
ରୋମଟାଙ୍କୁଡ଼ିବା, *v.* to stand on end (said of hair).
*ରୋମନ୍ଥ, *n.* ruminating; chewing of the cud.
*ରୋମନ୍ଥକ, *a.* ruminant;—*n.* an animal that ruminates.
ରୋମଶ, *a.* hairy.
*ରୋମହର୍ଷଣ, *a.* causing a thrill, awe-inspiring.
ରୋମାଞ୍ଚ, *ରୋମହର୍ଷ, *n.* bristling or standing on end of the hair.
ରୋମାଞ୍ଚିତ, *a.* having the hair erect through any sudden emotion.
*ରୋମାବଳୀ, *n.* the row of hair from the navel to the breast.
ରୋମାସ୍‌ସମ୍ପ୍ରଦାୟ, *n.* Romish Church.
ରୋୟଦାଦ୍, *n.* records of a case.
ରୋଲ, *n.* a ruler; *sound, rolling sound.
ରୋଶନି, ରୋଶନାଇ, *n.* an illumination; splendour. [fury.
ରୋଷ, *n.* wrath, anger, passion,
ରୋସୁମ୍, *n.* a fee, duties.
*ରୋଷାନ୍ୱିତ, *a.* angry, passionate.
ରୋଷାଇ, *n.* cooking.
ରୋଷାଇଘର, *n.* a cookroom.
ରୋହି, *n.* the *rohi* fish.
ରୋହିଣୀ, *n.* the 4th stellar mansion.
*ରୋହିତ, *a.* red;—*n.* the *rohi* fish; red colour; blood.

*ରୌଦ୍ର, *n.* sunshine, glare, heat.

*ରୌପ୍ୟ, *n.* silver;—*a.* made of silver.

ରୌରବ, *n.* a Hindu hell;—**a.* terrible.

ଲ.

ଲ, the 28th consonant.

ଲଉଡ଼, *n.* a stick, a cudgel.

ଲକ୍‌ଲକ୍, *n.* bubbling sound as in boiling rice, etc.

ଲଗା, *n.* a surety, bail;—*a.* planted, rooted.

ଲଗାଇବା, *v.* to apply to any purpose or work; to plant; to anoint; to bring into contact.

ଲଗାଣ, *n.* continuous rain.

ଲଗାମ, *n.* a bridle.

ଲଗାଲଗି, *a.* joined to each other.

ଲଗି, *n.* a hooked stick.

*ଲଗୁଡ଼, *n.* a club, bludgeon, staff.

ଲଗ୍ନ, *a.* attached to, connected with, clinging or sticking to;—*n.* a portion of time including the space which elapses between the first emersion of a sign of the zodiac above the horizon and its being completely above it.

*ଲଘିଷ୍ଠ, *a.* very light, very small.

ଲଘୁ, *a.* light, insignificant, small.

ଲଘୁଛନ୍ଦ, *n.* a cadence.

ଲଘୁତା, ଲଘୁତ୍ୱ, *n.* lightness, insignificance.

*ଲଘୁମୂଲ୍ୟ, *a.* low-priced;—*n.* a low price.

*ଲଘୁହସ୍ତ, *a.* ready or light-handed.

ଲଘୂକରଣ, *n.* reduction.

ଲଙ୍କା, *n.* Ceylon.

ଲଙ୍କାଧିପତି, *n.* *Rábana.*

ଲଙ୍କାମରିଚ, *n.* chillies.

ଲଙ୍ଗର୍, *n.* an anchor.

ଲଙ୍ଗଳ, *n.* a plough; a helm.

ଲଙ୍ଗଳଫାଳ, *n.* a ploughshare.

ଲଙ୍ଗଳମୁଣ୍ଡା, *n.* the head of a plough.

ଲଙ୍ଗଳା, *a.* naked.

ଲଙ୍ଗୁଳୀ, *a.* naked (ascetic).

ଲଙ୍ଘନ, *n.* leaping over, transgressing; fasting.

ଲଙ୍ଗା, *a.* naked, unsheathed.

ଲଜ୍ଜା, *n.* shame; modesty, shyness.

*ଲଜ୍ଜାକର, *a.* shameful, disgraceful.

*ଲଜ୍ଜାବାନ୍, *a.* ashamed, retiring, shy: *fem.* ଲଜ୍ଜାବତୀ ।

ଲଜ୍ଜାଳୁ, ଲଜ୍ଜାଶୀଳ, *a.* modest, bashful.

ଲଜ୍ଜାହୀନ, *a.* shameless, immodest.

ଲଜ୍ଜିତ, *a.* ashamed, put to shame.

*ଲଞ୍ଜ, *n.* a tail.

ଲଞ୍ଜତାରା, *n.* a comet.

ଲଟ୍, *n.* a fault, defect; responsibility.

ଲଟକାଇବା, *v.* to hang up, to suspend.

ଲଟଫଟ୍, *a.* intricate, perplexing, troublesome.

ଲଟପଟ୍, *a.* rolling about, wallowing.

ଲଟା, *n.* a creeper, vine, climbing plant.

ଲଟାଇବା, ଲଟେଇବା, *v.* to intertwine, to climb (as a creeper).

ଲଟୁ, ଲଟ୍ଟୁ, *n.* a toy of that name.

ଲଠି, ଲାଠି, *n.* a stick, walking stick.

ଲଡବଡିଆ, *a.* wavering, inconstant, moving.

ଲଡଲଡ, *a.* unsteady, movable.

ଲଡୁ, *n.* a sweetmeat ball.

ଲଢାଇ, *n.* a battle, fight, war.

ଲଢାଇବା, *v.* to cause to fight.

ଲଢାଳ, *n.* a fighter, warrior, boxer.

ଲଢିବା, *v.* to fight, to war.

ଲଣ୍ଠଣ୍, *n.* a lantern.

ଲଣ୍ଡଭଣ୍ଡ, *n.* confusion, disorder;—*a.* hurried.

ଲଣ୍ଡା, *a.* bald; lopped; shorn;—*n.* a bald-headed man.

ଲଣ୍ଡାବଘୁଲି, *n.* name of a medicinal plant and its seed.

ଲତା, *n.* a creeper, a vine.

ଲଦନ, *n.* loading; a load.

ଲଦାଇବା, *v.* to cause to be loaded or heaped up.

ଲଦାଲଦି, *n.* a loading and packing.

ଲଦବା, *v.* to load, to heap up.

*ଲପନ, *n.* mouth; speaking.

ଲବ, *n.* a morsel, atom, tittle, jot; (in *Arith.*) a numerator.

ଲବଙ୍ଗ, *n.* clove.

ଲବଣ, *n.* salt.

*ଲବଣାକ୍ତ, *a.* salted, steeped in salt.

ଲବଣୀ, *n.* butter.

ଲବ୍ଧ, *a.* obtained, gained, got.

ଲଭିବା, *v.* to obtain, to get.

ଲଭ୍ୟ, *n.* advantage, result;—**a.* obtainable.

ଲମ୍ପଟ, *a.* dissolute, immoral, lewd.

ଲମ୍ପଟତା, *n.* lasciviousness, lewdness.

*ଲମ୍ଫ, *n.* a jump, a leap.

ଲମ୍ବ, ଲମ୍ବା, *a.* long, tall, high.

ଲମ୍ବ, *n.* (in *Geom.*) a perpendicular.

ଲମ୍ବମାନ, *a.* hanging down, stretching.

ଲମ୍ବାଇ, *n.* length.

ଲମ୍ବାଇବା, *v.* to extend or lengthen.

ଲମ୍ବାଲମ୍ବି, *n.* the whole extent in length;—*ad.* lengthwise.

ଲୟ, *n.* destruction; meditation; equal time in music and dancing.

*ଲଳନା, *n.* a woman; tongue.

*ଲଳିତ, *a.* displaying charms, lovely.

ଲଲାଟ, *n.* the forehead; fate, destiny.

*ଲଲାମ, *n.* an ornament, an ornament for the head; anything that is the best of its kind;—*a.* charming, beautiful.

*ଲଶୁନ, ଲସୁନ, *n.* garlic.

ଲସା, *n.* pus, purulent matter.

ଲସି, *n.* juice (a liquid exuding from fruit broken off the tree).

ଲସ୍କର, *n.* an army; a soldier; ship's crew.

ଲହକା, *a.* weak; slim, slender.

ଲହଡା, ଲହରି, ଲହରୀ, *n.* a wave, billow.

ଲହର, *n.* continued talking or singing like the ceaseless roar of waves.

ଲହୁଣୀ, *n.* butter.

ଲକ୍ଷ, *a.* and *n.* one hundred thousand; 100,000.

ଲକ୍ଷଣ, *n.* mark, sign, characteristic.

*ଲକ୍ଷଣୀୟ, *a.* observable, noticeable, perceptible.

*ଲକ୍ଷିତ, *a.* indicated.

ଲକ୍ଷ୍ମୀ, *n.* the goddess of prosperity, wife of *Vishnu.*

ଲକ୍ଷ୍ମୀଛଡା, *a.* unfortunate.

ଲକ୍ଷ୍ମୀବନ୍ତ, *ଲକ୍ଷ୍ମୀବାନ୍, *a.* fortunate, prosperous.

ଲକ୍ଷ୍ୟ, *n.* a butt, aim;—*a.* noticeable, aimed.

ଲାଉ, *n.* a gourd, a pumpkin.

ଲାଉକରିବା, *v.* to carry (a man) on the back.

ଲାଏକ, *a.* proper, fit, competent; fertile.

ଲାଖ, *n.* lac, the lac insect; 100,000.

ଲାଖରାଜ, ଲାଖେରାଜ, *n.* freehold land.

ଲାଖରାଜଦାର, *n.* holder of free land.

ଲାଖିବା, *v.* see ଛାଖିବା ।

ଲାଗ୍‌ଲାଗ, *ad.* continuously, incessantly, repeatedly.

ଲାଗି, *ad.* on account of, for the sake of.

ଲାଗିବା, *v.* to touch, to adhere, to come in contact, to strike, to be engaged in.

ଲାଗୁଆ, *n.* a customer;—*a.* customary.

*ଲାଙ୍ଗଳ, *n.* a plough.

*ଲାଙ୍ଗଳଦଣ୍ଡ, *n.* the beam of a plough.

ଲାଙ୍ଗୁଡ, ଲାଙ୍ଗୁଳ, ଲାଙ୍ଗୂଳ, *n.* the tail of an animal.

ଲାଘବ, *n.* lightness, diminution.

ଲାଜ, *n.* shame, modesty.

*ଲାଜା, *n.* fried rice (see ଖଇ).

ଲାଜକୁଳା, ଲାଜକୁଡ଼, *a.* bashful, shame-faced.

ଲାଞ୍ଚ, *n.* a bribe.

ଲାଞ୍ଛନା, *ଲାଞ୍ଛନ, *n.* a stain, stigma, mark, sign.

*ଲାଞ୍ଛିତ, *a.* reproved; marked.

ଲାଞ୍ଜ, *n.* the tail of an animal.

ଲାଞ୍ଜି, *n.* the back part of a *dhinki.*

ଲାଟବନ୍ଦୀ, *n.* the due date for paying Government revenue, a sale-statement.

ଲାଠି, *n.* a club, stick, bludgeon.

ଲାତ, *n.* a kick.

ଲାବଣ୍ୟ, *n.* charm, beauty; *saltness.

ଲାଭ, *n.* gain, profit, advantage.

ଲାଭାଲାଭ, *n.* profit and loss.

*ଲାମ୍ପଟ୍ୟ, *n.* immorality, lewdness.

ଲାଳ, ଲାଳା, *n.* saliva, spittle.

ଲାଳନ, *n.* the careful nourishing of a child.

ଲାଳସା, *n.* desire. lust, covetousness.

*ଲାଳିତ, *n.* nursed, reared, caressed, fondled.

ଲାଳୁଆ, *a.* drivelling (boy); slippery.

ଲାଲ, *a.* red;—*n.* a horseshoe.

ଲାଲବନ୍ଦ, *n.* a farrier, horse-shoer.
ଲାଲିସ, *n.* a plaint, a lawsuit.
ଲାଶ, *n.* a corpse, a dead body.
ଲାହା, *ଲାକ୍ଷା, *n.* lac, sealing-wax.
ଲିଆ, *n.* parched rice (see ଖଇ).
ଲିଖ, *n.* a nit, louse.
ଲିଖନ, *n.* a writing.
ଲିଖିତ, *a.* written.
ଲିଙ୍ଗ, *n.* gender; *the penis, the Phallus
ଲିଚି, *n.* name of an edible fruit.
ଲିପା, *n.* smearing, plastering;—*a.* besmeared [letter.
*ଲିପି, *n.* a writing, a drawing; a
ଲିପିବଦ୍ଧ, *a.* mentioned by writing, written, recorded.
ଲିପିବା, *v.* to smear, to plaster over.
ଲିପ୍ତ, *a.* besmeared, tainted; joined; engaged in.
ଲିପ୍ସା, *n.* cupidity, covetousness.
*ଲିପ୍ସିତ, *a.* coveted, greedily sought after.
*ଲୀନ, *a.* united with, absorbed in.
ଲୀଳା, *n.* amorous sport, toying.
ଲୀଳାବତୀ, *n.* an arithmetical work; name of a female.
ଲୁକ୍କାୟିତ, *a.* concealed, hid.
ଲୁଗୁଣ, *a.* see ନଗୁଣ ।
ଲୁଗା, *n.* cloth, clothes, dress.
ଲୁଚୁଣ, *n.* a pilferer, a petty thief.
ଲୁଚାଇବା, *v.* to cause to hide.
ଲୁଚେ, ଲୁଚକ, ଲୁଚିଏ, ଲୁଚିକ, *a.* some, several;—*n.* a mass, a quantity.

ଲୁଚାଲୁଚି, *n.* hiding, secreting, covering up.
ଲୁଚିବା, *v.* to hide. [seek.
ଲୁଚକାଳି, *n.* the game of hide and
ଲୁଟ, ଲୁଟି, *n.* plunder, booty.
ଲୁଟାଇବା, *v.* to cause to be plundered, to cause to plunder.
ଲୁଟିଆର, *n.* a plunderer, a free-booter.
ଲୁଟିବା, *v.* to plunder, to loot.
ଲୁଣ, *n.* salt.
ଲୁଣିଆ, *n.* a dealer in salt;—*a.* saltish.
ଲୁଣିମାଛ, *n.* salt fish.
ଲୁଣ୍ଠନ, *n.* plundering; rolling about, wallowing.
ଲୁଣ୍ଠିତ, *a.* plundered; rolled about.
ଲୁଣ୍ଡା, *n.* a fire-wisp.
ଲୁଣ୍ଡି, *n.* thread stiffened with starch before weaving.
ଲୁପ୍ତ, *n.* effaced, extinct, obsolete.
*ଲୁବ୍ଧକ, *n.* a fowler, hunter.
ଲୁହ, *n.* a tear, tears.
ଲୁହା, *n.* iron.
ଲୁଇ, *n.* a kind of flannel.
*ଲୂତା, *n.* a spider.
*ଲୂତାତନ୍ତୁ, *n.* a spider's web, a cobweb.
ଲେଇ, *n.* paste, starch.
ଲେଉଟାଇବା, *v.* see ବେଉଟାଇବା ।
ଲେଉଟିଆ, *n.* a kind of spinage.
ଲେଉଟିବା, *v.* to turn, to turn back.
ଲେଖକ, *n.* a writer, a clerk.

ଲେଖନ, *n.* an iron pen, style or stylo; a writing.

ଲେଖନୀ, *n.* a pen, pencil, a graver.

ଲେଖା, *a.* written;—*n.* a writing.

ଲେଖାପଢା, *n.* writing and reading.

ଲେଖାଯୋଖା, *n.* accounts, reckonings.

ଲେଖାଲେଖି, *n.* written correspondence; the act of writing.

ଲେଖିତ, *a.* written, recorded.

ଲେଙ୍ଗଡା, *a.* lame, limping, crippled.

ଲେଣ୍ଡୁଆ, *n.* litter, rubbish;—*a.* unswept.

ଲେଜୁଆ, *n.* rheum of the eyes.

ଲେପ, *n.* an unguent, a plaster.

ଲେପନ, *n.* a smearing, a daubing.

ଲେଫାଫା, *n.* an envelope.

ଲେମ୍ବୁ, *n.* a lime, an orange.

ଲେଶ, *n.* minute particle; trace.

ଲେସଡା, *a.* waterish.

ଲେସିବା, *v.* to smear, to plaster.

*ଲେହନ, *n.* licking.

ଲେହୁ, *n.* paste.

*ଲେହ୍ୟ, *a.* (food) to be licked up.

ଲୋ, a vocative particle applied to women.

ଲୋଇ, *n.* serge cloth.

ଲୋକ, *n.* a person, people; world.

*ଲୋକନ, *n.* looking, surveying.

ଲୋକବାକ, *n.* servants and attendants; people.

*ଲୋକବାଦ, *n.* rumour, report, fame.

ଲୋକରଞ୍ଜନ, *n.* pleasing the world, popularity.

ଲୋକସାନ, *n.* loss, damage, mischief, injury.

ଲୋକାଚାର, *n.* general custom ways of the world.

ଲୋକାତୀତ, *a.* supernatural, extraordinary.

ଲୋକାନ୍ତର, *n.* another world, death.

ଲୋକାପବାଦ, *n.* public scandal, popular censure.

ଲୋକାରଣ୍ୟ, *n.* a crowd, multitude.

*ଲୋଚନ, *n.* the eye.

ଲୋଚା, *a.* libidinous, adulterous.

ଲୋଚାପଣିଆ, *n.* lechery, laciviousness.

ଲୋଟା, *n.* a metal water vessel.

ଲୋଟିବା, *v.* to tumble about, to wallow.

ଲୋଡା, *n.* need, occasion for, search;—*a.* necessary.

ଲୋଡାଲୋଡି, *n.* a general search.

ଲୋଡିବା, *v.* to search, to require.

ଲୋତକ, *n.* a tear, tears.

ଲୋଥ, *n.* see ନୋଥ ।

ଲୋଧ, *n.* a tree and its bark.

ଲୋପ, *n.* wiping out, extinction.

*ଲୋପ୍ୟ, *a.* effaceable.

ଲୋଭ, *n.* desire to get, covetousness.

ଲୋଭାଇବା, ଲୋଭେଇବା, *v.* to excite cupidity or covetousness.

ଲୋଭାସକ୍ତ, ଲୋଭୀ, *a.* greedy, covetous, desirous.

ଲୋମ, *n.* hair, down, wool.

ଲୋମକୂପ, *n.* root of the hair; pore of the skin.

*ଲୋମଶ, *a.* hairy, woolly, shaggy.
*ଲୋମହର୍ଷଣ, *a.* see ରୋମହର୍ଷଣ । [ing.
*ଲୋମାଞ୍ଚ, *n.* horripilation, thrill-
*ଲୋଲୁପ, *a.* very covetous, greedy.
*ଲୋଷ୍ଟ୍ର, *n.* a clod of earth.
*ଲୋହକାର, *n.* a blacksmith, iron-founder.
*ଲୋହକାନ୍ତ, *n.* a magnet, loadstone.
ଲୁହା, * ଲୋହ, *n.* iron. [cloth.
ଲୋହି, *n.* woollen wrapper, serge
*ଲୋହିତ, *a.* bloody, red, sanguine.
ଲୌକିକ, *a.* current, popular, world-
*ଲୌହ, *n.* iron. [ly.
*ଲୌହକାର, *n.* a blacksmith.
*ଲୌହବର୍ତ୍ମ, *n.* a railroad.

ଶ.

ଶ, *n.* the 29th consonant;—*a.* a hundred.
ଶତ, *a.* an *n.* one hundred; 100; c.
*ଶଂସିତ, *a.* spoken, said; praised, extolled.
ଶଁଷିବା, *v.* to curse, to use cutting language.
ଶଁଶଁ, *int.* sound of panting on account of great exertion.
*ଶକ, *n.* an era, epoch.
*ଶକଟ, *n.* a cart, waggon, hackery.
ଶକଡ଼ା, *a.* per hundred, per cent.
ଶକରକନ୍ଦ, *n.* the sweet potato.
ଶକାଳିବା, *v.* to feign to cry.
ଶକାବ୍ଦ, *n.* a year of the *Saka* era.
*ଶକୁନ, *n.* a bird; any omen presaging good or evil.
*ଶକୁନି, *n.* a vulture. [a noise.
ଶକଶକ, *a.* strongly desirous;—*n.*
ଶକ୍ତ, *a.* firm, hard, strong, austere.
ଶକ୍ତି, *n.* strength, power, ability.
ଶକ୍ତିମାନ, *a.* strong, powerful.
ଶକ୍ତିହୀନ, *a.* powerless, impotent.
*ଶକ୍ତୁ, *n.* a mushroom; parched and pulverized grain.
*ଶକ୍ୟ, *a.* practicable, possible.
*ଶକ୍ର, *n.* a name of *Indra.*
ଶଗଡ଼, *n.* a bullock-cart, a cart.
ଶଗଡ଼ିଆ, *n.* a bullock-cart driver.
ଶଙ୍କର, *n.* a name of *Siva*;—**a.* auspicious.
ଶଙ୍କା, *n.* terror, danger, peril.
ଶଙ୍କାକୁଳ, *a.* distressed with fear; suspicious.
ଶଙ୍କିତ, *a.* frightened, terrified.
ଶଙ୍କୁ, *n.* a stake, post or pole to mark some special place or boundary.
ଶଙ୍ଖ, *n.* conch. [falcon.
ଶଙ୍ଖଚିଲ, *n.* a large white hawk or
ଶଙ୍ଖଧ୍ୱନି, *n.* the sound of a conch.
ଶଙ୍ଖା, *n.* a shell bracelet.
ଶଙ୍ଖାରୀ, *n.* a shell-worker, the name of that caste.
ଶଙ୍ଖୁଳିବା, *v.* to visit a friend or relative; to comfort, to console.
ଶଚୀ, ଶଚି, *n.* wife of *Indra.*
ଶଜାରୁ, *n.* a porcupine.

ଶଠ, *a.* crafty, knavish, artful.
ଶଠତା, *n.* craftiness, knavery.
*ଶଣ, *n.* hemp, hemp plant.
*ଶଣ୍ଢ, ଶଣ୍ଡ, *n.* a eunuch; a bull.
ଶଣ୍ଢା, ଶଣ୍ଡା, *n.* the seed-stalk of an onion;—*a.* stout and strong.
ଶଣ୍ଢୁଆସି, *n.* a small pair of tongs.
ଶତ, *n.* a hundred.
ଶତଗୁଣ, *a.* and *n.* hundred-fold.
*ଶତପତ୍ର, *n.* a waterlily.
ଶତଭିଷା, *n.* 24th stellar mansion.
ଶତରଞ୍ଜ, ଶତରଞ୍ଜି, *n.* a carpet, floor-cloth; chessboard or cloth; a kind of play.
*ଶତାବରୀ, *n.* Indian climbing asparagus.
ଶତାବ୍ଦୀ, *n.* century.
ଶତାୟୁଃ, *a.* and *n.* centenary.
ଶତ୍ରୁ, *n.* an enemy, a foe, adversary.
*ଶତ୍ରୁଘ୍ନ, *a.* killing the enemy.
ଶତ୍ରୁତା, *n.* enmity, hostility.
*ଶତ୍ରୁତାପନ, *a.* overcoming or destroying one's foes.
ଶତ୍ରୁପକ୍ଷ, *n.* enemy's party, an oponent, antagonist.
ଶନି, *n.* the planet Saturn.
ଶନିବାର, *n.* Saturday.
ଶପଥ, *n.* an oath, imprecation.
*ଶପ୍ତ, *a.* cursed, anathematised.
*ଶଫରୀ, *n.* a small species of carp.
ଶପିନା, *n.* a subpœna.
ଶଫେଦ୍, *a.* white.
ଶବ, *n.* a corpse, a dead body.
ଶବଦାହ, *n.* burning a corpse.
*ଶବଯାନ, *n.* a bier, a hearse.
ଶବର, *n.* one of the aboriginal jungle tribes; *fem.* ଶବରୁଣୀ ।
ଶବ୍ଦ, *n.* a sound, noise, word, noun.
*ଶବ୍ଦକୋଷ, *n.* a dictionary, vocabulary.
ଶବ୍ଦବିଦ୍ୟା, ଶବ୍ଦଶାସ୍ତ୍ର, *n.* philology.
ଶବ୍ଦାର୍ଥ, *n.* the meaning of a word.
*ଶବ୍ଦାୟମାନ, *a.* sounding.
ଶବ୍ଦିତ, *a.* sounded, made to give out a sound, played upon (as a musical instrument).
*ଶମ, *n.* control of the senses.
*ଶମନ, *n.* the god of death; placidity; sacrificing.
ଶମିଆନା, *n.* a kind of awning.
*ଶମିତ, *a.* subdued, destroyed.
*ଶମ୍ବୁ, ଶମ୍ବୁକ, *n.* a snail, bivalve shell.
ଶମ୍ଭୁ, *n.* *Siva.*
ଶୟତାନ, *n.* Satan, the devil.
ଶୟତାନୀ, *a.* devilish, satanic;—*n.* devilishness.
ଶୟନ, *n.* lying down, sleeping.
ଶୟନଗୃହ, *n.* a bedroom.
*ଶୟାନ, *a.* sleeping, reclining, recumbent.
*ଶୟିତ, *a.* reclined, asleep.
ଶଯ୍ୟା, *n.* a bed, a thing to lie upon.
ଶଯ୍ୟାଗତ, *a.* bedridden, confined to bed.
ଶର, *n.* an arrow, a reed; cream.
ଶରଣ, *n.* shelter, protection, refuge.
ଶରଣାଗତ, ଶରଣାପନ୍ନ, *a.* sheltered;—*n.* a refuge.

ଶରତ୍, ଶରତ୍କାଳ, *n.* the autumn.
ଶରଚ୍ଚନ୍ଦ୍ର, *n.* the autumnal moon.
ଶରମ, *n.* shame, bashfulness, modesty.
ଶରବତ୍, *n.* sherbet, a beverage.
*ଶରବ୍ୟ, *n.* a butt, a mark.
ଶରା, *n.* a small earthen pot.
ଶରାଘାତ, *n.* a stroke by an arrow.
ଶରାବ, *n.* wine, spirits, liquor.
ଶରାବୀ, *a.* addicted to drinking.
*ଶରାସନ, *n.* a bow to shoot arrows from.
ଶରୀର, *n.* the body; matter. [death.
*ଶରୀରପତନ, *n.* fall of the body,
*ଶରୀରୀ, *a.* corporeal, bodied;—*n.* an animal.
*ଶର୍କରା, *n.* sugar, sugar-candy.
ଶର୍ତ୍ତ, *n.* terms of contract, stipula-
*ଶର୍ବରୀ, *n.* night. [tion.
ଶର୍ମ୍ମା, *n.* a Brahmanical surname; *pleasure.
ଶଳା, *n.* a wife's brother.
*ଶଳାକା, *n.* a skewer, a thin bar of metal or wood, an arrow, a ruler.
ଶଳିତା, *n.* a wick, wick of a lamp.
*ଶଲ୍ୟ, *n.* spear, blade, a crowbar, spit.
ଶଶା, *ଶଶ, ଶଶକ, *n.* a hare, rabbit.
ଶଶୀ, *ଶଶଧର, ଶଶାଙ୍କ, *n.* the moon.
ଶଶୁର, *n.* a father-in-law.
ଶସ, ଶାଁସ, *n.* kernel, nutritious part.
ଶସା, *n.* a cucumber.

ଶସ୍ତା, *a.* low-priced, cheap.
ଶସ୍ତ୍ର, *n.* a weapon, instrument, tool.
ଶସ୍ତ୍ରଧାରୀ, *ଶସ୍ତ୍ରପାଣି, *a.* bearing arms; —*n.* an armed man.
ଶସ୍ତ୍ରବିଦ୍ୟା, *n.* the science of arms.
ଶସ୍ୟ, *n.* corn, grain, kernel.
ଶସ୍ୟଶାଳୀ, *a.* abounding with corn.
ଶସ୍ୟକ୍ଷେତ୍ର, *n.* a corn-field.
ଶହର, *n.* a city, capital.
ଶହରିଆ, ଶହରୀ, *a.* belonging to a town, urban. [blue.
ଶାଁଳା, ଶାଁଳିଆ, *a.* azure, dark
ଶାଁଳାଶାଁଳି, *n.* coaxing, cajoling.
ଶାକ, *n.* greens, vegetables.
ଶାକର, *n.* a sweetened vegetable stew.
ଶାକ୍ତ, *n.* a worshipper of *Kali.*
ଶାକ୍ୟମୁନି, ଶାକ୍ୟସିଂହ, *n.* name of *Buddha.*
ଶାଙ୍କୋଳି, *n.* fetters, bonds.
ଶାଖା, *n.* a branch, a subdivision.
*ଶାଖୀ, *n.* a tree; a *Veda.*
ଶାଗ, *n.* greens (see ଶାକ) ।
ଶାଗୁଆ, *a.* green;—*n.* green colour.
*ଶାଟୀ, *n.* see ଶାଢୀ ।
*ଶାଠ୍ୟ, *n.* craftiness, deceitfulness.
ଶାଢୀ, *n.* a woman's cloth.
ଶାଣ, *n.* a whetstone.
*ଶାଣିତ, *a.* sharpened, whetted.
ଶାଦା, *a.* white; plain.
ଶାଦୀ, *n.* a marriage. [ment.
ଶାନି ତଜବିଜ, *n.* review of a judg-
ଶାନ୍ତ, *a.* ceased, tranquil, placid.

ଶାନ୍ତି, *n.* peace; relief.

ଶାପ, *n.* a curse, imprecation.

ଶାପଗ୍ରସ୍ତ, *a.* accursed, lying under a curse.

ଶାଫ୍, *a.* clean, pure.

ଶାଫ୍ସୁତୁର, *a.* clean, swept.

*ଶାବକ, *n.* the young of any animal.

ଶାବଳ, *n.* a crowbar.

ଶାବୁତ, ଶାବୁଦ, *n.* evidence, proof.

ଶାବୁନ, *n.* soap.

*ଶାବ୍ଦିକ, *a.* proficient in knowledge of words;–*n.* philologist; grammarian.

ଶାମୁକା, ଶାମୁକା, *n.* a snail, a bivalve.

*ଶାୟକ, *n.* an arrow.

ଶାରେଙ୍ଗା, *n.* a kind of lute.

ଶାରଦ, *n.* cold weather crop of paddy;—**a.* belonging or relating to autumn, autumnal.

ଶାରଦା, *n.* *Saraswati.*

*ଶାରଦୀୟ, *a.* autumnal.

ଶାରି, ଶାରିକା, ଶାରୀ, *n.* a parrot; a species of *myna.*

ଶାରୀରତତ୍ତ୍ୱ, *n.* physiology.

ଶାରୀରସ୍ଥାନ, *n.* anatomy.

ଶାରୀରିକ, *a.* bodily, corporeal.

*ଶାର୍ଙ୍ଗ, *n.* a bow made of horn;—*a.* made of horn.

*ଶାର୍ଦ୍ଦୂଳ, *n.* a tiger;—*a.* eminent.

ଶାଳ, *n.* the *sal* tree; a stable or shed.

ଶାଳଗ୍ରାମ, *n.* a stone worshipped as an emblem of *Vishnu.*

*ଶାଳନିର୍ଯ୍ୟାସ,, *n.* resin, gum of the *sal* tree.

ଶାଳା, ଶାଲ, *n.* a house, a building, a stable or shed.

ଶାଳି, *n.* paddy.

ଶାଳୀ, *n.* a wife's younger sister.

*ଶାଲ୍ମଳୀ, *n.* the silk-cotton tree (see ଶିମିଳି).

ଶାଲ୍, *n.* a shawl.

ଶାଲିଆନା, *a.* annual, yearly.

ଶାଲିସ୍, *n.* an arbitrator, an umpire.

ଶାଲିସି, *n.* arbitration.

ଶାଲୁ, *n.* a kind of fine red cloth.

ଶାଶୂ, *n.* a mother-in-law.

*ଶାସକ, *n.* a governor, a punisher.

ଶାସନ, *n.* reproof, correction, punishment; governing, government; a Bráhman village.

ଶାସନତନ୍ତ୍ର, ଶାସନପ୍ରଣାଳୀ, *n.* the system of government.

ଶାସିତ, *a.* governed; punished, brought under discipline.

ଶାସ୍ତି, *n.* punishment, correction, discipline.

ଶାସ୍ତ୍ର, *n.* a *shástra*, a sacred book.

ଶାସ୍ତ୍ରଜ୍ଞ, *a.* acquainted with the *shástras.*

*ଶାସ୍ତ୍ରବେତ୍ତା, *n.* one acquainted with the *shástras*, a philosopher.

ଶାସ୍ତ୍ରମତ, *a.* approved by the *shástras*;—*n.* doctrine of a *shástra.*

ଶାସ୍ତ୍ରୀ, *n.* a title given to a learned man; a pundit;—*a.* versed in the *shástras.*

ଶାସ୍ତ୍ରୀୟ, *a.* according to the *shástras.*
ଶାସ୍ତ୍ରୋକ୍ତ, *a.* declared in the *shástras.*
ଶିଆର, *n.* a furrow.
ଶିଆଳ, *n.* a jackal.
ଶିଉଳି, *n.* moss. [ଶିଶୁ).
*ଶିଂଶପା, *n.* name of a tree (see
ଶିଂଷା, ଶୀଂଷା, *n.* the spike of corn.
ଶିକଡ଼, *n.* a spreading root.
ଶିକା, *n.* a sling.
ଶିକାର, *n.* hnnting, the chase.
ଶିକାରୀ, *n.* a hunter, sportsman;—*a.* relating to hunting.
ଶିକୁଳି, *n.* a chain.
ଶିଖ, *n.* a mountain peak;–*a.* high.
ଶିଖର, *n.* top or point of anything.
*ଶିଖରୀ, *n.* a mountain. [crest.
ଶିଖା, *n.* a flame; spike of corn;
ଶିଖାଇବା, *v.* to teach, to train.
ଶିଖିବା, *v.* to learn. [fire.
*ଶିଖୀ, *a.* crested;—*n.* a peacock;
ଶିଙ୍ଗ, *n.* a horn; peak of a mountain.
ଶିଙ୍ଗଡ଼ା, *n.* an aquatic plant and its fruit.
ଶିଙ୍ଗା, *n.* a horn for cupping or blowing.
ଶିଙ୍ଗାଣି, ଶିଙ୍ଘାଣି, *n.* mucus of the nose.
ଶିଙ୍ଗାରୀ, *n.* a man appointed to decorate idols.
ଶିଙ୍ଗୀ, *n.* a species of fish.
ଶିଜୁ, ଶିଝୁ, *n.* several species of a milky plant.
ଶିଠା, *n.* dregs, sediment, dross.

ଶିଡ଼ି, *n.* a ladder, flight of steps or stairs.
ଶିଥିଳ, *a.* slack, relaxed, remiss.
ଶିଥିଳତା, *n.* slackness.
ଶିପ, *n.* burnt shells for lime.
ଶିବ, *n.* *Siva.* [*Siva.*
ଶିବରାତ୍ରି, *n.* a festival in honour of
*ଶିବା, *n.* *Durga*; a jackal.
*ଶିବିର, *n.* a tent, camp.
ଶିମିଳି, ଶିମୁଳୀ, *n.* the silk-cotton tree.
ଶିମ୍ବ, ଶିମ, *n.* a kidney-bean, legume.
ଶିର୍କା, *n.* vinegar.
ଶିର, ଶିରଃ, *n.* the head. [address.
ଶିରନାମା, ଶିରୋନାମା, *n.* superscription,
ଶିରପା, *n.* a cloth given as a reward.
*ଶିରଃପୀଡ଼ା, *n.* the head-ache.
*ଶିରସ୍ତ୍ରାଣ, *n.* helmet, hat, turban.
ଶିରା, *n.* a nerve, tendon, vein, artery.
ଶିରଷ, ଶିରସ, *n.* glue. [obeyed.
ଶିରୋଧାର୍ଯ୍ୟ, *a.* fit to be respected or
ଶିରୋଭୂଷଣ, *n.* a head-dress.
ଶିରୋମଣି, *n.* a jewel in the crest.
ଶିଳ, *n.* a stone, curry-stone.
ଶିଳପୁଆ, *n.* a muller for the above.
*ଶିଳା, *n.* stone; a hailstone.
ଶିଳାଜତୁ, *n.* bitumen.
ଶିଳାବୃଷ୍ଟି, *n.* hailstones, falling of hail.
ଶିଳ୍ପ, *n.* mechanical arts.
ଶିଳ୍ପକର, ଶିଳ୍ପକାର, ଶିଳ୍ପକାରୀ, *n.* an artificer, a mechanic.
ଶିଳ୍ପବିଦ୍ୟା, *n.* science of mechanics.

*ଶିଳ୍ପାଗାର, *n.* a workshop, manufactory.
ଶିଳ୍ପୀ, *n.* a workman;—*a.* working at a trade or manual arts.
ଶିଶି, *n.* a phial.
ଶିଶିର, *n.* dew, frost, hoar.
ଶିଶୁ, *n.* an infant, a young one.
ଶିଶୁ, ଶିଷୁ, *n.* name of a timber tree (*Dalbergia Sissoo*).
ଶିଶୁକ, ଶିଶୁମାର, *n.* porpoise. [hood.
ଶିଶୁକାଳ, ଶିଶୁତ୍ୱ, *n.* infancy, child-
*ଶିଶ୍ନ, *n.* the male organ, penis.
ଶିଷ୍ଟ, *a.* polite, civil, docile. [lity.
ଶିଷ୍ଟତା, *n.* politeness, docility, civi-
ଶିଷ୍ଟାଚାର, *n.* polite conduct.
ଶିଷ୍ୟ, *n.* a disciple, scholar, pupil.
ଶିକ୍ଷକ, *n.* a teacher. [trine.
ଶିକ୍ଷା, *n.* instruction, teaching, doc-
ଶିକ୍ଷାଗୁରୁ, *n.* a tutor, preceptor.
ଶିକ୍ଷିତ, *a.* educated, taught, studied, trained.
ଶୀଘ୍ର, *ad.* quickly, soon, rapidly.
ଶୀଘ୍ରତା, *n.* swiftness. [rapid.
ଶୀଘ୍ରଗାମୀ, ଶୀଘ୍ରଗତି, *a.* swift, fleet,
ଶୀତ, *n.* coldness, torpidity;—*a.* cold, apathetic, torpid.
ଶୀତକାଳ, *n.* cold season, winter.
ଶୀତଳ, *a.* cool, cold, refreshing.
ଶୀତଳପାଟୀ, *n.* a fine sort of Sylhet mat.
*ଶୀତାଂଶୁ, *n.* the moon.
ଶୀତାର୍ତ୍ତ, *a.* suffering from cold.
ଶୀର୍ଣ୍ଣ, *a.* emaciated, lean, shrivelled.

*ଶୀର୍ଷ, *n.* the head.
ଶୀର୍ଷକ, *n.* heading or superscription, title of any writing.
ଶୀଲ, an *affix* denoting joined, possessed or endowed with
ଶୀଲତା, *n.* politeness, civility, *tendency.
ଶୀଷ, *n.* a hiss, whistle. [seed.
ଶୁଁଆ, *n.* a kind of grass and its
ଶୁଁଶୁଁ, *n.* a snuffling sound. [sleep.
ଶୁଆ, *a.* sleeping;—*n.* a parrot; a
ଶୁଆଇବା, *v.* to cause to lie down or
ଶୁଆର, *n.* a cook. [sleep.
ଶୁଆରୀ, *n.* a vehicle, palkey, riding horse, etc. [*Byasa.*
ଶୁକ, *n.* a parrot; name of the son of
ଶୁଖାଇବା, *v.* to dry, to hang up to
ଶୁଖଲ, *a.* dried, withered. [dry.
ଶୁଖୁଆ, *n.* salted and dried fish.
ଶୁଷ୍କ, *a.* dried, withered, emaciated.
ଶୁଟ୍କି, *a.* dry, emaciated;—*n.* Bombay ducks.
ଶୁକ୍ତି, *n.* the loss in weight of rice or other grain through becoming dry; *a pearl oyster, a small shell.
ଶୁକ୍ର, *n.* the planet Venus; *semen.
ଶୁକ୍ରବାର, *n.* Friday.
ଶୁକ୍ଳ, *a.* bright, white, pure.
*ଶୁକ୍ଳତା, *n.* whiteness, purity.
ଶୁକ୍ଳପକ୍ଷ, *n.* the bright lunar fortnight.

ଶୁଖାଇବା, *v.* to dry up, to cause to dry or wither.
ଶୁଖିବା, *v.* to dry, to wither.
ଶୁଖିଲା, *a.* dry, sapless, withered, emaciated.
ଶୁଙ୍ଘାଇବା, ଶୁଙ୍ଘାଇବା, *v.* to cause to smell, to cause to be smelled, to apply perfumes.
ଶୁଙ୍ଘିବା, ଶୁଙ୍ଘିବା, *v.* to smell, to inhale by the nose.
ଶୁଚି, *a.* pure, virtuous, holy.
ଶୁଚିତା, *n.* purity, sanctity.
ଶୁଝିବା, *v.* to clear off (a debt), to pay back; to recompense; to retaliate.
ଶୁଝାଣ, *n.* a payment; recompense; retaliation
ଶୁଣାଇବା, *v.* to make known, to cause to hear.
ଶୁଣାଯାଇବା, *v.* to be told, to get to know.
ଶୁଣାଶୁଣି, *n.* common report.
ଶୁଣିବା, *v.* to hear, to listen.
ଶୁଣ୍ଠି, *n.* dried ginger.
ଶୁଣ୍ଡ, *n.* an elephant's proboscis.
ଶୁଣ୍ଡୀ, *n.* a distiller, dram-seller, name of the caste. [correct.
ଶୁଦ୍ଧ, *a.* pure, clean, unadulterated;
*ଶୁଦ୍ଧସତ୍ତ୍ୱ, *a.* perfect, righteous, pure. [tegrity.
*ଶୁଦ୍ଧତା, *n.* purity, correctness, in-
ଶୁଦ୍ଧାତ୍ମା, *a.* innocent, pure.
*ଶୁଦ୍ଧାତ୍ମ, *a.* pure of spirit or heart.
ଶୁଦ୍ଧି, *n.* purity, rectitude, sanctity; correctness. [docile.
ଶୁଧାର, *a.* grave, polite, well-bred,
ଶୁଧାଇବା, *v.* to cleanse, to purify; to correct.
ଶୁଧୁରିବା, *v.* to have one's defects or faults removed, to become good.
ଶୁବିଧା, *a.* good, easy.
ଶୁବେ, *n.* doubt, suspicion.
ଶୁଭ, *a.* auspicious, favourable.
ଶୁଭକର୍ମ, *n.* a good or auspicious act.
ଶୁଭକର, ଶୁଭଙ୍କର, ଶୁଭଙ୍କରକ, *a.* auspicious, propitious.
ଶୁଭଦୃଷ୍ଟି, *n.* a favourable glance.
ଶୁଭଲଗ୍ନ, *n.* auspicious moment.
ଶୁଭକ୍ଷଣ, *n.* an auspicious time.
*ଶୁଭଦୃଷ୍ଟ, *n.* good fortune, good luck. [sity.
ଶୁଭାଶୁଭ, *n.* prosperity and adver-
*ଶୁଭାନ୍ୱିତ, *a.* fortunate, lucky.
ଶୁଭିବା, *v.* to be audible.
ଶୁଭ୍ର, *a.* white, bright, shining.
ଶୁମାର, *n.* calculation, enumeration.
ଶୁଲୁପ, *n.* a sloop, a small ship.
*ଶୁଲ୍କ, *n.* port-duty, toll, fee.
ଶୁଶ୍ରୂଷା, *n.* attention, care, minding (specially used in regard to the sick).
ଶୁଷ୍କ, *a.* dry, sapless, withered.
ଶୁଷ୍କତା, *n.* dryness.
*ଶୂକର, *n.* a pig, a boar, a hog.

ଶୂଦ୍ର, *n.* the fourth Hindu caste—*Sudra.* [caste.
ଶୂଦ୍ରା, ଶୂଦ୍ରାଣୀ, *n.* a female of *Sudra*
ଶୂନ୍ୟ, *n.* a vacuum, a cipher, the atmosphere;—*a.* empty, void.
ଶୂନ୍ୟତା, *n.* emptiness, vacuity.
*ଶୂର, *n.* a hero, warrior;—*a.* heroic, brave.
*ଶୂର୍ପ, *n.* a winnowing tray, a *kulá.*
ଶୂଳ, *n.* colic pains, gripes;. a spit, a spear, a blade.
*ଶୂଳୀ, *n.* a spearman, pikeman.
ଶୃଗାଳ, *n.* a jackal. [order.
*ଶୃଙ୍ଖଳ, *n.* a chain, fetter, shackles;
ଶୃଙ୍ଖଳା, *n.* a series, an arrangement; concatenation.
ଶୃଙ୍ଗ, *n.* a horn, mountain-peak.
*ଶୃଙ୍ଗାର, *n.* love, copulation, passion,
*ଶୃଙ୍ଗୀ, *a.* horned; peaked.
ଶେଖର, *n.* a peak, a summit; a crest, a chaplet.
ଶେଠି, *n.* a surname of washermen.
ଶେତା, *a.* bloodless, anæmic.
ଶେମାହି, *a.* quarterly.
ଶେଯ, *n.* a bed.
ଶେଷ, *n.* end, result, limit;—*a.* ended, finished, last.
ଶେଷକାଳ, *n.* the latest time; death.
ଶେଷାବସ୍ଥା, *n.* old age, the last state.
*ଶୈତ୍ୟ, *n.* coldness, cold.
ଶୈଥିଲ୍ୟ, *n.* slackness, remissness.
ଶୈବ, *n.* a worshipper of *Siva.*
*ଶୈବାଳ, *n.* moss, weeds under water (see ଶିଉଳି) ।
*ଶୈଳ, *n.* a rock, a mountain.
ଶୈଳଜ, *n.* bitumen, storax, benzoin;—**a.* rock-born.
ଶୈଶବ, *n.* childhood, infancy.
ଶୋଇବା, *v.* to sleep, to lie down.
ଶୋକ, *n.* sorrow, grief, regret.
ଶୋକାର୍ତ୍ତ, ଶୋକାକୁଳ, *a.* grieved, sorrowful. [ing.
ଶୋକାକୃତ, *a.* sad, sorrowful, griev-
ଶୋଚନା, ଶୋଚନ, *n.* anxiety, grief, regret.
ଶୋଚନୀୟ, *ଶୋଚ୍ୟ, *a.* lamentable, deplorable.
ଶୋଟା, *n.* a stick, staff, club.
*ଶୋଣାମୁଖୀ, *n.* senna (see ସନାମୁଖି) ।
*ଶୋଣିତ, *n.* blood.
ଶୋଥ, *n.* swelling of the limbs.
*ଶୋଧ, *n.* purifying, correcting; payment. [taliation.
ଶୋଧନ, *n.* correction; paying, re-
ଶୋଧ୍ୱ, *n.* an arithmetical table of measures.
*ଶୋଧିତ, *a.* cleansed, purified.
ଶୋଧିବା, *v.* to give abuse, to vilify; to correct; to refine.
ଶୋଭନ, *a.* beautiful, handsome;—*n.* being comely or pleasant to the sight.
ଶୋଭନୀୟ, *a.* requiring to be adorned or beautified.
ଶୋଭା, *n.* lustre, beauty, elegance.

ଶୋଭାଯୁକ୍ତ, ଶୋଭିତ, *a.* beautiful, splendid.

ଶୋରା, *n.* nitre, saltpetre.

ଶୋଲ, *n.* the Indian pith-plant.

ଶୋଷ, *n.* thirst.

*ଶୋଷକ, *a.* absorbent, drying.

ଶୋଷଣ, *n.* suction, sucking up, absorption.

ଶୋଷିବା, *v.* to absorb, to suck, to imbibe.

ଶୋଷା, *a.* thirsty.

ଶୌଖିନ୍, *a.* fond of pleasure, jocose, gay.

ଶୌଚ, *n.* purification, ablution.

ଶୌଚାଚାର, *n.* work of purification.

*ଶୌଣ୍ଡିକ, *n.* a distiller, dealer in liquors.

*ଶୌରି, *n.* the planet Saturn; *Vishnu, Náráyan.*

*ଶୌର୍ଯ୍ୟ, *n.* heroism, bravery, prowess.

ଶ୍ମଶାନ, *n.* a cemetery, burning-place.

ଶ୍ମଶାନବାସୀ, *a.* living in a cemetery; —*n. Siva.*

*ଶ୍ମଶ୍ରୁ, *n.* the beard.

ଶ୍ୟାମଳ, ଶ୍ୟାମ, *a.* dark, azure, dark blue;—*n.* blue colour.

ଶ୍ୟାଳକ, *n.* a wife's brother.

*ଶ୍ୟେନ, *n.* a hawk, a falcon.

ଶ୍ରଦ୍ଧା, *n.* devotedness, devotion, fidelity; love, affection; respect, reverence; strong desire; a liking for.

ଶ୍ରଦ୍ଧାବାନ୍, *a.* believing, showing veneration.

ଶ୍ରଦ୍ଧାଳୁ, *a.* devoted to, attached, desirous, wishing or longing for.

ଶ୍ରବଣ, *n.* hearing, attending; *the ear.

ଶ୍ରବଣକର୍ତ୍ତା, *n.* a hearer, an auditor.

ଶ୍ରବଣା, *n.* the 22nd stellar mansion.

*ଶ୍ରବଣେନ୍ଦ୍ରିୟ, *n.* the ear, organ of hearing.

ଶ୍ରମ, *n.* exertion, diligence, labour.

ଶ୍ରମଜୀବୀ, *a.* earning a livelihood by industry, industrious.

*ଶ୍ରମଣ, *n.* a Buddhist ascetic.

*ଶ୍ରମବାରି, *n.* sweat, perspiration.

*ଶ୍ରମୀ, *a.* painstaking, industrious.

ଶ୍ରାଦ୍ଧ, *n.* Hindu ceremony for the dead.

ଶ୍ରାନ୍ତ, *a.* wearied, tired, exhausted.

*ଶ୍ରାନ୍ତି, *n.* weariness, fatigue, languor.

ଶ୍ରାବଣ, *n.* a month of that name, part of July and August.

*ଶ୍ରାବ୍ୟ, *a.* audible; fit to be heard.

ଶ୍ରୀ, *n. Lakshmi*; beauty, prosperity, elegance;—ଶ୍ରୀ, ଶ୍ରୀଯୁକ୍ତ, ଶ୍ରୀଯୁତ, used as the equivalent of "Mr." in English.

*ଶ୍ରୀକାତର, *a.* envious, invidious.

ଶ୍ରୀପଞ୍ଚମୀ, *n.* a Hindu festival held on the 5th day of the moon in *Mágha* (Jan.—Feb.).

*ଶ୍ରୀଫଳ, *n.* the *bel* fruit.

ଶ୍ରୀମାନ୍, *a.* prosperous, fortunate; beautiful; *fem.* ଶ୍ରୀମତୀ ।

ଶ୍ରୀଯୁକ୍ତ, ଶ୍ରୀଯୁତ, ଶ୍ରୀଳ, *a.* illustrious, prosperous, beautiful.

*ଶ୍ରୁତ, *a.* heard; having heard.

*ଶ୍ରୁତି, *n.* hearing, ear; the *Vedas.*

ଶ୍ରୁତିକଟୁ, *a.* harsh, discordant.

*ଶ୍ରୁତିପାଠ, *n.* studying the *Vedas.*

ସ୍ରୁକ୍, *n.* a sacrificial ladle.

ଶ୍ରେଣୀ, ଶ୍ରେଣି, *n.* a class, standard; a row, rank, tier.

ଶ୍ରେଣୀବଦ୍ଧ, *a.* arranged in lines.

ଶ୍ରେୟଃ, *n.* prosperity, beatitude, good result.

ଶ୍ରେୟସ୍କର, *a.* propitious.

ଶ୍ରେଷ୍ଠ, *a.* chief, best, preferable.

ଶ୍ରେଷ୍ଠତା, *n.* pre-eminence, excellence. [rump.

*ଶ୍ରୋଣି, ଶ୍ରୋଣୀ, *n.* the hip, loins,

*ଶ୍ରୋତବ୍ୟ, *a.* audible, fit to be heard.

ଶ୍ରୋତା, *n.* a hearer, auditor. [ear.

*ଶ୍ରୋତ୍ର, *n.* organ of hearing, the

*ଶ୍ଲଥ, *a.* slack, loose, flacid, remiss. [logy.

*ଶ୍ଲାଘା, *n.* praise, applause, a eu-

*ଶ୍ଲାଘ୍ୟ, *a.* praisworthy, laudable.

*ଶ୍ଲୀପଦ, *n.* elephantiasis.

*ଶ୍ଲେଷ୍ମଳ, *a.* expectorative.

ଶ୍ଲେଷ୍ମା, *n.* phlegm, serum, rheum.

ଶ୍ଲୋକ, *n.* a couplet, stanza, text.

*ଶ୍ୱପଚ, *n.* an outcaste;—*a.* of low caste.

*ଶ୍ୱବୃତ୍ତି, *n.* slavery, servitude.

ଶ୍ୱଶୁର, *n.* a father-in-law.

*ଶ୍ୱାନ, *n.* a dog.

*ଶ୍ୱାପଦ, *n.* carnivora.

ଶ୍ୱାସ, *n.* the breath; asthma.

*ଶ୍ୱିତ୍ର, *n.* a kind of leprosy.

*ଶ୍ୱେତ, *a.* white;—*n.* whiteness.

ଶ୍ୱେତପଦ୍ମ, *n.* the white lotus.

ଷ.

ଷ, the 30th consonant.

*ଷଟ୍, *a.* six.

*ଷଟ୍କର୍ଣ୍ଣ, *a.* known to three persons, *i e.*, to six ears.

*ଷଟ୍କର୍ମ, *n.* the six prescribed duties of a Bráhman.

*ଷଟ୍ପଦ, *n.* a bee.

*ଷଟ୍ପୁରୁଷ, *n.* six lineal ancestors.

ଷଠିଘର, *n.* ceremony on the sixth day after a child's birth.

ଷଡ୍ଭୁଜ, *a.* six-armed; hexagonal; —*n.* a hexagon.

ଷଡରସ, *ଷଡ୍ରସ, *n.* six kinds of juices.

ଷଡଷଡ, *n.* an imitative sound.

ଷଣ୍ଢ, ଷଣ୍ଡ, *n.* a bull; a eunuch.

*ଷଷ୍ଟି, *a.* sixty.

*ଷଷ୍ଠ, *a.* the sixth.

ଷଷ୍ଠୀ, *n.* sixth day of the moon.

ଷାଠିଏ, *a.* and *n.* sixty; 60; LX.

ଷାଣ୍ମାସିକ, *a.* half-yearly.

*ଷୋଡଶ, *a.* sixteen.

*ଷୋଡଶୋପଚାର, *n.* sixteen ingredients needed for worshipping an idol.

ଷୋଳ, *a.* and *n.* sixteen; 16; XVI.

*ଷୋଡଶୀ, *n.* a young woman.

ସ.

ସ, the 31st consonant.

ସଖି, ସଖୀ, *n.* a female friend or namesake.

ସଇସ, *n.* a groom, syce.

ସଉଆ, *n.* a quarter more.

ସଉଆଲ୍. ସଓଆଲ୍, *n.* a question, an interrogatory.

ସଉତୁଣୀ, *n.* a co-wife.

ସଉଦା, *n.* marketing, articles purchased.

ସଉଦାଗର, *n*, a merchant, trader.

ସଂ, a *prefix* meaning with, fully.

*ସଂକଳନ, *n.* compilation, collection, addition.

*ସଂକ୍ରମଣ, ସଙ୍କ୍ରମଣ, *n.* transition, transposition, the removing from one station to another.

ସଂକ୍ରମିତ, ସଙ୍କ୍ରମିତ, ସଂକ୍ରାମିତ, ସଙ୍କ୍ରାମିତ, *a.* passed from one station to another; connected with.

ସଂକ୍ରାନ୍ତ, *a.* concerning, relating to.

ସଂକ୍ରାନ୍ତି, *n.* sun's entrance into a sign.

ସଂକ୍ରାମକ, ସଙ୍କ୍ରାମକ, *a.* infectious, contagious.

ସଂକୁଡ, ସଙ୍କୁଡ, *n.* orts, refuse; cooked food.

ସଂଖ୍ୟା, *n.* a number, reckoning.

ସଂଗ୍ରହ, ସଙ୍ଗ୍ରହ, *n.* collection, compilation.

*ସଂଗ୍ରାମ, ସଙ୍ଗ୍ରାମ, *n.* conflict, war, battle.

ସଂଗୃହୀତ, ସଙ୍ଗୃହୀତ, *a.* collected, compiled.

*ସଂଗୋପନ, *n.* concealing, suppressing.

*ସଂଘଟନା, *n.* concurrence, conjuncture.

ସଂଜ୍ଞା, *n.* senses, a surname, name, term, idea; (in *Gram.*) a noun.

ସଂପ୍ରତି, *ad.* now, at present.

ସଂବତ୍, *n.* the era of *Vikramáditya*; era, year.

ସଂବତ୍ସର, *n.* a year, a full year.

ସଂବର, *n.* an elk.

ସଂବର୍ଦ୍ଧନା, *n.* honour, exaltation; *increase, advancement.

*ସଂବଳିତ, *a.* connected, met together.

ସଂବାଦ, *n.* news, intelligence, notice.

*ସଂବେଦନା, *n.* sympathy.

*ସଂବେଦ, *n.* perception, consciousness, conscience.

ସଂଯତ, *a.* restrained, self-controlled.

*ସଂଯମ, *n.* restraint, control, concentration of mind.

ସଂଯମୀ, *n.* one who subdues his passions, a sage, an ascetic;—*a.* controlling, subduing, continent.

ସଂଯୁକ୍ତ, *a.* connected with, related to; mixed.

ସଂଯୋଗ, *n.* connection, contact, union.

*ସଂଯୋଜିତ, *a.* joined, connected.

ସଂରକ୍ଷଣ, *n.* a preserving, a keeping, a guarding.

*ସଂରୁଦ୍ଧ, *a.* shut up, obstructed.

ସଂଲଗ୍ନ, *a.* stuck together, connected, joined.

ସଂଶୟ, *n.* doubt, hesitation, suspicion. [suspicious.

ସଂଶୟାତ୍ମା, *ସଂଶୟୀ, *a.* hesitating,

ସଂଶୋଧନ, *n.* correction, amendment; a cleansing, a cleansing by ablution.

*ସଂଶୋଧକ, *n.* a corrector, purifier, a reformer. [reformed.

ସଂଶୋଧିତ, *a.* corrected, purified,

*ସଂଶ୍ଳିଷ୍ଟ, *a.* united, embraced.

*ସଂଶ୍ଳେଷ, *n.* an embrace, union, junction, association.

*ସଂସଦ, *n.* an assembly, society.

ସଂସର୍ଗ, *n.* intercourse, living together. [intercourse.

* ସଂସର୍ଗୀ, *a.* social, maintaining

ସଂସାର, *n.* the world, secular state.

ସଂସାରୀ, *a.* worldly. [ed in.

*ସଂସୃଷ୍ଟ, *a.* united together; involv-

ସଂସ୍କାର, *n.* a purifying rite; habit; apprehension; reformation, consecration; perfection.

*ସଂସ୍କାରକ, *a.* purifying, reformative;—*n.* a purifier, a reformer.

ସଂସ୍କୃତ, *n.* Sanscrit;—**a.* consecrated, purified.

*ସଂସ୍ଥାନ, *n.* construction, form, shape; wealth. [settling.

ସଂସ୍ଥାପନ, *n.* establishing, fixing,

*ସଂସ୍ଥିତି, *n.* abode, standing, capital, wealth.

ସଂସ୍ପର୍ଶ, *n.* close contact, touch.

*ସଂସ୍ଫୁଟ, *a.* opened, disclosed.

ସଂସ୍ରବ, *n.* connection, union; contact, touch. [ted.

*ସଂହତ, *a.* destroyed; conglomera-

*ସଂହର୍ତ୍ତା, *n.* a murderer, a destroyer.

ସଂହାର, *n.* destruction, ruin.

ସଂହାରକ, *a.* destructive, ruinous;—*n.* a destroyer.

*ସଂହିତ, *a.* collected, compounded.

ସଂହିତା, *n.* an arrangement of the text of the *Vedas* into short sentences; *a compilation.

*ସଂକ୍ଷୟ, *n.* destruction, ruin.

ସଂକ୍ଷିପ୍ତ, *a.* abridged, condensed, brief.

ସଂକ୍ଷେପ, *n.* brevity, a compendium.

ସକଳ, *a.* all, entire, whole.

*ସକଳଙ୍କ, *a.* contaminated, defiled, rusty.

ସକାଉବା, *v.* to whimper, to snivel.

ସକାଳ, *n.* the early morning.

ସକାଶ, *ad.* near.

ସକାଶେ, ସକାଶ, *ad.* on account of, for.

ସଖା, *n.* a friend, companion.

ସଖୀ, *n.* a female friend.

*ସଖୀତ୍ୱ, *n.* friendship, intimacy.

*ସଖ୍ୟ, *n.* friendship.

*ସଗନ୍ଧ, *a.* having a fragrance.

ସଗର୍ବ, *a.* proud, haughty, arrogant.

*ସଗୁଣ, *a.* talented.

ସଗୋତ୍ର, *a.* of the same family.

ସଙ୍କଟ, *n.* difficulty; a strait, defile; —*a.* contracted, difficult.

ସଙ୍କଟସ୍ଥଳ, *n.* a place of danger; isthmus.

ସଙ୍କଟାପନ୍ନ, *a.* involved in difficulties.

*ସଙ୍କର, *n.* mixture, confusion or mixture of castes.

ସଙ୍କଳିତ, *a.* compiled, added, joined, blended, intermixed.

ସଙ୍କଳ୍ପ, *n.* will, intention, contrivance.

ସଙ୍କଳ୍ପିତ, *a.* wished for, intended, contrived.

ସଙ୍କୀର୍ଣ୍ଣ, *a.* narrow, crowded, contracted, strait.

ସଙ୍କୀର୍ତ୍ତନ, *n.* special religious gathering with music, celebrating, extolling.

ସଙ୍କୁଚିତ, *a.* contracted, straitened; ashamed.

ସଙ୍କେତ, *n.* beckoning, a sign, hint.

ସଙ୍କୋଚ, *n.* shyness; shrivelling, contracting.

*ସଙ୍କୋଚନ, *n.* a shrivelling up.

ସଙ୍କୋଚ୍ୟତା, *n.* compressibility.

ସଙ୍ଗାଳି, *n.* darling, beloved thing; joint stock.

ସଙ୍ଗୋଳିବା, *v.* to comfort, to console; to visit a friend or relative.

ସଙ୍ଗ, *n.* company, society.

ସଙ୍ଗତ, *a.* proper, relevant, probable; harmonious; consistent.

ସଙ୍ଗତି, *n.* fitness, applicability; competence.

ସଙ୍ଗମ, *n.* union, coming together.

ସଙ୍ଗାତ, *n.* a friend, companion, associate.

ସଙ୍ଗୀ, *n.* a companion, an attendant; —*a.* united with, attached or devoted to; *fem.* ସଙ୍ଗିନୀ ।

ସଙ୍ଗୀତ, *n.* choral music, singing.

ସଙ୍ଗୀନ, *n.* a bayonet;—*a.* weighty.

*ସଙ୍ଘ, *n.* an assemblage, a flock, heap.

ସଙ୍ଘର୍ଷଣ, *n.* friction, bragging; contact.

ସଚରାଚର, *a.* universal, current;—*n.* the creation.

ସଚଳ, *a* able to move, active.

ସଚ୍ଚ, ସଚ୍ଚା, *a.* genuine, real, true, right

ସଚିନ୍ତ, *a.* thoughtful, anxious.

*ସଚିବ, *n.* counsellor, friend, associate, mentor.

ସଚୀ, ସଚି, *n.* the wife of *Indra.*

ସଚେତନ, *a.* animate, vigilant, wary.

ସଚେଷ୍ଟ, *a.* bent upon, endeavouring, zealous, active.

ସଚ୍ଚିଦାନନ୍ଦ, *n.* ever existent, wise and happy, *i.e.*, the Supreme Spirit.

ସଜ, *a.* fresh, new;—*n.* apparatus.

ସଜନା, ସଜଣା, *n.* a tree the pods and leaves of which are used for culinary purposes.

*ସଜନୀ, *n.* a female companion.

ସଜଳ, *a.* watery, moist, wet.

ସଜା, *n.* punishment.

*ସଜାଗ, *a.* wakeful, vigilant, wary

ସଜାଡିବା, *v.* to put things in order, to arrange, to mend.

ସଜାତି, *a.* of the same tribe or class.

ସଜୀବ, *a.* alive, living, extant.

ସଜ୍ଜନ, *n.* a good or virtuous man.

ସଜ୍ଜା, *n.* outfit, armour, harness.

ସଜ୍ଜିତ, ସଜ୍ଜୀଭୂତ, *a.* armed, accoutred, dressed.

ସଞ୍ଚୟ, *n.* a heap, mass, hoard.

ସଞ୍ଚୟୀ, *n.* a collector, an accumulator.

ସଞ୍ଚା, *n.* a scar, a mark.

ସଞ୍ଚାଣ, *n.* a hawk, a falcon.

*ସଞ୍ଚାର, *n.* movement, a going; impulse.

ସଞ୍ଚିତ, *a.* gathered, accumulated.

ସଞ୍ଚିବା, ଛଞ୍ଚିବା, *v.* to accumulate, to gather.

ସଞ୍ଜ, *n.* evening.

ସଞ୍ଜୀବନୀ, *a.* life-giving (medicine).

*ସଟୀକ, *a.* with a commentary.

ସଡ଼କ, *n.* a highway, road, street.

ସଡ଼, ସଡ଼ା, *a.* rotten, putrid, tainted, musty.

ସଡ଼ାଇବା, ସଡ଼ାଇବା, *v.* to cause to putrify or rot.

ସଡ଼ିବା, ସଢ଼ିବା, *v.* to rot, to putrify.

ସଢ଼ୁ, ସଢ଼ୁ, *n.* husband of wife's sister.

ସତେଇ, *n.* cocoanut shell.

ସତତ, *ad.* incessantly, ever.

ସତର, *a.* and *n.* seventeen; 17; XVII.

ସତରଞ୍ଜ, *n.* the game of chess.

ସତରଞ୍ଜି, *n.* a carpet, floor-cloth.

ସତର୍କ, *a.* on the alert, vigilant, careful.

ସତୀ, *a.* chaste;—*n.* a good wife.

ସତୀତ୍ୱ, *n.* chastity, female purity.

*ସତୃଷ୍ଣ, *a.* thirsty, rapacious.

ସତେଜ, *a.* luxuriant, illustrious, vigorous.

ସତ୍, ସଦ୍, *a.* honest, virtuous, good, real, genuine, true.

ସତ୍କର୍ମ, *n.* a good act, piety, virtue.

ସତ୍କାର, *n.* hospitality, good work; homage; funeral rites.

ସତ୍କାର୍ଯ୍ୟ, *n.* religious duties, good works.

*ସତ୍କୁଳୋଦ୍ଭବ, *a.* sprung from a good caste.

*ସତ୍ତା, *n.* existence, entity; goodness; essence.

*ସତ୍ତ୍ୱ, *n.* goodness, holiness; entity; life, spirit, vitality; an embryo.

ସତ୍ତ୍ୱଗୁଣ, *n.* moral goodness.

ସତ୍ପଥ, *n.* a good way, good conduct.

ସତ୍ପୁତ୍ର, *n.* a good son.

ସତ୍ୟ, *a.* true, real, genuine, sincere; —*n.* truth.

ସତ୍ୟତା, *n.* truth, reality, certainty.

ସତ୍ୟବାଦୀ, *a.* truth-speaking, truthful.

ସତ୍ୟଯୁଗ, *n.* the first or golden age.

*ସତ୍ୟବ୍ରତ, *a.* devoted to truth, sincere.

ସତ୍ୟାନାଶ, *n.* ruin, destruction, perdition.

ସତ୍ୱର, *ad.* with quickness, quickly.

*ସଦନ, *n.* a house, dwelling.

ସଦୟ, *a.* compassionate, kind.
ସଦର, *a.* chief, supreme, main.
ସଦର୍‌ଦେୱାନୀ, *n.* the chief civil court.
ସଦର୍ପ, *a.* proud, vain; glorious.
ସଦସତ୍, *a.* good and evil.
ସଦସ୍ୟ, *n.* a spectator, a bystander; a delegate;—* *a.* social.
ସଦା, *ad.* always, perpetually.
ସଦାକାଳ, *ad.* at all times, for ever.
*ସଦାତ୍ମ, *a.* virtuous, good-spirited.
ସଦାଚାର, *n.* good conduct.
ସଦାନନ୍ଦ, *a.* happy, always joyful.
ସଦୃଶ, *ସଦୃକ୍ଷ, *a.* resembling, like.
ସଦୃଶତା, *n.* likeness, similarity.
ସଦ୍ଗତି, *n.* beatification, supreme bliss.
ସଦ୍‌ବକ୍ତା, *n.* a good speaker, an eloquent speaker.
*ସଦ୍‌ବୃତ୍ତ, *a.* well-behaved, amiable.
ସଦ୍ଭାବ, *n.* good disposition or intention; friendship.
*ସଦ୍ୟଃ, *ad.* instantly, forthwith.
*ସଦ୍ୟୋଜାତ, *a.* fresh, recent, new.
ସଧବା, *n.* a married woman. a wife.
ସଧର୍ମିଣୀ, *n.* a lawful wife.
ସନ, *n.* a year, the year.
ସନଦ, *n.* a deed of gift, a *sanad*.
*ସନାତନ, *a.* eternal, permanent.
*ସନାଥ, *a.* with a lord or master.
ସନ୍ତକ, *n.* a mark, sign (instead of signature).
ସନ୍ତତି, *n.* a child; offspring.
ସନ୍ତପ୍ତ, ସନ୍ତାପିତ, *a.* distressed, scorched, heated.

*ସନ୍ତରଣ, *n.* swimming, floating.
ସନ୍ତସ, *a.* damp (ground);—*n.* a kind of grass.
ସନ୍ତାପିବା, *v.* to cause grief; to inflame; to become wet or damp.
ସନ୍ତାନ, *n.* a child; offspring.
ସନ୍ତାପ, *n.* anguish, remorse, woe.
ସନ୍ତାପି ହେବା, *v.* to be pained or distressed.
ସନ୍ତୁଳା, *n.* vegetables when half-boiled.
ସନ୍ତୁଷ୍ଟ, *a.* pleased, gratified, satisfied.
ସନ୍ତୋଷ, *n.* gratification, pleasure.
ସନ୍ତ, *n.* a saint; a lesson given.
ସନ୍ଦର୍ଶନ, *n.* looking, viewing, meeting.
ସନ୍ଦିଗ୍ଧ, *ସନ୍ଦିହାନ, *a.* doubtful, suspicious.
ସନ୍ଦେଶ, *n.* news, information; a kind of sweetmeat.
*ସନ୍ଦେଶହର, *n.* a messenger, a spy.
ସନ୍ଦେହ, *n.* doubt, hesitation.
ସନ୍ଦେହୀ, *a.* doubting, sceptical.
ସନ୍ଧାନ, *n.* a tracing, seeking, a search.
ସନ୍ଧି, *n.* an alliance, peace; a joining; a narrow passage or opening.
ସନ୍ଧ୍ୟା, *n.* the evening, twilight.
ସନ୍ନିକଟ, *a.* near, close at hand.
ସନ୍ନିଧାନ, ସନ୍ନିଧି, *n.* nearness, proximity.
ସନ୍ନିପାତ, *n.* a dying state, coma; * total fall or ruin.

ସନ୍ନିବିଷ୍ଟ, *a.* absorbed or engrossed in; entered into. [inserting.

*ସନ୍ନିବେଶ, *n.* devotedness; nearness;

ସନ୍ନିବେଶିତ, *a.* introduced, inserted, put in.

*ସନ୍ନିହିତ, *a.* adjacent, close at hand.

ସନ୍ନ୍ୟାସ, *n.* asceticism, monastic life.

ସନ୍ନ୍ୟାସୀ, *n.* an ascetic, a devotee.

ସପ, *n.* a mat.

ସପତ୍ନୀ, *n.* a co-wife.

*ସପର୍ଯ୍ୟା, *n.* worship, adoration.

ସପରିବାର, *a.* with one's family.

ସପକ୍ଷ, *a.* of the same party.

ସପକ୍ଷତା, *n.* assistance.

*ସପିଣ୍ଡ, *n.* a kinsman. [men.

*ସପିଣ୍ଡୀକରଣ, *n.* *shráddha* for kins-

ସପିନା, *n.* a subpœna.

ସପୁରି, *n.* a pineapple.

ସପ୍ତ, *a.* seven; ସପ୍ତମ, seventh.

*ସପ୍ତତି, ସପ୍ତତିତମ, *a.* seventy.

ସପ୍ତଦଶ, *a.* seventeen.

ସପ୍ତମଙ୍ଗଳା, *a.* a bridal ceremony on the seventh day after marriage.

ସପ୍ତମୀ, *n.* the seventh day of the lunar fortnight. [major.

ସପ୍ତର୍ଷି, *n.* the constellation Ursa

ସପ୍ତାହ, *n.* a week, seven days.

ସପ୍ରମାଣ, *a.* authentic, self-evident.

ସଫଳ, *a.* fruitful; successful; efficacious.

ସଫା, *a.* white, pure, clear.

ସଫାଇ, *n.* white-washing; reliability, trustworthiness.

ସଫେଦା, *a.* white.

ସଫେଦ, *n.* white-washing.

ସବଂଶ, *a.* accompanied by the whole family.

ସବର୍ଣ୍ଣ, *a.* of the same class.

ସବଳ, *a.* strong, vigorous, energetic.

ସବାଖିଆଣି, *n.* a female of the *sabákhiá* tribe, an abusive expression to a woman.

ସବାଖିଆ, *n.* name of a low tribe, an abusive expression to a man.

ସବାଢାଲେ, *ad.* at once, at all.

ସବିନୟ, *a.* humble.

ସବିଶେଷ, *a.* special, circumstantial.

ସବୁ, *a.* all, whole.

ସବୁଜ, *a.* green.

*ସବ୍ୟ, *a.* left (opposite to right).

ସବ୍‌ଜି, *n.* vegetable.

ସଭୟ, *a.* timorous, fearful.

ସଭା, *n.* an assembly, a meeting.

ସଭାପତି, *n.* president of an assembly.

ସଭାସଦ, *n.* one of an assembly.

ସଭାସ୍ଥ, *a.* present at an assembly.

ସଭ୍ୟ, *a.* civilized, fit for company; —*n.* a member; a person of honourable parentage. [ners.

ସଭ୍ୟତା, *n.* politeness, good man-

*ସମ, *a.* even, level; similar.

ସମଶୀତୋଷ୍ଣ, *n.* (in *Geog.*) the temperate zone.

ସମକକ୍ଷ, *a.* equal, similar; rival.

ସମକାଳୀନ, *a.* contemporary, coeval.

ସମକୋଣ, *n.* a right angle. [whole.
ସମଗ୍ର, *a.* and *n.* all, entire, the
ସମଚତୁରସ୍ର, ସମଚତୁର୍ଭୁଜ, *n.* (in *Geom.*) a square.
ସମଚତୁର୍ଭୁଜ, *n.* (in *Geom.*) a rhombus. [hension.
ସମଝ, ସମଝ୍, *n.* knowledge, compre-
ସମଝିବା, ସମଝିବା, *v.* to understand, to know.
ସମତଳ, *n.* a plane surface;—*a.* level, even. [evenness.
ସମତା, *n.* sameness, similarity;
ସମତ୍ରିଭୁଜ, ସମବାହୁତ୍ରିଭୁଜ, *n.* an equilateral triangle.
ସମଦର୍ଶୀ, ସମଦୃଷ୍ଟି, *a.* viewing all alike. impartial.
ସମଧି, *n.* son's or daughter's father-in-law; *fem.* ସମଧୁଣୀ ।
ସମଦ୍ୱିବାହୁ, *a.* (in *Geom.*) isosceles (triangle). [sive.
ସମଧିକ, *a.* much, abundant, exces-
*ସମନ୍ୱୟ, *n.* connection, aggregation; company. [with.
*ସମନ୍ୱିତ, *a.* possessed of, endued
ସମବାହୁ, ସମଭୁଜ, *a.* (in *Geom.*) equilateral.
*ସମବେତ, *a.* collected, comprised.
ସମଭାବ, *n.* sameness, equability.
*ସମଭିବ୍ୟାହାର, *n.* intimacy, association, company. [ciate.
*ସମଭିବ୍ୟାହାରୀ, *n.* a companion, asso-
ସମଭୂମି, *n.* level ground, flat surface.
ସମୟ, *n.* time, season; leisure.

ସମୟୋଚିତ, *a.* proper for the season.
ସମର, *n.* war, battle, conflict.
ସମର୍ଥ, *a.* able, capable, strong.
ସମର୍ଥନ, *n.* confirmation, support.
ସମର୍ପଣ, *n.* making over, delivering.
ସମର୍ପଣପତ୍ର, *n.* a writing by which anything is transferred, deed of assignment. [ted to.
ସମର୍ପିତ, *a.* delivered over, commit-
*ସମର୍ଯ୍ୟାଦ, *a.* honourable, respectable.
*ସମଳ, *a.* dirty, filthy, squalid.
ସମଷ୍ଟି, *n.* the sum, total, entirety.
*ସମସରଳ, *a.* parallel.
*ସମସୂତ୍ରପାତ, *a.* in parallel lines.
ସମସ୍ତ *a.* all, whole;—*n.* an aggregate, the whole.
ସମକ୍ଷ, *a.* visible, evident, in sight.
*ସମାଂଶ, *n.* an equal share.
ସମାଗମ, *n.* a coming together.
ସମାଚାର, *n.* news, intelligence, tidings.
ସମାଜ, *n.* an association, a society, an assembly, a gathering.
ସମାଦର, *n.* respect, honour. [able.
*ସମାଦରଣୀୟ, *a.* honourable, vener-
*ସମାଦୃତ, *a.* respected, venerated, honoured. [sion.
ସମାଧା, *n.* settling, adjusting, deci-
ସମାଧାନ, *n.* the settling of an affair.
ସମାଧି, *n.* a burial; a grave; *meditation. [ground.
*ସମାଧି କ୍ଷେତ୍ର, ସମାଧି ସ୍ଥାନ, *n.* burial

ସମାନ, *a.* level; equal, on a par.
ସମାନୁପାତ, *n.* proportion (in *Arith.*)
ସମାନ୍ତର, ସମାନ୍ତରଳ, *n.* (in *Geom.*) a parallel.
*ସମାପକ, *a.* finishing, concluding.
ସମାପନ, *a.* completing, terminating.
ସମାପ୍ତ, *a.* finished, concluded.
ସମାପ୍ତି, *n.* a finishing, a conclusion.
ସମାବେଶ, *n.* abiding together, accommodation.
ସମାରୋହ, *n.* magnificence, pomp, grandeur.
ସମାଳିବା, *v.* see ସମ୍ଭାଳିବା। [pound.
ସମାସ, *n.* a compound noun, com-
ସମିଅନା, ସାମିଅନା, *n.* a canopy.
ସମିତି, *n.* a meeting, an assembly, an association, a society.
*ସମିଧ, *n.* fuel for a sacrifice. [per.
*ସମୀଚୀନ, *a.* good, right, real, pro-
ସମୀପ, *n.* vicinity, proximity.
*ସମୀର, *n.* wind, air.
ସମୁଚିତ, *a.* befitting, suitable, right.
*ସମୁଚ୍ଚୟ, *n.* a collection, assemblage.
ସମୁଦାୟ, *ସମୁଦୟ, *a.* all;—*n.* the aggregate.
ସମୁଦି, *n.* son's or daughter's father-in-law; *fem.* ସମୁଦୁଣୀ।
ସମୁଦ୍ର, *n.* the sea, the ocean.
*ସମୁଦ୍ରଯାନ, *n.* a ship, boat.
ସମୁଦ୍ରୀୟ, *a.* marine.
*ସମୁନ୍ନତ, *a.* elevated, exalted.
ସମୂଳ, *a.* with the roots.
ସମୂଳେ, *ad.* by the roots.
ସମୂହ, *n.* assemblage; the totality.
*ସମୃଦ୍ଧି, *n.* prosperity, wealth, increase. [with.
ସମେତ, *ad.* with, joined with, along
ସମ୍ପତ୍. ସମ୍ପଦ, *n.* property, wealth, affluence.
ସମ୍ପନ୍ନ, *a.* endowed with, possessed of; finished, completed.
ସମ୍ପର୍କ, *n.* connection, relationship.
ସମ୍ପର୍କୀୟ, *a.* related to, relative.
ସମ୍ପାଦକ, *n.* a secretary, an editor, a manager, one who accomplishes anything.
ସମ୍ପାଦନ, *n.* finishing, completing, effecting. [effected.
ସମ୍ପାଦିତ, *a.* accomplished, done,
ସମ୍ପାଦିବା, *v.* to keep carefully; to gather, to collect; to accomplish.
ସମ୍ପାଦ୍ୟ, *n.* (in *Geom.*) a problem.
ସମ୍ପୂର୍ଣ୍ଣ, *a.* filled, full, complete.
ସମ୍ପ୍ରତି, *ad.* now, at present.
ସମ୍ପ୍ରଦାନ, *n.* giving, conferring; (in *Gram.*) dative case.
ସମ୍ପ୍ରଦାୟ, *n.* community, a company, party, band; traditional doc-
*ସମ୍ବତ୍, *n.* era, year. [trine.
ସମ୍ବତ୍ସର, *n.* a year, a full year.
ସମ୍ବନ୍ଧ, *n.* connection, relation. [to.
ସମ୍ବନ୍ଧୀ, *a.* connected with, related
ସମ୍ବନ୍ଧୀୟ, *a.* relating to, relative.
ସମ୍ବରଣ, *n.* restraining, *a concealing.

ସମ୍ବର୍ଦ୍ଧନା, *n.* honour, respectful welcome. [stock.

ସମ୍ବଳ, *n.* provision for a journey;

ସମ୍ବାଦ, *n.* news, tidings, intelligence.

*ସମ୍ବେଶ, *n.* a dream, sleep.

ସମ୍ବୋଧନ, *n.* addressing; (in *Gram.*) vocative case.

ସମ୍ଭବ, *a.* possible, probable.

ସମ୍ଭାବନା, *n.* possibility, practicability.

*ସମ୍ଭାବ୍ୟ, ସମ୍ଭାବନୀୟ, *a.* possible.

ସମ୍ଭାର, *n.* fulness, multitude.

ସମ୍ଭାଳିବା, *v.* to restrain; to endure; to keep carefully.

ସମ୍ଭାଷଣ, *ସମ୍ଭାଷ, *n.* conversing; conversation, discourse. [from

ସମ୍ଭୂତ, *a.* born, produced, sprung

ସମ୍ଭିନ୍ନସମସ୍ଥାନ, *n.* an algebraical term.

ସମ୍ଭୋଗ, *n.* enjoyment, possession.

*ସମ୍ଭୋଗୀ, *a.* enjoying; cohabiting.

ସମ୍ଭ୍ରମ, *n.* honour, respect, reverence.

ସମ୍ଭ୍ରାନ୍ତ, *a.* honoured, respected.

ସମ୍ଭ୍ରାନ୍ତସମାଜ, *n.* the House of Lords; a highly respected or cultured community.

ସମ୍ମତ, *a.* of the same mind, willing.

ସମ୍ମତି, *n.* assent, acquiescence.

ସମ୍ମାନ, *n.* honour, esteem, respect.

ସମ୍ମିଳନ, *n.* union, concord, harmony.

ସମ୍ମୁଖ, *n.* front, place in front.

ସମ୍ମୁଖାସମ୍ମୁଖି, *ad.* face to face.

21

ସମ୍ମୁଖୀନ, *a.* lying in front of or before the face. [tion.

*ସମ୍ମୋହ, *n.* infatuation, stupefac-

*ସମ୍ୟକ୍, *a.* good, perfect; all;—*ad.* wholly, entirely; fitly.

ସମ୍ରାଟ୍, *n.* an independent sovereign, an emperor.

ସଯତ୍ନ, *a.* active, zealous.

ସର, *n.* cream, thick milk.

*ସରଃ, *n.* a tank, a pond.

ସରକାର, *n.* the Government.

ସରକାରି, *a.* belonging to the state.

ସରଜମୀନ୍, *n.* locality, particular spot.

ସରଞ୍ଜାମ, *n.* articles, things, furniture, materials.

ସରତା, *n.* betel-nut clippers.

ସରଦ, ସର୍ଦ, ସରଦି, ସର୍ଦି, *n.* a cold, a cough.

ସରଦାର, ସର୍ଦାର, *n.* a chieftain, headman, *Sardar*.

ସରପୋଷ, *n.* a cover or lid.

ସରବତ, ସର୍ବତ, *n.* *sherbet*, a beverage.

ସରବର, *n.* land of the best quality.

ସରବସ, *n.* rent, revenue.

ସରବସକାର, *n.* a collector of rents, an agent.

ସରମ, *n.* shame.

ସରଳ, *a.* upright, honest, sincere; straight.

ସରସ, *a.* juicy, fresh, tasty, racy.

ସରସା, *n.* a disease of the teeth;—*a.* more, better,

*ସରସୀ, *n.* a tank, a pond.
ସରସର, ସସସର, *a.* summary (judgment).
ସରସ୍ୱତୀ, *n.* the goddess of learning.
ସରହଦ, *n.* a boundary, border.
ସରାଇ, *n.* an inn; a baiting place, *sarai*.
ସରାଗ, *a.* with love or affection.
ସରି, *a.* alike, equal;—*n.* wheel ruts.
ସରିକ୍‌ଦାର, *n.* a sharer, a co-partner.
ସରିକି, *ad.* until, unto, whilst.
*ସରିତ୍, *n.* a river, stream.
ସରିସା, *a.* like, similar.
ସରୁ, *a.* thin, fine, slender.
*ସରୋବର, *n.* a tank, pond, lake.
*ସର୍ଗ, *n.* a chapter; creation; disposition.
*ସର୍ଜ୍ଜ, *n.* the *sal* tree.
*ସର୍ଜ୍ଜରସ, *n.* resin of the *sal* tree.
ସର୍ତ୍ତ, *n.* terms of contract, stipulation.
ସର୍ପ, *n.* a snake, serpent.
ସର୍ପରାଜ, *n.* *Básuki.*
ସର୍ବ, *a.* and *n.* all, universal, the whole.
ସର୍ବଜ୍ଞ, *a.* omniscient, all-knowing.
ସର୍ବତୋଭାବେ, *ad.* in every respect, wholly, fully.
ସର୍ବତ୍ର, *ad.* everywhere, in all places.
ସର୍ବଥା, *ad.* by all means, assuredly.
ସର୍ବଦର୍ଶୀ, *a.* omniscient, all-seeing.
ସର୍ବଦା, *ad.* always, at all times.
ସର୍ବନାମ, *n.* (in *Gram.*) a pronoun.
ସର୍ବନାଶ, *n.* total destruction.

*ସର୍ବବିତ୍, *a.* omniscient.
ସର୍ବବ୍ୟାପକ, ସର୍ବବ୍ୟାପୀ, *a.* all-pervading.
*ସର୍ବମୟ, *a.* universal, abounding in everything.
*ସର୍ବରୀ, *n.* the night.
ସର୍ବଶକ୍ତିମାନ୍, *a.* almighty, omnipotent.
ସର୍ବସୁଦ୍ଧା, *ad.* altogether, inclusively.
ସର୍ବସାଧାରଣ, *a.* general, common; —*n.* the public.
ସର୍ବସ୍ୱ, *n.* one's whole property.
ସର୍ବାଙ୍ଗ, *n.* the whole body.
ସର୍ବାଙ୍ଗସୁନ୍ଦର, *a.* completely beautiful.
ସର୍ବାଧିକାର, *n.* general control or superintendence.
*ସର୍ବାନ୍ତର୍ଯ୍ୟାମୀ, *a.* regulating the internal feelings of all;—*n.* the Supreme Spirit.
ସର୍ବାପେକ୍ଷା, *ad.* than all, beyond all.
ସର୍ବେନ୍ଦ୍ରିୟ, *n.* all organs of perception and action.
ସର୍ବୋପରି, *ad.* above all, supremely.
*ସର୍ଷପ, *n.* mustard, mustard-seed.
ସଳଖ, *a.* straight, even.
ସଳଖିବା, *v.* to straighten, to make even.
ସଲଜ୍ଜ, *a.* modest, bashful, ashamed.
*ସଲିଳ, *n.* water.
*ସଶରୀର, *a.* embodied.
*ସଶସ୍ତ୍ର, *a.* armed.
ସଶଙ୍କ, *a.* afraid, timid, doubtful.
ସସଜ୍ଜ, *a.* dressed, armed, accoutred.
*ସସତ୍ତ୍ୱା, *a.* pregnant, with child.
ସସ୍ତ୍ରୀକ, *a.* (a husband) with a wife.

ସହ, a *prefix*, meaning with, attending.

*ସହକାରିତା, *n.* assistance, co-operation.

ସହକାରୀ, *n.* a colleague, a fellow-labourer, one who assists;—*a.* co-operating.

*ସହଗମନ, *n.* a wife's death with her husband, contemporaneous death; a going with.

ସହଗାମୀ, *a.* going with;—*n.* a fellow-traveller.

ସହଚର, *n.* a companion;—*a.* walking with; *fem.* ସହଚରୀ ।

ସହଜ, *a.* easy; innate, natural.

*ସହଧର୍ମିଣୀ, *n.* a lawful wife.

ସହନଶୀଳ, *a.* longsuffering, patient.

ସହବର୍ତ୍ତୀ, *a.* being with, attending.

ସହବାସ, *n.* dwelling together, society.

ସହଭାଗିତା, *n.* co-partnership.

ସହଭାଗୀ, *n.* a co-partner, a sharer.

ସହଭୋଜନ, *n.* eating from the same dish.

ସହମରଣ, *n.* burning of a widow on the funeral pyre of her husband; see ସହଗମନ ।

ସହଯୋଗୀ, *a.* helping;—*n.* an assistant, a co-adjutor.

ସହର, *n.* a town, a city.

ସହରି, ସହରିଆ, *a.* belonging to a town;—*n.* a citizen.

ସହର୍ଷ, *a.* glad, pleased.

ସହସା, *ad.* suddenly, rashly, precipitately.

ସହସ୍ର, *a.* a thousand.

ସହାଧ୍ୟାୟୀ, *n.* a fellow student.

ସହାନୁଭୂତି, *n.* sympathy.

ସହାୟ, *n.* helper; an ally, a co-adjutor.

ସହାୟତା, *n.* co-operation, assistance, fellowship, help.

ସହିତ, *a.* being with, together with.

ସହିବା, *v.* to bear, to suffer.

ସହିଷ୍ଣୁ, *a.* enduring, patient, placable, forbearing.

ସହିଷ୍ଣୁତା, *n.* forbearance, patience.

ସହୀ, *n.* a female friend.

ସହୋଦର, *n.* an own brother; *fem.* ସହୋଦରା ।

ସହ୍ୟ, *a.* bearable.

ସକ୍ଷମ, *a.* capable, qualified.

ସାଆନ୍ତ, *n.* a master, lord.

ସାଆନ୍ତାଣୀ, *n.* a respectable woman, a lady; madam.

ସାଇ, ସାହି, *n.* a hamlet, division of a town.

ସାଇତିବା, *v.* to place in safety; to collect, to heap up.

ସାଉ, ସାହୁ, *n.* a surname; a trader.

ସାଉକାର, ସାହୁକାର, *a.* wealthy; liberal.

ସାଉଣ୍ଟିବା, *v.* to pick up, to collect together.

ସାଂସାରିକ, *a.* worldly, secular, fleshly, carnal.

ସାକର, *n.* a sweetened vegetable stew.

ସାକାର, *a.* having a form, bodily, corporeal.

ସାକାରପୂଜା, *n.* idolatry.

ସାକିନ୍, (। ସା।), *n.* particular place or village of dwelling.

ସାକ୍ଷୁଘରବା, *v.* to make a pretence of sorrow.

ସାଗର, *n.* the sea, the ocean.

ସାଗୁଣା, *n.* a vulture.

ସାଗୁଦାନା, *n.* sago.

ସାଙ୍କେତିକ, *a.* relating to signs.

ସାଙ୍ଖ୍ୟ, *n.* name of one of the *Darshanas.*

ସାଙ୍ଗ, *n.* company; a friend;—**a.* complete, concluded.

ସାଙ୍ଗୀ, *n.* a companion, an associate.

ସାଘାତିକ, *a.* deadly, fatal.

ସାଚ, *n.* treacle or molasses.

ସାଜ, *n.* outfit, armour, harness.

ସାଜିମାଟି, *n.* fuller's earth.

ସାଝି, *n.* a sharer, partner.

ସାଞ୍ଜୁ, ସାଞ୍ଜୁଆ, *n.* armour, coat of mail.

ସାଢେ, ସାଢ଼େ, *a.* with a half (as in one-and-a-half, two-and-a-half, etc., *i.e.*, ସାଢେ ଏକ, ସାଢେ ଦୁଇ) ।

ସାତ, *a.* and *n.* seven; 7; VII.

*ସାତ୍ତ୍ୱିକ, *a.* virtuous, well disposed.

ସାଥୀ, *n.* a companion, mate, comrade.

ସାଦରେ, *ad.* with respect or honour.

ସାଦା, *a.* white; plain.

ସାଦୃଶ୍ୟ, *n.* likeness, resemblance.

ସାଧ, ସାଦ, *n.* longing, desire, wish.

ସାଧକ, *a.* effecting;—*n.* a devout worshipper.

ସାଧନ, *n.* accomplishing, effecting.

ସାଧନା, *n.* effort, entreaty; worship.

*ସାଧନୀୟ, *a.* possible, accomplishable.

ସାଧାରଣ, *a.* common, general, universal.

ସାଧାରଣତନ୍ତ୍ର, *n.* a republic.

ସାଧିତ, *a.* accomplished, effected; overcome, subdued.

ସାଧୁ, *a.* pure; righteous.

ସାଧୁତା, *n.* righteousness, goodness.

ସାଧୁବାଦ, *n.* praise, eulogy.

ସାଧ୍ୟ, *a.* within one's power, possible.

ସାଧ୍ୟମତେ, *ad.* to the extent of one's power.

*ସାଧ୍ୱସ, *n.* fear, alarm.

ସାଧ୍ୱୀ, *n.* a virtuous woman; a faithful wife;—*a.* chaste.

ସାନ, *a.* small, little; youngest.

ସାନନ୍ଦ, *a.* joyful, happy, glad.

*ସାନୁକୂଳ, *a.* attended by favourable circumstances.

ସାନୁନୟ, *a.* courteous, civil.

ସାନ୍ତାଳ, *n.* name of a jungle tribe—*Santál.*

ସାନ୍ତ୍ୱନା, *n.* consolation, relief, comfort.

ସାନ୍ଧ୍ୟ, *a.* pertaining to the evening.

ସାନ୍ଧ୍ୟମିଳନ, *n.* evening party.

*ସାନ୍ନିଧ୍ୟ, *n.* nearness, proximity.

ସାପ, *n.* a snake, serpent.

ସାପକାତି, *n.* the cast-off skin of a snake.

ସାପୁଆ, ସାପୁଡ଼ିଆ, *n.* a snake-charmer.

ସାପେକ୍ଷ, *a.* having regard to, dependent on.

ସାଫ୍, *a.* clean, pure, pellucid.
ସାଫଲ୍ୟ, *n.* fruitfulness, success.
ସାବକ, *a.* original, old. [wife.
ସାବତଭାଇ, *n.* a half-brother by co-
ସାବତମା, *n.* a co-mother, a step-mother.
ସାବଧାନ, *a.* cautious, careful, wary.
ସାବଧାନତା, *n.* caution, care, atten-
*ସାବନ, *n.* a solar month. [tion.
ସାବାସ୍, *inter.* well done! bravo!
ସାବଡ଼, ସାବୁଡ଼, *a.* good, excellent.
ସାବିତ୍ରୀ, *n.* the *Gáyatri* or hymn to the sun.
ସାବୁଦ, ସାବୁତ, *n.* confirmation, proof.
ସାବୁନ, *n.* soap. [settled.
ସାବ୍ୟସ୍ତ, *a.* confirmed, established,
ସାମ, *n.* the third *Veda.*
ସାମଗ୍ରୀ, *n.* a thing, materials, goods.
ସାମନା, *a.* front, in front;—*n.* front part.
ସାମଞ୍ଜସ୍ୟ, *n.* fitness, congruity.
ସାମନ୍ତ, *n.* tributary chief; chief man or officer of a state.
*ସାମରିକ, *a.* military.
ସାମରିକ କର୍ଟମାର୍ଶଲ୍, *n.* court martial.
ସାମୟିକ, *a.* seasonable, temporary.
ସାମର୍ଥ୍ୟ, *n.* capability, capacity,
ସାମଲ, *n.* a surname. [power.
ସାମାଜିକ, *a.* belonging to a society or community, social.
ସାମାନ୍ୟ, *a.* common, ordinary, vul-
ସାମିଆନା, *n.* an awning. [gar.
ସାମିଲ, *a.* comprised, included.
ସାମୁଦ୍ରିକ, *a.* marine, relating to the sea;—**n.* a fortune-teller; the science of palmistry.
*ସାମ୍ବତ୍ସରିକ, *a.* yearly, annual.
ସାମ୍ୟ, *n.* similarity, equanimity.
ସାମ୍ରାଜ୍ୟ, *n.* empire, sovereign rule.
*ସାମ୍ପ୍ରଦାୟିକ, *a.* social. [tide.
ସାୟଂକାଳ, ସାୟାହ୍ନ, *n.* evening, even-
*ସାୟଂସମୀରଣ, *n.* evening breeze.
ସାର, *n.* essence, marrow; manure.
ସାରକୁଡ଼, *n.* a dunghill.
ସାରଗ୍ରାହୀ, *a.* able to comprehend.
ସାରଙ୍ଗୀ, *n.* a sort of fiddle.
ସାରଥି, *n.* a charioteer.
ସାରଦା, *n.* *Saraswati*; *Durgá.*
ସାରଭାଗ, *n.* quintessence, cream of anything.
ସାରମାଟି, *n.* manure.
*ସାରଲ୍ୟ, *n.* straightforwardness, sincerity. [tion.
ସାରସଂଗ୍ରହ, *n.* a compilation, collec-
*ସାରସ, *n.* the large Indian crane.
ସାରାତ୍ସାର, *n.* quintessence, best part.
ସାରାସାର, *n.* substance and vanity.
ସାରି, *n.* a line, row, range, tier.
ସାରି, ସାରିକା, ସାଳି, *n.* a talking *myna.*
ସାରିବା, *v.* to finish.
ସାରିନ୍ଦା, *n.* a musical instrument.
ସାରୁ, *n.* a kind of vegetable, *kachu, arum.*
ସାରୋଦ୍ଧାର, *n.* a compendium, drift.
ସାର୍ଥକ, *a.* answering an end, useful; successful.

*ସାର୍ଦ୍ଧ, *a.* increased by half, one half over.

*ସାର୍ବତ୍ରିକ, *a.* universal.

*ସାର୍ବଭୌମ, *n.* a universal sovereign; —*a.* universal.

ସାଳ, *n.* a kind of fish.

ସାଳଗ୍ରାମ, *n.* see ଶାଳଗ୍ରାମ ।

ସାଲ, *n.* a shawl; a year.

ସାଲସା, *n.* sarsaparilla.

ସାଲିଆନା, *a.* belonging to a year.

ସାଲିସ୍, *n.* compromise, settlement.

ସାଲୁ, *n.* a kind of red cloth.

*ସାଶ୍ରୁ, *a.* tearful, shedding tears.

*ସାହଙ୍କାର, *a.* proud, imperious, haughty.

ସାହସ, *n.* courage, boldness, daring.

ସାହସିକ, ସାହସୀ, *a.* courageous, bold, daring.

ସାହା, *n.* a helper, one who encourages.

ସାହାଯ୍ୟ, *n.* help, co-operation, assistance, alliance.

ସାହାସିଆ, *n.* a liar, a boaster; a bravo.

ସାହିତ୍ୟ, *n.* literature, belles-lettres.

*ସାହିତ୍ୟିକ, *a.* belonging to literature, literary, erudite;—*n.* one versed in literature, a literateur.

ସାହି, *n.* a village (see ସାଇ) ।

ସାହୁ, *n.* a trader; a surname.

ସାହୁକାର, *a.* rich, wealthy, opulent; —*n.* a rich man, a money-lender; a great man.

ସାହେବ, *n.* a lord, a master; used of Europeans.

ସାକ୍ଷାତ୍, *ad.* in the presence of;—*n.* interview, presence, sight.

ସାକ୍ଷାତ୍କାର, *n.* personal presence.

ସାକ୍ଷୀ, *n.* eyewitness, a witness.

ସାକ୍ଷ୍ୟ, *n.* testimony, evidence.

ସିଅ, *n.* a root fibre.

ସିଅଁ, *a.* sewn with a needle.

ସିଆହି, *n.* ink, blacking.

ସିଅଣା, ସିଆଣା, *a.* clever, knowing; mature.

ସିଇଁବା, *v.* to sew, to stitch, to seam.

ସିଂହ, *n.* a lion; a surname; sign Leo ;—*. chief.

ସିଂହଦ୍ୱାର, *n.* lion gate, main entrance.

ସିଂହନାଦ, *n.* a lion's roar; war-cry.

ସିଂହଳ, *n.* Ceylon.

ସିଂହଳୀ, *a.* belonging to or inhabiting Ceylon;—*n.* a native of Ceylon.

ସିଂହାଣି, ସିଙ୍ଘାଣି, ସିଙ୍ଗାଣି, *n.* mucous of the nose (see ଶିଙ୍ଘାଣି) ।

ସିଂହାସନ, *n.* a throne.

ସିଂହୀ, *n.* a lioness.

*ସିକତା, *n.* sand, sandy soil.

*ସିକତାମୟ, ସିକତିଲ, *a.* sandy.

ସିକଲଗର, *n.* a furbisher of metals.

*ସିକ୍ତ, *a.* wet, moistened.

ସିଝାଇବା, ସିଜାଇବା, *v.* to boil, to cook by boiling.

ସିଝିବା, ସିଝବା, *v.* to be boiled.

ସିଠା, *n.* dregs.

ସିଡ଼ି, *n.* a flight of steps, a ladder.

*ସିତ, *a.* white, fair, bright.

ସିତାର, ସିତାସ, *n.* see ସେତାର ।

ସିଦ୍ଧ, *a.* effected, perfected; boiled; —*n.* a saint.

ସିଦ୍ଧପୁରୁଷ, *n.* a perfect man.

ସିଦ୍ଧାନ୍ତ, *n.* final result, demonstration.

ସିଦ୍ଧି, *n.* accomplishment, fulfilment.

ସିଧା, *a.* straight; upright, honest.

ସିନା, an expletive meaning certainly, surely.

ସିନ୍ଦୁକ, *n.* a box, a chest.

ସିନ୍ଦୂର, *n.* vermillion, red-lead.

ସିନ୍ଧାଳ, *n.* a housebreaker.

ସିନ୍ଧି, *n.* a hole made in a wall by a thief.

ସିନ୍ଧିକାଠି, *n.* a housebreaker's tools.

ସିନ୍ଧୁ, *n.* the ocean; the river Indus.

ସିପାଇ, ସିପାହି, *n.* a sepoy or native soldier.

ସିପି, *n.* a cork, a bottle-stopper.

ସିରସ୍ତା, *n.* official records.

ସିରସ୍ତାଦାର, *n.* an officer in charge of official records.

ସିରକା, *n.* vinegar.

ସିରସ, *n.* glue.

ସୀତା, *n.* *Sitá*, wife of *Ráma* [*Chandra.*

*ସୀମନ୍ତ, *n.* parting of the hair down the centre.

*ସୀମନ୍ତିନୀ, *n.* a woman, one who thus parts her hair.

ସୀମା, ସୀମାନା, *n.* a boundary, limit, [border.

ସୀସା, *ସୀସକ, *n.* lead.

ସୁ, a *prefix* meaning good, easy.

ସୁଅ, *n.* a current, a stream.

ସୁଆଗ, ସୁହାଗ, *n.* excessive fondness.

ସୁଆଗା, ସୁହାଗା, *n.* borax.

ସୁଆଦିଆ, *a.* tasty.

ସୁଁଆବାଳିଆ, *n.* a hairy caterpillar.

*ସୁକର, *a.* easy to be done, practicable.

ସୁକାଳ, *n.* a time of plenty, a good time.

ସୁକୁମାର, *a.* soft, tender, delicate.

ସୁକୁମାରୀ, *a.* *fem.* of the above.

ସୁକୃତ, *n.* any good or virtuous act; righteousness.

ସୁକୃତି, *n.* an auspicious act, goodness.

ସୁକୃତୀ, *a.* virtuous, pious, happy.

ସୁଖ, *n.* happiness, pleasure.

ସୁଖକର, ସୁଖଦ, *a.* giving pleasure, pleasant.

ସୁଖଭୋଗ, *n.* the enjoyment of pleasure.

ସୁଖୀ, *a.* happy, at ease, well off.

ସୁଖ୍ୟାତ, *a.* of good repute, famed.

ସୁଖ୍ୟାତି, *n.* a good name, renown, fame.

ସୁଗଠନ, *a.* well-shaped, well-formed;—*n.* good workmanship.

ସୁଗନ୍ଧ, ସୁଗନ୍ଧି, *n.* fragrance;—*a.* fragrant, sweet-scented.

ସୁଗମ, *a.* easy, attainable, facile.

ସୁଘଞ୍ଚ, *a.* impervious, thick, close.

ସୁଡୋଉର, *a.* evident, clear, obvious.

ସୁଦିନ, *n.* auspicious event, good luck.

ସୁଚରିତ, *a.* virtuous, well-behaved; —*n.* good conduct, merit.

*ସୁଚାରୁ, *a.* charming, fascinating.

ସୁଜନ, *n.* a good or virtuous man, a benevolent man.

ସୁଜି, *n.* grits, coarse flour.

ସୁଜୀର୍ଣ୍ଣ, *a.* well-digested; worn out.

ସୁଝିବା, *v.* to refund, to repay.

ସୁଇ, *n.* a needle.

ସୁଡଙ୍ଗ, *n.* a subterranean hole or passage.

ସୁଡୌଲ, ସୁଢଗ, *a.* well-formed, handsome, graceful.

*ସୁତ, *n.* a son.

ସୁତରାଂ, *ad.* certainly, consequently, of course.

*ସୁତା, *n.* a daughter.

ସୁତୀକ୍ଷ୍ଣ, *a.* very keen or sharp.

ସୁଦ, ସୁଧ, ବଳନ୍ତର, *n.* interest.

ସୁଦର୍ଶନ, *n.* discus of *Vishnu*;—**a.* beautiful, good-looking.

ସୁଦିନ, *n.* a fine day, lucky day.

ସୁଦୀର୍ଘ, *a.* very long or extended.

ସୁଦୁର୍ଲଭ, *a.* very scarce or rare.

ସୁଦୂର, *a.* distant, very far off.

ସୁଦୃଢ, *a.* very firm, very hard.

ସୁଦୃଶ୍ୟ, *a.* good looking, handsome.

ସୁଦୃଷ୍ଟି, *n.* favour, kindness.

ସୁଦ୍ଧା, *conj.* inclusive, along with.

*ସୁଧା, *n.* nectar, ambrosia.

*ସୁଧାଂଶୁ, *n.* the moon.

*ସୁଧୀ, *n.* a learned man or Pandit; —*a.* learned, sensible, clever.

ସୁଧୀର, *a.* steady, deliberate, grave.

ସୁନା, *n.* gold.

ସୁନାମୁଖୀ, ସୁନାମଖେଇ, *n.* senna.

ସୁନାମୁଗ, *n.* a kind of pulse.

ସୁନାରି, *n.* a goldsmith; a flower very much like the laburnum.

ସୁନିଶ୍ଚିତ, *a.* ascertained, fixed, established.

ସୁନୀତି, *n.* good conduct, sound ethics.

ସୁନ୍ଦର, *a.* handsome, beautiful, fine.

ସୁନ୍ଦରତା, *n.* beauty, elegance.

ସୁନ୍ଦରୀ, *n. fem.* handsome, beautiful.

ସୁପକ୍ୱ, *a.* fully ripe, well-boiled.

ସୁପଥ, *n.* a good way, virtuous course.

ସୁପଥ୍ୟ, *n.* wholesome diet, regimen; —*a.* wholesome.

ସୁପାତ୍ର, *n.* a worthy person;—*a.* worthy, qualified.

ସୁପାରି, *n.* the betel-nut.

ସୁପାରିସ, *n.* a recommendation.

ସୁପୁତ୍ର, *n.* a fine, good or obedient son.

*ସୁପ୍ତ, *a.* asleep, sleeping.

ସୁପ୍ରଭାତ, *n.* a good morning, a fine morning.

*ସୁପ୍ରତିଷ୍ଠିତ, *a.* celebrated.

ସୁପ୍ରସନ୍ନ, *a.* very gracious.

ସୁବର୍ଣ୍ଣ, *n.* gold;—**a.* golden; fine coloured.

ସୁବର୍ଣ୍ଣମୟ, *a.* golden.

ସୁବା, *n.* a province; a governor.

ସୁବାସ, *n.* a fragrant scent; *a good residence.

ସୁବିଚାର, *n.* wise judgment, good counsel.

ସୁବିଧା, *n.* convenience, ease;—*a.* of a good kind; easy.

ସୁବୁଦ୍ଧି, *a.* intelligent, sensible.

ସୁବେ, *n.* doubt; *a province.

ସୁବେଦାର, *n.* an Indian military officer.

ସୁବୋଧ, *a.* intelligent, sensible.

ସୁବୋଧ୍ୟ, *a.* easily understandable.

*ସୁଭଗା, *n.* a beloved wife;—*a.* favoured.

ସୁଭଗ୍ୟ, *n.* good fortune.

*ସୁଭାଷିତ, *a.* well spoken.

ସୁଭିକ୍ଷ, *n.* a time of plenty.

ସୁମତି, *a.* very wise;—*n.* a good mind or disposition, benevolence.

ସୁମରିବା, *v.* (poetical) to recollect, remember.

ସୁମାର, *n.* enumeration.

ସୁମୁଖ, *a.* having good features, pretty.

ସୁମେରୁ, *n.* a fabulous mountain; the north pole.

ସୁମେରୁବୃତ୍ତ, *n.* arctic circle.

ସୁଯୋଗ, *n.* opportunity, convenient time.

*ସୁର, *n.* a god, demigod.

*ସୁରଙ୍ଗ, *a.* beautiful.

ସୁରତ, *a.* delighted, well-pleased.

ସୁରତହାଲ, *n.* a coroner's inquest, judicial investigation.

ସୁରତ, *n.* coition.

*ସୁରପତି, *n.* *Indra*.

*ସୁରପୁରୀ, *n.* *Indra's* capital, heaven.

*ସୁରବର୍ତ୍ମ, *n.* the firmament.

*ସୁରଲୋକ, *n.* the abode of the gods.

ସୁରସ, *a.* nice, savoury, sweet.

ସୁରା, *n.* strong liquor, spirits.

*ସୁରାପ, *n.* a drunkard, tippler.

*ସୁରାରି, *n.* an enemy of the gods, a Titan.

ସୁରୂପ, *a.* handsome, well-formed.

ସୁର୍ତ୍ତି, *n.* a lottery.

ସୁର୍ମା, *n.* collyrium, antimony.

ସୁଲଭ, *a.* easily attainable, cheap.

ସୁଲକ୍ଷଣ, *n.* a good sign;—*a.* having good signs, clearly distinguished by its characters.

*ସୁଲୋଚନ, *a.* having fine eyes.

ସୁଶୀଳ, *a.* good-natured, amiable.

ସୁଶୀଳତା, *n.* goodness of disposition.

ସୁଶୋଭିତ, *a.* comely, beautiful.

*ସୁଶୃଙ୍ଖଳ, *a.* well arranged, orderly.

*ସୁଶ୍ରାବ୍ୟ, *a.* pleasing to the ear, melodious, harmonious.

ସୁଶ୍ରୀ, *a.* handsome, beautiful, comely.

*ସୁଷମ, *a.* very lovely or beautiful.

*ସୁଷମା, *n.* exquisite beauty.

*ସୁଷୁପ୍ତ, *a.* fast asleep.

*ସୁଷୁପ୍ତି, *n.* profound repose, deep sleep.

*ସୁସଜ୍ଜ, *a.* well-armed, well-adorned.

ସୁସାଧ୍ୟ, *a.* easily practicable, easy.

ସୁସାର, *a.* well (in health); easy.

ସୁସ୍ଥ, *a.* well (in health), comfortable.

ସୁସ୍ଥତା, *n.* health, ease, comfort.
ସୁସ୍ଥି, *a.* indolent, lazy, dilatory.
ସୁସ୍ଥିର, *a.* settled, steady, established.
ସୁସ୍ପଷ୍ଟ, *a.* clear, distinct, intelligible.
ସୁସ୍ୱର, *n.* a melodious voice.
ସୁସ୍ୱାଦ, *n.* pleasant flavour.
ସୁହୃଦ, ସୁହୃଦ୍, *n.* a friend, associate, ally;— . friendly, affectionate.
ସୁହୃଦୟ, *a.* kind-hearted, friendly.
*ସୁହୃଦ୍ଭେଦ, *n.* breach of friendship.
ସୂକି, ସୂକ, *n.* a four-anna piece.
ସୂଚକ, *a.* pointing out, indicating; —*n.* an omen.
ସୂଚନା, *n.* information, an indication.
ସୂଚି, ସୂଚୀ, *n.* a needle; an index.
ସୂଚିତ, *a.* indicated, informed.
ସୂଚୀପତ୍ର, ସୂଚିପତ୍ର, *n.* a table of contents, an index.
*ସୂତ, *n.* a charioteer; a carpenter.
*ସୂତକ, *n.* impurity after childbirth.
ସୂତା, *n.* thread, yarn.
ସୂତିକା, *n.* a lying-in woman.
ସୂତୁଳି, *n*, twine, string.
ସୂତ୍ର, *n.* thread, a line; aphorism, rule, maxim.
*ସୂତ୍ରଧର, *n.* a carpenter, joiner.
ସୂତ୍ରପାତ, *n.* beginning, commencement; measuring, planning.
*ସୂନୃତ, *a.* true and pleasant;—*n.* true and agreeable speech.
ସୂପକାର, *n.* a cook.
*ସୂରି, *n.* a pundit, a poet.
ସୂର୍ଯ୍ୟ, *n.* the sun.
ସୂର୍ଯ୍ୟକାନ୍ତ, *n.* a crystal.
ସୂର୍ଯ୍ୟଗ୍ରହଣ, *n.* eclipse of the sun.
ସୂର୍ଯ୍ୟମଣ୍ଡଳ, *n.* the orb of the sun.
ସୂର୍ଯ୍ୟମୁଖୀ, *n.* the sun-flower.
ସୂର୍ଯ୍ୟାସ୍ତ, *n.* sunset.
ସୂର୍ଯ୍ୟୋଦୟ, *n.* sunrise.
ସୂକ୍ଷ୍ମ, *a.* fine, thin, delicate, small.
ସୂକ୍ଷ୍ମକୋଣ, *n.* an acute angle.
ସୂକ୍ଷ୍ମଦର୍ଶୀ, *a.* sharp-sighted, intelligent.
ସୂକ୍ଷ୍ମବୁଦ୍ଧି, *n.* sharp wit, acute intellect;-*a.* ingenious, keen, sharp.
*ସୃଗାଲ, ସୃଗାଳ, *n.* a jackal.
ସୃଜନ, *n.* a creating, producing.
ସୃଷ୍ଟ, *a.* created, formed, produced.
ସୃଷ୍ଟି, *n.* creation, formation, fabrication.
ସୃଷ୍ଟିକର୍ତ୍ତା, *n.* creator, maker; God.
ସୃଷ୍ଟିନାଶ, *n.* destruction of creation.
ସେ, *pron.* he, she, it, that.
ସେଯାବତ୍, *ad.* from that time.
ସେଉଳ, *n.* a kind of fish.
ସେକା, *n.* heat applied by fire or by hot water; baking;—*a.* baked.
ସେକାଲେ, *ad.* at that time, then.
ସେକିବା, *v.* to foment, to heat, to bake.
*ସେଚକ, *a.* watering;—*n.* one who waters a garden; a cloud.
ସେଚନ, *n.* sprinkling, irrigating.

ସେଠା, *a.* of or belonging to that place.
ସେଠାକୁ, *ad.* to that place, there.
ସେଠାରୁ, *ad.* from that place; thence.
ସେଠାରେ, *ad.* in that place, there.
ସେଠି, *ad.* in that place, there;—*n.* a surname.
ସେଣା, *n.* a bamboo basket used for raising water. [roof.
ସେଣି, *n.* rafters used in a thatched
ସେଣିକି, *ad.* there, on that side, aside.
ସେତଖାନା, *n.* a privy.
ସେତାର, *n.* a musical instrument with three strings. [mole.
*ସେତୁ, *n.* a bridge, embankment;
ସେନା, *n.* a soldier.
ସେନାପତି, *ସେନାନୀ, *n.* a general, a military commander.
ସେପରି, *a.* like that, same as that.
ସେପର୍ଯ୍ୟନ୍ତ, *ad.* till then, to that place.
ସେପାଖ, *ad.* and *n.* that side.
ସେପାରି, *ad.* and *n.* across, the other side of a river.
ସେପଟି, *n.* the other side, that side.
ସେପ୍ରକାର, *a.* of that kind.
ସେପ୍ରକାରେ, *ad.* in that way.
ସେବକ, *n.* a servant; *one who sews.
ସେବକା, *n.* a woman servant; a deaconess.
ସେବତୀ, *n.* the Indian white rose.
ସେବନ, *n.* taking (medicine etc.); *a serving, attending.

ସେବା, *n.* service, attendance.
ସେବାଇତ, *n.* an attendant; a *dhobá*, a barber.
*ସେବିତ, *a.* served, attended upon.
*ସେବ୍ୟ, *a.* worthy of being served.
ସେର, *n.* a *seer* (weight or measure); Cuttack seer 105 tolas; Balasore 80 tolas. [rich.
*ସେରନ୍ଧ୍ରା, *a.* having abundance,
ସେରୂପ, *a.* of that form.
ସେରୂପେ, *ad.* in that manner.
ସେହି, *pron.* he, she, it, that.
ସେହିକ୍ଷଣି, *ad.* immediately. [cal).
ସେହୁ, *pron.* he, she, it, that (poeti-
*ସୈକତ, *n.* a sand-bank;—*a.* consisting or made of sand.
ସୈନ୍ଧବ, *n.* rock-salt, fossil-salt.
ସୈନିକ, *a.* of an army, military;—*n.* a soldier.
ସୈନ୍ୟ, *n.* a soldier, an army.
ସୋଟା, ସୋଣ୍ଟା, *n.* a bludgeon, truncheon.
ସୋଦର, *n.* own brother;—*a.* uterine.
*ସୋପାନ, *n.* a step, staircase, ladder.
*ସୋମ, *n.* the moon.
ସୋମବାର, *n.* Monday.
ସୋମଲତା, . the moon-plant.
ସୋରା, *n.* nitre, saltpetre. [plant.
ସୋରିଷ, *n.* mustard-seed and its
ସୋହାଗ, *n.* fondness, affection, fondling.
ସୋହାଗା, *n.* borax.

ସୌଖୀନ, *a.* luxurious, foppish.
*ସୌଖ୍ୟ, *n.* pleasure, happiness, enjoyment.
*ସୌଗନ୍ଧ, *n.* a sweet scent.
ସୌଜନ୍ୟ, *n.* kindness, urbanity; honesty.
ସୌଦା, *n.* articles purchased, marketing; trade, commerce.
ସୌଦାଗର, *n.* a merchant, a trader.
*ସୌଦାମିନୀ, *n.* lightning.
*ସୌଧ, *n.* palace, mansion.
ସୌନ୍ଦର୍ଯ୍ୟ, *n.* beauty, elegance, neatness.
ସୌଭାଗ୍ୟ, *n.* good luck, fortune.
*ସୌଭ୍ରାତ୍ର, *n.* fraternal love.
*ସୌମ୍ୟ, *a.* handsome, pleasing.
*ସୌର, *a.* solar, relating to the sun.
ସୌରଜଗତ୍, *n.* the solar system.
*ସୌରଭ, *n.* fragrance, perfume, scent.
*ସୌଷ୍ଠବ, *n.* excellence, goodness, beauty.
*ସୌସାଦୃଶ୍ୟ, *n.* resemblance, similarity.
*ସୌହାର୍ଦ୍ଦ, ସୌହୃଦ୍ୟ, *n.* friendship, intimacy, amity.
*ସ୍କନ୍ଧ, *n.* the shoulder; a section.
*ସ୍ଖଳନ, *n.* tripping, slipping, erring
*ସ୍ଖଳିତ, *a.* slipped, mistaken, fallen.
ସ୍ତନ, *n.* the female breast.
ସ୍ତନବୃନ୍ତ, *n.* the nipple.
ସ୍ତନ୍ୟ, *n.* milk from the breast.
ସ୍ତନ୍ୟପାୟୀ, *a.* sucking the breast;—*n.* mamalia.
ସ୍ତବ, *n.* praise, a.eulogy.
*ସ୍ତବକ, *n.* bunch of flowers, a nosegay.
ସ୍ତବ୍ଧ, *a.* stiffened, paralysed, stopped.
*ସ୍ତମ୍ଭ, *n.* a pillar, post, column.
*ସ୍ତମ୍ଭନ, *n.* stupifying; a stupor.
ସ୍ତମ୍ଭିତ, ସ୍ତମ୍ଭୀଭୂତ, *a.* benumbed, insensible. fixed.
*ସ୍ତର, *n.* a str^tum, a layer of any substance.
*ସ୍ତାବକ, *n.* eulogizer, flatterer.
*ସ୍ତିମିତ, *a.* unmoved, motionless, fixed.
ସ୍ତୁତି, *n.* praise, eulogy, entreaty.
*ସ୍ତୁତିପାଠକ, *n.* a eulogist, panegyrist.
*ସ୍ତୁତିବାଦ, *n.* praise, eulogy.
*ସ୍ତୂପ, *n.* a pile, mound, heap.
*ସ୍ତୋକ, *n.* a little; a drop of water.
ସ୍ତୋତ୍ର, *n.* praise, flattery, entreaty.
ସ୍ତ୍ରୀ, *n.* a woman, wife, female.
ସ୍ତ୍ରୀଆଚାର, *n.* a woman's duties at marriage.
ସ୍ତ୍ରୀଗ୍ରହଣ, *n.* taking a wife, marrying.
ସ୍ତ୍ରୀତ୍ୱ, *n.* womanhood.
ସ୍ତ୍ରୀଧନ, *n.* a woman's private property.
ସ୍ତ୍ରୀଧର୍ମ, *n.* female duties; menses.
ସ୍ତ୍ରୀପୁରୁଷ, *n.* wife and husband, female and male.
ସ୍ତ୍ରୀଲିଙ୍ଗ, *n.* (in *Gram.*) feminine gender; *female organ, any mark of the female sex.
ସ୍ତ୍ରୀଲୋକ, *n.* a woman.
ସ୍ତ୍ରୀସଂସର୍ଗ, *n.* intercourse with women.

ସ୍ତ୍ରୀହରଣ, *n.* seduction, adultery, rape.

ସ୍ତ୍ରୈଣ, *a.* henpecked, effeminate.

ସ୍ଥଗିତ, *a.* postponed; stopped, ceased, obsolete.

*ସ୍ଥବିର, *a.* aged, steady;—*n.* an old man.

ସ୍ଥଳ, ସ୍ଥଳୀ, *n.* place, situation, dry land.

ସ୍ଥଳଚର, *a.* moving on dry land.

ସ୍ଥଳପଦ୍ମ, *n.* a beautiful flowering shrub and its flower; lily of the valley.

ସ୍ଥାନ, *n.* a place, spot, site, situation.

ସ୍ଥାନଚ୍ୟୁତ, ସ୍ଥାନଭ୍ରଷ୍ଟ, *a.* fallen from a place or situation.

ସ୍ଥାନାନ୍ତର, *n.* another place;—*ad.* elsewhere.

ସ୍ଥାନାବରୋଧକତା, *n.* resistance (in *Science*).

ସ୍ଥାନୀୟ, *a.* local.

ସ୍ଥାପକ, *n.* one who sets up, a founder;—*a.* placing, fixing.

ସ୍ଥାପନ, *n.* an establishing, a placing, setting up, fixing.

ସ୍ଥାପନା, *n.* an establishing, consecrating.

ସ୍ଥାପିତ, *a.* established, placed, set up, fixed.

*ସ୍ଥାବର, *a.* immovable, stable, fixed.

ସ୍ଥାୟୀ, *a.* permanent, enduring.

ସ୍ଥିତ, *a.* situated, fixed, placed.

ସ୍ଥିତି, *n.* fixed or settled state, stay, continuance.

ସ୍ଥିତିସ୍ଥାପକ, *a.* elastic (in *Science*).

ସ୍ଥିତିସ୍ଥାପକତା, *n.* elasticity (in *Science*).

ସ୍ଥିର, *a.* stable, firm, settled, fixed.

ସ୍ଥିରତା, *n.* firmness, durability.

ସ୍ଥିରବାକ୍ୟ, *n.* a man of his word;—*a.* exact.

ସ୍ଥିରୀକୃତ, *a.* established, confirmed.

ସ୍ଥୂଳ, *a.* thick, stout, gross, blunt.

ସ୍ଥୂଳକୋଣ, *n* an obtuse angle.

ସ୍ଥୂଳକୋଣୀ, *a.* (in *Geom.*) having an obtuse angle, obtuse-angled.

*ସ୍ଥୂଳଚାପ, *n.* a cotton-cleaner's bow.

ସ୍ଥୂଳତା, *n.* thickness; stupidity.

ସ୍ଥୂଳବୁଦ୍ଧି, *a.* dull, stupid, incapable.

*ସ୍ଥୈର୍ଯ୍ୟ, *n.* stability. firmness, certainty.

ସ୍ନାନ, *n.* bathing, ablution, washing.

ସ୍ନାନଯାତ୍ରା, *n.* the bathing festival.

ସ୍ନାୟୁ, *n.* nerve, a tendon.

ସ୍ନିଗ୍ଧ, *a.* soft, smooth, refreshing, cool; oily, unctuous.

ସ୍ନେହ, *n.* affection, love.

ସ୍ନେହପାତ୍ର, *n.* a favourite, beloved one, the object of affection.

ସ୍ନେହୀ, *a.* affectionate, agreeable.

*ସ୍ପନ୍ଦ, ସ୍ପନ୍ଦନ, *n.* throbbing, quivering, palpitation, pulsation.

ସ୍ପର୍ଦ୍ଧା, *n.* presumption; challenging.

ସ୍ପର୍ଶ, *n.* touch, touching, feeling.

ସ୍ପର୍ଶଜ୍ୟା, *n.* (in *Geom.*) a tangent.

ସ୍ପର୍ଶବର୍ଣ୍ଣ, *n.* from କ to ମ the 25 letters.

ସ୍ପର୍ଶମଣି, *n.* the philosopher's stone converting everything it touches into gold.

*ସ୍ପର୍ଶେନ୍ଦ୍ରିୟ, *n.* the organ or sense of touch, the skin.

ସ୍ପଷ୍ଟ, *a.* plain, manifest, clear.

ସ୍ପୃହା, *n.* longing, inclination, desire.

ସ୍ଫଟିକ, *n.* crystal, quartz.

*ସ୍ଫଟିକାରି, *n.* alum (see ଫିଟିକିରି) ।

*ସ୍ଫିଚ, *n.* the buttocks.

*ସ୍ଫୀତ, *a.* swollen, extended.

*ସ୍ଫୀତି, *n.* swelling, enlargement; prosperity.

*ସ୍ଫୁଟ, *a.* burst, opened, manifest.

*ସ୍ଫୁଟନ, *n.* a bursting, a cracking.

*ସ୍ଫୁଲିଙ୍ଗ, *n.* a spark of fire.

ସ୍ଫୂର୍ତ୍ତି, *n.* activity, a tremulous motion caused by surprise or joy, excitation.

*ସ୍ଫୂର୍ତ୍ତିମାନ୍, *a.* active, excited, palpitating.

*ସ୍ଫୋଟକ, *n.* a boil, tumour, abscess.

*ସ୍ଫୋଟନ, *n.* a rupture, a bursting.

*ସ୍ମର, *n.* the Hindu Cupid; recollecting.

ସ୍ମରଣ, *n.* remembrance, memory.

ସ୍ମରଣୀୟ, *a.* memorable.

*ସ୍ମାରକ, *a.* reminding; retentive.

ସ୍ମାର୍ତ୍ତ, *n.* a Brahman well versed in traditional law, name of a sect of Brahmans.

*ସ୍ମିତ, *a.* smiling;—*n.* a smile.

ସ୍ମୃତି, *n.* Hindu code; *recollection.

*ସ୍ୟୂତସନ୍ଧି, *n.* a seam, a joining; (in *Surgery.*) suture.

*ସ୍ରବ, ସ୍ରବଣ, *n.* a flow, flowing.

*ସ୍ରଷ୍ଟା, *n.* a creator, inventor, maker.

*ସ୍ରାବ, *n.* an oozing, a flowing, a trickling.

ସ୍ରୁଚ, ସ୍ରୁବ, *n.* a wooden sacrificial ladle.

ସ୍ରୋତ, ସ୍ରୋତଃ, *n.* a current, stream.

*ସ୍ରୋତସ୍ୱତୀ, *n.* a river, a flowing stream.

ସ୍ୱ, a *prefix* signifying own, self, indentity, individuality;—*n.* wealth, property (used in *Comp.* as ନିଜସ୍ୱ).

ସ୍ୱକର୍ମ, *n.* one's own affairs.

ସ୍ୱକୀୟ, *a.* own, peculiar.

*ସ୍ୱପକ୍ଷ, *n.* one's own party, partisans.

ସ୍ୱଗତ, *a.* confined to self, exclusive; —*n.* an aside.

ସ୍ୱଚ୍ଛ, *a.* transparent, pellucid, clear.

ସ୍ୱଚ୍ଛନ୍ଦ, *a.* easy, independent, voluntary;—*ad.* at one's own will or pleasure, voluntarily;—*n.* one's own will or choice.

ସ୍ୱଜନ, *n.* one's own family; a friend.

ସ୍ୱଜାତି, *n.* one's own caste, class or nation.

ସ୍ୱଜ୍ଞାନ, *n.* self-knowledge.

ସ୍ୱତନ୍ତ୍ର, *a.* independent, apart.

ସ୍ୱତଃ, *ad.* of itself.

ସ୍ୱତଃସିଦ୍ଧ, *a.* axiomatic, self-evident; —*n.* (in *Geom.*) an axiom.

ସ୍ୱତ୍ୱ, *n.* ownership, proprietary right.

ସ୍ୱତ୍ୱାଧିକାରୀ, *a.* having a right of property, wealthy;—*n.* a proprietor.

ସ୍ୱଦେଶ, *n.* native country, homeland.

ସ୍ୱଦେଶୀ, *a.* home-made, belonging to one's own country;—*n.* a fellow-countryman.

ସ୍ୱଧର୍ମ, *n.* one's own religious profession, nature, characteristics.

ସ୍ୱଧର୍ମତ୍ୟାଗ, *n.* apostacy.

ସ୍ୱନ, *n.* sound.

ସ୍ୱନାମ, *n.* own name.

ସ୍ୱପକ୍ଷ, *n.* one's own party.

ସ୍ୱପ୍ନ, *n.* dream, vision, sleep.

ସ୍ୱପ୍ନଦୋଷ, *n.* nocturnal impurity.

*ସ୍ୱବଶ, *a.* independent, uncontrolled.

ସ୍ୱଭାବ, *n.* nature, disposition, [character.

ସ୍ୱଭାବତଃ, *ad.* naturally, by nature.

ସ୍ୱୟଂ, *pron.* self, himself;—*ad.* in one's own person.

ସ୍ୱୟଂବର, ସ୍ୱୟମ୍ବର, *n.* a marriage in which the bride chooses the husband.

*ସ୍ୱୟଂବରା, ସ୍ୱୟମ୍ବରା, *n.* a girl choosing [a husband.

*ସ୍ୱୟଂଭୂ, ସ୍ୱୟମ୍ଭୂ, *n.* *Brahmá.* [God.

*ସ୍ୱୟଂଭୂ, ସ୍ୱୟଂମ୍ଭୂ, *a.* self-existent;—*n.*

ସ୍ୱର, *n.* voice, tune.

ସ୍ୱରବର୍ଣ୍ଣ, ସ୍ୱର, *n.* (in *Gram.*) the vowels. [voice.

ସ୍ୱରଭଙ୍ଗ, *n.* hoarseness; a shaking

ସ୍ୱରୂପ, *n.* sort, kind, species, a peculiar form of;—*a.* like, similar.

ସ୍ୱର୍ଗ, *n.* heaven, celestial abode.

ସ୍ୱର୍ଗୀୟ, *a.* heavenly, celestial.

ସ୍ୱର୍ଣ୍ଣ, *n.* gold.

*ସ୍ୱର୍ଣ୍ଣକାର, *n.* a goldsmith.

*ସ୍ୱଳ୍ପ, *a.* very little, very few.

ସ୍ୱସ୍ତି, *interj.* success! well done! be it so!

ସ୍ୱସ୍ତିକ, *n.* that which brings good fortune; a sign of good luck.

*ସ୍ୱାଗତ, *n.* a welcome, salutation.

*ସ୍ୱାତନ୍ତ୍ର୍ୟ, *n.* independence, wilfulness.

ସ୍ୱାତି, *n.* the 15th stellar mansion.

ସ୍ୱାଦ, *n.* flavour, taste; tasting.

ସ୍ୱାଦୁ, *a.* sweet, tasty, savoury, nice.

ସ୍ୱାଧିକାର, *n.* one's own right or title.

ସ୍ୱାଧୀନ, *a.* independent, free.

ସ୍ୱାଧୀନତା, *n.* independence. [cious.

ସ୍ୱାପଦ, *n.* a wild beast;—*a.* fero-

ସ୍ୱାଭାବିକ, *a.* natural, inherent, innate.

ସ୍ୱାମିତ୍ୱ, *n.* lordship, ownership.

ସ୍ୱାମୀ, *n.* a husband, master, owner.

*ସ୍ୱାୟତ୍ତ, *a.* independent.

*ସ୍ୱାର୍ଜିତ, *a.* self-acquired.

ସ୍ୱାର୍ଥ, *n.* one's own object or interest.

ସ୍ୱାର୍ଥପର, ସ୍ୱାର୍ଥପରାୟଣ, *a.* selfish, self-interested.

ସ୍ୱାର୍ଥପରତା, *n.* self-interestedness.

ସ୍ୱାସ୍ଥ୍ୟ, *n.* good health, relief, ease.

ସ୍ୱାହା, an exclamation;—*n.* the wife of *Agni.*

ସ୍ୱାକ୍ଷର, *n.* signature, autograph.

ସ୍ୱୀକାର, *n.* confession; consent, promise.

ସ୍ୱୀକାର୍ଯ୍ୟ, *n.* (in *Geom.*) a postulate.

ସ୍ୱୀକୃତ, *a.* agreed to; confessed.
*ସ୍ୱୀୟ, *a.* own, private, peculiar.
ସ୍ୱେଚ୍ଛା, *n.* one's own wish, impulse.
ସ୍ୱେଚ୍ଛାକ୍ରମେ, *ad.* voluntarily.
ସ୍ୱେଚ୍ଛାଚାରୀ, *a.* following one's own wish, unrestrained.
*ସ୍ୱେଦ, *n.* sweat.
*ସ୍ୱୈରୀ, *a.* unrestrained, self-willed.
*ସ୍ୱୈରଚାରିଣୀ, ସ୍ୱୈରିଣୀ, *n.* an unchaste woman.
ସ୍ୱୋପାର୍ଜ୍ଜିତ, *a.* self-acquired.

ହ.

ହ, the 32nd consonant.
ହଇ, *ad.* indeed, ay!
ହଇରାଣ, *n.* trouble, fag, difficulty; —*a.* troubled, put into difficulty,
ହଉ, *interj.* so be it, amen.
ହଁ, *interj.* assent, yes; well!
ହଂସ, *n.* a gander, drake; goose.
ହଂସଗାମିନୀ, *a.* (a woman) walking gracefully as a goose.
ହଂସା, *n.* the soul, breath of life.
ହଂସୀ, *n. fem.* a goose, a duck.
ହକ, *a.* just, true, right.
ହକଦାର, *n.* a proprietor.
ହକାର, *n.* a call (mainly used when a girl wife is called from her home to her husband's at the consummation of marriage).
ହକ୍କାହକ, *ad.* for nothing.
*ହକାରିବା, *v.* to call, to summon.
ହକିମ, *n.* a Muhammadan physician.
ହକ୍‌ସ୍ୱତ୍ୱ, *n.* right.
ହଗିବା, *v.* to relieve the bowels.
ହଗୁରା, *n.* one who has frequent stools;—*a.* timid, fearful.
ହଙ୍କାଇବା, *v.* to drive, to turn out, to lead away.
ହଙ୍ଗାମା, *n.* a quarrel, row, tumult.
ହଙ୍ଗାମୀ, *a.* noisy, riotous, quarrelsome.
ହଜମ, *n.* digestion.
ହଜମୀ, *a.* digestive;—*n.* digestive medicine.
ହଜା, *a.* lost.
ହଜାଇବା, *v.* to lose anything.
ହଜାମତ, *n.* shaving a person.
ହଜାର, *a.* and *n.* a thousand; 1000; [M.
ହଜିବା, *v.* to be lost.
ହଜୁର, *n.* presence; your honour.
ହଟ, *n.* teasing, importunity; diversion, fun.
ହଟହଟା, *n.* trouble; ridicule, general censure;—*a.* ridiculous, put to shame.
ହଟା, *n.* censure, dispraise; a market.
ହଟାଇବା, *v.* to take or push back.
ହଟୁଆ, *a.* amusing (person).
ହଟିବା, *v.i.* to retreat, draw back.
ହଠାତ୍, *ad.* accidentally, suddenly, easily.
ହଡ଼ବଡ଼, *n.* hurry, bustle, confusion.
ହଡ଼ବଡ଼ାଇବା, *v.* to be startled, to tremble, to be affrighted.

ହଡ଼ା, *n.* an old worn-out bullock.

ହଣାହଣି, *n.* mutual cutting or slaying, a repeated cutting or smiting.

ହଣ୍ଡା, *n.* a large earthen cooking vessel.

ହତ, *a.* killed, smitten, destroyed.

ହତଚିତ୍ତ, *a.* bereft of spirit or sense.

ହତଜ୍ଞାନ, *a.* senseless, stupid.

ହତଭାଗ୍ୟ, *a.* unfortunate, ill-fated.

ହତଶ୍ରୀ, *a.* bereft of fortune.

ହତା, *n.* an iron ladle; compound to a house; the joined palms.

ହତାଏ, *a.* (one) double handful.

ହତାଦର, *a.* bereft of respect or honour;—*n.* insult, disrespect, dishonour. •

ହତାଶ, *a.* disappointed, desponding.

ହତାହତ, *a.* killed and wounded.

ହତିଆର, *n.* a tool, implement, weapon.

ହତ୍ୟା, *n.* killing, murder, slaying.

*ହନନ, *n.* killing, beating, smiting.

ହନୁମାନ୍, *n.* the black-faced deified monkey; *Hanumán.*

ହନ୍ତା, *n.* a killer, slayer, murderer.

ହନ୍ତାଳିବା, *v.* to grope, to search.

ହପା, *n.* a wave, tide.

ହପ୍ତା, *n.* a week.

ହମ୍‌ହମ, *a.* ready to quarrel or strike.

ହମାନଦସ୍ତା, *n.* an iron pestle and mortar.

ହମାଳିବା, *v.* to low, to bellow.

ହମ୍ବାରଡ଼, ହମ୍ବାରବ, *n.* lowing, bellowing.

ହର, *n.* *Siva*; (in *Arith.*) a denominator.

ହରକତ, *n.* hindrance, impediment.

ହରକରା, *n.* a post peon or runner, a messenger.

ହରଶୋଭା, *n.* a kind of flower.

ହରଗୌରୀ, *n.* *Siva* and *Durgá* united.

ହରଘଡ଼ି, *ad.* at every hour.

ହରଡ, *n.* a kind of pulse.

ହରଣ, *n.* snatching, stealing, wasting; (in *Arith.*) division.

ହରଦର, *ad.* on an average, in the gross.

ହରଫ୍, *n.* a letter, a character.

ହରବର, *a.* troubled, bothered, perplexed;—*n.* confusion, perplexity.

ହରାଇବା, *v.* to lose.

ହରି, *n.* *Vishnu*; *a lion, horse, monkey.

ହରିକାଠ, *n.* wooden stocks.

ହରିଡା, *n.* a kind of medicinal fruit, the yellow myrobolan.

ହରିଣ, *n.* a deer, a buck.

ହରିଣୀ, *n.* a female deer, a doe.

ହରିତ, *a.* green, verdant.

*ହରିତକୀ, *n.* see ହରିଡା ।

ହରିତାଳ, *n.* sulphate of arsenic, yellow orpiment.

*ହରିଦ୍ରା, *n.* turmeric;—*a.* yellow.

ହରିବା, *v.* to take away, to steal; to divide.

ହରିବୋଲ, *n.* *Haribol*, a popular exclamation sometimes expressing joy as 'hurrah,' and at other times used as a prayer.

ହରେକ, *a.* every one; various.

*ହର୍ତ୍ତା, *n.* a thief, robber, plunderer.

ହର୍ତ୍ତାକର୍ତ୍ତା, *n.* the Absolute Disposer.

*ହର୍ମ୍ମ୍ୟ, *n.* a brick or stone house, palace.

ହର୍ଷ, *n.* delight, joy, gladness.

ହର୍ଷବିଷାଦ, *n.* sadness in joy.

ହର୍ଷିତ, *a.* delighted, glad, joyful.

ହଳ, *n.* a plough.

ହଳଦ, *n.* turmeric. [our.

ହଳଦିଆ, *a.* yellow;—*n.* yellow colour.

ହଳଦିବସନ୍ତ, *n.* name of a kind of yellow bird.

*ହଳଧର *n.* *Balarám*;—*a.* holding a plough.

ହଳନ୍ତ, *a.* see ହସନ୍ତ ।

ହଳା, ହଳାବିଡା, *n.* a bundle of paddy.

ହଳାହଳ, *n.* name of a deadly poison.

ହଳିଆ, ହଳୁଆ, *n.* a ploughman, a labourer; (also used as an adjective.)

ହଳେ, *n.* a pair.

ହଲକ, *n.* blood; life, spirit.

ହଲଫ, *n.* an oath.

ହଲହଲ, *a.* shaking, vibrating.

ହଲାଇବା, *v.* to shake, to move.

ହଲାଲଖୋର, *n.* a butcher. [and fro.

ହଲଚଲ, *n.* a shaking, a moving to

ହଲ୍ଲା, *n.* an uproar, a tumult.

ହସ, *n.* laughter; a laugh, grin, simper.

ହସନ୍ତ, *a.* (a letter) having the mark (୍) denoting that the inherent vowel is to be suppressed.

ହସାଇବା, *v.* to cause to laugh.

ହସିବା, *v.* to laugh.

ହସ୍ତ, *n.* the hand; a cubit; *elephant's trunk.

ହସ୍ତଗତ, *a.* come to hand subjected.

ହସ୍ତା, *n.* the 13th stellar mansion.

ହସ୍ତାନ୍ତର, *a.* transferred;—*n.* another's hand. [signature.

ହସ୍ତାକ୍ଷର, *n.* own hand-writing;

ହସ୍ତିଦନ୍ତ *n.* an elephant's tusk, ivory.

ହସ୍ତିନା, *n.* a name of ancient Delhi.

*ହସ୍ତିନୀ, *n.* a female elephant.

ହସ୍ତୀ, *n.* an elephant.

ହା, *interj.* oh ! alas ! well ! yes.

ହଁ, *ad.* yes, certainly, affirmatively.

ହାଇ, *n.* gaping, yawning.

ହାଉଁଯାଉଁ, *a.* anxious, troubled.

ହାଓଆ, *n.* air, wind.

ହାଉଡାଉ, *n.* abundance, plenty

ହାଉଡା, *n.* a stupid fellow, a blockhead; a dumb man; *fem.* ହାଉଡୀ ।

ହାଉଦା, *n.* a chair or seat on an elephant.

ହାଉହାଉ, *n.* a noise.

ହାକିମ, *n.* a governor, ruler, judge.

ହାକୁଟୀ, *n.* a hiccup.

ହାଙ୍ଗର, *n.* a shark.

ହାଜତ, *n.* custody (legal term).

ହାଜର୍, ହାଜିର୍, *a.* present, ready, willing. [pearance.

ହାଜରଜାମିନ୍, *n.* suretyship for ap-

ହାଜସ୍, ହାଜିସ୍, *n.* presence, attendance.

ହାଜିସ୍‌ବହି, *n.* attendance register.

ହାଜିରି, *n.* breakfast; attendance.

ହାଟ, *n.* a market, a fair.

ହାଟୁଆ, *n.* a market-man.

ହାଟୁଆଣୀ, *n.* a market-woman.

ହାଡ଼, *n.* a bone. [crane.

ହାଡ଼ଗିଳା, *n.* adjutant bird, gigantic

ହାଡ଼ଫୁଟା, *n.* the chicken-pox.

ହାଡ଼ଭଙ୍ଗା, *n.* breaking a bone; name of a medicinal climbing plant;—*a.* hard, wearisome; earned by hard labour.

ହାଡ଼ି, *n.* a sweeper, scavenger.

ହାଡ଼ିଆଣୀ, *n.* a female sweeper.

ହାଡ଼ୁଆ, *a.* bony.

ହାଣ, *n.* slaughter; a cutting, striking, digging, chopping.

ହାଣିବା, *v.* to cut, strike, dig, chop.

ହାଣ୍ଡି, *n.* an earthen cooking pot.

ହାଣ୍ଡିଆ, *n.* a kind of intoxicating liquid mostly used among *Sántáls* and *Konds.*

ହାଣ୍ଡିଖାଉ, *n.* a greedy woman.

ହାଣ୍ଡିଖିଆ, *a.* greedy, gluttonous;—*n.* a man who eats out of the handy. [miser.

ହାଣ୍ଡିଖଣା, *n.* a greedy person, a

ହାଣ୍ଡିଗିଳା, *n.* a gormandizer.

ହାଣ୍ଡିଶାଳ, *n.* a cooking-house.

ହାତ, *n.* the hand; a cubit.

ହାତଛଟା, *a.* given to thieving; ready to strike;—*n.* a thief; a striker.

ହାତକଡ଼ି, *n.* handcuffs, manacles.

ହାତକରତ, *n.* a hand-saw.

ହାତଯୋଡ଼ିବା, *v.* to join the hands or palms.

ହାତାହାତି, *n.* fisticuffs, boxing.

ହାତୀପଟ, *n.* a gable, gable end of a house.

ହାତୀଆଳ, *n.* an elephant driver.

ହାତୀଶୁଣ୍ଢ, *n.* an elephant's trunk.

ହାତୀ, *n.* an elephant.

ହାତୁଡ଼ା, ହାତୁଡ଼ି, *n.* a hammer.

ହାତୁଂହାତ, ହାତେହାତ, *ad.* instantly, from hand to hand.

ହାଡୁ, *interj.* away ! fie !

ହାନି, *n.* loss, injury, hurt.

ହାନିଲାଭ, *n.* loss and gain.

ହାପା, *n.* a kind of cake made of ground rice. [hand.

ହାପୁଡ଼ିବା, *v.* to sup or eat from the

ହାବଲି, ହାବେଲି, *n.* a kind of fire-work.

ହାବୁଡ଼ିବା, *v.* to collide, to meet.

ହାବେଲି, *n.* a palace or mansion; a kind of fire-work.

ହାମାନଦସ୍ତା, *n.* an iron mortar and pestle.

ହାମୁଡ଼ା, ହାମୁଡ଼ି, *n.* creeping, crawling.

ହାମୁଡାଇବା, ହାମୁଡାଇବା, ହାମୁଡବା, ହାମୁଡିବା, *v.* to crawl, to creep.

ହାମୁଡାଇଦେବା, ହାମୁଡାଇଦେବା, *v.* to cause to creep or crawl.

ହାୟ, *inter.* ah! alas!

ହାର, *n.* a necklace.

ହାରକ, *n.* a divisor; *a thief, robber.

ହାରାହାରି, *n.* average;—*ad.* on an average.

ହାରି, ହାରୁ, *n.* defeat, failure, foil.

ହାରିବା, *v.* to be defeated, to lose.

ହାର୍ଯ୍ୟ, *n.* a dividend;—**a.* liable to be taken away. [virus.

ହାଳାହଳ, *n.* deadly poison, venom;

ହାଲ୍, ହାଲତ, *n.* state or condition; bad circumstances. [modern.

ହାଲି, ହାଲୁ, *ad.* recently;—*a.* recent,

ହାଲ, *n.* an iron tyre.

ହାଲଚାଲ, *n.* state, circumstances; statistics; tidings.

ହାଲଅ, *n.* cold air or wind.

ହାଲି, *a.* recent, modern;—*ad.* recently.

ହାଲିଆ, *a.* debilitated, enfeebled by disease or trouble.

ହାଲିମ, *n.* garden cress. [gruel.

ହାଲୁଆ, *n.* a kind of sweetmeat,

ହାଲୁଇ, ହାଲେଇ, *n.* a confectioner.

ହାଲୁକା, *a.* light, thin, vain, empty.

ହାଲୁହାଲୁ, *n.* a tingling or throbbing sensation.

ହାସ, *n.* laughing, laughter.

ହାସିଆ, ହାଶିଆ, *n.* margin.

ହାସିଲ, *a.* effected, accomplished, successful.

ହାସ୍ୟ, *n*, laughing, laughter, smile.

ହାସ୍ୟମୁଖ, *n.* a smiling face. [larity.

ହାସ୍ୟରସ, *n.* facetiousness, jocu-

ହାସ୍ୟାସ୍ପଦ, *a.* ridiculous;—*n.* a butt of ridicule, laughing-stock.

ହାହା, *inter.* alas! alas!

ହାହାକାର, *n.* loud lamentation.

ହିଁହିଁ, *n.* sound of laughter; the neigh of horses.

ହିଂସକ, *a.* malicious, injurious.

ହିଂସା, *n.* malice, harm, injury.

ହିଂସିବା, *a.* see ହିଂସକ

ହିଂସ୍ର, ହିଂସୁକ, ହିଂସାଳୁ, *a.* malicious, mischievous.

ହିକ୍କା, *n.* hiccup.

ହିଙ୍ଗୁ, *n.* asafœtida.

ହିଙ୍ଗୁଳ, *n.* vermilion.

ହିଜଡା, *n.* a eunuch, hermaphrodite.

ହିଜଳ, *n.* name of a tree.

ହିଡ, *n.* a ridge round a field.

ହିଡମିଚ୍ଚ, *n.* name of a vegetable.

ହିତ, *n.* benefit, welfare, advantage. [sation.

ହିତକଥା, *n.* good advice or conver-

ହିତକର, *a.* favourable, useful, kind, friendly.

ହିତକାରୀ, *n.* a beneficent person;—*a.* beneficent. [cent.

ହିତଜନକ, *a.* advantageous, benefi-

ହିତବାଦୀ, *a.* giving good advice.

ହିତୈଷଣା, ହିତୈଷିତା, *n.* philanthropy.

ହିତୈଷୀ, *a.* desirous of benefit; benevolent;—*n.* one seeking another's welfare; *fem.* ହିତୈଷିଣୀ ।

ହିତୋପଦେଶ, *n.* good advice; a book containing moral teachings; the Book of Proverbs.

ହିଫାଜତ୍, *n.* care, custody.

ହିନ୍ଦୁ, *n.* a Hindu.

ହିନ୍ଦୁସ୍ଥାନ, *n.* Hindusthán.

ହିନ୍ଦୁସ୍ଥାନୀ, *a.* belonging to Hindusthán;—*n.* the Hindustani language.

ହିମ, *n.* snow, frost, cold;—*a.* frosty, cold.

ହିମକଟିବନ୍ଧ, *n.* frigid zone.

*ହିମକର, *n.* the moon.

ହିମକାଳ, *n.* winter, cold season.

*ହିମବାନ୍, *a.* snowy, frosty, cold, frigid, dewy;—*n.* Himalaya mountains.

*ହିମସଂହତି, *n.* a mass of snow or ice.

ହିମତ, *n.* spirit, daring, courage.

*ହିମାଂଶୁ, *n.* the moon.

*ହିମାନୀ, *n.* a mass or collection of snow, hoar-frost.

ହିମାଳୟ, *ହିମାଦ୍ରି, *n.* the Himàlaya mountains.

ହିୟା, *n.* (poetical) the heart, mind.

ହିୟାଦମ୍, *a.* stout-hearted, fearless.

ହିୟାଳି, *n.* a riddle, an enigma, a gibe.

*ହିରଣ୍ୟ, *n.* gold, silver, riches.

ହିସାବ, *n.* an account, a reckoning.

ହିସାବୀ, *a.* economical, thrifty, careful.

ହିସ୍ସା, ହିଂଶା, *n.* a share, lot, part.

ହିସ୍ସାଦାର, *n.* a sharer, a partner.

ହିସ୍ସାଦାରି, *n.* partnership.

ହୀନ, *a.* destitute, bereft of; mean, low.

ହୀନଜାତି, *n.* a low-caste.

ହୀନମାନ, *a.* destitute of honor, disrespected;—*n.* disesteem, contempt.

ହୀନମାନ୍ୟ, *a.* contemptible; parsimonious.

ହୀନସ୍ତା, *a.* low, wretched, destitute.

ହୀନୀ, *a.* mean, parsimonious.

ହୀର, *ହୀରକ, *n.* a diamond.

ହୀରାକସ, *n.* copperas, green vitriol.

ହୁଁ, *inter.* ha! aye; yes.

ହୁକୁମ୍, *n.* a command, an order, a decree.

ହୁକୁମତ୍, *n.* magisterial authority, sovereign dominion.

ହୁକୁମ୍ନାମା, *n.* a written command or order.

ହୁକୁମ୍ବରଦାର, *a.* obedient, obeying orders.

ହୁକ୍କା, *n.* the *huká.*

ହୁଗାଳିବା, *v.* to loosen, to slacken.

ହୁଗୁଳା, *a.* loose, shaky, slack.

ହୁଗୁଳିବା, *v.i.* to be slack, to be loosened; to get rid of.

ହୁଙ୍କା, *n.* a white ant hill.

ହୁଙ୍କାର, *n.* a loud and frightening sound.

ହୁଜତ୍, *n.* altercation, a quarrel; pertinacity.

ହୁଡ, *n.* a mistake.

ହୁଡା, *n.* the bank of a tank.

ହୁଡାଇବା, *v.* to cause to err; to lead astray.

ହୁଡିବା, *v.* to forget; to err; to go astray.

ହୁଡୁକା, *n.* an iron bolt, a fastening for a door.

ହୁଡୁମ, ହୁଡୁମ୍, *n.* a kind of parched rice.

ହୁଣ୍ଡା, *a.* foolish;—*n.* a foolish man; a hyena.

ହୁଣ୍ଡିଆ, *n.* one who takes or receives a bill of exchange.

ହୁଣ୍ଡୀ, *a.* foolish;—*n.* a foolish woman

ହୁଣ୍ଡି, *n.* a draft, bill of exchange.

*ହୁତାଶନ, *n.* fire, *Agni*, the god of fire.

ହୁଦା, *n.* a chuprasi's badge

ହୁଦାଦାର୍, *a.* having an official badge.

ହୁନର, *n.* skill, ingenuity, art, cleverness.

ହୁମ୍ହୁମ୍, *a.* ready to quarrel or fight.

ହୁରି, *n.* noise, shout, a crying out.

ହୁର୍ମତ୍, *n.* dignity, reputation, honour, chastity.

ହୁରୁସା, *a.* quarrelsome; vicious.

ହୁଳ, *n.* a sting, a sharp point.

ହୁଳହୁଳି, *n.* a sort of ululatus made by women on joyful occasions.

ହୁଳା, *n.* a sort of torch, a blaze.

ହୁଲି, *n.* the red-powder festival, *Doljátrá.*

ହୁଲିଆ, *n.* personal appearance; a description of a person.

ହୁଲିଆନାମା, *n.* a circulated description of a person.

ହୁଲୁଭଙ୍ଗା, *n.* a kind of small boat, a canoe.

ହୁସିଆର, *a.* attentive, clever, careful, vigilant, alert.

ହୁସିଆରି, *n.* sobriety, carefulness, vigilance.

*ହୃତ, *a.* seized; stolen; deprived of.

ହୃତ୍କମ୍ପ, *n.* palpitation of the heart.

ହୃତ୍ପିଣ୍ଡ, *n.* the heart.

ହୃଦପଦ୍ମ, *n.* the heart.

ହୃଦୟ, *n.* the heart, mind, breast.

ହୃଦୟଗ୍ରାହୀ, *a.* affecting, captivating.

ହୃଦୟଙ୍ଗମ, *a.* affecting, impressive.

ହୃଦୟବାନ୍, *a.* liberal, generous, good-hearted.

*ହୃଦ୍ୟ, *a.* beloved, dear, amiable.

ହୃଷ୍ଟ, *a.* rejoiced, glad, delighted.

*ହୃଷ୍ଟମାନସ, *a.* glad, glad-hearted.

ହୃଷ୍ଟପୁଷ୍ଟ, *a.* fat, sleek, plump.

ହେ, a vocative particle, oh! heigh!

ହେଂସ, *n.* a rush mat.

ହେଇ, ହେଇଟି, *ad.* here, near by;—*interj.* hark!

ହେକମତ, ହିକମତ୍, *n.* skill, cleverness, contrivance.

ହେଜ, *n.* memory, remembrance, recollection.

ହେଜିବା, *v.* to call to mind, to remember.

ହେଟ, ହେଠ, *a.* (poetical) bent, bowed down, humble.

ହେଟମୁଣ୍ଡ, ହେଠମୁଣ୍ଡ, *a.* (poetical) downcast, dejected.

ହେଟା, ହେଟାବାଘ, *n.* a hyena.

ହେଡା, *n.* flesh of a cow that has died of disease.

ହେଣ୍ଡିମାରିବା, *v.* to strike the sides with the elbows.

ହେଡା, ହୁଡା, *n.* compound to a house.

ହେତୁ, *n.* cause, reason, motive.

ହେତୁବାଦ, *n.* preamble, an expressed cause or reason.

ହେବା, *v.* to be, to become.

ହେମତ୍, *n.* courage, bravery.

ହେମନ୍ତ, *n.* winter, cold season.

ହେମାଳ, ହେମାଳିଆ, *a.* very cold.

ହେୟ, *a.* despicable, untenable.

ହେୟଜ୍ଞାନ, *n.* contempt, disesteem.

ହେରସା, *a.* without shame, immodest.

ହେରକା, *n.* etcetera;—*ad.* and the like, and so forth.

*ହେଳନ, *n.* disregard.

ହେଳମେଳ, *a.* familiar;—*n.* familiarity.

ହେଳା, *n.* trifling with, neglecting.

ହେଟପଣ, *a.* disturbed, distressed, troubled.

ହୋ, a vocative particle, oh! heigh!

*ହୋତା, *n.* a priest; sacrificer.

ହୋମ, *n.* offering oblations to gods by throwing ghee into the consecrated fire, a sacrifice; a burnt offering.

ହୋମକୁଣ୍ଡ, *n.* a hole in the ground for receiving the consecrated fire.

ହୋଶ୍, ହୋସ୍, *n.* sense.

ହ୍ରଦ, *n.* a lake, large sheet of water.

ହ୍ରସ୍ୱ, *a.* short, small, low in stature.

*ହ୍ରସ୍ୱତା, ହ୍ରସ୍ୱତ୍ୱ, *n.* shortness.

ହ୍ରାସ, *n.* decline, diminution.

କ୍ଷ.

କ୍ଷ, is a compound of କ and ଷ.

କ୍ଷଣ, *n.* a moment, a while.

କ୍ଷଣକେ, *ad.* in an instant.

କ୍ଷଣକୋପୀ, *a.* short-tempered;—*n.* a person whose temper or anger quickly passes and is without malice.

*କ୍ଷଣସ୍ଥାୟୀ, *a.* momentary, evanescent.

*କ୍ଷଣପ୍ରଭା, *n.* lightning.

କ୍ଷଣଭଙ୍ଗୁର, *a.* transient, frail, perishable.

କ୍ଷଣକ୍ଷଣ, *ad.* continually, perpetually.

କ୍ଷଣିକ, *a.* momentary, transient.

କ୍ଷତ, *n.* a wound, scar;—*a.* wounded.

*କ୍ଷତଜ, *n.* blood, pus, matter.

କ୍ଷତବିକ୍ଷତ, *a.* full of wounds and bruises.

କ୍ଷତି, *n.* loss, injury, harm, damage.

କ୍ଷତିକାରକ, କ୍ଷତିଜନକ, *a.* injurious, harmful, hurtful.

କ୍ଷତିଗ୍ରସ୍ତ, *a.* injured, damaged, suffering loss.

କ୍ଷତିପୂରଣ, *n.* compensation

କ୍ଷତ୍ରିୟ, କ୍ଷେତ୍ରିୟ, *କ୍ଷତ୍ର, *n.* one of the military or second caste.

*କ୍ଷନ୍ତବ୍ୟ, *a.* worthy of forgiveness, pardonable.

କ୍ଷମ, *a.* capable; patient; friendly.
କ୍ଷମତା, *n.* power, ability, authority.
କ୍ଷମତାପନ୍ନ, *a.* able, capable; authorised.
କ୍ଷମା, *n.* forgiveness, forbearance.
କ୍ଷମାବାନ୍, *a.* forbearing, forgiving.
*କ୍ଷମ୍ୟ, *a.* pardonable.
କ୍ଷୟ, *n.* wasting away, decline, consumption.
କ୍ଷୟକାଶ, *n.* the consumptive cough.
କ୍ଷୟମାସ, *n.* an intercalary month.
*କ୍ଷୟିତ, *a.* decayed, wasted, consumed.
*କ୍ଷରଣ, *n.* oozing, dripping, trickling.
କ୍ଷରିତ, *a.* leaked, oozed out.
କ୍ଷାନ୍ତ, *a.* ceased, quiet, tranquil, calm.
କ୍ଷାନ୍ତି, *n.* forbearance, desisting.
କ୍ଷାର, *n.* alkali, salt, ashes.
*କ୍ଷାଳନ, *n.* washing, rinsing, cleansing.
କ୍ଷାଳିତ, *a.* cleansed, washed.
*କ୍ଷିତି, *n.* the earth.
*କ୍ଷିତିପତି, କ୍ଷିତିପାଳ, *n.* a sovereign, a king.
କ୍ଷିପ୍ତ, *a.* distracted, mad; *thrown, cast.
କ୍ଷିପ୍ର, *ad.* rapid, quickly, soon.
କ୍ଷୀଣ, *a.* attenuated, thin; feeble.
କ୍ଷୀଣତା, *n.* slenderness, delicateness.
କ୍ଷୀଣଦେହ, *n.* emaciated body;—*a.* emaciated.
କ୍ଷୀର, *n.* milk; juice of certain plants.
କ୍ଷୀରସମୁଦ୍ର, *n.* sea of milk.
କ୍ଷୀରୀ, *n.* a cucumber.
କ୍ଷୀରି, କ୍ଷୀରସା, *n.* rice-milk, frumenty.
*କ୍ଷୀରୋଦ, *n.* see କ୍ଷୀରସମୁଦ୍ର ।
କ୍ଷୁଣ୍ଣ, *a.* perplexed, distressed; *powdered.
କ୍ଷୁଣ୍ଣମନା, *a.* distressed in mind, penitent, grieved.
କ୍ଷୁଦ୍ର, *a.* little, small, low, mean.
କ୍ଷୁଦ୍ରତା, *n.* smallness, littleness, meanness.
କ୍ଷୁଦ୍ରବୁଦ୍ଧି, *a.* miserly, penu-ions.
କ୍ଷୁଦ୍ରାଶୟ, *a.* narrowminded, mean.
କ୍ଷୁଧା, *n.* hunger, appetite.
କ୍ଷୁଧାତୁର, *a.* hungry, famished.
କ୍ଷୁଧାର୍ତ୍ତ, କ୍ଷୁଧିତ, *a.* hungry.
କ୍ଷୁବ୍ଧ, *a.* agitated, pained, distressed.
କ୍ଷୁର, *n.* a razor.
*କ୍ଷୁରପା, *n.* a short spud for grubbing up grass.
କ୍ଷେତ, କ୍ଷେତ୍ର, *n.* a field, a cornfield.
କ୍ଷେତ୍ର, *n.* a place of pilgrimage.
କ୍ଷେତ୍ରତତ୍ତ୍ୱ, *n.* geometry.
*କ୍ଷେତ୍ରପତି, *n.* a farmer, a landowner.
କ୍ଷେତ୍ରଫଳ, *n.* area.
କ୍ଷେପ, *n.* a load, a throw, a cast.
କ୍ଷେପଣ, *n.* spending; *throwing, casting.
*କ୍ଷେପଣୀ, *n.* an oar; a net.
*କ୍ଷୋଦିତ, *a.* engraved; powdered.
କ୍ଷୋଭ, *n.* perplexity, distress of mind.
କ୍ଷୋଭିତ, *a.* agitated, excited.
କ୍ଷୌର, *n.* shaving.

APPENDIX.

Scientific Names of Trees, Plants, &c.

Many of the following words occur in the body of the Dictionary; but as there are no corresponding terms by which to render many of them in English, they have been defined as a plant, tree, shrub, flower, &c.

ଅଅଳା, Phyllanthus emblica.
ଅକରକର, Pellitory.
ଅକସନ୍ଧ, Solanum fruitescens.
ଅକାଳବଲ୍ଲି, Cessampelos hexandra.
ଅଗବଥୁ, Premna spinosa and longi- [folia.
ଅଗୁରୁ, Amaris agallocha.
ଅଗ୍ନି Plumbago zeylanica.
ଅଗ୍ନିଶିଖା, ଲାଙ୍ଗଳିଆ, Gloriosa su- [perba.
ଅଜସନ୍ଧ, Solanum jacquini.
ଅଚ୍ୟୁଣ୍ଡ, Morinda tinctoria, used in dying.
ଅଜାଗର, Eclipta prostrata.
ଅଣସୋରିଷା, Cleome viscosa.
ଅଦା, Amomum zingiber.
ଅନନ୍ତମୂଳ, Periploca indica.
ଅପରାଜିତା, Clitoria ternatea.
ଅପାମାରଗ, ଅପାମାର୍ଗ, Achyranthes as- [pera.
ଅମ୍ଳିକା, Tamarindus indicus.
ଅମ୍ଳଲଡ, Oxales monodelpha.
ଅର୍କ, Asclepias gigantica.
ଅର୍ଜ୍ଜୁନ, Terminalia alata glabra.
ଅଳାଇଚ, Alpinia cardamomum.
ଅଶୋକ, Jonesia asoca.
ଅଶ୍ୱଗନ୍ଧା, Physalis flexuosa.
ଆକନ୍ଦ, Calotropis gigantia.
ଆକରୋଟ, Juglans regia.
ଆତ, Annona squamosa.
ଆମ୍ବଡା, Spondias mangifeera.
ଆମ୍ବ, Magnifera indica.
ଆୟାପାନ, Eupatorium Aya Pana.
ଆଲକୁଶୀ, Carpopogon pruriens.
ଇନ୍ଦୀବର, Nymphæ cœrulea.
ଇନ୍ଦ୍ରଯବ, Seed of Nerium Antidysen- [tericum.
ଇନ୍ଦ୍ରାଣୀ, Vitex negundo.
ଈଶ୍ୱରଜଟା, Hedysarum pictum.
ଉଅଉ, ଓଉ, Dillenia indica.
ଉଡୁମ୍ବର, Ficus glomerata.
ଉମ୍ବୁଟି, Ophioglossum vulgatum.
ଓଜଳା, Xiris indica, Verbena nodiflora, and Hibiscus esculenta.

ଓଡ଼ଫୁଲ, Hibiscus rosa sinensis.
ଓଜସମାଗ୍ଲ, Solanum pubescens.
ଓଲୁଅ, Arum campanulatum.
ଓସ୍ତ, ଅଶ୍ୱଥ, Ficus religioso.
କଇଁଫୁଲ, Nymphœa esculenta
କଇଥବେଲ, Feronia elephantium.
କଖାରୁ, Cucurbita pepo.
କଙ୍କସେଲ, Esox scolopax, Allangium hexapetalum.
କଚନାର, Bauhinia variegata and [purpurea.
କଞ୍ଜା, Guledupa indica.
କଟକଲେଜା, Cæsalpinia bonducella.
କଟୁଙ୍କା, Calotropis gigantea.
କଣ୍ଟକାଳ, Artocarpus integrifolia.
କଣ୍ଟାଅଳୁ, Dioscorea pentaphylla.
କଣ୍ଟ କୁସୁମ, Argemone Mexicana.
କଣ୍ଟାଗୋଲାପ, Rosa chinensis.
କଣ୍ଟାନେଉଟିଆ, Amaranthus spinosus.
କଣ୍ଟାବାଁଶ, Bambusa spino.
କଣ୍ଟାବେଲ, Jasminum multiflorum.
କଣ୍ଟାସାରୁ, Pothos lasia.
କଣ୍ଟାସୋଲ, Æschynomene paludosa.
କଦଳୀ, Musa sapientum.
କଦମ୍ବ, କୋଦମ, Nauclea orientalis.
କନକଚମ୍ପା, Pterospermum acerifolium.
କନେର, କନଅର, Nerium odorum.
କନ୍ଦମୂଳ, Convulvulus batatus.
କପା, Gossypium herbanum.
କମଳ, Nelumbium speciosum.
କମଳା, Citrus aurantium.
କରଞ୍ଜ, Guledupa ardorea.
କରଣ୍ଡା, ଖିରକୋଳି, Carrissa carondas.
କରବୀ, କରବୀର, Nerium odorum.
କରମଙ୍ଗା, Averrhoa carambola.
କଲମ, Convolvulus repens.
କଳାକସୁର, Capraria gratissima.
କଳାକାସୁନ୍ଦା, Cassia sophora.
କଳାଜିର, Nigella indica.
କଳାତୁଳସୀ, Ocymum sanctum.
କଳାମୁଗ, Phaseolus max.
କଳାଶିମ, Dolichos ensiformoides.
କଲରା, Momordica carantia.
କାଳିଅଣ୍ଟିଆ, Ardisia solcnacea.
କାକୁଡ଼ି, Cucumis uttissimus.
କାଙ୍ଗୁ, Panicum italicum.
କାଞ୍ଚନ, Bauhinia acuminata.
କାଣ୍ଡଶର, Saccharum sara.
କାନକୋଳି, Tizyphus napeca.
କାଶ, Saccharum spontaneum.
କିଆକଣ୍ଟା, Pandanus fœtidus.
କୁକୁରଅଳୁ, Dioscorea anguina.
କୁକୁରଛେଡ଼ା, Tetranthera monopetala.
କୁକୁରଶୁଙ୍ଗା, Conyza terebinthena.
କୁଞ୍ଜଲତା, Ipomea quamoclit.
କୁଡ଼କୁଚସ୍ପାଶିମ, Serratula cinerea.
କୁଦାଳିଆ, Hedysarum triflorum.
କୁନ୍ଦ, Jasminum grandiflorum.
କୁନ୍ଦୁରୁକା, Boswellia thurifera.
କୁମାରୀ, Aloe perfoliata.
କୁରୁବେଳ, Hibiscus tortuosus.
କୁଶ, Poa cynosuroides.
କୁସୁମ, କୁସୁମ୍ଭ, Carthamus tinctorius.
କୃମିଘ୍ନ, Serratula anthelmintica.
କୃଶାକୃ, Plumbago zeylanica.
କୃଷ୍ଣକେଳି, Mirabilis jalapa.

କୃଷ୍ଣଚୂଡା, Poinciana pulcherrima.
କୃଷ୍ଣପର୍ଣ୍ଣୀ, Hemiorites cordifolia.
କେତକୀ, Pandanus odoratissimus.
କେନ୍ଦୁ, Embryopteris glutinifera.
କେନ୍ଦୁଲି, Commelina nudiflora.
କେଳିକଦମ୍ବ, Nauclea cordifolia.
କେଶର, Stamina.
କେଶୁର, Verbesina calanduacila.
କୋଇଲେଖା, Barleria longifolia.
କୋଚିଲା, Strychnos nux vomica.
କୋଦାଳିଆ, Hedysarum triflorum.
କୋଳଥ, Dolichos biflorus.
କୋଳି, Zizyphus jujuba.
କୋଶଲା, Oldenlandiacry stallina.
ଖଇର, Mimosa catechu (khayár).
ଖଟାପାଳଙ୍ଗ, Rumex vesicarcus.
ଖଡ଼, Saccharum semidecumbens.
ଖମ୍ବଆଳୁ, Disoscorea alata.
ଖରଭୁଜ, ଖରମୁଜା, Cucumis melo.
ଖର୍ଜ୍ଜୁର, ଖର୍ଜ୍ଜୁରୀ, Phœnix sylvestris.
ଖସା, Sesamum orientale.
ଖୁଦଅଚଣା, Lathyrus sativus.
ଖୁଦଅଜାମ୍ବୁ, Antisdesma paniculata.
ଗଜପିପ୍ପଳୀ, Pothus officinabis.
ଗଞ୍ଜାଇ, ଘଡ, Cannabis sativa.
ଗଣ୍ଡିସାହାଡା, Ficus heterophylla.
ଗନ୍ଧବେଣା, Panicum strictum.
ଗନ୍ଧଭଦାଳି, Oldenlandia alata.
ଗନ୍ଧମାର, Artimisia indica.
ଗନ୍ଧମାଳତ, Echites caryophyllata.
ଗନ୍ଧରାଜ, Gardenia florida.
ଗବ, Ricinus communis.
ଗବଜଳ, Arundo bifaria.

ଗମ୍ଭାର, Gmelina arborea.
ଗୟାଓଷ୍ଠ, Ficus cordifolia.
ଘରଗଡ, Rhizophora.
ଗରଣ, Rhizophora decandra.
ଗରଣଆଳୁ, Dioscorea rubella.
ଗଲୁଡିଆ, Hedysarum lagopodsoides.
ଗର୍ଜ୍ଜନ, Dipterocarpus incana.
ଗହମ, Triticum æstivum.
ଗାଜର, Daucus carota.
ଗୁଆ, ଗୁବାକ, Areca-catechu.
ଗୁଆପାନମୂଳ, Ascleplias pseudosarsa.
ଗୁଗ୍ଗୁଳ, Bdellium.
ଗୁଡ, Leucocephala graminifolia
ଗୁଲଚିନା, Polyanthes tuberosa.
ଗୁଳୁଚି, Menispermum cordifolium.
ଗୁହ୍ୟଅବବୁର, Mimosa farnesiana.
ଗେଣ୍ଡୁ, Tagetes erecta.
ଗୋକ୍ଷୁର, Tribulus terrestris.
ଗୋଜହ୍ୱା, Hieracium Bruce.
ଗୋଲୁଡିଆ, Momordica monadelpha.
ଗୋଲାପଜାମ୍ବୁ, Eugenia jambos.
ଚୈଅନଳିତା, Corchorus capsularis.
ଘିକୁଆଁରୀ, Aloe perfoliata.
ଘୃତକୁମାରୀ, Aloe perfoliata; varsuc-
ଘେଁଟସାରୁ, Arum orixensis. [cotrina.
ଚଟ୍ଟା, Bauhinia accuminata.
ଚଣା, Pisum sativum.
ଚନ୍ଦ୍ରମଲ୍ଲୀ, Chrysanthemum indicum.
ଚମ୍ପା, Michelia champaca. [mus.
ଚମ୍ପାକେଉଟିଆ, Amaranthus polyga-
ଚମ୍ପାପଣସ, Artocarpus chaplasha.
ଚମ୍ବେଲ, Jasminum grandiflorum.
ଚକୁଣ୍ଡା, Cassia tora.

ଚାଲତା, Dillenia indica.
ଚିଙ୍ଗ୍ରାଦଳ, Nymphœa lotus.
ଚିତାମୂଳ, Plumbago zeylanica.
ଚିରଇତା, Gentiana cherayta.
ଚୁଆ, Celosia argentea.
ଚୋବଚିନି, Simlax china.
ଚୋରକଣ୍ଟା, Andrapogon aciculatum.
ଛତାରୁ, Asparagus racemosus.
ଛତଣା, Echites scholaris.
ଛୁନ୍ଛୁନିଆଶାଗ, Marsilea dentata.
ଜଙ୍ଗିହରଡା, Unripe fruit of Terminalia chebula.
ଜଟାମାଂସୀ, Valeriana jatamansi.
ଜଟାଶାଲପର୍ଣ୍ଣୀ, Hedysarum pulchellum.
ଜଡା, ଏରଣ୍ଡ, Ricinus communis.
ଜଳଖ, Leea.
ଜୟନ୍ତୀ, Æschynomene sesban.
ଜୟପାଳ, Croton riglium.
ଜରାଙ୍କୁଶ, Andropogon jwarancusa.
ଜଳପାଇ, Elæcarpus serrata.
ଜହ୍ନି, Luffa acutangula.
ଜାଇଫଳ, Myristica moschata.
ଜାଇଫୁଲ, ଜାଈ, Jasminum grandiflorum.
ଜାଦ୍ରୁମାରି, Cassia alata.
ଜାମ, Eugenia jambolana.
ଜାମରୁଲ, Eugenia alba.
ଜାରୁଲ, ଅଜ୍ଜ୍, Lagerstrœmia Regina.
ଜିଅଳ, Odina wordier.
ଜୀବକ, Celtis orientalis.
ଜୀର, Cuminum cyminum.
ଜୁଇ, Jasminum auriculatum.
ଜେଉଟ, Annona murieata.
ଝଙ୍କାଅଳୁ, Dioscorea golobosa.
ଝଙ୍କାପେଡ, Sida asiatica.
ଝାଉଁ, Tamarix indica.
ଝାଁଉର, Chara furcata.
ଝୁମକା, ଝୁମକ, Passiflora citrifolia.
ଟାଭା, Citrus medica.
ଟୋକାଉକୁଲିଆଉ, Trifolium officinale.
ଡେଙ୍ଗଗରଗଜ, Coix gigantea.
ଡାଲଚିନି, Laurus cinnamomum.
ଡାଳିମ୍ବ, Punica granatum.
ଡାଲପସାରୁ, Sagittaria.
ଡିମିରି, Ficus glomerata.
ତାଳ, Borassus flabelliformis.
ତରଡ, ତରୁଡ, Luffa acutangula.
ତଳାଭ, Corypha talliera.
ତମାଖୁ, Nicotiana tabacum.
ତରଙ୍ଗା, Alpinia allughas.
ତରଭୁଜ, Cucurbita citrullus.
ତରଲବାଉଁଶ, Bambusa tulda.
ତାଲମାଶବା, Mimosa dulcis.
ତାଲମୁଣ୍ଡି, Curculigo orchioides.
ତାଲମୂଳୀ, Curculigo orchioides.
ତନ୍ତୁଳି, Tamarindus indica.
ତିଳ, Sesamum orientale.
ତୁଳସୀ, Ocymum sanctum.
ତୁତ, Morus indica.
ତେଜପତ୍ର, Laurus cassia.
ଥଳପଦ୍ମ, Hibiscus mutabalis.
ଦନ୍ତୀ, Croton polyandrum.
ଦୟଣା, Artimisia indica.
ଦଳ, Panicum stagnium.
ଦସ୍ତା, Tutenag.
ଦାସକେରଣ୍ଡା, Melochia corchorifolia.
ଦ୍ୱିପହରଅ, Pentapetas phœnicea.

ଦ୍ୱିପାଟି, Impatiens balsamina.
ଦୁବ, Agrostis linearis.
ଦୁଧକଲ୍ମ, Convolvulus tarpethum.
ଦୁଧାଲି, Asclepias rosea.
ଦୁଲଭ, Hedysarum alhagi.
ଦୁଗଲଚମ୍ପା, Hedychium coronarium.
ଦେବଦାରୁ, Uvaria longifolia
ଦ୍ରାକ୍ଷାଲତା, Vitus vinifera.
ଧଣ୍ଡସ, Hibiscus culentus.
ଧନିଆ, ଧଣିଆ, Coriandrum sativum.
ଧବ, Grislea tomentosa.
ଧଳାକଳସୁର, Euphorbia thymifolia.
ଧଳାଧାନ, Andropogon verticellata.
ଧଳାନେଉଟିଆ, Amaranthus olérace-
ଧଳାବଚ, Acorus calamus. [us.
ଧଳାବାଡଅଁଳା, Sida rhomboidœa.
ଧଳାମୁଗ, Phaseolus sublobatus.
ଧାତୁକୀଫୁଲ, Grisler tomentosa.
ଧାନ, Oryza sativa.
ଧାନୁଆମରିଚ, Capsicum minimum.
ଧୂତୁରା, ଧତୁରା, Datura metel.
ଧୂନ୍ଦୁଲ, Luffa pentandra.
ନଟା, Guilandina bonduccella.
ନଟାସିଜୁ, Euphorbia antiquorum.
ନଡ଼ିଆ, Cocos nucifera. [speciosum.
ନଳ, Arundo tibialis, Nelumbium
ନଳଦ, Veleriana jatamansi.
ନଖୁଣିଆସିମ, Dolichos gladiatus.
ନାଗଦମଣୀ, Artemisia vulgaris.
ନାଗଫେଣୀ, Cactus indicus.
ନାଗବଲ୍ଲୀ, Bauhinia anguina.
ନାଗରମୁଥା, Cyperus pertenuis.
ନାଗେଶର, Mesua ferrea.

ନାକୁଚ, Mimosa pudica.
ନାକଛିକଣୀ, Artemisia sternutatoria.
ନାରଙ୍ଗା, Citrus aurantium.
ନାଲବାଡଅଁଳା, Sida rhombifolia.
ନାଲିମୁଗ, Phaseolus calcaratus.
ନିର୍ବିଷା, Kempferia angustifolia.
ନିମ, Melia azaddirachta.
ନିମୁଖା, Cissampelos hexandra.
ନିର୍ମଳୀ, Strychnos potatorum.
ନୀଳ, Indigofera tinctoria.
ନୀଳପଦ୍ମ, Nymphæ cyanea.
ନୁଣନଳିଆ, Leea aequata.
ନୁଣନୁଣିଆକୋଳି, Solanum indicum.
ନୁଣିଆଶାଗ, Portulaca oleracea.
ନେଉଆ, Annona reticulata. [laris.
ପଟ, Corchorus olitorius and capsu-
ପଟୋଳ, Trichosanthes dioica.
ପଣସ, Artocarpus integrifolia.
ପଣା, Pistia stratiotes.
ପତୁରିଅସିଜୁ, Castus indica.
ପଥରଖଟ, Saccharum.
ପଥରଚୂର, Plectranthus aromaticus.
ପଦ୍ମ, Nelumbium speciosum. [sum.
ପଦ୍ମଗୁଲଚି, Menispurmum tomento-
ପପସ୍ୱା, ଅମୃତଭଣ୍ଡା, Carica papaya.
ପରଶପିପ୍ପଳୀ, Hibiscus populneoides.
ପଳାଶ, Butea frondosa.
ପାକଡ଼, Ficus venosa.
ପାଟଳୀ, Bignonia suaveolens.
ପାଣିଅଁଳା, Flacourtia cataphracta.
ପାଣିଫଳ, Trapa bicornis.
ପାଣିମରିଚ, Polygonum flacidum.
ପାଣିଶିଉଳି, Vallisneria octandra.

ପାନସରଜ, Coix lacryma.
ପାନଶିଉଳି, Grewia sepiaria.
ପାଲଙ୍ଗଶାଗ, Beta Bengalensis.
ପାଲଧୁଆ, Erythrina indica.
ପିଆଜ, Allium ascalonicum.
ପିଆଶାଲ, Pentaptera tomentosa.
ପିଠାଳିମ୍ବା, Trewia nudiflora.
ପିଭଙ୍ଗ, Trigonella corniculata.
ପିତାକୋରେଇ, Echites antedysenterica.
ପିତାଲରଭା, Trichosanthes lobata.
ପିତାନଳିତା, Corchorus fuscus.
ପିତାଲାଉ, Cucurbita lagenaria.
ପିତାଶାଗ, Pharnaceum mollugo.
ପିଜୁଳି, Psidium phriferum.
ପିପ୍ପଳୀ, Piper longum.
ପିୟାଳ, Buchanania latifolia.
ପୁଣ୍ଡରୀକ, Nelumbium speciosum.
ପୁଦିନା, ପୋଦିନା, Mentha sativa.
ପୁନାଙ୍ଗ, Rottlera tinctoria.
ପୁରୁଣୀ, Boerhaavia precumbens, the red variety.
ପୋଇଶାଗ, Basella lucida.
ପୋକସୁଙ୍ଗା, Cotyledon laciniata.
ପୋଲବାଉଁଶ, Bambusa balcooa.
ଫାରସାକୋଲି, Grewia asiatica.
ଫୁଟି, Cucumis momordica.
ଫୁଲସୋଲ, Æschy nomeneaspera.
ଫେସି, Linum usitatissimum.
ବଁଇଚ, Flacourtia sapida.
ବକମ, Cœsalpinia sappan.
ବକୁଳ, ବଉଳ, Memusops elengi.
ବଚ, Acorus calamus.
ବଟ, ବର, Ficus indica.
ବଡକନଅର, Euphorbia hirta.
ବଡଗୋଖରୁ, Pedalium murex.
ବଡମେଥି, Trigonella fœnum grecum
ବଦରୀ, Zizyphus jujuba.
ବଦାମ, Terminalia catappa.
ବନଅଦା, Zingiber cassumunar.
ବନକପା, Hibiscus vitifolius.
ବନବେତ୍ର, Flagellaria indica.
ବନଗୋମୁଗ, Cucumis Madras patanus.
ବନଛଣପଟ, Crotalaria verrucosa.
ବନଜାମ୍ବୁ, Eugenia fruticosa.
ବନଛତୁଡ, Phyllanthus multiflorus.
ବନକାରଙ୍ଗ, Gemium lanceolatum.
ବନମରିଚ, Ammannia vesicatoria.
ବନଲବଙ୍ଗ, Ludwigia parviflora.
ବନହଳଦୀ, Curcuma zedoaria.
ବବୁର, ବବୁରି, Mimosa arabica, or acacia arabica.
ବରମହାଟି, Clematis.
ବରଲ୍ଲି, Asclepias acida.
ବସୁଦ୍ଧକାନ୍ତା, Lycopodium imbricatum.
ବରୁଣ, Capparis trifoliata.
ବସୁଗୋଲାବ, Rosa centifolia.
ବାଇଗବା, Jatropha curcas.
ବାଇଡଙ୍କ, Carpopogon pruriens.
ବାଘନଖିଆ, Alangium hexapetalum.
ବାଡିଅଁଳା, Sida cordifolia.
ବାତାବଲେମ୍ବୁ, Citrus decumana.
ବାସଙ୍ଗ, Justicia adhatoda.
ବାହାଡା, Terminalia belerica.
ବିଛୁଆତି, Tragia involucrata.
ବିଉଙ୍ଗ, Erycibe paniculata.
ବିଷଭାଡକ, Convolvulus argenteus.

ବୁହ, Phaseolus max.
ବେଉଁଶକଣ୍ଟା, Bambusa spinosa.
ବେଣା, Andropogon muricatus.
ବେତ, Calamus rotang.
ବେଲ, Ægle marmelos.
ବୋଇତିକଖାରୁ, Cucurbita melopepo.
ଭାଣ୍ଟି, Volkameria odorata.
ଭଗଶୋଲ, Smithia aspera.
ଭଲିଆ, Semecarpus anacardium.
ଭୃଙ୍ଗରାଜ, Verbesina scandens.
ଭୂଇଁକଖାରୁ, Convolvulus paniculatus
ଭୂଇଁଚମ୍ପା, Kempferia rotunda.
ଭୂଇଁଜାମୁ, Ardisia solanacea.
ଭୂଇଁଡାଲିମ୍ବ, Careya herbacea.
ଭୂଇଁନିମ୍ବ, Justicia paniculata.
ଭୂତକେଶ, Premna serratifolia.
ଭୂତସଜ, Ophioglossom flexuosum.
ମଁୟଣ, Vangueria spinosa.
ମଁୟଣସାରୁ, ମାଣସାରୁ, Arum indicum.
ମଁଜୁଆତ, ମେଁଦ, ମେହେନ୍ଦି, Lawsonia inermis.
ମଞ୍ଜିଷ୍ଠା, Rubia munjeet.
ମନ୍ତ୍ରାଫଳ, Vangueria spinosa.
ମନ୍ଦାର, Hibiscus rosa sinensis.
ମରିଚ, Piper nigrum.
ମଲଙ୍ଗ, Epidendrum.
ମଲ୍ଲଟୀ, Thumbergia grandiflora.
ମଲ୍ଲି, ମଲ୍ଲୀ, Jasminum zambac.
ମସୁର, Ervum lens.
ମହାକାଳ, Cucumis colocynthus.
ମହୁରି, ସାଜମହୁରି, Pimpinella anisum.
ମହୁଲ, ମହୁଲା, Bassia latifolia.
ମହୋତ୍ପଳ, Nelumbium speciosum.
ମାକଡଜାଳି, Panicum ciliare.
ମାଣ୍ଡିଆ, Eleusine coracana
ମାଧବୀଲତା, Gærtnera recemosa.
ମାଳତୀ, Echites caryophyllata, and Jasminum grandiflorum.
ମୁଚକୁନ୍ଦ, Pterospermum suberifolium.
ମୁଥା, Cyperus rotundus.
ମୁରଗା, Celosia cristata.
ମୁଳା, Raphanus sativus.
ମୁଷାକାଣି, Salvinia cuculata.
ମେଥି, Trigonella fœnum graecum.
ମେସ୍ତପାଟ, Hibiscus cannabis.
ମୋଚରସ, Bombax heptaphyllum.
ଯଜ୍ଞଡୁମୁର, Ficus glomerata.
ଯାଦୁମାରି, Cassia alata.
ଯାଷ୍ଟିମଧୁ, Glycyrrhiza glabra.
ଯୁଆଣି, Ligusticum ajowan.
ଯୂଥୀ, ଯୂଥିକା, Jasminum arriculatum.
ରକ୍ତଚନ୍ଦନ, Pterocarpus santalinus.
ରକ୍ତପଦ୍ମ, Nelumbium speciosum.
ରକ୍ତପିତ୍ତ, Ventilago Madras patensis.
ରଙ୍ଗାକାଞ୍ଚନ, Bauhinia variegata.
ରଙ୍ଗାଚିତାମୂଳ, Plumbago rosea.
ରଙ୍ଗାପୁରୁଣୀ, Boerhaavia precumbens (the white variety).
ରଙ୍ଗାଫୁଲ, Æschynomene grandiflora.
ରଙ୍ଗାମୁରଗାଇ, Celosia cristata.
ରସୁଣ, Allium sativum.
ଭସୁଣିଆ, Spilanthus oleracia.
ରାଇଶୋରଷ, Sinapis dichotoma.
ରାମକଦଳୀ, Musa sapientum (Banana)
ରାମତୁଳସୀ, Ocimum gratissimum.
ରାମବାଇଗଣ, Solanum hirsutum.
ଲଜ୍ଜା, Mimoso octandra.

ରିଠା, Sapindus detergens.
ରୁଁଜ, କାଇଁଚ, Abrus precatorius.
ରୁପଗଛ, Convolvulus argenteus.
ରୁଦ୍ରାକ୍ଷ, Eleocarpus ganitrus.
ଲଙ୍କାସିଜୁ, Euphorbia tirucalli.
ଲଟକଣ, Bixa, orellana (Anotta).
ଲଣ୍ଡାବଗୁଲ୍, ଇଣ୍ଡାବଗୁଲ୍, Plantago ispaghul.
ଲବଙ୍ଗ, Eugenia caryophyllata.
ଲବାନ୍, Boswellia thurifera.
ଲୋଧ, Symplocos racemosa.
ଶଙ୍କରଜଟା, Hedysarum pictum.
ଶଣ, Crotolaria juncea.
ଶର, Saccharum sara.
ଶାଳ, Shorea robusta.
ଶାଳପର୍ଣ୍ଣୀ, Hedysarum gangeticum.
ଶିଙ୍ଗାରହାର, Nyctanthes arbortristis.
ଶିମୁଳୀ, Bombax heptaphylla.
ଶିଶୁ, Dalbergia sissoo.
ଶୁଲଫା, Anethum sowa.
ଶୋଣ, Bignonia indica. [purpurea.
କୋଜ, ଦେବକାଞ୍ଚନ, କଚନାର, Bauhinia
ଶ୍ୟାମଲତା, Echites frutescents.
ଶ୍ୱେତମୁରଗାଛ, Celosia argentea.
ସଜନା, Hyperanthera morunga.
ସପୁରୀପଣସ, Bromelia ananas.
ସପ୍ତପର୍ଣ୍ଣୀ, Echites scholaris.
ସରଳକାଠ, Pinus longifolia.
ସମରାଜ. Vernonia anthelmintica.
ସର୍ବଜୟା, Cana indica.
ସଲସବୋଲି, Capparis sepiaria.
ସାଗୁଆନ୍, Tectona grandis.
ସାଇଁଶୁଦ, Ophioxylon serpentinum.
ସାଳସାଲୁକ, Nymphea stellata.
ସାଜଦୁଲକସା, Phlomis esculenta.
ସ୍ୱାରକନ୍ଦ, (?), Arum nymphæi fol- [ium.
ସାରୁ, Arum colocasia.
ସାଲଗମ୍, Brassica rapa.
ସାଲମିସିରି, Salep or Orchis mascula.
ସାଲସା, Sarsaparilla.
ସାଲୁକ, କଇଁ, Nymphæa lotus.
ସାହାଡା, Trophis aspera.
ସଁଉତ, Rosa glandulifera.
ସିଙ୍ଗଡା, Trapa bispinosa.
ସିଜୁ, Euphorbia neriifolia or lingularia.
ସିରସ, Mimosa seereessa.
ସୁଗନ୍ଧା, Ocimum caryophllatum.
ସୁନାମୁଗ, Phaseolus aureus.
ସୁନାରି, Cassia fistula.
ସୁନିସୁନିଆଶାଗ, Marsilea dentata.
ସୁନସ୍ତ, Sterculia argentea.
ସୁଲଫାଶାଗ, Fumaria parviflorum.
ସୂର୍ଯ୍ୟମଣି, Hibiscus phœniceus.
ସୂର୍ଯ୍ୟମୁଖୀ, Helianthus annuus.
ସେବତୀ, Rosa glandulifera.
ସୋମଲତା, Asclepias acida.
ସୋରିଷ, Sinapis dichotoma.
ସୋଲ, Æschynomene paludosa.
ସୋଲା, ବୁଁଟ, Cicer arietinum.
ସୋପ, ସଉପ, Anethum sowa.
ସ୍ଥଳପଦ୍ମ, Hibiscus matabilis.
ହଡାସୁଣ୍ଡ, Lycopodium imbricatum.
ହେନ୍ତାଳ, Phœnix paludosa.
ହରଡ, Cytisus calan.
ହରିଡା, Terminalia chebula.

ହଳଦୀ, Curcuma longa.
ହଲ୍‌କସା, ଗଇଘସ, Pholmis zeylanica.
ହାଡ଼ଯୋଡ଼ା, Cissus quandrangularis.
ହାତଶୁଣ୍ଢା, Heliotropium indicum.
ହାପରମାଳି, Echites dichotoma.
ହାଲିମ, Lepidium sativum.
ହିଙ୍ଗୁ, ହେଙ୍ଗୁ, Fercula asafœtida.
ହିଜଳିବଦାମ, Anacardium occidentale.
ହିଜ୍ଜଳ, Eugenia acutangula.
ହିଡ଼ମିଚ୍ଛ, Hengtsba repens.
ହିମସାଗର, Cotyledon laciniata.
ହୋଗଳା, Typha elephantinum.
ଷେତପାପଡ଼ା, Oldenlandia biflora.

Names of Diseases.

ଅଗ୍ରମାଂସ, Liver disease.
ଅଙ୍ଗଗ୍ରେଥନ, Convulsions.
ଅଜୀର୍ଣ୍ଣ, Indigestion.
ଅଣ୍ଟାବାତ, Lumbago.
ଅତିସାର, Dysentery.
ଅଧାକପାଳୀ, Hemicrania.
ଅନ୍ତ୍ରବୃଦ୍ଧି, Rupture.
ଅପସ୍ମାର, ମୃଗୀରୋଗ, Epilepsy.
ଅମ୍ଳପିତ୍ତ, Syphilis.
ଅର୍ଦ୍ଧାଙ୍ଗ, Hemiplegia.
ଅର୍ଶ, Piles.
ଅବୁ, Wen.
ଅକ୍ଷିପକ, Sore-eye.
ଅକ୍ଷିପୁଷ୍ପ, Cataract.
ଅକ୍ଷିରୋଗ, Ophthalmia.
ଉନ୍ମାଦ, Insanity.
ଉହା, Polypus of the nose.
କଣକଟା, Whitlow.
କମ୍ପଜ୍ୱର. Ague.
କାଛୁ, କୁଣ୍ଡିଆ, Itch.
କାମଳ, Jaundice.
କାଶ, ଦାଷ, Cough.
କୃମି, Worms.
କେମ୍ପା, ଖେଞ୍ଚ, Cramp, Spasms.
କୋଢ଼, କୁଷ୍ଠ, Leprosy.
କୋଷବୃଦ୍ଧି, Hydrocele.
ଗଣ୍ଠିବାତ, Rheumatism.
ଗଣ୍ଡମାଳା, King's evil.
ଗଳଗଣ୍ଡ, Bronchocele.
ଗୋଦର, Elephantiasis.
ଝଦ୍ଦଣା, Diarrhœa.
ଘା, Sore.
ଘିମ୍ପିର, Prickly heat.
ଛର୍ଦ୍ଦି, ବାନ୍ତି, ଅଲ, Vomiting.
ଛାଲୁ, Thrush.
ଜଡ଼ୁ, ଆଲୁଅ, Wart.
ଜର, ଜ୍ୱର, Fever.
ଜଳୋଦର, Dropsy.
ଦାଦୁ, Ringworm.
ନରସୁର, Fistula.
ଝାଡ଼ାବାନ୍ତି, ଝାଡ଼ାକଲ, ଓଲାଉଠା, Cholera.
ତଣ୍ଟିଘା, Sore throat.
ତଣ୍ଟିବଥା, Quinsy.
ଦାନ୍ତଟଣା, Toothache.

ଦାହ, Inflammation.
ଦୁର୍ବଳତା, Debility.
ଧ୍ୱଜଭଙ୍ଗ, Impotency.
ପଥରୀ, Stone.
ପକ୍ଷାଘାତ, Palsy.
ପାଦସ୍ଫୋଟ, Kibe.
ପାଳିଜ୍ୱର, Intermittent fever.
ପାର୍ଶ୍ୱଶୂଳ, Pleurisy.
ପିତ୍ତ, Bile, Bilious.
ପିଳେହାର, ପିଲୋଇ, Spleen.
ପୂଜ, Pus.
ପେଟବଥା, Belly-ache.
ପେଟମୋଡା, Gripes.
ପ୍ରଦର, Menorrhagia.
ପ୍ରମେହ, ଧାତୁଭଙ୍ଗ, Gonorrhœa.
ପ୍ରଳାପ, Delirium.
ଫୁଟ୍‌କୁଣି, Pimple.
ଫୁଲ, Swelling; Albugo.
ବଥ, ବାଳମୂଳିଆ, Boil.
ବରଣ, Tumour, pustule.
ବସନ୍ତ, Smallpox.
ବହୁମୂତ୍ର, Diabetes.
ବାଘି, Bubo.
ବାତ, Gout, rheumatism.
ବାୟୁଶୂଳ, Colic.
ବଉଁଶ, A scabby disease.
ବ୍ରଣ, A boil, carbuncle.
ଭଗନ୍ଦର, Fistula (in ano).
ଭେଦ, Looseness.
ମହୁଢ, Plague.
ମଳବନ୍ଧ, Costiveness.
ମିଳିମିଳା, Measles.
ମୁଣ୍ଡଘୂର୍ଣ୍ଣ, Vertigo.
ମୁଣ୍ଡବଥା, Headache.
ମୂତ୍ରକୃଚ୍ଛ୍ର, Strangury.
ମୂର୍ଚ୍ଛା, Fainting
ମୋତିଆବନ୍ଧ, Gutta serena.
ଯକ୍ଷ୍ମା, Pulmonary Consumption.
ରକ୍ତାତିସାର, Bloody flux.
ସ୍ୱଜଳୁଷ୍ଟ, St. Anthony's fire.
ଶୋଥ, Intumescence.
ଶ୍ୱାସ, Shortness of breath.
ଶ୍ୱାସକାସ, Asthma.
ସର୍ଦ୍ଦି, A cold.
ସ୍ୱରଭଙ୍ଗ, Hoarseness.
ହାମଫୁଟି, Chickenpox.
କ୍ଷୟକାସ, Consumption.

Fractions.

ପାଏ or ପା, a quarter, is thus represented	୲
ଅଧ, ଅଧେ, ଅର୍ଦ୍ଧ, ଅର୍ଦ୍ଧେକ, half	୳
ପାଉଣେ, or ତିନିପା, three-quarters	୴
ଦେଢ଼, one and a half	୧୳
ଅଢ଼ାଇ, two and a half	୨୳

These are irregular. In all other cases a quarter more than an even number is expressed by prefixing ସଉଆ, to the number; a half by prefixing ସାଢ଼େ; and three-quarters by prefixing ପାଉଣେ to the even number. *Exam.* ସଉଆ ତିନି, three and a quarter; ସାଢ଼େ ତିନି, three and a half; ପାଉଣେ ଚାରି, three and three-quarters, viz., a quarter less than four.

Fractional parts are generally expressed by dividing the Rupee into sixteen annas or parts. *Exam.* ସାତ ଅଣା, seven annas, or seven-sixteenths; ଦଶ ଅଣା, ten annas, or ten-sixteenths.

The signs are as follow:—

୵	୶	୷	୲	୲୵	୲୶	୲୷	୳	୳୵	୳୶	୳୷	୴	୴୵	୴୶	୴୷	୧
$\frac{1}{16}$	$\frac{1}{8}$	$\frac{3}{16}$	$\frac{1}{4}$	$\frac{5}{16}$	$\frac{6}{16}$	$\frac{7}{16}$	$\frac{1}{2}$	$\frac{9}{16}$	$\frac{10}{16}$	$\frac{11}{16}$	$\frac{3}{4}$	$\frac{13}{16}$	$\frac{14}{16}$	$\frac{15}{16}$	1

Days of the Week.

					Muhammadan.
Sunday,	ରବିବାର,	from the	Sun,	ରବି ।	ଏତ୍ୱାର୍ ।
Monday,	ସୋମବାର,	,,	Moon,	ସୋମ ।	ପୀର୍ ।
Tuesday,	ମଙ୍ଗଳବାର,	,,	Mars,	ମଙ୍ଗଳ ।	ମଙ୍ଗଲ୍ ।
Wednesday,	ବୁଧବାର,	,,	Mercury,	ବୁଧ ।	ବୁଧ ।
Thursday,	ଗୁରୁବାର,	,,	Jupiter,	ବୃହସ୍ପତି ।	ଜୁମେରାତ୍ ।
Friday,	ଶୁକ୍ରବାର,	,,	Venus,	ଶୁକ୍ର ।	ଜୁମ୍ମା ।
Saturday,	ଶନିବାର,	,,	Saturn,	ଶନି ।	ଶନିଚର୍ ।

A day is divided into two parts, ଦିନବେଳ, viz., the time from sun-rising to sun-setting; and ରାତ୍ରିକାଳ, the time from sun-setting to sun-rising. Each of these is sub-divided into four equal parts called ପ୍ରହର, or watches, one of which is nearly equal to three English hours, but varying with the season.

Of the Hindu Months.

The Hindu months always begin at what they call the ସଂକ୍ରାନ୍ତି, viz., the moment of the sun's entering any sign of the Zodiac.

ବୈଶାଖ,	Baisákha	part of	April	and	May.	Sign, ମେଷ ।
ଜ୍ୟେଷ୍ଠ,	Jesthha	,,	May	,,	June.	ବୃଷ ।
ଆଷାଢ,	Ashárdha	,,	June	,,	July.	ମିଥୁନ ।
ଶ୍ରାବଣ,	Srábaña	,,	July	,,	August.	କର୍କଟ ।
ଭାଦ୍ରବ,	Bhádraba	,,	August	,,	September.	ସିଂହ ।
ଆଶ୍ୱିନ,	Ashwina	,,	September	and	October.	କନ୍ୟା ।
କାର୍ତ୍ତିକ,	Kártika	,,	October	,,	November.	ତୁଳା ।
ମାର୍ଗଶିର,	Márgashira	,,	November	,,	December.	ବୃଶ୍ଚିକ ।
ପୌଷ,	Pousha	,,	December	,,	January.	ଧନୁ ।
ମାଘ,	Mághha	,,	January	,,	February.	ମକର ।
ଫାଲ୍ଗୁନ,	Phálguna	,,	February	,,	March.	କୁମ୍ଭ ।
ଚୈତ୍ର,	Chaitra	,,	March	,,	April.	ମୀନ ।

The month is divided into two ପକ୍ଷ, or sides (of the moon); the time from change (ଅମାବାସ୍ୟା) to the full moon (ପୌର୍ଣ୍ଣିମା), is called the ଶୁକ୍ଳପକ୍ଷ, bright side; and from the full to the change କୃଷ୍ଣପକ୍ଷ, the dark. A lunar day is called ତିଥି ।